Lecture Notes in Computer Science　　10500

Commenced Publication in 1973
Founding and Former Series Editors:
Gerhard Goos, Juris Hartmanis, and Jan van Leeuwen

More information about this series at http://www.springer.com/series/7408

Joost-Pieter Katoen · Rom Langerak
Arend Rensink (Eds.)

ModelEd, TestEd, TrustEd

Essays Dedicated to Ed Brinksma
on the Occasion of His 60th Birthday

 Springer

Editors
Joost-Pieter Katoen (ID)
RWTH Aachen University
Aachen
Germany

and

University of Twente
Enschede
The Netherlands

Rom Langerak
University of Twente
Enschede
The Netherlands

Arend Rensink
University of Twente
Enschede
The Netherlands

ISSN 0302-9743   ISSN 1611-3349   (electronic)
Lecture Notes in Computer Science
ISBN 978-3-319-68269-3   ISBN 978-3-319-68270-9   (eBook)
DOI 10.1007/978-3-319-68270-9

Library of Congress Control Number: 2017954907

LNCS Sublibrary: SL2 – Programming and Software Engineering

This Springer imprint is published by Springer Nature
The registered company is Springer International Publishing AG
The registered company address is: Gewerbestrasse 11, 6330 Cham, Switzerland

Ed Brinksma

Foreword

This Festschrift is a birthday salute to Ed Brinksma, who recently celebrated his 60th birthday. It contains contributions by a number of Ed's colleagues, former PhD students, and researchers with whom Ed has been collaborating intensively. Ed has been very active in academic research; about 12 years ago he became Director of the Embedded Systems Institute followed by many years as Rector of the University of Twente, a job he fulfilled until the end of 2016 with full devotion and great enthusiasm.

The Festschrift is a tribute to the various seminal contributions of Ed Brinksma. Ed studied mathematics at the Rijksuniversiteit Groningen and completed his studies in the field of mathematical logics under the supervision of Johan van Benthem, one of the contributors to this Festschrift. In 1982, he took up an assistant professorship at the University of Twente, those days called the Technische Hogeschool Twente. It seems Twente is the right place for Ed, as he is still employed at this university! In 1988, Ed received a doctoral degree from Twente for his dissertation entitled "On the Design of Extended LOTOS," which he completed under the supervision of Chris Vissers. As a 34-year-old researcher he got a full professorship in Twente in 1991; those days Ed was one of the youngest professors (if not the youngest) in computer science in The Netherlands.

Ed's research is in the field of formal methods, or as he likes to phrase it, applied mathematics in computer science. In his research philosophy, formal methods research is based on a carefully balanced interaction between foundational aspects on the one hand, and software tool support and applications on the other. His research reflects this. Ed is perhaps most well-known for his work on the modelling formalism LOTOS (language of the temporal ordering of events), the only process algebra that made it into an international standard (in 1989) for describing communication protocols and distributed systems.

Ed recognized that a language in itself is insufficient. Together with Chris Vissers, Pippo Scollo, and Marten van Sinderen, he developed various specification techniques — in current jargon one would nowadays probably call them "patterns" — to assist the design process of distributed systems. The so-called constraint-oriented specification style is a prominent example of such pattern. He complemented this with a vision on transformational design that he developed for, amongst others, interface refinement, decomposition of processes into distributed ones, and the transformational design of cache coherency protocols.

Ed has been one of the pioneers of systematic and rigorous testing of implementations of (distributed) systems. His identification of the so-called canonical tester and the accompanying test derivation algorithms constitute the basis for modern model-based testing and have been important inputs to the ISO standard on testing. Together with Jan Tretmans, one of his first PhD students, he developed this further. Jan's contribution to this Festschrift gives a nice account of how this approach today has evolved into a practical one.

Another area that Ed pioneered has been the integration of performance and reliability aspects into formal methods. In the mid-1990s, he equipped process algebras
with probabilities and time; later he developed algorithms for timed automata enriched
with prices. His early aim, the full integration of performance and reliability analysis
into a single framework, has formed the basis of current flourishing research areas such
as probabilistic model checking. Quantitative extensions of modelling formalisms and
semantic models are still an active area of research. Various contributions in this
Festschrift give a good indication of what has been achieved so far.

Other topics Ed intensively considered are true concurrency semantics, first for
LOTOS, and later for the sake of simplifying the verification. Later, he became
increasingly interested in modelling where the central question is where good and
adequate models come from. The contribution of Bernhard Steffen and his co-authors
to this Festschrift shows how learning can be applied to synthesize such models in a
semi-automated manner. A fascinating development on this topic can be witnessed in
the last few decades.

It is worth to mentioning that Ed played a decisive role in establishing international
conferences in the field of formal methods. He has been one of the key players in the
establishment of the conference series Formal Description Techniques (FORTE) and
Protocol Specification, Verification, and Testing (PSTV). He also took the initiative to
set up the first meetings on formal testing, resulting in the International Workshop on
Protocol Test Systems (IWPTS), and actively stimulated the birth of the conference
series on Quantitative Evaluation of Systems (QEST). FORTE and QEST still exist;
IWPTS has been the trendsetter for various other workshops and conferences in testing.
In 1995, together with Rance Cleaveland, Kim Guldstrand Larsen, and Bernhard
Steffen, Ed took the initiative to launch the TACAS (Tools and Algorithms for the
Construction and Analysis of Systems) workshop. This European counterpart to the (at
that time) US-dominated CAV conference has over the years evolved into one of the
most prominent conferences on formal verification and tools.

Ed's vision of science, something he discusses in an extremely passionate manner
and with extensive (and lengthy) motivation, has inspired many of his pupils and
fellow researchers. In particular, his search for simplicity — in his inauguration speech
in 1991, Ed summarized this as, "the development of formal methods makes no sense
when this is not accompanied by a dedicated effort to present ideas in a crystal clear and
simple manner"[1] — has always been a key element in his view.

Besides being our example of an excellent researcher, inspiring mentor, and a great
boss, Ed first and foremost is our friend. We could have filled yet another book with
anecdotes about trips – do you still remember Crete, Aalborg, Beijing, and Australia,
Ed? Just to mention a few – and stories about Lotosphere dinners, entertaining evenings
(nights?) in bars and restaurants. Thanks for all the wonderful times, and thanks for
being a great friend and colleague. Ed, many congratulations on your 60th birthday!
Have a good one.

---

[1] De ontwikkeling van formele methoden is zinloos wanneer deze niet wordt begeleid door gerichte
inspanning om de presentatie van de ideeen zo helder en eenvoudig mogelijk te houden.

We thank Springer, in particular Alfred Hofmann, Anna Kramer, and Ingrid Haas, for their support, and thank Harold Bruintjes for his assistance in generating the final version of the Festschrift. Thomas Noll is thanked for his reviewing efforts and Ida den Hamer for the local organization.

August 2017

Joost-Pieter Katoen
Rom Langerak
Arend Rensink

Contents

Modeling and Semantics

From LOTOS to LNT

Hubert Garavel[1,2,3](✉), Frédéric Lang[1,2,3], and Wendelin Serwe[1,2,3]

[1] INRIA, Grenoble, France
{hubert.garavel,frederic.lang,wendelin.serwe}@inria.fr
[2] Univ. Grenoble Alpes, LIG, 38000 Grenoble, France
[3] CNRS, LIG, 38000 Grenoble, France
http://convecs.inria.fr

Abstract. We revisit the early publications of Ed Brinksma devoted, on the one hand, to the definition of the formal description technique LOTOS (ISO International Standard 8807:1989) for specifying communication protocols and distributed systems, and, on the other hand, to two proposals (Extended LOTOS and Modular LOTOS) for making LOTOS a simpler and more expressive language. We examine how this scientific agenda has been dealt with during the last decades. We review the successive enhancements of LOTOS that led to the definition of three languages: E-LOTOS (ISO International Standard 15437:2001), then LOTOS NT, and finally LNT. We present the software implementations (compilers and translators) developed for these new languages and report about their use in various application domains.

Keywords: Abstract data type · Algebraic specification · Concurrency theory · E-LOTOS · Formal description technique · Formal method · Formal specification · LOTOS · LNT · Process algebra · Process calculus · Specification language

1 Introduction

The present article was written in honor of Ed Brinksma and included in a collective *Festschrift* book offered to him at the occasion of his 60th birthday.

The first part of Ed Brinksma's research career has been devoted to the design of formal methods for the specification of communication protocols and distributed systems, the LOTOS language being the common theme and vital lead for the scientific contributions. This first part approximately extends over twelve years, between 1984 (as dated by the conference article [14]) and 1995 (as dated by the book chapter [9]). It was directly succeeded, with some chronological overlap, by a second part centered on conformance testing for protocols (with a first paper [16] published in 1991) and a third part centered on real time and performance evaluation (with early papers, e.g., [15] published in 1995).

In the present article, we focus on this first part, in which we distinguish two different threads of work: (i) the definition of the LOTOS language, which culminated with its adoption by ISO (International Standard 8807:1989) and (ii)

© Springer International Publishing AG 2017
J.-P. Katoen et al. (Eds.): Brinksma Festschrift, LNCS 10500, pp. 3–26, 2017.
DOI: 10.1007/978-3-319-68270-9_1

the elaboration of two proposals for enhancing LOTOS, by introducing valuable features not present in the standard, either because they were not ready on time when it was adopted or because they did not reach international consensus.

The present article is organized as follows. Section 2 recalls the contributions of Ed Brinksma to the definition of LOTOS and gives a brief account of the impact of this language in academia and industry. The two next sections review two early languages proposed by Ed Brinksma for enhancing LOTOS, namely Extended LOTOS (Sect. 3) and Modular LOTOS (Sect. 4). The three next sections present three more recent languages that, between 1993 and now, have been proposed to supersede LOTOS, namely E-LOTOS (Sect. 5), LOTOS NT (Sect. 6), and LNT (Sect. 7), with some discussion about the actual impact of these languages. Finally, Sect. 8 gives a few concluding remarks.

2   LOTOS

Among all publications of Ed Brinksma related to the definition of LOTOS, we highlight three key contributions, each of a different nature and scope:

– Obviously, the ISO Draft International Standard defining LOTOS [58] occupies a place of choice. Even if earlier drafts of LOTOS had circulated before (e.g., Ed Brinksma's first tutorial on LOTOS [10] given in 1985) and even if experiments with LOTOS had already been done at some universities (e.g., the model-checking verification of protocols in 1986 [33, 34]), this Draft International Standard published in 1987 was the first complete, coherent definition of LOTOS made available to the international community. Two years after, this document reached its final status by being approved as the ISO International Standard 8807:1989 [60].
  The definition of LOTOS was a collective achievement done within an ISO committee (project 97.21.20.2) under the leadership of Ed Brinksma, who was the editor in charge of producing the standard. Tommaso Bolognesi, Günter Karjoth, Luigi Logrippo, Jan de Meer, Elie Najm, Juan Quemada, Pippo Scollo, Alaister Tocher, Jan Tretmans, and Chris Vissers participated, among others, in this committee.
  The resulting LOTOS language was an audacious combination of the most recent innovations in formal methods at that time. To describe and manipulate data structures, the LOTOS committee selected abstract data types—more precisely, a dialect of the algebraic language ACT ONE [25, 26, 80]. To describe the behaviour of concurrent processes, the committee retained the key ideas of process algebra, blending into a single language the best features of several calculi, namely CCS [82], TCSP [17], and Circal [81]; LOTOS also brought original ideas, such as its "disable" operator, which models nondeterministic disruption (e.g., crashes and failures), and its "enable" operator, which allows value-passing sequential continuation after the termination of a group of parallel processes.
  The definition of LOTOS provided in the ISO standard was fully formal, much in line with the longstanding Dutch tradition of computer-language

definitions. The syntax was given as a BNF grammar; the static semantics was specified as a set of mathematical constraints and functions defined by induction over syntactic constructs; the semantics of data types was expressed as a many-sorted term algebra obtained by quotienting the algebra generated by a derivation system; finally the behavioural semantics of processes was defined operationally using a set of structured operational semantics rules. This formal definition was followed by annexes providing informal explanations and complementary information.

- Jointly written with Tommaso Bolognesi, Ed Brinskma's tutorial on LOTOS [6] is also a highly cited publication. Written in a lively style and illustrated with a wealth of examples, this tutorial targets the end users of LOTOS. It is orthogonal and complementary to the (somewhat dry) ISO standard definition, primarily oriented towards language implementers and semanticists.
- Another insightful contribution is Ed Brinskma's 1989 paper on constraint-oriented specification [12]. It is well-known that the decomposition of a computer system into concurrent/parallel tasks may take two forms: it is either *physical* if the decomposition closely reflects the actual distribution of tasks over processors, or *logical* otherwise, if the decomposition is rather intended to provide the system with a modular structure that does not necessarily correspond to its actual topology. Ed Brinksma develops the latter approach in the framework of the LOTOS multiway rendezvous, which enables two or more processes to synchronize, negotiate, and exchange data values during one atomic event. The paper formulates the fundamental intuition of *parallel composition as conjunction*, meaning that the multiway rendezvous achieves the logical conjunction of all the individual constraints expressed by a set of processes running concurrently. This idea enables a certain degree of "declarative" programming (namely, constraint solving) to be introduced in the framework of a fundamentally "operational" (i.e., constructive, imperative) language such as LOTOS. The usefulness of the approach is demonstrated on realistic examples of communication protocols [12], but it is also relevant to other application domains, e.g., hardware circuits ([41] shows how the complex arbitration protocol of the SCSI-2 bus can be concisely modelled using an eight-party LOTOS rendezvous) or robotics ([47] illustrates how a software controller for an entire manufacturing plant can be obtained as the parallel composition of many simple controllers, one for each device or degree of freedom of a device in the plant).

Retrospectively, the international effort invested in LOTOS was successful in several respects:

- Although LOTOS is a committee-designed language based on two very different concepts (algebraic data types and process calculi), it achieves a suitable compromise and a fair integration between its various elements. All its language constructs (perhaps with the exception of the **choice** and **par** operators on gate lists) derive from concrete needs and are useful in practice.
- LOTOS is clearly more abstract and higher level than the two other standardized languages it was competing with (namely, Estelle [59] and SDL [18]), and

proved that a specification language could be formal and executable at the same time.

- The design of LOTOS made it clear that process calculi were not only mathematical notations for studying concurrency theory, but that they could be turned into computer languages used to model real-life systems. LOTOS was indeed the first process calculus in which large specifications of complex systems (e.g., protocols and services of OSI and ISDN networks) were produced. Later, it was shown that the high abstraction level of LOTOS makes it also suitable to other application domains, e.g., multiprocessor architectures and asynchronous circuits.
- The LOTOS community put strong emphasis on software tools, often in the framework of European projects such as SEDOS, LOTOSphere, SPECS, EUCALYPTUS-1 and -2, etc. Today, most of these tools are no longer available, but the CADP toolbox[1] [45] is still actively maintained. Also, many ideas present in early LOTOS tools would certainly benefit from modern developments in symbolic execution and verification technology.

On the negative side, one can point out two main shortcomings of LOTOS:

- Despite its status of international standard, LOTOS did not manage to unite the academic community working on process calculi. Not only the preexisting algebras/calculi ACP, CCS, and CSP remained, but new languages appeared, e.g., μCRL. This resulted in fragmented efforts and a lack of critical mass that became apparent in the mid-90s.
- LOTOS also failed to gain wide industrial acceptance, mostly due to its so-called "steep learning curve". Because it is an abstract, expressive, and flexible language based on concepts absent from mainstream languages, LOTOS is best used by high-level experts rather than average software programmers: this is unfortunately a fatal flaw as far as dissemination is concerned.

3   Extended LOTOS

As soon as the definition of LOTOS was frozen as an ISO standard, it appeared that the language was not fully satisfactory and that some of its features could be redesigned in a better way. Ed Brinksma's role as the editor of the LOTOS standard did not prevent him from suggesting enhancements to LOTOS.

His first contribution in this respect is his PhD thesis [11], defended in 1988, which proposes a language named "Extended LOTOS" that significantly differs from LOTOS. Concerning data specifications, Extended LOTOS keeps the abstract data types of LOTOS, but adds better support for modules. Concerning behavioural specifications (namely, concurrent processes), Extended LOTOS brings deeper changes:

- It introduces a notion of *action product* inspired from SCCS [83], whereas LOTOS only has simple actions.

---

[1] http://cadp.inria.fr.

- Extended LOTOS attempts at unifying in one single operator both forms of sequential composition (action prefix and "enable") that exist in LOTOS.
- Extended LOTOS breaks with the algebraic style of LOTOS and other process calculi by replacing unary and binary operators with n-ary constructs having a fully bracketed syntax, e.g., "**sel** B_1 [] B_2 [] ... [] B_n **endsel**" for nondeterministic choice or "**par** $B_1 \parallel B_2 \parallel ... \parallel B_n$ **endpar**" for parallel composition.
- Extended LOTOS proposes other desirable features, among which a **par** operator ranging over a finite domain of values.

Although Extended LOTOS has never been actually implemented, these ideas had the merit to point out the main shortcomings of LOTOS and made it clear that the language, despite its status of international standard, still deserved major enhancements.

4 Modular LOTOS

Published three years later, a deliverable (edited by Ed Brinksma) of the LOTO-Sphere project [13] adopts a point of view orthogonal to that of Extended LOTOS: leaving aside all ideas for improving the behaviour part of LOTOS, this deliverable focuses on enhancements to the data part of LOTOS, in which usability problems have been identified as most crucial, and proposes a new language called "Modular LOTOS", two synthetic presentations of which can also be found in [9,90]. Modular LOTOS suggests the following enhancements:

- Distinction between *constructors* and *functions*, whereas LOTOS made no difference between these two forms of operations;
- Introduction of *partial functions*, whereas LOTOS only allowed totally defined operations;
- Support for *built-in types* (e.g., natural numbers, integer numbers, strings) and *generic data structures* (e.g., lists, sets, arrays, etc.);
- Introduction of *modules* gathering data and/or behaviour definitions, namely, types, constructors, functions, and processes;
- Introduction of module interfaces (called *descriptions*) that can be used to hide certain definitions contained in modules;
- Introduction of *renaming* to avoid name clashes between different modules;
- Support for *generic modules* parameterized by descriptions.

To our knowledge, Modular LOTOS has never been implemented, although key ideas (namely, distinction between constructors and functions, partial functions, and splitting of large LOTOS specifications into multiple files) were already supported in the CÆSAR.ADT compiler for LOTOS [35]. At this point, Ed Brinskma shifted his research interests to other topics, but the LOTOS reform movement he had initiated expanded rapidly.

5   E-LOTOS

Between 1993 and 2001, an ISO committee gathered under the lead of Juan Quemada to revise the LOTOS standard. Arnaud Février, Hubert Garavel, Alan Jeffrey, Guy Leduc, Luc Léonard, Luigi Logrippo, José Mañas, Elie Najm, Mihaela Sighireanu, and Jacques Sincennes participated in this committee as regular contributors, with the help of more than twenty occasional contributors [89].

At the beginning, the proposed changes were modest, trying to repair rather than replace LOTOS; as time passed, it appeared that more radical enhancements were desirable. This work eventually resulted in a new language named E-LOTOS (for "Enhanced LOTOS") approved as ISO/IEC International Standard 15437:2001 [61]. Tutorials on E-LOTOS can be found in [101], [56,57,70]. Compared to LOTOS, E-LOTOS brings deep changes that aim at greater expressiveness and/or better user-friendliness:

- Concerning the data types, E-LOTOS goes far beyond the ideas suggested for Modular LOTOS. Rather than enhancing ACT-ONE, E-LOTOS removes it, replacing abstract data types with a functional language—an approach also explored in [5], which proposes a concurrent language combining a process calculus (CCS) and a functional language (ML). E-LOTOS goes even further by giving its functional language an imperative flavour: in particular, E-LOTOS variables can be assigned and E-LOTOS functions can have output (i.e., call by result) parameters to return multiple results, which, in conventional functional languages, is usually done by returning tuple values.
- E-LOTOS data types can be records (with named or unnamed fields) or (possibly recursive) types defined by a list of constructors. E-LOTOS also provides predefined types (Booleans, naturals, integers, rationals, floating-point reals, characters, and strings) and abbreviations for declaring enumerated types, records, sets, and lists.
- Contrary to LOTOS, in which the data and behaviour parts are two entirely different sub-languages, E-LOTOS tries to unify functions and processes; functions can be seen as particular cases of processes that only do local calculations before terminating, do not perform any observable or invisible action, and do not let time elapse. Consequently, functions and processes share a number of common constructs, among which: variable assignments, if-then-else conditionals, case with pattern matching, while loops, for loops, etc.
- In both its data and behaviour parts, E-LOTOS introduces a unique sequential composition operator, which unifies the action-prefix and "enable" operators present in the behaviour part of LOTOS.
- E-LOTOS provides support for exception handling. In the data part of E-LOTOS, exceptions bring a convenient solution to the need for partial functions. In the behaviour part, exceptions allow some involved communication protocols to be described compositionally—see [49] for an advocacy paper on exceptions in process calculi.
- Gates (i.e., communication ports) are explicitly typed in E-LOTOS, whereas they are untyped in LOTOS—see [36] for an introduction to gate typing,

which leads to more readable specifications, detects communication mismatches at compile time rather than at run time, and provides a simple solution to the "structured events" issue in the constraint-oriented style.

- To express *quantitative time* aspects, the behaviour part of E-LOTOS allows to specify constraints on the duration of actions and/or the instant(s) at which they may occur. Such features are required to describe isochronous protocols and real-time systems precisely, and many timed extensions of LOTOS have been proposed, e.g., ET-LOTOS [71,72] and RT-LOTOS [22].
- The behaviour part of E-LOTOS introduces a *n*-ary parallel operator [51] that generalizes the three binary parallel composition operators of LOTOS. This new operator is easier to use, more readable, and enables *m*-among-*n* synchronization (in particular, the 2-among-*n* synchronization of CCS).
- The behaviour part of E-LOTOS also introduces new operators, such as *rename* (which allows to change the name of observable actions and exceptions, to merge or split gates, and to add or remove offers from actions) and *suspend/resume* (which generalizes the "disable" operator of LOTOS by allowing resumable interrupts to be modelled).
- Finally, E-LOTOS provides *modules* that may contain types, functions, and/or processes. Modules can be imported and exported; they have *interfaces* for information hiding and can be *generic*.

Due to its new features resulting from multiple, sometimes conflicting influences, and despite the unification between functions and processes, E-LOTOS is a complex language, with an impressive number of semantic rules. The E-LOTOS standard has 120 pages (+80 pages of annexes), while the LOTOS standard has only 70 pages (+70 pages of annexes). It is therefore unclear whether E-LOTOS brings a satisfactory answer to the "steep learning curve" issue with LOTOS.

This probably explains why E-LOTOS only had a marginal impact in practice. Very few case studies have been done using E-LOTOS; one can mention [96,99] (which compares LOTOS and E-LOTOS on a common example), [21,24,92,93]. To our knowledge, E-LOTOS has never been implemented in software tools (except perhaps [24] or [74]) nor taught in university classes.

In some sense, the shift from LOTOS to E-LOTOS is reminiscent of the shift from Algol 60 to Algol 68: a simple, elegant, yet limited language was replaced by a larger, more expressive, formally defined language, which, because of its growth in complexity, failed to build a sufficient momentum of interest among its potential users.

6   LOTOS NT

6.1   Design of LOTOS NT

In 1997, when it became manifest that E-LOTOS was getting too large and too complex, INRIA Grenoble started investigating a fallback solution. This led to the design of LOTOS NT (where "NT" stands for "New Technology"), a simplified dialect of E-LOTOS that could be feasibly implemented and provide an actual replacement solution for LOTOS.

It was decided to not introduce in LOTOS NT some questionable features that significantly contribute to the complexity of E-LOTOS, among which: type synonyms, anonymous tuples (i.e., the possibility, borrowed from ML, that any list of values put between parentheses creates a new value having a valid, yet undeclared tuple type), extensible records, type equality relation based on structure equivalence (rather than name equivalence), subtyping relation based on record subtyping, etc.

For the same reasons, two features present in E-LOTOS but absent from LOTOS, the suspend-resume operator and the support for quantitative time, were not introduced in LOTOS NT, as it was felt that the potential applications of such features were already covered by competing formalisms such as timed automata [2] and were not worth the effort/impact ratio.

The formal definition of LOTOS NT (syntax, static semantics, and dynamic semantics) was given in [94]. Rationale for the design of LOTOS NT (and of E-LOTOS as well, since LOTOS NT influenced the latest evolutions of E-LOTOS) can be found in [50].

6.2   Implementation of LOTOS NT

To implement this language, a compiler named TRAIAN[2] [95] has been developed at INRIA Grenoble since 1997. It is built using the SYNTAX [7] and FNC-2 [63] compiler-generation tools designed at INRIA Rocquencourt. Unfortunately, FNC-2 ceased to be maintained in 1999, which prevented TRAIAN from being completed; as a consequence, TRAIAN only handles the data part of LOTOS NT (i.e., types and functions) but not the behaviour part (i.e., processes and channels).

As it is, TRAIAN performs lexical analysis, syntactic analysis, abstract syntax tree construction, static semantics analysis of LOTOS NT data specifications, and translates these into C programs, which can in turn be compiled and executed. TRAIAN has been regularly maintained and enhanced: ten releases have been issued since 1998, the latest version of TRAIAN (dated 2016) containing 55,500 lines of FNC-2 and C code.

6.3   Applications of LOTOS NT

Although TRAIAN only supports a fragment of LOTOS NT, it has useful applications in compiler construction. Our approach [44] consists in using the SYNTAX compiler generator for the lexical and syntactic analyses, together with LOTOS NT for semantical aspects, in particular the definition, construction, and traversals of abstract trees. Some involved parts of the compiler can be written directly in C if necessary, but most of the compiler is usually written in LOTOS NT, which is then translated into C code by TRAIAN.

---

[2] http://vasy.inria.fr/traian.

The combined use of SYNTAX, LOTOS NT, and TRAIAN proves to be satisfactory, as regards both the rapidity of development and the quality of resulting compilers. So far, twelve compilers have been developed at INRIA Grenoble using this approach: AAL [75], ATLANTIF [97], CHP2LOTOS [46], CTRL2BLK [76], EVALUATOR 4.0 [79], EXP.OPEN 2.0 [67], FSP2LOTOS [68], GRL2LNT [62], LNT2LOTOS [19], NTIF [43], PIC2LNT [77], and SVL [23,42,66].

7 LNT

7.1 Design of LNT

Because of the limitations of TRAIAN, LOTOS NT does not provide a replacement solution for LOTOS. The need for a better language based on process calculi remains [38,39], even if all prior attempts have failed to provide a usable solution.

In 2005, a new opportunity was found to progress this agenda: the Bull company was interested in using the CADP toolbox to formally verify multiprocessor architectures, but was reluctant to use LOTOS as a modelling language, mostly due to the verbosity of the LOTOS data part. To ease the writing of large specifications by Bull, still using the existing CADP tools, INRIA Grenoble undertook the development of a translator to convert LOTOS NT data types and functions into LOTOS ones. This made it possible to produce specifications combining a data part written in LOTOS NT (more concise and less error-prone than LOTOS) and a behaviour part written in LOTOS. The translator converted such composite specifications into plain LOTOS ones, which then could be analyzed by the CADP tools.

A first version of this translator was delivered to Bull in July 2005. Since then, the translator has been constantly improved and extended to handle new LOTOS NT features. In 2007, support for the behaviour part of LOTOS NT was added; this progressively removed the need for composite specifications, as it became possible to write entire specifications in LOTOS NT, with no LOTOS code at all.

Due to the rapid evolution of this translator, its input language gradually diverged from the original LOTOS NT implemented in TRAIAN, which remained quite stable in comparison. To avoid ambiguities, it was decided in 2014 to give this input language a new name ("LNT"), while reserving the name "LOTOS NT" for the language accepted by TRAIAN—such a distinction was not made in papers published before Spring 2014, in which LOTOS NT and LNT were used as synonyms.

The current definition of LNT is given in [19]. In a nutshell, LNT combines, in a single language with an Ada-like syntax designed to favour readability, selected features borrowed from imperative languages, functional languages, and value-passing process calculi:

– An LNT specification is a set of *modules*, each of which may import other modules and define *types*, *functions*, *channels*, and/or *processes*.

- A *type* is either predefined (namely, **bool**, **nat**, **int**, **real**, **char**, and **string**), defined by specifying the *free constructors* that generate its domain of values, or defined using the *type combinators* **array**, **list**, **range**, **set**, **sorted list**, **sorted set**, and **where** (the latter enabling predicate subtyping).
- A *function* is either predefined (namely, logical, arithmetical, and relational operations on predefined types), automatically generated for some user-defined type (such as free constructors, but also equality, order relations, field accessors and selectors, etc., which are generated if the user requests them), or have a handwritten definition provided by the user.
- A *channel* is a gate type that, following the ideas of [36], specifies the types of values to be sent or received during interactions on a given gate. There exist two special channels: **none**, which expresses that no value can be sent or received (this is useful for pure synchronization and exceptions), and **any**, which permits all values to be sent or received (this allows gates to be "untyped", as in LOTOS, thus ensuring backward compatibility).
- A *process* is a program fragment that, as in LOTOS and other process calculi, executes and communicates with its environment by sending and/or receiving values on a set of gates.

Globally, LNT has four different kinds of routines, of increasing complexity:

- A *constructor* has only **in** parameters (call by value), no explicit definition, and does not raise exceptions.
- A *pure function* has only **in** parameters, an implicit or explicit definition, and may raise exceptions if needed (this provides for partially-defined functions).
- A *procedural function* (or *procedure*, for short) may have **in**, **out** (call by result), or **in-out** (call by value-result) parameters; unlike constructors and pure functions, it does not necessarily return a result; it usually has an explicit definition and may raise exceptions.
- A *process* may also have **in**, **out**, or **in-out** parameters; it has an explicit definition, may raise exceptions [49], and interacts with its environment by means of gates. The key difference between processes and other routines is that the execution of processes can be nondeterministic and let time elapse (the execution semantics is that of process calculi and labelled transition systems) whereas the three former kinds of routines execute deterministically and atomically (the execution semantics is that of functional languages).

LNT possesses three main concepts for denoting computation:

- An *expression* corresponds to the usual notion of expression in imperative programming languages. It is an algebraic term built using constants, variables, and calls to constructors and pure functions. The evaluation of each expression is deterministic (it always returns the same result or raises the same exception), atomic (it is expected to terminate and take a negligible amount of time), and free from side effects (it does not modify variables).
- An *instruction* corresponds to the usual notion of statement in imperative programming languages. Instructions serve to explicitly define the bodies of

LNT functions. Basic instructions include: **null** (which does nothing), assignment to a variable or an array element, **return** of a function result, **raise** of an exception, procedure call, **assert**, etc. Instructions can be combined using structured-programming constructs, such as sequential composition, **if-then-else** conditionals, **case** with pattern matching, **for** and **while** loops, loops with **break** clauses, and declarations of variables with a limited scope. Because instructions manipulate and modify a store, the semantics of LNT relies on static analysis to prohibit all situations where uninitialized variables could be used; this way, instructions have an imperative-programming syntax and a functional-programming semantics. Like the evaluation of expressions, the execution of instructions is deterministic and atomic.

– A *behaviour* is the LNT equivalent of a LOTOS "behaviour expression". Behaviours serve to define the bodies of LNT processes. Behaviours can be seen as a superset of instructions since they contain all instructions (except **return**) but also include additional constructs specific to process calculi: **stop** (deadlock), communication on a gate (possibly with sending and/or receiving values), assignment of a non-deterministic value to a variable, process call, forever loop without **break** clause, non-deterministic choice (which is n-ary, rather than binary), parallel composition (which is n-ary and *graphical* [51], i.e., explicitly describes the communications/synchronizations between concurrent behaviours), gate hiding, and disruption (i.e., the "disable" operators of LOTOS). Unlike instructions, the execution of behaviours is nondeterministic, non-atomic, and may never terminate.

In the design of LNT, one main attainment is the integration in a single language of two very different models of computations: imperative/functional languages and process calculi. This was not the case with LOTOS, nor with its competitors Estelle and SDL, both of which clumsily amalgamate state machines with another formalism for data computation. Such a unification, which had been tried without success in E-LOTOS, is now effective in LNT. A key issue was the status of sequential composition [40], which led to question and discard some well-established habits of process calculi, especially the action-prefix operator of CCS and LOTOS, and the use of dynamic semantics in place of static semantics.

7.2   Implementation of LNT

Contrary to the four aforementioned languages (Extended-LOTOS, Modular LOTOS, E-LOTOS, and LOTOS NT), the definition and implementation of which were planned as two successive steps (the latter being never undertaken or never completed), LNT was designed in a radically different way, using an "agile" approach. Every new language feature was first implemented and assessed on a growing base of non-regression tests before being adopted for LNT.

Initially designed as a standalone tool, the translator from LNT to LOTOS became an integral part of the CADP toolbox in 2010. Actually, this translator is not one single tool, but comprises three complementary tools:

- LPP[3] ("LNT PreProcessor") is a small translator (2000 lines of C and Lex code) that expands the user-friendly LNT notations for literal constants (numbers, characters, strings, etc.) into algebraic terms making use of predefined LOTOS sorts and operations defined in custom libraries.
- LNT2LOTOS[4] is a rather complex translator developed using the aforementioned SYNTAX/TRAIAN technology (3800 lines of SYNTAX code, 35,500 lines of LOTOS NT, and 2900 lines of C code). LNT2LOTOS translates an LNT specification into LOTOS code, possibly augmented with some little C code fragments.
- LNT.OPEN[5] is a small utility (400 lines of shell script) that provides a top-level entry point for processing LNT specifications with the CADP tools and, more specifically, with the CÆSAR.ADT [35] and CÆSAR [48] compilers for LOTOS, and the OPEN/CÆSAR framework [37] for simulation, verification, and testing. Taking as input an LNT specification and an OPEN/CÆSAR application program, LNT.OPEN first translates (the various modules composing) the LNT specification into LOTOS by calling LPP and LNT2LOTOS, then compiles the generated LOTOS specification by calling CÆSAR.ADT and CÆSAR, and finally invokes the OPEN/CÆSAR application program to explore and analyze the corresponding state space on the fly.

Without exposing in full detail the algorithms implemented in LNT2LOTOS, these are some key principles underlying the translation:

- The main guideline is to keep the translation as simple as possible, so as to swiftly upgrade the translator each time the definition of LNT evolves. Consequently, duplication of work between the translator and the LOTOS compilers is avoided, meaning that the translator does not implement certain static semantics checks at the LNT level if the same checks are later performed at the LOTOS level. In particular, the translator makes no attempt to infer and check the types of LNT value expressions, deferring these tasks to the LOTOS compilers operating on the generated code.
- The channels used for typing LNT gates raise a specific problem because, on the one hand, the LNT2LOTOS translator is not intended to perform type checking and, on the other hand, LNT gates, which are typed, are translated into LOTOS gates, which are untyped, so that type-checking errors at the LNT level cannot be detected at the LOTOS level. To address this problem, LNT2LOTOS generates, for each LNT channel C, one or several overloaded LOTOS constant functions f_C, which take as parameters the expected typed values specified for C and always return true. For each LNT action involving some gate G whose channel is C, a LOTOS Boolean guard is generated, which invokes function f_C with the input or output offers of the action, thus expressing in LOTOS the type-checking constraints arising from the definition of C. If the action is not well-typed at the LNT level, the corresponding

---

[3] http://cadp.inria.fr/man/lpp.html.

[4] http://cadp.inria.fr/man/lnt2lotos.html.

[5] http://cadp.inria.fr/man/lnt.open.html.

guard will provoke at the LOTOS level a type-checking error at compile time; otherwise, the guard will evaluate to true at run time.

- The LNT2LOTOS translator performs, on LNT functions and processes, static analyses not done at the LOTOS level; for instance, it rejects (or warns about) unused variables, variables used without being assigned before, variables assigned but never used, variables shared between concurrent processes, etc. Such checks are either required by the LNT semantics (see [40] for a discussion) or suitable to ensure that LNT specifications remain as simple as possible, so as to increase readability and efficiency of verification.

- The predefined types of LNT (**bool**, **nat**, etc.) are implemented using base libraries written in LOTOS and C code. The user-defined types (built using free constructors or type combinators) are translated into LOTOS abstract data types (possibly with some additional C code meant for efficiency), together with their associated functions (equality, order relations, field accessors and selectors, etc.).

- Although, in LNT, user-defined functions and processes have the same functional/imperative style and share many constructs (e.g., assignments, **assert**, **raise**, **if-then-else**, pattern-matching **case**, **for** and **while** loops, loops with **break**, etc.), the two algorithms that translate, respectively, these functions and processes into LOTOS are very different, due to the fundamental asymmetry, in the target language, between the data part (based on abstract data types) and the behaviour part (based on process calculi).

- Our algorithm for translating LNT functions generalizes the one proposed in [88], which translates into Horn clauses a small subset of C functions with only integer and list types. Our algorithm translates LNT functions into LOTOS (non-constructor) operations, which are defined using algebraic equations considered as conditional term-rewrite rules. The translation takes advantage of the rewrite strategy implemented in the CÆSAR.ADT compiler, which assumes a decreasing priority between equations. Notice that each LNT function having **out** parameters (call by result) or **in-out** parameters (call by value-result) translates to several LOTOS functions. The translation of certain LNT constructs (**assert**, **case**, and loops) also generates auxiliary LOTOS functions.

- Our algorithm for translating LNT processes takes its roots in our prior works on the translation to LOTOS of three modelling languages for hardware and software systems: the CHP2LOTOS translator [46] for CHP, the FLAC translator [4] for Fiacre, and the FSP2LOTOS translator [68] for FSP. The algorithm is involved, but four main points are worth being highlighted.

(i) Certain behavioural LNT constructs directly map to equivalent LOTOS ones. For instance, each LNT gate translates to a corresponding LOTOS gate and each LNT process translates to a corresponding LOTOS process. The algorithm benefits from the fact that both LOTOS and LNT have an *action-based* (rather than *state-based*) semantics and share a common semantic model (namely, labelled transition systems). Thanks to action-based semantics, the translation can freely introduce auxiliary LOTOS processes and variables, still preserving the semantic model (which would not be possible with state-based semantics); in particular, execution traces are identical at the LOTOS and LNT levels, which avoids the usual need for a reverse translation of diagnostics from the target to the source level.

(ii) Certain behavioural LNT constructs are too powerful to be expressed using only the behaviour part of LOTOS; for such constructs, the data part of LOTOS must also be used, by generating auxiliary sorts, operations, and algebraic equations. For instance, the **case** construct present in LNT processes is translated using both the behaviour part of LOTOS (nondeterministic choice and Boolean guards are used to express the selection between the various **case** branches) and the data part of LOTOS (equations, considered as rewrite rules, are used to express pattern matching, which is not supported by the behaviour part of LOTOS).

(iii) An involved part of the algorithm translates the LNT parallel composition operator, which is n-ary, into an algebraic combination of LOTOS parallel composition operators, which are binary. Such a translation does not always succeed, meaning that certain network topologies specified in LNT cannot be expressed in LOTOS [51]; however, we never faced this problem in real-life case studies. Also, it was not possible to introduce in LNT the concept of n-among-m synchronization proposed in [51], because it is not supported in LOTOS; such a limitation is more annoying in practice, e.g., for the specification of Web services, which quite often require 2-among-m synchronization.

(iv) Another involved part of the algorithm translates the LNT sequential composition operator (which is unique, symmetric, atomic, and lets all values of variables assigned on its left-hand side flow implicitly to its right-hand side [40]) into one of the two LOTOS sequential composition operators, either the action-prefix operator (which is asymmetric, atomic, and lets variable values flow implicitly from its left- to its right-hand side) or the "enable" operator (which is symmetric, non-atomic as it generates a τ-transition, and forbids variable values to flow from its left- to its right-hand side except if these variables are explicitly listed in an **accept** clause). Following the principles set for the CHP2LOTOS translator [46], we chose to generate action prefix as much as possible and "enable" only when unavoidable, which produces better LOTOS code at the expense of a more involved translation. To fight state-space explosion and preserve strong equivalence between the LNT and LOTOS specifications, we slightly deviated from LOTOS semantics by adding a special pragma "(*! atomic *)" that instructs the LOTOS compiler not to generate a τ-transition when implementing the "enable" operator. There are many other algorithmic subtleties, such as the creation of auxiliary "continuation" processes for those LNT behaviours following loops and conditionals (i.e., **case**, **if**, and **select**), the translation of parallel composition occurring on the left-hand side of sequential composition where each parallel branch computes the values of different variables, the translation of **out** and **in-out** parameters of LNT processes into **exit** results returned by LOTOS processes, the need to respect the strict typing rules set by LOTOS "functionality" constraints, the optimization of tail-recursive process instantiations, etc.

In addition to the above tools, which ultimately translate an LNT specification into a sequential C program, there also exists a compiler named DLC ("Distributed LNT Compiler") [31,32] that translates an LNT specification into a set of C programs executing concurrently and communicating through TCP sockets; to produce such a distributed implementation, the DLC compiler exploits the concurrent architecture defined by the parallel composition operators present in the LNT specification.

7.3   Applications of LNT

The usability of the LNT language gradually increased with the progress of its translator to LOTOS. As of mid-2009, this translator was sufficiently complete and robust to allow a total shift from LOTOS to LNT at INRIA Grenoble, where no LOTOS code has been manually written since then, LNT being now the preferred high-level language for modelling concurrent systems and analyzing them using the CADP tools.

At Grenoble INP and Université Grenoble-Alpes, LNT has also replaced LOTOS to teach master students the fundamentals of concurrency theory. We observed that LNT enables students to better focus on high-level concepts, rather than getting lost in low-level details of LOTOS syntax and static semantics.

The LNT language and its tools have been used for many case studies, at INRIA Grenoble and in other academic or industrial labs as well (we only mention those not affiliated with the authors' institutions):

- *Avionics*: verification of an equipment failure management protocol[6] and of a ground-plane communication protocol[7] [52,98] provided by Airbus;
- *Cloud computing*: verification of self-configuration protocols[8] [27] (Orange Labs), of the Synergy reconfiguration protocol for component-based systems[9] [8], and of dynamic management protocol for cloud applications[10] [1];
- *Distributed algorithms*: verification and performance evaluation of mutual exclusion protocols[11] [78], verification of multiway synchronization protocols[12] [28,30,32], specification and rapid prototyping of Stanford's RAFT distributed consensus algorithm[13] [29,32], and performance evaluation of concurrent data structures[14] [102] (RWTH Aachen, Germany and Chinese Academy of Sciences, Beijing, China);
- *Hardware design*: formal analysis and co-simulation of a dynamic task dispatcher[15] [69] (STMicroelectronics), formal analysis of ARM's ACE cache

---

[6] http://cadp.inria.fr/case-studies/09-k-failure-management.html.
[7] http://cadp.inria.fr/case-studies/09-h-tftp.html.
[8] http://cadp.inria.fr/case-studies/11-i-selfconfig.html.
[9] http://cadp.inria.fr/case-studies/11-h-synergy.html.
[10] http://cadp.inria.fr/case-studies/13-g-dynamic-management.html.
[11] http://cadp.inria.fr/case-studies/10-f-mutex.html.
[12] http://cadp.inria.fr/case-studies/13-d-multiway.html.
[13] http://cadp.inria.fr/case-studies/15-g-raft.html.
[14] http://cadp.inria.fr/case-studies/16-b-concurrent.html.
[15] http://cadp.inria.fr/case-studies/11-g-dtd.html.

coherency protocol[16] [64,65] (STMicroelectronics), verification and rapid prototyping of an asynchronous model of the Data Encryption Standard[17] [91], verification of a fault-tolerant routing algorithm for a network-on-chip[18] [103] (University of Utah, USA);

- *Human-computer interaction*: specification and validation of graphical user interfaces for a prototype control room of a nuclear power plant[19] [85] and of plastic user interfaces exploiting domain ontologies[20] [20] (Toulouse, France);
- *Industrial systems*: model-based testing of the CANopen field bus and EnergyBus architecture[21] [53] (Saarland University, Germany), formal specification and rapid prototyping of a software controller for a metal processing plant[22] [47].

Another indication of the practical usefulness of LNT is given by its use as a target language in a growing number of translators, which implement various languages by translating them to LNT. Indeed, LNT suitably replaces LOTOS for automatically-generated code as well as for handwritten code, since the translation to LNT is much easier than the translation to LOTOS, and because it is now preferable to let the LNT2LOTOS translator take in charge all algorithmic subtleties required to produce valid and efficient LOTOS code. We are aware of the following tools (again, we do not mention the authors' institutions):

- The BPMN2Py/Py2LNT translators[23] [55,86] for analyzing choreographies of Web services specified in WS-CDL (Université de Nantes, France);
- The CMT translator [73] for the BPEL/WSDL specification languages for Web services (Tsinghua University, Beijing, China and MIT, Cambridge, MA, USA), and another, more complete algorithm for translating BPEL/WDSL/Xpath/XML Schema to LNT [98];
- The DFTCalc tool[24] [3,54] for Dynamic Fault Trees (University of Twente, The Netherlands);
- The EB³2LNT translator[25] [100] for the EB³ specification language for information systems (Université Paris Est, France);
- The GRL2LNT translator[26] [62] for the GRL specification language for GALS (*Globally Asynchronous Locally Synchronous*) systems;
- The OCARINA tool[27] [84] for the AADL architecture description language (ISAE, Toulouse, France and University of Sfax, Tunisia);

---

[16] http://cadp.inria.fr/case-studies/13-e-ace.html.
[17] http://cadp.inria.fr/case-studies/15-f-des.html.
[18] http://cadp.inria.fr/case-studies/13-f-utahnoc.html.
[19] http://cadp.inria.fr/case-studies/14-d-hmi.html.
[20] http://cadp.inria.fr/case-studies/15-d-plastic-user-interfaces.html.
[21] http://cadp.inria.fr/case-studies/14-c-energybus.html.
[22] http://cadp.inria.fr/case-studies/17-a-production-cell.html.
[23] http://cadp.inria.fr/software/12-e-choreography.html.
[24] http://cadp.inria.fr/software/12-i-dftcalc.html.
[25] http://cadp.inria.fr/software/13-a-eb3.html.
[26] http://cadp.inria.fr/software/14-c-grl.html.
[27] http://cadp.inria.fr/software/15-b-ocarina.html.

- The PIC2LNT translator[28] [77] for the applied π-calculus (an extension of the π-calculus with typed data values);
- the VBPMN translator[29] [87] for the BPMN language for describing business processes (Université Paris Ouest, France).

8 Conclusion

Computer systems handling asynchronous concurrency are inherently complex and cannot be reliably designed without adequate specification languages supported by sound analysis tools. Ed Brinksma contributed to this agenda in two significant ways: (i) by leading the definition and standardization of the LOTOS language, which exposed the key ideas of process calculi to a large audience and sparkled considerable interest in academia and industry; (ii) by sending a clear signal that LOTOS, despite its qualities, was not the end of the road and that further enhancements were possible and desirable.

The present paper provided a retrospective account of the evolution of the LOTOS-based family of specification languages, starting from LOTOS itself, reviewing the successive proposals for enhancing LOTOS (Extended LOTOS, Modular LOTOS, E-LOTOS, and LOTOS NT), and ending with LNT, the most recent descendent, which preserves the most valuable ideas of process calculi but entirely modifies the shape of the language to make it compatible with mainstream programming languages. The feedback acquired by using LNT for the design of complex industrial systems suggests that LNT provides a viable and effective replacement for LOTOS. Quoting STMicroelectronics engineers: "Although modeling the [Dynamic Task Dispatcher] in a classical formal specification language, such as LOTOS, is theoretically possible, using LNT made the development of a formal model practically feasible" [69].

Concerning future work, we can highlight two main research directions:

- The LNT language is not yet frozen and can still be further enhanced. For instance, the unification of exceptions across functions and processes is almost complete. We now consider equipping processes with optional **return** behaviours, so that functions become a strict subset of processes. We also plan to introduce, beyond assertions that already exist in LNT, pre-conditions, post-conditions, and loop invariants that would allow the application of mainstream theorem provers and static analyzers to LNT specifications.
- The current implementation of LNT by translation to LOTOS is justified by the reuse of existing LOTOS tools. It is intellectually challenging, but sometimes overly complex: for instance, LNT functions, written in a functional/imperative style, are first translated to LOTOS algebraic equations, and then compiled back to imperative C code. A native implementation of LNT would certainly be simpler and more efficient; it would also overcome

---

[28] http://cadp.inria.fr/software/13-d-pic2lnt.html.
[29] http://cadp.inria.fr/software/16-a-vbpmn.html.

certain LOTOS limitations that currently prevent useful constructs, such as the **trap** operator for exception catching [49] and the n-among-m synchronization pattern in parallel composition [51], from being added to LNT.

References

1. Abid, R., Salaün, G., Bongiovanni, F., De Palma, N.: Verification of a dynamic management protocol for cloud applications. In: Van Hung, D., Ogawa, M. (eds.) ATVA 2013. LNCS, vol. 8172, pp. 178–192. Springer, Cham (2013). doi:10.1007/978-3-319-02444-8_14

2. Alur, R., Dill, D.L.: A theory of timed automata. Theor. Comput. Sci. **126**(2), 183–235 (1994)

3. Arnold, F., Belinfante, A., Van der Berg, F., Guck, D., Stoelinga, M.: DFTCalc: a tool for efficient fault tree analysis. In: Bitsch, F., Guiochet, J., Kaâniche, M. (eds.) SAFECOMP 2013. LNCS, vol. 8153, pp. 293–301. Springer, Heidelberg (2013). doi:10.1007/978-3-642-40793-2_27

4. Berthomieu, B., Bodeveix, J.P., Farail, P., Filali, M., Garavel, H., Gaufillet, P., Lang, F., Vernadat, F.: FIACRE: an intermediate language for model verification in the TOPCASED environment. In: Laprie, J.C. (ed.) Proceedings of the 4th European Congress on Embedded Real-Time Software (ERTS 2008), Toulouse, France, January 2008

5. Berthomieu, B., Le Sergent, T.: Programming with behaviors in an ML framework — the syntax and semantics of LCS. In: Sannella, D. (ed.) ESOP 1994. LNCS, vol. 788, pp. 89–104. Springer, Heidelberg (1994). doi:10.1007/3-540-57880-3_6

6. Bolognesi, T., Brinksma, E.: Introduction to the ISO specification language LOTOS. Comput. Netw. ISDN Syst. **14**(1), 25–59 (1988)

7. Boullier, P., Jourdan, M.: A new error repair and recovery scheme for lexical and syntactic analysis. Sci. Comput. Program. **9**(3), 271–286 (1987)

8. Boyer, F., Gruber, O., Salaün, G.: Specifying and verifying the SYNERGY reconfiguration protocol with LOTOS NT and CADP. In: Butler, M., Schulte, W. (eds.) FM 2011. LNCS, vol. 6664, pp. 103–117. Springer, Heidelberg (2011). doi:10.1007/978-3-642-21437-0_10

9. Brinksma, E., Leih, G.: Enhancements of LOTOS. In: Bolognesi, T., Lagemaat, J., Vissers, C. (eds.) LOTOSphere: Software Development with LOTOS, pp. 453–466. Kluwer Academic Publishers, Dordrecht (1995)

10. Brinksma, E.: A tutorial on LOTOS. In: Diaz, M. (ed.) Proceedings of the 5th IFIP International Workshop on Protocol Specification, Testing and Verification (PSTV 1885), Moissac, France, pp. 171–194. North-Holland, Amsterdam, June 1985

11. Brinksma, E.: On the design of Extended LOTOS - a specification language for open distributed systems. Ph.D. thesis, University of Twente, November 1988

12. Brinksma, E.: Constraint-oriented specification in a constructive formal description technique. In: de Bakker, J.W., de Roever, W.-P., Rozenberg, G. (eds.) REX 1989. LNCS, vol. 430, pp. 130–152. Springer, Heidelberg (1990). doi:10.1007/3-540-52559-9_63

13. Brinksma, E.: Task 1.4 Deliverable on Language Enhancements, LOTOSphere (ESPRIT Projet 2304) Document ref. Lo/WP1/T1.4/N0016/V3, 146 p., April 1992

14. Brinksma, E., Karjoth, G.: A specification of the OSI transport service in LOTOS. In: Yemini, Y., Strom, R.E., Yemini, S. (eds.) Proceedings of the 4th IFIP International Workshop on Protocol Specification, Testing and Verification, Skytop Lodge, PA, USA, pp. 227–251. North-Holland, Amsterdam, June 1984

15. Brinksma, E., Katoen, J.P., Langerak, R., Latella, D.: A stochastic causality-based process algebra. Comput. J. **38**(7), 552–565 (1995)

16. Brinksma, E., Tretmans, J., Verhaard, L.: A framework for test selection. In: Jonsson, B., Parrow, J., Pehrson, B. (eds.) Proceedings of the IFIP WG6.1 9th International Symposium on Protocol Specification, Testing and Verification, Stockholm, Sweden. pp. 233–248. North-Holland, Amsterdam, June 1991

17. Brookes, S.D., Hoare, C.A.R., Roscoe, A.W.: A theory of communicating sequential processes. J. ACM **31**(3), 560–599 (1984)

18. CCITT: Specification and Description Language. Recommendation Z.100, International Consultative Committee for Telephony and Telegraphy, Geneva, March 1988

19. Champelovier, D., Clerc, X., Garavel, H., Guerte, Y., McKinty, C., Powazny, V., Lang, F., Serwe, W., Smeding, G.: Reference Manual of the LNT to LOTOS Translator (Version 6.7), INRIA, Grenoble, France, July 2017

20. Chebieb, A., Ameur, Y.A.: Formal verification of plastic user interfaces exploiting domain ontologies. In: Zhiqiu, H., Jun, S. (eds.) Proceedings of the International Symposium on Theoretical Aspects of Software Engineering (TASE 2015), Nanjing, China, pp. 79–86. IEEE Computer Society, Washington, D.C. (2015)

21. Clark, R.G., Moreira, A.: Use of E-LOTOS in adding formality to UML. J. Univers. Comput. Sci. **6**(11), 1071–1087 (2000)

22. Courtiat, J., Santos, C.A.S., Lohr, C., Outtaj, B.: Experience with RT-LOTOS, a temporal extension of the LOTOS formal description technique. Comput. Commun. **23**(12), 1104–1123 (2000)

23. Crouzen, P., Lang, F.: Smart reduction. In: Giannakopoulou, D., Orejas, F. (eds.) FASE 2011. LNCS, vol. 6603, pp. 111–126. Springer, Heidelberg (2011). doi:10. 1007/978-3-642-19811-3_9

24. de Souza, W.L., et al.: Design of distributed multimedia applications (DAMD). In: Hutter, D., Stephan, W., Traverso, P., Ullmann, M. (eds.) FM-Trends 1998. LNCS, vol. 1641, pp. 77–91. Springer, Heidelberg (1999). doi:10.1007/ 3-540-48257-1_4

25. Ehrig, H., Fey, W., Hansen, H.: An algebraic specification language with two levels of semantics. Bericht No. 83-03, Fachbereich 20-Informatik, Technische Universität Berlin (1983)

26. Ehrig, H., Mahr, B.: Fundamentals of Algebraic Specification 1: Equations and Initial Semantics. EATCS Monographs on Theoretical Computer Science, vol. 6. Springer, Heidelberg (1985). doi:10.1007/978-3-642-69962-7

27. Etchevers, X., Salaün, G., Boyer, F., Coupaye, T., Palma, N.D.: Reliable self-deployment of distributed cloud applications. Softw. Pract. Exp. **47**(1), 3–20 (2017)

28. Evrard, H.: Génération automatique d'implémentation distribuée à partir de modèles formels de processus concurrents asynchrones. Thèse de Doctorat, Université de Grenoble, July 2015

29. Evrard, H.: DLC: compiling a concurrent system formal specification to a distributed implementation. In: Chechik, M., Raskin, J.-F. (eds.) TACAS 2016. LNCS, vol. 9636, pp. 553–559. Springer, Heidelberg (2016). doi:10.1007/ 978-3-662-49674-9_34

30. Evrard, H., Lang, F.: Formal verification of distributed branching multiway synchronization protocols. In: Beyer, D., Boreale, M. (eds.) FMOODS/FORTE - 2013. LNCS, vol. 7892, pp. 146–160. Springer, Heidelberg (2013). doi:10.1007/978-3-642-38592-6_11

31. Evrard, H., Lang, F.: Automatic distributed code generation from formal models of asynchronous concurrent processes. In: Aldinucci, M., Daneshtalab, M., Leppänen, V., Lilius, J. (eds.) Proceedings of the 23rd Euromicro International Conference on Parallel, Distributed and Network-based Processing - Special Session on Formal Approaches to Parallel and Distributed Systems (PDP/4PAD 2015), Turku, Finland, pp. 459–466. IEEE Computer Society Press, Washington, D.C., March 2015

32. Evrard, H., Lang, F.: Automatic distributed code generation from formal models of asynchronous processes interacting by multiway rendezvous. J. Log. Algebr. Methods Program. **88**, 121–153 (2017)

33. Garavel, H.: Utilisation du système CESAR pour la vérification de protocoles spécifiés en LOTOS. Rapport SPECTRE C2, Laboratoire de Génie Informatique - Institut IMAG, Grenoble, December 1986

34. Garavel, H.: Vérification de programmes LOTOS à l'aide du système QUASAR. Master's thesis, Institut National Polytechnique de Grenoble, September 1986

35. Garavel, H.: Compilation of LOTOS abstract data types. In: Vuong, S.T. (ed.) Proceedings of the 2nd International Conference on Formal Description Techniques FORTE 1989, Vancouver BC, Canada, pp. 147–162. North-Holland, Amsterdam, December 1989

36. Garavel, H.: On the introduction of gate typing in E-LOTOS. In: Dembinski, P., Sredniawa, M. (eds.) Proceedings of the 15th IFIP International Workshop on Protocol Specification, Testing and Verification (PSTV 1995), Warsaw, Poland, pp. 283–298. Chapman & Hall, New York, June 1995

37. Garavel, H.: OPEN/CÆSAR: an open software architecture for verification, simulation, and testing. In: Steffen, B. (ed.) TACAS 1998. LNCS, vol. 1384, pp. 68–84. Springer, Heidelberg (1998). doi:10.1007/BFb0054165

38. Garavel, H.: Défense et illustration des algèbres de processus. In: Mammeri, Z. (ed.) Actes de l'Ecole d'été Temps Réel ETR 2003, Toulouse, France. Institut de Recherche en Informatique de Toulouse, September 2003

39. Garavel, H.: Reflections on the future of concurrency theory in general and process calculi in particular. In: Palamidessi, C., Valencia, F.D. (eds.) Proceedings of the LIX Colloquium on Emerging Trends in Concurrency Theory, Ecole Polytechnique de Paris, France, 13–15 November 2006. Electronic Notes in Theoretical Computer Science, vol. 209, pp. 149–164. Elsevier Science Publishers, Amsterdam, April 2008. Also available as INRIA Research Report RR-6368

40. Garavel, H.: Revisiting sequential composition in process calculi. J. Log. Algebr. Methods Program. **84**(6), 742–762 (2015)

41. Garavel, H., Hermanns, H.: On combining functional verification and performance evaluation using CADP. In: Eriksson, L.-H., Lindsay, P.A. (eds.) FME 2002. LNCS, vol. 2391, pp. 410–429. Springer, Heidelberg (2002). doi:10.1007/3-540-45614-7_23

42. Garavel, H., Lang, F.: SVL: a scripting language for compositional verification. In: Kim, M., Chin, B., Kang, S., Lee, D. (eds.) FORTE 2001. IIFIP, vol. 69, pp. 377–392. Kluwer Academic Publishers, Dordrecht (2002). doi:10.1007/0-306-47003-9_24

43. Garavel, H., Lang, F.: NTIF: a general symbolic model for communicating sequential processes with data. In: Peled, D.A., Vardi, M.Y. (eds.) FORTE 2002. LNCS, vol. 2529, pp. 276–291. Springer, Heidelberg (2002). doi:10.1007/3-540-36135-9_18

44. Garavel, H., Lang, F., Mateescu, R.: Compiler construction using LOTOS NT. In: Horspool, R.N. (ed.) CC 2002. LNCS, vol. 2304, pp. 9–13. Springer, Heidelberg (2002). doi:10.1007/3-540-45937-5_3

45. Garavel, H., Lang, F., Mateescu, R., Serwe, W.: CADP 2011: a toolbox for the construction and analysis of distributed processes. Int. J. Softw. Tools Technol. Transf. (STTT) 15(2), 89–107 (2013). Springer

46. Garavel, H., Salaün, G., Serwe, W.: On the semantics of communicating hardware processes and their translation into LOTOS for the verification of asynchronous circuits with CADP. Sci. Comput. Program. 74(3), 100–127 (2009)

47. Garavel, H., Serwe, W.: The unheralded value of the multiway rendezvous: illustration with the production cell benchmark. In: Hermanns, H., Höfner, P. (eds.) Proceedings of the 2nd Workshop on Models for Formal Analysis of Real Systems (MARS 2017), Uppsala, Sweden, vol. 244, pp. 230–270. Electronic Proceedings in Theoretical Computer Science, April 2017

48. Garavel, H., Sifakis, J.: Compilation and verification of LOTOS specifications. In: Logrippo, L., Probert, R.L., Ural, H. (eds.) Proceedings of the 10th IFIP International Symposium on Protocol Specification, Testing and Verification (PSTV 1990), Ottawa, Canada, pp. 379–394. North-Holland, Amsterdam, June 1990

49. Garavel, H., Sighireanu, M.: On the introduction of exceptions in LOTOS. In: Gotzhein, R., Bredereke, J. (eds.) Proceedings of the IFIP Joint International Conference on Formal Description Techniques for Distributed Systems and Communication Protocols, and Protocol Specification, Testing, and Verification (FORTE/PSTV 1996), Kaiserslautern, Germany, pp. 469–484. Chapman & Hall, New York, October 1996

50. Garavel, H., Sighireanu, M.: Towards a second generation of formal description techniques - rationale for the design of E-LOTOS. In: Groote, J.F., Luttik, B., Wamel, J. (eds.) Proceedings of the 3rd International Workshop on Formal Methods for Industrial Critical Systems (FMICS 1998), Amsterdam, The Netherlands, pp. 187–230. CWI, Amsterdam, May 1998. Invited lecture

51. Garavel, H., Sighireanu, M.: A graphical parallel composition operator for process algebras. In: Wu, J., Chanson, S.T., Gao, Q. (eds.) Formal Methods for Protocol Engineering and Distributed Systems. IAICT, vol. 28, pp. 185–202. Kluwer Academic Publishers, Dordrecht (1999)

52. Garavel, H., Thivolle, D.: Verification of GALS systems by combining synchronous languages and process calculi. In: Păsăreanu, C.S. (ed.) SPIN 2009. LNCS, vol. 5578, pp. 241–260. Springer, Heidelberg (2009). doi:10.1007/978-3-642-02652-2_20

53. Graf-Brill, A., Hermanns, H., Garavel, H.: A model-based certification framework for the EnergyBus standard. In: Ábrahám, E., Palamidessi, C. (eds.) FORTE 2014. LNCS, vol. 8461, pp. 84–99. Springer, Heidelberg (2014). doi:10.1007/978-3-662-43613-4_6

54. Guck, D., Spel, J., Stoelinga, M.: DFTCalc: reliability centered maintenance via fault tree analysis (tool paper). In: Butler, M., Conchon, S., Zaïdi, F. (eds.) ICFEM 2015. LNCS, vol. 9407, pp. 304–311. Springer, Cham (2015). doi:10.1007/978-3-319-25423-4_19

55. Güdemann, M., Salaün, G., Ouederni, M.: Counterexample guided synthesis of monitors for realizability enforcement. In: Chakraborty, S., Mukund, M. (eds.)

ATVA 2012. LNCS, vol. 7561, pp. 238–253. Springer, Heidelberg (2012). doi:10. 1007/978-3-642-33386-6_20

56. Huecas, G., Llana-Díaz, L., Quemada, J., Robles, T., Verdejo, A.: Process calculi: E-LOTOS. In: Bowman, H., Derrick, J. (eds.) Formal Methods for Distributed Processing: A Survey of Object-Oriented Approaches, pp. 77–104. Cambridge University Press, Cambridge (2001)

57. Huecas, G., Llana-Díaz, L., Robles, T., Verdejo, A.: E-LOTOS: an overview. In: Marsan, M.A., Quemada, J., Robles, T., Silva, M. (eds.) Proceedings of the Workshop on Formal Methods and Telecommunications (WFMT'99), Zaragoza, Spain, pp. 94–102. Prensas Universitarias de Zaragoza, September 1999

58. ISO/IEC: LOTOS - A Formal Description Technique Based on the Temporal Ordering of Observational Behaviour. Draft International Standard 8807, International Organization for Standardization - Information Processing Systems - Open Systems Interconnection, Geneva, July 1987

59. ISO/IEC: ESTELLE - A Formal Description Technique Based on an Extended State Transition Model. International Standard 9074, International Organization for Standardization - Information Processing Systems - Open Systems Interconnection, Geneva, September 1988

60. ISO/IEC: LOTOS - A Formal Description Technique Based on the Temporal Ordering of Observational Behaviour. International Standard 8807, International Organization for Standardization - Information Processing Systems - Open Systems Interconnection, Geneva, September 1989

61. ISO/IEC: Enhancements to LOTOS (E-LOTOS). International Standard 15437:2001, International Organization for Standardization - Information Technology, Geneva, September 2001

62. Jebali, F., Lang, F., Mateescu, R.: Formal modelling and verification of GALS systems using GRL and CADP. Formal Asp. Comput. **28**(5), 767–804 (2016)

63. Jourdan, M., Parigot, D.: Application development with the FNC-2 attribute grammar system. In: Hammer, D. (ed.) CC 1990. LNCS, vol. 477, pp. 11–25. Springer, Heidelberg (1991). doi:10.1007/3-540-53669-8_71

64. Kriouile, A., Serwe, W.: Formal analysis of the ACE specification for cache coherent systems-on-chip. In: Pecheur, C., Dierkes, M. (eds.) FMICS 2013. LNCS, vol. 8187, pp. 108–122. Springer, Heidelberg (2013). doi:10.1007/978-3-642-41010-9_8

65. Kriouile, A., Serwe, W.: Using a formal model to improve verification of a cache-coherent system-on-chip. In: Baier, C., Tinelli, C. (eds.) TACAS 2015. LNCS, vol. 9035, pp. 708–722. Springer, Heidelberg (2015). doi:10.1007/ 978-3-662-46681-0_62

66. Lang, F.: Compositional verification using SVL scripts. In: Katoen, J.-P., Stevens, P. (eds.) TACAS 2002. LNCS, vol. 2280, pp. 465–469. Springer, Heidelberg (2002). doi:10.1007/3-540-46002-0_33

67. Lang, F.: Exp.Open 2.0: a flexible tool integrating partial order, compositional, and on-the-fly verification methods. In: Romijn, J., Smith, G., van de Pol, J. (eds.) IFM 2005. LNCS, vol. 3771, pp. 70–88. Springer, Heidelberg (2005). doi:10. 1007/11589976_6. Full version available as INRIA Research Report RR-5673

68. Lang, F., Salaün, G., Hérilier, R., Kramer, J., Magee, J.: Translating FSP into LOTOS and networks of automata. Formal Asp. Comput. **22**(6), 681–711 (2010)

69. Lantreibecq, E., Serwe, W.: Formal analysis of a hardware dynamic task dispatcher with CADP. Sci. Comput. Program. **80**(Part A), 130–149 (2014)

70. Leduc, G., Jeffrey, A., Sighireanu, M.: Introduction à E-LOTOS. In: Cavalli, A. (ed.) Ingénierie des protocoles et qualité de service. Collection IC2, chap. 6, pp. 213–253. Hermès, Paris (2001)

71. Léonard, L., Leduc, G.: An introduction to ET-LOTOS for the description of time-sensitive systems. Comput. Netw. ISDN Syst. **29**(3), 271–292 (1997)
72. Léonard, L., Leduc, G.: A formal definition of time in LOTOS. Formal Asp. Comput. **10**(3), 248–266 (1998)
73. Li, X., Madnick, S., Zhu, H., Fan, Y.: Improving data quality for web services composition. In: Proceedings of the 7th International Workshop on Quality in Databases (QDB 2009), Lyon, France, August 2009
74. Massetto, F.I., de Souza, W.L., Zorzo, S.D.: Simulator for E-LOTOS specifications. In: Proceedings of the 35th Annual Simulation Symposium (SS 2002), San Diego, California, USA, pp. 389–394. IEEE Computer Society, Washington, D.C., April 2002
75. Mateescu, R.: A generic framework for model checking software architectures. In: Augusto, J.C., Ultes-Nitsche, U. (eds.) Proceedings of the 2nd International Workshop on Verification and Validation of Enterprise Information Systems (VVEIS 2004), Porto, Portugal. INSTICC Press, April 2004. Keynote presentation
76. Mateescu, R., Monteiro, P.T., Dumas, E., de Jong, H.: Computation tree regular logic for genetic regulatory networks. In: Cha, S.S., Choi, J.-Y., Kim, M., Lee, I., Viswanathan, M. (eds.) ATVA 2008. LNCS, vol. 5311, pp. 48–63. Springer, Heidelberg (2008). doi:10.1007/978-3-540-88387-6_6
77. Mateescu, R., Salaün, G.: PIC2LNT: model transformation for model checking an applied pi-calculus. In: Piterman, N., Smolka, S.A. (eds.) TACAS 2013. LNCS, vol. 7795, pp. 192–198. Springer, Heidelberg (2013). doi:10.1007/978-3-642-36742-7_14
78. Mateescu, R., Serwe, W.: Model checking and performance evaluation with CADP illustrated on shared-memory mutual exclusion protocols. Sci. Comput. Program. **78**(7), 843–861 (2013)
79. Mateescu, R., Thivolle, D.: A model checking language for concurrent value-passing systems. In: Cuellar, J., Maibaum, T., Sere, K. (eds.) FM 2008. LNCS, vol. 5014, pp. 148–164. Springer, Heidelberg (2008). doi:10.1007/978-3-540-68237-0_12
80. de Meer, J., Roth, R., Vuong, S.: Introduction to algebraic specifications based on the language ACT ONE. Comput. Netw. ISDN Syst. **23**(5), 363–392 (1992)
81. Milne, G.J.: CIRCAL and the representation of communication, concurrency, and time. ACM Trans. Progr. Lang. Syst. **7**(2), 270–298 (1985)
82. Milner, R. (ed.): A Calculus of Communicating Systems. LNCS, vol. 92. Springer, Heidelberg (1980). doi:10.1007/3-540-10235-3
83. Milner, R.: Calculi for synchrony and asynchrony. Theor. Comput. Sci. **25**, 267–310 (1983)
84. Mkaouar, H., Zalila, B., Hugues, J., Jmaiel, M.: From AADL model to LNT specification. In: de la Puente, J.A., Vardanega, T. (eds.) Ada-Europe 2015. LNCS, vol. 9111, pp. 146–161. Springer, Cham (2015). doi:10.1007/978-3-319-19584-1_10
85. Oliveira, R., Dupuy-Chessa, S., Calvary, G., Dadolle, D.: Using formal models to cross check an implementation. In: Luyten, K., Palanque, P. (eds.) Proceedings of the 8th ACM SIGCHI Symposium on Engineering Interactive Computing Systems (EICS 2016), Brussels, Belgium, pp. 126–137. ACM, New York, June 2016
86. Poizat, P., Salaün, G.: Checking the realizability of BPMN 2.0 choreographies. In: Proceedings of the 27th Symposium On Applied Computing (SAC 2012), Riva del Garda, Italy. ACM Press, New York, March 2012
87. Poizat, P., Salaün, G., Krishna, A.: Checking business process evolution. In: Kouchnarenko, O., Khosravi, R. (eds.) FACS 2016. LNCS, vol. 10231, pp. 36–53. Springer, Cham (2017). doi:10.1007/978-3-319-57666-4_4

88. Ponsini, O., Fédèle, C., Kounalis, E.: Rewriting of imperative programs into logical equations. Sci. Comput. Program. **56**(3), 363–401 (2005)
89. Quemada, J.: E-LOTOS Has Born, February 1997. Email announcement available from ftp://ftp.inrialpes.fr/pub/vasy/publications/elotos/announce-97.txt
90. Roth, R., de Meer, J., Storp, S.: Data specifications in Modular LOTOS. In: Bolognesi, T., Lagemaat, J., Vissers, C. (eds.) LOTOSphere: Software Development with LOTOS, pp. 467–479. Kluwer Academic Publishers, Dordrecht (1995)
91. Serwe, W.: Formal specification and verification of fully asynchronous implementations of the Data Encryption Standard. In: van Glabbeek, R., Groote, J.F., Höfner, P. (eds.) Proceedings of the International Workshop on Models for Formal Analysis of Real Systems (MARS 2015), Suva, Fiji. Electronic Proceedings in Theoretical Computer Science, vol. 196. Open Publishing Association (2015)
92. Shankland, C., Verdejo, A.: Time, E-LOTOS, and the FireWire. In: Marsan, M.A., Quemada, J., Robles, T., Silva, M. (eds.) Proceedings of the Workshop on Formal Methods and Telecommunications (WFMT 1999), Zaragoza, Spain, pp. 103–119. Prensas Universitarias de Zaragoza, September 1999
93. Shankland, C., Verdejo, A.: A case study in abstraction using E-LOTOS and the FireWire. Comput. Netw. **37**(3/4), 481–502 (2001)
94. Sighireanu, M.: Contribution à la définition et à l'implémentation du langage "Extended LOTOS". Thèse de Doctorat, Université Joseph Fourier (Grenoble), January 1999
95. Sighireanu, M., Catry, A., Champelovier, D., Garavel, H., Lang, F., Schaeffer, G., Serwe, W., Stoecker, J.: LOTOS NT User's Manual (Version 2.8), INRIA/CONVECS, Grenoble, France, 109 p. ftp://ftp.inrialpes.fr/pub/vasy/traian/manual.pdf
96. Sighireanu, M., Turner, K.: Requirement capture, formal description and verification of an invoicing system. Research Report RR-3575, INRIA, Grenoble, December 1998
97. Stöcker, J., Lang, F., Garavel, H.: Parallel processes with real-time and data: the ATLANTIF intermediate format. In: Leuschel, M., Wehrheim, H. (eds.) IFM 2009. LNCS, vol. 5423, pp. 88–102. Springer, Heidelberg (2009). doi:10.1007/978-3-642-00255-7_7
98. Thivolle, D.: Langages modernes pour la vérification des systèmes asynchrones. Thèse de Doctorat, Université Joseph Fourier, Grenoble, France and Universitatea Politehnica din Bucuresti, Bucharest, Romania, April 2011
99. Turner, K.J., Sighireanu, M.: (E)-LOTOS: (enhanced) language of temporal ordering specification. In: Frappier, M., Habrias, H. (eds.) Software Specification Methods: An Overview Using a Case Study, pp. 166–190. Springer, London (2001). doi:10.1007/978-1-4471-0701-9_10
100. Vekris, D., Lang, F., Dima, C., Mateescu, R.: Verification of EB3 specifications using CADP. Formal Asp. Comput. **28**(1), 145–178 (2016)
101. Verdejo, A.: E-LOTOS: Tutorial and Semantics. Master's thesis, Departamento de Sistemas Informáticos y Programación, Universidad Complutense de Madrid, Spain, June 1999
102. Wu, H., Yang, X., Katoen, J.-P.: Performance evaluation of concurrent data structures. In: Fränzle, M., Kapur, D., Zhan, N. (eds.) SETTA 2016. LNCS, vol. 9984, pp. 38–49. Springer, Cham (2016). doi:10.1007/978-3-319-47677-3_3
103. Zhang, Z., Serwe, W., Wu, J., Zheng, T.Y.H., Myers, C.: An improved fault-tolerant routing algorithm for a network-on-chip derived with formal analysis. Sci. Comput. Program. **118**, 24–39 (2016)

LOTOS-Like Composition of Boolean Nets and Causal Set Construction

Tommaso Bolognesi$^{(\boxtimes)}$ (iD)

CNR-ISTI, Pisa, Italy
`t.bolognesi@isti.cnr.it`

Abstract. In the context of research efforts on causal sets as discrete models of physical spacetime, and on their derivation from simple, deterministic, sequential models of computation, we consider *boolean nets*, a transition system that generalises cellular automata, and investigate the family of causal sets that derive from their computations, in search for interesting emergent properties. The choice of boolean nets is motivated by the fact that they naturally support compositions via a LOTOS-inspired parametric parallel operator, with possible interesting effects on the emergent structure of the derived causal sets.

More generally, we critically reconsider the whole issue of algorithmic causet construction and expose the limitations suffered by these structures w.r.t. to the requirements of Lorentz invariance that even *discrete* models of physical spacetime, as recently shown, can and should satisfy. We conclude by hinting at novel ways to add momentum to the bold research programme that attempts to identify the natural with the computational universe.

Keywords: Boolean nets · Causal sets · Discrete spacetime · Parallel composition · LOTOS

1 Introduction

This paper is dedicated to Ed Brinksma and is largely motivated by a desire to explore possible bridges between the topics investigated by Ed and friends in 'those good-old LOTOS days' – process-algebraic languages and operators, formal specification styles and structuring principles, etc.[1] – and the new research field that the author has joined after quitting the formal methods community, around 2005. This new area of activity deals with the emergent properties of the

---

[1] Of course the range of Ed's activities is broader, as suggested by the Festschrift title 'ModelEd, TestEd, TrustEd'. Indeed, the addition of 'randomisEd' wouldn't be completely inappropriate, in light of an episode which involved a small group of 'LOTOS-eaters' during a relaxing late-evening walk in a forgotten European city. On that occasion Prof. Brinksma, dissatisfied with the manipulations performed on the Rubik Magic Rings puzzle by the author – dismissed as insufficiently random – gave a public, truly brilliant demonstration of his unexpected randomisation skills.

© Springer International Publishing AG 2017
J.-P. Katoen et al. (Eds.): Brinksma Festschrift, LNCS 10500, pp. 27–47, 2017.
DOI: 10.1007/978-3-319-68270-9_2

computations of simple programs, and with discrete models of physical space-time. The occasion gives us also the opportunity for a critical assessment of some of the steps taken in these directions.

Causal Sets. Causality among events in spacetime is regarded by many theoretical physicists as a most fundamental aspect of nature, and represents a key notion in the *continuum* spacetime of Special and General Relativity. When revisited under the assumption of spacetime discreteness – a feature often imagined to manifest itself at the Plank scale $(10^{-35}\,\mathrm{m}, 10^{-44}\,\mathrm{s})$ – the idea of causality finds a simple realisation in terms of causal sets [10,28,30]. A *causal set*, or *causet*, is a partially ordered set of events $(S, \preceq)$ with the additional property of being *finitary*, which means that all *order intervals* $I[s,t] = \{x | s \preceq x \preceq t\}$, for any pair of elements s and t (the *source* and the *sink*) must be finite. A causet can be represented by a directed acyclic graph. Most efforts in the Causal Set Programme are concerned with identifying adequate counterparts, in the discrete setting, of concepts and features of continuous spacetime [29], such as lightcones, Lorentz invariance [12], dimensionality [22], curvature [1].

The most direct way to obtain a causet of solid, physical realism is to directly derive it, using the *stochastic sprinkling technique* to be introduced later, from a solid, continuous, Lorentzian manifold (e.g. flat Minkowski or positively-curved De Sitter space-time) guaranteed to satisfy the Einstein field equations. However, an attractive challenge for those who support the conjecture of an ultimately discrete, computational and deterministic nature of the universe, is to derive realistic causets directly from the computations of simple, discrete, deterministic models, without resorting to predefined continuum solutions, as *sprinkling* does. This idea has been first proposed by Wolfram [34], under the whimsical name of 'universe hunting', and has been further investigated by the author since 2010, often referred to as 'algorithmic causet construction' [3–5].

Bridges. How can we establish a bridge between algorithmic causal sets and process algebra? A possible link is suggested by the observation that partially ordered structures of events are such general and flexible mathematical objects that, unsurprisingly, they find application in a number of diverse fields of science and technology, including Computer Science. For example, roughly in the same period during which the Causal Set Programme for Quantum Gravity started to use these structures as discrete models of spacetime, in Theoretical Computer Science, in the areas of Concurrency Theory and Formal Methods, the 'true concurrency semantics' research effort started to devise mappings from process algebras to event structures somewhat analogous to causets [32,33].

An important difference between the two types of event set, from Physics and from Computer Science, is that in the former *all* events are expected to take place, while in the latter, as a reflection of choice operators in the syntax, special relations indicate that some events are in conflict. In Bundle Event Structures [20], for example, relation $e \# e'$ means that there is no system run in which both e and e' occur: some portions of the event structure remains 'unvisited'.

However, a difference between the two structures that is more interesting for our purposes here is that we cannot hope to detect emergent, macroscopic, possibly regular patterns in stochastic causets - by the very definition of stochastic process - while in the event structures from Computer Science this is certainly possible, since structure and order are inherited from the syntax itself. This fact, abstractly represented in Fig. 1, makes event structures from process algebraic specifications potentially interesting under a quantum gravity or computational universe perspective.

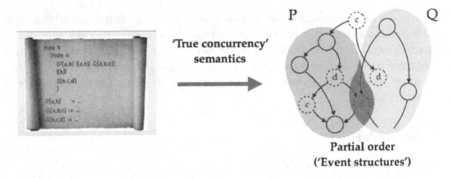

Fig. 1. The true-concurrency semantics of a process-algebraic specification maps a formal piece of syntax into a highly structured set of partially ordered events. The structure found in the semantic object on the r.h.s. is inherited from the structure in the syntactic object on the l.h.s.

Indeed, our initial plan was to investigate the emergent properties of the event structures obtained by the 'true concurrency semantics' of LOTOS [20] for large corpora of specifications, possibly generated at random. The unavailability of a fully automated semantics for a sufficiently large subset of the language – one including recursion – and the limited resources at our disposal, prevented us from following this path. We have therefore opted for a conceptually simpler labelled transition system – boolean nets – and have studied the causets that originate from their computations. Interestingly, it is straightforward to export to this state transition model the LOTOS parametric parallel composition operator, that represents a key structuring construct of the language: this is attractive, in light of the importance that we attribute to the emergence of macro/structures in causets.

Paper Plan. In Sect. 2 we introduce boolean nets, their synchronous and asynchronous executions, and the global graphs derived in the two cases. In Sect. 3 we contrast stochastic vs. deterministic causet construction techniques, recalling the main technique of the first type – manifold *sprinkling* – and mentioning two alternative approaches – *indirect* and *direct* – for building causets of the second type. In Sect. 4 we address the derivation of causets from (unstructured) asynchronous computations of boolean networks, under three different execution policies, and we study a peculiar property of the obtained graphs that has to do with Lorentz invariance. This leads us to critically reconsider the *indirect* approach to algorithmic causet construction in its generality. In Sect. 5 we consider the parametric parallel composition of (asynchronous) boolean nets, and take a preliminary look at the associated causets. In Sect. 6 we mention a few aspects in which, in our opinion, research and experimentation on 'universe hunting' could find new momentum and better results in term of emergent complexity.

2 Boolean Networks: Sync and Async Execution

Boolean networks, abbreviated *bool nets* in the sequel, are a sequential dynamical system based on a finite set of boolean variables, each controlled by a different boolean function. Random bool nets have been originally developed by Stuart Kauffman for modelling genetic regulatory networks [19], and have found application, more recently, in *Integrated Information Theory*, as abstract models of neural networks [25].

2.1 The Model

An (N, k)-bool net is a pair $(G(B, E), F)$ where:

– $G(B, E)$ is a directed graph with N vertices $B = \{b_1, \ldots, b_N\}$, and $N \cdot k$ edges E that specify the k input arguments: $b_{i,1} \to b_i, \ldots, b_{i,k} \to b_i$ for every $b_i \in B$.
– $F = \{f_1, \ldots f_N\}$ is a set of N boolean functions of k arguments.

Each vertex $b_i \in B$ is a boolean variable controlled by boolean function $f_i(b_{i,1} \ldots b_{i,k}) \in F$. The ordered k-tuple of arguments $(b_{i,1} \ldots b_{i,k})$ identifies the bits in B that f_i reads, and corresponds to k directed edges in E, namely edges $b_{i,1} \to b_i, \ldots, b_{i,k} \to b_i$. Thus, there is a total of $|E| = N * k$ edges.[2] The $G(B, E)$ graph of a $(N5, k3)$-bool net is provided, as an example, in Fig. 2-left. The numeric codes of the boolean functions associated to each node are indicated in parentheses. Note that there are 2^{2^k} boolean functions of k variables – 256 for this example.

There are two ways in which a boolean net can be executed:

Synchronous execution. This criterion naturally combines with a *discrete time* assumption: at each time step, or clock tick $t = 0, 1, 2 \ldots$, each function f_i reads the values of its k arguments – the bits $b_{i,1}, \ldots, b_{i,k}$ identified by the incoming edges of node b_i – and fires, assigning the computed value to its controlled node, i.e. to variable b_i. All functions fire together. Under this synchronous firing policy, boolean nets are a generalisation of cellular automata [17].

We assume deterministic functions $F = \{f_1, \ldots f_N\}$, thus synchronous evolution is itself *deterministic*: each global state has only one successor. Thus, placing deterministic bool nets with synchronous evolution in the wider context of probabilistic system - viewing them as special, limit cases of that

---

[2] Note that, unless decorated with appropriate edge priority assignments, the graph is not sufficient for correctly identifying the order of function arguments: this is disambiguated in F.

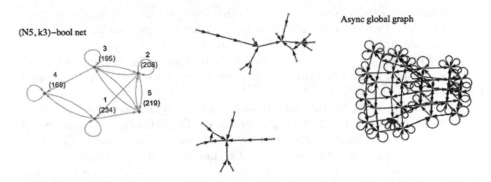

Sync global graph

(N5, k3)–bool net

Async global graph

Fig. 2. $G(B, E)$ directed graph for a $(N5, k3)$-bool net (left). Numbers in parentheses near each node identify the boolean function of three variables that controls the node bit. Each node has three incoming arcs, identifying the argument bits. Global graphs for the same net under sync (middle) and async (right) execution.

family - we can represent them by *causal graphs* [26], since they fulfill the requirement that the state at time $t + 1$ of each variable b_i, denoted b_i^{t+1}, is conditionally independent of b_j^{t+1}, for every other variable b_j, given the global state B^t of the system at time t: $prob(b_i^{t+1}|B^t, b_j^{t+1}) = prob(b_i^{t+1}|B^t)$. Each bit/function $b_i = f_i(b_{i,1} \ldots b_{i,k})$ can thus be interpreted as an individual causal element within the system [26].

Asynchronous execution. Although we assume deterministic functions $F = \{f_1, \ldots f_N\}$, asynchronous evolution admits both *deterministic* and *nondeterministic* variants.

The *nondeterministic* form naturally combines with a *continuous time* assumption: we imagine function firing to be an instantaneous random event, occurring independently from other firings. In continuous time, the probability of two firings to occur simultaneously is zero, thus we assume that all these events occur one at a time, in an interleaving fashion. Correspondingly, each global state may have multiple successors – as many as the number N of bits. The continuous time postulate that no two firings occur simultaneously actually introduces a causal dependency between the individual bits $b_i \in B$. While the global transitions of the system from its current state B_t to its next state B_{t+1} may still be interpreted as a global mechanism, the states of individual bits within system B are not conditionally independent on the past. The next state of an individual bit may depend on the next state of other bits b_j in addition to the current state of its parents $\{b_{i,1} \ldots b_{i,k}\}$. For this reason, asynchronously updated bool nets cannot be interpreted as a system composed of individual causal elements [25], and thus do not readily fit into the framework of causal graphs [26].

Two types of *deterministic*, asynchronous bool nets shall be introduced later.

2.2 Global Graphs

Bool nets, either sync or async, are *finite* transition systems, thus we can capture their behaviour by a directed, global, state transition graph in which each node is a global state, i.e. a tuple of bits. For a complete characterisation of the bool net behaviour we do not refer to a specific initial global state, but create all global states and find all transitions that emanate from each of them. In general the graph may be disconnected.

Two global graphs, for the same boolean net but with sync or async execution, are illustrated in Fig. 2. The sync graph in the middle has two connected components, each featuring a three-node cyclic attractor. The layout of the async graph on the right exhibits some degree of symmetry, and may give the impression of a 3-D assembly of cubic frames: this is a consequence of the transition interleaving policy, by which a group of transitions may fire in all possible orderings. (In a simple setting, with just two transitions, interleaving yields the typical diamond shape.)

3   Stochastic vs. Deterministic Causets

Started in the late 1980's [10], the Causal Set Programme has always been concerned with techniques for building realistic causets, able to reproduce or approximate features of physical, continuous spacetime. Invariably, all the considered techniques have been of *stochastic* nature. The primary technique, in this group, is *sprinkling*.

By the *sprinkling technique* one can derive a causet from a Lorentzian manifold M provided with a volume measure, in two steps. First one creates a uniform, Poisson distribution of points - to become the causet nodes - in a finite region of M, with density δ, so that the expected number of points in a volume V is δV, and the probability to find exactly n points in that portion is:

$$P(n) = \frac{(\delta V)^n e^{-\delta V}}{n!}. \tag{1}$$

Then the causet edges are created by letting the sprinkled points inherit the causal structure of M: in M two points/events are causally related when their squared Lorentz distance L^2 is positive (time-like relation) or null (light-like relation), and are causally unrelated when L^2 is negative (space-like relation).[3] In the sequel we shall conveniently call these objects *sprinkled causets*. Sprinkled causets can be regarded as the most direct discrete versions of 'real', continuous forms of physical spacetime (e.g. Minkowski and De Sitter).

As mentioned in the introduction, a challenging goal of causet-based quantum gravity research is to build causets of physical significance without resorting to an underlying continuum, with the manifold obtained a posteriori, as an asymptotic approximation.

---

[3] In four dimensional, Minkowski spacetime M^{1+3}, with time dimension t and spatial dimensions x, y, z, the squared Lorentz distance between events $e_1(t_1, x_1, y_1, z_1)$ and $e_2(t_2, x_2, y_2, z_2)$ is $L^2(e_1, e_2) = +(t_2 - t_1)^2 - (x_2 - x_1)^2 - (y_2 - y_1)^2 - (z_2 - z_1)^2$.

The first experiments with *deterministic* techniques for causet construction, as opposed to *stochastic* techniques, have been carried out by Wolfram [34], although some preliminary ideas can be found in [16].

The rationale for this alternative approach is, in our opinion, quite strong, although still controversial in the community of theoretical physicists: as widely shown by Wolfram with cellular automata and other simple models [34], the richness and variety of patterns that emerge from suitable (and, typically, graphical) representation of deterministic computations, ranging from regular, periodic behaviours to fractal structures, from pseudo-randomness to 'digital particles', is far beyond the reach of purely stochastic models. Furthermore, the assumption of a physical universe fundamentally fuelled, at its lowest spacetime scales, by a digital computation rather than by differential equations, has appealed several physicists (and non-physicists) in the last decades [15,21,31,36] and may be, at present, the best candidate for explaining the peculiar mix of order and disorder found in nature. (For a comprehensive collection of papers on these issues, see [13].)

Following Wolfram's pioneering steps, we have carried out a number of additional experiments with algorithmic causet construction [3–8], investigating properties such as dimensionality, curvature, and Lorentz invariance in the discrete setting.

We distinguish two main techniques for algorithmic causet construction.

Indirect. Reflecting Wolfram's original ideas, a causet is obtained by considering the computation of a sequential model (e.g. an n-dimensional Turing machine), by viewing the computation steps as the events (nodes) of the causet, and by inferring the causal relations among events from the write and read operations carried out at each step on the state variables of the model (e.g. the tape cells and the state of the Turing machine head). A concrete example of application of this technique is provided in Sect. 4.

Direct. In this case we devise an algorithm that directly creates and manipulates the graph representing the causet.

As the reader may have already realised, there is an abundant degree of arbitrariness in these constructions, and no clear guiding principle for their choice, other than, perhaps, conceptual simplicity. The exploration of the computational universe, as conceived by Wolfram, is fundamentally a blind experimental activity: run virtually all instances of the model at hand and see what happens. One may also object that, under the assumption of a computational universe, the choice of a specific Turing-universal model from which to derive causets is irrelevant, since all of them are equivalent, at least in terms of computing power. In practice, however, different models perform quite differently when it comes to concretely spotting interesting properties. Cellular automata diagrams, for example, are more convenient than many other models for detecting, by direct visual inspection, interesting emergent patterns such as digital particles. Thus, we still consider it interesting to explore families of causets derived from different models of computation.

4   Causets from Async Bool Nets

What type of causet can be derived from the computation of a bool net, following the 'indirect' construction approach of Sect. 3?

Let $A = (G(B,E),F)$ be a (N,k)-bool net, and let us conveniently restrict here to the case of *asynchronous* execution (see Subsect. 2.1), in which step w of the sequential computation corresponds to the application of just one boolean function $f_i \in F$, that we write $f_i^w(b_{i,1},\ldots b_{i,k})$ for stressing its position w in the sequence of steps. We shall directly say that *event w has written bit b_i after reading bits $b_{i,1},\ldots b_{i,k}$.* We have chosen to address asynchronous rather than synchronous bool nets because they are closer to the LOTOS execution model, and because the derivation of causets from them is easier and more in line with our past experiments.

Following the general technique described in [4], to which the reader is referred for more details, a causet $C = (S, \preceq)$ is readily obtained from the selected computation of bool net A as follows:

- S is the set of computation steps, identified only by their temporal order of occurrence w – a natural number;
- $v \preceq w$, where $v, w \in S$, whenever one of the arguments $b_{i,1},\ldots b_{i,k}$ of function $f_i^w(b_{i,1},\ldots b_{i,k})$, say $b_{i,j}$, sees event v as its *most recent writer event*, meaning that no other event between v and w has written $b_{i,j}$. We say that $b_{i,j}$ is the *causality mediator* between v and w.

For obtaining and comparing multiple causet types from the same basic model we consider three different bool net (async) execution policies:

Nondeterministic - At each step the choice of which function to fire it taken uniformly at random.

Deterministic - bit cycling - The N bits of the net are updated one after the other, from left to right, in cycles.

Deterministic - label cycling - Function firings are enriched by labels, which turn out to be particularly useful when used in conjunction with LOTOS-like parallel composition of bool nets. These labels are assigned by a deterministic mechanism: each function $f_i(b_{i,1},\ldots b_{i,k})$, controlling bit b_i of net A has an associated one-to-one *labelling function* $\alpha : \{0,1\}^k \to L$, which returns a different symbol of alphabet L for each different k-tuple of bits read by f_i. L thus includes 2^k symbols; furthermore, it is ordered.[4] A pointer scans L from left to right, and stops at the first label that is represented in one of the transitions: this is the transition to be fired. When multiple transitions share that label, the one corresponding to the bit with lowest index is chosen. This labelling policy is just a simple implementation of the idea that a transition label should depend on the current state of the system, but there are

---

[4] For $k = 3$, for example, we typically set $\alpha(0,0,0) = 0$, $\alpha(0,0,1) = 1,\ldots, \alpha(1,1,1) = 7$, with $L = \{0\ldots7\}$ ordered in the natural way. In the sequel we shall also create a different labelling function for each different bool net bit by considering different rotations of the range tuple $(0\ldots7)$.

clearly many other ways to reflect this requirement, or even to dismiss it. Our choice has been, admittedly, quite arbitrary, and we cannot exclude that other labelling techniques might yield more interesting causets; indeed, a certain degree of arbitrariness seems unavoidable, in 'Wolfram-style' explorations of the huge universe of deterministic computations.

Which causet properties are we going to analyse?

In [8] we have considered several statistical indicators meant to characterise causets obtained from various techniques, and to measure their closeness to the ideal Lorentzian causets – the sprinkled causets mentioned in Sect. 3. Here we focus on just one indicator, which refers to the out-degrees of causet nodes.[5]

The importance of looking at the growth rate of causet node out-degrees is well explained by Rideout [27]:

"The 'usual' discrete structures which we encounter, e.g. as discrete approximations to spatial geometry, have a 'mean valence' of order 1. e.g. each 'node' of a Cartesian lattice in three dimensions has six nearest neighbors. [...] Such discrete structures cannot hope to capture the noncompact Lorentz symmetry of spacetime. Causal sets, however, have a 'mean valence' which grows with some finite power of the number of elements in the causal set. It is this 'hyper-connectivity' that allows them to maintain Lorentz invariance in the presence of discreteness."

Thus, an important requirement for a causet to support Lorentz invariance is that the number of outgoing links from the generic causet node should grow with the size of the causet (see also [9]).

In [11] Bombelli et al. mention that, considering the causet $C[s,t]$ obtained from uniformly sprinkling points in an order interval $I[s,t]$ of height T of d-dimensional Minkowski space (T being the Lorentz distance between s and t), the number of nearest neighbors of the root node s – the number of outgoing links – grows like $Log(T)$ for $d = 2$, and like T^{d-2} for $d \geq 3$, provided that the sprinkling density is kept constant. Again, the essential feature here is that the out-degree of *each* node in a sprinkled causet will grow, possibly slowly, but unbounded, as new nodes are added.

Can we expect this feature to be satisfied by the causets derived from the three variants of bool net computation just introduced? The answer depends on whether we adopt a nondeterministic or deterministic execution and, in the second case, it depends on the type of algorithm.

Let us clarify the issue in the wider context of causets derived from the sequential steps of virtually any model of computation, following the 'indirect' technique in which causality is induced by the mediation of state variables.

Consider some generic sequential model of computation and let X be the possibly dynamic set of state variables that can be read, written, created or

---

[5] Recall that we always consider the causet in its transitively reduced form, or Hasse diagram, whose edges are often called 'links'.

destroyed by the computation steps. Recall that we establish a direct correspondence between the steps and the causet nodes, so that we can sloppily attribute read/write or create/destroy operations to the ones or the others.

Here is what may happen in terms of causet link creation and node out-degree growth:

- If event w *reads* variable $x \in X$, then a new edge $v \to w$ is created, where event v is the most recent writer of x.
- If event w *creates* variable x, it acquires the opportunity to see its own outgoing edges grow in number, thanks to all future events, if any, that read x before some other event writes or destroys x.
- If event w *writes* or *destroys* x, it permanently prevents node v – the most recent writer of x until w – to collect further outgoing edges.

If follows that the only circumstance in which a causet node v can see its out-degree grow unbounded is when v creates/writes x, and in the subsequent events, x is read infinitely often but never rewritten.

As a consequence, any *fair* sequential model in which each state variable is always eventually updated yields causets in which *all* nodes exhibit an O(1) growth of their out-degrees. This is clearly the case of our *nondeterministic*, async bool net computations, that behave fairly by definition!

How about *deterministic* bool net computations? The 'advantage' of these computations is that they may behave unfairly in a number of creative ways!

Let us then consider Fig. 3. In these plots we compare four types of causets in terms of their node degree growth. They are: causets from sprinkling in 2D space (see Sect. 3), causets from nondeterministic bool nets, and causets from deterministic bool nets with bit-cycling or label-cycling.

Each plot refers to the growth of a single 300-node causet, and collects 300 function plots, each describing the out-degree growth of a different node as the causet develops.

The two plots in the upper row, with their random-like traits, reflect the nondeterministic nature of the computations from which they originate, but differ in a fundamental aspect: in a sprinkled causet (upper-left) – the structure of reference for Lorentz invariance – each node out-degree grows slowly but unbounded; in a causet from an infinite, nondeterministic async bool net computation, each node reaches, with probability 1, a constant, permanent out-degree, for the reasons we have discussed, although ever bigger constants may be achieved, as the computation unfolds.

The two plots in the lower row are from the two deterministic variants of async bool net computations: bit-cycling and label-cycling. Not surprisingly, the bit-cycling policy, being maximally fair with respect to bit choice, prevents the growth of node out-degrees beyond N, the number of bits in the net, since, in the causet construction process, no event can play the role of most recent bit writer for more than N steps. On the contrary, the label-cycling policy, exerting only an indirect control on the choice of the bit to update, leaves room, in a few cases, to 'unfair' behaviours, thus to unbounded node out-degree growth, as clearly visible in the lower-right plot of Fig. 3.

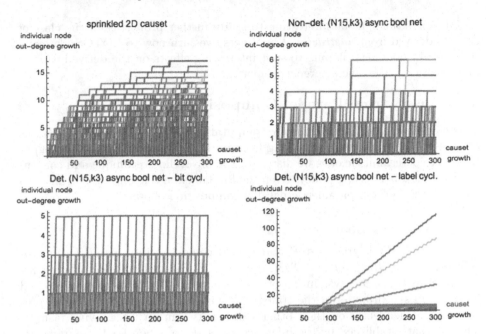

Fig. 3. Individual growth rates, as a function of causet size, of the out-degree of *all* nodes in causets of four types: sprinkled causet of dimensions $d = 2$ (upper-left), causet from nondeterministic async bool net (upper-right), from deterministic async bool net with bit cycling (lower-left), and from deterministic async bool net with label cycling (lower-right).

Indeed, we can cheaply establish a limitation also for the deterministic causets from label-cycling bool net computations: the number of causet nodes with unbounded node degree must be *finite*, and smaller than N, the total number of bits. The reason is as follows. Recalling that each event writes precisely one bit of the net, if we had more than N events exhibiting unbounded out-degree growth, by the pigeon-hole principle at least two of them, e_x and e_y, would be in charge of the same bit, implying that the occurrence of the most recent of them in the sequential computation, say e_y, would obscure e_x as most recent writer of that bit, stopping permanently the out-degree growth of e_x.

This circumstance indicates that these toy causets cannot compete with sprinked causets in terms of physical realism. Still, the examples above seem to demonstrate that, when focusing on the much desired property of unbounded out-degree growth, a deterministic approach to causet construction may offer advantages w.r.t. a nondeterministic one – excluding of course sprinkling itself, which directly derives its good properties from an underlying manifold of guaranteed physical significance.

Discussion on the limits of causets obtained by the 'indirect' technique shall be resumed in the closing section.

Although it might be interesting to study further properties of the class of causets derived from *unstructured* bool nets, we turn now to LOTOS-like *compositions* of bool nets, hoping to spot interesting effects on the derived causets in terms of macroscopic emergent properties.

5   Causets from Parallel Compositions of Bool Nets

This section deals with deterministic computations of LOTOS-like compositions of bool nets. In this case, for moving from potentially nondeterministic computations to deterministic ones we disregard the bit-cycling technique and concentrate on the label-cycling policy, given the fundamental role played by transition labels in the LOTOS parametric parallel composition operator.

5.1   Composing Bool Nets

When two LOTOS processes P and Q are composed in a *parallel composition expression* '$P|[syncLabs]|Q$', where *syncLabs* is a set of labels, the resulting labelled transition system is obtained by forcing the processes to proceed jointly – in synchrony – on the transitions with labels in *syncLabs*, while proceeding independently on their other transitions – in an interleaving fashion. This is what established by the inference rules of transition for the parametric parallel composition operator:

$$\frac{P \xrightarrow{x} P' \wedge x \notin syncLabSet}{P|[syncLabSet]|Q \xrightarrow{x} P'|[syncLabSet]|Q} \qquad (left \ \ interleaving) \qquad (2)$$

$$\frac{Q \xrightarrow{x} Q' \wedge x \notin syncLabSet}{P|[syncLabSet]|Q \xrightarrow{x} P|[syncLabSet]|Q'} \qquad (right \ \ interleaving) \qquad (3)$$

$$\frac{P \xrightarrow{x} P' \wedge Q \xrightarrow{x} Q' \wedge x \in syncLabSet}{P|[syncLabSet]|Q \xrightarrow{x} P'|[syncLabSet]|Q'} \qquad (synchronisation) \qquad (4)$$

The derivation of a *global transition graph* from an async bool net (unstructured) was discussed in Subsect. 2.2. Since the semantics rules (2)–(4) for LOTOS parallel composition are applicable to *labelled transition systems*, it is perfectly feasible to apply them to the composition of boolean nets P and Q. The only missing elements are transitions labels!

For assigning labels to the individual transitions of async bool nets P and Q, we use the deterministic labelling policy described in Sect. 4, based on a labelling function α. On this basis, the application of rules (2)–(4) becomes possible, and the expression $P|[syncLabs]|Q$ formally identifies all possible transitions of the composite system also when P and Q are bool nets.

Thus, expression $P|[syncLabs]|Q$ denotes a composite system in which P and Q may execute their respective transitions independently form each other, or jointly, when both are labelled by an element of *syncLabs*, thus involving a mix of synchrony and asynchrony. We shall use the LOTOS notation '$P|||Q$' for the case $syncLabs = \phi$ ('pure interleaving'). Of course, the composite transition system can be further composed with additional async nets.

5.2   Derived Causets

For exploring the class of causets associated with deterministic computations of composite bool nets, we start from most elementary instances of the model. We shall therefore consider bool net compositions of form $P[N3, k3] ||| Q[N3, k3]$.

Figure 4 illustrates four typical pairs of graphs for this type of composition. Each pair consists of a *raw* causet and its transitively reduced form, next to each other. All four *reduced* causets – the proper causets of interest here – collapse to a trivial tree form that basically washes away the structure of the raw graph.

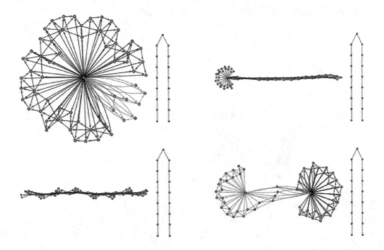

Fig. 4. Causets from deterministic computations of randomly generated bool nets $P[N3, k3]$ and $Q[N3, k3]$ composed by disjoint (interleaving) parallel composition $P|||Q$. The computation is made deterministic by the cycling label policy described in the text. The four (transitively reduced) causets share the same trivial tree-like form, and are shown, for clarity, with fewer nodes than the corresponding raw graph. In the raw graphs, the causal edges created by transitions of P and Q are rendered, respectively, in black and grey. The central node with high out-degree in the upper-left graph corresponds to the initial event of the computation, which initialises all 6 bits of P and Q. The different shapes of the raw graphs essentially depend on the number of nodes that succeed to permanently keep the role of last writer for some bit of P or Q.

It is easy to realise that, by using the $P|||Q$ composition, the causet events generated by the independent transitions of P and Q can only be arranged in two independent total orders: when $N = k$, as in this case, each event e of P reads *all* bits of P, thus it causally depends on the immediately preceding event e' of P, no matter which bit e' has written. Likewise for Q.

It is important not to confuse global transition graphs, not shown here, with causets. First, the global transition graph contains all transitions among all possible global system states, while a causet corresponds to one particular execution path on the global graph, and reveals its intrinsic partial order, if any.

Second, a causet *node* represents an event corresponding to a *transition* in the global graph.[6]

Figure 5 refers to two bool net compositions of form $P[N3, k3]|\{a\}|Q[N3, k3]$, in which P and Q must synchronise on just one label ('a'), out of the $2^k = 8$ labels of alphabet L. This simple change is sufficient to induce a change in the derived causets, which appear on the r.h.s. of the figure: now some causet events correspond to synchronisations between P and Q, and the causets appear as two separate causal paths that periodically share these events. In spite of the extreme simplicity of these patterns, we may regard them as a first, rudimentary demonstration of how to promote the appearance of macrostructures – the intertwined causal paths of P and Q – in a causet.

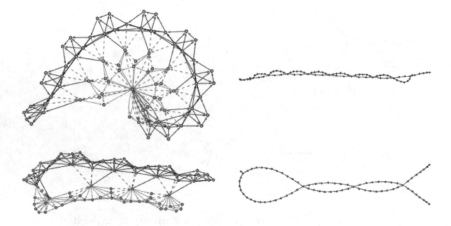

Fig. 5. Causets from deterministic computations of randomly generated bool nets $P[N3, k3]$ and $Q[N3, k3]$ composed by parallel composition $P|\{a\}|Q$. Raw and reduced causet forms are shown next to each other. Again, the different growth patterns of the raw causets (circular vs. linear) are not retained in the reduced causets, which appear essentially equivalent.

The inspection of causets from $P(N3, k3)|[syncLabs]|Q(N3, k3)$ bool net compositions with increasing coupling, i.e. larger set *syncLab*, does not reveal any qualitatively different causet structure, except for an increased probability of deadlock – a bool net waiting to synchronise its transition on a label not available in the transitions of the other. (Note that talking about deadlock *probability* corresponds to the fact that we are creating *random* instances of bool nets, for the given parameter settings, i.e. random sets of boolean functions.)

---

[6] In the graphical rendering of causets, we may render differently (black/gray/dashed) the edges that point to a node, depending on whether that node corresponds to a transition from P, from Q, or from both. This is the criterion adopted for Figs. 4 and 5. As an alternative, we may directly paint the causets node differently, as done for the subsequent figures.

Moving now to higher parameter values we find causets (in their transitively reduced form!) of higher complexity. A curious phenomenon observed here is the dependence of the causet overall shape, or growth symmetry – again, circular or linear – on the coupling factor $|syncLabs|$. Figure 6 shows the causets obtained from $P[N15, k3]\|[syncLabs]\|Q[N15, k3]$ compositions of a fixed pair of bool nets, with $|syncLabs|$ ranging from 0 to 8, the alphabet size.

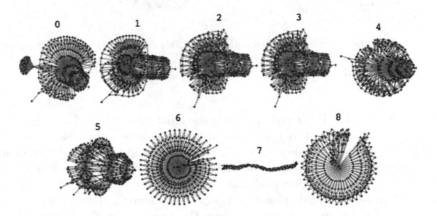

Fig. 6. Causets from parallel compositions $P[N15, k3]\|[syncLabs]\|Q[N15, k3]$ of two bool nets, with coupling factor $|syncLabs|$ ranging from 0 to 8, as indicated on top of each graph. Only for coupling factor 7 does the causet assume a linear shape.

Curiously, with 7 synchronisation labels the causet develops linearly rather than circularly. Note that with the $(N15, k3)$ parameter setting, deadlocks end up being much less frequent, due to the increased offer of labeled transitions by the two interacting nets.

Our primary motivation for exploring causets from structured, *composite* bool net systems was to spot the emergence of corresponding macro structures in the causets themselves, and the possibility to identify a partition into distinguishable regions. Graph and network theories certainly provide an abundance of tools that might prove useful for formally characterising or measuring 'interesting' causet partitions, but their consideration is beyond the scope of this paper. On the other hand, a simple way to help identifying regions by direct visual inspection is to paint causet nodes with different colors, following some predefined criterion. In the case of bool net parallel compositions an obvious criterion, implicitly suggested already in Fig. 1, is to differentiate among nodes corresponding to independent transitions of P, of Q, and of P and Q jointly. In Fig. 7 we provide two examples (one of them is the second element in the upper row of Fig. 6) in which the three types of causet node are painted, respectively, in white, black and pink.

With respect to the construction of realistic discrete models of physical spacetime, the experiments we have carried out with interacting bool nets, some

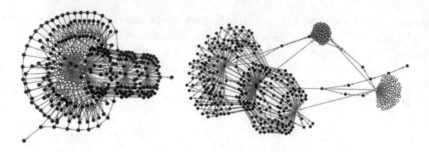

Fig. 7. Painting causet nodes. White and black nodes correspond to transitions performed in interleaving by bool nets P and Q, respectively. Pink nodes correspond to joint transitions of the two bool nets. (Color figure online)

of which have been illustrated here, suggest that the value of the algorithmic causets obtained in this way is mainly metaphorical. The case of cellular automata is somewhat analogous: very few people believe that those automata can, in themselves, fully explain or actually *generate* the whole physical universe, but more people may be convinced that the surprising emergent properties they exhibit, often resembling patterns and processes found in nature, hint at the existence of some deep connection between the computational and the natural universe. Our causets from bool nets indicate that it is possible to obtain some form of macro-structure from deterministic, sequential computations. However, an important limitation of this approach is that the macrostructure is not genuinely *emergent*, in the same way as digital particles unpredictably emerge in some cellular automata, but is an expected consequence of the structure built into the process by us.

This and other limitations of the 'algorithmic causet' effort are discussed in the next, closing section, where we also hint at possible solutions and mention some promising developments.

6   Conclusions

The limitations affecting the causets discussed in this paper represent only a part (and not the most problematic!) of the difficulties that experiments with algorithmic causet construction have faced in the last 15 years. Let us briefly summarise the issues, placing them in a temporal perspective.

The first derivation of causets (or 'causal networks') from the computations of a sequential model, namely a *mobile automaton* operating on a one-dimensional array of cells, has been proposed by Wolfram (see [34], p. 489, and the interactive demo [24]). The crucial limitation of those graphs is that the transitively reduced causet is *totally ordered*, corresponding to a sequence of nodes with both in-degree 1 (except for the root) and out-degree 1. According to the findings on Lorentz invariance in the discrete setting [9,11,27], this is bad.

The total order of events is a direct consequence of the short steps taken by the automaton on the cell array: some of the three (or more) cells read at each step must have been written in the immediately preceding step, yielding events that are causally linked one after the other. (A way to avoid the total order is to consider 'jumping mobile automata' [4].)

The same total-order limitation is suffered by causets derived from Turing Machines (TM), also investigated by Wolfram and others (see demo [35]). A jumping policy would not be effective here, since it is now also the state of the machine head that inevitably plays the role of causality mediator between any pair of adjacent events.

Some of the features exhibited by the *raw* causets derived from the above models appear potentially interesting, even under a Physics perspective. In [4], for example, we have classified the raw causets from the computations of the 4096 elementary TM's – those with 2 states and binary tape. The large majority of them cannot escape the dull fate of a trivial, one-dimensional growth, as in case 7 of Fig. 6, but, interestingly, the toy spacetime produced in 12 cases is two-dimensional and planar: it is flat (Euclidean) for 8 of them, and negatively curved (hyperbolic) for the remaining 4.

It is frustrating to discover elaborate patterns in algorithmic, raw causet, and see them vanish completely after transitive reduction. To mitigate the problem, in [3] we have shown that when transitive reduction is applied to a local area of the raw causet, rather than globally, some patterns in that area may survive, notably digital particles.

Another important limitation that affects the raw and, a fortiori, the reduced causets from several simple models of computation is *planarity*. In [4] it is proved that the causets from general, one-dimensional TMs, from two variants of mobile automata on tape, from string rewrite systems, and from tag systems and cyclic tag systems are all planar, a feature that conflicts with the four dimensions of conventional spacetime.

One way to obtain causets of higher dimensionality consists in increasing the dimensionality of the support on which their parent computation operates, based on the idea that a d-dimensional support should yield a $(d+1)$-dimensional causet, due to the expected contribution of the intervened time dimension. For this reason, causets from two-dimensional TM's and from *network mobile automata* [2] – a model analogous to mobile automata on tape, but operating by rewrite rules on planar, trivalent networks – have been widely investigated in [3], yielding examples of three-dimensional causets. Some improved results were obtained by dropping the planarity requirement for the support network, and by using genetic algorithms [6].[7]

In light of the Occam's razor principle, however, a technique by which the desired causet features (high dimensionality or macro-regions) emerge

---

[7] Several techniques are available for measuring the dimension of a graph [23]. Unfortunately their estimates may disagree! For the mentioned example we have used the 'node shell growth rate' technique, which provided a dimension 3 estimate but only relative to the node shells centered a the causet root.

spontaneously from a simple and abstract computation should be preferred over ones by which they are built explicitly into the process.

In this paper we have focused on a specific feature of algorithmic causets related to Lorentz invariance: node out-degree growth, as a function of causet size. In this respect, the status of the various classes of algorithmic causets can be summarised as follows, in order of increasing interest.

- Out-degree $= 1$ for all causet nodes. This is the trivial case of totally ordered causets, which would not even deserve mention if it were not the norm for most of the initial experiments in the field.
- $O(1)$ out-degree growth for all nodes. Causet nodes are related by a proper partial order, but none of their out-degrees can grow beyond a constant value. Graphs assume a typical, uninteresting 'polymer-like', linear structure. When using the indirect causet construction technique in which causality is induced by read-write operations on state variables, an $O(1)$ growth is observed whenever these operations interest all variables in a fair manner. Examples include the discussed causets from bool net computations using the cycling-bit policy, but also many causets from our past experiments with network mobile automata.
- The out-degree grows unbounded (polynomially) for a *finite* number of nodes. An example, referring to bool net computations using the cycling-label policy, was illustrated in Fig. 3, in the lower-right plot.
- The out-degree grows unbounded for an unboundedly growing number of nodes, although not for *all* of them. This feature cannot be observed with causets derived from computations involving a finite and constant number of state variables, like the bool nets considered in the paper, but may be satisfied by dropping that limitation: when new state variables are constantly created, some of them may end up being read infinitely often without being rewritten, thus inducing unbounded growth in the out-degree of their last writer event. Clearly this privilege cannot be enjoyed by *all* causet nodes, since any write operation (we assume they never cease) will permanently stop the out-degree growth of some causet node, as explained in the paper. In network mobile automata, state variables – represented by the faces of the dynamic, planar network – are constantly created by one of the two employed rewrite rules, thus the feature in question can be potentially observed, although in the referenced papers we have not investigated it. Note that the above limitations may affect the causets from virtually any sequential model of computation, given the general validity of the arguments we have provided.
- The out-degree grows unbounded for *all* causet nodes. This is the ideal case observed with stochastic, sprinkled causets, consistent with the Lorentz-invariance requirement. With the *indirect* causet construction technique of concern in this paper, this feature cannot be achieved. On the contrary, it can with an algorithmic, *direct* causet construction technique such as the one described in [8].

Coming now to a more general assessment of the results obtained so far with algorithmic causets and other analogous efforts, in our opinion the most serious problem that this research faces today is that the powerful phenomenon of emergence in computation has never succeeded to ignite a multi-layered cascade of hierarchical levels of emergence, beyond the first level. With Wolfram's ECA's [34], for example, the ground level 0 consists of the boolean functions defining the automata, and a level 1 may emerge from it, e.g. with the digital particles of ECA 110: no level 2 in turn emerges from the interactions of these particles.

This persistent failure to achieve a multi-layered architecture of emergence from simple models of computation seems to indicate that radically new and even more 'creative' ingredients must be involved in the process. We tentatively list three of them, not completely disjoint from one another.

Self-modifying code. Rather that being static, the algorithm that fuels the simulated universe from the bottom could modify itself as it evolves. This is certainly a substantial paradigmatic change, and a well-known concept in Computer Science, but we are not aware of any successful experiments with it in the area of interest here.

Top-down causation. This is regarded as one of the key factors for boosting complexity and variety in the biosphere: the upper level – e.g. a collectivity – induces changes back to the lower level – e.g. the individuals. George Ellis has recently shown how effective and pervasive top-down causation can be, beyond the realm of biology [14].

Emergent causality. Under the usual, reductionist interpretation of the natural world, or of complex artificial systems, all the causal power resides at the lowest, most reduced level of description, leaving no room for causation at the upper levels. But very recent work has shown [18], precisely in the context of the boolean networks described in Subsect. 2.1, and using a formal notion of *Effective Information* based on relative entropy (or 'Kullback-Leibler divergence'), that in some cases the upper levels can supersede the lower ones in causal power.

We hope to witness, in the near future, a new wave of experiments on algorithmic causet construction and 'universe hunting' able to fruitfully incorporate some of the concepts listed above. The task is demanding, its potential results groundbreaking: not only might they reveal a whole new generation of emergent, computation-based phenomena of relevance for complexity studies and fundamental physics, but they could also shed light on the mechanisms at the roots of agency and, ultimately, of consciousness [25].

Acknowledgements. The author expresses his warmest gratitude to Larissa Albantakis for many stimulating exchanges and discussions on notions of causality, Effective Information, Integrated Information. Lack of time has prevented us from completing our joint investigation of the possible applications of these recently proposed informational measures to the synchronous/asynchronous, deterministic/nondeterministic, unstructured/composite boolean networks considered here. This will be the subject of a forthcoming paper.

This work has been partially funded by FQXi Mini-Grant number: FQXi-MGA-1702.

References

1. Benincasa, D.M.T., Dowker, F.: The scalar curvature of a causal set. Phys. Rev. Lett. **104**, 181301 (2010). http://arxiv.org/abs/1001.2725
2. Bolognesi, T.: Planar trinet dynamics with two rewrite rules. Complex Syst. **18**(1), 1–41 (2008)
3. Bolognesi, T.: Algorithmic causets. In: Space, Time, Matter - Current Issues in Quantum Mechanics and Beyond - Proceedings of DICE 2010. IOP (2011). J. Phys. - Conf. Ser
4. Bolognesi, T.: Causal sets from simple models of computation. Int. J. Unconvn. Comput. (IJUC) **7**, 489–524 (2011)
5. Bolognesi, T.: Algorithmic causal sets for a computational spacetime. In: Zenil, H. (ed.) A Computable Universe. World Scientific, Singapore (2013)
6. Bolognesi, T.: Do particles evolve? In: Zenil, H. (ed.) Irreducibility and Computational Equivalence. Springer, Heidelberg (2013). doi:10.1007/978-3-642-35482-3_12
7. Bolognesi, T.: Spacetime computing: towards algorithmic causal sets with special-relativistic properties. In: Adamatzky, A. (ed.) Advances in Unconventional Computing. ECC, vol. 22, pp. 267–304. Springer, Cham (2017). doi:10.1007/978-3-319-33924-5_12
8. Bolognesi, T.: Simple indicators for lorentzian causets. Class. Quantum Gravity **33**(18), 185004 (2016). (41 p.)
9. Bombelli, L., Henson, J., Sorkin, R.D.: Discreteness without symmetry breaking: a theorem May 01 2006. Mod. Phys. Lett. A **24**, 2579–2587 (2009). doi:10.1142/S0217732309031958
10. Bombelli, L., Lee, J., Meyer, D., Sorkin, R.D.: Space-time as a causal set. Phys. Rev. Lett. **59**(5), 521–524 (1987)
11. Bombelli, L., Lee, J., Meyer, D., Sorkin, R.D.: Reply to comment on 'space-time as a causal set'. Phys. Rev. Lett. **60**(7), 656 (1988)
12. Dowker, F., Henson, J., Sorkin, R.: Quantum gravity phenomenology, Lorentz invariance and discreteness. Mod. Phys. Lett. A **19**, 1829–1840 (2004)
13. Zenil, H. (ed.): A Computable Universe. World Scientific, Singapore (2013)
14. Ellis, G. (ed.): How Can Physics Underlie the Mind?. TFC. Springer, Heidelberg (2016). doi:10.1007/978-3-662-49809-5
15. Fredkin, E.: Five big questions with pretty simple answers. IBM J. Res. Dev. **48**(1), 31–45 (2004)
16. Gacs, P., Levin, L.A.: Causal nets or what is a deterministic computation? Inf. Control **51**, 1–19 (1981)
17. Gardner, M.: Mathematical games: the fantastic combinations of John Conway's new solitaire game 'Life'. Sci. Am. **223**(4), 120–123 (1970)
18. Hoel, E.P., Albantakis, L., Tononi, G.: Quantifying causal emergence shows that macro can beat micro. PNAS **110**(49), 19790–19795 (2013)
19. Kauffman, S.A.: Metabolic stability and epigenesis in randomly constructed genetic nets. J. Theoret. Biol. **22**, 437–467 (1969)
20. Langerak, R.: Bundle event structures: a non-interleaving semantics for LOTOS. In: Diaz, M. Groz, R. (eds) FORTE. IFIP Transactions, vol. C-10, pp. 331–346. North-Holland, Amsterdam (1992)
21. Lloyd, S.: Universe as quantum computer. Complexity **3**(1), 32–35 (1997)
22. Meyer, D.A.: The dimension of causal sets. Ph.D. thesis, MIT (1989)
23. Nowotny, T., Requardt, M.: Dimension theory of graphs and networks, July 1997. http://arxiv.org/abs/hep-th/9707082

24. Nussey, A., Tafjord, O.: Causal network generated by a mobile automaton. The Wolfram Demonstrations Project. http://demonstrations.wolfram.com/Cau salNetworkGeneratedByAMobileAutomaton/
25. Masafumi, O., Larissa, A., Giulio, T.: From the phenomenology to the mechanisms of consciousness: integrated information theory 3.0. PLoS Comput. Biol. **10**(5), e1003588 (2014)
26. Pearl, J.: Causality: Models, Reasoning and Inference, vol. 29. Cambridge University Press, Cambridge (2000)
27. Rideout, D.P.: HomePage. University of California, San Diego, valid March 2016. http://www.math.ucsd.edu/~drideout/
28. Rideout, D.P., Sorkin, R.D.: A classical sequential growth dynamics for causal sets. Phys. Rev. D **61**, 024002 (1999). http://arxiv.org/abs/gr-qc/9904062 [gr-qc]
29. Saravani, M., Aslanbeigi, S.: On the Causal Set-Continuum Correspondence, 25 May 2014. arXiv:1403.6429v1 [hep-th]
30. Sorkin, R.D.: Causal sets: discrete gravity. In : Gomberoff, A. Marolf, D. (eds.) Proceedings of the Valdivia Summer School, September 2003. http://arxiv.org/abs/gr-qc/0309009
31. Hooft, G.: The cellular automaton interpretation of quantum mechanics, June 2014. http://arxiv.org/abs/1405.1548 [quant-ph]
32. Winskel, G.: Event structures. In: Brauer, W., Reisig, W., Rozenberg, G. (eds.) ACPN 1986. LNCS, vol. 255, pp. 325–392. Springer, Heidelberg (1987). doi:10.1007/3-540-17906-2_31
33. Winskel, G.: An introduction to event structures. In: de Bakker, J.W., de Roever, W.-P., Rozenberg, G. (eds.) REX 1988. LNCS, vol. 354, pp. 364–397. Springer, Heidelberg (1989). doi:10.1007/BFb0013026
34. Wolfram, S.: A New Kind of Science. Wolfram Media Inc., Champaign (2002)
35. Zeleny, E.: Turing machine causal networks. The Wolfram Demonstrations Project. http://demonstrations.wolfram.com/TuringMachineCausalNetworks/
36. Zuse, K.: Calculating space. Technical report, Proj, MAC, MIT, Cambridge, Mass (1970). Technical Translation AZT-70-164-GEMIT. Original title: "Rechnender Raum"

Problem Solving Using Process Algebra Considered Insightful

Jan Friso Groote$^{(\boxtimes)}$ [ID] and Erik P. de Vink [ID]

Department of Mathematics and Computer Science,
Eindhoven University of Technology, Eindhoven, The Netherlands
{J.F.Groote,E.P.d.Vink}@tue.nl

Abstract. Process algebras with data, such as LOTOS, PSF, FDR, and mCRL2, are very suitable to model and analyse combinatorial problems. Contrary to more traditional mathematics, many of these problems can very directly be formulated in process algebra. Using a wide range of techniques, such as behavioural reductions, model checking, and visualisation, the problems can subsequently be easily solved. With the advent of probabilistic process algebras this also extends to problems where probabilities play a role. In this paper we model and analyse a number of very well-known – yet tricky – problems and show the elegance of behavioural analysis.

1 Introduction

There is great joy in solving combinatorial puzzles. Numerous books have appeared describing those [13,33]. And although some of the puzzles are easy to solve once properly understood, they are real brain teasers for most people.

Many of these puzzles are about behaviour. Classical mathematics and logic hardly provides an effective context to solve such problems systematically. This is apparent if one considers classical analysis. But also fields like graph theory, combinatorics, combinatorial optimisation, probability theory, and even logic all require a translation of the problem to the mathematical domain that is generally not completely straightforward.

This is where process algebras come in. Process algebras are very suited to describe the behaviour often present in the puzzles mentioned. In the last decades numerous tools have been developed to provide insight in the behaviour denoted in a process algebra expression as it quickly became clear that the behaviour described in such an expression can be rather intricate. This gave rise to hiding of actions, behavioural reductions, various visualisation techniques, as well as modal logics to express and validate properties about behaviour.

The early 1970s can be seen as the period when process algebra was born. Both Milner and Bekič wrote a treatise expressing that actions were important to study behaviour [2,25,27]. It was the seminal work of Milner in 1981 that put process algebras on the map [28]. This had quite some effect. For instance Hoare presented CSP in 1978 as an advanced programming language [21], whereas

© Springer International Publishing AG 2017
J.-P. Katoen et al. (Eds.): Brinksma Festschrift, LNCS 10500, pp. 48–63, 2017.
DOI: 10.1007/978-3-319-68270-9_3

he presented it in 1985 as a process algebra [22]. The work on CSP has been developed into the impressive family of tools, FDR, that are based on failure divergence refinement [14, 31].

The work on CCS also inspired the design of the language LOTOS [24] as a language to model communication services and protocols. A major role in its development was played by the Technische Hogeschool Twente (now Twente University) first in the completely formal standardisation of the language, with Brinksma as main editor, and later in activities to build tools around it. Notable are the extensive formal specifications of standard protocols, but also those of manufacturing systems, that were developed at the time [5, 7, 32]. The CADP toolset stems from this period [12]. It is the only major toolset still capable of analysing LOTOS specifications. Furthermore, it has become quite powerful throughout the years.

The Algebra of Communicating Processes (ACP) was developed in Amsterdam [3, 4] around the same time. In order to model practical systems first PSF (Protocol Specification Formalism) was designed [26], which was followed by the simpler formalism μCRL [18], later renamed to mCRL2, which was also directed towards analysis of practical specifications [17]. All these LOTOS-like formalisms use data based on abstract equational datatypes. mCRL2 also supports time and these days also probabilities.

An important feature of mCRL2 is the support for a modal logic with time and data, which is very useful to investigate properties of the described behaviour. Temporal logic, with the operators $[F]$ and $[P]$, stems from [30]. Pnueli pointed to the applicability of formal logics to analyse behaviour [29]. For mCRL2 we are using the modal mu-calculus which is essentially Hennessy-Milner logic [20] with fixed points [23]. An alternative is the use of linear time logic (LTL [29]) or computational tree logic (CTL [8]), but these are far less expressive than the modal mu-calculus [15].

In this paper we show process algebraic models of a number of well-known mathematical puzzles. Most people find them hard to solve when they are confronted with them for the first time. We show that the puzzles can straightforwardly be modelled into process algebra and using the standard analysis tools, such as behavioural reduction, model checking, and visualisation, the solutions to these puzzles are easy to obtain.

The major observation is that process algebra is an industrious mathematical discipline in itself due to its capacity to understand worldly phenomena. Traditionally, there is a tendency to think that process algebras, or more generally formal methods, are intended to analyse software, protocols, and complex distributed algorithms. But the application to examples as in this paper shows that process algebra has an independent stand.

In this paper we use the language mCRL2, as we are acquainted with it, and it offers all we need, namely the capacity to express behaviour, data structures, probabilities, time (although we do not exploit time here), and modal formulas. mCRL2 has a very rich toolset offering a whole range of analysis methods, far more than we use for the examples in this article. In the following we do not explain the tool nor the formalism. For this we refer to [17] or the webpage www.mcrl2.org. The examples in this article are part of the mCRL2 distribution downloadable from this website.

2   The Problem of the Wolf, Goat, and Cabbage

A problem that is well-known, at least to the people in Western Europe, is the problem of the wolf, the goat, and the cabbage: A traveller walks through stretched Russian woods together with a friendly wolf, a goat, and a cabbage. Hungry and worn out, this companionship arrives at a river that they must cross. There is a small boat only sufficient to carry our traveller and either the wolf, the goat, or the cabbage. More than two do not fit. Crossing is complex as when left unsupervised by the traveller, the wolf will eat the goat, while the goat will eat the cabbage. The question to answer is whether it is possible to cross the river without the goat or the cabbage being eaten.

This problem is quite old. It already appeared in a manuscript from the eighth century A.D. [1]. Dijkstra wrote one of his well-known EWDs addressing this problem [10]. The description in mCRL2 can be found in Table 1. The description uses two shores, *left* and *right*, which are essentially sets of 'items', i.e. sets of wolf, goat, and/or cabbage, resting at that shore. The opposite shore is given by a function *opp*. An update function is used to remove items from one side and add it to the other.

The behaviour of crossing the river is given by the process *WGC*. It has two parameters, namely the shores s comprised of the sets of items at each side of the river, and the current position p of the traveller. Observe that mCRL2 accommodates the use of data types such as sets which allows to neatly describe the shores as a pair of sets containing items. The first two pairs of lines of the *WGC* process express that if the wolf and the goat, or the goat and the cabbage are at the side opposite of the traveller, something is eaten, expressed by the action is_eaten. The symbol δ indicates that the process stops after this action. Note that actions are typeset in a different font for easy recognition.

The third group of lines of the process expresses that the traveller can move to the other shore alone, by performing the move action. To reduce the number of transitions somewhat, we only allow this when no item can be eaten. The fourth group of lines expresses that the traveller can transport one item from one shore to the other. The last group of lines states that if the complete companionship arrives at the right shore, the action done can take place. Initially, the traveller, wolf, goat, and cabbage are at the left shore.

As the state space of this behaviour is small, it can nicely be visualised. See Fig. 1. At the top we find the initial state, which is green. The goal state is coloured blue at the bottom. All states where an action is_eaten can be done are coloured red. They go to the white deadlocked state. All labels is_eaten are removed for readability. States where nothing is eaten are green, yellow, or blue. It is easy to see that there are paths from the green to the blue state through yellow states by moving counter clock wise through the graph. One of such paths is

Table 1. An mCRL2 description of the problem of the wolf, the goat, and the cabbage

```
sort  Item = struct wolf | goat | cabbage;
      Position = struct left | right;
      Shores = struct shores(Set(Item), Set(Item));

map   opp : Position → Position;
      items : Shores × Position → Set(Item);
      update : Shores × Position × Item → Shores;

var   s, t : Set(Item);
      i : Item;
eqn   opp(left) = right, opp(right) = left;
      items(shores(s, t), left) = s, items(shores(s, t), right) = t;
      update(shores(s, t), right, i) = shores(s − {i}, t + {i});
      update(shores(s, t), left, i) = shores(s + {i}, t − {i});

proc  WGC(s : Shores, p : Position) =
          {wolf, goat} ⊆ items(s, opp(p)) →
              is_eaten(goat)·δ +
          {goat, cabbage} ⊆ items(s, opp(p)) →
              is_eaten(cabbage)·δ +
          ¬({wolf, goat} ⊆ items(s, opp(p))) ∧ ¬({goat, cabbage} ⊆ items(s, opp(p))) →
              move(opp(p))·WGC(s, opp(p)) +
          Σ_{i:Item} ·(i ∈ items(s, p)) →
              move(opp(p), i)·WGC(update(s, opp(p), i), opp(p)) +
          items(s, right) ≈ {wolf, goat, cabbage} →
              done·δ;

init  WGC(shores({wolf, goat, cabbage}, ∅), left);
```

$$move(right, goat) \cdot move(left) \cdot move(right, wolf) \cdot move(left, goat) \cdot$$
$$move(right, cabbage) \cdot move(left) \cdot move(right, goat) \cdot done.$$

Inspection of the state space also reveals that there is one other essential solution to this problem, namely one where the places of the wolf and the cabbage are exchanged. This is no surprise as the wolf and the cabbage have symmetrical roles. Note that it is also clear why this puzzle is considered tricky. Each solution requires the counter intuitive step of moving the goat three times across the river, an insight that requires humans to overcome their default mental set.

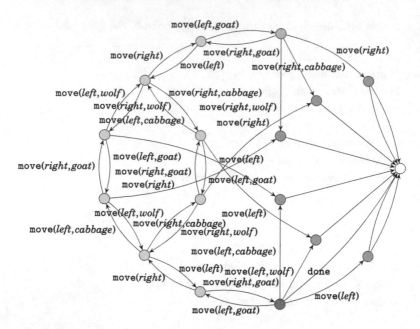

Fig. 1. The state space of the problem with the wolf, the goat and the cabbage (Color figure online)

For this puzzle we are lucky that the number of states is sufficiently small to be depicted. In general this is not the case. Fortunately, modal formulas are a marvellous tool to investigate properties of behaviour. In this case we want to know whether there is a path from the initial state to a state where the action done is possible, while no action is_eaten is possible in any of the states on this path. In the modal mu-calculus as available in the mCRL2 toolset this is expressed by

$$\mu X.(((\langle\text{true}\rangle X \vee \langle\text{done}\rangle\text{true}) \wedge \neg\langle\exists\text{i: } \textit{Item}.\texttt{is\_eaten}(i)\rangle\text{true}).$$

The use of the minimal fixed point guarantees that the action done must be reached in a finite number of steps. The modality ⟨true⟩ says that an arbitrary action can be done. Checking this formula instantly yields true confirming that the traveller can safely reach the other shore with all the companions intact.

3   Crossing a Rope Bridge in the Dark

The second problem is similar in nature to the first but not as well-known. Four people of different age arrive at a rope bridge across a canyon in the night. They need to cross the bridge as quickly as possible. Each person has its own time to cross the bridge, namely, 1, 2, 5, and 10 min. Unfortunately, the bridge can only carry the weight of two persons simultaneously. To make matters worse, they

Table 2. The problem of crossing a rope bridge specified in mCRL2

sort *Position* = **struct** *this_side* | *far_side* ;
         Person = **struct** p_1 | p_2 | p_3 | p_4 ;

map *travel_time* : *Person* → ℕ;
        initial_location : *Person* → *Position* ;
        other_side : *Position* → *Position* ;
        max_time : ℕ;

var *p* : *Person* ;
eqn *initial_location(p)* = *this_side* ;
        travel_time(p_1) = 1; *travel_time*(p_2) = 2;
        travel_time(p_3) = 5; *travel_time*(p_4) = 10;
        other_side(this_side) = *far_side* ;
        other_side(far_side) = *this_side* ;
        max_time = 20;

proc *X*(*light_position* : *Position*, *location* : *Person* → *Position*, *time* : ℕ) =
         time ≤ *max_time* ∧ ∀*p*:*Person*.*location*(*p*) ≈ *far_side* →
             ready(*time*)·δ +
         Σ*p*:*Person* ·
             time ≤ *max_time* ∧ *location*(*p*) ≈ *light_position* →
                 move(*p*,*other_side*(*location*(*p*)))·
                     X(*other_side*(*light_position*),
                         location[*p* → *other_side*(*location*(*p*))],
                         time + *travel_time*(*p*)) +
         Σ*p*,*p*′:*Person* ·
             p ≉ *p*′ ∧ *time* ≤ *max_time* ∧ *location*(*p*) ≈ *light_position* ∧
                 location(*p*′) ≈ *light_position* →
             move(*p*,*p*′,*other_side*(*location*(*p*)))·
                 X(*other_side*(*light_position*),
                     location[*p* → *other_side*(*location*(*p*))][*p*′ → *other_side*(*location*(*p*′))],
                     time + **max**(*travel_time*(*p*),*travel_time*(*p*′)));

init *X*(*this_side*,*initial_location*,0);

only carry one flashlight. Crossing without the flashlight is impossible. So, the flashlight needs to be returned for others to cross. The question is to find the minimal time in which the group of people can cross the bridge.

The problem is modelled in mCRL2 in Table 2. The location of each person is now given by a function *location*: *Person* → *Position*. The function update construction is used to change a function. The expression *location*[*p* → *s*] represents a new function which is equal to *location* except that person *p* is now mapped to position s. The parameter *time* records the total time to cross the bridge and *light_position* keeps track of the place of the flashlight.

The behaviour consists of three summands, and is a direct translation of the problem. The first summand expresses that if all people are at the far side, a **ready** action is done, reporting the time to cross. The second summand expresses that one person crosses the bridge, and the third summand indicates that two people move to the other side together.

Natural numbers in mCRL2 are specified using abstract data types and have no upper bound. This means that the state space of this problem is infinite as there are inefficient crossing strategies that can take arbitrarily large amounts of time. Although not strictly necessary, as mCRL2 is very suitable to investigate infinite state spaces, it is generally a wise strategy to keep state spaces finite and even as small as reasonably possible. Solving the problem naively, quickly leads to a crossing time of 19 min. We therefore limit the maximal crossing time to 20 min and focus on in the question whether crossing under 19 min is possible.

The generated state space is somewhat larger, namely 470 states and 1607 transitions, which disallows inspection as an explicit graph. Fortunately, we can use the tool `ltsview`, which can visualise the structure of large transition systems [16], in some case up to millions of states. Pictures made by `ltsview` appear to be rather pointless pieces of art at first glance, but when investigated, provide remarkable insight in the depicted behaviour.

The behaviour of crossing the rope bridge is depicted in Fig. 2 at the left. The initial state is at the top. The layering corresponds to the number of crossings of the bridge. The individually visible states and structures that grow to the side of the picture indicate deadlocks, i.e., states where the crossing time exceeds 20. For instance, the states at the end of the outward moving structure at the top right indicate that the bound of 20 min can be exceeded in three crossings. The red disk (the one but lowest) is the disk containing the action **ready**(17). There are no **ready** actions with a lower argument. This indicates that the bridge cannot be crossed in less than 17 min.

`ltsview` is not the most efficient way to inspect which **ready** actions are possible. By searching for actions while generating the state space it becomes immediately clear that the actions **ready**(17), **ready**(19) and **ready**(20) are possible. A trace to **ready**(17) is

$$\mathtt{move}(p_2, p_1, \mathit{far\_side}) \cdot \mathtt{move}(p_1, \mathit{this\_side}) \cdot \mathtt{move}(p_4, p_3, \mathit{far\_side}) \cdot$$
$$\mathtt{move}(p_2, \mathit{this\_side}) \cdot \mathtt{move}(p_2, p_1, \mathit{far\_side}) \cdot \mathtt{ready}(17).$$

This trace shows why this puzzle is hard to solve. The idea to save time to let the two slowest persons cross simultaneously does not easily come to mind for most people.

Using modal logics we can also easily check that 17 is the most optimal crossing time. The next formula, which says that there is a path to the action **ready**(17) and not to any action **ready**(n) for any $n < 17$, is readily proven to hold:

$$\langle \mathtt{true}^\star \cdot \mathtt{ready}(17) \rangle \, \mathtt{true} \wedge \forall n{:}\mathbb{N}.(n < 17 \rightarrow [\mathtt{true}^\star \cdot \mathtt{ready}(n)] \, \mathtt{false}).$$

Fig. 2. An `ltsview` visualisation of crossing a rope bridge and the game tic-tac-toe (Color figure online)

4   A Winning Strategy in Tic-tac-toe

Finding winning strategies in games can also be neatly expressed and studied in process theory. One of the simplest well-known games that can be analysed in this way is tic-tac-toe. Essentially, tic-tac-toe consists of a 3 by 3 board where two players alternatingly put a naught or cross at empty positions on the board. The first player that has three of naughts or crosses in a row, horizontally, vertically or diagonally, wins the game.

Table 3 contains a rather natural formalisation of this game. The playing board is given by a function from pairs of naturals to pieces. A less elegant formulation uses lists of lists of pieces, but for state space generation this is much faster. A player moves by putting its own piece at an empty position on the board using the action put. The action win is used to indicate that one of the players did win. The most complex function is $did\_win(p, b)$, checking whether player p, represented by a piece, did win the game. In the formalisation we use $c \rightarrow p \diamond q$ denoting 'if c then p else q'.

The total behaviour of this game has 5479 states and 17109 transitions, which is not very large. This behaviour is depicted in Fig. 2 at the right. The red dot at the right middle indicates where player 'naught' can win. There are more such states two disks lower, but they are hardly visible in the figure.

Although the transition system for this game is relatively small, it makes no sense to investigate it directly to determine whether the player that starts the game has a winning strategy. Fortunately, modal formulas come to the rescue.

Table 3. An mCRL2 formalisation of tic-tac-toe

sort *Piece* = **struct** *empty* | *naught* | *cross* ;
   Board = $\mathbb{N}^+ \rightarrow \mathbb{N}^+ \rightarrow$ *Piece* ;

map *empty_board* : *Board* ;
   did_win : *Piece* × *Board* $\rightarrow$ $\mathbb{B}$;
   other : *Piece* $\rightarrow$ *Piece* ;

var *b* : *Board* ;
   p : *Piece* ;
   i, j : $\mathbb{N}^+$;

eqn *empty_board*(*i*)(*j*) = *empty* ;
   other(*naught*) = *cross* ; *other*(*cross*) = *naught* ;
   did_win(*p, b*) =
      $(\exists i : \mathbb{N}^+ . (i \leqslant 3 \land b(i)(1) \approx p \land b(i)(2) \approx p \land b(i)(3) \approx p)) \lor$
      $(\exists j : \mathbb{N}^+ . (j \leqslant 3 \land b(1)(j) \approx p \land b(2)(j) \approx p \land b(3)(j) \approx p)) \lor$
      $(b(1)(1) \approx p \land b(2)(2) \approx p \land b(3)(3) \approx p) \lor$
      $(b(1)(3) \approx p \land b(2)(2) \land p \approx b(3)(1) \approx p)$;

proc *TicTacToe*(*board* : *Board*, *player* : *Piece*) =
      did_win(*other*(*player*), *board*) $\rightarrow$
         win(*other*(*player*))·δ
      $\diamond$ $(\Sigma_{i,j:Pos} . (i \leqslant 3 \land j \leqslant 3 \land board(i)(j) \approx empty) \rightarrow$
         put(*player*, *i*, *j*)·
            TicTacToe(*board*[*i* $\rightarrow$ *board*(*i*)[*j* $\rightarrow$ *player*]], *other*(*player*)));

init *TicTacToe*(*empty_board*, *cross*);

The following formula expresses that player 'cross' has a winning strategy. It says that there is a way to put a cross on the board after which player 'cross' wins, or for every counter move by player 'naught', X must hold again, saying that also in that case player 'cross' has a winning strategy. This formula is invalid. There is no winning strategy for the player 'cross', and due to symmetry neither for player 'naught'.

$$\mu X. \langle \exists i, j : \mathbb{N}^+ . \text{put}(cross, i, j) \rangle \, (\langle \text{win}(cross) \rangle \text{true} \lor$$
$$([\exists i, j : \mathbb{N}^+ . \text{put}(naught, i, j)] \, X \, \land \, \langle \text{true} \rangle \text{true}))$$

Note that we use of a minimal fixed point operator expressing that winning must happen within a finite number of steps. As there are only a limited number of moves in tic-tac-toe this is always satisfied, hence a maximal fixed point operator could also have been used.

5   The Monty Hall Problem

Processes algebras have seen various extensions. One of these extensions is the addition of probabilities, which gives rise to the interesting combination of nondeterministic and probabilistic behaviour. This opens up the field of probabilistic puzzles to be modelled. The Monty Hall problem is a very nice example, because when understood is it very simple, yet most people fail to solve it properly.

Table 4. An mCRL2 specification of the Monty Hall quiz

---

sort *Doors* = **struct** $d_1 \mid d_2 \mid d_3$;
init **dist** *door_with_prize* : *Doors* [1/3].
    dist *initially_selected_door_by_player* : *Doors* [1/3].
        player_collects_prize(*initially_selected_door_by_player* $\not=$ *door_with_prize*)·δ;

The Monty Hall problem is a tv-quiz from the 1960s. A player can win a prize when he opens one of three doors with the prize behind it. Initially, the player selects a door with probability $\frac{1}{3}$. Subsequently, the quizmaster opens one of the remaining doors showing that it does not hide the prize. The question is whether the player should switch doors to optimise his winning probability.

The problem is expressed in the specification in Table 4. The process only consists of a single action player_collects_prize(b) where the boolean argument b is true if a prize is collected. The **dist** keyword is used to indicate a probability distribution. The process **dist** $x : S[D(x)].p$ indicates that variable x of sort S is selected with probability distribution $D(x)$. One of the doors hides the prize. This door is represented by the variable *door_with_prize* which can have values d_1, d_2, or d_3, each with a probability of $\frac{1}{3}$. Initially, the player selects a door. If the player decides to switch doors after the quizmaster opened a door, the player has a prize if and only if the initially chosen door did *not* carry the prize. This is expressed by the use of not equal sign ($\not=$) in the argument of the action. If the player decides to stick to the door that was initially selected, the not equal sign should be replaced by equality.

The resulting state space has 9 transitions each with a probability $\frac{1}{9}$. It is convenient to apply a probabilistic bisimulation reduction on the transition system. This leads to the reduced transition system in Fig. 3. It is clearly visible that the action player_collects_prize(true) can be done with probability $\frac{2}{3}$. Thus, when switching doors the probability of obtaining a prize is $\frac{2}{3}$, opposed to $\frac{1}{3}$ when not switching doors.

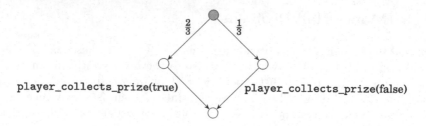

Fig. 3. The reduced probabilistic transition system for the Monty Hall problem

6   The Problem of the Lost Boarding Pass

More complex probabilistic problems can become rather hard even with the full strength of probability theory at ones disposal. Yet modelling the problem in mCRL2 is again pretty straightforward. The tools can subsequently help to obtain the required answer.

A particularly intriguing puzzle is that of the lost boarding pass as it has a remarkable answer, defying the intuition of most people trying to solve the problem: There is a plane with 100 seats. The first passenger boarding the plane lost his boarding ticket and selects a random seat. Each subsequent passenger will use his own seat unless it is already occupied. In that case he also selects a random seat. The question is what the probability is that the *last* passenger entering the plane will sit in his own seat.

The behaviour is modelled in Table 5. The number N is the number of seats, which is set to 100. The behaviour of entering the plane is characterised by two parameters. The parameter *number_of_empty_seats* indicates how many seats are still empty in the plane. The parameter *everybody_has_his_own_seat* indicates that all remaining seats correspond exactly with the places for all passengers that still have to board the plane. Except if the number of empty seats is 0. In that case it indicates whether the last passenger got its own seat.

Initially the first passenger selects his seat at random. With probability $\frac{1}{N}$ he will end up at his own seat. This corresponds with the situation where b is true. In the main process *Plane*, when all passengers have boarded the plane, the action last_passenger_has_his_own_seat indicates by its argument whether the last passenger got his own seat. If not all passengers boarded the plane yet, a next passenger enters (indicated by the action enter) and then it can either be that he finds his own seat free (b_0 is true) or occupied (b_0 is false). If everybody is sitting at is own seat this next passenger will for sure find his own seat free. Otherwise, he finds his own seat free with probability $1 - 1/number\_of\_empty\_seats$ as exactly one person is sitting on a wrong seat.

When this next passenger finds his own seat free he can sit down. This is done by the action select_seat with two parameters. But if his own seat is occupied, he must randomly select a seat for himself. If he selects the seat such

Table 5. An mCRL2 specification of the lost boarding pass

map $N : \mathbb{N}^+$;
eqn $N = 100$;

proc *Plane*(*everybody_has_his_own_seat* : $\mathbb{B}$, *number_of_empty_seats* : $\mathbb{N}$) =
      (*number_of_empty_seats* ≈ 0) $\rightarrow$
        last_passenger_has_his_own_seat(*everybody_has_his_own_seat*)·δ
      $\diamond$ (enter·
        dist b_0 : $\mathbb{B}$[*if*(*everybody_has_his_own_seat*, *if*(b_0, 1, 0),
             if(b_0, $1 - 1$/*number_of_empty_seats*, 1/*number_of_empty_seats*))].
        b_0 $\rightarrow$ select_seat·
        Plane(*everybody_has_his_own_seat*, *number_of_empty_seats* $- 1$)
        $\diamond$ **dist** b_1 : $\mathbb{B}$[*if*(b_1, 1/*number_of_empty_seats*, $1-1$/*number_of_empty_seats*)].
        select_seat·
        Plane(*if*(*number_of_empty_seats*≈ 1, *everybody_has_his_own_seat*, b_1),
          number_of_empty_seats $- 1$));

init **dist** b : $\mathbb{B}$[*if*(b, 1/N, $(N-1)$/N)].*Plane*(b, $N - 1$);

that all passengers are sitting on their assigned seats (modulo a permutation) this is indicated in the variable b_1, where this passenger has probability

$$1/number\_of\_empty\_seats$$

of doing this.

The generated state space turns out to be linear in the size of the number of seats. It has 791 states and 790 transitions. Modulo strong probabilistic bisimulation there are 399 states and 398 transitions. It has the shape of a long sequence, as depicted in Fig. 4. Detailed exploration of this figure indicates that whence all the remaining passengers correspond to the remaining seats the last passenger will certainly get his own seat. Yet it is not obvious what the probability for the last passenger to get his own seat is. For this we use two – at present experimental – tools[1]. The first one applies a probabilistic weak trace reduction. The obtained state space, see Fig. 5, is rather non-exciting but indicates clearly that the probability of the last passenger to end up at its own seat is $\frac{1}{2}$. The remarkable property of this exercise is that this probability is independent of the number of seats.

---

[1] The tools are by Olav Bunte (evaluation of modal formulas on probabilistic transition systems) and Ferry Timmers (probabilistic trace reduction).

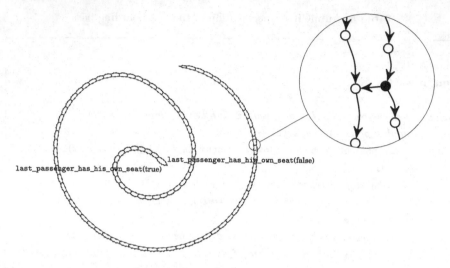

Fig. 4. The state space of the problem of the lost boarding pass with 100 passengers

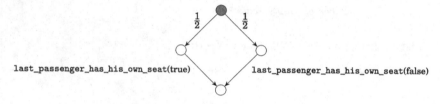

Fig. 5. The state space of the lost boarding pass problem modulo weak trace equivalence

There is another way to obtain this probability by employing modal formulas over reals. These formulas are derived from the modal mu-calculus but deliver a real number, instead of a boolean. In this case the formula is just

$$\langle \text{true}^{\star} \cdot \text{last\_passenger\_has\_his\_own\_seat}(\text{true}) \rangle \, \text{true}$$

which is possible as the state space is deterministic. Needless to say that the verification of this formula yields $\frac{1}{2}$ as well.

7   Concluding Remarks

Process algebra is generally well-suited to solve many behaviour-oriented mathematical puzzles. In this paper we have used the process algebraic framework of mCRL2 to show how to model a number of such puzzles. Subsequently, the standard analysis tools available in mCRL2 (and occasionally an experimental one) were used for behavioural reduction, model checking and visualisation. From this it is clear that process algebra has a wider scope than the usual fields of software analysis and distributed computing in which it finds many applications.

Process algebra focuses on behavioural aspects of the subject of study. The underpinning algebraic and equational theory allows to relate to logics, in particular modal logics [6], as descriptions of properties or requirements over space, time, and probabilities. Logical characterisations and their assessment via model checking are a valuable replacement in situations where visual techniques, highlighted for the puzzles discussed here, become impractical.

Also other authors indicated that a notion of behaviour or state space is required for proper conditional reasoning, especially in the probabilistic setting. In [19] the distinction is made between 'naive' and 'sophisticated' space. For the Monty Hall puzzle this amounts to the three doors for the naive space, and to sequences of events for the sophisticated space. In the process algebraic modelling of the problem, it is exactly the latter that is determined by the specified behaviour, thus making the underlying protocol explicit.

Although we defend the use of process algebra as a qualitatively better approach to solving behavioural problems, this is a subjective opinion, influenced by our experience with process algebras. To substantiate this in a more objective manner one should measure how much time people need to solve particular problems with particular techniques, for instance by psychological tests.

If process algebraic techniques become commonplace, it might be that the nature of 'tricky' puzzles will shift where the proper behaviour is not directly obvious. Nice examples are for instance Freudenthal problems, containing knowledge, like the Muddy Children puzzle [11]. Translating knowledge into behaviour often requires a twist. In such cases dynamic epistemic logic might be more suitable [9].

Acknowledgment. The authors are grateful to the reviewers for their constructive and inspiring comments.

References

1. Hadley, J., Singmaster, D.: Problems to sharpen the young. Math. Gaz. **76**(475), 102–126 (1992). doi:10.2307/3620384
2. Bekič, H.: Towards a mathematical theory of processes. Technical report TR25.125, IBM Laboratory, Vienna (1971). Also appeared in Jones, C.B. (ed.) Programming Languages and Their Definition, Lecture Notes in Computer Science, vol. 177. Springer (1984)
3. Bergstra, J.A., Klop, J.W.: Fixed point semantics in process algebras. Report IW 206, Mathematisch Centrum, Amsterdam (1982)
4. Bergstra, J.A., Klop, J.W.: Process algebra for synchronous communication. Inf. Comput. **60**(1/3), 109–137 (1984)
5. Biemans, F., Blonk, P.: On the formal specification and verification of CIM architectures using LOTOS. Comput. Ind. **7**(6), 491–504 (1986)
6. Blackburn, P., van Benthem, J., Wolter, F. (eds.): Handbook of Modal Logic. Studies in Logic and Practical Reasoning, vol. 3. Elsevier, Amsterdam (2007)
7. Brinksma, E., Karjoth, G.: A specification of the OSI transport service in LOTOS. In: Yemini, Y., Strom, R.E., Yemini, S. (eds.) Protocol Specification, Testing and Verification IV, pp. 227–251. North-Holland, Amsterdam (1984)

8. Clarke, E.M., Emerson, E.A.: Design and synthesis of synchronization skeletons using branching time temporal logic. In: Kozen, D. (ed.) Logic of Programs 1981. LNCS, vol. 131, pp. 52–71. Springer, Heidelberg (1982). doi:10.1007/BFb0025774
9. van Ditmarsch, H., van der Hoek, W., Kooij, B.: Dynamic Epistemic Logic. Studies in Epistemology, Logic, Methodology, and Philosophy of Science, vol. 337. Springer, Heidelberg (2008). doi:10.1007/978-1-4020-5839-4
10. Dijkstra, E.W.: Pruning the search tree. EWD1255. www.cs.utexas.edu/users/EWD/transcriptions/EWD12xx/EWD1255.html. Accessed June 2017
11. van Emde Boas, P., Groenendijk, J., Stokhof, M.: The conway paradox: its solution in an epistemic framework. In: Groenendijk, J., Janssen, T.M.V., Stokhof, M. (eds.) Truth, Interpretation, and Information: Selected Papers from the Third Amsterdam Colloquium, pp. 159–182. Foris Publications, New York (1984)
12. Garavel, H., Lang, F., Mateescu, R., Serwe, W.: CADP 2011: a toolbox for the construction and analysis of distributed processes. Int. J. Softw. Tools Technol. Transf. 15(2), 89–107 (2013)
13. Gardner, M.: My Best Mathematical and Logic Puzzles. Dover, Downers Grove (1994)
14. Gibson-Robinson, T., Armstrong, P., Boulgakov, A., Roscoe, A.W.: FDR3 — a modern refinement checker for CSP. In: Ábrahám, E., Havelund, K. (eds.) TACAS 2014. LNCS, vol. 8413, pp. 187–201. Springer, Heidelberg (2014). doi:10.1007/978-3-642-54862-8_13
15. Cranen, S., Groote, J.F., Reniers, M.A.: A linear translation from CTL* to the first-order modal μ-calculus. Theoret. Comput. Sci. 412(28), 3129–3139 (2011)
16. Groote, J.F., van Ham, F.: Interactive visualization of large state spaces. Int. J. Softw. Tools Technol. Transf. 8(1), 77–91 (2006)
17. Groote, J.F., Mousavi, M.R.: Modeling and Analysis of Communication Systems. The MIT Press, Cambridge (2014). (See for the toolset www.mcrl2.org)
18. Groote, J.F., Ponse, A.: The syntax and semantics of μCRL. Report CS-R9076, CWI, Amsterdam (1990)
19. Grünwald, P., Halpern, J.Y.: Updating probabilities. In: Darwiche, A., Friedman, N. (eds.) Uncertainty in Artificial Intelligence, pp. 187–196. Morgan Kaufman, Burlington (2002)
20. Hennessy, M., Milner, R.: On observing nondeterminism and concurrency. In: de Bakker, J., van Leeuwen, J. (eds.) ICALP 1980. LNCS, vol. 85, pp. 299–309. Springer, Heidelberg (1980). doi:10.1007/3-540-10003-2_79
21. Hoare, C.A.R.: Communicating sequential processes. Commun. ACM 21(8), 666–677 (1978)
22. Hoare, C.A.R.: Communicating Sequential Processes. Prentice Hall International, Upper Saddle River (1985)
23. Kozen, D.: Results on the propositional μ-calculus. Theoret. Comput. Sci. 27, 333–354 (1983)
24. ISO 8807:1989. Information processing systems - Open Systems Interconnection - LOTOS - A formal description technique based on the temporal ordering of observational behaviour. ISO/IECJTC1/SC7 (1989)
25. Milner, R.: An approach to the semantics of parallel programs. In: Proceedings Convegno di Informatica Teorica, pp. 283–302, Pisa (1973)
26. Mauw, S., Veltink, G.J.: A process specification formalism. Fundam. Inform. XIII, 85–139 (1990)
27. Milner, R.: Processes: a mathematical model of computing agents. In: Rose, H.E., Shepherdson, J.C. (eds.) Proceedings Logic Colloquium 1972, pp. 158–173. North-Holland, Amsterdam (1973)

28. Milner, R. (ed.): A Calculus of Communicating Systems. LNCS, vol. 92. Springer, Heidelberg (1980)
29. Pnueli, A.: The temporal logic of programs. In: Foundations of Computer Science, pp. 46–57. IEEE, Piscataway (1977)
30. Prior, A.N.: Time and Modality. Oxford University Press, Oxford (1957)
31. Roscoe, A.W.: Understanding Concurrent Systems. Springer, Heidelberg (2010). doi:10.1007/978-1-84882-258-0
32. van Sinderen, M., Ajubi, I., Caneschi, F.: The application of LOTOS for the formal description of the ISO session layer. In: Turner, K.J. (ed.) Formal Description Techniques, pp. 263–277. North-Holland, Amsterdam (1989)
33. Winkler, P.: Mathematical Puzzles. A Connaisseur's Collection. A.K. Peters, Natick (2004)

Delayed-Choice Semantics for Pomset Families and Message Sequence Graphs

Clemens Dubslaff[✉] and Christel Baier

Faculty of Computer Science, Technische Universität Dresden, Dresden, Germany
{clemens.dubslaff,christel.baier}@tu-dresden.de

Abstract. Message sequence charts (MSCs) are diagrams widely used to describe communication scenarios. Their higher-order formalism is provided by graphs over MSCs, called message sequence graphs (MSGs), which naturally induce a non-interleaving linear-time semantics in terms of a pomset family. Besides this pomset semantics, an operational semantics for MSGs was standardized by the ITU-T as an interleaving branching-time semantics using a process-algebraic approach. A key ingredient in the latter semantics is *delayed choice*, formalizing that choices between communication scenarios are only made when they are inevitable. In this paper, an approach towards branching-time semantics for pomset families that follows the concept of delayed choice is proposed. First, *transition-system semantics* are provided where global states comprise cuts of pomsets represented either by suffixes or prefixes of family members. Second, an *event-structure semantics* is presented those benefit is to maintain the causal dependencies of events provided by the pomset family. These semantics are also investigated in the context of pomset families generated by MSGs.

1 Introduction

During the last decades, much effort has been put into developing models for concurrent systems to specify and reason about communication protocols. *Message sequence charts (MSCs)* provide an intuitive formalism to describe scenarios for asynchronously communicating processes. They are standardized by the ITU [18] and have been also included into the current UML 2.0 specification [11] as *sequence diagrams*. An MSC comprises time lines for each process on which events of the respective process are totally ordered, and message arrows that connect corresponding send and receive events between the processes. Two communication scenarios given by MSCs can be composed by extending the time lines of the first MSC by the time lines of the same process in the second MSC. This naturally allows for specifying collections of MSCs by graphs over MSCs, called *message sequence graphs (MSGs)*: an MSG describes all those MSCs that arise from sequential compositions of MSCs along paths in the MSG.

The authors are supported by Deutsche Telekom Stiftung, by the DFG through the Collaborative Research Center SFB 912 – HAEC, the Excellence Initiative by the German Federal and State Governments (cluster of excellence cfAED), the DFG-projects BA-1679/11-1 and BA-1679/12-1, and the 5G Lab Germany.

© Springer International Publishing AG 2017
J.-P. Katoen et al. (Eds.): Brinksma Festschrift, LNCS 10500, pp. 64–84, 2017.
DOI: 10.1007/978-3-319-68270-9_4

Example 1. In Fig. 1, an example MSG is depicted that contains two non-empty MSCs, both describing a communication scenario where process s sends data to process r and waits for an acknowledgment. The left scenario branch models the case where a failure during the transmission of data occurred, imposing a timeout at process s. Then, s resends the data to r, being either unsuccessful again (see the self loop at the left box) or being successful (switching to the right box). In the latter case, when r successfully received all data, an acknowledgement is sent to s and the communication between s and r terminates.

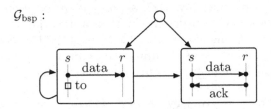

Fig. 1. An example MSG for sender-receiver communication scenarios

Semantics for MSGs. In the taxonomy of models for concurrent systems [34], different abstraction levels of semantics are provided along two orthogonal axes: one distinguishes between non-interleaving and interleaving and the other between branching-time and linear-time semantics. Non-interleaving semantics model causal dependencies and the independence of actions in an explicit way. Within branching-time semantics, the information when choices are made during an execution of the system can be modeled, while linear-time semantics abstract away from the points where these choices are made. To this end, non-interleaving branching-time semantics can be seen as the most general semantics in this taxonomy and interleaving linear-time semantics as the most abstracted ones.

MSCs naturally induce a non-interleaving linear-time semantics in terms of a *partially-ordered multiset (pomset)* [30], provided by the total time-line orderings and the fact that any send event has to precede its corresponding receive event [1]. The composition of MSCs is defined syntactically by gluing process time lines together. This corresponds to the *local concatenation* of pomsets [30] where events of the same process are assumed to depend on each other. Thus, a non-interleaving linear-time semantics for MSGs is naturally defined by a family of pomsets comprising the MSCs that arise from concatenating pomsets of MSCs along paths in the MSG. This semantics for MSGs is widely accepted in the literature and often used to reason about MSGs (cf., e.g., [2,5,19,21,26,28] and surveys [9,27]).

Although the pomset semantics for MSGs is very natural, the standard semantics for MSGs specified by the international telecommunication union (ITU-T) in [17] is an interleaving branching-time semantics, defined through a process-algebraic approach. Besides historical reasons, the choice of this approach has been mainly motivated by providing an operational semantics for

MSGs that allows to reason about the step-wise behavior of systems specified by MSGs [23,31]. The basic building blocks of the process-algebraic semantics are process terms for MSCs [22] defined over atomic actions, standard concatenation ·, and standard choice +. These process terms have an interleaving branching-time semantics. The standardized process-algebraic semantics for MSGs is obtained by a well-known standard transformation from automata theory, leading to a regular expression over process terms for MSCs [31]. Within this regular expression, special operators for concatenation, choice and recursion [17,23,24,31][1] are employed:

- Concatenation is provided by *weak sequential composition* borrowed from [33] those purpose is to transfer the local concatenation on pomsets [30] to the world of interleaving branching-time semantics. The definition of weak sequential composition is based on a *permission relation* that specifies how process terms can be influenced by firing actions not contained in the process term itself but in its context.
- The choice operator is given by *delayed choice* [3], an intrinsic linear-time operator where choices between MSC fragments are delayed until they are inevitable. According to [3], "the delayed-choice operator acts as a deterministic choice in the context of strong bisimulation by unifying process-algebra terms with a common prefix".
- Recursion is defined by adapting the recursion operator of [4] for MSGs with rules for weak sequential composition and delayed choice [31].

The main challenge within the process-algebraic approach towards an operational semantics for MSGs comes into play when interpreting recursion on process terms that involve weak sequential composition and delayed choice, as their definition requires negative premises in the operator-defining rules. It is well known that negative premises in operator-specifying rules impose several difficulties when aiming towards fixed points [10]. Reniers, one of the authors of the standardized process-algebraic semantics [17], noticed in his doctoral thesis [31] that "the definition of the permission relation on recursive equations is extremely difficult and no solution is found there yet" (see page 160 of [31]). Although [31] adapted the standardized semantics to avoid recursive equations, his process-algebraic semantics still contains negative premises in operator-specifying rules. Besides others, this raises the question whether an operational semantics for MSGs could be defined without sophisticated operators in terms of weak sequential composition and delayed choice but where the main concepts of the standardized process-algebraic semantics are maintained.

Our Contribution. Following the concept of delayed choice but avoiding sophisticated process-algebraic operators, we define branching-time semantics for pomset families. During the presentation of our semantics, we exemplify

---

[1] The cited papers focus on *high-level MSCs*, i.e., MSGs which in addition allow for a hierarchical structure and parallel composition. As high-level MSCs can be unfolded into an MSG [2] without changing their operational semantics, we disregard the parallel composition operator and focus solely on MSGs in this paper.

their application to MSGs using the running example from the introduction. We first aim towards interleaving branching-time semantics (as within the process-algebraic approach defining delayed choice [3]) and present two different views on defining transition systems for pomset families:

(1) **Suffix transition systems** arise from interpreting delayed choice on pomset families that, similar to the process-algebraic approach, contain all possible future behaviors of pomset-family members. This semantics is used as a reference model for all other semantics in this paper.

(2) **Prefix transition systems** interpret delayed choice based on the past behaviors of the pomset family members. They are deterministic and bisimilar to the corresponding suffix transition system (1).

The purpose of suffix transition systems (1) is to closely follow the process-algebraic approach for defining delayed-choice semantics in the context of pomset families. Prefix transition systems (2) complete the picture of our approach and extend the delayed-choice semantics for MSGs provided in [8] towards arbitrary pomset families. This semantics thus provides the connection of the semantics defined throughout this paper to the approach by [8]. Every MSG naturally induces a pomset family where each member is an MSC. Thus, suffix and prefix transition systems also provide delayed-choice semantics for MSGs.

We furthermore present a non-interleaving branching-time semantics for pomset families in terms of a prime event structure [29]:

(3) **Pomset event structures** maintain the causality information between the events in the pomset family members. For pomsets generated by MSGs, the transition system induced by the pomset event structure is isomorphic to the corresponding prefix transition system (2).

As far as we know, pomset event structures (3) provide the first non-interleaving branching-time semantics for MSGs that follows the concept of delayed choice.

As intended by the authors of [33], it is quite natural that the weak sequential composition operator corresponds to the local concatenation of pomsets in our setting, not requiring the sophisticated definition of the permission relation that imposes difficulties within recursion. We show that the process-algebraic delayed-choice operator corresponds to the standard union operation in the setting of pomset families.

Further Related Work. The process-algebraic approach for the standard operational semantics for MSGs [17,23,24,31] uses interleaved models of MSCs as basic building blocks. Based on these process terms for MSCs, sophisticated operators of weak sequential composition and delayed choice are used to mimic the linear-time behavior of MSGs in the branching-time setting. This is in contrast to our approach, where we use the pomset semantics for MSCs as basic building blocks and exploit standard linear-time operators *before* interleaving pomset families towards a branching-time semantics.

Besides using the process-algebraic approach, a transition-system semantics for MSGs has been presented in [7] also based on the pomset semantics for MSGs but not obeying delayed choice in the sense as we establish in this paper. In particular, the transition system of [7] is not deterministic. Most related to our pomset event structure (3) is the prime-event-structure semantics for MSGs presented in [12]. However, their recursive definition employs the standard choice operator instead of delayed choice, inducing a transition-system semantics that is non-deterministic and infinitely branching. Further branching-time semantics not following the concept of delayed choice have been presented as graphs with synchronization points [21], or Petri-net components [14].

In order to reason about quantitative aspects of MSGs, our previous work in [8] presented a transition-system semantics for MSGs that essentially corresponds to the prefix transition-system semantics (cf. (2) above).

2   Preliminaries

In this section, we recall basic concepts of models for concurrency, communication systems and notations used throughout this paper. By $\mathbb{N}$ we denote the set of non-negative integers. For any set X, we denote by 2^X the power set of X.

2.1   Models for Concurrency

The models we use throughout this paper mainly follow the taxonomy detailed in the introduction (cf., e.g., [34]), comprising linear-time models in terms of *formal languages* (interleaving) and *pomsets* (non-interleaving), and branching-time models in terms of *transition systems* (interleaving) and *event structures* (non-interleaving). Furthermore, we follow the principle of atomic *actions*, i.e., tasks of the system indivisible on the abstraction level of the model, where we denote by Σ the alphabet of all actions. Instances of actions are *events* from a set E that are labeled by its corresponding action name via a labeling function $\lambda \colon E \to \Sigma$.

Formal Languages. We denote by $\Sigma^\star$ and Σ^+ the set of all finite and non-empty finite words over Σ, respectively. By ε we denote the empty word. A *language* over Σ is a subset of $\Sigma^\star$. By $w[i]$ we denote the $(i+1)$-st symbol of a word w and by $|w|$ the length of w.

Pomsets. A labeled partial order is a tuple $\mathcal{P} = (E, \leqslant, \lambda)$, where $\leqslant$ is a partial order over a set of events E and $\lambda \colon E \to \Sigma$ is the labeling function. We identify isomorphic labeled partial orders, i.e., we treat them as *pomsets* [30]. We call a pomset *basic* if λ is injective and *finite* if E is a finite set. If not stated differently, we assume any pomset to be finite. Furthermore, we restrict ourselves to pomsets that are not autoconcurrent, i.e., for all $e, e' \in E$ with $\lambda(e) = \lambda(e')$ we have either $e \leqslant e'$ or $e \geqslant e'$. The empty pomset is denoted by $\oslash$. The set of pomsets over Σ is denoted by $\mathbb{PO}_\Sigma$. A linearization of $\mathcal{P}$ is a word $w \in \Sigma^\star$ for which there is a bijection $\xi \colon \{0, ..., |w|-1\} \to E$ with $\lambda(\xi(i)) = w[i]$ and $\xi(i) \not> \xi(j)$

for all $i \leqslant j < |w|$. $\mathcal{P}$ is *total* if for all $e, e' \in E$ with $e \neq e'$ we have either $e < e'$ or $e > e'$. With abuse of notations, we identify total orders with their linearization. For a set of events F, we denote by $\mathcal{P}|_F$ the projection of $\mathcal{P}$ onto F, i.e., the pomset $(E \cap F, \leqslant_F, \lambda_F)$, where $e \leqslant_F e'$ iff $e, e' \in E \cap F$ and $e \leqslant e'$, and where $\lambda_F(e) = \alpha$ iff $e \in F \cap E$ and $\lambda(e) = \alpha$. The *upward closure* on F is defined as $\uparrow F = \{e \in E : \exists e' \in F.e \geqslant e'\}$. A pomset $\mathcal{P}'$ for which there is an upward closed F with $\mathcal{P}' = \mathcal{P}|_F$ is called *suffix* of $\mathcal{P}$. $\mathcal{P}'$ is an α-*suffix* of $\mathcal{P}$ if furthermore $E \backslash F = \{e\}$ with $\lambda(e) = \alpha$. The set of all (α-) suffixes of $\mathcal{P}$ is denoted by $\mathrm{Suff}(\mathcal{P})$ ($\mathrm{Suff}_\alpha(\mathcal{P})$, respectively). Accordingly, we define the notions of *downward closure* $\downarrow F$, and *prefixes* $\mathrm{Pref}(\mathcal{P})$ and $\mathrm{Pref}_\alpha(\mathcal{P})$. A *pomset family* is a set of pomsets, where we denote the set of all pomset families over Σ by $\mathbf{POF}_\Sigma = 2^{\mathbf{PO}_\Sigma}$. Notations for pomsets defined above extend to pomset families $\mathfrak{P} \in \mathbf{POF}_\Sigma$ as expected, e.g., for some $\alpha \in \Sigma$, $\mathrm{Suff}_\alpha(\mathfrak{P}) = \bigcup_{\mathcal{P} \in \mathfrak{P}} \mathrm{Suff}_\alpha(\mathcal{P})$. The notion of α-suffixes is generalized to pomset families $\mathrm{Suff}_w(\mathfrak{P})$ of w-suffixes of $\mathfrak{P}$ for $w \in \Sigma^\star$ by defining $\mathrm{Suff}_\varepsilon(\mathfrak{P}) = \mathfrak{P}$ and $\mathrm{Suff}_{w\alpha}(\mathfrak{P}) = \mathrm{Suff}_\alpha(\mathrm{Suff}_w(\mathfrak{P}))$, for $w \in \Sigma^\star$, $\alpha \in \Sigma$.

Transition Systems. A *transition system* over an alphabet Σ is a tuple $\mathcal{T} = (S, \longrightarrow, \iota, \mathrm{Term})$ where S is a countable set of states, $\longrightarrow \subseteq S \times \Sigma \times S$ a transition relation, $\iota \in S$ an initial state, and $\mathrm{Term} \subseteq S$ a set of *termination states*. A *path* for a word $w = \alpha_0 \alpha_1 \cdots \alpha_{n-1}$ is a sequence $\pi = s_0 \alpha_0 s_1 \alpha_1 \ldots \alpha_{n-1} s_n$, where $s_0 = \iota$ and $s_i \xrightarrow{\alpha_i} s_{i+1}$ for all $i < n$. π is an *execution* for w if $s_n \in \mathrm{Term}$. $\mathcal{T}$ is *finite* if its reachable part $\{s \in S : \iota \longrightarrow^\star s\}$ is finite. $\mathcal{T}$ is *deterministic* if for all $s, t, t' \in S$ reachable in $\mathcal{T}$ and $\alpha \in \Sigma$ with $s \xrightarrow{\alpha} t$ and $s \xrightarrow{\alpha} t'$ we have $t = t'$. The set of all transition systems over Σ is denoted by $\mathbf{TS}_\Sigma$.

Event Structures. As a branching-time non-interleaving model we rely on *(labeled) prime event structures* [29] and amend a notion of termination. A prime event structure is a tuple $\mathcal{E} = (E, \leqslant, \lambda, \#)$ that extends a possibly infinite pomset $(E, \leqslant, \lambda)$ with an irreflexive and symmetric *conflict relation* $\# \subseteq E \times E$ such that the following conditions hold:

(Principle of finite causes) $\downarrow e$ is finite for all $e \in E$, and
(Conflict heredity) $e\#e'$ and $e' \leqslant e''$ implies $e\#e''$ for all $e, e', e'' \in E$.

A *configuration* of $\mathcal{E}$ is a finite subset of events $C \subseteq E$ that is

Downward-closed, i.e., $\downarrow C = C$, and
Conflict-free, i.e., for all $e, e' \in C$ we never have $e\#e'$.

The set of configurations of $\mathcal{E}$ is denoted by $\mathrm{Conf}(\mathcal{E})$. A *prime event structure with termination* is a pair $(\mathcal{E}, \mathrm{Term})$, where $\mathcal{E}$ is a prime event structure and $\mathrm{Term} \subseteq \mathrm{Conf}(\mathcal{E})$ is a set of *termination configurations*. To simplify notations, we use the notion of an *event structure* instead of "prime event structure with termination". We denote the set of all event structures over Σ by $\mathbf{ES}_\Sigma$.

2.2 Relations Between Models for Concurrency

Following [34], we introduce mappings between the models of the last section:

- $\mathfrak{ts} \colon \mathbf{ES}_\Sigma \;\to\; \mathbf{TS}_\Sigma$ is the function that assigns the transition system $\mathfrak{ts}(\mathcal{E}) = \big(\mathrm{Conf}(\mathcal{E}), \varnothing, \longrightarrow, \mathrm{Term}\big)$ to an event structure $\mathcal{E} = (E, \leqslant, \lambda, \#, \mathrm{Term})$, where $C \xrightarrow{\alpha} D$ iff $D = C \cup \{e\}$ for some $e \in E$ with $\lambda(e) = \alpha$.
- $\mathfrak{pof} \colon \mathbf{ES}_\Sigma \to \mathbf{POF}_\Sigma$ is the function that assigns the pomset family $\mathfrak{pof}(\mathcal{E}) = \big\{ (C, \leqslant|_C, \lambda|_C) : C \in \mathrm{Term} \big\}$ to an event structure $\mathcal{E} = (E, \leqslant, \lambda, \#, \mathrm{Term})$.
- $\mathfrak{lang} \colon \mathbf{TS}_\Sigma \to \Sigma^*$ is the function that assigns the language $\mathfrak{lang}(\mathcal{T})$ to a transition system $\mathcal{T}$ comprising all words for which there is an execution in $\mathcal{T}$.
- $\mathfrak{lang} \colon \mathbf{POF}_\Sigma \to \Sigma^*$ is the function that assigns the language $\mathfrak{lang}(\mathfrak{P}) = \bigcup_{\mathcal{P} \in \mathfrak{P}} \mathrm{Lin}(\mathcal{P})$ to a pomset family $\mathfrak{P}$, where $\mathrm{Lin}(\mathcal{P})$ denotes the set of linearizations of $\mathcal{P}$.[2]

It is well known that these functions commute, i.e., for any event structure $\mathcal{E}$ we have $\mathfrak{lang}\big(\mathfrak{ts}(\mathcal{E})\big) = \mathfrak{lang}\big(\mathfrak{pof}(\mathcal{E})\big)$.

Bisimulation. Bisimilarity is a central concept to compare the behavior of branching-time models [25]. A *bisimulation* between two transition systems $\mathcal{T} = (S, \iota, \longrightarrow, \mathrm{Term})$ and $\mathcal{T}' = (S', \iota', \longrightarrow', \mathrm{Term}')$ is a binary relation $\equiv \subseteq S \times S'$ where $\iota \equiv \iota'$,

(a) for all $s \in \mathrm{Term}$ there is an $s' \in \mathrm{Term}'$ with $s \equiv s'$, and
(a') for all $s' \in \mathrm{Term}'$ there is an $s \in \mathrm{Term}$ with $s \equiv s'$,

and where for all $s \in S$ and $s' \in S'$ with $s \equiv s'$ we have that

(b) for all $t \in S$ with $s \xrightarrow{\alpha} t$ there is a $t' \in S'$ with $s' \xrightarrow{\alpha}{}' t'$ and $t \equiv t'$, and
(b') for all $t' \in S'$ with $s' \xrightarrow{\alpha}{}' t'$ there is a $t \in S$ with $s \xrightarrow{\alpha} t$ and $t \equiv t'$.

If there exists a bisimulation between $\mathcal{T}$ and $\mathcal{T}'$, then $\mathcal{T}$ and $\mathcal{T}'$ are called *bisimilar*. A *bisimulation for* $\mathcal{T}$ is a bisimulation $\equiv$ between $\mathcal{T}$ and $\mathcal{T}$. We shall often use the well-known fact that bisimilarity coincides with trace equivalence for deterministic transition systems.

Lemma 1. *If $\mathcal{T}$ and $\mathcal{T}'$ are deterministic transition systems, then $\mathcal{T}$ and $\mathcal{T}'$ are bisimilar iff $\mathfrak{lang}(\mathcal{T}) = \mathfrak{lang}(\mathcal{T}')$.*

2.3 Modeling Communication Systems

Let P denote a finite set of *processes* and let Λ be a finite alphabet of *data labels*. To model communication between processes, we consider a special instance of the alphabet Σ. That is, we consider the set of communication actions $Act = \bigcup_{p \in P} Act_p$, where Act_p comprises all actions a process $p \in P$ may perform, i.e., send actions $p!q(m)$ (process p sends a message m to process q), receive actions $p?q(m)$ (p receives m from q), and local actions $p(l)$ (p performs a local

---

[2] Note that we overload the function $\mathfrak{lang}$ for transition systems and pomset families.

action l), for processes $q \in P$, and data labels $m, l \in \Lambda$. *Events* are instances of actions collected in a set E to which we assign actions by a labeling function $\lambda \colon E \to Act$. Given a set of events $F \subseteq E$, we denote by $F_!$ the set of send events, i.e., $F_! = \{e \in F : \exists p, q \in P, m \in \Lambda . \lambda(e) = p!q(m)\}$, and by $F_?$ the set of receive events, i.e., $F_? = \{e \in F : \exists p, q \in P, m \in \Lambda . \lambda(e) = p?q(m)\}$. Furthermore, for a process $p \in P$ and pomset $\mathcal{P} = (F, \leqslant, \lambda)$, we define $F_p = \{e \in F : \lambda(e) \in Act_p\}$.

Message Sequence Charts. The ITU-T standard [15] introduced *message sequence charts (MSCs)* as visual formalism for communication scenarios. Here, we recall the definition of MSCs based on pomsets [20].

Definition 1. *An MSC is a pomset* $\mathcal{M} = (E, \leqslant, \lambda)$ *for which* $\mathcal{M}|_p$ *is total for each* $p \in P$ *and where* $\leqslant = \left(<_\mu \cup \bigcup_{p \in P} \leqslant|_{E_p} \right)^\star$. *Here,* $<_\mu = \{(e, \mu(e)) : e \in E_!\}$ *denotes the binary relation defined for a bijection* $\mu \colon E_! \to E_?$ *with* $\lambda(e) = p!q(m)$ *and* $\lambda(\mu(e)) = q?p(m)$ *for all* $e \in E_!$.

The mapping μ in the above definition guarantees that the action labels are compatible with the interpretation of send and receive events, i.e., matches every receive event with a corresponding send event. The requirement that the events of a process are totally ordered formalizes the time-line ordering. We denote by $\mathbb{MSC}$ the set of all MSCs and by $\mathbb{bMSC}$ the set of all basic MSCs, i.e., MSCs $(E, \leqslant, \lambda)$ where λ is injective.

Example 2. Let us return to the introductory Example 1 that models a simple set of communication scenarios over processes $P = \{s, r\}$. The MSC depicted on the left-hand side models a scenario with some timeout event, formalized by $\mathcal{M}_t = (E_t, \leqslant_t, \lambda_t)$ with $E_t = \{!, ?, to\}$, $\leqslant_t = \{(!, ?), (!, to)\}$, and $\lambda_t(!) = s!r(data)$, $\lambda_t(?) = r?s(data)$, and $\lambda_t(to) = s(to)$. Likewise, we formalize the MSC on the right-hand side by $\mathcal{M}_a = (E_a, \leqslant_a, \lambda_a)$, where $E_a = \{!d, ?d, !a, ?a\}$, $\leqslant_a = \{(!d, ?d), (!a, ?a), (?d, !a)\}^\star$, and where λ_a is given by $\lambda_a(!d) = s!r(data)$, $\lambda_a(?d) = r?s(data)$, $\lambda_a(!a) = r!s(ack)$, and $\lambda_a(?a) = s?r(ack)$. Note that both MSCs are basic.

Composition. Pomsets over Act are composed by performing a local concatenation where events of the same process depend on each other [30]. Formally, we define $\odot \colon \mathbb{PO}_{Act} \times \mathbb{PO}_{Act} \to \mathbb{PO}_{Act}$ as follows: Let $\mathcal{X} = (X, \leqslant_X, \lambda_X)$ and $\mathcal{Y} = (Y, \leqslant_Y, \lambda_Y)$ be pomsets over Act with $X \cap Y = \varnothing$. Then, $\mathcal{X} \odot \mathcal{Y}$ is defined as the smallest pomset $\mathcal{Z} = (Z, \leqslant, \lambda)$ where $Z = X \cup Y$, $\leqslant|_X = \leqslant_X$, $\leqslant|_Y = \leqslant_Y$, and where for all $p \in P$, $e \in X_p$, $e' \in Y_p$ we have $e \leqslant e'$. The composition operation is extended to sequences of pomsets by $\odot \colon \mathbb{PO}_{Act}^\star \to \mathbb{PO}_{Act}$, where $\odot \varepsilon = \varnothing$ and $\odot(\pi \mathcal{P}) = (\odot \pi) \odot \mathcal{P}$ for any $\pi \in \mathbb{PO}_{Act}^\star$ and $\mathcal{P} \in \mathbb{PO}_{Act}$. For a language over pomset sequences $L \subseteq \mathbb{PO}_{Act}^\star$, we define $\odot L = \{\odot \pi : \pi \in L\}$.

In case the pomsets to be composed are MSCs, it is easy to see that composition again yields an MSC. Intuitively, composing MSCs corresponds to "gluing" their process lines together.

Message Sequence Graphs. Whereas MSCs model single communication scenarios, *message sequence graphs (MSGs)* were introduced in [16] as the standard higher-order formalism to specify collections of communication scenarios, i.e., sets of MSCs.

Definition 2. *An* MSG *is a tuple* $\mathcal{G} = (B, b_0, \hookrightarrow, \beta)$, *where B is a finite set of boxes, $b_0 \in B$ an initial box, $\hookrightarrow \subseteq B \times B$ a transition relation, and $\beta \colon B \to$ bMSC a labeling function that assigns basic MSCs to boxes.*

Note that we allow β for assigning the empty MSCs $\oslash$ to some box. We extend β towards $\beta \colon B^\star \to$ MSC by inductively defining $\beta(\varepsilon) = \oslash$ and $\beta(\pi b) = \beta(\pi) \odot \beta(b)$ for $\pi \in B^\star$ and $b \in B$. A box sequence $\pi = b_0 b_1 \ldots b_n \in B^\star$ is called a *path in* $\mathcal{G}$ if $b_i \hookrightarrow b_{i+1}$ for all $i < n$. If π cannot be prolonged in $\mathcal{G}$, i.e., there is no $b \in B$ such that $b_n \hookrightarrow b$, we call π an *execution* of $\mathcal{G}$ and define by $\mathcal{B}[\mathcal{G}]$ the *box language* of $\mathcal{G}$ as the set of executions of $\mathcal{G}$. In the following, we assume that any path in $\mathcal{G}$ can be prolonged towards an execution of $\mathcal{G}$. An MSC $\mathcal{M}$ is *accepted by* $\mathcal{G}$ if $\mathcal{M}$ arises from a composition along an execution of $\mathcal{G}$. The *pomset semantics* of $\mathcal{G}$ is the set of all MSCs accepted by $\mathcal{G}$, denoted by $\mathfrak{P}[\mathcal{G}] = \beta(\mathcal{B}[\mathcal{G}])$.

Example 3. The the MSG $\mathcal{G}_{\text{bsp}}$ from Example 1 is formalized by

$$\mathcal{G}_{\text{bsp}} = \big(\{\iota, t, a\}, \iota, \{(\iota, t), (\iota, a), (t, t), (t, a)\}, \beta\big)$$

with $\beta(\iota) = \oslash$, $\beta(t) = \mathcal{M}_t$, and $\beta(a) = \mathcal{M}_a$ where $\mathcal{M}_t$ and $\mathcal{M}_a$ are the MSCs defined as in Example 2. The set of paths in $\mathcal{G}_{\text{bsp}}$ is the regular language given by the regular expression $\varepsilon + \iota t^\star(a + \varepsilon)$. The box language $\mathcal{B}[\mathcal{G}_{\text{bsp}}]$ is given by the regular expression $\iota t^\star a$. The communication scenario arising from the execution $\iota t a \in \mathcal{B}[\mathcal{G}_{\text{bsp}}]$ is the MSC $(E, \leqslant, \lambda) = \beta(\iota) \odot \beta(t) \odot \beta(a) = \mathcal{M}_t \odot \mathcal{M}_a$, i.e., $E = E_t \cup E_a$, $\leqslant = \big(\leqslant_t \cup \leqslant_a \cup\{(to, !d), (?, ?d)\}\big)^\star$, and $\lambda = \lambda_t \cup \lambda_a$.

3 Transition Systems for Pomset Families

In this section, we present transition systems for pomset families that follow the concept of delayed choice. For this, let us fix an alphabet of actions Σ. Although we do not consider process algebras in detail here, let us support the intuition behind delayed choice operator $\mp$ by providing the process-algebraic rules of [3], where $\mp$ has been defined first. A *process term* stands for a possible future behavior of the system, where reductions on the terms are made through firing actions. The operational semantics of $\mp$ is provided by the rules **(DC1)**, **(DC2)**, **(DC3)**, and symmetric rules with exchanged roles for process terms x and y (and process terms x' and y', respectively). In these rules, $x \xrightarrow{\alpha} y$ stands

$$\frac{\text{term}(x)}{\text{term}(x \mp y)} \text{ (DC1)} \qquad \frac{x \xrightarrow{\alpha} x' \quad y \xrightarrow{\alpha}}{(x \mp y) \xrightarrow{\alpha} x'} \text{ (DC2)} \qquad \frac{x \xrightarrow{\alpha} x' \quad y \xrightarrow{\alpha} y'}{(x \mp y) \xrightarrow{\alpha} (x' \mp y')} \text{ (DC3)}$$

for an execution of an action $\alpha \in \Sigma$ in x, $x \stackrel{\alpha}{\nrightarrow}$ expresses that action α is not executed by x, and term(x) stands for x having the option to terminate. Hence, **(DC1)** states that $x \mp y$ can terminate if x can. The other rules illustrate exactly the intuitive behavior of delayed choice: the choice between two process terms x and y is not resolved when they perform the same actions (cf., **(DC3)**), but when from x an action is performed that is not enabled in y (cf., **(DC2)**).

Operational Semantics for Pomset Families. To specify the operational behavior of systems described by some pomset family $\mathfrak{P}$, a central aspect is to identify the global state of the system and to describe the step-wise behavior from each of the states. For a single pomset $\mathcal{P} = (E, \leqslant, \lambda)$, a global state is traditionally defined by a *cut*, i.e., a partition of the events E into past events U and future events $V = E \backslash U$. Thus, every cut of $\mathcal{P}$ can be specified by either the set of past events U or future events V – the respective other set of events follows from the fixed set of events E. From a cut, action α can be performed when there is a minimal future event $e \in V$ labeled by α. After performing α, the event e from the set of future events V is moved to the set of past events U.

Having the interpretation of delayed choice in mind, where process terms describe future behaviors, we may describe cuts by their future events and amend the partial order and labeling inherited from the given pomset. This yields a formalization of the stepwise behavior $\stackrel{\alpha}{\leadsto}$ of executing an action α over (future) pomsets $\mathcal{Y} \in \mathbb{PO}_\Sigma$ by $\mathcal{Y} \stackrel{\alpha}{\leadsto} \mathrm{Suff}_\alpha(\mathcal{Y})$.[3] The principle of the operational behavior for single pomsets can be generalized towards pomset families by $\leadsto \subseteq \mathbb{POF}_\Sigma \times \Sigma \times \mathbb{POF}_\Sigma$, where the standard union on pomset families serves as delayed choice within the step-wise behavior $\leadsto$ described above. That is, for a pomset family $\mathfrak{X} \in \mathbb{POF}_\Sigma$, we have $\mathfrak{X} \stackrel{\alpha}{\leadsto} \mathfrak{Y}$ iff $\mathfrak{Y} = \mathrm{Suff}_\alpha(\mathfrak{X})$. It is easy to check that the rules for delayed choice specified for process algebra terms are fulfilled by $\leadsto$ (cf. **(DC2)** and **(DC3)**), replacing $\stackrel{\alpha}{\rightarrow}$ by $\stackrel{\alpha}{\leadsto}$ and using pomset families instead of process terms. Here, $\mathfrak{X} \stackrel{\alpha}{\nleadsto}$ denotes that $\mathrm{Suff}_\alpha(\mathfrak{X}) = \varnothing$. Furthermore, the empty pomset $\oslash \in \mathfrak{X}$ naturally serves as candidate for term$(\mathfrak{X})$ (cf. **(DC1)**).

Formalizing the approach with the step-wise operational behavior for pomset families described above, we obtain *suffix transition systems* where cuts of the pomset family members are represented by the pomset of future events. To complete the picture, we further present *prefix transition systems* for pomset families where cuts are represented by pomsets of past events.

For the remainder of this section, let us fix a pomset family $\mathfrak{P} \in \mathbb{POF}_\Sigma$.

3.1 Suffix Transition Systems

Definition 3. *The* suffix transition system *of $\mathfrak{P}$ is given by*

$$\mathcal{T}_{\mathrm{suff}}[\mathfrak{P}] \quad = \quad \left(2^{\mathrm{Suff}(\mathfrak{P})}, \mathfrak{P}, \leadsto, \mathfrak{T} \right)$$

where $\mathfrak{T} = \{ \mathfrak{X} \subseteq \mathrm{Suff}(\mathfrak{P}) : \oslash \in \mathfrak{X} \}$, and where for $\mathfrak{X}, \mathfrak{Y} \subseteq \mathrm{Suff}(\mathfrak{P})$ we have $\mathfrak{X} \stackrel{\alpha}{\leadsto} \mathfrak{Y}$ iff $\mathfrak{Y} = \mathrm{Suff}_\alpha(\mathfrak{X})$.

---

[3] Note that $\mathrm{Suff}_\alpha(\mathcal{Y})$ is a singleton as we assume pomsets to be not autoconcurrent.

Note that states of the suffix transition system of $\mathfrak{P}$ might be an infinite pomset family in case $\mathfrak{P}$ is infinite.

Example 4. Let us return to our running example, i.e., let us consider the MSG $\mathcal{G}_{\mathrm{bsp}}$ from Example 3. By the definition of the pomset semantics for MSGs, we have $\mathfrak{P}[\mathcal{G}_{\mathrm{bsp}}] = \{\mathcal{M}_t \odot \ldots \odot \mathcal{M}_t \odot \mathcal{M}_a\}$. For illustration purposes, we extend the definition of $\odot$ towards pomset families by $\mathcal{X} \odot \mathfrak{Y} = \{\mathcal{X} \odot \mathcal{Y} : \mathcal{Y} \in \mathfrak{Y}\}$. Using this abbreviation and with $\mathfrak{P} = \mathfrak{P}[\mathcal{G}_{\mathrm{bsp}}]$, Fig. 2 shows a fragment of the suffix transition system $\mathcal{T}_{\mathrm{suff}}[\mathfrak{P}]$ with initial state $\mathfrak{P}$ and one termination state $\{\varnothing\}$. $\mathcal{T}_{\mathrm{suff}}[\mathfrak{P}]$ contains cycles and is infinite since for all $k \in \mathbb{N}$ the pomset family

$$\underbrace{\mathcal{M}_t|_{\{?\}} \odot \ldots \odot \mathcal{M}_t|_{\{?\}}}_{k \text{ times}} \odot \left((\mathcal{M}_t|_{\{?,to\}} \odot \mathfrak{P}) \cup \{\mathcal{M}_a|_{\{?d,!a,?a\}}\}\right)$$

is a reachable state in $\mathcal{T}_{\mathrm{suff}}[\mathfrak{P}]$.

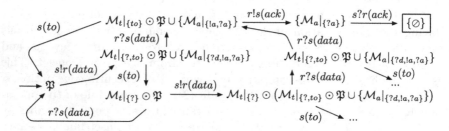

Fig. 2. Fragment of the suffix transition system for $\mathfrak{P}[\mathcal{G}_{\mathrm{bsp}}]$

Proposition 1 (Properties of $\mathcal{T}_{\mathrm{suff}}[\mathfrak{P}]$). *Given $\mathfrak{P} \in \mathbb{POF}_\Sigma$,*

(a) $\mathcal{T}_{\mathrm{suff}}[\mathfrak{P}]$ is deterministic, and
(b) $\mathrm{lang}(\mathcal{T}_{\mathrm{suff}}[\mathfrak{P}]) = \mathrm{lang}(\mathfrak{P})$.

Proof. It is easy to see by the definition of $\mathrm{Suff}_\alpha(\cdot)$ that $\mathcal{T}_{\mathrm{suff}}[\mathfrak{P}]$ is deterministic[4]. Let us now show language equality of $\mathcal{T}_{\mathrm{suff}}[\mathfrak{P}]$ and $\mathfrak{P}$:

$(\Rightarrow)$ Let $w \in \mathrm{lang}(\mathcal{T}_{\mathrm{suff}}[\mathfrak{P}])$, i.e., there is an execution $\mathfrak{X}_0 \alpha_0 \mathfrak{X}_1 \alpha_1 \ldots \alpha_{n-1} \mathfrak{X}_n$ of $\mathcal{T}_{\mathrm{suff}}[\mathfrak{P}]$ with $\mathfrak{X}_0 = \mathfrak{P}$, $\mathfrak{X}_n \in \mathfrak{T}$ and $w = \alpha_0 \alpha_1 \ldots \alpha_{n-1}$. Then, by the definition of $\mathfrak{T}$, $\varnothing \in \mathfrak{X}_n$. Furthermore, by the definition of $\mathrm{Suff}_\alpha(\cdot)$, there is a $\mathcal{P} \in \mathfrak{X}_0$ such that for all $i < n$ there is $\mathcal{P}_i \in \mathfrak{X}_i$ with $\mathcal{P}_0 = \mathcal{P}$, $\mathcal{P}_n = \varnothing$ and $\mathcal{P}_{i+1} = \mathrm{Suff}_{\alpha_i}(\mathcal{P}_i)$. We show that w is a linearization of $\mathcal{P}_0 = (E, \leqslant, \lambda)$, i.e., there is a bijection $\xi: \{0, \ldots, n-1\} \to E$ with $\lambda(\xi(i)) = \alpha_i$ and $\xi(i) \not> \xi(j)$ for all $i \leqslant j < n$. For $i < n$, let $\xi(i)$ be the uniquely defined event in $\mathcal{P}_i \setminus \mathcal{P}_{i+1}$. Then, since $\mathcal{P}_{i+1} = \mathrm{Suff}_{\alpha_i}(\mathcal{P}_i)$, $\lambda(\xi(i)) = \alpha_i$ for all $i < n$. Towards a contradiction, assume that there are $i \leqslant j$ such that $\xi(i) > \xi(j)$. Then, by the definition of suffixes, $\mathcal{P}_j$ is upward closed and thus, $\xi(i) \in \mathcal{P}_j$. Hence, by the definition of $\mathrm{Suff}_\alpha(\cdot)$, for all $k \geqslant i$ we have $\xi(i) \in \mathcal{P}_k$, which yields $\xi(i) \notin \mathcal{P}_i \setminus \mathcal{P}_{i+1}$, contradicting the definition of ξ.

---

[4] Recall that determinism depends only on the reachable part in $\mathcal{T}_{\mathrm{suff}}[\mathfrak{P}]$.

($\Leftarrow$) Let $w \in \text{lang}(\mathfrak{P})$, i.e., there is some $\mathcal{P} \in \mathfrak{P}$ such that $w \in \text{Lin}(\mathcal{P})$. With $w = \alpha_0 \alpha_1 \ldots \alpha_{n-1}$ and $\mathcal{P} = (E, \leqslant, \lambda)$ there is thus a bijection $\xi \colon \{0, \ldots, n-1\} \to E$ with $\lambda(\xi(i)) = \alpha_i$ and $\xi(i) \not> \xi(j)$ for all $i \leqslant j < n$. Let $\mathcal{P}_i$ for $i \leqslant n$ be inductively defined by $\mathcal{P}_0 = \mathcal{P}$ and $\mathcal{P}_{i+1} = \mathcal{P}_i \backslash \{\xi(i)\}$. Then for all $i < n$ we have that $\xi(i)$ is a minimal event in $\mathcal{P}_i$ and thus, by the definition of suffixes, $\mathcal{P}_{i+1} = \text{Suff}_{\alpha_i}(\mathcal{P}_i)$. Thus, there is a path $\pi = \mathfrak{X}_0 \alpha_0 \mathfrak{X}_1 \alpha_1 \ldots \alpha_{n-1} \mathfrak{X}_n$ in $\mathcal{T}_{\text{suff}}[\mathfrak{P}]$ with $\mathfrak{X}_0 = \mathfrak{P}$ and where $\mathcal{P}_i \in \mathfrak{X}_i$ for all $i \leqslant n$. As $\oslash = \mathcal{P}_n$, we have that $\oslash \in \mathfrak{X}_n$ and hence, π is an execution in $\mathcal{T}_{\text{suff}}[\mathfrak{P}]$. This directly yields $w \in \text{lang}(\mathcal{T}_{\text{suff}}[\mathfrak{P}])$. $\square$

Motivated by the last proposition and the fact that the step-wise behavior and the termination states satisfy the rules for delayed choice on suffix pomset families as illustrated in the introductory argumentation of this section, we use suffix transition systems as a reference model for delayed-choice semantics on pomset families.

Definition 4. *A transition system $\mathcal{T}$ for a pomset family $\mathfrak{P}$ obeys delayed choice if $\mathcal{T}$ is deterministic and bisimilar to $\mathcal{T}_{\text{suff}}[\mathfrak{P}]$.*

3.2 Prefix Transition Systems

We now define prefix transition systems, where states are given by prefixes of a pomset family. Intuitively, any prefix stands for the partially ordered history of an execution of the system. Prefix transition systems generalize the transition-system semantics for MSGs of [8] towards arbitrary pomset families (possibly not generated by MSGs).

Definition 5. *The prefix transition system semantics of $\mathfrak{P}$ is given by*

$$\mathcal{T}_{\text{pref}}[\mathfrak{P}] \quad = \quad \left(2^{\text{Pref}(\mathfrak{P})}, \{\oslash\}, \rightharpoonup, \mathfrak{T}\right),$$

where $\mathfrak{T} = \{\mathfrak{X} \subseteq \text{Pref}(\mathfrak{P}) : \mathfrak{X} \cap \mathfrak{P} \neq \varnothing\}$ and where for $\mathfrak{X}, \mathfrak{Y} \subseteq \text{Pref}(\mathfrak{P})$ we have $\mathfrak{X} \overset{\alpha}{\rightharpoonup} \mathfrak{Y}$ iff $\mathfrak{X} = \text{Pref}_\alpha(\mathfrak{Y})$.

Example 5. In Fig. 3, a fragment of the prefix transition system $\mathcal{T}_{\text{pref}}[\mathfrak{P}[\mathcal{G}_{\text{bsp}}]]$ is depicted where $\mathcal{G}_{\text{bsp}}$ is as in Example 3. Note that in this example, every reachable pomset family is a singleton.

Proposition 2 (Properties of $\mathcal{T}_{\text{pref}}[\mathfrak{P}]$). *Given $\mathfrak{P} \in \text{POF}_\Sigma$,*

(a) $\mathcal{T}_{\text{pref}}[\mathfrak{P}]$ is acyclic,
(b) $\mathcal{T}_{\text{pref}}[\mathfrak{P}]$ is deterministic, and
(c) $\text{lang}(\mathcal{T}_{\text{pref}}[\mathfrak{P}]) = \text{lang}(\mathfrak{P})$.

Proof. In order to show that $\mathcal{T}_{\text{pref}}[\mathfrak{P}]$ is acyclic, we rely on the fact that for all $\mathfrak{X} \subseteq \text{Pref}(\mathfrak{P})$ reachable in $\mathcal{T}_{\text{pref}}[\mathfrak{P}]$ we have that $\mathcal{X}, \mathcal{Y} \in \mathfrak{X}$ implies $|\mathcal{X}| = |\mathcal{Y}|$. Let now $\#(\mathfrak{X})$ denote the number of events contained in each $\mathcal{X} \in \mathfrak{X}$. Then, for all reachable $\mathfrak{X}, \mathfrak{Y} \subseteq \text{Pref}(\mathfrak{P})$ with $\mathfrak{X} \overset{\alpha}{\rightharpoonup} \mathfrak{Y}$ we have $\#(\mathfrak{Y}) = \#(\mathfrak{X}) + 1$. Thus, $\mathcal{T}_{\text{pref}}[\mathfrak{P}]$ is acyclic. For any $\mathfrak{Y} \subseteq \text{Pref}(\mathfrak{P})$ and $\alpha \in \Sigma$, $\mathfrak{X} = \text{Pref}_\alpha(\mathfrak{Y})$ is uniquely defined and by the definition of $\overset{\alpha}{\rightharpoonup}$, we directly obtain that $\mathcal{T}_{\text{pref}}[\mathfrak{P}]$ is deterministic. Let us now show language equality of $\mathcal{T}_{\text{pref}}[\mathfrak{P}]$ and $\mathfrak{P}$:

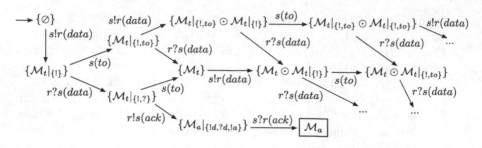

Fig. 3. Fragment of the prefix transition system for $\mathfrak{P}[\mathcal{G}_{\mathrm{bsp}}]$

($\Rightarrow$) Let $w \in \mathrm{lang}(\mathcal{T}_{\mathrm{pref}}[\mathfrak{P}])$, i.e., there is an execution $\mathfrak{X}_0 \alpha_0 \mathfrak{X}_1 \alpha_1 \ldots \alpha_{n-1} \mathfrak{X}_n$ of $\mathcal{T}_{\mathrm{pref}}[\mathfrak{P}]$ with $\mathfrak{X}_0 = \{\varnothing\}$, $\mathfrak{X}_n \in \mathfrak{T}$ and $w = \alpha_0 \alpha_1 \ldots \alpha_{n-1}$. Then, by the definition of $\mathfrak{T}$, there is some $\mathcal{P}_n = (E, \leqslant, \lambda) \in \mathfrak{X}_n$ such that $\mathcal{P}_n \in \mathfrak{P}$. Furthermore, by the definition of $\mathrm{Pref}_\alpha(\cdot)$, for all $i < n$ there is $\mathcal{P}_i \in \mathfrak{X}_i$ with $\mathcal{P}_i = \mathrm{Pref}_{\alpha_i}(\mathcal{P}_{i+1})$. We show that w is a linearization of $\mathcal{P}$, i.e., there is a bijection $\xi \colon \{0, \ldots, n-1\} \to E$ with $\lambda(\xi(i)) = \alpha_i$ and $\xi(i) \not> \xi(j)$ for all $i \leqslant j < n$. For $i < n$, let $\xi(i)$ be the uniquely defined event in $\mathcal{P}_{i+1} \setminus \mathcal{P}_i$. Then, since $\mathcal{P}_i = \mathrm{Pref}_{\alpha_i}(\mathcal{P}_{i+1})$, $\lambda(\xi(i)) = \alpha_i$ for all $i < n$. Towards a contradiction, assume that there are $i \leqslant j$ such that $\xi(i) > \xi(j)$. Then, by the definition of prefixes, $\mathcal{P}_{i+1}$ is downward closed and thus, $\xi(j) \in \mathcal{P}_{i+1}$. Hence, by the definition of $\mathrm{Pref}_\alpha(\cdot)$, for all $k > i$ we have $\xi(j) \in \mathcal{P}_k$, which yields $\xi(j) \notin \mathcal{P}_{j+1} \setminus \mathcal{P}_j$, contradicting the definition of ξ.

($\Leftarrow$) Let $w \in \mathrm{lang}(\mathfrak{P})$, i.e., there is some $\mathcal{P} \in \mathfrak{P}$ such that $w \in \mathrm{Lin}(\mathcal{P})$. With $w = \alpha_0 \alpha_1 \ldots \alpha_{n-1}$ and $\mathcal{P} = (E, \leqslant, \lambda)$ there is thus a bijection $\xi \colon \{0, \ldots, n-1\} \to E$ with $\lambda(\xi(i)) = \alpha_i$ and $\xi(i) \not> \xi(j)$ for all $i \leqslant j < n$. Let E_i for $i \leqslant n$ be inductively defined by $E = \varnothing$ and $E_{i+1} = E_i \cup \{\xi(i)\}$. Furthermore, let $\mathcal{P}_i = \mathcal{P}|_{E_i}$ for all $i \leqslant n$. Since $\xi(i) \not> \xi(j)$ for all $i \leqslant j < n$, all $\mathcal{P}_i$ are downward closed and thus, by the definition of prefixes, $\mathcal{P}_i = \mathrm{Pref}_{\alpha_i}(\mathcal{P}_{i+1})$. Thus, there is a path $\pi = \mathfrak{X}_0 \alpha_0 \mathfrak{X}_1 \alpha_1 \ldots \alpha_{n-1} \mathfrak{X}_n$ in $\mathcal{T}_{\mathrm{pref}}[\mathfrak{P}]$ with $\mathfrak{X}_0 = \{\varnothing\}$ and where $\mathcal{P}_i \in \mathfrak{X}_i$ for all $i \leqslant n$. As $\mathcal{P}_n = \mathcal{P}$, we have that $\mathcal{P} \in \mathfrak{X}_n$ and hence, $\mathfrak{X}_n \cap \mathfrak{P} \neq \varnothing$. Thus, π is an execution in $\mathcal{T}_{\mathrm{pref}}[\mathfrak{P}]$ and hence, $w \in \mathrm{lang}(\mathcal{T}_{\mathrm{pref}}[\mathfrak{P}])$. □

The above proposition in combination with Proposition 1 and Lemma 1 directly yields that $\mathcal{T}_{\mathrm{pref}}[\mathfrak{P}]$ is a delayed-choice semantics for $\mathfrak{P}$:

Theorem 1. $\mathcal{T}_{\mathrm{pref}}[\mathfrak{P}]$ *obeys delayed choice, i.e.,* $\mathcal{T}_{\mathrm{pref}}[\mathfrak{P}]$ *is deterministic and bisimilar to* $\mathcal{T}_{\mathrm{suff}}[\mathfrak{P}]$.

3.3 Comparison and Discussion

To further illustrate the differences between suffix and prefix transition systems, let us consider a simple example issuing a pomset family $\mathfrak{P} = \{\mathcal{X}, \mathcal{Y}\}$ that comprises the pomsets $\mathcal{X} = (\{e, e'\}, \{(e, e')\}, \{(e, a), (e', a')\})$ and $\mathcal{Y} =$

$(\{e, e'\}, \varnothing, \{(e, \alpha), (e', \alpha')\})$. Figure 4 depicts the resulting suffix and prefix transition systems for $\mathfrak{P}$. When executing α followed by α', the choice between $\mathcal{X}$ and $\mathcal{Y}$ is delayed, i.e., this execution could follow either $\mathcal{X}$ or $\mathcal{Y}$. However, when executing α' first, the choice between $\mathcal{X}$ and $\mathcal{Y}$ is resolved towards $\mathcal{Y}$. Whereas in the case of the suffix transition system there is only one termination state, the prefix transition system contains the history of the execution and has two termination states. Note that both transition systems contain states which comprise more than one pomset.

$$(1) \qquad\qquad (2)$$

Fig. 4. The (1) prefix and (2) suffix transition system for $\mathfrak{P} = \{\mathcal{X}, \mathcal{Y}\}$

Using the process algebra introduced in [17,31], we can describe $\mathfrak{P}$ by the process-algebraic term $(\alpha \| \alpha') \mp (\alpha \cdot \alpha')$. Using the rules specified in [31], we obtain the transition system depicted in (1) of Fig. 5, which corresponds to the prefix transition system for $\mathfrak{P}$. Identifying bisimilar process-algebraic terms using the bisimulation $\leftrightarrow$ provided in [31] yields a transition system corresponding to the suffix transition system for $\mathfrak{P}$, depicted in (2) of Fig. 5.

$$(1) \qquad\qquad (2)$$

Fig. 5. Transition system of $(\alpha \| \alpha') \mp (\alpha \cdot \alpha')$ (1) and its quotient w.r.t. $\leftrightarrow$ (2)

Note that in contrast to the prefix transition system $\mathcal{T}_{\mathrm{pref}}[\mathfrak{P}[\mathcal{G}_{\mathrm{bsp}}]]$ detailed in Example 5, $\mathcal{T}_{\mathrm{pref}}[\mathfrak{P}]$ contains reachable states that are not singletons.

Lemma 2. *For all MSGs $\mathcal{G}$, the reachable states of $\mathcal{T}_{\mathrm{pref}}[\mathfrak{P}[\mathcal{G}]]$ are singletons.*

Proof. As $\mathcal{T}_{\mathrm{pref}}[\mathfrak{P}[\mathcal{G}]]$ is deterministic (see Proposition 2b), every action sequence $w \in Act^\star$ for which there is a path yields a uniquely defined state that we denote by $\mathcal{X}_w$. Towards an induction on w, the statement holds for $w = \varepsilon$ as then, $\mathcal{X}_w = \{\varnothing\}$. Let w be such that $\mathcal{X}_w = \{(E, \leqslant, \lambda)\}$. Consider an $\alpha \in Act_p$ for a process $p \in P$ such that there is an α-transition in $\mathcal{X}_w$ leading to $\mathcal{X}_{w\alpha}$. Let $\mathcal{X} \in \mathcal{X}_{w\alpha}$ with $\mathcal{X} = (E \cup \{e\}, \leqslant \cup (X \times \{e\}), \lambda \cup \{(e, \alpha)\})$ for $X \subseteq E$. This can be assumed w.l.o.g. due to the definition of $\text{Pref}_\alpha(\cdot)$. If α is a local or send event, then $X = \downarrow E_p \times \{e\}$ due to the definition of $\odot$ and the fact that local and send events have at most one direct predecessor in an MSC. Let $\alpha = p?q(m)$ and k denote the number of α-events in E. Since every receive event is mapped to a send event in a basic MSC, this mapping takes over to MSCs in $\mathfrak{P}[\mathcal{G}]$ by the definition of $\odot$. Thus, the kth event labeled by $q!p(m)$ on the process line E_q is a direct predecessor of e in $\mathcal{X}$. Since every receive event has at most two direct predecessors, we obtain $X = \downarrow\hat{e} \cup \downarrow E_p$ again by the definition of $\odot$. Hence, X is uniquely defined through $(E, \leqslant, \lambda)$ and α, leading to $\mathfrak{X}_{w\alpha}$ being a singleton. $\square$

4   An Event Structure for Pomset Families

In this section, we present a branching-time semantics for pomset families that is non-interleaving, i.e., models causal dependencies and independence explicitly. Throughout this section, we fix a pomset family $\mathfrak{P}$ over Σ. Similar to concepts of [32], we define an event structure for $\mathfrak{P}$ where events are pomsets that arise from the downward closure of an event in some pomset of $\mathfrak{P}$. More formally, for a pomset $\mathcal{P} \in \mathfrak{P}$ with $\mathcal{P} = (F, \preceq, \nu)$ and $e \in F$, we consider the *pomset downward closure* of e as $\mathcal{P}|_{\downarrow e}$ with $\downarrow e = \{e' \in F : e' \preceq e\}$.

Definition 6. *The* pomset event structure $\mathcal{E}[\mathfrak{P}]$ *is given by* $(E, \leqslant, \lambda, \#, \text{Term})$ *where*

- $E = \{\mathcal{P}|_{\downarrow e} : \mathcal{P} = (F, \preceq, \nu) \in \mathfrak{P}, e \in F\}$
- $\mathcal{X} \leqslant \mathcal{Y}$ *iff* $\mathcal{X} \in \text{Pref}(\mathcal{Y})$
- $\lambda(\mathcal{P}|_{\downarrow e}) = \nu(e)$ *for* $\mathcal{P} = (F, \preceq, \nu) \in \mathfrak{P}, e \in F$
- $\mathcal{X} \# \mathcal{Y}$ *iff there is no* $\mathcal{P} \in \mathfrak{P}$ *with* $\mathcal{X}, \mathcal{Y} \in \text{Pref}(\mathcal{P})$
- $\mathcal{X} \in \text{Term}$ *iff there is* $\mathcal{P} = (F, \preceq, \nu) \in \mathfrak{P}$ *such that* $\mathcal{X} = \{\mathcal{P}|_{\downarrow e} : e \in F\}$

To show that $\mathcal{E}[\mathfrak{P}]$ is well defined, we note that $(E, \leqslant, \lambda)$ is a (possibly infinite) pomset as the prefix relation on any pomset family is a partial order, and $\#$ is clearly irreflexive and symmetric. Furthermore, the principle of finite causes holds as $\mathcal{P} = (F, \preceq, \nu) \in \mathfrak{P}$ is finite and thus, $\text{Pref}(\mathcal{P}|_{\downarrow e})$ is also finite for all $e \in F$. To show that conflict heredity holds, let $\mathcal{X}, \mathcal{Y}, \mathcal{Z} \in E$ and $\mathcal{X} \# \mathcal{Y}$, $\mathcal{Y} \leqslant \mathcal{Z}$ and assume that $\mathcal{X} \# \mathcal{Z}$ does not hold. Then, there is $\mathcal{P} \in \mathfrak{P}$ such that $\mathcal{X}, \mathcal{Z} \in \text{Pref}(\mathcal{P})$. By the definition of $\leqslant$, $\mathcal{Y} \in \text{Pref}(\mathcal{Z}) \subseteq \text{Pref}(\mathcal{P})$, which contradicts $\mathcal{X} \# \mathcal{Y}$ as there should be no $\mathcal{Q} \in \mathfrak{P}$ with $\mathcal{X}, \mathcal{Y} \in \text{Pref}(\mathcal{Q})$, violated by $\mathcal{Q} = \mathcal{P}$. It is left to show that $\text{Term} \subseteq \text{Conf}(\mathcal{E}[\mathfrak{P}])$, which is a direct consequence of the following lemma.

Lemma 3. *For all* $\mathcal{P} = (F, \preceq, \nu) \in \text{Pref}(\mathfrak{P})$, $C = \{\mathcal{P}|_{\downarrow e} : e \in F\}$, *we have* $C \in \text{Conf}(\mathcal{E}[\mathfrak{P}])$ *and* $\mathcal{P} = (C, \leqslant|_C, \lambda|_C)$.

Proof. Towards an induction on $n = |F|$, the statement is clearly fulfilled for $n = 0$ by $\varnothing \in \text{Conf}(\mathcal{E}[\mathfrak{P}])$. Now, let $|F| = n+1$ and assume that the statement holds for all $\mathcal{Q} \in \text{Pref}(\mathfrak{P})$ with an event space containing n elements. In particular, for all $\alpha \in \Sigma$ with $\mathcal{P}' = (F', \preceq|_{F'}, \nu|_{F'}) \in \text{Pref}_\alpha(\mathcal{P})$ there is an $f \in F$ with $\nu(f) = \alpha$

such that $F \setminus F' = \{f\}$. Since we assume pomsets to be not autoconcurrent, f is uniquely defined if it exists. We first show that $C = C' \cup \{\mathcal{P}|_{\downarrow f}\} \in \mathrm{Conf}(\mathcal{E}[\mathfrak{P}])$ with $C' = \{\mathcal{P}'|_{\downarrow e} : e \in F'\}$. Since $\mathcal{P} \in \mathrm{Pref}(\mathfrak{P})$ we have $\mathcal{P}|_{\downarrow f} \in E$. Furthermore, $C' \in \mathrm{Conf}(\mathcal{E}[\mathfrak{P}])$ by induction hypothesis and thus $C \subseteq E$. C is conflict-free with $\mathcal{P}$ as witness. Now assume that C is not downward-closed, i.e., there is an $\mathcal{X} \in E \setminus C$ with $\mathcal{X} \leqslant \mathcal{P}|_{\downarrow f}$. By the definition of $\leqslant$ we have $\mathcal{X} \in \mathrm{Pref}(\mathcal{P}|_{\downarrow f})$. Thus, there is an $x \in F$ with $\mathcal{X} = \mathcal{P}|_{\downarrow x}$. If $x \neq f$, then $\mathcal{X} \in C'$ and if $x = f$, then $\mathcal{X} = \mathcal{P}|_{\downarrow f}$. Hence, $\mathcal{X} \in C$, contradicting $\mathcal{X} \in E \setminus C$. Now we show that $\mathcal{P} = (C, \leqslant|_C, \lambda|_C)$. By induction hypothesis, we have $\mathcal{P}' = (C', \leqslant|_{C'}, \lambda|_{C'})$. Thus, it suffices to show that for all $e \in F$ we have $e \preceq f$ iff $\mathcal{P}|_{\downarrow e} \leqslant \mathcal{P}|_{\downarrow f}$:

($\Rightarrow$) It follows directly that $\downarrow e \subseteq \downarrow f$ and thus, $\mathcal{P}|_{\downarrow e} \in \mathrm{Pref}(\mathcal{P}|_{\downarrow f})$.
($\Leftarrow$) From $\mathcal{P}|_{\downarrow e} \in \mathrm{Pref}(\mathcal{P}|_{\downarrow f})$, we get $\downarrow e \subseteq \downarrow f$ and thus, $e' \preceq f$ for all $e' \in \downarrow e$. $\square$

4.1 Properties of Pomset Event Structures

In the general case, pomset event structures do not induce a deterministic transition system such they do not obey delayed choice in the sense of Definition 4. We illustrate this fact by the following example.

Example 6. Let us reconsider the example of Sect. 3.3. On the left of Fig. 6, the pomset event structure of $\{\mathcal{X}, \mathcal{Y}\}$ is depicted (1), where the arrow connects causal dependent events and the dashed line conflicting ones. On the right of Fig. 6, the induced transition system is shown (2). Note that this transition system is non-deterministic in the configuration $\{\mathcal{Y}|_{\{e\}}\}$.

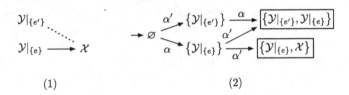

(1)   (2)

Fig. 6. $\mathcal{E}\ \{\mathcal{X}, \mathcal{Y}\}$ (1) and induced transition system ts $\mathcal{E}[\{\mathcal{X}, \mathcal{Y}\}]$ (2)

We now present a further lemma that intuitively provides the backward direction of Lemma 3:

Lemma 4. *For all $C \in \mathrm{Conf}(\mathcal{E}[\mathfrak{P}])$ we have $(C, \leqslant|_C, \lambda|_C) \in \mathrm{Pref}(\mathfrak{P})$.*

Proof. Since C is conflict-free there is a $\mathcal{P} = (F, \preceq, \nu) \in \mathrm{Pref}(\mathfrak{P})$ such that $\mathcal{X} \in \mathrm{Pref}(\mathcal{P})$ for all $\mathcal{X} \in C$. Thus, there is a function $\xi \colon C \to F$ such that for all $\mathcal{X} \in C$ we have $\mathcal{X} = \mathcal{P}|_{\downarrow \xi(\mathcal{X})}$. Clearly, ξ is injective and it is left to show that $\mathcal{P}|_{\xi(C)} = (C, \leqslant|_C, \lambda|_C)$. We do so by showing that for all $\mathcal{X}, \mathcal{Y} \in C$ we have $\xi(\mathcal{X}) \preceq \xi(\mathcal{Y})$ iff $\mathcal{X} \leqslant \mathcal{Y}$:

($\Rightarrow$) From $\downarrow \xi(\mathcal{X}) \subseteq \downarrow \xi(\mathcal{Y})$, we get $\mathcal{P}|_{\xi(\mathcal{X})} \in \mathrm{Pref}(\mathcal{P}|_{\xi(\mathcal{Y})})$ and hence, $\mathcal{X} \in \mathrm{Pref}(\mathcal{Y})$.

($\Leftarrow$) As $\mathcal{X} \in \mathrm{Pref}(\mathcal{Y})$, we have $\mathcal{P}|_{\xi(\mathcal{X})} \in \mathrm{Pref}(\mathcal{P}|_{\xi(\mathcal{Y})})$ and thus, $\downarrow\xi(\mathcal{X}) \subseteq \downarrow\xi(\mathcal{Y})$. Hence, for all $e' \in \downarrow\xi(\mathcal{X})$ we get $e' \preceq \xi(\mathcal{Y})$ and in particular $\xi(\mathcal{X}) \preceq \xi(\mathcal{Y})$.   □

Mainly relying on Lemmas 3 and 4 above, we show compatibility of $\mathcal{E}[\mathfrak{P}]$ with its generating pomset $\mathfrak{P}$:

Theorem 2 (Compatibility Theorem). $\mathfrak{pof}(\mathcal{E}[\mathfrak{P}]) = \mathfrak{P}$.

Proof. ($\subseteq$) For all $\mathcal{P} \in \mathfrak{pof}(\mathcal{E}[\mathfrak{P}])$ there is some $C \in \mathrm{Term}$ with $\mathcal{P} = (C, \leqslant |_C, \lambda|_C)$. By Lemma 4 we have $\mathcal{P} \in \mathrm{Pref}(\mathfrak{P})$ and due to the definition of Term in $\mathcal{E}[\mathfrak{P}]$, we finally obtain $\mathcal{P} \in \mathfrak{P}$.

($\supseteq$) Let $\mathcal{P} = (F, \preceq, \nu) \in \mathfrak{P}$ and $C = \{\mathcal{P}|_{\downarrow e} : e \in F\}$. Then, due to Lemma 3, $\mathcal{P} = (C, \leqslant |_C, \lambda|_C)$ and $C \in \mathrm{Term}$. Thus, by the definition of $\mathfrak{pof}$, we get $\mathcal{P} \in \mathfrak{pof}(\mathcal{E}[\mathfrak{P}])$.   □

4.2   Pomset Event Structures for MSGs

As any MSG $\mathcal{G}$ induces a pomset semantics $\mathfrak{P}[\mathcal{G}]$, an event structure semantics for $\mathcal{G}$ is naturally defined through $\mathcal{E}[\mathfrak{P}[\mathcal{G}]]$.

Example 7. Let us consider the running example with the MSG $\mathcal{G}_{\mathrm{bsp}}$ from Example 3 and denote its event structure by $\mathcal{E}[\mathfrak{P}[\mathcal{G}_{\mathrm{bsp}}]] = (E, \leqslant, \lambda, \#, \mathrm{Term})$. Figure 7 shows a fragment of $\mathcal{E}[\mathfrak{P}[\mathcal{G}_{\mathrm{bsp}}]]$. Arrows indicate direct successors, i.e., $e \to e'$ iff $e < e'$ and there is no $e'' \in E$ with $e < e'' < e'$. Dashed lines connect minimal conflicting events, i.e., $e \dashdash e'$ iff $e\#e'$ and there is no $e'' \in E$ with $e\#e'' < e'$ or $e'\#e'' < e$. All other conflicting events can be derived from these minimal conflicting events through conflict heredity. Note that, e.g., the event $\mathcal{M}_a$ has no successor and is in conflict with every event of the upper branch of Fig. 7. Thus, the configuration $C = \{\mathcal{M}_t|_{\{!\}}, \mathcal{M}_t|_{\{!,?\}}, \mathcal{M}_a|_{\{!d,?d,!a\}}, \mathcal{M}_a\}$ is maximal in the sense that it cannot be extended by any other event. Furthermore, $C \in \mathrm{Term}$ as $\mathcal{M}_a \in \mathfrak{P}$.

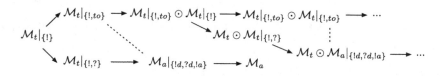

Fig. 7. Fragment of the event structure for $\mathfrak{P}[\mathcal{G}_{\mathrm{bsp}}]$

Note that the basis for our construction in Definition 6 is provided by pomset downward closures, which in the setting of MSGs correspond to p-views for processes $p \in P$ [13]. Although the transition system induced by a pomset event structure does neither need to be deterministic nor bisimilar to the corresponding suffix transition system (see Example 6), it obeys delayed choice in the setting of MSGs:

Theorem 3. *Let $\mathcal{G}$ be an MSG. Then, $\mathsf{ts}\big(\mathcal{E}[\mathfrak{P}[\mathcal{G}]]\big)$ is isomorphic to $\mathcal{T}_{\mathrm{pref}}\big[\mathfrak{P}[\mathcal{G}]\big]$.*

Proof. Let us denote $\mathcal{E}\big[\mathfrak{P}[\mathcal{G}]\big]$ by $\mathcal{E} = (E, \leqslant, \lambda, \#, \mathrm{Term})$ and the transition relation of $\mathsf{ts}(\mathcal{E})$ by $\longrightarrow$. Furthermore, let $\mathcal{T}_{\mathrm{pref}}\big[\mathfrak{P}[\mathcal{G}]\big] = (S, \{\varnothing\}, \rightsquigarrow, \mathfrak{T})$. Lemma 4 induces a mapping $\xi\colon \mathrm{Conf}(\mathcal{E}) \to \mathrm{Pref}(\mathfrak{P}[\mathcal{G}])$ by $\xi(C) = (C, \leqslant|_C, \lambda|_C)$ for all $C \in \mathrm{Conf}(\mathcal{E})$. Due to Lemma 3, ξ is bijective. Since every reachable state $\mathfrak{X}$ in $\mathcal{T}_{\mathrm{pref}}\big[\mathfrak{P}[\mathcal{G}]\big]$ is a singleton (see Lemma 2), it suffices to show that for all $\alpha \in Act$ and $C, D \in \mathrm{Conf}(\mathcal{E})$ we have $C \xrightarrow{\alpha} D$ iff $\{\xi(C)\} \xrightarrow{\alpha} \{\xi(D)\}$.

($\Rightarrow$) For $C \xrightarrow{\alpha} D$ there is an event $e \in E$ such that $D = C \cup \{e\}$ and $\lambda(e) = \alpha$. By the definition of prefixes and the fact that we only consider pomsets that are not autoconcurrent, we thus obtain $\{(C, \leqslant|_C, \lambda|_C)\} = \mathrm{Pref}_\alpha(\{(D, \leqslant |_D, \lambda|_D)\})$. Hence, $\{\xi(C)\} \xrightarrow{\alpha} \{\xi(D)\}$.

($\Leftarrow$) Let $\{\xi(C)\} \xrightarrow{\alpha} \{\xi(D)\}$. Then $\{(C, \leqslant|_C, \lambda|_C)\} = \mathrm{Pref}_\alpha(\{(D, \leqslant|_D, \lambda|_D)\})$ and thus, there is an event $e \in D$ with $\lambda(e) = \alpha$ such that $(C, \leqslant|_C, \lambda|_C) = (D \backslash \{e\}, \leqslant|_{D \backslash \{e\}}, \lambda|_{D \backslash \{e\}})$. By Lemma 3 we obtain $C = D \backslash \{e\}$ and hence, the definition of $\mathsf{ts}(\cdot)$ yields $C \xrightarrow{\alpha} D$.

It is left to show that $C \in \mathrm{Term}$ iff $\{\xi(C)\} \in \mathfrak{T}$. Due to Theorem 2, we have $C \in \mathrm{Term}$ iff $\xi(C) \in \mathfrak{P}[\mathcal{G}]$. By the definition of $\mathcal{T}_{\mathrm{pref}}\big[\mathfrak{P}[\mathcal{G}]\big]$ and Lemma 2, $\{\mathcal{X}\} \in \mathfrak{T}$ iff $\mathcal{X} \in \mathfrak{P}[\mathcal{G}]$. The statement follows directly since ξ is a bijection. $\square$

As a direct consequence of the above theorem and Theorem 1, we obtain that $\mathcal{E}\big[\mathfrak{P}[\mathcal{G}]\big]$ can be seen as a delayed-choice semantics for $\mathcal{G}$. Thus, our definition of pomset event structures covers the first non-interleaving branching-time semantics for MSGs that follows the delayed-choice principle.

Corollary 1. *$\mathsf{ts}\big(\mathcal{E}[\mathfrak{P}]\big)$ obeys delayed choice, i.e., $\mathsf{ts}\big(\mathcal{E}[\mathfrak{P}]\big)$ is deterministic and bisimilar to $\mathcal{T}_{\mathrm{suff}}[\mathfrak{P}]$.*

5   Conclusion

The main contribution of this paper is that we provided a semantical framework of branching-time semantics for pomset families and MSGs following the delayed-choice principle. In contrast to the original definition of delayed choice based on process algebras, we circumvented the intrinsic linear-time operators in terms of delayed choice [3] and weak sequential composition [33] by operating directly on pomset families. Within this approach, delayed choice corresponds to the standard union operation on pomset families that arise from removing minimal events of pomset family members, and weak sequential composition corresponds to local concatenation of pomsets [30] (as intended by [33]). We thus avoid difficulties within the definition of the standard operational semantics for MSG [17, 31] that require fixed points over operator-defining rules with negative premises. As a reference semantics, we defined suffix transition systems, which closely follow the process-algebraic approach in the sense that states represent future behaviors. The prefix transition-system semantics provides a connection to the branching-time semantics defined in [8], where quantitative aspects for MSGs have been investigated. Whereas previously presented event-structure semantics for MSGs [12] do not follow the delayed-choice principle, we constructed an event structure that is consistent with our transition-system semantics, i.e., those transition system is deterministic and bisimilar to our reference semantics.

We illustrated that our event structure semantics follows the delayed-choice principle by referring to its induced transition system. It naturally arises the question whether there is a reasonable definition of delayed choice directly on event structures, possibly relying on deterministic event structures [32]. This question and the problem of defining an event structure obeying delayed choice for arbitrary pomset families is left for further work. Towards an application of our semantical framework, extending LOTOS [6] with a delayed-choice operator could enable reasoning about delayed-choice semantics for pomsets and MSGs.

Acknowledgments. The authors thank Arend Rensink and Joost-Pieter Katoen for their valuable comments on this paper.

References

1. Alur, R., Holzmann, G.J., Peled, D.: An analyzer for message sequence charts. In: Software Concepts and Tools, pp. 304–313 (1996)
2. Alur, R., Yannakakis, M.: Model checking of message sequence charts. In: Baeten, J.C.M., Mauw, S. (eds.) CONCUR 1999. LNCS, vol. 1664, pp. 114–129. Springer, Heidelberg (1999). doi:10.1007/3-540-48320-9_10
3. Baeten, J.C.M., Mauw, S.: Delayed choice: an operator for joining message sequence charts. In: Hogrefe, D., Leue, S. (eds.) FORTE 1994. IFIPAICT, pp. 340–354. Springer, Boston (1994)
4. Bergstra, J.A., Bethke, I., Ponse, A.: Process algebra with iteration and nesting. Comput. J. **37**(4), 243 (1994)
5. Bollig, B., Kuske, D., Meinecke, I.: Propositional dynamic logic for message-passing systems. Log. Methods Comput. Sci. **6**(3:16), 1–31 (2010)
6. Bolognesi, T., Brinksma, E.: Introduction to the ISO specification language LOTOS. Comput. Netw. **14**, 25–59 (1987)
7. Chakraborty, J., D'Souza, D., Narayan Kumar, K.: Analysing message sequence graph specifications. In: Margaria, T., Steffen, B. (eds.) ISoLA 2010. LNCS, vol. 6415, pp. 549–563. Springer, Heidelberg (2010). doi:10.1007/978-3-642-16558-0_45
8. Dubslaff, C., Baier, C.: Quantitative analysis of communication scenarios. In: Sankaranarayanan, S., Vicario, E. (eds.) FORMATS 2015. LNCS, vol. 9268, pp. 76–92. Springer, Cham (2015). doi:10.1007/978-3-319-22975-1_6
9. Genest, B., Muscholl, A.: Message sequence charts: a survey. In: ACSD, pp. 2–4 (2005)
10. Groote, J.F.: Transition system specifications with negative premises. Theor. Comput. Sci. **118**(2), 263–299 (1993)

11. OM Group: Unified modeling language (UML): Superstructure version 2.4.1, August 2011. http://www.omg.org/spec/UML/2.4.1/Superstructure/PDF/
12. Hélouët, L., Jard, C., Caillaud, B.: An event structure based semantics for high-level message sequence charts. Math. Struct. Comput. Sci. **12**(4), 377–402 (2002)
13. Henriksen, J.G., Mukund, M., Kumar, K.N., Sohoni, M., Thiagarajan, P.S.: A theory of regular MSC languages. Inf. Comput. **202**, 1–38 (2005)
14. Heymer, S.: A semantics for MSC based on Petri-net components. In: Proceedings of the 2nd Workshop of the SDL Forum Society on SDL and MSC, SAM 2000 (2000)
15. ITU-T. Message Sequence Chart (MSC). Z.120 v1.0 (1993)
16. ITU-T: Message Sequence Chart (MSC). Z.120 v2.0 (1996)
17. ITU-T: Annex B: Formal semantics of Message Sequence Charts. Z.120 v2.2 (1998)
18. ITU-T: Message Sequence Chart (MSC). Z.120 v5.0 (2011)
19. Katoen, J., Lambert, L.: Pomsets for message sequence charts. In: 8th GI/ITG-Fachgespraech, pp. 197–207. Shaker Verlag (1998)
20. Levin, V., Peled, D.: Verification of message sequence charts via template matching. In: Bidoit, M., Dauchet, M. (eds.) CAAP 1997/TAPSOFT 1997. LNCS, vol. 1214, pp. 652–666. Springer, Heidelberg (1997). doi:10.1007/BFb0030632
21. Madhusudan, P.: Reasoning about sequential and branching behaviours of message sequence graphs. In: Orejas, F., Spirakis, P.G., van Leeuwen, J. (eds.) ICALP 2001. LNCS, vol. 2076, pp. 809–820. Springer, Heidelberg (2001). doi:10.1007/3-540-48224-5_66
22. Mauw, S., Reniers, M.A.: An algebraic semantics of basic message sequence charts. Comput. J. **37**, 269–277 (1994)
23. Mauw, S., Reniers, M.A.: Operational semantics for MSC'96. Comput. Netw. **31**(17), 1785–1799 (1999)
24. Mauw, S., Reniers, M.A.: High-level message sequence charts. In: SDL Forum, pp. 291–306 (1997)
25. Milner, R.: Communication and Concurrency. PHI Series in Computer Science. Prentice Hall, Upper Saddle River (1989)
26. Muscholl, A., Peled, D.: Message sequence graphs and decision problems on Mazurkiewicz traces. In: Kutyłowski, M., Pacholski, L., Wierzbicki, T. (eds.) MFCS 1999. LNCS, vol. 1672, pp. 81–91. Springer, Heidelberg (1999). doi:10.1007/3-540-48340-3_8
27. Muscholl, A., Peled, D.: Deciding properties of message sequence charts. In: Leue, S., Systä, T.J. (eds.) Scenarios: Models, Transformations and Tools. LNCS, vol. 3466, pp. 43–65. Springer, Heidelberg (2005). doi:10.1007/11495628_3
28. Muscholl, A., Peled, D., Su, Z.: Deciding properties for message sequence charts. In: Nivat, M. (ed.) FoSSaCS 1998. LNCS, vol. 1378, pp. 226–242. Springer, Heidelberg (1998). doi:10.1007/BFb0053553
29. Nielsen, M., Plotkin, G., Winskel, G.: Petri nets, event structures and domains. Theor. Comput. Sci. **13**(1), 85–108 (1981)
30. Pratt, V.: Modeling concurrency with partial orders. Int. J. Parallel Program. **15**, 33–71 (1986)
31. Reniers, M.A.: Message sequence chart: Syntax and semantics. Ph.D. thesis, Eindhoven University of Technology, June 1999
32. Rensink, A.: A complete theory of deterministic event structures. In: Lee, I., Smolka, S.A. (eds.) CONCUR 1995. LNCS, vol. 962, pp. 160–174. Springer, Heidelberg (1995). doi:10.1007/3-540-60218-6_12

33. Rensink, A., Wehrheim, H.: Weak sequential composition in process algebras. In: Jonsson, B., Parrow, J. (eds.) CONCUR 1994. LNCS, vol. 836, pp. 226–241. Springer, Heidelberg (1994). doi:10.1007/978-3-540-48654-1_20
34. Winskel, G., Nielsen, M.: Models for concurrency. In: Abramsky, S., Gabbay, D.M., Maibaum, T.S.E. (eds.) Handbook of Logic in Computer Science, vol. 4, pp. 1–148. Oxford University Press, Oxford (1995)

Testing

On the Existence of Practical Testers

Jan Tretmans[1,2]([⊠])

[1] TNO - Embedded Systems Innovation, Eindhoven, The Netherlands
jan.tretmans@tno.nl
[2] Radboud University, Nijmegen, The Netherlands

Abstract. Model-based testing is one of the promising technologies to increase the efficiency and effectiveness of software testing. This paper outlines the evolution of model-based testing based on labelled transition systems, from purely theoretical developments in the eighties to industrially applicable tools now: from *canonical testers* to *practical testers*. We present TORXAKIS as an example of a practical model-based tester, founded in the testing theory for labelled transition systems, and now being introduced in the daily practice of testing.

Keywords: Software testing · Model-based testing · Labelled transition systems · Model-based testing tools

1 Model-Based Testing

Software Testing. Systematic testing plays an important role in the quest for improved quality and reliability of software systems. Software testing, however, is often an error-prone, expensive, and time-consuming process. Estimates are that testing consumes 30–50% of the total software development costs. The tendency is that the effort spent on testing is still increasing due to the continuing quest for better software quality, and the ever growing size and complexity of systems. The situation is aggravated by the fact that the complexity of testing tends to grow faster than the complexity of the systems being tested, in the worst case even exponentially. Whereas development and construction methods for software allow the building of ever larger and more complex systems, there is a real danger that testing methods cannot keep pace with these construction and development methods. This may seriously hamper the development and testing of future generations of software systems.

Model-Based Testing. Model-based testing (MBT) is one of the promising technologies to meet the challenges imposed on software testing. With MBT a system under test (SUT) is tested against an abstract model of its required behaviour. The main virtue of model-based testing is that it allows test automation that goes well beyond the mere automatic execution of manually crafted test cases. It

This work has been supported by NWO-TTW project 13859: SUMBAT – Supersizing Model-Based Testing.

© Springer International Publishing AG 2017
J.-P. Katoen et al. (Eds.): Brinksma Festschrift, LNCS 10500, pp. 87–106, 2017.
DOI: 10.1007/978-3-319-68270-9_5

allows for the algorithmic generation of large amounts of test cases, including test oracles (expected results), completely automatically from the model of required behaviour. If this model is valid, i.e., expresses precisely what the system under test should do, all these tests are provably valid, too.

From an industrial perspective, model-based testing is a promising approach to detect more bugs faster and cheaper. The current state of practice is that test automation mainly concentrates on the automatic execution of tests, but that the problem of test generation is not addressed. Model-based testing aims at automatically generating high-quality test suites from models, thus complementing automatic test execution.

From an academic perspective, model-based testing is a formal-methods approach to testing that complements formal verification and model checking. Formal verification and model checking intend to show that a system has specified properties by proving that a model of that system satisfies these properties. Thus, any verification is only as good as the validity of the model on which it is based. Model-based testing, on the other hand, starts with a (verified) model, and then aims at showing that the real, physical implementation of the system behaves in compliance with this model. Due to the inherent limitations of testing, testing can never be complete: testing can only show the presence of errors, not their absence [26].

Benefits of Model-Based Testing. Model-based testing makes it possible to generate test cases automatically, enabling the next step in test automation. It makes it possible to generate more, longer, and more diversified test cases with less effort, whereas, being based on sound algorithms, these test cases are provably valid.

Making models for MBT usually already leads to better understanding of system behaviour and requirements and to early detection of specification and design errors. Moreover, constructing models for MBT paves the way for other model-based methods, such as model-based analysis, model checking, and simulation, and it forms the natural connection to model-based system development that is becoming an important driving force in the software industry.

Test suite maintenance, i.e., continuously adapting test cases when systems are modified, is an important challenge of any testing process. In MBT, maintenance of a multitude of test cases is replaced by maintenance of one model. Finally, various notions of (model-) coverage can be automatically computed, expressing the level of completeness of testing, and allowing better selection of test cases.

Sorts of Model-Based Testing. There are different kinds of testing, and thus of model-based testing, depending on the kind of models being used, the quality aspects being tested, the level of formality involved, the degree of accessibility and observability of the system being tested, and the kind of system being tested. In this contribution we consider model-based testing as *formal, specification-based, active, black-box, functionality testing* of *reactive systems*. It is *testing*, because it involves checking some properties of the SUT by systematically performing experiments on the real, running SUT. The kind of properties being checked are concerned with *functionality*, i.e., testing whether the system correctly does what it should do in terms of correct responses to given stimuli. We do *specification-based, black-box* testing, since the externally observable behaviour of the system, seen as a *black-box*, is compared with what has been specified. The testing is *active*, in the sense that the tester controls and observes the SUT in an active way by giving stimuli and triggers to the SUT, and observing its responses, as opposed to passive testing, or monitoring. Our SUTs are *dynamic, data-intensive, reactive systems*. Reactive systems react to external events (stimuli, triggers, inputs) with output events (responses, actions, outputs). In dynamic systems, outputs depend on inputs as well as on the system state. Data-intensive means that instances of complex data structures are communicated in inputs and outputs, and that state transitions may involve complex computations and constraints. Finally, we deal with *formal testing*: there is a formal, well-defined theory underpinning models, SUTs, and correctness of SUTs with respect to models, which enables formal reasoning about *soundness* and *exhaustiveness* of generated test suites.

A Theory for Model-Based Testing. A theory for model-based testing must, naturally, first of all define the models that are considered. The modelling formalism determines the kind of properties that can be specified, and, consequently, the kind of properties for which test cases can be generated. Secondly, it must be precisely defined what it means for an SUT to conform to a model. Conformance can be expressed using an *implementation relation*, also called *conformance relation* [15]. Although an SUT is a black box, we can assume it could be modelled by some model instance in a domain of implementation models. This assumption is commonly referred to as the *testability hypothesis*, or *test assumption* [32]. The testability hypothesis allows reasoning about SUTs as if they were formal models, and it makes it possible to define the implementation relation as a formal relation between the domain of specification models and the domain of implementation models. Soundness, i.e., do all correct SUTs pass, and exhaustiveness, i.e., do all incorrect SUTs fail, of test suites is defined with respect to an implementation relation.

In the domain of testing reactive systems there are two prevailing 'schools' of formal model-based testing. The oldest one uses Mealy-machines, also called finite-state machines (FSM); see [20, 46, 51]. In this paper we concentrate on the other one that uses *labelled transition systems* (LTS) for modelling. A labelled transition system is a structure consisting of states with transitions, labelled with actions, between them. The states model the system states; the labelled transitions model the actions that a system can perform. There is a rich and well-understood theory for MBT with LTS, on which we elaborate in Sect. 2.

Labelled transition systems form a well-defined semantic basis for modelling and model-based testing, but they are not suitable for writing down models explicitly. Typically, realistic systems have more states than there are atoms on earth (which is approximately 10^{50}) so an explicit representation of states is impossible. What is needed is a language to represent large labelled transition systems. *Process algebras* have semantics in terms of labeled transition systems, they support different ways of composition such as choice, parallelism, sequencing, etc., and they were heavily investigated in the eighties [41, 42, 48]. They are a good candidate to serve as a notation for LTS models.

Model-Based Testing Challenges. Software is anywhere, and ever more systems depend on software: software controls, connects, and monitors almost every aspect of systems, be it a car, an airplane, a pacemaker, or a refrigerator. Consequently, overall system quality and reliability are more and more determined by the quality of the embedded software. Typically, such software consists of several million lines of code, with complex behavioural control-flow as well as intricate data structures, with distribution and a lot of parallelism, having complex and heterogeneous interfaces, and controlling diverse, multidisciplinary processes. In addition, systems continuously evolve and are composed into larger systems and systems-of-systems, whereas system components may come from heterogeneous sources: there can be legacy, third-party, out-sourced, off-the-shelf, open source, or newly developed components.

For model-based testing, these trends lead to several challenges. First, the size of the systems implies that making complete models is often infeasible so that MBT must deal with partial and under-specified models and abstraction, and that partial knowledge and uncertainty cannot be avoided. Secondly, the combination of complicated state-behaviour and intricate input and output-data structures, and their dependencies, must be supported in modelling. Thirdly, distribution and parallelism imply that MBT must deal with concurrency in models, which introduces additional uncertainty and non-determinism. In the fourth place, since complex systems are built from sub-systems and components, and systems themselves are more and more combined into systems-of-systems, MBT must support compositionality, i.e., building complex models by combining simpler models. Lastly, since complexity leads to an astronomical number of potential test cases, test selection, i.e., how to select those tests from all potential test cases that can catch most, and most important failures, within constraints of testing time and budget, is a key issue in model-based testing.

In short, to be applicable to testing of modern software systems, MBT shall support partial models, under-specification, abstraction, uncertainty, state & data, concurrency, non-determinism, compositionality, and test selection. Though several academic and commercial MBT tools exist, there are not that many tools that support all of these aspects.

Goal. The goal of this paper is to sketch the evolution from *the existence of canonical testers* [11] to *the existence of a practical tester*. It is not the aim to present a formal treatment, nor to give definitions or algorithms – we refer to the literature for this – but we intend to give an overview of the steps that have led from the formal *canonical-tester* theory to practical model-based testing tools, which, on the one hand, have a well-founded theoretical basis, and, on the other hand, are now being introduced in the daily practice of testing, thus demonstrating that "Theory can be practical!" [14].

More in particular, we will show the practical tester TORXAKIS, an MBT tool that uses a number of the discussed testing and modelling theories [56]. Moreover, TORXAKIS deals with most of the challenges posed in the previous paragraph: it supports modelling of state-based control flow together with complex data, it deals with non-determinism, abstraction, partial models and under-specification, concurrency, and composition of complex models from simpler models. TORX-AKIS is a research MBT tool that is being developed by the Radboud University Nijmegen, the University of Twente, and TNO-ESI (NL), and that has been applied to various systems, ranging from smart-cards [49] to large, high-tech embedded systems.

Overview. This section, Sect. 1, introduced and discussed model-based testing and set the context and goal for the remaining sections. Section 2 will describe the evolution of testing theory for labelled transition systems starting from testing equivalences and canonical testers up to the implementation relations that are used in TORXAKIS. Section 3 demonstrates the existence of a practical tester: it presents TORXAKIS, the theories underpinning it, and two small examples starting with the obligatory *Hello World!* example. Finally, Sect. 4 recapitulates and briefly looks at some future open problems.

2   Testing Transition Systems

Labelled transition systems (LTS) and its variants constitute a powerful semantic model for describing and reasoning about dynamic, reactive systems. LTS-based testing theory has developed over the years from a theory-oriented approach for defining LTS equivalences to a theory that forms a sound basis for real testing and industrially viable testing tools. In this section we sketch the evolution of LTS-based testing theory, and thus provide an update of [18].

Testing Equivalences. Testing theory for LTS started with using testing to formalize the notion of behavioural equivalence for LTS. Two LTSs show equivalent behaviour if there is no test that can observe the difference between them. By defining appropriate formalizations for test and observation this led to the theory of testing equivalences and preorders for LTS [24,25]. Different equivalences can then be defined by choosing different formalizations of test and observation: more powerful testers lead to stronger equivalences, and the other way around. In the course of the years, many such variations were investigated, with testers that can observe the occurrence of actions, the refusal of actions, or the potentiality of doing actions, testers that can undo actions, that can make copies of the system state, or that can repeat tests indefinitely. Comparative concurrency semantics systematically compares these and other equivalences and preorders defined over LTS [1,33,34,45,53]. Crucial in these equivalences is the notion of *non-determinism*, i.e., that after doing an action in an LTS the subsequent state is not uniquely determined. For deterministic systems almost all equivalences coincide [29].

Test Generation. Whereas the theory of testing equivalences and preorders is used to define semantic relations over LTS using all possible tests, actual testing turns this around: given an LTS s (the specification) and a relation **imp** over LTS (the implementation relation), determine a (minimal) set of tests $T_{\mathbf{imp}}(s)$ that characterizes all implementations i with i **imp** s.

First steps towards systematically generating such test suites (sets of tests) from a specification LTS were made by Brinksma et al. in [11,12,17] leading to the *canonical tester* theory for the implementation relation **conf**. The intuition of **conf** is that after traces, i.e., sequences of actions, that are explicitly specified in the specification LTS, the implementation LTS shall not unexpectedly refuse actions, i.e., the implementation may only refuse a set of actions if the specification can refuse this set, too. This introduces *under-specification*, in two ways. First, after traces that are not in the specification LTS, anything is allowed in the implementation. Second, the implementation may refuse less than the specification. In this approach, models were represented using the process algebraic specification language LOTOS [7,16,42].

Inputs and Outputs. The canonical tester theory and its variations make an important assumption about the communication between the SUT and the tester, viz. that this communication is synchronous and symmetric. Each communication event is seen as a joint action of the SUT and the tester, inspired by the parallel composition in process algebra. This also means that both the tester and the SUT can block the communication, and thus stop the other from progressing. In practice, however, it is different: actual communication between an SUT and a tester takes place via inputs and outputs. Inputs are initiated by the tester, they trigger the SUT, and they cannot be refused by the SUT. Outputs are produced by the SUT, and they are observed and cannot be refused by the tester.

A first approach to a testing theory with inputs and outputs was developed by interpreting each action as either input or output, and by modelling the communication medium between SUT and tester explicitly [38,61]. Later this was generalized by just assuming that inputs cannot be refused by the SUT – the SUT is assumed to be *input-enabled*, i.e., in each state there is a transition for all input actions – and outputs cannot be refused by the tester, akin to I/O-automata [47]. Adding these assumptions to the concepts of the canonical tester theory and **conf** – refusal sets of the implementation shall be refusal sets of the specification, but only for explicitly specified traces – leads to a new implementation relation that was coined **ioconf** [58]. The assumptions that the SUT cannot refuse inputs and the tester cannot refuse outputs makes that the only relevant refusal that remains is refusing all possible outputs by the SUT, which is called *quiescence* [62]. Intuitively, quiescence corresponds to observing that there is no output of the SUT, which is an important observation in testing theory as well as in practical testing.

In **ioconf** the test will stop after observing quiescence, i.e., during each test run quiescence occurs at most once, as the last observation. Phalippou noticed that in practical testing quiescence is observed as a time-out during which no output from the SUT is observed, and that after such a time-out testing continues with providing a next input to the SUT, so that quiescence can occur multiple times during a test run [52]. Inspired by this observation, *repetitive quiescence* was added to **ioconf**, leading to the implementation relation **ioco** [59]. Theoretically, **ioco** is akin to failure-trace preorder with inputs and outputs [45]. Intuitively, **ioco** expresses that an SUT conforms to its specification if the SUT never produces an output that cannot be produced by the specification in the same situation, i.e., after the same trace. *Quiescence* is treated as a special, virtual output, actually expressing the absence of real outputs.

For **ioco**-testing there is a test generation algorithm that was proved to be *sound* – all **ioco**-correct SUTs pass all generated tests – and *exhaustive* – all **ioco**-incorrect SUTs are eventually detected by some generated test. The implementation relation **ioco** is the basis for a couple of MBT tools, such as TGV [43], the AGEDIS TOOL SET [36], TORX [5], JTORX [4], Uppaal-Tron [40], Axini Test Manager (ATM) [2], and TORXAKIS (Sect. 3).

A couple of variations have been proposed for **ioco**, such as **uioco** dealing more accurately with under-specification [6], **mioco** for multiple input and output channels [39], **wioco** that diminishes the requirements on input enabledness [64], various variants of timed-**ioco** [9,40,44], and **sioco** for LTS with data [30,31].

Data. The **ioco**-testing theory for labelled transition systems mainly deals with the dynamic aspects of system behaviour, i.e., with state-based control flow. The static aspects, such as data structures, their operations, and their constraints, which are part of almost any real system, are not covered. Symbolic Transition Systems (STS) add (infinite) data and data-dependent control flow, such as guarded transitions, to LTS, founded on first order logic [31]. Symbolic **ioco** (**sioco**) lifts **ioco** to the symbolic level. The semantics of STS and **sioco** is given directly in terms of LTS; STS and **sioco** do not add expressiveness but they provide a way of representing and manipulating large and infinite transition systems symbolically. Test generation in TORXAKIS uses STS following the algorithm of [30].

3 A Practical Tester: TorXakis

TORXAKIS is an experimental tool for on-line model-based testing. This section gives a light-weight introduction to TORXAKIS, the underlying theory, its models, and its usage, illustrated with two examples: the obligatory *Hello World!* example and a more elaborate *Job-Dispatcher* example. TORXAKIS is freely available under a BSD3 license [56].

3.1 Theory

Test Generation Algorithm. TORXAKIS implements the **ioco**-testing theory [59,60] for labelled transition systems. More precisely, it implements test generation for symbolic transition systems following the on-the-fly **ioco**-test generation algorithm described in [30].

TORXAKIS is an on-the-fly (on-line) MBT tool which means that it combines test generation and test execution: generated test steps are immediately executed on the SUT and responses from the SUT are immediately checked and used when calculating the next step in test generation.

Currently, only random test selection is supported, i.e., TORXAKIS chooses a random action among the possible inputs to the SUT in the current state. This involves choosing among the transitions of the STS and choosing a value from the (infinite, constrained) data items attached to the transition. The latter involves constraint solving.

Modelling. TORXAKIS uses its own language to express models. The language is strongly inspired by the process-algebraic language LOTOS [7,42], and incorporates ideas from EXTENDED LOTOS [12] and mCRL2 [35]. The semantics is based on STS, which in turn has a semantics in LTS. The process-algebraic part is complemented with a data specification language based on algebraic data types (ADT) and functions like in functional languages. In addition to user-defined ADTs, predefined data types such as booleans, unbounded integers, strings, and regular expressions over strings are provided.

Having its roots in process algebra, the language is compositional. It has several operators to combine processes: sequencing, choice, parallel composition with and without communication, interrupt, disable, and abstraction (hiding). Communication between processes can be multi-way, and actions can be built using multiple labels.

Implementation. TORXAKIS builds on the model-based testing tools TORX [5] and JTORX [4]. The main additions are data specification and manipulation with algebraic data types, and its own, well-defined modelling language. Like TORX and JTORX, TORXAKIS generates tests by first unfolding the process expressions from the model into a *behaviour tree*, on which primitives are defined for generating test cases. Unlike TORX and JTORX, TORXAKIS does not unfold data into all possible concrete data values, but it keeps data symbolically. Unfolding of process expressions is similar to the LOTOS simulators HIPPO [28,57] and SMILE [27].

In order to manipulate symbolic data and solve constraints for test-data generation, TORXAKIS uses SMT solvers (Satisfaction Modulo Theories) [23]. Currently, Z3 and CVC4 are used via the SMT-LIBv2.5 standard interface [3, 22,50]. Term rewriting is used to evaluate data expressions and functions.

The well-defined process-algebraic basis with **ioco** semantics makes it possible to perform optimizations and reductions based on equational reasoning with testing equivalence, which implies **ioco**-semantics.

The core of TORXAKIS is implemented in the functional language Haskell [37], while parts of TORXAKIS itself have been tested with the Haskell MBT tool QuickCheck [21].

Innovation. Compared to other model-based testing tools TORXAKIS offers support for test generation from non-deterministic models, under-specification, dealing with uncertainty, concurrency, parallelism, and abstraction, and the combination of constructive modelling in transition systems with property-oriented specification via data constraints.

3.2 Usage

In order to use TORXAKIS we need a system under test (SUT), a model specifying the allowed behaviour of the SUT, and probably an adapter (test harness, wrapper) to connect the actual SUT to TORXAKIS.

System Under Test. The SUT is the actual program or system that we wish to test. The TORXAKIS view of an SUT is a black-box communicating with messages on its interfaces, i.e., on its input and output channels. An input is a message sent by the tester to the SUT on an input channel; an output is the observation by the tester of a message from the SUT on an output channel. A behaviour of the SUT is a possible sequence of input and output actions. The goal of testing is to compare the actual behaviour that the SUT exhibits with the behaviour specified in the model.

Technically, channels are implemented as plain old sockets where messages are line-based strings, or string-encodings of some typed data. So, the TORXAKIS view of an SUT is a black-box communicating strings on a couple of sockets.

There is a caveat: sockets have asynchronous communication whereas models and test generation assume synchronous communication. This may lead to race conditions if a model offers the choice between an input and an output. If this occurs the asynchronous communication of the sockets must be explicitly modelled, e.g., as queues in the model.

Model. The model is written in the TORXAKIS modelling language. A (collection of) model file(s) contains all the definitions necessary for expressing the model: channel, data-type, function, constant, and process definitions, which are all combined in a model definition. In addition, the model file contains some testing specific aspects: connections and en/decodings. A connection definition defines how TORXAKIS is connected to the SUT by specifying the binding of model channels to sockets. En/decodings specify the mapping of abstract messages (ADTs) to strings and vice versa. The next subsections will explain the details of modelling using two examples.

Adapter. TORXAKIS communicates with the SUT via sockets, so either the SUT must offer a socket interface – which a lot of real-life SUTs don't do – or the SUT must be connected via an adapter, wrapper, or test harness that interfaces the SUT to TORXAKIS, and that transforms the native communication of the SUT to the socket communication that TORXAKIS requires. Usually, such an adapter must be manually developed. Sometimes it is simple, e.g., transforming standard IO into socket communication using standard (Unix) tools like `netcat` or `socat`, as the example below shows. Sometimes, building an adapter can be quite cumbersome, e.g., when the SUT provides a GUI. In this case tools like

SELENIUM [54] or SIKULI [55] may be used to adapt a GUI or a web interface to socket communication. An adapter is not specific for MBT but is required for any form of automated test execution. If traditional test automation is in place then this infrastructure can quite often be reused as adapter for MBT.

Testing. Once we have an SUT, a model, and an adapter, we can use TORXAKIS to run tests. The tool performs on-the-fly testing of the SUT by automatically generating test steps from the model and immediately executing these test steps on the SUT, while observing and checking the responses from the SUT. A test case may consist of thousands of such test steps, which makes it also suitable for reliability testing, and it will eventually lead to a verdict for the test case.

Other functionality of TORXAKIS includes calculation of data values, constraint solving for data variables, exploration of a model without connecting to an SUT (closed simulation), and simulation of a model in an environment, i.e., simulation while connected to the outside world (open simulation).

3.3 Hello World!

Traditionally, the first program, in this case the first model, made in a new language is the famous *Hello World!* program. Here, we take a slight variation of *Hello World!*: our system first gets a name as input and then outputs "Hello ⟨name⟩!", repeating these two actions indefinitely. Our SUT is an executable program claiming to show this behaviour. Our task is to test whether the SUT indeed behaves as prescribed. So, the first task is to express the required behaviour in a model; see Fig. 1 for the TORXAKIS model.

The model contains 4 definitions. First, `CHANDEF` defines two channels with messages of type `String`.

Secondly, the `PROCDEF` defines a process, named `helloName`, which has two channels of type `String` and no parameters. Process `helloName` specifies the following behaviour: first there is an action on channel `Inp`, followed by an action on channel `Outp`, followed by a recursive call of `helloName` to express the indefinite repetition. The operator `>->` denotes sequencing of actions. In the action on `Inp`, a message with name `name` is communicated, which must be of type `String`, the type of `Inp`. Moreover, the message must satisfy the constraint given between `[[` and `]]`. This regular expression constraint requires that `name` starts with a capital letter followed by one or more small letters. The following action on channel `Outp` is uniquely constructed from the concatenation `"Hello"` `++` `name` `++` `"!"`, where `name` refers to the value that `name` obtained in the preceding action.

Thirdly, the complete model is defined in `MODELDEF`. It specifies which channels are inputs, which are outputs, and the behaviour of the model using the process `helloName` defined earlier.

The `CNECTDEF` specifies that the tester connects as client to the SUT (the server) via sockets. It binds the channel `Input`, which is an input of the model and of the SUT, thus an *output* of TORXAKIS, to the socket ⟨localhost, 7890⟩. Moreover, an encoding of actions to strings on the socket can be defined, but in

```
CHANDEF   Chans
  ::=
       Input   ::  String ;
       Output  ::  String
ENDDEF

PROCDEF   helloName [Inp, Outp :: String] ()
  ::=
            Inp ? name [[ strinre(name, REGEX('[A-Z][a-z]+')) ]]
       >->  Outp ! "Hello " ++ name ++ " !"
       >->  helloName [Inp, Outp] ()
ENDDEF

MODELDEF   Hello
  ::=
       CHAN IN    Input
       CHAN OUT   Output

       BEHAVIOUR
             helloName [Input, Output] ()
ENDDEF

CNECTDEF   Sut
  ::=
       CLIENTSOCK

       CHAN OUT   Input    HOST "localhost" PORT 7890
       ENCODE     Input    ? s  ->  ! s

       CHAN IN    Output   HOST "localhost" PORT 7891
       DECODE     Output   ! s  <-  ? s
ENDDEF
```

Fig. 1. TORXAKIS model of *Hello World!*

this case, the encoding is trivial. Analogously, outputs from the SUT, i.e., inputs to TORXAKIS, are read from socket ⟨localhost, 7891⟩ and decoded.

The next step is to develop an adapter. This is not part of the TORXAKIS model. Assuming that our SUT is called `helloWorld`, and that it communicates on standard input/output, this means that we have to convert input/output communication to socket communication. In a Linux-like environment this may be done using utilities like `netcat nc` or `socat`, like:

```
$ nc -l 7890 | ./helloWorld | nc -l 7891
```

Now we can perform a test by running the SUT with its adapter and TORX-AKIS as two separate processes; see Fig. 2 for a run of TORXAKIS. User inputs in TORXAKIS are marked <<; responses from TORXAKIS are marked >>.

After having started TORXAKIS, we start the tester with `tester Hello Sut`, expressing that we wish to test with model `Hello` and SUT connection `Sut`, shown in the model file in Fig. 1. Then we can test 6 test steps with `test 6` and, indeed, after 6 test steps it stops with verdict **PASS**. A test run of 6 steps is rather small; we could have run for 100,000 steps or more. TorXakis generates inputs to the SUT, such as (`Input, ["Zp"]`), with names satisfying the regular expression constraint. These input names are generated from the constraint by the SMT solver. Some extra functionality has been added in TORXAKIS in order to generate quasi-random inputs, which is not normally provided by an SMT solver. Moreover, it is checked that the outputs, such as (`Output, ["Hello Zp !"]`), are correct.

```
$ torxakis HelloWorld.txs

TXS >>   TorXakis :: Model-Based Testing
TXS >>   input files parsed: HelloWorld.txs
TXS <<   tester Hello Sut
TXS >>   tester started
TXS <<   test 6
TXS >>   ....1: IN:  Act { { ( Input, [ "Zp" ] ) } }
TXS >>   ....2: OUT: Act { { ( Output, [ "Hello Zp !" ] ) } } }
TXS >>   ....3: IN:  Act { { ( Input, [ "Cpkqk" ] ) } }
TXS >>   ....4: OUT: Act { { ( Output, [ "Hello Cpkqk !" ] ) } } }
TXS >>   ....5: IN:  Act { { ( Input, [ "Bhapj" ] ) } }
TXS >>   ....6: OUT: Act { { ( Output, [ "Hello Bhapj !" ] ) } } }
TXS >>   PASS
TXS <<
```

Fig. 2. TORXAKIS test run of *Hello World!*

3.4 Example: Job Dispatcher

The *Job-Dispatcher* is a system that distributes jobs over available processors. Jobs arrive in a dispatcher, are queued, and when a processor is available, the job is forwarded to that processor. When job processing is finished, the job is delivered. The TORXAKIS model is given in Figs. 3 and 4. We explain some aspects of the model.

The *Job-Dispatcher* has two typed channels for communication with the outside world. The types are user-defined algebraic data types. A value of type JobOut is either a JobOut with 3 fields, or an Error (which is not further used in this example). Type JobList defines a list of JobData in the standard recursive way. It is used in process dispatcher to queue the Job requests.

Functions can be defined in a standard, functional style, with recursion. Functions and expressions are strongly typed and overloading is allowed. The function isValidJob defines a constraint on JobData which is used when messages of type JobData are communicated to restrict the domain of valid messages.

Process dispatcher uses the choice process operator ## to specify the choice between receiving a new job request, which is then added to the queue, or dispatching the first element of the queue to one of the processors if the queue is not empty. A processor processes a job by calculating the greatest common divisor using the function gcd. Process processors starts pnum processor-instances by 'forking' them. This is achieved by the parallel operator |||: a processor is started in parallel with more processors with decreased pnum until pnum == 1.

Finally, the behaviour of model Disp is defined as a dispatcher with empty initial queue in parallel with 4 processors. These communicate via channel Job2Proc: the dispatcher sends the jobs via this channel non-deterministically to one of the processors, but the dispatcher cannot influence which processor will take the job. By using the HIDE constructor, the channel Job2Proc is hidden for the outside world, i.e., actions on this channel are abstracted away. From the outside, it can only be observed that after some time the job appears on channel Finish.

```
CHANDEF   Channels
 ::=
      Job    :: JobData ;
      Finish :: JobOut
ENDDEF

TYPEDEF   JobData
 ::=
      JobData { jobId    :: Int
              ; jobDescr :: String
              ; x, y     :: Int
              }
ENDDEF

FUNCDEF   isValidJob ( jobdata :: JobData ) :: Bool
 ::=
          ( jobId(jobdata) > 0 )
      /\  ( (jobId(jobdata) % 2) == 0 )
      /\  strinre(jobDescr(jobdata), REGEX('[A-Z]{2}[0-9]*'))
      /\  ( x(jobdata) > 0 )
      /\  ( y(jobdata) > 0 )
ENDDEF

TYPEDEF   JobOut
 ::=
      JobOut  { jobId     :: Int
              ; processor :: Int
              ; gcd       :: Int
              }
   | Error   { reason    :: String
              }
ENDDEF

TYPEDEF   JobList
 ::=
      Nil
    | Cons    { hd    :: JobData
              ; tl    :: JobList
              }
ENDDEF

FUNCDEF   ++ (ll :: JobList; job :: JobData) :: JobList
 ::=
      IF    isNil(ll) THEN Cons(job, Nil)
                      ELSE Cons(hd(ll), tl(ll) ++ job)
      FI
ENDDEF

FUNCDEF   gcd (a, b :: Int) :: Int
 ::=
      IF a == b THEN a
                ELSE IF a > b THEN gcd (a - b, b)
                              ELSE gcd (a, b - a)
                     FI
      FI
ENDDEF
```

Fig. 3. The *Job-Dispatcher* model: channels, types, and functions.

In the SUT connection the predefined functions `toString` and `fromString` are used to convert between the abstract data types on the model channels `Job` and `Finish` and a standard `String` representation on the socket. The user

```
PROCDEF   dispatcher [Job :: JobData; Dispatch :: JobData] (queue :: JobList)
  ::=
              Job ? job :: JobData [[isValidJob(job)]]
          >-> dispatcher [Job, Dispatch] (queue ++ job)
       ##
          [[ not(isNil(queue)) ]]
          =>> Dispatch ! hd(queue)
          >-> dispatcher [Job, Dispatch] (tl(queue))
ENDDEF

PROCDEF   processor [Start :: JobData; Finish :: JobOut] (pid :: Int)
  ::=
              Start ? job :: JobData
       >-> Finish ! JobOut(jobId(job), pid, gcd(x(job),y(job)))
       >-> processor [Start, Finish] (pid)
ENDDEF

PROCDEF   processors [Start :: JobData; Finish :: JobOut] (pnum :: Int)
  ::=
              processor [Start, Finish] (pnum)
       |||
              [[ pnum > 1 ]] =>> processors [Start, Finish] (pnum - 1)
ENDDEF

MODELDEF Disp
  ::=
        CHAN IN     Job
        CHAN OUT    Finish

        BEHAVIOUR  HIDE [Job2Proc :: JobData]
                   IN
                          dispatcher [Job, Job2Proc]  (Nil)
                   |[ Job2Proc ]|
                          processors [Job2Proc, Finish] (4)
                   NI
ENDDEF

CNECTDEF  Sut
  ::=
        CLIENTSOCK

        CHAN OUT    Job                        HOST "localhost" PORT 7890
        ENCODE      Job     ? jd          ->   ! toString(jd)

        CHAN IN     Finish                     HOST "localhost" PORT 7890
        DECODE      Finish ! fromString(s)  <- ? s
ENDDEF
```

Fig. 4. The *Job-Dispatcher* model: processes, model, and SUT connection.

can also define her own converting functions or use the standard to/ fromXML functions.

Figure 5 gives the first 16 steps of a TORXAKIS test run with the *Job-Dispatcher* on an SUT not shown here. The first parameter of both JobData and JobOut gives the JobId. It is clear that the jobs are not processed in order of arrival, and that sometimes there is no job being processed (e.g., after step 2 and after step 16), and sometimes there are 4 (e.g., after step 10).

```
$ torxakis JobDispatcher.txs

TXS >>   TorXakis :: Model-Based Testing
TXS >>   input files parsed: JobDispatcher.txs
TXS <<   tester Disp Sut
TXS >>   tester started
TXS >>   ....1: IN:   Act { { ( Job, [ JobData(56,"MX7",13,42) ] ) } }
TXS >>   ....2: OUT:  Act { { ( Finish, [ JobOut(56,2,1) ] ) } }
TXS >>   ....3: IN:   Act { { ( Job, [ JobData(50,"KH",35,46) ] ) } }
TXS >>   ....4: IN:   Act { { ( Job, [ JobData(38,"KC00000",55,14) ] ) } }
TXS >>   ....5: OUT:  Act { { ( Finish, [ JobOut(50,4,1) ] ) } }
TXS >>   ....6: IN:   Act { { ( Job, [ JobData(66,"KK0804",22,36) ] ) } }
TXS >>   ....7: IN:   Act { { ( Job, [ JobData(72,"PP839",57,41) ] ) } }
TXS >>   ....8: IN:   Act { { ( Job, [ JobData(36,"GC280",10,85) ] ) } }
TXS >>   ....9: OUT:  Act { { ( Finish, [ JobOut(38,3,1) ] ) } }
TXS >>   ...10: IN:   Act { { ( Job, [ JobData(22,"AD36",87,2) ] ) } }
TXS >>   ...11: OUT:  Act { { ( Finish, [ JobOut(22,4,1) ] ) } }
TXS >>   ...12: OUT:  Act { { ( Finish, [ JobOut(36,3,5) ] ) } }
TXS >>   ...13: OUT:  Act { { ( Finish, [ JobOut(72,1,1) ] ) } }
TXS >>   ...14: IN:   Act { { ( Job, [ JobData(90,"PK00",54,70) ] ) } }
TXS >>   ...15: OUT:  Act { { ( Finish, [ JobOut(66,2,2) ] ) } }
TXS >>   ...16: OUT:  Act { { ( Finish, [ JobOut(90,3,2) ] ) } }
```

Fig. 5. TORXAKIS test run of *Job-Dispatcher*.

4   Concluding Remarks

From Canonical to Practical Testers. We have shown the developments from testing equivalences, via canonical testers, **conf**, **ioconf**, **ioco**, **sioco**, and TORXAKIS, to practical testers, i.e., how formal theory from the eighties constitutes the foundation for practical approaches to model-based testing that are now being introduced in the daily practice of testing. In addition, models for MBT are expressed using the principles of process algebra also investigated during that era. Thus, the road from theory to practical applications may take a while.

It should be noted that, apart from the developments described in this paper, MBT tool development also benefited a lot from other developments, in particular from the availability of powerful tools supporting symbolic methods, such as SMT solvers [23].

TorXakis. The main features of the MBT tool TORXAKIS were illustrated using two simple examples. TORXAKIS implements **ioco**-test generation for symbolic transition systems, and it supports state-based control flow together with complex data structures, on-the-fly testing, partial and under-specification, nondeterminism, abstraction, random test selection, concurrency, and model compositionality. TORXAKIS is an experimental MBT tool, used in applied research, education, case studies, and experiments in the (embedded systems) industry. TORXAKIS currently misses good usability, scalability does not always match the requirements of complex systems-of-systems, and test selection is still only random, but more sophisticated test selection strategies are being investigated [8]. TORXAKIS supports state & data but no probabilities, real-time, or hybrid systems, yet.

Future Theory. Current MBT algorithms and tools can potentially generate many more tests from a model than can ever be executed. Consequently, *test selection* is one of the major research issues in model-based testing. Test selection concerns the problem of finding criteria for selecting from the astronomical number of potential test cases those tests that have the largest chance of detecting most, and the most important bugs, with the least effort.

Random approaches, which are often used for small systems, do not suffice for large and complex systems: the probability of completely randomly selecting an important test case within the space of all possible behaviours converges to zero. At the other end from random there is the explicit specification of test purposes, i.e., a tester specifies explicitly what (s)he wishes to test, but that requires a lot of manual effort, and, moreover, how should the tester know what to test. Different approaches have been identified for determining what the "most important behaviours" are, such as testing based on system requirements, code coverage, model coverage, risk analysis, error-impact analysis, or expected user behaviour (operational profiles).

A framework for formalizing test selection can be given using measure theoretic approaches and introducing abstract test-cost and error-weight functions [10,13,19]. However, it turns out to be a major challenge to give concrete instances of such cost and weight functions that satisfy the abstract requirements, reflect human intuition of what important errors are, and are practically computable.

Related to apriori test selection, is aposteriori coverage, quality, and confidence in the tested system. Since exhaustive testing is practically impossible, the question pops up what has been achieved after testing: can the coverage of testing, the quality of the tested SUT, or the confidence in correct functioning of the SUT, somehow be formalized and quantified? It is not to be expected that these fundamental research questions will soon be completely solved.

Future Practice. New software testing methodologies are needed if testing shall keep up with software development and meet the challenges imposed on it, otherwise we may not be able to test future generations of systems. Model-based testing looks like a promising candidate, but if it is not MBT, what else?

MBT is an interesting technique once a model of the SUT is available. Availability of behavioural models, however, is one of the issues that currently prohibits the widespread application of MBT. In the first place there is the question of making and investing in models: there is reluctance against investing in making models, being considered as yet another software artifact. Secondly, mastering the art of behavioural modeling requires education and experience that is not always available. Thirdly, the information necessary to construct a model, in particular for legacy, third-party, or out-sourced systems or components, is not always (easily) available.

These issues lead to the question whether models can be generated automatically, e.g., for use in regression testing or testing systems after refactoring. Model generation from an SUT, a kind of black-box reverse engineering, (re)constructs a model by observing the behaviour of the SUT, either passively from system logs, or actively by performing special tests. This activity is called *model learning*, also known as test-based modeling, automata learning, or grammatical inference, and it is currently a popular research topic [63].

Acknowledgements. I wish to thank Piërre van de Laar for many discussions and for co-developing TORXAKIS. Piërre van de Laar, Petra van den Bos, and Ramon Janssen are thanked for proofreading this paper.

This contribution was written in honour of Ed Brinksma for the *Festschrift* on the occasion of his 60th birthday. It gives a survey of the developments in formal approaches to testing, showing the important role of Ed's work and ideas in shaping this area of scientific as well as applied research: the definition and application of formal methods, process-algebraic modelling, the formalization of testing concepts, and the canonical tester theory as its theoretical foundation. Also my own work on model-based testing is for an important part inspired and influenced by Ed's work. I wish to thank Ed Brinksma for his inspiration, guidance, and support during many years, both at the University of Twente and at ESI. Ed, thank you, and congratulations with your 60th birthday.

References

1. Abramsky, S.: Observational equivalence as a testing equivalence. Theoret. Comput. Sci. **53**(3), 225–241 (1987)
2. Axini: Testautomatisering. http://www.axini.com
3. Barrett, C., Conway, C., Deters, M., Hadarean, L., Jovanović, D., King, T., Reynolds, A., Tinelli, C.: CVC4. In: Gopalakrishnan, G., Qadeer, S. (eds.) CAV 2011. LNCS, vol. 6806, pp. 171–177. Springer, Heidelberg (2011). doi:10.1007/978-3-642-22110-1_14
4. Belinfante, A.: JTorX: a tool for on-line model-driven test derivation and execution. In: Esparza, J., Majumdar, R. (eds.) TACAS 2010. LNCS, vol. 6015, pp. 266–270. Springer, Heidelberg (2010). doi:10.1007/978-3-642-12002-2_21
5. Belinfante, A., Feenstra, J., de Vries, R., Tretmans, J., Goga, N., Feijs, L., Mauw, S., Heerink, L.: Formal test automation: a simple experiment. In: Csopaki, G., Dibuz, S., Tarnay, K. (eds.) International Workshop on Testing of Communicating Systems, vol. 12, pp. 179–196. Kluwer Academic Publishers, Dordrecht (1999)
6. van der Bijl, M., Rensink, A., Tretmans, J.: Compositional testing with IOCO. In: Petrenko, A., Ulrich, A. (eds.) FATES 2003. LNCS, vol. 2931, pp. 86–100. Springer, Heidelberg (2004). doi:10.1007/978-3-540-24617-6_7
7. Bolognesi, T., Brinksma, E.: Introduction to the ISO specification language LOTOS. Comput. Netw. ISDN Syst. **14**, 25–59 (1987)
8. van den Bos, P., Janssen, R., Moerman, J.: *n*-complete test suites for IOCO. In: Cavalli, A., Yenigün, H., Yevtushenko, N. (eds.) IFIP International Conference on Testing Software and Systems - ICTSS 2017. LNCS, Springer, Heidelberg (2017). To be published
9. Brandán Briones, L., Brinksma, E.: A test generation framework for *quiescent* real-time systems. In: Grabowski, J., Nielsen, B. (eds.) FATES 2004. LNCS, vol. 3395, pp. 64–78. Springer, Heidelberg (2005). doi:10.1007/978-3-540-31848-4_5
10. Briones, L.B., Brinksma, E., Stoelinga, M.: A semantic framework for test coverage. In: Graf, S., Zhang, W. (eds.) ATVA 2006. LNCS, vol. 4218, pp. 399–414. Springer, Heidelberg (2006). doi:10.1007/11901914_30

11. Brinksma, E.: On the existence of canonical testers. Memorandum INF-87-5, University of Twente, Enschede (1987)

12. Brinksma, E.: A theory for the derivation of tests. In: Aggarwal, S., Sabnani, K. (eds.) Protocol Specification, Testing, and Verification VIII, pp. 63–74. North-Holland (1988)

13. Brinksma, E.: On the coverage of partial validations. In: Nivat, M., Rattray, C., Rus, T., Scollo, G. (eds.) AMAST1993. Workshops in Computing, pp. 245–252. Springer, London (1994). doi:10.1007/978-1-4471-3227-1_25

14. Brinksma, E.: Formal methods for conformance testing: theory can be practical. In: Halbwachs, N., Peled, D. (eds.) CAV 1999. LNCS, vol. 1633, pp. 44–46. Springer, Heidelberg (1999). doi:10.1007/3-540-48683-6_6

15. Brinksma, E., Alderden, R., Langerak, R., van de Lagemaat, J., Tretmans, J.: A formal approach to conformance testing. In: de Meer, J., Mackert, L., Effelsberg, W. (eds.) Second International Workshop on Protocol Test Systems, pp. 349–363. North-Holland (1990)

16. Brinksma, E., Karjoth, G.: A specification of the OSI transport service in LOTOS. In: Protocol Specification, Testing, and Verification IV. North-Holland (1984)

17. Brinksma, E., Scollo, G., Steenbergen, C.: LOTOS specifications, their implementations and their tests. In: van Bochmann, G., Sarikaya, B. (eds.) Protocol Specification, Testing, and Verification VI, pp. 349–360. North-Holland (1987)

18. Brinksma, E., Tretmans, J.: Testing transition systems: an annotated bibliography. In: Cassez, F., Jard, C., Rozoy, B., Ryan, M.D. (eds.) MOVEP 2000. LNCS, vol. 2067, pp. 187–195. Springer, Heidelberg (2001). doi:10.1007/3-540-45510-8_9

19. Brinksma, E., Tretmans, J., Verhaard, L.: A framework for test selection. In: Jonsson, B., Parrow, J., Pehrson, B. (eds.) Protocol Specification, Testing, and Verification XI, pp. 233–248. North-Holland (1991)

20. Chow, T.: Testing software design modeled by finite-state machines. IEEE Trans. Softw. Eng. 4(3), 178–187 (1978)

21. Claessen, K., Hughes, J.: QuickCheck: a lightweight tool for random testing of haskell programs. In: International Conference on Functional Programming 2000. ACM Press (2000)

22. Cok, D.: The SMT-LIBv2 Language and Tools: A Tutorial. GrammaTech Inc., Ithaca (2011)

23. De Moura, L., Bjørner, N.: Satisfiability modulo theories: introduction and applications. Commun. ACM 54(9), 69–77 (2011)

24. De Nicola, R.: Extensional equivalences for transition systems. Acta Informatica 24, 211–237 (1987)

25. De Nicola, R., Hennessy, M.: Testing equivalences for processes. Theoret. Comput. Sci. 34, 83–133 (1984)

26. Dijkstra, E.W.: Notes On Structured Programming – EWD249. Technische Hogeschool Eindhoven, Eindhoven, The Netherlands, T.H. Report, 70-WSK-03 (1969)

27. Eertink, H.: Executing LOTOS specifications: the SMILE tool. In: Bolognesi, T., van de Lagemaat, J., Vissers, C. (eds.) LOTOSphere: Software Development with LOTOS, pp. 221–234. Kluwer Academic Publishers, Dordrecht (1995)

28. van Eijk, P.: Software tools for the specification language LOTOS. Ph.D. thesis, University of Twente, Enschede, The Netherlands (1988)

29. Engelfriet, J.: Determinacy → (observation equivalence = trace equivalence). Theoret. Comput. Sci. 36(1), 21–25 (1985)

30. Frantzen, L., Tretmans, J., Willemse, T.A.C.: Test generation based on symbolic specifications. In: Grabowski, J., Nielsen, B. (eds.) FATES 2004. LNCS, vol. 3395, pp. 1–15. Springer, Heidelberg (2005). doi:10.1007/978-3-540-31848-4_1

31. Frantzen, L., Tretmans, J., Willemse, T.A.C.: A symbolic framework for model-based testing. In: Havelund, K., Núñez, M., Roşu, G., Wolff, B. (eds.) FATES/RV -2006. LNCS, vol. 4262, pp. 40–54. Springer, Heidelberg (2006). doi:10.1007/11940197_3

32. Gaudel, M.C.: Testing can be formal, too. In: Mosses, P.D., Nielsen, M., Schwartzbach, M.I. (eds.) CAAP 1995. LNCS, vol. 915, pp. 82–96. Springer, Heidelberg (1995). doi:10.1007/3-540-59293-8_188

33. van Glabbeek, R.J.: The linear time - branching time spectrum. In: Baeten, J.C.M., Klop, J.W. (eds.) CONCUR 1990. LNCS, vol. 458, pp. 278–297. Springer, Heidelberg (1990). doi:10.1007/BFb0039066

34. Glabbeek, R.J.: The linear time – branching time spectrum II (the semantics of sequential systems with silent moves). In: Best, E. (ed.) CONCUR 1993. LNCS, vol. 715, pp. 66–81. Springer, Heidelberg (1993). doi:10.1007/3-540-57208-2_6

35. Groote, J., Mousavi, M.: Modeling and Analysis of Communicating Systems. MIT Press, Cambridge (2014)

36. Hartman, A., Nagin, K.: The AGEDIS tools for model based testing. In: International Symposium on Software Testing and Analysis – ISSTA 2004, pp, 129–132. ACM Press, New York (2004)

37. Haskell: an advanced, purely functional programming language. https://www.haskell.org

38. Heerink, A.: A bounded queue model relating synchronous and asynchronous communication. Master's thesis, University of Twente, Enschede, The Netherlands (1993)

39. Heerink, L.: Ins and outs in refusal testing. Ph.D. thesis, University of Twente, Enschede, The Netherlands (1998)

40. Hessel, A., Larsen, K.G., Mikucionis, M., Nielsen, B., Pettersson, P., Skou, A.: Testing real-time systems using UPPAAL. In: Hierons, R.M., Bowen, J.P., Harman, M. (eds.) Formal Methods and Testing. LNCS, vol. 4949, pp. 77–117. Springer, Heidelberg (2008). doi:10.1007/978-3-540-78917-8_3

41. Hoare, C.: Communicating Sequential Processes. Prentice-Hall, Upper Saddle River (1985)

42. ISO: Information Processing Systems, Open Systems Interconnection, LOTOS - A Formal Description Technique Based on the Temporal Ordering of Observational Behaviour. International Standard IS-8807, ISO, Geneve (1989)

43. Jard, C., Jéron, T.: TGV: theory, principles and algorithms: a tool for the automatic synthesis of conformance test cases for non-deterministic reactive systems. Softw. Tools Technol. Transf. **7**(4), 297–315 (2005)

44. Krichen, M., Tripakis, S.: Black-box conformance testing for real-time systems. In: Graf, S., Mounier, L. (eds.) SPIN 2004. LNCS, vol. 2989, pp. 109–126. Springer, Heidelberg (2004). doi:10.1007/978-3-540-24732-6_8

45. Langerak, R.: A testing theory for LOTOS using deadlock detection. In: Brinksma, E., Scollo, G., Vissers, C.A. (eds.) Protocol Specification, Testing, and Verification IX, pp. 87–98. North-Holland (1990)

46. Lee, D., Yannakakis, M.: Principles and methods for testing finite state machines - a survey. Proc. IEEE **84**(8), 1090–1123 (1996). August

47. Lynch, N., Tuttle, M.: An introduction to input, output automata. CWI Q. **2**(3), 219–246 (1989). Technical report MIT/LCS/TM-373 (TM-351 revised), Massachusetts Institute of Technology, Cambridge, USA (1988)

48. Milner, R.: Communication and Concurrency. Prentice-Hall, Upper Saddle River (1989)
49. Mostowski, W., Poll, E., Schmaltz, J., Tretmans, J., Wichers Schreur, R.: Model-based testing of electronic passports. In: Alpuente, M., Cook, B., Joubert, C. (eds.) FMICS 2009. LNCS, vol. 5825, pp. 207–209. Springer, Heidelberg (2009). doi:10.1007/978-3-642-04570-7_19
50. de Moura, L., Bjørner, N.: Z3: an efficient SMT solver. In: Ramakrishnan, C.R., Rehof, J. (eds.) TACAS 2008. LNCS, vol. 4963, pp. 337–340. Springer, Heidelberg (2008). doi:10.1007/978-3-540-78800-3_24
51. Petrenko, A.: Fault model-driven test derivation from finite state models: annotated bibliography. In: Cassez, F., Jard, C., Rozoy, B., Ryan, M.D. (eds.) MOVEP 2000. LNCS, vol. 2067, pp. 196–205. Springer, Heidelberg (2001). doi:10.1007/3-540-45510-8_10
52. Phalippou, M.: Relations d'Implantation et Hypothèses de Test sur des Automates à Entrées et Sorties. Ph.D. thesis, L'Université de Bordeaux I, France (1994)
53. Phillips, I.: Refusal testing. Theoret. Comput. Sci. **50**(2), 241–284 (1987)
54. Selenium - Browser Automation. http://www.seleniumhq.org
55. Sikuli Script. http://www.sikuli.org
56. TorXakis. https://github.com/torxakis
57. Tretmans, J.: HIPPO: a LOTOS simulator. In: van Eijk, P., Vissers, C., Diaz, M. (eds.) The Formal Description Technique LOTOS, pp. 391–396. North-Holland (1989)
58. Tretmans, J.: Test generation with inputs, outputs, and quiescence. In: Margaria, T., Steffen, B. (eds.) TACAS 1996. LNCS, vol. 1055, pp. 127–146. Springer, Heidelberg (1996). doi:10.1007/3-540-61042-1_42
59. Tretmans, J.: Test generation with inputs, outputs and repetitive quiescence. Softw. Concepts Tools **17**(3), 103–120 (1996)
60. Tretmans, J.: Model based testing with labelled transition systems. In: Hierons, R.M., Bowen, J.P., Harman, M. (eds.) Formal Methods and Testing. LNCS, vol. 4949, pp. 1–38. Springer, Heidelberg (2008). doi:10.1007/978-3-540-78917-8_1
61. Tretmans, J., Verhaard, L.: A queue model relating synchronous and asynchronous communication. In: Linn, R., Uyar, M. (eds.) Protocol Specification, Testing, and Verification XII, pp. 131–145. No. C-8 in IFIP Transactions, North-Holland (1992)
62. Vaandrager, F.: On the relationship between process algebra and input/output automata. In: Sixth Annual IEEE Symposium on Logic in Computer Science, pp. 387–398. IEEE Computer Society Press (1991)
63. Vaandrager, F.: Model learning. Commun. ACM **60**(2), 86–95 (2017)
64. Volpato, M., Tretmans, J.: Towards quality of model-based testing in the IOCO framework. In: International Workshop on Joining AcadeMiA and Industry Contributions to Testing Automation - JAMAICA 2013, pp. 41–46. ACM, New York (2013)

Compositional Testing of Real-Time Systems

Kim G. Larsen[1]([⊠]), Axel Legay[2], Marius Mikučionis[1], Brian Nielsen[1],
and Ulrik Nyman[1]

[1] Department of Computer Science, Aalborg University, Aalborg, Denmark
{kgl,marius}@cs.aau.dk
[2] INRIA, Rennes, France

Abstract. In this paper we revisit the notion of compositional testing in the setting of real-time systems. In particular, we introduce crucial notions of real-time conformance testing and compositional verification of real-time systems. We illustrate these notions on a Small University example, and show how the tools UPPAAL TRON, UPPAAL ECDAR and UPPAAL SMC provide strong support for an efficient compositional testing methodology.

1 Introduction

The goal of testing is to gain confidence in a physical computer based system by means of executing it. More than one third of typical project resources is spent on testing embedded and real-time systems, but still it remains ad-hoc, based on heuristics, and error-prone. Therefore systematic, theoretically well-founded and effective automated real-time testing techniques are of great practical value had have been received great attention over the years.

Model-Based Testing. In this paper we make a small investigation of model-based testing for real-time systems. In general testing conceptually consists of three activities: test case generation, test case execution and verdict assignment. Using model based testing, a behavioral model can be interpreted as a specification S that defines the required and allowed observable (real-time) behavior of the implementation I. It can therefore be used for generation of sound and (theoretically) complete test suites. In this setting, the notion of input/output conformance testing [26] has been particular successful as a notion of correct behaviour of an implementation with respect to a given specification.

On-Line Testing. Test cases can be generated off-line from the specification model S, i.e. the complete set of test scenarios and verdicts are computed apriori and before execution. Another approach is online (on-the-fly) testing that combines test generation and execution: only a single test primitive is generated from the model S at a time which is then immediately executed on the implementation I under test. Then the produced output by I as well as its time of occurrence are checked against S, a new test primitive is produced and so

---

Three methods for managing a small university.

© Springer International Publishing AG 2017
J.-P. Katoen et al. (Eds.): Brinksma Festschrift, LNCS 10500, pp. 107–124, 2017.
DOI: 10.1007/978-3-319-68270-9_6

forth until it is decided to end the test, or an error is detected. An observed test run is a trace consisting of an alternating sequence of (input or output) actions and time delays. There are several advantages of online testing: (1) testing may potentially continue for a long time (hours or even days), and therefore long, intricate, and stressful test cases may be executed; (2) the state-space-explosion problem experienced by many offline test generation tools is reduced because only a limited part of the state-space needs to be stored at any point in time; (3) online test generators often allow more expressive specification languages, especially wrt. allowed non-determinism in real-time models. In particular for real-time system on-line testing of timed input/output conformance (rtioco) with respect to (networks of) timed automata specifications is supported by the tool UPPAAL TRON.

Compositional Testing. On-line conformance testing is applicable to both individual components (unit-testing) as well as to composite systems (integration testing). Now for composite systems, where it is possible to test the components in isolation, the notion of compositional testing has been considered and recently reinvestigated.

In [27] it is stated that: "compositional testing concerns the testing of systems that consist of communicating components which can also be tested in isolation. Examples are component based testing and interoperability testing. We show that, with certain restrictions, the ioco-test theory for conformance testing is suitable for compositional testing, in the sense that the integration of fully conformant components is guaranteed to be correct. As a consequence, there is no need to re-test the integrated system for conformance."

In [9] the authors show that "exploiting the compositional structure of system specifications considerably reduce the effort in model-based testing. Moreover, inferring properties about the system from testing its individual components allows the designer to reduce the amount of integration testing."

Most recently Ken McMillan[1] investigated a compositional testing framework for hardware systems: "In this methodology each component of a system is given a formal specification and it is proved formally that these specifications guarantee system-level correctness. The components are then rigorously tested against their formal specifications. This approach has the advantages of unit testing in covering component behaviors, while at the same time exposing all system-level errors to testing. Moreover, it can expose latent bugs in components that are not stimulated in the given system but may occur when the component is re-used in a different environment."

Within the family of UPPAAL tools, the branch UPPAAL ECDAR supports compositional development and stepwise refinement of real-time systems using timed input/output automata as the underlying specification theory. Now in combination with UPPAAL TRON for online conformance testing and UPPAAL SMC for statistical model checking, we shall in the following present a tool-supported methodology for compositional testing and verification of real-time systems.

---

[1] Invited tutorial at ETAPS 2017.

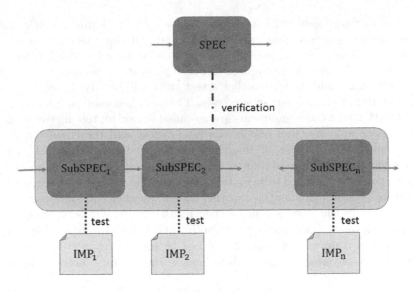

Fig. 1. Compositional testing

2 Methodology

As stated, the goal of compositional model-based testing is to enable the developer to prove from testing of the individual components against their component models that the composed system satisfies the system requirements model, see Fig. 1.

Formally, given a number of implementation components $I_1 \ldots I_i, \ldots I_n$, the associated component sub-specifications $S_1 \ldots S_i, \ldots S_n$, and an overall system specification S, the compositional testing methodology can be formulated as follows:

$$I_1 \preceq S_1 \ldots I_i \preceq S_i \ldots I_n \preceq S_n \;\; \wedge \;\; (S_1 \parallel \ldots S_i \ldots \parallel S_n) \preceq S$$

$$\implies (I_1 \parallel \ldots I_i \ldots \parallel I_n) \preceq S$$

Here, $\preceq$ denotes that a refinement holds between two system models, and $\parallel$ denotes parallel composition of two system models. These ingredients will be formalised in Sect. 4.

Normally, implementations I_i are black-box physical artefacts, and consequently, the refinement $I_i \preceq S_i$ must be established using testing techniques involving execution, simulation, and observation of I_i. In contrast, the models of the components S_i and system S are known formal objects, and determining refinement among such artefacts are amenable to a variety of formal verification or heuristic simulation based techniques. This will be further described and exemplified in Sects. 6 and 7.

Hence, system test may be conducted by, in principle, two easier steps: component testing and system specification verification.

Compositional testing methods thereby potentially have several advantages. First, compositionality is a key technique for scaling up testing to large systems.

Automated test case generation usually employs different kinds of static analysis (reachability analysis, constraint solving, etc.) of the specification model. For models with large state-spaces, this computation may become infeasible or cause impractically slow or incomplete test case generation. Second, with smaller components, it is easier to ensure that a test suite will satisfy a given coverage criterion of the model and/or source code. Third, it becomes possible to make re-use of testing effort as components are modified or added; testing can focus on the changed components and possible its integration, and thereby avoid retesting the whole system. Worse, all manually written system-wide test cases must be reviewed and possibly updated to reflect the change. Fourth, diagnosis and debugging caused by a failed test run becomes easier because the search space for the problem becomes smaller, i.e., smaller model, smaller code-base, or shorter test cases. Finally, the tester's ability to control the component is typically better when the component can be accessed directly rather than through a big context of other system components. This should not be underestimated for embedded real-time cyber-physical systems, where sensor and timing uncertainties often arise.

We see three main limiting factors for the deployment of compositional testing. One is that the system should be constructed from well-defined identifiable components. However, many systems are not developed with a rigorous component architecture in mind, or have a big non-component based legacy. In networked protocol applications, components are often easier to identify and isolate.

Another potential limiting factor is the lack of available models for the system and component models: it is well-known from model-based development and verification that these models are not systematically created a priori, and may be hard to come by afterwards.

Finally, there is a lack of available effective tools with solid theoretical foundations. The tools need to enable specification, refinement check, composition, component testing, and should further be integrated around the same sufficiently expressive specification language.

2.1   Related Work

Whilst the overall idea of compositional testing is often used in an ad-hoc way, formal compositional testing is still far from state-of-the-art.

A compositional testing theory were first proposed by [27]. Here it is presented how labelled transition systems and the IoCo relation used with certain restrictions on the involved specifications, and hiding and composition operators.

This work was later expanded on by Nickovic et al. in [9]. Inspired by game and interface theory, they defined two alternative composition and hiding operations that address the limitations of the basic IoCo theory. We share the use of concepts from games and interface theory, but we focus on adding real-time. A co-algebraic characterization of compositional testing with IoCo is presented in [1].

The problems of compositionality of real-time io-conformance was discussed by Tripakis in [22], and by Briones in [5]. Supporting composition and testing re-use, Larsen et al. developed the relativized real-time conformance relation in [20]. In context of finite state machines compositional testing has been investigated in [3].

In the present work, we not only discuss theoretical properties of real-time conformance relations, but also demonstrate an end-to-end tool testing and verification tool suite.

3   Timed I/O Automata

In the branches UPPAAL TRON, UPPAAL ECDAR and UPPAAL SMC, we have introduced Timed I/O Automata as the foundation for a compositional specification formalism, with semantics given in terms of (stochastic) Time I/O Transition Systems. In particular, we have introduced notions and constructs for conformance, refinement, consistency, logical and structural composition, all indispencial ingredients of a testing and a compositional design methodology.

In the following we give an informal description of the specification formalism of Timed I/O Automata through a small (but important) example: A Small University. For complete and formal definitions we refer to [18].

Small University. Universities operate under increasing pressure and competition. One of the popular factors used in determining the level of national funding is that of societal impact, which is approximated by the number of patent applications filed. Clearly one would expect that the number (and size) of grants given to a university has a (positive) influence on the amount of patents filed for.

Figure 2 gives the insight as to the organisation of a very Small University comprising three components Administration, Machine and Researcher.

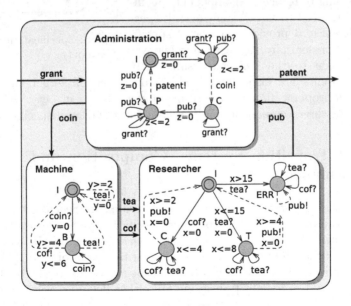

Fig. 2. Overview of a Small University

The **Administration** is responsible for interaction with society in terms of aquiring grants (**grant**) and filing patents (**patent**). However, the other components are necessary for patents to be obtained. The **Researcher** will produce the crucial publications (**pub**) within given time intervals, provided timely stimuli in terms of coffee (**cof**) or tea (**tea**). Here coffee is clearly prefered over tea. The beverage is provided by a **Machine**, which given a coin (**coin**) will provide either coffee or tea within some time interval, or even the possibility of free tea after some time.

In more detail, the **Machine** specification is a timed (input/output) automaton [2] (TIOA), with a single clock **y** and two locations **I** and **B**. A distinguishing property of a TIOA is that it is input-enabled reflected by **coin?** transitions in both locations. Having accepted a **coin?**, the **B** location has an invariant **y<=6** which ensures that some beverage will be produced within 6 s. The guard **y>=4** on the **cof!** transition insists that coffee will only be available after at least 4 s. Similarly the absence of a guard on the **tea!** transitions reflects that in a valid implementation of **Machine**, tea could be ready at any point.

In Fig. 2, the three components are specifications each allowing for a multitude of incomparable, actual implementations differing with respect to exact timing behavior (e.g. at what time are publications actually produced by the **Researcher** given a coffee) and exact output produced (e.g. does the **Machine** offer tea or coffee given a coin).

As a main property, we may want to show that the composition of arbitrary implementations conforming to respective component specification is guaranteed to satisfy some overall specification. Here Fig. 3 provides an overall specification **Spec** – essentially saying that whenever grants are given to the University sufficiently often then patents are also guaranteed within a certain upper time-bound.

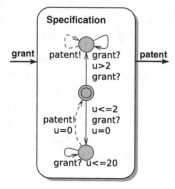

Fig. 3. Specification for Small University.

Checking this property amounts to establishing a refinement between the composition of the three component specifications and the overall specification.

4   Timed Transition Systems, Composition and Conformance

Timed Transition Systems Semantics. As described in Sect. 3, we are using TIOA as a mean of syntactically expressing specifications. Semantically a TIOA describes a timed labelled transition systems, with states being pairs (ℓ, ν), where ℓ is a location of the TIOA and ν is a valuation for the clocks of the TIOA. E.g. in our Small University example $(B, y = 3.2)$ will be a state of the TIOA **Machine**. As usual for timed automata transitions are either delay transitions or action transitions. Thus, the following transition sequence is possible in **Machine**:

$$(\mathsf{B}, \mathsf{y} = 3.2) \xrightarrow{2.3} (\mathsf{B}, \mathsf{y} = 5.5) \xrightarrow{\mathsf{cof!}} (\mathsf{I}, \mathsf{y} = 5.5).$$

Within UPPAAL ECDAR and UPPAAL SMC, the assumption is that TIOA are deterministic and input-enabled. Also, specifications are assumed to have satisfy the property of independent progress, i.e. in any reachable state $s = (\ell, \nu)$ either $s \xrightarrow{d}$ for any non-negative delay d, or $s \xrightarrow{d} \xrightarrow{o}$ for some delay d and output o. Independent progress is one of the central properties in our specification theory: it reflects that an implementation cannot ever get stuck in a state where it is up to the environment to guarantee progress by providing an input. So in every state, there is either an output transition (which is controlled by the implementation) or an ability to delay until an output is possible. Otherwise a state can delay indefinitely. An implementation cannot wait for an input from the environment without letting time pass. One can easily check that all three components of the Small University satisfy these properties.

Composition. The parallel composition $S_1 \parallel S_2$ of two TIOA specifications S_1 and S_2 is essentially a classical product construction, where the two components synchronize on corresponding inputs/outputs (in a broadcast manner) as well as on delay. In our Small University example the composition Machine‖Researcher will have the following transition sequence:

$$[(\mathsf{B}, \mathsf{y} = 3.2), (\mathsf{I}, \mathsf{x} = 0)] \xrightarrow{2.3} [(\mathsf{B}, \mathsf{y} = 5.5), (\mathsf{I}, \mathsf{x} = 2.3)] \xrightarrow{\mathsf{cof!}} [(\mathsf{I}, \mathsf{y} = 5.5), (\mathsf{C}, \mathsf{x} = 0)].$$

In Fig. 4 UPPAAL SMC provides a sample simulation of the Small University for 100 s. Here the states of the three components Machine, Researcher and Administration are given as time-dependent functions. E.g. at time 50, the Machine is in the B (brewing) state (having the value 1), the Researcher is the I (idle) state (having value 4) and the Administration is in the C (having just offered a coin) state (having value 10).

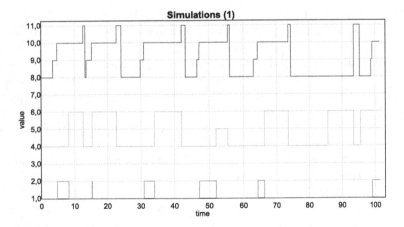

Fig. 4. Simulation of Small University for 100 s. Machine: ($\mathsf{I} = 1$, $\mathsf{B} = 2$). Researcher: ($\mathsf{I} = 4$, $\mathsf{C} = 5$, $\mathsf{T} = 6$, $\mathsf{ERR} = 7$). Administration: ($\mathsf{I} = 8$, $\mathsf{G} = 9$, $\mathsf{C} = 10$, $\mathsf{P} = 11$)

Conformance. Conformance or refinement between TIOA specifications is the crucial part of our specification theory. Refinement between specifications S_1 and S_2 should reflect an inclusion between the corresponding two sets of implementations. In our specification theory, implementations are essentially specifications that cannot be refined any further. As an example, consider the alternative specification Machine' in Fig. 5.

It should be obvious, that Machine' must be a refinement of the original specification Machine in Fig. 2 in that it allows less behaviour of a potential implementation: free tea is now only allowed after 4 time-units; after insertion of a coin the only option for beverage is coffee and in a much more narrow time-interval (between 4 and 5 s compared with between 4 and 6 s). In general, the refinement between two TIOA's is similar to an alternating game, but for deterministic TIOA refinement it simplifies to that of timed language inclusion, i.e.:

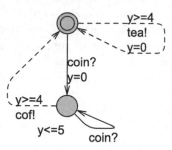

Fig. 5. Machine'.

$$S_1 \preceq S_2 \overset{\Delta}{=} \mathsf{TTr}(S_1) \subseteq \mathsf{TTr}(S_2)$$

where $\mathsf{TTr}(S) = \{\omega \in (\mathbb{R} \cup I \cup O)^* \mid S \overset{\omega}{\to}\}$, i.e. $\mathsf{TTr}(S)$ are all timed words for which S has a transition sequence. Given this definition, it is easy to see that indeed Machine' $\preceq$ Machine.

Clearly, timed refinement (conformance) $\preceq$ is transitive. Most importantly, $\preceq$ is a precongruence with respect to parallel composition of specifications. Thus if $S_i \preceq T_i$ ($i = 1, 2$), then also $S_1 \| S_2 \preceq T_1 \| T_2$.

5   Component Test

In 2004 the branch UPPAAL TRON was introduced offering the possibility of performing on-line conformance testing of real real-time systems with respect to timed input-output automata [24,25]. UPPAAL TRON implements a sound and (theoretically) complete randomized testing algorithm, and uses a formally defined notion of correctness to assign verdicts: i.e. – as presented in the previous Sect. 4 – (relativized) timed input/output conformance providing a timed generalization of Jan Tretmans ioco [26]. Using online testing, events are simultaneously generated, executed on the system under test and the correctness of the responses are checked against the timed automata model. UPPAAL TRON has been successfully applied to a number of industrial case studies including an advanced electronic thermostat regulator sold world-wide in high volume by the Danish company Danfoss [23].

Now continuing our Small University example, Fig. 6 shows a coffee machine prototype, where a controller is connected to a sensor and an actuator. The sensor senses the coin presence and provides inputs to the controller, whereas the controller produces outputs "coffee" or "tea" displayed on the LED screen.

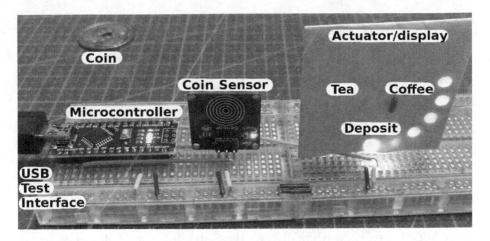

Fig. 6. A coffee machine prototype from https://youtu.be/rnwF0aB7mJA. (Color figure online)

```
void loop() {                          bool waitForCoin(const uint32_t d) {
  if (waitForCoin(3000)) {               uint32_t t = 0;
    if (coffee) makeCoffee();            uint8_t sense = readSensor();
    else makeTea();                      while (sense != HIGH && t < d) {
    coffee = !coffee;                      sleep(dt); sense = readSensor();
  } else {    // no coin, time-out        t += dt;
    makeTea();      // purge water       }
    while (readSensor() != HIGH)         if (sense != HIGH) return false;
      sleep(dt);                         digitalWrite(LED_BUILTIN, HIGH);
  }                                      strip.set(8, L, L, 0);
}                                        strip.render();        // show coin
void makeCoffee() {                      while (sense == HIGH) {
  for (int i=15; i>=8; --i) {              sleep(dt); sense = readSensor();
    strip.set(i, L, 0, 0);               }
    strip.render();                      digitalWrite(LED_BUILTIN, LOW);
    sleep(500); // 8*500ms=4s            showDeposit();
  }                                      return true;
  Serial.write("c\n"); // output       }
  strip.zeros(); strip.render();
}
```

Fig. 7. Coffee machine C code.

The display in picture shows deposit as one golden light at the bottom and 5 out of 8 lights of progress on the right for producing coffee. The display can show a similar green progress on the left for tea outputs. For testing purposes, the inputs and outputs are multiplexed with a serial line over USB port.

Figure 7 shows an excerpt from the implementation code. The main loop consists of a simple code of waiting for a coin and then producing coffee or tea.

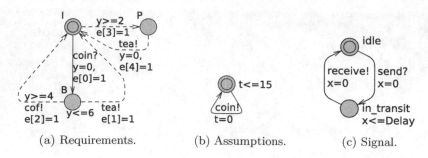

(a) Requirements.   (b) Assumptions.   (c) Signal.

Fig. 8. Online test specification.

The wait for coin has a 7 s timeout to purge the water and preserve the energy. The *makeCoffee()* procedure displays the 8-step progress of 500 ms each and finally produces coffee signal when done. The *waitForCoin(d)* function monitors the coin sensor which returns **HIGH** when the coin is inserted and **LOW** when dropped. The function returns **true** if the coin is inserted and **false** if no coin was registered and the specified time-out **d** has elapsed.

We have connected our coffee machine to UPPAAL TRON via USB interface and successfully tested its conformance against the **Machine** model shown in Fig. 8a using the test environment shown in Fig. 8b. The coffee machine in Fig. 8a differs from the **Machine** in Fig. 2 by an extra location **P** which allows the machine to commit producing **tea** without being interrupted by **coin** inserts in case **tea** and **coin** are produced at the very same time. In general, the input and output interleaving may happen in between the tester and the implementation and thus they might disagree on the order of events, therefore such possibility needs to be reflected in the specification. Adding the signal traveling processes (e.g. template in Fig. 8c) is a systematic way of modeling the communication delay and interleaving. The requirement specification also has annotations **e[X]=1** which track the test coverage of the edge **X**.

Once we are confident with our implementation, we inspect the fault detection capability by mutating the coffee production step delay from 500 ms to 800 ms, which will produce coffee only after $8 \cdot 0.8\,s = 6.4\,s$ hence stressing the invariant **u<=6**. Figure 9 shows a log from the resulting online test. The log consists of initialization details, a configuration, a sequence of test events, diagnostics and final verdict.

The test event lines are prefixed by "TEST" and tell that UPPAAL TRON received **tea** at 7488303 μs, which is at (7;8) in model time units, i.e. some time between 7 and 8 time units. UPPAAL TRON then chose to offer a **coin** at (9;10), and received **cof** somewhere at (16;17) time units. Notice that the time delay between the second **coin** and **cof** is strictly between 6 and 8, which makes it strictly greater than 6, and thus may potentially violate the invariant **u<=6** in **B** (provided that the implementation was indeed in this location). After observing **cof** UPPAAL TRON announced diagnostics and the "test failed" verdict. The diagnostics includes the last symbolic state estimate implying that the specification

```
./tron —F 100 —u 4000,4000 —v 10 coffee.xml —I coffee.so — /dev/serial/by-id/usb—1a86_USB2.0—
      Serial—if00—port0
UPPAAL TRON 1.5 using UPPAAL 4.1.2 (rev. 4352), June 2009
Compiled with g++—4.3.3 —Wall —DNDEBUG —O2 —ffloat—store —march=pentiumpro —DTIGA_MERGE_STATES
      —DBOOST_DISABLE_THREADS
Copyright (c) 1995 — 2009, Uppsala University and Aalborg University.
All rights reserved.
Options for UPPAAL TRON:
  Search order is breadth first
  Using no space optimisation
  State space representation uses minimal constraint systems
  Observation uncertainties: 0, 4000, 0, 4000 (microseconds).
  Scheduling latency: 0 microseconds
  Future precomputation: closure(100 mtu).
  Input delay extended by: 0
  OS scheduler: non—real—time.
  Emulation invariants: Tester.
  Timeunit: 1000000us
  Timeout: 1000mtu
  Inputs:  coin()
  Outputs: cof(), tea()
TEST: tea()@7488303us at (7;8) on 1
TEST: coin()@[9666106us;9667407us] at (9;10) on 2
TEST: cof()@16465269us at (16;17) on 2
Short post—mortem analysis based on last good stateSet(2):
1)
( Machine.B Tester._id3 )
#t>9, Machine.y<=6, Machine.y—Tester.t<=0, Machine.y—#t<—9, Tester.t<=6, Tester.t—Machine.y<=0,
      Tester.t—#t<—9, #t<16, #t—Machine.y<10, #t—Tester.t<10 e[0]=1 e[1]=0 e[2]=0 e[3]=1 e[4]=1
2)
( Machine.P Tester._id3 )
Machine.y>=2, #t>9, Machine.y<18, Machine.y—Tester.t<3, Machine.y—#t<—7, Tester.t<=15, Tester.t—
      Machine.y<=—2, Tester.t—#t<—9, #t<25, #t—Machine.y<8, #t—Tester.t<10 e[0]=0 e[1]=0 e[2]=0 e
      [3]=1 e[4]=1

  Options for input    : coin()@(9;25)
  Options for output   : tea()@(9;25), cof()@(13;16)
  Options for internal: (empty)
  Options for delay    : until 25)
  Last time—window     : (16;17)
Got unacceptable output: cof()@16465269us at (16;17)
Expected outputs were: tea()@(9;25), cof()@(13;16)
Observed LATER than expected.
TEST FAILED: IUT produced output too late
Time elapsed: 16 tu = 16.465742s
Time     left: 984 tu = 983.534258s
Random  seed: 1498152656
```

Fig. 9. Failed online test of a mutated coffee machine.

was expecting tea at (9;25) or cof at (13;16) which is earlier than observation at (16;17), alternatively it could have also accepted another tea if machine moved to P and ignored the coins, but that was not what has been observed. The state estimate also includes the values of coverage variables e[] which encode the information about the traversed edges. The two symbolic states agree that the tea!-edge has been covered (e[3]==1 and e[4]==1), but disagree if coin? has been handled (state of e[0]). UPPAAL TRON matched the observation of cof with the possible event cof! but with differing timing and thus concluded that this output was issued too late.

We have run 100 online tests and 95 terminated with the failed verdict exactly like in Fig. 9, while the remaining 5 tests failed with "Observed unacceptable

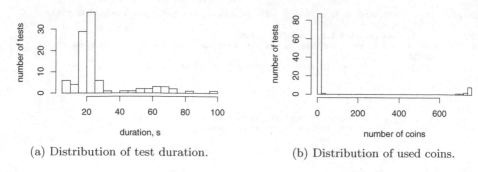

(a) Distribution of test duration.   (b) Distribution of used coins.

Fig. 10. Online tests statistics.

output" `cof` because UPPAAL TRON was offering more `coins` at a point where `y<=6` was already violated (location `P` was the only candidate) and hence `cof` was not among possible outputs, but `tea` was.

Figure 10 shows the distribution of time duration and the number of coins used in online tests. On average tests took 26.5 s and 92.7 coins. Most (over 80) tests were very short of up to 30 s and took up to 10 coins, but UPPAAL TRON also tried some 12 extreme runs flooding with more than 600 coins which just prolonged testing (there were no tests in between). We conclude that UPPAAL TRON is fast and efficient at finding timing errors.

6 Compositional Verification

In 2010 the branch UPPAAL ECDAR was introduced supporting a scalable methodology for compositional development and stepwise refinement of real-time systems [17, 18]. The underlying specification theory is that of timed I/O automata being essentially timed games (with inputs being controllable, and outputs being uncontrollable) equipped with suitable methods for refinement checking (in terms of an alternating simulation between two timed game specifications), consistency checking, logical as well as structural composition. The UPPAAL ECDAR branch relies heavily on the UPPAAL TIGA engine to solve various games that arise in the computing of the various composition operators and refinements. For a full account of UPPAAL ECDAR we refer the reader to the tutorial [16].

In the setting of our running example, we apply UPPAAL ECDAR to validate whether our component specifications working in parallel will satisfy the overall specification of the system. We check the following refinement using UPPAAL ECDAR:

```
refinement: (Administration || Machine || Researcher) <= Spec
```

This refinement check examines if the parallel composition of the three components `Administration`, `Machine` and `Researcher` conforms to the university specification `Spec`. But much to our surprise when first constructing the running example this turned out not to be the case.

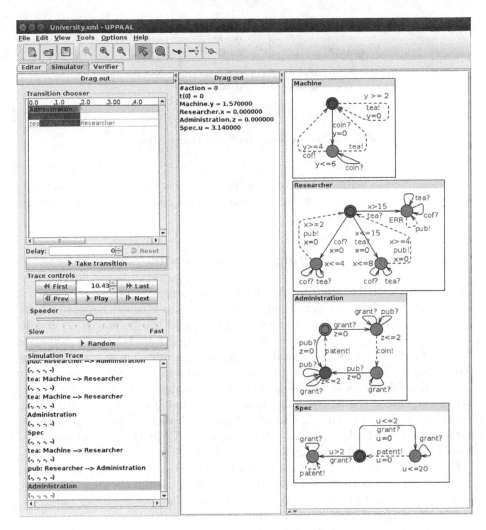

Fig. 11. Screenshot showing a longer counterexample generated by UPPAAL ECDAR.

Figure 11 shows the counter example strategy, which proves that there is a way in which the parallel components can violate the specification. The surprising fact is that it is a rather simple counterexample.

The shortest trace to disprove the refinement consists of three steps. The Machine can produce tea by just waiting 2 time units, which will enable the Researcher to produce a publication which is communicated on the pub! channel. This can in turn allow the Administration to produce a patent!. This is in violation of the specification, Spec, as it does not allow the productions of patents from the initial location.

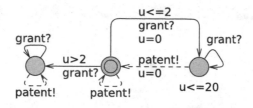

Fig. 12. Modified version `SpecFixed` of `Spec`.

Fortunately the solution to fixing the refinement is rather straight forward. We just need to ad a single **patent!** self-loop to the initial location of `Spec` as seen in Fig. 12.

7   Conformance Checking via Simulation

One of most recent branches of the UPPAAL tool suite – UPPAAL SMC introduced in 2011 – allows for performance evaluation the much richer formalisms of stochastic hybrid automata and games [14,15] and has by now been widely applied to analysis of a variety of case studies ranging from biological examples [13], schedulability for mixed-critical systems [4,11], evaluation of controllers for energy-aware buildings [10], social-technical attacks in security [19] as well as performance evaluation of a variety of wireless communication protocols [28]. Also the statistical model checking engine of UPPAAL SMC is supported by a distributed implementation [8], and allows for the statistical model checking of a large subset of MITL [6,7]. For a full account of UPPAAL SMC we refer the reader to the recent tutorial [12].

The modeling formalism of UPPAAL SMC is based on a stochastic interpretation and extension of the timed automata formalism used in the classical model checking version of UPPAAL. For individual components the stochastic interpretation replaces the nondeterministic choices between multiple enabled transitions by probabilistic choices (that may or may not be user-defined). Similarly, the non-deterministic choices of time-delays are refined by probability distributions, which at the component level are given either uniform distributions in cases with time-bounded delays or exponential distributions (with user-defined rates) in cases of unbounded delays.

In the setting of real-time conformance (refinement) checking between specifications, UPPAAL SMC may be used as inexpective, simulation-based alternative to the considerably more expensive symbolic and game-based conformance checking offered by UPPAAL ECDAR as we described and applied in the previous Sect. 6.

To illustrate this, we reconsider our running Small University Example. First we construct in Fig. 13(a) a TIOA `SpecComp` which will be used to monitor an arbitrary behaviour and detect when it violates the original university specification `Spec`. Essentially (as indicated by the name) `SpecComp` is the complement of

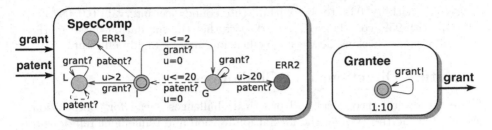

Fig. 13. (a) complement of `Spec` and (b) stochastic environment component `Grantee`

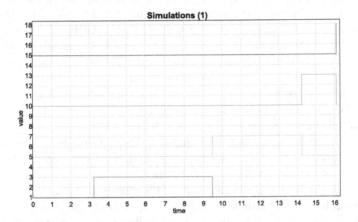

Fig. 14. A concrete run demonstrating that the Small University is not a refinement of `Spec`. Machine: $(\mathtt{I}=1, \mathtt{B}=2, \mathtt{T}=3)$, Researcher: $(\mathtt{I}=5, \mathtt{C}=6, \mathtt{T}=7, \mathtt{ERR}=8)$; Administration: $(\mathtt{I}=10, \mathtt{G}=11, \mathtt{C}=12, \mathtt{P}=13)$; SpecComp: $(\mathtt{I}=15, \mathtt{G}=16, \mathtt{L}=17, \mathtt{ERR1}=18, \mathtt{ERR2}=19)$.

`Spec` with the two locations **ERR1** and **ERR2** serving as error states to be reached upon violation[2].

Now we combine the Small University, i.e.

$$\text{Machine}\,|\,\text{Researcher}\,|\,\text{Administration}$$

with `SpecComp` form Fig. 13(a) as a monitor, and additionally with the component `Grantee` from Fig. 13(b) for stochastically generating `grant`'s (here according to an exponential distribution with rate $\frac{1}{10}$). Figure 14 illustrates a random run of the complete composition obtained by UPPAAL SMC. As can be seen, this run provides a counter-example to the desired conformance between the Small University and `Spec`. In fact this failing run was found already after 26 random runs, and UPPAAL SMC estimates the probability of reaching an

---

[2] In contrast to general timed automata, complementation is possible due to the assumption that TIOA's are deterministic.

error-state within 200 s to be within the confidence interval [0.000973288, 0.19637] with 95% confidence. This indicates that the simulation-based method for conformance checking between specification may be highly efficient.

8   Future Directions and Challenges

There are several theoretical and practical challenges ahead for compositional testing. On the theory side, the formal foundation and refinement relations are still mostly concerned with basic functionality. These must be extended to cope with various quantitative properties, e.g., performance, soft real-time, hybrid discrete/continuous behavior, and security. They must be able to capture the underlying assumptions and guarantees. We believe that relativized io-conformance testing is a good foundation for further development. Component based and model-based development techniques should match better. Model-based tools and techniques need to support both architectural and behavioral models explicitly that match real component models and software development. In contrast, these should be enhanced with solid theoretical semantics, clean execution model, and a formal notion of interfaces.

Industrial take-up is another challenge. Industrial engineers are often not aware of the available techniques and tools, and their full potential. There is a big element of training, where engineers need to be educated to think more in terms of components and composability. They often lack the skills needed to design and implement systems with "nice" composability properties that match the underlying theory. In particular, it is a challenge to create the abstractions needed to break the overall system model into several sub-specification models (or conversely, to find and model the requirements for a system model composed from components). With current state-of-art, these specification models must be crafted manually. On the other hand, the tools should be packaged in such a way that well-skilled and well-trained industrial engineers will able to apply them without too often encountering the idiosyncrasies of the underlying formalisms and analysis tools. The formal analysis tools too often under-performs when not applied by expert users. In these respects, UPPAAL ECDAR needs further development. In contrast, approximate simulation based techniques are often more directly applicable, as exemplified by the refinement check computed by UPPAAL SMC in Sect. 7. In particular, in the first early development cycles of non-highly critical systems, a fast statistical check may be preferred to the potentially time consuming full analysis.

As mentioned, it is often difficult for companies to develop software with a clean component model because of a large legacy. At the same time, however, many distributed systems are becoming increasingly service-oriented and increasingly constructed by composing these services. This is especially true in the Internet-of-things domains. A particular theoretical challenge here will be to support the dynamic binding that takes place in the brokerage phase.

A compositional method for verification and testing for the future applications is thus very necessary, and further research and dissemination to industrial practice is indispensable.

References

1. Aiguier, M., Boulanger, F., Kanso, B.: A formal abstract framework for modelling and testing complex software systems. Theoret. Comput. Sci. **455**, 66–97 (2012). International Colloquium on Theoretical Aspects of Computing (2010)
2. Alur, R., Dill, D.L.: A theory of timed automata. Theoret. Comput. Sci. **126**(2), 183–235 (1994)
3. Kanso, B., Chebaro, O.: Compositional testing for FSM-based models. Int. J. Softw. Eng. Appl. (IJSEA) **5**(3) (2014)
4. Boudjadar, A., David, A., Kim, J.H., Larsen, K.G., Mikucionis, M., Nyman, U., Skou, A.: Degree of schedulability of mixed-criticality real-time systems with probabilistic sporadic tasks. In: 2014 Theoretical Aspects of Software Engineering Conference, TASE 2014, Changsha, China, 1–3 September 2014, pp. 126–130. IEEE Computer Society (2014)
5. Briones, L.B.: Assume-guarantee reasoning with ioco testing relation. In: Proceedings of the 22nd IFIP International Conference on Testing Software and Systems (2010)
6. Bulychev, P., David, A., Larsen, K.G., Legay, A., Li, G., Poulsen, D.B.: Rewrite-based statistical model checking of WMTL. In: Qadeer, S., Tasiran, S. (eds.) RV 2012. LNCS, vol. 7687, pp. 260–275. Springer, Heidelberg (2013). doi:10.1007/978-3-642-35632-2_25
7. Bulychev, P., David, A., Guldstrand Larsen, K., Legay, A., Li, G., Bøgsted Poulsen, D., Stainer, A.: Monitor-based statistical model checking for weighted metric temporal logic. In: Bjørner, N., Voronkov, A. (eds.) LPAR 2012. LNCS, vol. 7180, pp. 168–182. Springer, Heidelberg (2012). doi:10.1007/978-3-642-28717-6_15
8. Bulychev, P., David, A., Guldstrand Larsen, K., Legay, A., Mikučionis, M., Bøgsted Poulsen, D.: Checking and distributing statistical model checking. In: Goodloe, A.E., Person, S. (eds.) NFM 2012. LNCS, vol. 7226, pp. 449–463. Springer, Heidelberg (2012). doi:10.1007/978-3-642-28891-3_39
9. Daca, P., Henzinger, T.A., Krenn, W., Nickovic, D.: Compositional specifications for ioco testing. In: Seventh IEEE International Conference on Software Testing, Verification and Validation, ICST, 31 March 2014–4 April 2014, Cleveland, Ohio, USA, pp. 373–382. IEEE Computer Society (2014)
10. David, A., Du, D., Larsen, K.G., Mikucionis, M., Skou, A.: An evaluation framework for energy aware buildings using statistical model checking. Sci. China Inf. Sci. **55**(12), 2694–2707 (2012)
11. David, A., Larsen, K.G., Legay, A., Mikučionis, M.: Schedulability of herschel-planck revisited using statistical model checking. In: Margaria, T., Steffen, B. (eds.) ISoLA 2012. LNCS, vol. 7610, pp. 293–307. Springer, Heidelberg (2012). doi:10.1007/978-3-642-34032-1_28
12. David, A., Larsen, K.G., Legay, A., Mikucionis, M., Poulsen, D.B.: Uppaal SMC tutorial. STTT **17**(4), 397–415 (2015)
13. David, A., Larsen, K.G., Legay, A., Mikucionis, M., Poulsen, D.B., Sedwards, S.: Statistical model checking for biological systems. STTT **17**(3), 351–367 (2015)
14. David, A., Larsen, K.G., Legay, A., Mikučionis, M., Poulsen, D.B., van Vliet, J., Wang, Z.: Statistical model checking for networks of priced timed automata. In: Fahrenberg, U., Tripakis, S. (eds.) FORMATS 2011. LNCS, vol. 6919, pp. 80–96. Springer, Heidelberg (2011). doi:10.1007/978-3-642-24310-3_7

15. David, A., Larsen, K.G., Legay, A., Mikučionis, M., Wang, Z.: Time for statistical model checking of real-time systems. In: Gopalakrishnan, G., Qadeer, S. (eds.) CAV 2011. LNCS, vol. 6806, pp. 349–355. Springer, Heidelberg (2011). doi:10. 1007/978-3-642-22110-1_27

16. David, A., Larsen, K.G., Legay, A., Nyman, U., Traonouez, L., Wasowski, A.: Real-time specifications. STTT **17**(1), 17–45 (2015)

17. David, A., Larsen, K.G., Legay, A., Nyman, U., Wąsowski, A.: ECDAR: An Environment for Compositional Design and Analysis of Real Time Systems. In: Bouajjani, A., Chin, W.-N. (eds.) ATVA 2010. LNCS, vol. 6252, pp. 365–370. Springer, Heidelberg (2010). doi:10.1007/978-3-642-15643-4_29

18. David, A., Larsen, K.G., Legay, A., Nyman, U., Wasowski, A.: Timed I/O automata: a complete specification theory for real-time systems. In: Johansson and Yi [21], pp. 91–100

19. David, N., David, A., Hansen, R.R., Larsen, K.G., Legay, A., Olesen, M.C., Probst, C.W.: Modelling social-technical attacks with timed automata. In: Bertino, E., You, I. (eds.) Proceedings of the 7th ACM CCS International Workshop on Managing Insider Security Threats, MIST 2015, Denver, Colorado, USA, 16 October 2015, pp. 21–28. ACM (2015)

20. Hessel, A., Larsen, K.G., Mikucionis, M., Nielsen, B., Pettersson, P., Skou, A.: Testing real-time systems using UPPAAL. In: Hierons, R.M., Bowen, J.P., Harman, M. (eds.) Formal Methods and Testing. LNCS, vol. 4949, pp. 77–117. Springer, Heidelberg (2008). doi:10.1007/978-3-540-78917-8_3

21. Johansson, K.H., Yi, W. (eds.): Proceedings of the 13th ACM International Conference on Hybrid Systems: Computation and Control, HSCC 2010, Stockholm, Sweden, 12–15 April 2010. ACM (2010)

22. Krichen, M., Tripakis, S.: Conformance testing for real-time systems. Form. Methods Syst. Des. **34**(3), 238–304 (2009)

23. Larsen, K.G., Mikucionis, M., Nielsen, B., Skou, A.: Testing real-time embedded software using uppaal-tron: an industrial case study. In: Proceedings of the 5th ACM International Conference on Embedded Software, EMSOFT 2005, pp. 299–306. ACM, New York (2005)

24. Larsen, K.G., Mikucionis, M., Nielsen, B.: Online testing of real-time systems using UPPAAL. In: Grabowski, J., Nielsen, B. (eds.) FATES 2004. LNCS, vol. 3395, pp. 79–94. Springer, Heidelberg (2005). doi:10.1007/978-3-540-31848-4_6

25. Mikučionis, M., Larsen, K.G., Nielsen, B.: T-uppaal: online model-based testing of real-time systems. In: Proceedings of the 19th IEEE International Conference on Automated Software Engineering, ASE 2004, pp. 396–397. IEEE Computer Society, Washington, DC, USA (2004)

26. Tretmans, J.: A formal approach to conformance testing. In: Rafiq, O. (ed.) Protocol Test Systems, VI, Proceedings of the IFIP TC6/WG6.1 Sixth International Workshop on Protocol Test Systems, Pau, France, 28–30 September 1993. IFIP Transactions, vol. C-19, pp. 257–276. North-Holland (1993)

27. van der Bijl, M., Rensink, A., Tretmans, J.: Compositional testing with IOCO. In: Petrenko, A., Ulrich, A. (eds.) FATES 2003. LNCS, vol. 2931, pp. 86–100. Springer, Heidelberg (2004). doi:10.1007/978-3-540-24617-6_7

28. van Glabbeek, R.J., Höfner, P., Portmann, M., Tan, W.L.: Modelling and verifying the AODV routing protocol. Distrib. Comput. **29**(4), 279–315 (2016)

Model-Based Testing Without Models: The TodoMVC Case Study

Alexander Bainczyk[✉], Alexander Schieweck[✉], Bernhard Steffen,
and Falk Howar

Dortmund University of Technology, Dortmund, Germany
{alexander.bainczyk,alexander.schieweck,bernhard.steffen,
falk.howar}@tu-dortmund.de

Abstract. Web applications define the interface to many of the businesses and services that we interact with and use on a daily basis. The technology stack enabling these applications is constantly changing and applications are accessed from a plethora of different devices. Automated testing of the behavior of applications is a promising strategy for reducing the manual effort that has to be spent on ensuring a consistent user experience across devices. Unfortunately, specifications or models of the desired behavior often do not exist. Model-based testing without models (aka learning-based testing) tries to overcome this hurdle by integrating model learning and model-based testing. In this paper, we sketch the ALEX tool [1,11] for learning-based testing of web application and demonstrate its operation on benchmarks from the TodoMVC project. Our learning-based conformance analysis reveals that 7 of 27 Todo-apps exhibit behavior that differs from the majority of implementations.

Keywords: Active automata learning · Model-based testing · Specification mining · Conformance testing

1 Introduction

Web applications define the interface to many of the businesses and services that we interact with and use on a daily basis. The technology stack enabling these applications is constantly changing and steadily growing — for more than two decades by now — forcing developers and operators to adapt to new technologies and replace old ones frequently. At the same time, applications are accessed from a plethora of different devices, running different browsers in many different versions. Application developers have to work very hard in order to maintain a consistent user experience on different platforms and with changing underlying technology.

Different browsers with various implementations of HTML, CSS and JavaScript [21] interpretations require special care and turn the barrier-free implementation even of comparatively simple web applications into a challenge. Hundreds of JavaScript frameworks have been developed to ease the life of developers

© Springer International Publishing AG 2017
J.-P. Katoen et al. (Eds.): Brinksma Festschrift, LNCS 10500, pp. 125–144, 2017.
DOI: 10.1007/978-3-319-68270-9_7

and to provide a more structured way to deal with those hurdles. While these frameworks often aim at unique behavior across different client platforms, this remains a vision for the most part to this day. Companies have to employ testers who ensure the consistency of the user experience.

Automated testing of the behavior of applications in different browsers is a promising strategy for reducing the manual effort that has to be spent in this area. There exist testing frameworks that allow record-and-replay testing of web applications. Selenium [10] probably is the most widely known such tool. Web-testing often relies on information and structure in the DOM-trees of web pages (i.e., the tree-structure of nested HTML elements in the corresponding HTML document) for navigating pages and applying test inputs. While this works well for pages produced in one technology stack, in many instances it can not be used for testing regressions between different stacks.

What is needed, is an approach to testing web applications at a behavioral level and that can scale across many client platforms as well as across many back-end technologies. Since the user interface of many web applications is stateful (login from a landing page, then sequences of dialogues realize use cases, etc.), model-based testing seems to be a natural candidate formal method. Unfortunately, unlike in more classic infrastructure domains (e.g., telephony), interfaces of web applications are not strongly regulated or standardized. Specifications or models of the desired behavior do not exist.

Model-based testing without models (aka learning-based testing) tries to overcome this hurdle by integrating model learning [43] and model-based testing [15]. A model of the application under testing is learned from test cases and then becomes the basis for model-based testing. Divergences of the modeled behavior can be used to refine the initial learned model. Such an approach is directly applicable in settings where multiple models are being learned, either across many client platforms or for many consecutive versions of an applications. In such a scenario, models can be used to identify behavioral outliers and regressions.

In this paper, we demonstrate the ALEX tool [1, 11] for learning-based testing — using a set of web applications as benchmarks. The ALEX tool aims at automating learning-based testing. It provides a graphical user interface in which users can simply define (model-level) actions from atomic operations on a web-page (e.g., filling a field in a form, clicking a button, or following a link). The ALEX tool then uses those actions as a basis for generating test cases (i.e., sequences of actions) and inferring a model of the application.

We use applications from the TodoMVC project [2] as benchmarks. The TodoMVC project invites developers to provide implementations in their favorite framework for a quite simple, standardized todo application whose requirements are given by a textual requirements document and 30 test cases. A "todo application" allows users to manage a simple list of todo items. The project's name is TodoMVC as developers are encouraged to use the model-view-controller (MVC) pattern. Currently, the TodoMVC website lists 71 corresponding TodoMVC implementations, 27 of which are client-side JavaScript implementations which can be operated using Selenium [10] and are classified stable. This repository of slightly different implementations is a perfect basis for simulating the application of learning-based testing over the lifetime of a web application. We use learning-based testing to analyze to which extent these 27 Todo implementations coincide in their user-level behavior, and whether they satisfy the TodoMVC requirements. Our learning-based examination reveals that 7 of the 27 implementations differ from the majority regarding the user-level behavior.

Key to our approach is a common behavioral language of inputs that is shared between all applications. This common language then is mapped to 27 different implementations. ALEX simplifies this style of comparative conformance testing of web applications, in particular, by easing construction of mappings to different concrete implementations. It can be done in a web browser almost without programming. We have made ALEX and the entire setup of this case study openly available on the web [1], so readers can easily replay, modify or extend the experiments, or even design her own new learning-based testing setups.

Our main contribution is a small qualitative study of the effectiveness and efficiency of automated and tool-supported learning-based testing for ensuring the consistent behavior of a web application over time and in different browsers. We analyze the effort spent on test automation using the ALEX tool and report on discovered divergences in the behavior of the analyzed applications.

Related Work. Learning-based testing relies on model learning and model-based testing. Model learning is based on active automata learning [8]. Testing is based on methods for testing transition systems [15]. Used testing methods range from simplistic random sampling, over model-based methods [40] to proper conformance tests [18]. Basis for the integration of the two approaches is the insight that both are merely different sides of the same coin as has been observed in multiple publications [13,41]; central to both worlds are access sequences and distinguishing sequences that allow entering and discriminating states. ALEX is based on active learning for Mealy machines [39], which allows to capture input/output behavior, and can be configured to use different testing strategies in the spectrum sketched above.

Model-based testing without models (aka learning-based testing) is developed by different sets of authors using different concrete techniques in varying settings. One of the earliest practical applications of active automata learning was testing of telecommunication systems [23,24] and web applications [36]. In recent years this line of application has been continued for several different types of systems. Argyros et al. [9] use automata learning techniques to infer models of regular expressions behind HTML encoders from different programming languages and websites in order to check them for equivalence and idempotence. Dinca and co authors develop an approach for generating test-suites for event-b models through active automata learning [19]. Choi et al. use active automata learning for testing the behavior of the graphical user interfaces of android applications [17]. Shahbaz and Groz infer models of embedded components and use these models as a basis for test case generation [38]. Meinke and Sindhu present LBTest, a tool for learning-based testing of reactive systems, integrating model checking, active automata learning, and random testing [34]. Windmüller and co-authors and the Active Continuous Quality Control presented in [44], which aims at controlling the impact of version change. The authors of [6] evaluate different combinations of learning and testing on a set of slightly different implementations of the bounded retransmission protocol.

We have developed in ALEX in the spirit of such testing tools as TorX [42] or its successor JTorX [12] that are underpinned by a sound theoretic framework but make the theory easily applicable. From a user's perspective, the big difference to these tools is that in ALEX no specification has to be provided. Instead, a model of the observed behavior of a system is learned from (automatically generated) tests.

Outline. We start by describing learning-based testing and the ALEX tool in the next section. Section 3 presents the TodoMVC project, some requirements and use cases of the tested applications, and the common behavioral language which we use during testing. In Sect. 4, we provide detailed results of the case study, before concluding in Sect. 5.

2   Background

Learning-based testing is based on active automata learning and model-based testing. We provide a brief introduction to automata learning here and describe how model-based testing methods are integrated. We also briefly describe how ALEX uses this theoretic framework for testing web applications.

2.1   Model Learning

Active automata learning [8,39] aims to reveal exactly the states of a reactive system by building a model, or to be more precise a Mealy machine [33] of a reactive system. This is done automatically by posing carefully constructed test cases to a *system under learning (SUL)* and observing the output behavior. In this process, three different parties are involved (cf. Fig. 1). A *learner* passes input

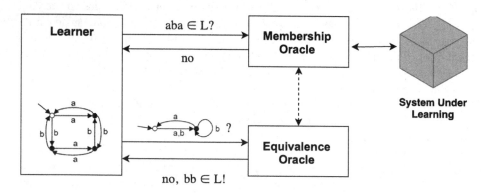

Fig. 1. Active automata learning of a language L with alphabet $\Sigma = \{a, b\}$.

sequences to a *membership oracle* which executes them on the SUL and returns the output behavior. From these observations the learner builds a *hypothesis* (cf. e.g. Fig. 5) which aims to reflect the behavior of the SUL. To verify whether the hypothesis represents the actual behavior of the SUL, an *equivalence oracle* is asked. In theory, this oracle either answers with yes or no and in the latter case delivers a counterexample which is used by the learner to refine the hypothesis.

In practice however, due to the nature of black-box systems, such an oracle does not exist. Thus, one typically has to approximate *equivalence queries* by posing multiple *membership queries*, i.e., via testing. *LearnLib*[1] [30,35,37], an open source learning framework provides various alternatives for this kind of approximation, ranging from techniques using random test generation to conformance tests [4,5,18,22]. So-called "lifelong learning" has been proposed for applications in which counterexamples can be obtained through monitoring [14,29]. In learning-based testing, equivalence queries are simply used to switch from model learning to model-based testing and back.

2.2 Model-Based Testing Without Models

The tool ALEX (*Automata Learning EXperience*)[2], presented in [11], can be understood as a graphical user interface to *LearnLib* that allows users to infer Mealy machines of web applications and HTTP based web APIs at ease. ALEX allows users to define a set of model-level input actions from atomic operations on a web page (e.g., filling forms or clicking on elements). These input actions are then used by learning and testing algorithms in LearnLib as a basis for learning a model of a web application.

For the alphabet modeling, a user first defines an abstract input alphabet (cf. Fig. 2a) via a simple web form. Then, for each abstract input symbol, he models the concrete logic as a sequence of parametrized Selenium[3]-based actions (cf. Fig. 2b) that are executed in a real browser during the learning process. Therefore, a broad range of atomic interactions with the browser-based user interface of a web application is provided.

In the experiment setup, a user selects the symbols that should be included in the input alphabet, chooses one of several learning algorithms, a strategy to find counterexamples and the web browser in which the tests should be executed in. With these specifications, ALEX will then automatically generate tests based on these inputs and produce a model of the tested web application. The generated tests form a conformance test suite as is discussed in [13]. Then, the tool allows investigations such as the calculation of the symmetric difference between two models and the manual specification of counterexamples. Further, statistical values that are characteristic for a learning experiment are gathered automatically (cf. Table 2) in the learning process.

---

[1] http://learnlib.de/.
[2] http://learnlib.github.io/alex/.
[3] http://www.seleniumhq.org/.

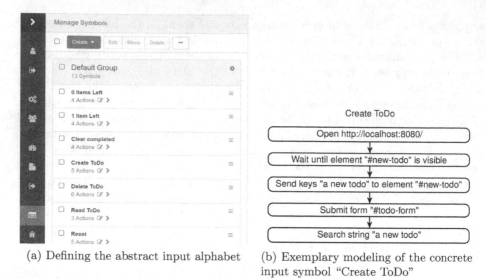

(a) Defining the abstract input alphabet

(b) Exemplary modeling of the concrete input symbol "Create ToDo"

Fig. 2. Specifying test inputs with ALEX [11].

3   A Language for Testing TodoMVC

TodoMVC[4] is a project consisting of several JavaScript implementations of a simple todo application that should look the same and behave according to a given textual specification [3]. Independent developers can provide implementations of TodoMVC in their favorite JavaScript framework. The catch of the project is that a different JavaScript framework is used for every implementation with the goal to allow developers to easily compare and choose a framework for their own next project.

In January of 2017, there were 36 implementations considered stable and 35 versions that were denoted beta. Moreover, all these implementations have been developed with a different frontend library. The remainder of this section describes the different TodoMVC implementations that we used as a basis for our study as well as the common behavioral language that was used as a basis for testing.

3.1   TodoMVC Implementations

The simple todo applications share a common user interface shown in Figure 3 which is also provided by TodoMVC. It allows to create new tasks, edit and delete them. Furthermore, tasks can be marked as completed and it is possible to show only active or completed tasks. Also there is a button to mark all tasks

---

[4] http://todomvc.com/.

Fig. 3. The common UI of TodoMVC.

as completed and another one to delete all completed tasks. A specification [3] describes all the visual elements and their behavior as well as the expected work flow in the application.

For our study, we have selected 27 out of the 36 stable versions of TodoMVC, modeled, learned and analyzed them with ALEX in order to find possible deviations from the specification. It has to be noted that we skipped some applications: *Ember.js*, *TroopJS+RequireJS*, *GWT*, *Elm*, *Regent* and *AngularDart*. The first because it is not accessible, the others because there have been problems with Selenium when learning models. Those problems are also known issues of the TodoMVC project. Furthermore we skipped *SocketStream*, *Firebase + AngularJS* and *Express + gcloud-node* because they are the only implementations that rely on a backend server and they automatically connect to a global accessible server. This means that it is not easily possible to learn those variants in an isolated test environment. The complete list of learned variants can be seen in Table 1.

3.2   Common Behavioral Language for TodoMVC

We define an abstract alphabet based on the use cases of the TodoMVC project that are given in the specification [3].

Inputs. For the inputs to an applications this results in the following 12 alphabet symbols:

{Create, Read, Update, Delete} Todo. A todo item can be created, updated and deleted. Further, one can check if the todo item is displayed in the list of all visible todos.

Table 1. Todo implementations and modeling time for test inputs.

No.	Framework	Modeling based on	Modeling time	No. of changes
1	AngularJS	-	2 h 56 min 22 s	-
2	Backbone	AngularJS	6 min 47 s	11/13
3	Ampersand	AngularJS	3 min 13 s	1/13
4	Vue	Backbone	1 min 48 s	0/13
5	Polymer	AngularJS	2 min 12 s	1/13
6	React	Backbone	1 min 52s	0/13
7	VanillaJS	Backbone	1 min 59 s	0/13
8	JQuery	Polymer	1 min 17s	0/13
9	KnockoutJS	Polymer	1 min 25 s	0/13
10	Mithril	Polymer	1 min 27 s	0/13
11	Knockback	Backbone	1 min 13 s	0/13
12	CanJS	Polymer	0 min 57 s	0/13
13	Dojo	Angular	1 min 41 s	1/13
14	Marionette	Polymer	0 min 59 s	0/13
15	Dart	Backbone	1 min 24 s	1/13
16	Flight	Polymer	1 min 21 s	1/13
17	VanillaES6	Backbone	3 min 24 s	3/13
18	Spine	Polymer	0 min 57 s	0/13
19	Closure	Polymer	1 min 2 s	0/13
20	ScalaJS + React	Backbone	1 min 15 s	0/13
21	ScalaJS + Scala.bind	Backbone	1 min 1 s	0/13
22	Seranade	Angular	1 min 15 s	3/13
23	TypeScript + React	Backbone	1 min 8 s	0/13
24	TypeScript + Angular	Backbone	1 min 3 s	0/13
25	TypeScript + Backbone	Backbone	0 min 57 s	0/13
26	js_of_ocaml	Backbone	0 min 59 s	0/13
27	Humble+GopherJS	Backbone	1 min 2 s	0/13

Toggle Done. A todo item is either marked as *active* or as *done*, this symbol toggles the state of the todo item.

Toggle Done All. With a single click, the status of all visible todo items is toggled.

Clear Done. Delete all todo items that are marked as done at once.

View {All, Active, Done}. The user can display all todo items or filter items based on their state.

{0 items, 1 item} Left. There is a counter that displays how many todo items are active. We differentiate between zero and one item because we only operate on a single item.

These 12 symbols are sufficient to capture all the requirements in the specification except for data persistence, which is, in fact, a non-regular property and can therefore not be modeled by Mealy machines. In addition it should be noted that ALEX requires an additional symbol for a system reset leading to an overall size of the learning alphabet of 13. In order to test different implementations, these abstract inputs have to be mapped to (implemented as) concrete sequences of actions on a DOM-tree as is described below.

Outputs. Further, we capture the output behavior of the web application using two symbols: *OK* indicates that all actions, that an input symbol consists of, could be executed on the system without throwing an error. An error might e.g. occur if a button, that can be accessed by a unique CSS selector, should be clicked on, but due to the current state of the system, is not visible. In such a case we encode the output as *FAILED(n)* where $n \geq 1$ points to the n-th action in the concrete mapped implementation of the previously executed input symbol.

3.3   Mapping the Behavioral Language to Implementations

We have implemented concrete versions of the abstract test inputs for 27 applications. For one, these 27 applications became the basis for our testing experiments. But, the implementation allowed us to also evaluate the software engineering aspect of our approach: In the envisioned scenario of learning-based regression testing and user experience testing, the behavioral language has to be implemented and adapted multiple times (using ALEX).

In order to study the complexity of this task, we have picked a single TodoMVC application, namely *AngularJS*, and have started modeling the first input alphabet implementation with our tool ALEX. After this first alphabet was modeled and a first learning run against the *AngularJS* implementation was performed, we validated that the model and the implementation works as intended. Afterwards we went on with the second application: *Backbone* but did not start from scratch implementing another input alphabet. Instead, we reused the alphabet we obtained from *AngularJS* and only modified those parts where the two applications differ. During the successive treatment of the 27 alphabet implementations the number of adaptations grew, thus enlarging the pool from which future adaptation could profit, which results in the hierarchy depicted in Fig. 4.

Remark. The differences meant here are not of behavioral nature, but have a structural background. An HTML document is structured as a *document object model (DOM)* where the relationship between two elements can be expressed with a parent- child or sibling relation. In this tree, each element can be accessed via a *CSS selector* (a unique identifier, which represents the path from the root node to the specific element). Although TodoMVC provides a common HTML template that the libraries should use, some developers modified the selectors to their own will. This does not result in a different user interface, but how each element is accessed by a selector. So, for example, the same element that

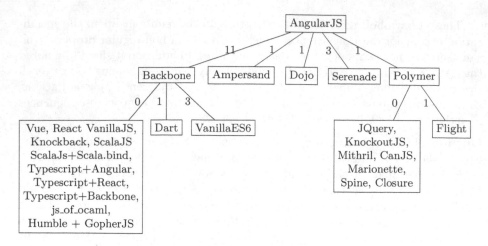

Fig. 4. The hierarchy of derived input alphabets. The edge labels denote the number symbols that had to be modified.

is accessed in *AngularJS* with a unique ID via *#todo-list > li:nth-child(1)* (the first item in the list) is accessed via *.todo-list > li:nth-child(1)* in *Backbone*. As a result, the selectors have to be adjusted accordingly in the new input alphabet implementation. All required adaptations of the alphabet implementations were of this kind: they only concerned the selectors, and not the action itself.

3.4   Analysis of Implementation Effort

In order to analyze the reuse effect, the two main developers of ALEX carefully measured the manual effort for these adaptations using a stopwatch. The corresponding measurements and the order in which implementations were realized can be seen in Table 1.

The initial task of modeling the input alphabet for *AngularJS* took the developers about three hours, which includes the familiarization with the TodoMVC specification, modeling alphabet implementation itself, testing and debugging our modeling. *Backbone*, which was treated next, required to adjust the selectors of eleven (out of 13) symbols, which was possible in less than 7 min using ALEX. As one goes down the rows of the table, one can see that with time and the growing pool of alphabets to choose from, we have gotten more and more practice selecting and adjusting the alphabets to the corresponding applications. As a result, it only took the developers about one to one and a half minutes for a new application in the end.

The choice of which available alphabet was used as a basis for a new application was made by a short check of the source code of the targeted application to determine as basis the existing alphabet of an application with structural similarities. The required time is also included in the measurements.

The information given in Table 1 directly translates to an alphabet reuse-hierarchy that is shown in Fig. 4. As you can see there, two of the nodes represent implementations that did not require any change. Thus we ended up having only nine different alphabet implementations in total.

4 Testing the Behavior of Todo MVC Apps

We have used the implementation of the behavioral language to apply learning-based testing to 27 todo applications. The experiments reveal several behavioral outliers and violations of the specification.

4.1 Experimental Setup

Our experiments are conducted in two series. In the first series, we establish a common input alphabet that covers the use cases of the TodoMVC specification for our 27 candidates. In order to guarantee a regular behavior, we sequentialize create, read, update and delete operations by learning models that at most one task at any given time may exist per state.[5] Then, we examine the automatically inferred models in order to reveal possible differences in the user-level behavior of the applications.

In the second series, we extend and refine the set of test inputs to allow the presence of up to two todo items at the same time. The point of the second series is to provide a feeling of the impact of the restriction to disallow the concurrent treatment of todo items. For this series, we analyze a representative sample of applications that behave identically in the first series.

All experiments have been executed on a machine with an Intel Core i5 6600k (4×3.50 GHz), 16 GB of main memory and a 128 GB SSD. For the operating system, Linux Mint 18.1 64bit has been used. Furthermore, the tests have been executed in Google Chrome v55 in combination with the Chromedriver v2.27[6].

ALEX offers a user to choose from a variety of learning-based algorithms. In this study we use the TTT algorithm [29] which had the best performance profile.

On our homepage[7] we provide all the material that is required to replay our experiments and step-by-step instructions that guides a user through the first learn process.

Originally, we had planned to end the learning-based testing process for each of the 27 TodoMVC implementations with a W-method conformance test [18] that could identify a maximum of three additional states. However, already a test suite that assumed a maximum of two additional states turned out to be impractical in terms of the execution time: The testing of a single TodoMVC

---

[5] This has been enforced by adding code to the implementations of test inputs that checks whether a task is absent or created, but currently not visible — similar to a test purpose.

[6] https://sites.google.com/a/chromium.org/chromedriver/.

[7] http://learnlib.github.io/alex/book/1.2/contents/examples/todomvc/index.html.

implementation finished after about two days, without finding new states. We therefore decided to continue with an extended random test, which we configured, depending on the phase, to take about 30–60 min for each of the learning processes. We considered this as sufficient, as it constitutes about 90% of the overall time taken for equivalence queries in each of the learning experiments. Indeed, the equivalence queries providing a new counterexample typically only ran for less than half a minute. Of course, there is no guarantee that we succeeded to infer the entire behavior.

4.2 Results of Testing with Sequential Tasks

The results of our learning-based evaluation with ALEX are presented in Table 2. For each implementation, we measured the execution time, the number of system

Table 2. Statistics of testing TodoMVC implementations. The table shows results for both series. Highlighted rows mark outliers within a series.

No.	Framework	Runtimes [hh:mm:ss]			Resets			Inputs			EQs	States
		MG	MBT	Total	MG	MBT	Total	MG	MBT	Total		
1	AngularJS	00:18:45	00:36:11	00:54:56	476	102	578	3372	5772	9144	5	9
2	Backbone	00:21:29	00:38:44	01:00:14	510	76	586	3454	4339	7793	4	9
3	Ampersand	00:19:50	00:35:46	00:55:36	509	100	609	3569	5662	9231	5	9
4	Vue	00:18:06	00:35:58	00:54:04	476	102	578	3372	5772	9144	5	9
5	Polymer	00:20:13	00:35:53	00:56:06	509	100	609	3597	5662	9259	5	9
6	React	00:19:11	00:37:10	00:56:21	447	76	553	3253	4270	7523	5	9
7	VanillaJS	00:19:50	00:35:44	00:55:35	509	100	609	3569	5662	9231	5	9
8	JQuery	00:43:46	00:36:41	01:20:27	854	223	1077	7102	12596	19698	6	13
9	KnockoutJS	00:17:53	00:36:42	00:54:35	447	76	553	3253	4270	7523	5	9
10	Mithril	00:20:13	00:36:03	00:56:16	509	100	609	3569	5662	9231	5	9
11	Knockback	00:18:18	00:36:47	00:55:06	447	76	553	3253	4270	7523	5	9
12	CanJS	00:13:15	00:35:52	00:49:07	354	70	424	2384	3928	6312	4	7
13	Dojo	02:57:58	00:40:47	03:38:46	2329	216	2545	19128	12160	31288	12	31
14	Marionette	00:24:01	00:37:00	01:01:01	689	147	836	5115	8384	13499	7	12
15	Dart	00:20:48	00:35:50	00:56:38	509	100	609	3569	5662	9231	5	9
16	Flight	00:59:39	00:37:37	01:37:17	1469	229	1698	10660	13053	23713	11	22
17	VanillaES6	00:24:31	00:36:43	01:01:14	508	113	621	3585	6376	9961	6	9
18	Spine	00:18:09	00:36:00	00:54:09	476	102	578	3372	5772	9144	5	9
19	Closure	00:18:03	00:36:00	00:54:03	476	102	578	3372	5772	9144	5	9
20	ScalaJS+React	00:19:55	00:36:47	00:56:42	506	76	582	3532	4351	7883	4	9
21	ScalaJS+Scala.bind	00:18:12	00:36:42	00:54:56	477	76	553	3253	4270	7523	5	9
22	Seranade	00:17:57	00:36:56	00:54:53	477	76	553	3253	4270	7523	5	9
23	TypeScript+React	00:20:22	00:36:01	00:56:24	509	100	609	3569	5662	9231	5	9
24	TypeScript+Angular	00:18:10	00:36:40	00:54:51	477	76	553	3253	4270	7523	5	9
25	TypeScript+Backbone	00:20:08	00:35:51	00:55:59	509	100	609	3569	5662	9231	5	9
26	js_of_ocaml	00:17:41	00:36:45	00:54:27	477	76	553	3253	4270	7523	5	9
27	Humble+GopherJS	00:22:46	00:36:09	00:58:55	509	100	609	3569	5662	9231	5	9
With determinized hashing policy												
1	AngularJS	00:58:44	00:57:22	01:56:06	1317	110	1427	10924	6186	17110	7	20
2	Backbone	00:59:09	00:57:57	01:57:07	1317	110	1427	10924	6186	17110	7	20
3	Ampersand	00:57:57	00:57:23	01:55:21	1317	110	1427	10924	6186	17110	7	20
9	KnockoutJS	01:02:08	01:00:20	02:02:29	1317	110	1427	10924	6186	17110	7	20
15	Dart	00:59:22	00:57:32	01:56:54	1317	110	1427	10924	6186	17110	7	20
17	VanillaES6	00:57:27	00:57:18	01:54:46	1317	110	1427	10924	6186	17110	7	20
22	Seranade	02:57:39	01:42:09	04:39:49	3567	164	3731	36728	9235	45963	10	43

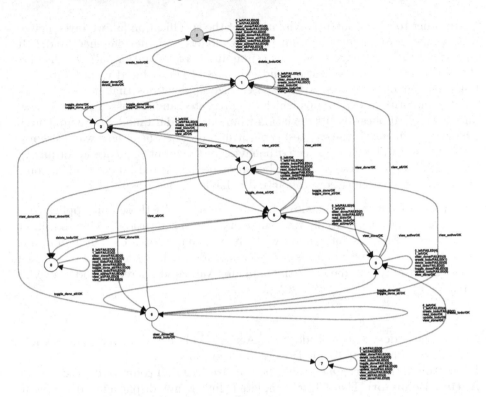

Fig. 5. Reference hypothesis of TodoMVC.

resets as well as the number of inputs that have been posed to the system during the model generation (MG) and the model based testing (MBT). In nearly all cases, with *Polymer* being the exception, the outliers within a series can be identified directly by looking at the state space of the resulting model. 22 of the 27 learned implementations of TodoMVC resulted in a model with nine states, and, indeed, all but *Polymer* have the same final hypothesis which is depicted in Fig. 5. We consider these 21 implementations of TodoMVC as reference implementations, because they do not only satisfy the specification [3] but are also state minimal. Besides *Polymer*, the 22nd 9-state implementation, also *JQuery*, *CanJS*, *Dojo*, *Marionette* and *Flight* deviate from this reference behavior. This does, however, not automatically imply that they do not satisfy the specification.

Strictly speaking, *CanJS* is the specification-conforming implementation with the smallest model and would therefore be the candidate of choice according to the Occam's razor principle. The 21 correct implementations with 9 states satisfy an additional constraint which can be regarded as a convention: one should not accidentally change the status of the view. We took their behavioral model as reference, and considered the omission of this additional constraint as a typical problem of incomplete specifications.

In order to reveal potential violations of the specification [3], we investigated the symmetric difference between these 6 models and the reference model. It turned out that, indeed, all the 6 corresponding implementations allow behaviors that differ from the specification and can possibly be reduced to programming bugs. By our observations, we can categorize applications that do not behave like the majority in two groups which are presented and discussed in the following. For each application, its deviation from our standard model is documented. The input sequence is the shortest separating word, i.e. the easiest way to reproduce the issue. Then, the expected behavior of the input sequence according to the specification is presented. And because the here listed inputs lead to some violation of the specification, the actual behavior is described as well.

Violation of the Specification. In this group, we list those four applications that violate the specification. We define that the specification is violated, if, at some point during the interaction with the user interface, a certain action, e.g. an operation on a todo item, is not possible, although it should be (according to the input/output behavior of the manually validated reference model) or vice versa.

Dojo

Input Sequence: Create Todo, View Active, Update Todo, Toggle Done, Clear Done, Create Todo, Toggle Done All, Clear Done.
Expected Behavior: One should be able to delete all completed tasks.
Actual Behavior: The 'Clear completed' link is not displayed and therefore one can not delete the task. Additionally, the counter that displays the number of open tasks shows that there is still one entry left.

Flight

Input Sequence: Create Todo, View Active, Update Todo, View Active, Read Todo
Expected Behavior: Clicking on the 'active' filter link multiple times should be idempotent and thus reading the entry again should be possible.
Actual Behavior: The todo item disappears. Also, the item does not appear in any other view, even after a browser refresh.

Marionette

Input Sequence: Create Todo, View Done, Toggle Done All, View Active, Toggle Done All, 1 Item Left.
Expected Behavior: The counter of open tasks should display that still one entry is open.
Actual Behavior: The last 'Toggle Done All' action is not performed and the counter still shows '0 items left'. The action is only fired when clicking the button twice. All other states result from that misbehavior.

Polymer

Input Sequence: Create Todo, Toggle Done, 0 Items left.
Expected Behavior: The counter should show the string '0 items left'.
Actual Behavior: The actual text of the counter is '0 item left' should be '0 items left'.

Let us now discuss these observations in more detail from an observational perspective starting with the most severe bug. This bug, which is found in *Flight*, is severe for two reasons. First, after the second 'View Active' action all visible todo items disappear, irreversibly. Even future created todo items disappear permanently. By playing around with the application in this state, we found that this behavior persists even after a browser restart. The only way to get back to the initial state of *Flight* is to remove all client side storage in the web browser manually, which is a long-winded process for non-expert end users. Second, even putting the first aspect aside, the specification [3] is clearly violated in many other cases as well, as required create, read, update and delete operations on the todo items are not possible after there sudden disappearance.

As one can read from the description of the actual behavior above, all erroneous applications except *Polymer* come in a state where an action should be executable but is not. For *Dojo*, after the input sequence, a completed todo item is present on the page, but the 'Clear completed'-button is not visible although it should be according to the specification. For *Marionette* the first toggle action switches the state from active to completed, the second reverses this. Still, the counter is not updated. These errors can be resolved by further interaction with the applications, by refreshing the page or restarting the browser.

Finally, *Polymer* seems to just have a spelling error.

Other Behavioral Outliers. Besides the applications that directly violate the specification by our means at some point, two applications show a different behavior than the majority, although they do not contradict the specification. The description of the expected behavior therefore only states what other TodoMVC implementations do given the corresponding input sequence and what a user would expect after working with other implementations:

CanJS

Input Sequence: Create Todo, Toggle Done, View Done, Delete Todo, Create Todo, Read Todo.
Expected Behavior: One should not be able to read the new todo item, because the application should still only show completed tasks.
Actual Behavior: The new todo item is visible in the list. The implementation switches from the 'active' or 'completed' view to the 'all' view as soon as one creates a new todo item.

JQuery

Input Sequence: Create Todo, Toggle Done, View Done, Clear Done, Create Todo, Read Todo.

Expected Behavior: One should not be able to read the new entry, because the application should still only show completed tasks.

Actual Behavior: The new task is readable. This implementation switches from the completed view to the all view as soon as a new entry is created.

Input Sequence: Create Todo, View Active, Toggle Done, Toggle Done All.

Expected Behavior: The button to toggle all todo items should be visible.

Actual Behavior: The button is not displayed and therefore can not be clicked in case the task list is empty.

In *CanJS*, if the user creates a new todo item, the routing mechanism automatically switches to the view where all todo items are listed, no matter which filter is currently active. Since the specification does not draw a connection between creating todo items and the filter functionality and the application behaves consistently in this behavior, this seems to be a matter of the developers dedicated choice of implementation. So technically, the model of *CanJS* with its seven states is the minimal specification conforming solution. One may argue, however, that this solution does not conform to unspoken conventions.

JQuery has, in fact, the same anomaly as *CanJS*, and it additionally deviates form the reference behavior concerning toggling. Here, the specification states that there has to be a button to toggle the state of all todo items at once, but not that the button has to be displayed also if the todo item list is empty. The other applications implemented this differently by making this action available in all possible use cases.

4.3   Results of Testing with Concurrent Tasks

In the second series, we took 7 of the 21 TodoMVC implementations that proved to have equivalent models in the first series and extended their input alphabets in a way that they allow a maximum of two todo items to be present at the same time instead of just one. This refinement serves the purpose of learning models of the applications that better approximate their actual behavior.

The results of the second series are listed at the bottom of Table 2. As indicated by the corresponding headline, they were obtained using an updated version of ALEX which now better supports repeatability of learning experiments by determinizing the access of elements in a hash map where the mapping of abstract to concrete input symbols is defined. The (by default random) order in which elements are read from that mapping influences the total amount of resets and inputs the learner has to make.

As one can see, only the numbers of *Serenade* deviate from the others. Investigating the corresponding symmetric differences reveals that the behavior of *Serenade* deviates from the other implementations essentially because of the following error:

Serenade

Input Sequence: Create Todo, Toggle Done, Create Todo, View Active, Delete Todo, 0 Items Left.

Expected Behavior: The view that displays all active todo items should be empty.

Actual Behavior: The todo item that has been created as a second is still in the list.

The misbehavior that *Serenade* shows would not have been detected if we did not conduct the second phase. It presents a clear violation against the TodoMVC specification, since the todo item is not deleted correctly. It is also the only application that actually throws an internal error. A closer look at the developer console of the web browser reveals the following message: *"Uncaught TypeError: Cannot read property 'length' of undefined"*. This indicates that an access to the underlying todo item array happens although the array has not been initialized at the time of the access. Luckily for the user, the application does not transition into an application breaking error state, but works as intended after switching between the todo item filters.

5   Conclusion

We have shown how to systematically compare technologically different Todo list implementations via learning-based testing. Our two phase learning-based examination of the 27 stable, Selenium-accessible, client-side implementations of the TodoMVC collection has revealed seven behavioral outliers. Enabler for this comparison was the underlying abstract common behavioral language which made their technical difference transparent. Our learning-based approach to validating that different implementations of the same functionality are in fact behaviorally equivalent has a wide range of applications: most mobile "apps" come in numerous implementations to cover the market of smart phones/watches and tablets and change the underpinning framework once at times.

A major goal of ALEX is simplicity [32]: Using ALEX, much of the usual manual quality assurance effort can be automated. We are planning to further increase automation using techniques like [20,25,27,31] for automatically inferring optimal alphabet abstractions. We also plan to evaluate, how much productivity of domain experts can be increased by using ALEX during testing.

ALEX currently only supports the inference of regular models. In future work, we plan to investigate Isberner's technology for learning visibly pushdown automata [7,26] (e.g., to capture repetitive task treatment). An extension of ALEX that uses learning of extended finite state machines [16,28] is also foreseen (e.g., for treating data persistence).

References

1. Automata learning experience (2016). http://learnlib.github.io/alex/. Accessed 23 Oct 2016
2. Todomvc (2016). http://todomvc.com/. Accessed 23 Oct 2016
3. Todomvc specification (2016). https://github.com/tastejs/todomvc/blob/master/app-spec.md. Accessed 21 Oct 2016

4. Aarts, F., Jonsson, B., Uijen, J.: Generating models of infinite-state communication protocols using regular inference with abstraction. In: Petrenko, A., Simão, A., Maldonado, J.C. (eds.) ICTSS 2010. LNCS, vol. 6435, pp. 188–204. Springer, Heidelberg (2010). doi:10.1007/978-3-642-16573-3_14

5. Aarts, F., Kuppens, H., Tretmans, J., Vaandrager, F., Verwer, S.: Improving active mealy machine learning for protocol conformance testing. Mach. Learn. **96**(1), 189–224 (2014)

6. Aarts, F., Kuppens, H., Tretmans, J., Vaandrager, F.W., Verwer, S.: Learning and testing the bounded retransmission protocol. In: Proceedings of the Eleventh International Conference on Grammatical Inference, ICGI 2012. University of Maryland, College Park, USA, 5–8 September 2012, pp. 4–18 (2012)

7. Alur, R., Madhusudan, P.: Visibly pushdown languages. In: Proceedings of the Thirty-sixth Annual ACM Symposium on Theory of Computing, STOC 2004, pp. 202–211. ACM, New York, NY, USA (2004)

8. Angluin, D.: Learning regular sets from queries and counter examples. Inf. Comput. **75**(2), 87–106 (1987)

9. Argyros, G., Stais, I., Kiayias, A., Keromytis, A.D.: Back in black: towards formal, black box analysis of sanitizers and filters. In: 2016 IEEE Symposium on Security and Privacy (SP), pp. 91–109, May 2016

10. Avasarala, S.: Selenium WebDriver Practical Guide. Packt Publishing, Birmingham (2014). ISBN 9781782168850

11. Bainczyk, A., Schieweck, A., Isberner, M., Margaria, T., Neubauer, J., Steffen, B.: ALEX: mixed-mode learning of web applications at ease. In: Margaria, T., Steffen, B. (eds.) ISoLA 2016. LNCS, vol. 9953, pp. 655–671. Springer, Cham (2016). doi:10.1007/978-3-319-47169-3_51

12. Belinfante, A.: JTorX: a tool for on-line model-driven test derivation and execution. In: Esparza, J., Majumdar, R. (eds.) TACAS 2010. LNCS, vol. 6015, pp. 266–270. Springer, Heidelberg (2010). doi:10.1007/978-3-642-12002-2_21

13. Berg, T., Grinchtein, O., Jonsson, B., Leucker, M., Raffelt, H., Steffen, B.: On the correspondence between conformance testing and regular inference. In: Cerioli, M. (ed.) FASE 2005. LNCS, vol. 3442, pp. 175–189. Springer, Heidelberg (2005). doi:10.1007/978-3-540-31984-9_14

14. Bertolino, A., Calabrò, A., Merten, M., Steffen, B.: Never-stop learning: continuous validation of learned models for evolving systems through monitoring. ERCIM News **2012**(88), 28–29 (2012)

15. Brinksma, E., Tretmans, J.: Testing transition systems: an annotated bibliography. In: Cassez, F., Jard, C., Rozoy, B., Ryan, M.D. (eds.) MOVEP 2000. LNCS, vol. 2067, pp. 187–195. Springer, Heidelberg (2001). doi:10.1007/3-540-45510-8_9

16. Cassel, S., Howar, F., Jonsson, B., Steffen, B.: Active learning for extended finite state machines. Formal Aspects Comput. **28**(2), 233–263 (2016)

17. Choi, W., Necula, G., Sen, K.: Guided GUI testing of android apps with minimal restart and approximate learning. SIGPLAN Not. **48**(10), 623–640 (2013)

18. Chow, T.S.: Testing software design modeled by finite-state machines. IEEE Trans. Softw. Eng. **SE–4**(3), 178–187 (1978)

19. Dinca, I., Ipate, F., Mierla, L., Stefanescu, A.: Learn and test for event-B – A rodin plugin. In: Derrick, J., Fitzgerald, J., Gnesi, S., Khurshid, S., Leuschel, M., Reeves, S., Riccobene, E. (eds.) ABZ 2012. LNCS, vol. 7316, pp. 361–364. Springer, Heidelberg (2012). doi:10.1007/978-3-642-30885-7_32

20. Drews, S., D'Antoni, L.: Learning symbolic automata. In: Legay, A., Margaria, T. (eds.) TACAS 2017. LNCS, vol. 10205, pp. 173–189. Springer, Heidelberg (2017). doi:10.1007/978-3-662-54577-5_10

21. Flanagan, D.: JavaScript: The Definitive Guide: Activate Your Web Pages (Definitive Guides), 6th edn. O'Reilly Media, Sebastopol (2011)
22. Fujiwara, S., von Bochmann, G., Khendek, F., Amalou, M., Ghedamsi, A.: Test selection based on finite state models. IEEE Trans. Softw. Eng. **17**(6), 591–603 (1991)
23. Hagerer, A., Hungar, H., Niese, O., Steffen, B.: Model generation by moderated regular extrapolation. In: Kutsche, R.-D., Weber, H. (eds.) FASE 2002. LNCS, vol. 2306, pp. 80–95. Springer, Heidelberg (2002). doi:10.1007/3-540-45923-5_6
24. Hagerer, A., Margaria, T., Niese, O., Steffen, B., Brune, G., Ide, H.-D.: Efficient regression testing of CTI-systems: testing a complex call-center solution. Ann. Rev. Commun. Int. Eng. Consortium (IEC) **55**, 1033–1040 (2001)
25. Howar, F., Steffen, B., Merten, M.: Automata learning with automated alphabet abstraction refinement. In: Jhala, R., Schmidt, D. (eds.) VMCAI 2011. LNCS, vol. 6538, pp. 263–277. Springer, Heidelberg (2011). doi:10.1007/978-3-642-18275-4_19
26. Isberner, M.: Foundations of active automata learning: an algorithmic perspective. Ph.D. thesis. TU Dortmund University, October 2015
27. Isberner, M., Howar, F., Steffen, B.: Inferring automata with state-local alphabet abstractions. In: Brat, G., Rungta, N., Venet, A. (eds.) NFM 2013. LNCS, vol. 7871, pp. 124–138. Springer, Heidelberg (2013). doi:10.1007/978-3-642-38088-4_9
28. Isberner, M., Howar, F., Steffen, B.: Learning register automata: from languages to program structures. Mach. Learn. **96**, 1–34 (2013)
29. Isberner, M., Howar, F., Steffen, B.: The TTT algorithm: a redundancy-free approach to active automata learning. In: Bonakdarpour, B., Smolka, S.A. (eds.) RV 2014. LNCS, vol. 8734, pp. 307–322. Springer, Cham (2014). doi:10.1007/978-3-319-11164-3_26
30. Isberner, M., Howar, F., Steffen, B.: The open-source learnlib. In: Kroening, D., Păsăreanu, C.S. (eds.) CAV 2015. LNCS, vol. 9206, pp. 487–495. Springer, Cham (2015). doi:10.1007/978-3-319-21690-4_32
31. Maler, O., Mens, I.-E.: Learning regular languages over large alphabets. In: Ábrahám, E., Havelund, K. (eds.) TACAS 2014. LNCS, vol. 8413, pp. 485–499. Springer, Heidelberg (2014). doi:10.1007/978-3-642-54862-8_41
32. Margaria, T., Steffen, B.: Simplicity as a driver for agile innovation. Computer **43**(6), 90–92 (2010)
33. Mealy, G.H.: A method for synthesizing sequential circuits. Bell Syst. Tech. J. **34**(5), 1045–1079 (1955)
34. Meinke, K., Sindhu, M.A.: Lbtest: a learning-based testing tool for reactive systems. In: Sixth IEEE International Conference on Software Testing, Verification and Validation, ICST 2013, Luxembourg, 18–22 March 2013, pp. 447–454 (2013)
35. Merten, M., Steffen, B., Howar, F., Margaria, T.: Next generation learnlib. In: Abdulla, P.A., Leino, K.R.M. (eds.) TACAS 2011. LNCS, vol. 6605, pp. 220–223. Springer, Heidelberg (2011). doi:10.1007/978-3-642-19835-9_18
36. Raffelt, H., Merten, M., Steffen, B., Margaria, T.: Dynamic testing via automata learning. Int. J. Softw. Tools Technol. Trans. (STTT) **11**(4), 307–324 (2009)
37. Raffelt, H., Steffen, B., Berg, T., Margaria, T.: LearnLib: a framework for extrapolating behavioral models. Int. J. Softw. Tools Technol. Trans. (STTT) **11**(5), 393–407 (2009)
38. Shahbaz, M., Groz, R.: Analysis and testing of black-box component-based systems by inferring partial models. Softw. Test. Verif. Reliab. **24**(4), 253–288 (2014)
39. Steffen, B., Howar, F., Merten, M.: Introduction to active automata learning from a practical perspective. In: Bernardo, M., Issarny, V. (eds.) SFM 2011. LNCS, vol. 6659, pp. 256–296. Springer, Heidelberg (2011). doi:10.1007/978-3-642-21455-4_8

40. Timmer, M., Brinksma, E., Stoelinga, M.: Model-based testing. In: Software and Systems Safety - Specification and Verification, pp. 1–32. IOS Press (2011)
41. Tretmans, J.: Model-based testing and some steps towards test-based modelling. In: Bernardo, M., Issarny, V. (eds.) SFM 2011. LNCS, vol. 6659, pp. 297–326. Springer, Heidelberg (2011). doi:10.1007/978-3-642-21455-4_9
42. Tretmans, J., Brinksma, E.: Torx: automated model-based testing. In: Hartman, A., Dussa-Ziegler, K. (ed.) First European Conference on Model-Driven Software Engineering, pp. 31–43, December 2003
43. Vaandrager, F.: Model learning. Commun. ACM **60**(2), 86–95 (2017)
44. Windmüller, S., Neubauer, J., Steffen, B., Howar, F., Bauer, O.: Active continuous quality control. In: Proceedings of the 16th International ACM Sigsoft Symposium on Component-based Software Engineering, CBSE 2013, pp. 111–120. ACM New York, NY, USA (2013)

Diagnosis and Testing: How is Their Relation? Can They Be Combined?

Laura Brandán Briones[1]([✉]) and Agnes Madalinski[2]

[1] CONICET and Fa.M.A.F., Universidad Nacional de Córdoba, Córdoba, Argentina
lbrandan@famaf.unc.edu.ar
[2] Chair of Software Engineering, Otto-von-Guericke-University Magdeburg,
Magdeburg, Germany
amadalin@gmail.com

Abstract. Diagnosis and testing have coexisted for a long time, even though they have not been combined, mostly because they consider errors in a different manner. In this paper we present a novel framework that combines fault diagnosis with **ioco**-passive testing. To do so in a proper manner we initially present a formal definition of testability for transition system models, as well as for model-based testing. Later, we enrich our framework so that it captures possible attacks from malicious users. Finally, we consider a weighted failure model that can inform about the severity of a failure. We conclude that diagnosis and testing can be combined in a profitable manner.

1 Introduction

Today, we are facing a *smart* world where embedded devices with electronic and software functions, making systems more and more complex. Many of these systems are critical and require the highest dependability standards since a system failure might cause injuries or even deaths. A real challenge is to ensure that a system operates properly during its functioning, i.e. according to its specification. To identify any dysfunction due to an error occurrence is a demanding task. Therefore, early fault detection is the key to support system performances, ensuring system safety, and increasing system life.

Fault diagnosis deals with unobservable faults that are considered inherent to the system [1]. Such faults cannot be ruled out at design time and normally we only desire to know about their existence to at least deploy some prevention mechanism to handle them. The word diagnosis comes from the medical context where a diagnosis is the process of identifying a disease by its symptoms. Thus, diagnosis is performed by analyzing observed event sequences of the system. To be able to do correct diagnosis without ambiguity, faults should be diagnosable. The diagnosability property describes the system ability to determine whether a given fault has effectively occurred based on system observations in a finite time. The seminal work of Sampath et al. in [2] copes with the identification of such anticipated but unobservable faults. These can be explained by a given observable sequence of events based on the system model, which includes both

© Springer International Publishing AG 2017
J.-P. Katoen et al. (Eds.): Brinksma Festschrift, LNCS 10500, pp. 145–165, 2017.
DOI: 10.1007/978-3-319-68270-9_8

normal and expected faulty behavior. Therefore, a system is diagnosable if it is always possible to determine whether a fault occurred in finite time without ambiguity.

Testing is a well known practice in industry as well as in research. The aim of testing is to execute a system implementation to find failures (a manifestation of a fault in the implementation), i.e. to find a discrepancy between the actual behavior and the intended behavior described by a specification. In particular, the model-based testing approach formally describes the system to be tested with a specification model that expresses its correct behavior. Two advantages are achieved with this practice: first, formal techniques can be applied to the model and second, the testing process can be automated. There are two complementary approaches to test implementations: (a) active testing, where test cases are derived from the specification and then executed in its implementation checking if the implementation conforms to (w.r.t. a given relation) the specification; and (b) passive testing, where a monitor passively observes the implementation without disturbing it and checks if the sequences of observed events conform to (again, w.r.t. a given relation) the specification. These two approaches are usually applied in different states of the implementation process. Normally active testing is performed before the implementation is delivered, in order to realize if some changes should be done on it. While passive testing is done when the implementation is already in use, because testing infinitely is impossible or because the system is already in use. Particularly, our research is based on model-based testing (MBT), i.e. the research area that comprises the usage of models to automate test activities and generate tests from the model [3].

Model checking and testing have been combined several times, but these approaches operate over different types of systems. Model checking operates over models while testing operates over the real systems that are functioning (implementation), of course, each of them have their benefits. In this paper we try to combine diagnosis with testing, which are two approaches that operate over the same type of systems, i.e. implementations. However, little consideration is given in the literature to the fact that both testing and diagnosis have similar objectives and methods even though they are, normally, done in separate domains. Although they are complementary, both can be model-based approaches (using a specification model, a correct and a faulty model of the system, an observation model, etc.) and commonly rely on model-checking techniques ensuring formally that some given properties are satisfied by the model. Both diagnosis and passive testing try to realize if the behavior of a system is correct, based on the system observations. This is a crucial and challenging task, both approaches have similar properties, albeit complementary in their application. They both require the systematic exploration of the system being analyzed, and they both reason about single traces of events.

In this paper we first establish a formal definition for testability over transition system models. Normally, in testing the testability hypothesis is used in order to be able to perform tests, meaning that, the word testability is used to describe when and how a test can be executed in a system. However, our concern in this paper is how testability of a fault is defined to ensure that a failure is produced. Preliminary insights were presented in our paper [4] where the manifestability property is presented. Fault manifestability represents a weak requirement on faults occurrences and observations for having a chance to be identified on-line. This property can be verified at the design stage. Later, we analyze fault testability for model-based testing.

We present a novel framework that integrates fault diagnosis with passive testing identifying fault conditions to be caught. While testing failures we are simultaneously performing fault diagnosis with a common engine called Advanced-proxy. We focus on **ioco** model-based testing theory [5,6]. Recall that complete test suites are infinite, and thus, not practically executable. Hence, possibly some incorrect implementations are not discovered by the testing performed before delivering. Yet, these failures, when they occur, can be detected by the Advanced-proxy. This gives an extensive inside of the erroneous behavior of the monitored system. Moreover, we show that the set of faults that we can expose is larger than normally is done in diagnosis, because we combine the diagnosable faults caught usually by diagnosis with the testable faults that are not diagnosable.

Finally, we expand our framework to also involve a weighted fault model. We use this model to represent the severity of an unexpected event. This, in turn, gives a clue about the gravity of the occurred errors, i.e. what impact such a failure has on the system and the urgency on fixing it.

The Paper is Organized as Follows. Following Sect. 2 with some related work, Sect. 3 presents our motivation. In Sect. 4 we present a theoretical background where we introduce the faulty input-output transition system (FIOTS) and some notions related to our approach. Later, we make a short introduction to diagnosis in Sect. 5 and testing in Sect. 6, where we define the testability property for FIOTS and for MBT. In Sect. 7 the Advanced-proxy is defined, and we prove several properties for our proposal framework. Moreover, in Sect. 8 we present an extended model with weighted failures. Finally, in Sect. 9 conclusions are drawn and future works are presented. Throughout the paper we illustrate the presented notions with examples.

2   Related Work

Fault diagnosis of discrete event systems has become an active research area in recent years. A formal foundation for fault diagnosis based on models that include both nominal and faulty behavior was introduced in [1,2] (which also included a diagnosability analysis). The system is modeled by a classical automaton with observable and unobservable events. Intuitively, its observable events correspond to controller commands and sensor readings, while the unobservable ones correspond to internal activity that is not recorded by sensors. The faults are also unobservable otherwise it would be trivial to detect them. The diagnosis problem deals with identifying which unobservable faults, if any, explain a given observed sequence of events based on the model of the system. If a system is diagnosable, it is always possible to determine whether some fault occurred in finite time without ambiguity.

Many extensions of [2] have been adopted and further developed by many groups. For example, to improve efficiency the twin plant approach has been introduced in [7,8]. Many modeling formalisms have been used such as automata, timed automata [9], its probability extensions [10] and Petri nets [11–13]. Additionally modular and distributed approaches have been proposed [14–16]. For a review on this topic refer to [17].

A weaker property, called manifestability has been presented in [4], which describes the capability of a system to manifest (i.e. to be distinguishable from any non faulty behavior) a fault occurrence in at least one context (i.e. one future behavior). This is in contrast to diagnosability, where all future behaviors of all fault occurrences should be distinguishable from all normal behaviors. Manifestability is the weakest property that requires the system to have a chance of identify the fault occurrence under fairness assumption over the branching chosen.

The theory of testing has become a strong subject of research, in particular, the application of formal methods in the area of model-driven testing has led to a better understanding of the notion of conformance between implementations and specifications. Automated generation methods for test suites from specifications have been developed [3,5,18,19], which have led to a new generation of powerful test generation and execution tools such as SpecExplorer [20], TorX [21] and TGV [22].

A clear advantage of a formal approach for testing is the provable soundness of the generated test suites, i.e. the property that each generated test suite will only reject implementations that do not conform to the given specification. In many cases an exhaustiveness result is obtained, i.e. the property that for each non-conforming implementation a test case can be generated that will expose all errors (cf. [5]). In practice, the above notion of exhaustiveness is usually problematic, since exhaustive test suites will contain infinitely many tests. This raises the question of test selection, i.e. the selection of well chosen, finite test suites that can be generated (and executed) within the available resources [23]. However, it is clear that some tests will not be executed before product delivery (maybe the longer ones or the non common ones, etc.).

On the other hand passive testing offers a continuous monitoring for systems under test without disturbing them while they are in operation. The **ioco** passive testing approach was introduced in [6], where traces are extracted by means of a proxy-tester which represents an intermediary between client applications and the implementation (i.e. without running in the same environment as the implementation). A combination of **ioco** passive testing and runtime verification was presented in [24].

The testability and diagnosability metrics standard (IEEE Std 1522) has been introduced in [25] to provide a formal foundation to the test community. A purpose of this standard is to provide a common basis for discussing and comparing testability/diagnosability characteristics of a given system. Although, there is not any formal definition of fault testability.

3   Motivation

Our research arose from the fact that diagnosis and testing consider faults in a different manner. As a starting point both consider faults as unobservable events. However, diagnosis considers expected faults, i.e. it considers that faults belong to the specification, while testing does not. Diagnosability (what is done before a diagnosis can be done) studies how do we have to modify the specification of a system in a way that these unobservable expected faults become diagnosable (meaning it does not look at the cause of a failure, but it considers that some observations imply that a fault occurred). On the other side, testing considers unexpected faults and it studies how we can realize that a fault occurred by observing the manifestation (i.e. failure) of that unexpected fault.

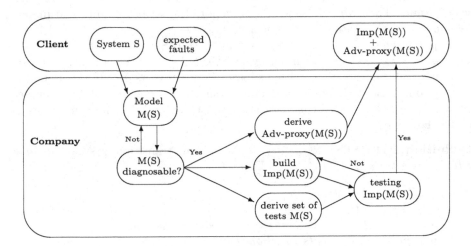

Fig. 1. Motivation

The idea behind our proposed framework is illustrated in Fig. 1. Suppose a client orders a system to be diagnosable for a set of faults already known that can occur (Why? Because the customer needs a means to check for possible problems to avoid major crashes). A company builds such a system from the given specification. Note that, if necessary, the specification has to be modified (by adding more observation, i.e. sensors) to satisfy the diagnosability property in order to achieve a correct diagnosis. This is followed by the testing phase, where a set of tests is derived but only a finite subset can be executed. Meanwhile, an Advanced-proxy (the passive Testing engine and the Diagnoser) is derived. Finally, after testing has been successfully performed the implemented system and the Advanced-proxy are delivered to the client. With the Advanced-proxy the client is able to perform, tests for failures from an incorrect implementation (which had not been caught in the inherently incomplete testing) and to diagnose inherent unobservable faults.

The famous *m-consecutive-k-out-of-n system* can benefit from our approach. This system consists of a sequence of n ordered components along a line such that the system works if and only if less than k consecutive components in the system fail [26], but if more than k consecutive components do fail, the system stops working. A real-life example of this kind of system is a gas pipe going upward with several pumps.

Therefore, in the specification of this system, the failing of k consecutive components is a diagnosable fault, however, if a larger number of consecutive components fails then a failure is observed and the system stops working.

4 Preliminaries

We use standard definitions for labeled transition systems. Let Σ be a finite set of events. Then, with Σ^* and Σ^ω we denote the set of all finite and infinite sequences over Σ. With $\sigma \sqsubseteq \rho$ we denote that $\sigma \in \Sigma^*$ is a prefix of $\rho \in \Sigma^*$.

A *faulty input-output transition system* is a FIOTS with the set of observable events, Σ_{obs}, subdivided into input events Σ_I and output events Σ_O; and a set of unobservable events $\Sigma_{\neg obs}$ with a subset of faulty events Σ_F. In this paper, to simplify our presentation we consider that there is only one type of fault denoted f, i.e. $\Sigma_F = \{f\}$, as in [2] this restriction can be extended to multiple types of faults. Formally:

Definition 1 (FIOTS). *A faulty input-output transition system, denoted FIOTS, is a tuple $L = \langle Q, q_0, \Sigma_{obs}, \Sigma_{\neg obs}, T \rangle$, where*

- *Q is a finite set of states;*
- *$q_0 \in Q$ is the initial state;*
- *$T \subseteq Q \times \Sigma \times Q$ is a finite branching transition relation;*
- *Σ is a finite set of events partitioned into: a set of observable events Σ_{obs}, subdivided in a set of input events Σ_I and output events Σ_O (i.e. $\Sigma_{obs} = \Sigma_I \cup \Sigma_O$ & $\Sigma_I \cap \Sigma_O = \emptyset$); and a set of unobservable events $\Sigma_{\neg obs}$ containing a subset of fault events Σ_F (i.e. $\Sigma_F \subseteq \Sigma_{\neg obs}$). With $\Sigma = \Sigma_{obs} \cup \Sigma_{\neg obs}$ and $\Sigma_{obs} \cap \Sigma_{\neg obs} = \emptyset$.*

We use '?' to denote input events ($a? \in \Sigma_I$) and '!' to denote outputs events ($a! \in \Sigma_O$). With τ we denote the unobservable events and in case we like to specify that it is a fault we denote it by f.

Figure 2(a) depicts an example $FIOTS = \langle \{q_1, q_2, q_3, q_4, q_5, q_6, q_7, q_8\}, q_1, \{a?, c?, b!, c!\}, \{f\}, \{(q_1, a?, q_2), (q_2, a?, q_5), (q_5, b!, q_2), (q_1, f, q_3), (q_3, a?, q_6), (q_6, a?, q_7), (q_7, c!, q_6), (q_3, c?, q_8), (q_8, c!, q_8), (q_8, c!, q_4), (q_4, c!, q_4), (q_1, c?, q_4)\} \rangle$, which will be used throughout this paper as a running example.

Definition 2. *Let $L = \langle Q, q_0, \Sigma_{obs}, \Sigma_{\neg obs}, T \rangle$ be a FIOTS, then*

- *A path in L is a sequence $\rho = q_0 a_0 q_1 a_1 \ldots$ such that for all i we have $(q_i, a_i, q_{i+1}) \in T$. We denote by $\mathsf{paths}(q)$ the set of paths starting in q. The set $\mathsf{cycle}(L)$ is the set of all cycle that occur in L, where a cycle is a paths starting and ending in the same state. The trace σ of a path ρ, is the sequence $\sigma = a_0 a_1 \ldots$ of events in Σ occurring in ρ, so $\sigma \in \Sigma^*$;*
- *We write $q \xrightarrow{a} q'$ in case $(q, a, q') \in T$, we use $q \xrightarrow{a}$ to denote that there exists a state q' such that $q \xrightarrow{a} q'$, and we use $q \rightarrow$ to denote that there exists event a and a state q' such that $q \xrightarrow{a} q'$;*
- *We write $q \overset{\epsilon}{\Rightarrow} q'$ in case $q = q'$ or there exist states $q_1, \cdots, q_{n-1}$ and unobservable events $a_1, \cdots, a_n \in \Sigma_{\neg obs}$ such that $q \xrightarrow{a_1} q_1, \cdots, q_{n-1} \xrightarrow{a_n} q'$ (note that a_i can be a f). For a given an event $a \in \Sigma$ we write $q \overset{a}{\Rightarrow} q'$ if there exist q_1, q_2 such that $q \overset{\epsilon}{\Rightarrow} q_1, q_1 \xrightarrow{a} q_2, q_2 \overset{\epsilon}{\Rightarrow} q'$. And also, for a given observable event $a \in \Sigma_{obs}$ we write $q \overset{a}{\Rightarrow}_F q'$ if there exist q_1, q_2 such that $q \overset{\epsilon}{\Rightarrow} q_1, q_1 \xrightarrow{f} q_2, q_2 \overset{a}{\Rightarrow} q'$. Moreover, given a trace $\sigma = a_1 \ldots a_n$ we write $q \overset{\sigma}{\Rightarrow} q'$ if exist states $q_1 \cdots q_{n-1}$ such that $q \overset{a_1}{\Rightarrow} q_1 \ldots q_{n-1} \overset{a_n}{\Rightarrow} q'$;*
- *In case σ is finite, with $|\sigma|$ we denote the length of the trace σ. Given $n \in \mathbb{N}$ and a trace $\sigma \in \mathsf{traces}(L)$ with $n \leq |\sigma|$, we denote by σ^n the initial n sequence $a_0 a_1 \ldots a_n$ of events in Σ occurring in σ;*
- *The observable trace of a trace σ, denoted $obs(\sigma)$, is the sequence $a_0 a_1 \ldots$ of events in Σ_{obs} occurring in σ;*
- *We denote by $\mathsf{traces}^F(L)$ the set of traces in L that end with a fault, i.e. $\mathsf{traces}^F(L) = \{\sigma \in \mathsf{traces}(L) \mid \sigma \in \Sigma^* \Sigma_F\}$, $\mathsf{traces}^\omega_F(L)$ the set of all infinite traces in L with at least one fault, i.e. $\mathsf{traces}^\omega_F(L) = \{\sigma \in \mathsf{traces}(L) \mid \sigma \in \Sigma^\omega \wedge \exists \sigma' \in \mathsf{traces}^F(L) \wedge \sigma' \sqsubseteq \sigma\}$, $\mathsf{traces}^\omega_{\neg F}(L)$ the set of all infinite traces in L without any fault, i.e. $\mathsf{traces}^\omega_{\neg F}(L) = \{\sigma \in \mathsf{traces}(L) \mid \sigma \in \Sigma^\omega \wedge f \notin \sigma\}$;*
- *Given a natural number $k \in \mathbb{N}$ we denote by $\mathsf{traces}^{F,k}(L)$, the set of all traces σ such that there exists another trace σ' that ends in a fault and σ extends σ' with at least $|\sigma'| + k$ events, i.e. $\mathsf{traces}^{F,k}(L) = \{\sigma \in \mathsf{traces}(L) \mid \exists \sigma' \in \mathsf{traces}^F(L) \wedge |\sigma'| + k \leq |\sigma| \wedge \sigma' \sqsubseteq \sigma\}$;*
- *Given a trace $\sigma \in \mathsf{traces}(L)$, we write L **after** σ to denote all the states that we can reach after the observable events of σ, i.e. L **after** $\sigma = \{q \in Q \mid q_0 \overset{\sigma}{\Rightarrow} q\}$.*

For example, in Fig. 2(a), $\pi_1 = q_1 a?q_2 a?q_5 b!q_2$ is a path, $\pi_2 = q_2 a?q_5 b!q_2$ is a cycle, $\mathsf{trace}(\pi_1) = a?a?b!$ and $|\mathsf{trace}(\pi_1)| = 3$. Moreover, if $\sigma = fa?a?c!a?c!$ then its initial sequence until 3 is $\sigma^3 = fa?a?$, its observable trace is $obs(\sigma) = a?a?c!a?c!$ and $f \in \sigma$ denotes that there is an error event in this trace.

We restrict our work to *convergent* and *live* FIOTS, meaning that for all $L \in$ FIOTS, each cycle has at least one observable event and for all states there exists a transition initiated in that state, i.e.

$$\forall \pi \in \mathsf{cycle}(L) : \exists a \in \Sigma_{obs} : a \in \pi \tag{1}$$

$$\forall q \in Q : q \rightarrow \tag{2}$$

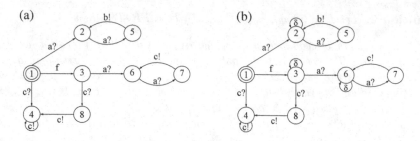

Fig. 2. (a) Faulty input-output transition system, (b) FIOTS with δ-transitions

5   Diagnosis and Diagnosability

Diagnosis is the process of observing the system in order to recognize if a fault occurred. This is based on the assumption that to be able to do diagnosis the observations that assure a fault existence are known [1,2]. The fact that in this paper we consider only one type of fault, does not imply that systems can have only one fault, systems can have several instances of that type of fault. To perform a correct fault diagnosis (without ambiguity) faults must be diagnosable. The fault diagnosability property determines which observation sequence of a system, if any, explains a given anticipated fault (modeled us an unobservable event). The idea is that, if the system is diagnosable, each fault occurrence generates a unique sequence of observable events that explains that fault. The notion of diagnosability was introduced in [2]. Informally, a fault f is diagnosable if it is possible to detect it using a record of observed events, in a finite delay. On the contrary, a fault is not diagnosable if there exist two infinite paths from the initial state with the same infinite sequence of observable events but only one of them contains the fault and the other does not. In such a case it cannot be concluded whether a fault has or has not occurred.

Definition 3 (Diagnosability). *Let L be a FIOTS, then L is* diagnosable *if and only if the following holds,* $\forall f \in \Sigma_F : \exists n \in \mathbb{N} : \forall \rho \in \text{traces}^{F,n}(L)$:

$$\forall \alpha \in \text{traces}(L) : obs(\rho) = obs(\alpha) : f \in \alpha$$

To verify the diagnosability property the twin-plant method was presented in [7], where a polynomial check is done in contrast to the initial exponential approach [2]. The verification of diagnosability is done by putting two observers of the system in parallel. An observer is a non-deterministic system with the same set of observable traces as the initial system with states which estimate the possible system states. The states of an observer are reached by taking only observable transitions.

In order to perform a correct fault diagnosis (without ambiguity) the fault system specification (given as FIOTS) must be diagnosable. Once we ensure that all faults in a system are diagnosable (if it is necessary some sensors are added [1]) the idea is to build a Diagnoser, a system that recognizes whether some traces happen, that imply a fault occurrence. Following the ideas presented in [2], given a fault diagnosable system the diagnosis will be without ambiguity, i.e. it gives a correct explanation of fault occurrence.

Let L be a FIOTS, then a Diagnoser of L is a deterministic FIOTS that can be seen as an extension of a deterministic observer of L, which gives: (1) an estimate of the current state of the system after the occurrence of every observable event; (2) an information on potential past fault occurrences in the form of fault labels attached to the state estimation. Label F is used to denote states that can be reached by a trace containing some event $f \in \Sigma_F$, whereas label N is used for states that can be reached by a trace that does not contain any event in Σ_F.

Definition 4 (Diagnoser). *Given $S = \langle Q^S, q_0^S, \Sigma_{obs}^S, \Sigma_{\neg obs}^S, T^S \rangle$ a FIOTS, its Diagnoser $D = \langle Q^D, q_0^D, \Sigma_{obs}^D, \Sigma_{\neg obs}^D, T^D \rangle$ is defined as follows*

- $Q^D \subseteq \mathcal{P}(Q^S \times \{N, F\})$;
- $q_0^D = \{(q_0^S, N)\}$;
- $\Sigma_{obs}^D = \Sigma_{obs}^S$;
- $\Sigma_{\neg obs}^D = \emptyset$;
- $T^D = \{(Q, a, Q') | \exists\, q_1, q_2 \in Q^S : (q_1, l) \in Q : \forall\, (q_2, l') \in Q' :$
  $\qquad (q_1 \overset{a}{\Rightarrow}_F q_2 \in T^S \wedge l' = F) \vee (q_1 \overset{a}{\Rightarrow} q_2 \in T^S \wedge (l = F \wedge l' = F))$
  $\qquad \vee (q_1 \overset{a}{\Rightarrow} q_2 \in T^S \wedge q_1 \overset{a}{\not\Rightarrow}_F q_2 \in T^S \wedge (l = N \wedge l' = N))\}$

Particularly, if a state Q is reached in a Diagnoser D after a trace σ, i.e. $Q = (D \text{ after } \sigma)$, such that for a diagnosable f with n the number that makes f diagnosable, i.e. $\sigma \in \text{traces}^{F,n}(S)$, then

$$\nexists\, q' \in Q^S : (q', N) \in Q.$$

Figure 3 presents a Diagnoser for our example from Fig. 2(a). The Diagnoser performs diagnosis while it observes on-line the behavior of the system. Faults are diagnosed by comparing the labels associated with the state estimation. For example in Fig. 2(a) observing $a?a?c!$ we can conclude that a fault occurred, because the reached state has only a label F. Note that observing just $a?a?$ we are not certain yet if some fault occurred or not, because we have label N and label F.

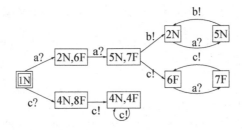

Fig. 3. Diagnoser for our running example

Generally, diagnosability is a very strong property that requires a high number of sensors. Consequently, it is not rare that developing a diagnosable system is too expensive.

6   Testing and Testability

Testing is the process of executing an implementation trying to realize if a failure occurred. Testing should produce observable, unambiguous and consistent results. If a failure occurred it is assumed that there exists a fault that produced that failure. Following this idea, we treat faults as unobservable and failures as observations that tell us that an unobservable fault occurred.

As an example consider the system in Fig. 2(a), clearly the fault f is not diagnosable, because for any k value some traces with k events after a f occurrence we are not able to realize if the fault occurred or not. However if we observe $a?\ \widehat{a?c}!$ we can be sure that fault f occurred. Therefore, we try to define testability as the property that describes this type of situations.

Testability. We consider that a failure is the manifestation of a fault occurrence. So, if a testing procedure is not able to contemplate a given failures then the fault that produces it is not testable with that procedure. For example, if a testing procedure only contemplates events and not timing, it can not test a delay. Then, we consider fault testability as the fault ability to be tested.

We formally define the testability property over $FIOTS$ as the property a fault has to have such that its existence can be detected. Thus, we consider a fault f testable if there exists an observation (a failure) that tells us that each time we see that observation we can be sure that f occurs.

Definition 5 (Testability). *Let L be a $FIOTS$ we say that a fault f is testable in L if and only if*

$$\exists\ \sigma \in \text{traces}^F(L) : \exists\ \sigma' \in \text{traces}(L) : \sigma \sqsubseteq \sigma' : \forall\ \sigma'' \in \text{traces}(L) :$$
$$\text{if } obs(\sigma') = obs(\sigma'') \text{ then } f \in \sigma''$$

Moreover we call σ' the failure that denotes the presence of f.

It may be advantageous to realize which faults we can not test, i.e. when a fault f is not *testable*. A fault f is not testable if and only if

$$\forall\ \sigma \in \text{traces}^F(L) : \forall\ \sigma' \in \text{traces}(L) : \sigma \sqsubseteq \sigma' : \exists\ \sigma'' \in \text{traces}(L) : obs(\sigma')$$
$$= obs(\sigma'') \land f \notin \sigma''$$

This means that there exists a fault that, for all traces that contain that fault those traces always have another trace, with the same observability, that does not contain that fault. In other words it is not possible to observe a behavior that shows that a fault occurred, without ambiguity; then that fault is not testable.

Theorem 1. *If fault f is diagnosable in FIOTSL, then it is testable in L.*

Proof. Because f is diagnosable lets k be the natural number that makes f diagnosable in L. So, we know from diagnosability definition that $\forall \sigma \in \text{traces}^{F,k}(L)$: $\forall \sigma' \in \text{traces}(L) : obs(\sigma) = obs(\sigma') : f \in \sigma'$ then we know that at least one trace has all its continuations with f, what is exactly the requirement for the testability definition. □

6.1 Model-Based Testing

Model-based testing (MBT) relies on models of the system under test and its specification to automate test case derivation, test verdict, etc. The idea is that the testing process tries to find a discrepancy between the specification model and the implementation.

We redefine testability but now in MBT. We consider that there exists an unobservable fault in the implementation that produces an observable failure and it shows a discrepancy with respect to the specification, i.e. there is no trace observably equivalent in the specification, we consider this discrepancy a failure.

Definition 6 (MB-testability). *Let S be a specification and P an implementation both in FIOTS then we say that a fault f is MBtestable in P if and only if*

$$\exists \sigma \in \text{traces}^F(P) : \exists \sigma' \in \text{traces}(P) : \sigma \sqsubseteq \sigma' : \nexists \sigma'' \in \text{traces}(S) : obs(\sigma') = obs(\sigma'')$$

Moreover we call σ' the failure that denotes the presence of f.

The biggest difference here is that fault testability concerns the observability of the implementation and the model specification.

Lemma 1. *Given a specification $S \in FIOTS$ and an implementation $P \in FIOTS$ then if f is MBtestable in P then there exists a failure in P.*

Proof. Because f is MBtestable we know that there exists a trace $\sigma \in \text{traces}^F$ $(P) : \exists \sigma' \in \text{traces}(P)$ with $\sigma \sqsubseteq \sigma'$ such that does not exist $\sigma_S \in \text{traces}(S)$ with $obs(\sigma') = obs(\sigma_S)$. Therefore σ' is the failure, because it proves that the implementation shows a behavior not specified. □

6.2 The ioco Model-Based Testing

We recall the basic theory about test derivation from faulty input-output transition systems similarly as it was initially defined in [5] for input-output transition systems. Although, our approach follows the **ioco** testing theory, it can be applied to any testing relation with tree-shape tests.

An important contribution of the **ioco** testing theory is the quiescence concept, i.e. the absence of outputs events in a given state. Trace inclusion with the quiescence concept is more powerful than simple trace inclusion. Thus, we incorporate quiescence in specifications, by adding a self-loop $q \xrightarrow{\delta} q$ labeled with a special label δ to each quiescent state q, i.e.

$$\forall\, q \in Q \text{ with } \forall\, a \in \Sigma_{O,\tau} : q \xrightarrow{a} \quad\quad (3)$$

and consider δ as an output event. From now on we assume that $FIOTS$ can perform a δ event as an output event, i.e. for a given system L we consider δ is in Σ_O^L. In cases we need to denote that a $FIOTS$ is not extended with δ transitions, we specially denoted as $S_{\neg\delta}$. Note that because faults are not observable we consider them as τ transitions.

So, from now on we assume that systems can perform a δ event as an output event, and we consider our systems extended with δ-transitions as in Fig. 2(b). Moreover, we lift all concepts and notations (e.g. traces, etc.) that have been defined for $FIOTS$s to $FIOTS$s extended with δ-events. Then $\sigma = a?\delta a?$ is a trace in our example from Fig. 2(b).

Definition 7. *Let* $L = \langle Q, q_0, \Sigma_{obs}, \Sigma_{\neg obs}, T \rangle$ *be a FIOTS, then given a set of states* $Q' \subseteq Q$, *we write* $out(Q')$ *to the set of output events that are allowed in all states of the set* Q', *i.e.* $out(Q') = \{a! \in \Sigma_O | \exists\, q \in Q' : q \xrightarrow{a!}\} \cup \{\delta | \exists\, q \in Q' : q \xrightarrow{\delta}\}$.

As normally is done in model-based testing, we restrict our work to *input-enabling FIOTS* implementations, meaning that for every P implementation all inputs are accepted in all states, i.e.

$$\forall\, q \in Q : \forall\, a? \in \Sigma_I : q \xrightarrow{a?} \quad\quad (4)$$

We adapt the **ioco** testing relation to relate an input-enabled implementation with a specification modeled as $FIOTS$, where the output of the implementation should be a subset of the allowed specification outputs.

Definition 8. *Given a specification* $S \in FIOTS$ *and an input-enabled implementation* $P \in FIOTS$ *then:*

P **ioco** S *if and only if* $\forall\, \sigma \in \mathsf{traces}(S) : out(P \text{ after } \sigma) \subseteq out(S \text{ after } \sigma)$

In this definition we consider that traces can contain δ, which are called δ-Straces (meaning that δ is considered as a normal event). Note, that as in the initial **ioco** definition in [5] our traces contain: observable events ($\Sigma_{I,O}$), unobservable events (τ and f) and δ-events (δ included in Σ_O).

The **ioco** test cases are adaptive, that is, the next event to be performed (observe the system, stimulate the system or stop the test) may depend on the test history, i.e. the trace observed so far. If, after a trace σ, the Tester decides to stimulate the system with an input $a?$, then the new test history becomes $\sigma a?$. If, after a trace σ, the Tester decides for an observation, the test accounts for all possible continuations $\sigma b!$ with $b! \in \Sigma_O$ an output event (again including quiescent event). The Tester contains two special states $pass$ and $fail, pass \neq fail$, so that a Tester can stop the recursion using the $pass$ state, and in case that an output event is not accepted by the specification the Tester uses the $fail$ state to denote it. The **ioco** theory requires that tests are *fail fast,* i.e. stop after the discovery of the first failure, and never fail immediately after an input. Formally, a test case consists of the set of all possible test histories obtained in this way.

Definition 9

– A test case *(or test) t for an FIOTS L is a finite, prefix-closed subset of Σ^* such that*
  - *if $\sigma a? \in t \wedge a? \in \Sigma_I$, then $\sigma b \notin t$ for any $b \in \Sigma$ with $a? \neq b$;*
  - *if $\sigma a! \in t \wedge a! \in \Sigma_O$, then $\sigma b! \in t$ for all $b! \in \Sigma_O$;*
  - *if $\sigma \notin \mathsf{traces}(L)$, then no proper extension of σ is contained in t.*
– *The length $|t|$ of test t is the length of the longest trace in t, i.e. $|t| = \max_{\sigma \in t} |\sigma|$.*

Note that in this definition we consider that δ belongs to Σ_O.

Figure 4 shows tree different tests of the specification presented in Fig. 2(b). The failure states are represented as an octagon with a cross meaning that the system is in a failure if it arrives to that state, we call them error-states.

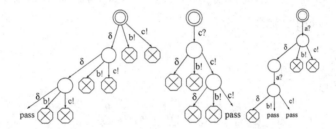

Fig. 4. Tests

Because **ioco**-testing is proven [5] to be sound and exhaustive we know that all failures can be exposed by its tests. This means that if a fault is testable then it can be detected by the **ioco**-testing.

7   Advanced-Proxy

The idea of our Advanced-proxy is to combine diagnosis checking of modeled faults with testing of failures. We propose to augment the Diagnoser with error transitions that will end up in failure states. In a sense we treat all kinds of errors, i.e. expected unobservable faults and failures from unexpected unobservable faults. One of the main advantages of our method is that we extend the testing phase, approaching us to exhaustive testing.

Since we propose to do passive testing in a proxy style, we do not interfere with the normal behavior of the system. We only require logs of the observable information to conclude if an expected fault or an unexpected failure happens. Following some ideas from passive testing of [6], we observe the system to be checked without any interaction with it.

Given that the Diagnoser is a deterministic model of the system with more information in their states, we can augment it with the information of where to go (to an error-state) when a unexpected event comes, i.e. an output event not allowed by the implementation or an input event not expected by the specification. First, we add to the Diagnoser an error-state that subsumes all outputs events that were not allowed by the specification. Second, we add another state, called M-state, that subsumes all input events that were not expected by the specification. Note that, because we consider implementations as input-enabled our second M-state will inform us about an input event that is allowed by the implementation but should not be there, meaning that the implementation is used incorrectly. The following definition explains our augmented procedure to create the Advanced-proxy. It is important to note that the Diagnoser used in our construction of the Advanced-proxy is the Diagnoser from the specification before its δ-extension, i.e. $D(S_{\neg\delta})$. But to build the proxy-tester part we consider that specifications are extended with δ-events.

Definition 10 (Advanced-proxy). *Given* $D(S_{\neg\delta}) = \langle Q^D, q_0^D, \Sigma_{obs}^D, \Sigma_{\neg obs}^D, T^D \rangle$ *a Diagnoser checker of the specification* $S = \langle Q^S, q_0^S, \Sigma_{obs}^S, \Sigma_{\neg obs}^S, T^S \rangle$, *then its Advanced-proxy* $A = \langle Q^A, q_0^A, \Sigma_{obs}^A, \Sigma_{\neg obs}^A, T^A \rangle$ *is defined as follows:*

- $Q^A = Q^D \cup \{E\} \cup \{M\}$;
- $q_0^A = q_0^D$;
- $\Sigma_{obs}^A = \Sigma_{obs}^D$;
- $\Sigma_{\neg obs}^A = \Sigma_{\neg obs}^D = \emptyset$;
- $T^A = T^D \cup$

$$\{(Q, a!, E)| \forall\, a! \in \Sigma_O^S \cup \{\delta\} : \forall\, Q \in Q^D : \forall\, q' \in Q^S : q' \in Q \underset{a!}{\wedge} q' \overset{a!}{\not\to}\} \cup$$
$$\{(Q, a?, M)| \forall\, a? \in \Sigma_I^S : \forall\, Q \in Q^D : \forall\, q' \in Q^S : q' \in Q \wedge q' \overset{a?}{\not\to}\}$$

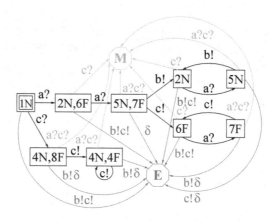

Fig. 5. Diagnoser($S_{\neg\delta}$) + Tester(S) = Advanced-proxy

Figure 5 shows the Advanced-proxy for our running example. The idea of considering the M-state becomes interesting when we think that implementations can interact with a malicious user that is trying to take advantage of the implementation input-enabled property.

Given that we consider the δ extension of our specification an interesting question arises: why we do not consider that after observing a δ event in the first state (q_1) we can be sure that a fault occurred? Even this is right, in this case we are doing diagnosis where we only diagnose faults that are diagnosable as in Definition 3, and in this case f is not diagnosable. This situation is very similar to the one considered in our previous paper [4] where we do not consider all futures but only some of them to be sure a fault occurred.

Corollary 1. *Given $S = \langle Q^S, q_0^S, \Sigma_{obs}^S, \Sigma_{\neg obs}^S, T^S \rangle$ a FIOTS specification, with the Advanced-proxy $A = \langle Q^A, q_0^A, \Sigma_{obs}^A, \Sigma_{\neg obs}^A, T^A \rangle$ of S and f is a diagnosable fault in S, then*

$$\exists\, \sigma \in \mathsf{traces}(S) : \exists\, Q \in Q^A : Q = (A \text{ after } \sigma) \text{ and } \nexists\, q' \in S : (q', N) \in Q$$

Proof. Suppose $\sigma \in \mathsf{traces}^{F,n}(S)$ with n be the number that makes f diagnosable in S. Given $D = \langle Q^D, q_0^D, \Sigma_{obs}^D, \Sigma_{\neg obs}^D, T^D \rangle$ the Diagnoser for $S_{\neg \delta}$, then by Definition 4 we know that σ is in $\mathsf{traces}(D)$. Moreover, we have that for any state $Q \in Q^D$ such that $Q = (D \text{ after } \sigma)$ then does not exists any state q' in the specification S such that (q', N) is in Q.

Now, by Definition 10 we know that A has the same transition as D plus some new transition going to states M and E. So we know that if σ is in D then σ is in A. Moreover because system A do not modify labels on states we can be sure that for all state $Q \in Q^A$ such that $Q = (A \text{ after } \sigma)$ then does not exists any state q' in the specification S such that (q', N) is in Q. $\square$

Corollary 1 proves that if a specification has a diagnosable fault it could be caught by the Advanced-proxy by arriving to a state where all the labels will be with F.

Lemma 2. *Given $P = \langle Q^P, q_0^P, \Sigma_{obs}^P, \Sigma_{\neg obs}^P, T^P \rangle$ be a FIOTS implementation of $S = \langle Q^S, q_0^S, \Sigma_{obs}^S, \Sigma_{\neg obs}^S, T^S \rangle$ a FIOTS specification, with the Advanced-proxy $A = \langle Q^A, q_0^A, \Sigma_{obs}^A, \Sigma_{\neg obs}^A, T^A \rangle$ of S, and P i̸oco S then*

$$\exists\, \sigma \in \mathsf{traces}(P) : \sigma = \sigma' a \wedge \sigma' \in \mathsf{traces}(S) \wedge$$
$$\sigma \notin \mathsf{traces}(S) \wedge \sigma \in \mathsf{traces}(A) \wedge E = (A \text{ after } \sigma)$$

Proof. Given that the **ioco** testing theory is proven to be sound and exhaustive [5] to prove this lemma it is enough to prove that given any test t derived from S with the **ioco** algorithm then for any trace σ that ends in a *fail* state in that test t this trace is in A and $E = (A \text{ after } \sigma)$.

Now because σ in not a specification trace it means that $\sigma = \sigma' a$ with $a \in \Sigma_O(S)$, $\sigma' \in \mathsf{traces}(S)$ and $a \notin out(S \text{ after } \sigma')$. By Definition 10 we know that if σ' is in $\mathsf{traces}(S)$ then $\sigma' \in \mathsf{traces}(A)$ and because $a \notin out(S \text{ after } \sigma')$ then $E = (A \text{ after } \sigma)$. $\square$

Lemma 2 shows that if a system implementation is **ioco** incorrect with respect to a specification then it could be caught by the Advanced-proxy by arriving to the E state.

Lemma 3. *Given* $S = \langle Q^S, q_0^S, \Sigma_{obs}^S, \Sigma_{\neg obs}^S, T^S \rangle$ *a FIOTS specification, with the Advanced-proxy* $A = \langle Q^A, q_0^A, \Sigma_{obs}^A, \Sigma_{\neg obs}^A, T^A \rangle$ *of* S, *and* $\exists \ \sigma \in \mathrm{traces}(S)$: $\exists \ a? \in \Sigma_I^S : \sigma a? \notin \mathrm{traces}(S)$ *then*

$$\sigma a? \in \mathrm{traces}(A) \wedge M = (A \ \textbf{after} \ \sigma a?)$$

Proof. Because $\sigma \in \mathrm{traces}(S)$ we know that $\sigma \in \mathrm{traces}(A)$ and because $\sigma a? \notin \mathrm{traces}(S)$ using Definition 10 we know that for all inputs that are not specified the Advance-proxy will end up in the M state, i.e. $M = (A \ \textbf{after} \ \sigma a?)$.   □

Lemma 3 proves that for inputs that are not specified in the specification the Advanced-proxy will manifest them by arriving to the M state.

Composition. The integration of an implementation with our Advanced-proxy can be modeled by putting the components in parallel while synchronizing on their common events. Note that here we do not relate inputs with outputs and we do not make them outputs as normally it is done in the literature. Instead we relate the same events, inputs with inputs and outputs with outputs. We take this decision with the idea to be as transparent as we can be with the proxy, so that a user of the implementation does not notice the proxy presence. This is done in that way so that the existence of this proxy does not interrupt the normal behavior of our system. The synchronization between an implementation P and an Advanced-proxy A is denoted by $P||A$.

Definition 11 (composition). *Given* $P = \langle Q^P, q_0^P, \Sigma_{obs}^P, \Sigma_{\neg obs}^P, T^P \rangle$ *be a FIOTS implementation of* $S = \langle Q^S, q_0^S, \Sigma_{obs}^S, \Sigma_{\neg obs}^S, T^S \rangle$ *a FIOTS specification and* $A = \langle Q^A, q_0^A, \Sigma_{obs}^A, \Sigma_{\neg obs}^A, T^A \rangle$ *the Advanced-proxy of* S, *the parallel composition* $P||A = \langle Q^{P||A}, q_0^{P||A}, \Sigma_{obs}^{P||A}, \Sigma_{\neg obs}^{P||A}, T^{P||A} \rangle$ *is defined as follows:*

- $Q^{P||A} = \{q_1||Q_2 : q_1 \in Q^P \wedge Q_2 \in Q^A\}$;
- $q_0^{P||A} = q_0^P||q_0^A$;
- $\Sigma^{P||A} = \Sigma^P$;
- $T^{P||A}$ *is the minimal set satisfying the following inference rules* $(a \in \Sigma_{I,O,\tau}^{P||A})$:

$$\begin{array}{ll} q_1 \xrightarrow{a} q_1', a \notin \Sigma_{I,O}^A & \vdash q_1||Q_2 \xrightarrow{a} q_1'||Q_2 \\ q_1 \xrightarrow{a} q_1', Q_2 = \{E\} & \vdash q_1||Q_2 \xrightarrow{a} q_1'||Q_2 \\ q_1 \xrightarrow{a} q_1', Q_2 = \{M\} & \vdash q_1||Q_2 \xrightarrow{a} q_1'||Q_2 \\ Q_2 \xrightarrow{a} Q_2', a \notin \Sigma_{I,O}^P & \vdash q_1||Q_2 \xrightarrow{a} q_1||Q_2' \\ q_1 \xrightarrow{a} q_1', Q_2 \xrightarrow{a} Q_2', a \neq \tau \vdash q_1||Q_2 \xrightarrow{a} q_1'||Q_2' \end{array}$$

Note that, because our Advanced-proxy does not have internal transitions, i.e. τ, it is output enabled and the implementation is input-enabled then $(Q_2 \xrightarrow{a} Q_2')$ does not happen. Another important part of this definition is that if the Advanced-proxy arrives to states E or M it does not block the implementation but it stays in the same state.

8 Advanced-Proxy over Weighted Fault Model

We can extend our Advanced-proxy with the idea that specifications are models that, not only, provide the expected behaviour but also they can provide the unexpected behaviour. Moreover, they can give a severity of the unexpected events. Following the ideas from [23] we present the weighted fault models.

Definition 12 (WFM). *A* weighted fault model *over* Σ_{obs} *is a function* $w : \Sigma_{obs}^* \to \mathbb{R}^{\geq 0}$ *such that*

$$0 \leq \sum_{\sigma \in \Sigma_{obs}^*} w(\sigma)$$

Thus, a WFM w assigns a non-negative error weight to each trace $\sigma \in \Sigma_{obs}^*$. If $w(\sigma) = 0$, then σ represents a correct system behaviour; if $w(\sigma) > 0$, then σ represents an incorrect behaviour and $w(\sigma)$ denotes the severity of the error. The higher $w(\sigma)$, the worse that error. We sometimes refer to traces $\sigma \in \Sigma_{obs}^*$ with $w(\sigma) > 0$ as *error traces* and traces with $w(\sigma) = 0$ as *correct traces*.

An Enriched Specification is a FIOTS L augmented with a state weight function r. The FIOTS L is the behavioral specification of the system, i.e. its traces represent the correct system behaviours. Hence, these traces will be assigned error weight 0; traces not in L are erroneous and get an error weight through r, as explained below.

Definition 13 (ES). *An Enriched Specification E is a pair (S, r), where $S = \langle Q^S, q_0^S, \Sigma_{obs}^S, \Sigma_{\neg obs}^S, T^S \rangle$ is a FIOTS and $r : Q^S \times \Sigma_O \to \mathbb{R}^{\geq 0}$. We require that, if $r(q, a) > 0$, then there is no a-successor of q in E, i.e. there is no $q' \in Q^S$ such that $(q, a, q') \in T$.*

We denote the components of E by S_E and r_E and leave out the subscript E if it is clear from the context. We lift all concepts and notations (e.g. traces, paths, etc.) that have been defined for FIOTSs to Es.

We wish to create a WFM from the ES E, using r to assign weights to traces not in L. If there is no outgoing a-transition in q, then the idea is that, for a trace σ ending in q, the (incorrect) trace σa gets weight $r(q, a)$.

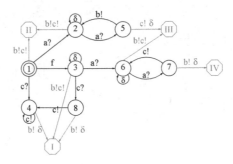

Fig. 6. Spec + faults + failures + weights = Enriched Spec

Definition 14 (w_E). *Given an enriched specification $E = (S, r)$ we define the function $w_E : \Sigma^* \to \mathbb{R}^{\geq 0}$ by*

$$w_E(\varepsilon) = 0 \qquad w_E(\sigma a) = \begin{cases} min\{r(q, a) \mid q_0 \overset{\sigma}{\Rightarrow} q\} & \text{if } \exists\, r(q, a) \\ 0 & \text{otherwise} \end{cases}$$

It is proven that given an enriched specification E then, if $w_E(\sigma a) > 0$, then $\sigma \in \mathsf{traces}(E)$, but $\sigma a \notin \mathsf{traces}(E)$. So, we create our Enriched-advanced-proxy similarly as we did the Advanced-proxy but for all erroneous outputs from the specification instead of going to the E-state now they go to a state that represents the severity of producing that output accordingly with the specification.

Figure 6 shows the Enriched Specification for our running example, where to simplify the figure we use roman numbers, so $r(q_1, c!) = 2, r(q_1, b!) = 2$, $r(q_5, \delta) = 3$, etc. It consists of the specification of expected behavior and the severity of unexpected output events.

Definition 15 (Enriched-advanced-proxy). *Given a Diagnoser checker $D = \langle Q^D, q_0^D, \Sigma_{obs}^D, \Sigma_{\neg obs}^D, T^D \rangle$ of a system $S = \langle Q^S, q_0^S, \Sigma_{obs}^S, \Sigma_{\neg obs}^S, T^S \rangle$ and $E = (S, r)$ a enriched specification, $A = \langle Q^A, q_0^A, \Sigma_{obs}^A, \Sigma_{\neg obs}^A, T^A \rangle$ the Enriched-advanced-proxy is defined as follows:*

- $Q^A = \bigcup_{\forall\, r(q,a)=k} k \cup Q^D \cup \{M\}$;
- $q_0^A = q_0^D$;
- $\Sigma_{obs}^A = \Sigma_{obs}^D$;
- $\Sigma_{\neg obs}^A = \Sigma_{\neg obs}^D = \emptyset$;
- $T^A = T^D \cup$
  $\{(Q, a!, k) | \forall_a a! \in \Sigma_O^S \cup \{\delta\} : \forall\, Q \in Q^D : \forall\, q' \in Q^S : q' \in Q : k = min$
  $\{r(q', a!) | q' \not\rightarrow\}\}$
  $\cup \{(Q, a?, M) | \forall\, Q \in Q^D : \forall\, a? \in \Sigma_I^S : \forall\, q' \in Q^S : q' \in Q \land q' \overset{a?}{\not\rightarrow}\}$

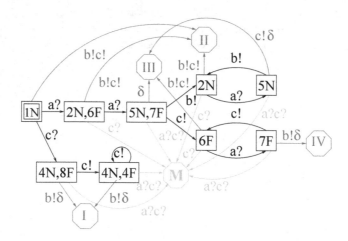

Fig. 7. Enriched Advanced-proxy

Figure 7 shows the Enriched-advanced-proxy for our running example. Note that if an output δ event is observed in state $[5N, 7F]$ then the severity of that error is the minimum between the severity of doing δ in state 5 and doing it in state 7 from our enriched specification from Fig. 6.

In our Enriched-advanced-proxy we have a diagnoser for predictable faults, an informer that tells us when the implementation is trying to be used differently as it was expected, plus a tester that informs us not only when an output was not expected but also the severity of producing that output.

Our Enriched advanced-proxy has the same power of a normal Diagnoser, with the power of a passive Tester, plus the power to know the severity of a possible **ioco** testing error. With the Diagnoser we expect to catch all the unobservable faults to be able to react and prevent major problems. With the Tester we expect to be able to be as close as we can to infinite nature of the formal testing approach, and moreover, with the severity knowledge we expect to be able to inform not only when a error happens but also to quantified how many problems this error makes.

9   Conclusions

The activities of diagnosis and testing are complementary: diagnosis tries to check for anomalies that show the presence of faults (inherent to the system) in order to take measures about it; while testing tries to detect failures, i.e. discrepancies between the actual behavior and the intended one described by the specification. In this paper we presented a formal definition of testability in general, as well as in the model-based context. Then, we presented a monitoring engine called Advanced-proxy, where we combine diagnosis and passive testing so that they can be performed simultaneously. Thus we can identify predictable faults of the system and failures from incorrect implementations (which had been missed by the inherently incomplete testing). Also, we can capture if a malicious user is triggering the implementation with an input that was not specified. Moreover, we consider a weighted failure model that can inform about the severity of a failure and extended our Advanced-proxy with this resource.

Referring to the questions in our title we conclude that the relation between diagnosis and testing is very robust and that they can be combined as in our Advanced-proxy, where we profit from both manners of considering errors.

We thank the anonymous reviewers and Joost-Pieter Katoen for their careful reading of our manuscript and their many insightful comments and suggestions.

References

1. Sampath, M., Sengupta, R., Lafortune, S., Sinnamohideen, K.: Failure diagnosis using discrete-event models. IEEE Trans. Control Syst. Technol. **4**(2), 105–124 (1996)
2. Sampath, M., Sengupta, R., Lafortune, S., Sinnamohideen, K., Teneketzis, D.: Diagnosability of discrete events systems. IEEE Trans. Autom. Control **40**(9), 1555–1575 (1995)

3. De Nicola, R., Hennessy, M.C.B.: Testing equivalences for processes. Theoret. Comput. Sci. **34**, 83–133 (1984)
4. Ye, L., Dague, P., Longuet, D., Brandán Briones, L., Madalinski, A.: Fault manifestability verification for discrete event systems. In: ECAI 2016, pp. 1718–1719 (2016)
5. Tretmans, J.: Test generation with inputs, outputs and repetitive quiescence. In: TR-CTIT-96-26, CTIT Technical Report Series. Centre for Telematics and Information Technology (CTIT), University of Twente, Enschede, The Netherlands (1996)
6. Salva, S.: Passive testing with proxy-testers. Int. J. Softw. Eng. Appl. **5**(4), 1–16 (2011)
7. Jiang, S., Huang, Z., Chandra, V., Kumar, R.: A polynomial algorithm for testing diagnosability of discrete event systems. IEEE Trans. Autom. Control **46**, 1318–1321 (2000)
8. Tae-Sic, Y., Lafortune, S.: Polynomial-time verification of diagnosability of partially observed discrete-event systems. IEEE Trans. Autom. Control **47**(9), 1491–1495 (2002)
9. Bouyer, P., Chevalier, F., D'Souza, D.: Fault diagnosis using timed automata. In: Sassone, V. (ed.) FoSSaCS 2005. LNCS, vol. 3441, pp. 219–233. Springer, Heidelberg (2005). doi:10.1007/978-3-540-31982-5_14
10. Barigozzi, A., Magni, L., Scattolini, R.: A probabilistic approach to fault diagnosis of industrial systems. IEEE Trans. Control Syst. Technol. **12**(6), 950–955 (2004)
11. Fabre, E., Benveniste, A., Haar, S., Jard, C.: Distributed monitoring of concurrent and asynchronous systems*. Discrete Event Dyn. Syst. **15**(1), 33–84 (2005)
12. Genc, S., Lafortune, S.: Distributed diagnosis of place-bordered Petri nets. IEEE Trans. Autom. Sci. Eng. **4**(2), 206–219 (2007)
13. Madalinski, A., Khomenko, V.: Diagnosability verification with parallel LTL-X model checking based on Petri net unfoldings. In: 2010 Conference on Control and Fault-Tolerant Systems (SysTol), pp. 398–403. October 2010
14. Brandán Briones, L., Madalinski, A. Ponce de León, H.: Distributed diagnosability analysis with Petri nets. CoRR, abs/1502.07744 (2015)
15. Pencolé, Y., Cordier, M.-O.: A formal framework for the decentralised diagnosis of large scale discrete event systems and its application to telecommunication networks. Artif. Intell. **164**(1–2), 121–170 (2005)
16. Schumann, A., Pencolé, Y., Thiébaux, S.: A decentralised symbolic diagnosis approach. In: Proceedings of 19th European Conference on Artificial Intelligence, ECAI 2010, Lisbon, Portugal, 16–20 August 2010, pp. 99–104 (2010)
17. Zaytoon, J., Lafortune, S.: Overview of fault diagnosis methods for discrete event systems. Annu. Rev. Control **37**(2), 308–320 (2013)
18. Tretmans, J., Brinksma, E.: TorX: automated model-based testing. In: Hartman, A., Dussa-Ziegler, V. (eds.) First European Conference on Model-Driven Software Engineering, pp. 31–43, December 2003
19. Briones, L.B., Brinksma, E.: A test generation framework for *quiescent* real-time systems. In: Grabowski, J., Nielsen, B. (eds.) FATES 2004. LNCS, vol. 3395, pp. 64–78. Springer, Heidelberg (2005). doi:10.1007/978-3-540-31848-4_5
20. Veanes, M., Campbell, C., Grieskamp, W., Schulte, W., Tillmann, N., Nachmanson, L.: Model-based testing of object-oriented reactive systems with spec explorer. In: Hierons, R.M., Bowen, J.P., Harman, M. (eds.) Formal Methods and Testing. LNCS, vol. 4949, pp. 39–76. Springer, Heidelberg (2008). doi:10.1007/978-3-540-78917-8_2

21. Belinfante, A., Frantzen, L., Schallhart, C.: Tools for test case generation. In: Model-Based Testing of Reactive Systems, pp. 391–438 (2004)
22. Jard, C., Jéron, T.: TGV: theory, principles and algorithms: a tool for the automatic synthesis of conformance test cases for non- deterministic reactive systems. Int. J. Softw. Tools Technol. Transf. **7**, 297–315 (2005)
23. Briones, L.B., Brinksma, E., Stoelinga, M.: A semantic framework for test coverage. In: Graf, S., Zhang, W. (eds.) ATVA 2006. LNCS, vol. 4218, pp. 399–414. Springer, Heidelberg (2006). doi:10.1007/11901914_30
24. Salva, S., Cao, T.D.: A model-based testing approach combining passive conformance testing and runtime verification application to web service compositions deployed in clouds. In: Lee, R. (ed.) Software Engineering Research, Management and Applications. SCI, vol. 496, pp. 99–116. Springer, Heidelberg (2014). doi:10.1007/978-3-319-00948-3_7
25. Sheppard, J.W., Kaufman, M.: Formal specification of testability metrics in IEEE P1522. In: IEEE AUTOTESTCON, Pennsylvania (2001)
26. Kontoleon, J.: Reliability determination of r-successive-out-of-n: F system. Trans. Reliab. **29**(5), 600–602 (1980). IEEE

Analysis

Verifying Properties of Systems Relying on Attribute-Based Communication

Rocco De Nicola[1]([✉]), Tan Duong[2], Omar Inverso[2], and Franco Mazzanti[3]

[1] IMT School for Advanced Studies Lucca, Lucca, Italy
`rocco.denicola@imtlucca.it`
[2] Gran Sasso Science Institute, L'aquila, Italy
`{tan.duong,omar.inverso}@gssi.it`
[3] ISTI CNR, Pisa, Italy
`franco.mazzanti@isti.cnr.it`

Abstract. AbC is a process calculus designed for describing collective adaptive systems, whose distinguishing feature is the communication mechanism relying on predicates over attributes exposed by components. A novel approach to the analysis of concurrent systems modelled as AbC terms is presented that relies on the UMC model checker, a tool based on modelling concurrent systems as communicating UML-like state machines. A structural translation from AbC specifications to the UMC internal format is provided and used as the basis for the analysis. Three different algorithmic solutions of the well studied stable marriage problem are described in AbC and their translations are analysed with UMC. It is shown how the proposed approach can be exploited to identify emerging properties of systems and unwanted behaviour.

1 Introduction

In the eighties much work was devoted to formalisms for the specification and verification of concurrent systems. It was already clear that this class of systems was going to become more and more important even if the Internet, as we know it today, was not yet available[1]. In that period in Twente University there was a group of researchers working on the theory of concurrent systems. That theory was based on the explicit synchronization and message passing primitives proposed by Milner [25] and Hoare [19], and the researchers wanted to improve its usability. Indeed, they gave a great contribution to the development of the language LOTOS that in [8] is introduced as "a specification language that has been specifically developed for the formal description of the OSI (Open systems Interconnection) architecture, although it is applicable to distributed, concurrent systems in general. In LOTOS a system is seen as a set of processes which interact and exchange data with each other and with their environment."

---

[1] Just consider that the email address(es) of the friend to whom this volume is dedicated were something like `uucp: mcvax!utinu1!infed` and `earn: hiddink@hentht5`.

© Springer International Publishing AG 2017
J.-P. Katoen et al. (Eds.): Brinksma Festschrift, LNCS 10500, pp. 169–190, 2017.
DOI: 10.1007/978-3-319-68270-9_9

The main actor behind the effort was Ed Brinskma, who contributed to both the definition of the language and to the proof techniques to verify conformance of communication network protocols implementations with their abstract specifications [9,15].

Since then, communication networks have dramatically changed our world and we are now working with autonomous agents that roam over the Internet, adapt to changing situations and environments, interact with other agents or humans and control essential components of our daily life. It is more and more common that such autonomous agents interact anonymously and form groups of peers dynamically according to specific features, or attributes, that the different peers expose. For instance, members of a social network interested in language exchange activities can use their own location and favourite languages to find suitable people nearby.

Thus, the old formalisms and especially their communication primitives, based on broadcast or direct one-to-one, communication are not appropriate anymore for selecting partners and programming so called collective adaptive systems. New formalisms based on alternative communication paradigms and supported by new proof techniques are on demand for dealing with them. Prompted by the needs outlined above, we have defined AbC [4] a novel process calculus that relies on *attribute-based communication* and formalises the above intuition by combining actor-style concurrency with one-to-many message passing. Traditional linguistic approaches struggle in the presence of highly-dynamical environments often seen in real-world situations, from social networks to stock exchanges. AbC can instead cope with these systems quite naturally, usually keeping the specifications compact and intuitively easy to follow [11].

The effectiveness of this new formalism has so far been assessed mostly from a programming standpoint, with prototype implementations of the proposed interaction mechanisms in Java [5] and Erlang [11]. However, the potential benefits of AbC when reasoning about system properties have only been hinted at, through proof-of-concept verification of simple properties of formal models manually built from AbC specifications [10].

In this paper, we report our first attempt to the systematic analysis and verification of attribute-based communication systems. The initial step in our verification approach consists in mechanically translating the AbC specification of a given system into a UML-like state machine. In AbC the supported communications primitives require some kind of global view of the attributes of all the components of a system. The most direct way to model this global status is to see it as the internal status of a nondeterministic state machine, in which the behaviour of a single process term is captured by one or more state machine transitions. In this way, each process can have access to the values of the attributes of the other processes to effectuate AbC-style communication. In order to preserve the structure of the AbC process, we explicitly keep track of the execution point of each process and use to guard the transitions. Depending on the properties of interest, relevant structural and behavioural aspects of the state machine can be made observable and accessible to the logical verification engine, through the definition of specific abstractions rules.

For system analysis, our approach relies on the UMC verification framework [20]. UMC is specifically oriented towards the early analysis of (likely wrong) initial system designs, that trades the capacity of dealing with very large systems with the capacity of helping users to easily understand the source of design errors. This is achieved, among the other things, by providing interactive explanations of the results of the evaluations and by allowing the user to observe and reason on systems at a high level of abstraction without being distracted, if not overwhelmed, by all the details of the specification.

We illustrate the impact of our approach by considering three variants of the well studied stable marriage problem (SMP) [17] that can be naturally expressed in terms of partners' attributes. Solving the SMP problem amounts to finding a stable matching between two equally sized sets of elements given an ordering of preferences for each element. Thus, one has to find an algorithm for pairing each element in one set to an element in the other set in such a way that there are no two elements of different pairs which both would rather have each other than their current partners. When no such pair of elements exists, the set of pairs is deemed stable. The classical algorithm of [17] goes through a sequence of proposals initiated by members of one group (*the initiators*) according to their preferences. Members of the other group (*the responders*) after receiving a proposal, do choose the best initiator between their current partner and the one making advances. It can be proved that such an algorithm guarantees existence of a unique stable matching.

Our variants of SMP allow initiators and responders to express their interests in potential partners by using their attributes rather than their identities ordered by means of an explicit preference list. Member's preferences are represented as predicates over the attributes of potential partners. For one variant, we follow the classical algorithm where initiators first propose to the responder they prefer most and then relax their expectations if no partner is willing to accept their proposal. In the other variant, initiators start proposing with the lowest requirements, to make sure to get a partner, and gradually increase their expectations hoping to find better partners.

We experimented our verification methodology on the three above mentioned algorithmic solutions to SMP by considering a number of properties of interest, such as stability of the matching and its completeness, existence of a unique solution, level of satisfaction of the components. These properties are first described informally and then rendered as logical formulae to be formally checked against the generated models. The outcome of our verification allows us to make some considerations both on the different algorithms and on the used tools.

Indeed, the results of our experiments have shown that systems relying on attribute-based communications can be particularly complex to design and analyse. However, by exhaustively verifying a specification over all possible inputs, despite the small problem size considered, we have experienced that many non-trivial emerging properties and potential problems can indeed be discovered by following our methodology.

The rest of the paper is organised as follows. We briefly introduce the AbC process calculus and the UMC model checker in Sect. 2. We describe our translation from AbC process terms into UMC textual description of UML-like state machines in Sect. 3. In Sect. 4, we show how to specify in AbC solutions for both classical SMP and its attribute-based variants, and then present fragments of the result of our verification and discuss their outcomes. Finally, Sect. 5 contains some concluding remarks.

2   Background

The AbC Calculus. AbC [4] is a process calculus centered on the attribute-based communication paradigm. Its core syntax is reported in Fig. 1. An AbC system consists of independent components (C). A component can be either a process (P) and an attribute environment (Γ) or a parallel composition of components $C_1 \parallel C_2$. The behaviour of a component is modeled by process P executing actions in the style of process algebra, while its attributes are used to encode some domain aspects (e.g. battery level, component role, identity, ...) and are stored in the component's environment Γ which is a partial mapping from attribute names to their values. Since attributes play a key role in interactions, AbC assumes that their names are agreed in advance among components [4].

$$
\begin{array}{ll}
\text{(Components)} & C ::= \Gamma : P \mid C_1 \parallel C_2 \\
\text{(Processes)} & P ::= 0 \mid (E)@\Pi.P \mid \Pi(x).P \mid [a := E]P \mid \langle \Pi \rangle P \\
& \quad \mid P_1 + P_2 \mid P_1 \vert P_2 \mid K \mid \mathbf{\Pi?P_1\_\_P_2} \\
\text{(Expressions)} & E ::= v \mid x \mid a \mid this.a \\
\text{(Predicates)} & \Pi ::= \text{tt} \mid E_1 \bowtie E_2 \mid \Pi_1 \wedge \Pi_2 \mid \neg\Pi
\end{array}
$$

Fig. 1. AbC syntax

A process P can be either an inactive process 0, a prefixing process $\alpha.P$, an update process $[a := E]P$, an awareness process $\langle \Pi \rangle P$, a choice process $P_1 + P_2$, a parallel process $P_1 \vert P_2$, or a process call K (under the assumption that each process has a unique definition $K \triangleq P$).

We often omit the inactive process for convenience. The prefixing process executes the action α and continues as P. The update process sets the attribute a to the value of expression E and behaves like P. The awareness process blocks the execution of process P until predicate Π becomes true. The choice process can behave either like P_1 or P_2. The parallel process interleaves the executions of P_1 and P_2. For modelling communication AbC relies on two prefixing actions:

$(E)@\Pi$ is the *attribute-based output* that is used to send the value of expression E to those components whose attributes satisfy predicate Π;

$\Pi(x)$ is the *attribute-based input* that binds to the variable x the message received from any component whose attributes, and possibly the communicated values, satisfy the receiving predicate Π.

The semantics of output actions are asynchronous and non-blocking while that of input actions are blocking. The receiving predicates can also be specified over the message content, in addition to the attributes of sending components. Parallel components communicate using these two primitives, while parallel processes within a component simply interleave their executions. An update operation is performed atomically with the following action, given that the component under the updated environment can perform that action. In some cases, to model an update operation alone $[a := E]$, we exploit an empty send action $()@(\text{ff})$ to obtain $[a := E]()@(\text{ff})$.

An expression E may be a constant value v, a variable x, an attribute name a, or a reference *this.a* to attribute a in the local environment. Predicate Π can be either tt, a comparison between two expressions $E_1 \bowtie E_2$, a logical conjunction of two predicates $\Pi_1 \wedge \Pi_2$ or a negation of a predicate $\neg \Pi$. We write $\Gamma \models \Pi$ to state that predicate Π holds in environment Γ.

All the above mentioned constructs have already been introduced in [4], and we refer the interested reader to this paper for the definition of the operational semantics of the full calculus.

There is however a new operator that we introduce for the first time in this paper and is very important to support processes in taking decisions depending on the conditions of the context they are operating in. We have called the new operator, the *awareness operator*:

$$\Pi?P_1 \_ P_2$$

relies on a sort of global awareness and allows the executing system to proceed as P_1 if the environment contains at least one component whose attributes satisfy predicate Π, and as P_2 otherwise. Its operational semantics is modelled by the following inference rules:

$$\frac{\exists\, C : \Gamma(C) \models \Pi \quad P_1 \xrightarrow{\alpha} P_1'}{\Pi?P_1 \_ P_2 \xrightarrow{\alpha} P_1'} \qquad \frac{\nexists\, C : \Gamma(C) \models \Pi \quad P_2 \xrightarrow{\alpha} P_2'}{\Pi?P_1 \_ P_2 \xrightarrow{\alpha} P_2'}$$

The main difference between the local awareness operator and the global one is that the predicate appearing in the latter can refer to the attributes of external components.

In fact, the attribute-based communication primitives have been introduced while abstracting from the selection mechanism of communication partners, e.g., ignoring how predicates are evaluated and how components address each other. When it comes to practical settings, both for programming and verifying AbC systems, one has to take into consideration those issues which in turn raise the problem of designing a communication infrastructure. Existing implementations of AbC paradigm [5,10] do rest on a centralized component which plays the role of a global registration and a message forwarder. This component has global knowledge of the system while other components are not aware of each other and only interact with this centralized one. In this paper, we also assume that there is a such global component in an AbC system. While this assumption guides our translation strategy which will be presented in Sect. 3, one important benefit is that it allows implementing operators like $\Pi?P_1 \_ P_2$, needing global awareness.

The UMC Model Checker. UMC [20] is one of the model checkers belonging to the KandISTI [6] formal verification framework used for analyzing functional properties of concurrent systems. In UMC, a system is represented as a set of communicating UML-like state machines, each associated with an active object in the system. UMC adopts doubly-labelled transition systems (L2TS) [14] as semantic model of the system behaviour. A L2TS is essentially a directed graph in which nodes and edges are labelled with sets of predicates and of events, respectively. The model checker allows to interactively explore this graph and to verify behavioral properties specified in the state-event based UCTL [16] logics. UCTL allows to express state predicates over (the labelling of) system states, event predicates over (the labelling of) single-step system evolutions, and combine these with temporal and boolean operators in the style of CTL and ACTL. A UML-like state machine is described in UMC in the form of a class declaration structured as below:

```
class Name is
  Signals:
  -- asynchronous signals accepted by this class
  Vars:
  -- local variables of this object
  Transitions:
  -- transitions that determine the behaviour of the class
  end Name
```

where a list of `Signals` summarises the set of events to which an active object may react[2]. A signal denotes an asynchronous event that may trigger the transitions of an object. An object can send signals to itself by executing `self.signal_name`. The `Vars` section contains the private, non statically-typed, local variables of the class and optionally their initial value. Values can denote object names, boolean values, integer values or, recursively, (dynamically sized) sequences of values. The `Transitions` section declares a set of transition rules which describe the behaviour of the class and have the following general form:

```
source -> target {trigger [guard] / actions}
```

to denote a state transition from state `source` to state `target`. The transition is triggered by a suitable trigger event `trigger` (which is a signal name) and if the `guard` expression is satisfied, all actions inside the transition body are executed. The execution of actions may in turn change the state of the object or

---

[2] UMC also supports an `Operations` section for the definition of synchronous events, which is however not relevant in our study.

trigger other transitions. In fact, UMC supports a fairly rich language to specify actions and guards. For more details we refer to the UMC website [2] and the documentation therein.

While the structure of the semantic in terms of L2TS of an UMC specification is directly defined by the system behaviour, the labels associated to nodes and edges of the graph are specified by *abstraction* rules that allow the designer to define the relevant internal aspects of the system. These rules are defined inside the `Abstractions` section:

```
Abstractions {
  Action: <internal event> -> <edge label>
  ...
  State:  <internal system state> -> <node label>
  ...
}
```

The possibility of obtaining an L2TS which focuses only the aspects of the system that are considered relevant is particularly useful in many cases. For example one can visualize a compact summary of the computation trees, factorized via appropriate behavioural equivalence notions. Or he can model check abstract L2TS (without any knowledge of the underlying UMC), and reason on systems without a detailed knowledge of the underlying concrete implementation.

3   Transforming AbC Models into UMC Models

In this section we describe a mechanical translation from AbC specifications into to UML-like state machines. The main effort in this part lays in the careful modelling of the attributes and of their visibility, which implicitly require some sort of global view of the the system. In fact, since our target modelling language has no concept of global data, a simple solution would require at least implementing shared states and appropriate synchronisation. We avoid that by gathering all the processes in the initial system along with their attributes into a unique object in the translated model, where the behaviour described by a single process term is captured by one or more transitions. This successfully provides a direct access to attributes to every process. However, some ingenuity is required to respect the process structure of the input system and its precise semantics. We thus introduce an explicit tracking mechanism for the execution points of the processes. This amounts to dynamically labelling new terms while visiting the process structure, and to introducing appropriate guards for the transitions, to guarantee that at any point of the evolution of the system only feasible transitions are allowed. Labels and guards can be combined to model sequentialisation, non-deterministic choice, and parallel composition.

We now describe the translation in detail. Our input system is a collection of AbC components, where the specification for the i-th component, denoted with

$$C_i ::= \Gamma_i : \langle D_i, P_{init_i} \rangle$$

includes an attribute environment Γ_i, a set D_i of process declarations, and an initial behaviour P_{init_i} which refers to the processes defined in D_i. We adopt the following notational conventions. Expressions can be vectors with relevant operators in the UMC style [3], e.g., given a vector v, we can write $v.head, v.tail, v[i]$ for the first element, the rest and the ith element of v, respectively. Predicates can contain tests of membership relation between an element and a vector (denoted by $\in, \notin$). We further assume that the specified system consists of a fixed number of components, and that the parallel operator does not occur inside a recursive definition. The only allowed exception is the definition of a process of the form $P := Q|P$, where $|$ is replaced by its bounded version $|^m$, i.e. the number of parallel instances to be created. For example: $P := Q |^2 P$ is interpreted as three processes $P := Q_1 | Q_2 | Q_3$.

The output of our translation is a UMC class whose general structure is depicted in Fig. 2. It includes fixed code snippets such as the necessary signals and data structures to model AbC input and output actions. It also contains vectors to model attribute environments, one for each attribute.

```
1   Class AbCSystem is
2   Signals: allowsend(i:int),
3             bcast(tgt,msg,j:int);
4   Vars:
5       RANDOMQUEUE;
6       receiving:bool := false;
7       pc:int[];
8       bound:obj[];
9       /* Attributes vectors */
10      att1:int[]; att2:int[]; ...
11  State Top Defers allowsend(i)
12  Transitions:
13      /* Initial movement of the system */
14      init -> SYS {- /
15        for i in 0..pc.length-1 {
16            self.allowsend(i);
17      }}
18      /* Transitions of all components */
19      S[[⟨D₁, P_{init1}⟩]]
20      S[[⟨D₂, P_{init2}⟩]]
21      ...
22  end AbCSystem
```

Fig. 2. Translation of AbC specifications.

The system state is a UML parallel state (SYS), where each component is modelled by its own region (Ck). Attribute input and output semantics are modelled with the help of unique events. The bcast(tgt,msg,j) event, which triggers all the receive actions in all components and contains the actual set tgt of components allowed to receive the message, the actual message msg, and the index j of the sending component. The `allowsend(i)` event, where i denotes a component index used to schedule the components through interleaving when sending messages. According to the semantics of AbC, *receive* actions are blocking and executed together, and *send* actions of all the components should be handled in an interleaved way. To accommodate this, we use the event queue of the state machine to store a set of `allowsend(i)` signals, one for each AbC component i. These signals are declared in the top state of the system as `Defers`, to prevent them from being removed from the events queue when they do not trigger any transition. Moreover, the queue is defined as `random` so that the relative ordering of signals is not considered relevant. In this way, at each step in which an AbC *send* operation has to be performed, a single `allowsend` signal is nondeterministically selected from the queue, allowing a single component to proceed.

The `Transitions` section collects all the transitions generated from the process terms while visiting the process structure. Transitions have the following form:

```
SYS.Ck.s0 -> Ck.s0 {Trigger[... & pc[k][p]=CNT]/
    -- transition body
    pc[k][p]:=CNT + 1;
}
```

where `CNT` is a *program counter* initially set to 1 and incremented as new transitions are produced. This provides a unique label associated with the transition, its *entry point*. Additionally, `pc[k][p]` is the *execution point* of process `p` in component `k`. The guard on the transitions makes sure that its entry point matches the execution point of the corresponding component and process. At the end of a transition, `pc[k][p]` is assigned a new value, referred to as its *exit point*, in order to correctly enable the next set of feasible transitions. The values of `k`, `p`, `CNT`, and the full guards are worked out according to the structural mapping procedure described below.

Structural Mapping. Let us denote with $\mathcal{S}[\![P]\!]^{k,p,v}_{\rho}$ the function that maps a process term P into a set of UMC transitions, where k is the component index, p the process index, and v the entry value. At the beginning, P is the init behaviour of the component and p, v are both initialised with 1. The information carried while traversing the process structure is stored in ρ. Figure 3 presents our translation rules from AbC process terms to UMC transitions, while Fig. 4(b)–(d) gives an idea of how transitions are glued together according to the process structure. The translation maintains two variables: the current number of processes *procs* and a program counter *cnt*[p] for a process with index p, both calculated dynamically while visiting the input.

Inaction. An inaction process is translated into nothing.

Update. The translation of $[a := E]P$ accumulates the update expression $[a := E]$ into variable *upd* of ρ and returns the translation of P under the new environment.

Awareness. The translation of $\langle \Pi \rangle P$ accumulates predicate Π into variable *aware* of ρ and returns the translation of P under the new environment.

$$\mathcal{S}[\![nil]\!]^{k,p,v}_\rho = \emptyset$$

$$\mathcal{S}[\![a := E]P]\!]^{k,p,v}_\rho = \mathcal{S}[\![P]\!]^{k,p,v}_{\rho'}$$

where $\rho' = \rho\{upd \mapsto \rho(upd) \cup [a := E]\}$

$$\mathcal{S}[\![\langle \Pi \rangle P]\!]^{k,p,v}_\rho = \mathcal{S}[\![P]\!]^{k,p,v}_{\rho'}$$

where $\rho' = \rho\{aware \mapsto \rho(aware) \cup \Pi\}$

$$\mathcal{S}[\![P_1 + P_2]\!]^{k,p,v}_\rho = \mathcal{S}[\![P_1]\!]^{k,p,v}_\rho; \mathcal{S}[\![P_2]\!]^{k,p,v}_\rho$$

$$\mathcal{S}[\![P_1 | P_2]\!]^{k,p,v}_\rho = \mathcal{S}[\![P_1]\!]^{k,p_1,1}_{\rho'}; \mathcal{S}[\![P_2]\!]^{k,p_2,1}_{\rho'}$$

where $p_1 = procs, \; p_2 = procs + 1,$
$\qquad \rho' = \rho\{parent \mapsto \rho(parent) \cup (p, v)\},$
$\qquad procs = procs + 2, cnt[p_1] = 1, cnt[p_2] = 1$

$$\mathcal{S}[\![K]\!]^{k,p,v}_\rho = \begin{cases} \mathcal{B}[\![\emptyset]\!]^{k,p,exit}_\rho & \text{if } \rho(K_{\text{visit}}) = \text{true} \\ \mathcal{S}[\![P]\!]^{k,p,v}_{\rho'} & \text{otherwise} \end{cases}$$

where $exit = \rho(K_{\text{entry}}), P = D_k(K),$
$\qquad \rho' = \rho\{K_{\text{visit}} \mapsto true, K_{\text{entry}} \mapsto v\}$

$$\mathcal{S}[\![(E)@(\Pi).P]\!]^{k,p,v}_\rho = \mathcal{B}[\![(E)@(\Pi)]\!]^{k,p,v}_\rho; \mathcal{S}[\![P]\!]^{k,p,v'}_{\rho'}$$

where $v' = cnt[p] + 2, cnt[p] = cnt[p] + 2$
$\qquad \rho' = \rho\{upd \mapsto \emptyset, aware \mapsto \emptyset, parent \mapsto \emptyset\}$

$$\mathcal{S}[\![\Pi(x).P]\!]^{k,p,v}_\rho = \mathcal{B}[\![\Pi(x)]\!]^{k,p,v}_\rho; \mathcal{S}[\![P]\!]^{k,p,v'}_{\rho'}$$

where $v' = cnt[p] + 1, cnt[p] = cnt[p] + 1$
$\qquad \rho' = \rho\{upd \mapsto \emptyset, aware \mapsto \emptyset, parent \mapsto \emptyset\}$

Fig. 3. Structural translation of processes: semicolon $(;)$ denotes the completion of a left translation before starting a new one, $\rho(x)$ is the value of variable x in ρ

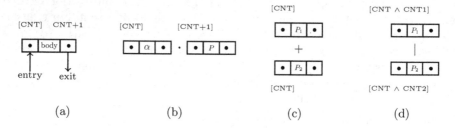

(a)   (b)   (c)   (d)

Fig. 4. Structural mapping to combine generated UMC transitions: (a) graphical representation of a transition; (b) an action prefixing process $\alpha.P$ has the entry point of α as CNT, and the entry point of P as CNT + 1; (c) a choice process $P_1 + P_2$ has the same entry point on both sub-processes P_1, P_2; (d) the entry points of sub-processes P_1, P_2 in a parallel process $P_1|P_2$ contain also the exit point of $P_1|P_2$

Nondeterministic Choice. The translation of $P_1 + P_2$ is a sequence of two translations of sub-processes with the same set of parameters and the same environment.

Parallel Composition. The translation of $P_1 | P_2$ is a sequence of two translations of the sub-processes. It generates two new processes indices p_1 and p_2 which are calculated from the current number of processes *procs*, and initialises two new global counters $cnt[p_1]$, $cnt[p_2]$. In the case of parallel composition, the entry points of sub-processes P_1, P_2 does contain not only their own counters but also the counter of the spawning process $P_1 | P_2$. Therefore, the translations of P_1, P_2 store the exit point of the parent process (p, v) in variable *parent* which will be used as an additional guard for prefixing actions of P_1 and of P_2.

Process Call. The translation of a process call K looks up its definition P in the process declarations D_k and returns a translation of P. If process K is already translated, function $\mathcal{B}$ generates a dummy transition whose exit point is equal to the entry point of K. Otherwise, it remembers K is visited and stores this fact together with the entry point value of K into ρ for (possibly) later recursions.

Action-Prefixing. The translation of $\alpha.P$ is a behavioural translation of α and a translation of the continuation process P. The translation of α is done by the function $\mathcal{B}$, as it will be presented shortly. The translation of P is parameterised with a new environment where the previous accumulated information is reset, and a new entry value v', calculated from the value of program counter $cnt[p]$, is added. In fact, we need two UMC transitions for an output action, thus the value of $cnt[p]$ is increased by two.

Accumulated Information. In the above generated transitions, guards may include the accumulated awareness predicates and the transition body may include accumulated update commands. We omit the details for conciseness.

Global Awareness. Finally, the global awareness construct $\Pi?P_1\_\_P_2$ is treated as a process whose structure is $\beta.(P_1 + P_2)$ where the transition of β simply evaluates the global predicate Π to enable transitions of P_1 and P_2 (via additional guards) appropriately.

Behavioural Mapping. We now describe the function $\mathcal{B}[\![\alpha]\!]_\rho^{k,p,v}$ which generates the actual UMC code for a specific action α according to the information accumulated in the environment ρ and the parameter set.

We model the output action in two steps that are forced to occur in a strict sequence: the sending to self of the `bcast` event that dispatches to all the parallel components and the discarding of this very message, as illustrated by the code snippet below. Variable `receiving` works as a lock, to guarantee the correct ordering of the two transitions. Here the (main) transition is guarded by conditions on the execution point of the action and by awareness predicates, while the transition body includes update commands, the computation of potential receivers and a sending operation.

$$\mathcal{B}[\![(E)@\Pi]\!]_\rho^{k,P,v} =$$

```
SYS.Ck.s0 -> Ck.s0 {
    allowsend(i)[i=k & receiving=false & pc[k][p]=v & [[ρ(parent)]]] & [[ρ(aware)]]]/
    [[ρ(update)]];
    for j in 0..pc.length-1 {
        if ([[Π]]) then {tgt[j]:=1;} else {tgt[j]:=0;}
    };
    receiving:=true;
    self.bcast(tgt,[[E]],k);
    pc[k][p] = v + 1;
}
SYS.Ck.s0 -> Ck.s0 {
    bcast(tgt,msg,j)[pc[k][p] = v + 1]/
    receiving:=false;
    self.allowsend(k);
    pc[k][p] = v + 2;
}
```

An input action is translated into the following transition, triggered by signal bcast(tgt,msg,j) from some sender. It is enabled, for a component k, if the message is for it, the receiving predicate Π and, possibly, the preceding awareness predicates are satisfied. Variable binding is done by assigning the received message msg to vector bound. Similarly to the output action, the transition guard might contain awareness predicates; the transition body might contain update commands.

$$\mathcal{B}[\![\Pi(x)]\!]_\rho^{k,P,v} =$$

```
SYS.Ck.s0 -> Ck.s0 {
    bcast(tgt,msg,j)[tgt[k]=1 & pc[k][p]=v & [[ρ(parent)]]] & [[ρ(aware)]] & [[Π]]]/
    [[ρ(update)]];
    bound[k][p] = msg;
    pc[k][p] = v + 1;
}
```

4   A Case Study

The Stable Marriage Problem (SMP) [17] is a well studied problem that has applications in a variety of real-world situations, such as assigning students to colleges or appointing graduating medical students to their first hospital. SMP that has been initially formulated in terms of peers that make offer to potential partners by taking into account a preference list is easily adaptable to a context in which partners are selected according to their attributes. Indeed, due to its simple formulation and its intrinsically concurrent nature, SMP has been already used to show the advantages of AbC as a very high-level formalism to describe complex systems [10, 11]. In this section, we use it to show how our framework can be used to reason about properties of attribute based systems.

We apply our verification methodology to three possible algorithmic solutions of stable marriage in order to check a selection of properties of interest. For each solution, we provide a short informal description along with the resulting formal specifications in AbC. Similarly, we present a number of properties first informally and then as a precise logical property of the state machines generated (see Sect. 3) from the formal specifications. We show how to instrument these state machines for property checking. As we go along, we also consider a few additional program-specific properties that we used as a guidance to refine the formal specifications themselves.

The idea of stable marriage is to find a stable matching between two equally sized sets of elements (men and women in the original formulation, whence the word marriage) given an ordering of preferences for each element. Providing a solution to SMP amounts to devising an algorithm for pairing each element in one set to an element in the other set in such a way that there are no two elements of different pairs which both would rather have each other than their current partners. When no such pair of elements exists, the set of pairs is deemed stable. The classical algorithm of [17] goes through a sequence of proposals initiated by members of one group (*the initiators*) according to their preference lists. Members of the other group (*the responders*) after receiving a proposal, do choose the best initiator between their current partner and the one making advances. Our first algorithm implements the classical solution, where preferences are represented as complete ordered lists of identifiers. Initiators and responders are programmed as individual processes that interact using their local preference lists in a point-to-point fashion using their identity. The other two programs adapt the classical solution to the context of attribute-based communication, where partners are selected by considering predicates over the attributes of the potential partners. The two new solutions differ for the way initiators choose their potential partners. They can start by either making proposals to the responder they prefer most and then relax their expectations or making proposals with the lowest requirements, to make sure to get a partner, and gradually increase their expectations.

4.1 Specifications

Classical Stable Marriage. In the classical solution to stable marriage, each initiator actively proposes himself to the most favourite responder according to its preference list. In case it gets a refusal or is dropped, it tries again with the next element in the list. A responder waits for incoming proposals, accepting any proposal when single, or choosing between its current partner and the new proposer according to its preferences. The algorithm terminates when there is no more activity.

AbC Specification. Our first AbC program is based on the idea presented in [5]. Initiators and responders are AbC components whose attributes are the identifier *id*, the preference list *prefs*, and the current *partner*. The behaviour of an individual initiator is specified by process M. It updates attribute *partner* to the first element of *prefs*, and then sends a *propose* message to components whose *id* equals to *partner*. The continuation process Wait waits for a *no* message to reset the *partner*, before restarting with M:

$$\text{M} \triangleq [\textit{this.partner} := \textit{this.prefs.head}, \textit{this.prefs} := \textit{this.prefs.tail}]$$
$$(\textit{propose}, \textit{this.id})@(\textit{id} = \textit{this.partner}).\text{Wait}$$
$$\text{Wait} \triangleq [\textit{this.partner} := 0](\$msg = no)(\$msg).\text{M}$$

The behaviour of a responder is specified by process W. In process Handle a responder waits for incoming proposals, and behaves either like A if the responder finds the new initiator is better or like R otherwise. W is composed in parallel with n instances (where n is the problem size) so that it can receive new messages while processing the current one. Notice that both R and A use a reversed form of preference lists to compare the current partner with a new initiator:

$$W \triangleq \text{Handle} \mid^n W$$

$$\text{Handle} \triangleq (\$msg = propose)(\$msg, \$id).(A(\$id) + R(\$id))$$

$$A(\text{id}) \triangleq \langle \text{this}.prefs[\text{this}.partner] < \text{this}.prefs[\$id] \rangle$$

$$[\$ex := \text{this}.partner, \text{this}.partner := \$id](no)@(id = \$ex)$$

$$R(\text{id}) \triangleq \langle \text{this}.prefs[\text{this}.partner] > \text{this}.prefs[\$id] \rangle (no)@(id = \$id)$$

Top-Down Stable Marriage. In this case preferences are expressed as predicates over the attributes of partners rather than as lists of people. For example, a person might be interested in finding a partner from a specific country who speaks a specific language. A suitable communication predicate would be $country = \text{this}.favcountry \ \wedge \ language = \text{this}.favlanguage$, where $language$ and $country$ are two attributes of initiators and responders, and $favcountry$ and $favlanguage$ are used to express preferences.

Following the above idea, in the top-down solution to SMP the initiator starts by making offers to responders that satisfy its highest requirements, i.e., have all wanted attributes. In case nobody satisfy these requirements, the initiator retries after weakening the predicate by eliminating one of the preferred attributes and waits for a reaction. The system then evolves as follows.

A single initiator that receives a *yes* considers himself engaged and sends out a *confirm* message; it keeps proposing if a *no* is received. An engaged initiator that receives a *yes* notifies the interested responder that meanwhile another partner has been found by sending a *toolate* message. An engaged initiator dropped by its current partner with a *bye* message restarts immediately proposing.

An engaged responder reacts upon receiving a proposal by comparing the new initiator with the current partner. If the new proposer is not better, it will receive a *no* message. Otherwise, the responder sends a *yes* to notify the proposer her availability, and waits for a reply. Upon receiving a *confirm*, the responder changes partner and sends *bye* to the ex partner; in case a *toolate* message is received the responder continues without changes.

AbC Specification. We model a scenario where each participant exposes two characteristics besides their identifiers: $\{id, w, b\}$ for proposers and $\{id, e, h\}$ for responders. Furthermore, participants have their own preferences on which are modeled by $\{pe, ph\}$ and $\{pw, pb\}$. The behaviour of a proposer is modeled as process P, used to make proposals, composed in parallel with process M_{Handle} for handling replies.

$$M \triangleq P \mid M_{\text{Handle}}$$

$$P \triangleq \langle \text{this}.partner = 0 \wedge \text{this}.proposed = 0 \rangle [\text{this}.proposed := 1] P_1$$

$$P_1 \triangleq \Pi_{\{\neg bl, pe, ph\}} ?(\tilde{v})@\Pi_{\{\neg bl, pe, ph\}}.P_{--} (\Pi_{\{\neg bl, pe\}} ?(\tilde{v})@\Pi_{\{\neg bl, pe\}}.P_{--} (\tilde{v})@\Pi_{\{\neg bl\}}.P)$$

Process P, guarded by two conditions this.$partner = 0$ and this.$proposed = 0$, becomes actives when a single proposer has not yet sent a proposal. After that, it sets the flag $proposed$ and continues as P_1. To model the adaptive behaviour of proposers needed to relax their preferences, we use the new global awareness operator (see Sect. 2) in the definition of P_1 where we use $\Pi_{\{\neg a_1, a_2, a_3\}}$ to denote the predicate in the form $id \notin a_1 \wedge e = a_2 \wedge h = a_3$ and $\tilde{v}$ denotes the sent message, i.e., $\{propose, this.id, this.w, this.b\}$. It is important to add an attribute bl which is a list of responders that the proposer does not want to contact. The list is updated when a proposer receives a no or a bye message. This allows them to know when to relax their requirements.

A proposer may receive multiple replies; process M_{Handle} takes care of this according to the message type: Wait is used to handle bye and no messages while Yes handles yes messages.

$$M_{\text{Handle}} \triangleq \text{Yes} \mid \text{Wait} \qquad \text{Yes} \triangleq \text{Loop} \mid^n \text{Yes} \qquad \text{Wait} \triangleq \text{Loop}_1 \mid^n \text{Wait}$$

$$\text{Loop} \triangleq (\$msg = yes)(\$msg, \$id).\text{Ans}(\$id)$$

$$\text{Ans}(id) \triangleq \langle this.partner = 0\rangle [this.partner := \$id, this.bl := this.bl + [\$id]]$$
$$(confirm)@(id = this.partner).\text{Loop}$$
$$+ \langle this.partner \neq 0\rangle(toolate)@(id = \$id).\text{Loop}$$

$$\text{Loop}_1 \triangleq [this.partner := 0, this.proposed := 0](\$msg = bye)(\$msg, \$id).\text{Loop}_1$$
$$+ (\$msg = no)(\$msg, \$id).$$
$$[this.proposed := 0, this.bl := this.bl + [\$id]]()@(\texttt{ff}).\text{Loop}_1$$

The behaviour of a responder is specified by W_{Handle}. On receiving a proposal, a responder can behave like A (accept), R (reject) or D (discard). The local attribute bl is updated in A and R while D uses it to avoid unnecessary processing. Acceptance and rejection of a proposal are dealt with similarly as in the classical case, except that the extra message acknowledgement requires an attribute $lock$, to process sequentially possibly parallel messages.

$$W_{\text{Handle}} \triangleq (\$msg = propose)(\$msg, \$id, \$w, \$b).$$
$$(R(\$id, \$w, \$b) + A(\$id, \$w, \$b) + D(\$id))$$

$$R(id, w, b) \triangleq \langle \$id \notin this.bl \wedge (new\_init\_is\_not\_better)\rangle$$
$$[this.bl := this.bl + [\$id]](no, this.id)@(id = \$id).W_{\text{Handle}}$$

$$A(id, w, b) \triangleq \langle \$id \notin this.bl \wedge this.lock = 0 \wedge (new\_init\_is\_better)\rangle$$
$$[this.lock := 1, this.bl := this.bl + [\$id]]$$
$$(yes, this.id)@(id = \$id).\text{Wait}(\$id, \$w, \$b)$$

$$\text{Wait}(id, w, b) \triangleq [this.ex := this.partner, this.partner := \$id,$$
$$this.cw := \$w, this.cb := \$b](\$msg = confirm)(\$msg).$$
$$[this.lock := 0](bye)@(id = this.ex).W_{\text{Handle}}$$
$$+ [this.lock := 0, this.bl := this.bl - [\$id]]$$
$$(\$msg = toolate)(\$msg).W_{\text{Handle}}$$

$$D(id) \triangleq \langle \$id \in this.bl\rangle()@(\texttt{ff}).W_{\text{Handle}}$$

In the above specifications, the pair (cw, cb) denotes the characteristics of current partner, which is used by the responder to compare him with a new proposer. For example, predicate *new_init_is_better* is encoded as:

$$(\text{this}.partner = 0) \lor (\$w = \text{this}.pw \land \text{this}.cw \neq \text{this}.pw) \lor$$
$$(\$w = \text{this}.cw \land \$b = \text{this}.pb \land \text{this}.cb \neq \text{this}.pb)$$

Bottom-Up Stable Marriage. We have also experimented with another approach to SMP, where proposers start looking for the less-liked partner and try to incrementally improve their level of satisfaction by continuously proposing themselves even after finding a partner in the attempt to find someone they like more then their current one. In this case both proposers and responders can be dropped by their current partner if a more appreciated option pops up.

We have implemented this protocol in AbC using a slightly different approach. We used an extra process in components Proposer and Responder that plays the role of a message queue manager. This process appends every incoming messages to the tail of queue, while another process implementing the main behaviour retrieves messages from the queue and processes them sequentially.

Due to space limit, we omit the presentation of this specification. The interested reader can refer to [1] for full specifications of case studies.

4.2 Formal Analysis

UMC Models and Annotations. We have developed a tool [1] to implement the translation rules presented in Sect. 3. This tool has been used to translate the three AbC solutions for SMP into UMC models. The number of UMC code lines varies depending on specification and on the input instances. For example, in the classical case, the number of UMC lines are the same for component M, while it increases proportionally with the size of the problem for component W due to the use of operator $|^n$.

The actual UMC model used for the analysis is composed by two objects: an object, triggered by a *start*(<inputdata>) event, modelling the behaviour of the AbC specification with the given input data, and an object which generates all the possible input data and activates the AbC model with them. For checking the generic (i.e. for all inputs) validity of a formula ϕ we in practice evaluate the formula A[{not *start*} W {*start*} ϕ], which says that ϕ holds in the initial state of any of the possible scenarios. The number of generated system states reported in the rest of this section refers to the cumulative data over the whole input domain.

In order to verify our properties of interests, we have annotated the generated UMC models with abstraction rules to make observable labels on states and actions.

```
Abstractions {
    State id[0]=$1 and partner[0]=$2 -> haspartner($1,$2)
    State id[1]=$1 and partner[1]=$2 -> haspartner($1,$2)
    ...
    Action sending($1,$2) -> send($1,$2)
    Action received($1,$2,$3) -> received($1,$2,$3)
    -- Other instrument
    Action m_decr -> m_decr
    Action w_decr -> w_decr
}
```

Here rules starting with `States` expose labels $haspartner(\$1, \$2)$ in all system states, where $\$1$ is the identifier of a component (proposer or responder) and $\$2$ is the matching partner. We assume that the identifiers of initiators and responders are in the ranges $[1 \ldots n]$ and $[n + 1 \ldots 2n]$ respectively, with n being the problem size. Rules starting with `Actions` instead expose *send* and *receive* labels on all transitions denoting attribute send and receive actions.

We have additionally instrumented the models with more involved annotations. In particular, we store the current level of satisfaction of people, computed when a component updates its partner. In classical SMP, the level of satisfaction of initiators and responders is determined by the position of the current partner in the preference list. In the attribute-based variant, this number is calculated based on the similarity between one's own preferences and the characteristics of partners. The procedure issues a signal `decr` if the current computed satisfaction level is smaller than the previous one.

Solution-Independent Properties. For all the three AbC specifications, we are interested in checking the following properties:

F_1 *(convergence)* The system converges to final states:
AF FINAL [3]

F_{2a} *(completeness of matching)* Everybody has a partner:
AF (FINAL implies not $haspartner(*,0)$)

F_{2b} *(uniqueness of matching)* There exists only one final matching:
AG (((EF(FINAL and $haspartner(1,4)$)) implies AF (FINAL and $haspartner(1,4)$))
and ((EF(FINAL and $haspartner(1,5)$)) implies AF(FINAL and $haspartner(1,5)$))
and ((EF(FINAL and $haspartner(1,6)$)) implies AF(FINAL and $haspartner(1,6)$))))

F_{2c} *(symmetry of matching)* The matchings are symmetric:
AG (FINAL implies (($haspartner(1,4)$ implies $haspartner(4,1)$)
and ($haspartner(1,5)$ implies $haspartner(5,1)$)
and ($haspartner(1,6)$ implies $haspartner(6,1)$)))

F_3 *(satisf. of responders)* The level of satisfaction of responders always increases:
A[{not w_decr} U FINAL]

F_4 *(satisf. of proposers)* The level of satisfaction of proposers always increases:
A[{not m_decr} U FINAL].

---

[3] FINAL is a shortcut for "not EX {true} true".

Table 1. Verification results of three algorithmic solutions

Property	F_1	F_{2a}	F_{2b}	F_{2c}	F_3	F_4
Classical	✓	✓	✓	✓	✓	×
Top-down	✓	✓	×	✓	✓	×
Bottom-up	×	×	×	✓	×	×

We performed the analysis for the three proposed solutions on the whole input space using a machine with an Intel Core i5 2.6 GHz, 8 GB RAM, running OS X and UMC v4.4. For the classical case, we considered problems of 3 (i.e., three proposers and three responders). For the attribute-based variants we considered problems of size 2, where each person has four attributes (two for expressing their preferences about partners, and two for modelling their features), each having two possible values. The results of our verification are reported in Table 1. A [✓] means that the formula is satisfied by all possible inputs, while a [×] means that the formula does not hold for at least one input.

By looking at these results we can attempt some considerations:

Classical. Formulae $F_1, F_{2a}, F_{2b}, F_{2c}$ do hold, confirming that the classical algorithm always returns a unique and complete matching. The fact that formula F_3 holds while F_4 does not hold further reflects that a responder keeps trading up its partners for better ones, while proposers can be dropped at any time.

Top-Down. Since formula F_{2a} does hold and F_{2b} does not, we can conclude that the top-down strategy will in general return multiple but complete matchings. This is not surprising, since attribute-based stable marriage is a general case of stable marriage with ties and incomplete list (SMTI) [11], and it is known that one instance of SMTI may have multiple matchings [23]. When verifying F_3 and F_4, we obtain the same results of the classical case.

Bottom-Up. F_1 does not hold indicating that this approach is not guaranteed to converge. This happens in any configuration containing a cycle in the preferences which makes partners chasing each other. Formula F_{2b} does not hold because there might be two proposers competing for one responder w.r.t. their lowest requirements, thus one of the two remains single. We also verified that both formulas F_3, and F_4 do not hold. This reflects that the satisfaction levels of components may decrease because partners from both sides may drop them for better ones at any moment.

Solution-Dependent Properties. In addition to previous properties, we also considered a few protocol-related properties to increase to double check the correctness of the specifications derived from informal requirements.

In particular, we verified the following property of the classical solution:

F_5. After a proposer receives a *no*, it will eventually send a new proposal[4]:
　　AG ([received($1,no$,*)] AF {send(%1,*propose*)} true)

As expected, UMC answered true when verifying F_5. This guarantees that the proposer will send a proposal again, thus confirming that our specification in that regard meets the informal requirements.

As we have specified a communication protocol for matching entities, the following properties of the top-down solution are important to determine whether the implementation conforms to the requirements:

F_6. If a proposer receives a *bye*, it will always eventually send a new proposal:
　　AG([received($1, bye, *$)] AF{send(%1, *propose*)} true)

F_7. If a responder sends *yes* it will eventually receive a *toolate* or *confirm*:
　　AG[send($1, yes$)] AF{received(%1, *confirm*, *) or received(%1, *toolate*, *)}

F_8. After sending a proposal an initiator does not send further proposals until it receives a *no*:
　　AG[send($1, propose$)] A[{*not* send(%1, *propose*)} W{received(%1, *no*, *)}]

By verifying the above properties, we have found out that F_7 holds, while F_6 and F_8 do not. Formula F_8 can be false, because, after sending a proposal, an initiator may receive a *yes*, and then a *bye* message which forces it to send a new proposal. F_6 does not always hold because a initiator after receiving a *bye* message from his partner, may immediately receive a *yes* message from another responder. In this case, it can confirm the new responder without the needs of sending new proposals.

Notice that the informal description of the top-down strategy is not quite rigorous. We have two statements somewhat in contrast, one statement saying that after a *yes* an initiator without a partner should send a *confirm*, and another statement saying that after a *bye* an initiator should send a new proposal. When a *bye* and a *confirm* arrive in sequence, the informal description is not clear in describing the intended behaviour. The formalisation of this requirement in terms of a logical formula, its verification w.r.t. the formal specification of the system, and the observation of the generated counter-example has allowed us to detect and understand this kind of ambiguities.

State Space. Among others, the top-down solution requires the largest number of states with almost 18 millions in the worst case, compared with 0.5 and 4 millions states of the classical and of the bottom-up solution, respectively.

One of the main reasons for this is in the different size of the input space. The attribute-based variant of stable marriage used four attributes with two possible values for each, the space of problems of size 2 has $16^4 = 65536$ configurations. In the classical solution, each agent is characterised by its preference list and thus the space of problems of size 3 only has $3^6 = 729$ configurations.

The complexity of the top-down specification is also a reason for its state explosion, which stems from the use of attribute-based send. In fact, initiators

---

[4] id and %id are used to match the identities of the sending and receiving components.

and responders consist of parallel components performing more actions than their classical counterparts: after sending a proposal message, a proposer needs extra acknowledgment messages for selecting his partner. This greatly increases the interleaving of actions by the sub-processes of the components and thus the state space.

5 Concluding Remarks

We have presented a model-checking approach to the verification of attribute-based communication systems. Starting from informal requirements, we have devised formal specifications in AbC. We have then shown how to systematically translate these into verifiable models accepted by UMC. We have exploited the approach for analysis of an algorithmic solution to the classical stable matching problem, as well as for two variants that extend the problem by introducing attribute-based communication among components. We have considered a set of interesting properties for the above programs and described them first informally and then as explicit properties of the generated models.

The results of our experiments have shown that systems relying on attribute-based communications can be particularly complex to design and analyse. However, by exhaustively verifying a specification over all possible inputs, despite the small size of the problem considered, we have experienced that many non-trivial emerging properties and potential problems can indeed be discovered by following our methodology. This confirms once more that concurrency bugs can be detected by only considering a very small number of processes [22].

Experiments with different implementations of SMP in AErlang, an attribute-based extension of Erlang, have been presented in [11]. Also in some previous work [10], we modeled and verified an example instance of stable marriage using attributes. However there the translation was done manually and the verification considered only one configuration.

The analysis of concurrent systems modelled by process algebras has been thoroughly investigated in [18] by relying on powerful abstractions techniques. Other research groups [13,24,26] have taken an approach similar to ours and perform verification by translating a specification formalism into a verifiable one that could make use of existing model checkers.

Techniques for constructing a model for stable marriage and analyzing its convergence has been presented in [7]. There, the authors encoded classical SMP in a DTMC model and analyzed it with the tools provided by PRISM to study different instances of stochastic matching markets.

There are interesting future directions for this work. An extensive experimentation with additional case studies would certainly contribute to refine our approach [21]. Extending AbC with new constructs to model the spatial and mobility aspects of components would allow handling larger classes of systems [12]. Extending our verification approach to quantitative reasoning will improve usefulness, while investigating state reduction techniques will improve tractability.

References

1. AbC2UMC. http://github.com/ArBITRAL/AbC2UMC
2. UMC. http://fmt.isti.cnr.it/umc
3. UMC Docs. http://fmt.isti.cnr.it/umc/DOCS
4. Abd Alrahman, Y., De Nicola, R., Loreti, M.: On the power of attribute-based communication. In: Albert, E., Lanese, I. (eds.) FORTE 2016. LNCS, vol. 9688, pp. 1–18. Springer, Cham (2016). doi:10.1007/978-3-319-39570-8_1
5. Abd Alrahman, Y., De Nicola, R., Loreti, M.: Programming of CAS systems by relying on attribute-based communication. In: Margaria, T., Steffen, B. (eds.) ISoLA 2016. LNCS, vol. 9952, pp. 539–553. Springer, Cham (2016). doi:10.1007/978-3-319-47166-2_38
6. ter Beek, M.H., Gnesi, S., Mazzanti, F.: From EU projects to a family of model checkers. In: De Nicola, R., Hennicker, R. (eds.) Software, Services, and Systems. LNCS, vol. 8950, pp. 312–328. Springer, Cham (2015). doi:10.1007/978-3-319-15545-6_20
7. Biró, P., Norman, G.: Analysis of stochastic matching markets. Int. J. Game Theo. **42**(4), 1021–1040 (2013)
8. Bolognesi, T., Brinksma, E.: Introduction to the ISO specification language LOTOS. Comput. Netw. **14**, 25–59 (1987). https://doi.org/10.1016/0169-7552(87)90085-7
9. Brinksma, E.: On the design of extended LOTOS, Doctoral Dissertation. University of Twente (1988)
10. De Nicola, R., Duong, T., Inverso, O., Trubiani, C.: AErlang at work. In: Steffen, B., Baier, C., Brand, M., Eder, J., Hinchey, M., Margaria, T. (eds.) SOFSEM 2017. LNCS, vol. 10139, pp. 485–497. Springer, Cham (2017). doi:10.1007/978-3-319-51963-0_38
11. De Nicola, R., Duong, T., Inverso, O., Trubiani, C.: AErlang: empowering erlang with attribute-based communication. In: Jacquet, J.-M., Massink, M. (eds.) COORDINATION 2017. LNCS, vol. 10319, pp. 21–39. Springer, Cham (2017). doi:10.1007/978-3-319-59746-1_2
12. De Nicola, R., Gorla, D., Pugliese, R.: On the expressive power of KLAIM-based calculi. Theor. Comput. Sci. **356**(3), 387–421 (2006)
13. De Nicola, R., Lluch Lafuente, A., Loreti, M., Morichetta, A., Pugliese, R., Senni, V., Tiezzi, F.: Programming and verifying component ensembles. In: Bensalem, S., Lakhneck, Y., Legay, A. (eds.) ETAPS 2014. LNCS, vol. 8415, pp. 69–83. Springer, Heidelberg (2014). doi:10.1007/978-3-642-54848-2_5
14. De Nicola, R., Vaandrager, F.W.: Three logics for branching bisimulation. J. ACM **42**(2), 458–487 (1995). http://doi.acm.org/10.1145/201019.201032
15. Brinksma, E., Giuseppe Scollo, C.S.: LOTOS specifications, their implementations and their tests. In: Proceedings of IFIP WG6.1, Protocol Specification, Testing, and Verification VI, pp. 349–360 (1987)
16. Fantechi, A., Gnesi, S., Lapadula, A., Mazzanti, F., Pugliese, R., Tiezzi, F.: A logical verification methodology for service-oriented computing. ACM Transactions on Software Engineering and Methodology (TOSEM) (2012)
17. Gale, D., Shapley, L.S.: College admissions and the stability of marriage. Am. Math. Mon. **69**(1), 9–15 (1962)
18. Groote, J.F., Reniers, M.A.: Algebraic process verification. Eindhoven University of Technology, Department of Mathematics and Computing Science (2000)

19. Hoare, C.A.R.: Communicating Sequential Processes. Prentice-Hall Inc., Upper Saddle River (1985)
20. ter Beek, M.H., Fantechi, A., Gnesi, S., Mazzanti, F.: A state/event-based model-checking approach for the analysis of abstract system properties. Sci. Comput. Program. **76**(2), 119–135 (2011)
21. Kümmel, M., Busch, F., Wang, D.Z.: Taxi dispatching and stable marriage. Proc. Comput. Sci. **83**, 163–170 (2016)
22. Lu, S., Park, S., Seo, E., Zhou, Y.: Learning from mistakes: a comprehensive study on real world concurrency bug characteristics. In: ACM Sigplan Notices, vol. 43, pp. 329–339. ACM (2008)
23. Manlove, D.F., Irving, R.W., Iwama, K., Miyazaki, S., Morita, Y.: Hard variants of stable marriage. Theor. Comput. Sci. **276**(1–2), 261–279 (2002)
24. Mateescu, R., Salaün, G.: Translating Pi-calculus into LOTOS NT. In: Méry, D., Merz, S. (eds.) IFM 2010. LNCS, vol. 6396, pp. 229–244. Springer, Heidelberg (2010). doi:10.1007/978-3-642-16265-7_17
25. Milner, R. (ed.): A Calculus of Communicating Systems. LNCS, vol. 92. Springer, Heidelberg (1980)
26. Song, H., Compton, K.J.: Verifying π-calculus processes by promela translation. Technical report CSE-TR-472-03 (2003)

How Much Are Your Geraniums?
Taking Graph Conditions Beyond First Order

Arend Rensink[(✉)]

University of Twente, Enschede, The Netherlands
arend.rensink@utwente.nl

Abstract. Previous work has shown how first-order logic can equivalently be expressed through nested graph conditions, also called *condition trees*, with surprisingly few ingredients. In this paper, we extend condition trees by adding set-based operators such as sums and products, calculated over operands that are themselves characterised by first-order logic formulas. This provides a greatly improved way to specify computations such as: *given that the price of a geranium plant equals 2 per flower petal, return the average price of all geraniums with at least one flower*.

We claim the same level of expressive equivalence as before between (extended) condition trees and a certain class of logic formulas; we show that the latter go beyond what can be expressed in first-order logic.

On the practical side, we evaluate the performance and usability of set-based operators by specifying and comparing the example geranium property, with and without set-based operators, in the graph transformation tool GROOVE.

1 Introduction

Graph transformation is a formalism that can be used for different purposes: to define graph languages (as a generalisation of string grammars; see for instance [8]), to define binary relations and functions over graphs (as a generalisation of term rewriting; see for instance [22]) or as a rule-based formalism to describe the behviour of a system (as a generalisation of, for instance, Petri nets; see [18]). In each of these settings, it is of interest how powerful the graph transformation rules are. Here a balance must be struck between sticking to the simplest kind of rules, which have very well-defined properties but provide only low-level building blocks, and allowing more elaborate, powerful rules, which enable one to specify the language, relation or dynamic system at hand more directly and concisely but whose effect is correspondingly harder to analyze.

In this paper, we follow the algebraic approach to graph transformation pioneered by the late Hartmut Ehrig.[1] A good reference work for the theoretical

---

[1] Ehrig was also a leading researcher in *algebraic data specification*, i.e. [7]; in that capacity he was one of the founders of ACT-ONE, the data type specification language of LOTOS, the standardisation of which in [20] was one of Ed Brinksma's early scientific achievements.

© Springer International Publishing AG 2017
J.-P. Katoen et al. (Eds.): Brinksma Festschrift, LNCS 10500, pp. 191–213, 2017.
DOI: 10.1007/978-3-319-68270-9_10

background of the approach in general is the book [5]. The simplest kind of rules, working on the simplest kind of graphs, consist only of a *left hand side* and a *right hand side*, both of which are graphs. Applying such a rule to a given *host graph* roughly consists of the following two steps:

- Finding a match of the left hand side to the host graph, in the form of a graph morphism;
- Replacing the image of the left hand side in the host graph that was identified by the match by a copy of the right hand side, while preserving some context.

From the point of view of analyzability, one of the advantages of these simple rules is that the condition for their applicability as well as the scope of their application are fixed by the left hand side: the rule tests for the presence of a certain substructure in the host graph, and all ensuing changes are applied within this substructure. This, however, is simultaneously a disadvantage when one wants to specify a transformation consisting of an a priori unknown number of small, identical changes. A good example is the effect of firing a transition in a Petri net: in this situation, *all* input places should contain a token which, moreover, should be consumed; and *all* output places should receive a token. There is no bound on the number of input places or output places a transition in an actual Petri net may have; so to achieve the desired effect using only simple graph transformation rules, one has to take refuge to one of the following solutions:

- Devise a fairly complicated protocol of simple rule applications in which the input places are individually tested for the presence of a token, after which those are also individually removed and tokens are placed on the individual output places.
- Create one rule for every combination of m input places and n output places. However, apart from the fact that this gives rise to an infinitary family of rules, one also has to ensure that the rule for $i \times j$ input/output places is not applicable to a transition with $m \times n$ input/output places with $m > i$ or $n > j$. This requires a test for the absence, rather than the presence, of certain structures in the host graph, which in itself is beyond our simple rules as well.

Because limitations of this kind were found to severely hamper the practical use of graph transformation in practice, mechanisms to generalise and extend both the applicability condition of rules as well as their effect have been studied for quite some time. For instance:

- [14] proposes to enrich rules with so-called *negative application conditions* (NACs) that test for the absence of structure, nullifying one of the obstacles to the second solution discussed above.
- [6,23] generalise NACs to *nested graph conditions*, using which any first-order property of graphs can be used as a rule applicability condition. In particular, the nesting structure mimics the concept of *alternating quantifiers*.

- [12,26] study the concept of *amalgamation* of rules, which is a composition mechanism that allows building complex rules such as the Petri net firing rule out of arbitrarily many copies of small "simple" rules. Such composed rules are sometimes called *multi-rules*.
- [24,25] present *nested rules*, which can be seen as a marriage of nested graph conditions and amalgamation: in terms of [26], the proof of the nested graph condition serves as the amalgamation scheme. A nested rule can contain universal quantification not only within its applicability condition, but also within sub-rules, which then have an effect wherever in the host graph the corresponding applicability sub-condition is satisfied.

However, first-order logic has its limitations, and there are in fact applicability conditions and multi-rules that can still not easily be expressed using any of the above techniques. For instance, there are cases where it is relevant to know or compute a *collective* value for a set of sub-graphs characterised by some property. This is where the current paper comes in. As an example, consider the following task:

> Given that the price of a geranium plant equals 2 per flower petal, compute the average price of all geraniums with at least one flower.

In mathematical notation, this can be expressed as follows:

$$(\sum_{g \in G} price(g))/|G| \quad \text{where} \quad \begin{aligned} & price : g \mapsto \sum_{f \in F_g} 2 * petals(f) \\ & G = \{g \mid \mathbf{Geranium}(g) \wedge F_g \neq \varnothing\} \\ & F_g = \{f \mid \mathbf{Flower}(f) \wedge \mathsf{has}(g, f)\} \end{aligned} \tag{1}$$

This has the following noteworthy features:

- $\mathbf{Geranium}(x)$, $\mathbf{Flower}(y)$ and $\mathsf{has}(x, y)$ are predefined predicates expressing, respectively, that x is a geranium, y is a flower, and y is a flower of x,
- $petals(x)$ is a predefined partial function returning the number of petals of x, if x is a $\mathbf{Flower}$.
- G and F_g (for $g \in G$) are defined as sets of, respectively, all geraniums and all flowers of geranium g;
- $price(g)$ is the price of geranium g, defined as twice the number of petals of all flowers of g.

The need to use sets of entities (G and F_g) and set-based operators ($\sum$ and the cardinality $|G|$) take this beyond what can be expressed in first-order logic. Consequently, the computation of a formula such as the above is essentially as tricky to specify using graph transformation, even with nested rules as in [25], as is the firing of a Petri net transition is with only simple rules: again, one has to sum up first the flower petals and subsequently the individual geranium prices one by one.

This paper proposes a way to directly support set-based operators. We present this in three aspects: 1. a generalisation of nested graph conditions; 2. an extension of first-order logic; 3. an experiment showing the performance and conciseness gain with respect to the encoding of (1) using simple rules. We claim that this extension is not just theoretically interesting but also practically useful: in the course of time, we have received multiple feature requests for our graph transformation tool GROOVE [11] to support functionality of this kind, most lately in the context of [16].

The remainder of this paper is structured as follows: in Sect. 2 we present the necessary background from algebra and graph theory; in Sect. 3 we recall the theory behind nested graph conditions. Section 4 contains the main technical contribution, viz. the extension to set-based operators. In Sect. 5 we report on the experiment of encoding formula (1) above in terms of set-based operators; and in Sect. 6 we summarise the findings and present related and future work.

2   Definitions

In this section, we set the stage by recalling some basic notions from algebra, graph theory and logic that we need to present our contribution.

2.1   Algebra

We restrict ourselves to the domain of integers. This means we work with a fixed signature Σ with consisting of the standard arithmetic operators, such as add (addition), mul (multiplication) and div (division). Each operator has an *arity* $\nu(o) \in \mathbb{N}$. Constants are included as nullary operators. We also use a universe of variables $\mathcal{V}$. From these ingredients, we define *terms* through the following grammar:

$$t ::= x \mid o(t_1, \ldots, t_{\nu(o)}) \tag{2}$$

where $x \in \mathcal{V}$ and $o \in \Sigma$. The set of terms over a given set of variables $V \subseteq \mathcal{V}$ is denoted $\mathbb{T}(V)$.

Definition 1 (algebra, homomorphism). *An algebra is a tuple $A = \langle D, (F^o)_{o \in \Sigma} \rangle$ consisting of*

- *a value domain D;*
- *a partial function $F^o \colon D^{\nu(o)} \to D$ for each $o \in \Sigma$.*

Given two algebras A_1, A_2, a homomorphism $h \colon A_1 \to A_2$ is a partial function $h \colon D_1 \to D_2$ such that for all operators $o \in O$ and all $v_i \in D$ $(1 \leq i \leq \nu(o))$:

$$h(F_1^o(v_1, \ldots, v_{\nu(o)})) = F_2^o(h(v_1), \ldots, h(v_{\nu(o)}))$$

provided that all function applications are defined.

The functions F^o are allowed to be partial so that division by zero can be accounted for. Henceforth we identify an algebra A with its value domain and just talk about the values of A, rather than of the domain of A. In fact, in this paper we restrict ourselves to two particular (families of) algebras:

- The term algebra $\mathbb{T}(V)$ for arbitrary finite sets of variables $V \subseteq \mathcal{V}$, where each function F^o is total and constructs a new term by applying the corresponding operator o to the operand terms.
- The natural algebra $\mathbb{I}$ consisting of the "actual" integers and the "actual" functions for addition, multiplication, etc. (and division by 0 is undefined).

2.2   Attributed Graphs

In the following, $\mathcal{N}$ denotes a universe of nodes, and $\mathcal{L}$ a universe of graph (edge) labels.

Definition 2 (graph, morphism). *A graph is a tuple $G = \langle N, E \rangle$ where*

- *$N \subseteq \mathcal{N}$ is a set of nodes;*
- *$E \subseteq N \times \mathcal{L} \times N$ is a set of edges.*

Graph G is called attributed *over an algebra A if $A \subseteq N_G$. The class of all graphs is denoted* **Graph** *and the subclass of attributed graphs* **Graph**^{A}.

Given two graphs G_1, G_2, a morphism $f : G_1 \to G_2$ is a function $f : N_1 \to N_2$ such that:

$$f : (n_1, a, n_2) \mapsto (f(n_1), a, f(n_2)).$$

Morphism f is called attributed *if the G_i are attributed over A_i ($i = 1, 2$) and $f \upharpoonright A_1$ is a homomorphism from A_1 to A_2. The class of all morphism is denoted* **Morph**.

Morphism f is called injective *if $f(n_1) = f(n_2)$ implies $n_1 = n_2$.*

We use $src(e)$, $lab(e)$ and $tgt(e)$ to denote the source, label and target of an edge e, and $dom(f)$, $cod(f)$ to denote the domain and codomain of a morphism f. If G is attributed over A, we call the elements of $A \subseteq N_G$ data nodes and the elements of $N_G \setminus A$ pure nodes. We also refer to a graph that is not attributed as a *pure graph*.

Note that the node set of an attributed graph is typically infinite, because algebra domains are. The only data nodes of such a graph we are usually interested in (and that are included in figures) are those that are connected by some edge to a pure node.

In practice, the only attributed morphisms f we will consider are such that either $dom(f)$ and $cod(f)$ are graphs over $\mathbb{T}(V_1)$ and $\mathbb{T}(V_2)$ for some $V_1 \subseteq V_2 \subseteq \mathcal{V}$ and $f \upharpoonright \mathbb{T}(V_1)$ is the identity homomorphism, or such that $dom(f)$ is attributed over $\mathbb{T}(V)$ for some $V \subseteq \mathcal{V}$ and $cod(f)$ is attributed over $\mathbb{I}$.

2.3   First-Order Logic

In its purest form, first-order logic (**FOL**) reasons about arbitrary structures, using formulas composed from some predefined set of n-ary predicates. Here we restrict to binary predicates, which coincide with the set of edge labels $\mathcal{L}$ introduced above.

Furthermore, we also use a set of variables $\mathcal{X}$, which for now is not connected to the data variables $\mathcal{V}$ used above. The grammar of **FOL** is then given by:

$$\phi ::= a(x, y) \mid \phi_1 \vee \phi_2 \mid \phi_1 \wedge \phi_2 \mid \neg\phi \mid \forall x : \phi \mid \exists x : \phi \qquad (3)$$

for arbitrary $a \in \mathcal{L}$ and $x, y \in \mathcal{X}$. We also use the notation $Q X : \phi$ with $Q \in \{\exists, \forall\}$ and finite $X \subseteq \mathcal{X}$ to denote the simultaneous existential or universal quantification over all variables in X. We use $fv(\phi)$ to denote the free variables of a formula ϕ, defined in the usual way; we call formula ϕ *closed* if $fv(\phi) = \varnothing$.

Formulas are evaluated over *interpretations*, which define a domain of discourse as well as actual relations for all predicate symbols. In our setting, interpretations coincide with graphs, although in keeping with tradition we will denote them I rather than G: for a given predicate symbol $a \in \mathcal{L}$, the actual binary relation as defined by a given interpretation (i.e., graph) I is nothing but the set of pairs $(src(e), tgt(e))$ for all edges $e \in E_I$ with $lab(e) = a$.

We also need the concept of an *assignment* α, which is a partial mapping $\alpha \colon \mathcal{X} \to N_G$ mapping at least all free variables of ϕ to nodes in the interpretation. For given assignments α, β, we use the following constructions:

$$\alpha[x \leftarrow n] \colon y \mapsto \begin{cases} n & \text{if } x = y \\ \alpha(y) & \text{otherwise.} \end{cases} \qquad \alpha[\beta] \colon y \mapsto \begin{cases} \beta(y) & \text{if } y \in dom(\beta) \\ \alpha(y) & \text{otherwise.} \end{cases}$$

The semantics of **FOL** is given by a relation $I, \alpha \vDash \phi$ expressing "I satisfies ϕ under α," defined as follows:

$$
\begin{array}{ll}
I, \alpha \vDash a(x, y) & \text{if } (\alpha(x), a, \alpha(y)) \in E_I \\
I, \alpha \vDash \phi_1 \wedge \phi_2 & \text{if } I, \alpha \vDash \phi_1 \text{ and } I, \alpha \vDash \phi_2 \\
I, \alpha \vDash \phi_1 \vee \phi_2 & \text{if } I, \alpha \vDash \phi_1 \text{ or } I, \alpha \vDash \phi_2 \\
I, \alpha \vDash \neg\phi & \text{if not } I, \alpha \vDash \phi \\
I, \alpha \vDash \forall x : \phi & \text{if } I, \alpha[x \leftarrow n] \vDash \phi \text{ for all } n \in N_I \\
I, \alpha \vDash \exists x : \phi & \text{if there is a } n \in N_I \text{ such that } I, \alpha[x \leftarrow n] \vDash \phi.
\end{array}
$$

α may be omitted if ϕ is closed.

3   Nested Graph Conditions

In this section, we recall nested graph conditions and their equivalence (in expressive power) to **FOL**.

3.1   Conditions as Graphs

In order to understand in what sense a graph can represent a property also expressible in **FOL**, consider that any graph C can be seen as a pattern that occurs or does not occur in another graph G—where "occurring in" means that there exists a morphism $\gamma \colon C \to G$. For an equivalent **FOL** formula, we first have to establish a correspondence of nodes (of C) to variables (in $\mathcal{X}$). For this purpose, we fix a mapping $\xi \colon \mathcal{N} \to \mathcal{X}$ that associates a variable with every node.

Definition 3 (condition graph). *A condition graph is a graph C such that ξ is injective on N_C.*

We use $\xi_C = \xi \restriction N_C$ to denote the restriction of ξ to the nodes of condition graph C (hence ξ_C^{-1} is well-defined). We also denote $x_n = \xi(n)$.

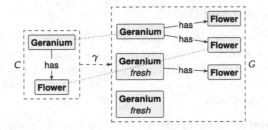

Fig. 1. Example graph condition with satisfying morphism γ (The dotted lines indicate the node mapping)

Whether or not a function $\gamma\colon N_C \to N_G$ is a morphism from C to G is a property of G that is equivalently expressed by the following formula, evaluated over $I = G$ with assignment $\alpha = \gamma \circ \xi_C^{-1}$:

$$\phi_C := \bigwedge\nolimits_{e \in E_C} lab(e)(x_{src(e)}, x_{tgt(e)}) \tag{4}$$

This equivalence is formally stated by the following proposition.

Proposition 1. *Let C be a condition graph, G a graph and α an assignment to N_C.*

1. *$\alpha \circ \xi_C$ is a morphism from C to G if and only if $G, \alpha \vDash \phi_C$.*
2. *There exists a morphism from C to G if and only if $G \vDash \exists\, \xi(N_C) : \phi_C$.*

Clearly, morphisms in the satisfaction of condition graphs take over the role of assignments in the satisfaction of **FOL** formulas, viz., to bind nodes of the target graph [the interpretation] to nodes [variables] of the source graph [the formula].

Example 1. As an example, consider the graphs C and G in Fig. 1. Inscribed node labels are syntactic sugar for self-edges with that label. C specifies that there is a flowering geranium, which is equivalently expressed by

$$\exists x, y : \mathbf{Geranium}(x, x) \land \mathbf{Flower}(y, y) \land \mathsf{has}(x, y).$$

(In keeping with the decision to restrict **FOL** to binary predicates, this uses **Geranium**(x, x) rather than **Geranium**(x) as in (1) to express that x is a geranium; however, there is no conceptual difference between the two.) G actually has 3 pairs of **Geranium**-**Flower**-pairs that satisfy this condition, one of which is identified by the morphism γ in the figure.

The compositional definition of $\vDash$ over **FOL** gradually builds up the assignment α. To also take pre-existing bindings into account in the case of graphs, we will use graph morphisms, rather than graphs, both for the conditions themselves and for the combination of interpretation and assignment.

3.2   Morphisms as Conditions

In the following we consider morphisms $g \colon B \to G$, where B stands for the *bound graph*, which can be seen as a sub-pattern of a condition graph that has already been "found". The nodes of B will turn out to correspond to free variables in the formula to be checked. Accordingly, rather than just condition graphs C, we consider *condition morphisms*.

Definition 4 (condition morphism). *A condition morphism is an injective morphism $c \colon B \to C$ between condition graphs, such that $\xi_B = \xi_C \circ c$.*

Morphism $g \colon B \to C$ satisfies condition morphism $c \colon C \to D$ if (just as in the case of condition graphs, see Proposition 1) a third morphism $\gamma \colon C \to G$ exists, which however (in addition) satisfies $\gamma \circ c = g$; in other words, γ has to respect the image of the bound graph. This is represented by the commuting diagram.

$$
\begin{array}{ccc}
 & B & \\
c \swarrow & & \searrow g \\
C & \dashrightarrow{\gamma} & G
\end{array}
$$

Notationally, this is expressed by the (overloaded) relation $\vDash$:

$$g \vDash c \text{ if there is some } \gamma \colon cod(c) \to cod(g) \text{ such that } \gamma \circ c = g. \tag{5}$$

In fact, γ is a *witness* or *proof* that c exists in (the codomain of) g. We also use $[\![c]\!]$ to denote the semantic function of c that maps any $g \colon B \to G$ to the set of proofs of c on g, thus:

$$[\![c]\!] \colon g \mapsto \{\gamma \in \textbf{\textit{Morph}} \mid \gamma \circ c = g\}. \tag{6}$$

A condition morphism $c \colon B \to C$ is equivalent to the following formula:

$$\phi_c := \exists \xi(N_C \setminus c(N_B)) \colon \phi_C \tag{7}$$

The equivalence is formally stated by the following proposition:

Proposition 2 (condition morphism equivalence). *Let $c \colon B \to C$ be a condition morphism and $g \colon B \to G$ a morphism; then $g \vDash c$ if and only if $G, g \circ \xi_B^{-1} \vDash \phi_c$.*

It should be noted that the injectivity of c is required for this to work: if there were distinct $n_1, n_2 \in N_B$ such that $c(n_1) = c(n_2)$, then ϕ_c would have to include a predicate equating x_{n_1} and x_{n_2}. For simplicity we have chosen to omit equality from the version of **FOL** used in this paper and restrict condition morphisms to injective ones; in the conclusions we briefly discuss what would be required to generalise the setup.

Vice versa, (we claim without proof that) any formula ϕ from the following fragment of **FOL** can be easily encoded into an equivalent graph condition:

$$\phi ::= a(x, y) \mid \phi_1 \wedge \phi_2 \mid \exists x \colon \phi.$$

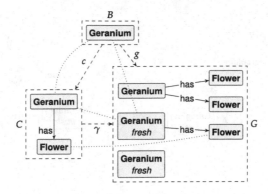

Fig. 2. Example condition morphism with satisfying morphism: $g \vDash c$

Example 2. Figure 2 is a variation on Fig. 1 where the bound graph B pre-identifies the particular **Geranium** of which we want to know whether it has a **Flower**. A proof γ of the satisfaction of c on g is drawn in.

3.3   Trees as Conditions

In the following, we use *diagrams*, which are special kinds of graphs, of which the nodes are labelled with elements of **Graph** and the edges are labelled with elements of **Morph** with domain and codomain corresponding to the edge source and target. We will apply the usual trick of identifying diagram nodes and edges with their labels; in the context of this paper this will not give rise to ambiguities. If G is a node in a diagram D, $out_D(G) = \{f \in D \mid dom(f) = G\}$ denotes the set of morphisms in D with domain G. Such a diagram D is *tree-shaped* if it is acyclic and has a single node $rt(D)$ with no incoming edges, whereas all other nodes have precisely one incoming edge. If D is tree-shaped, then for any node G of D we use $D[G]$ to denote the subtree of D rooted in G.

Definition 5 (condition tree). *A condition tree C is a tree-shaped diagram consisting of condition graphs and condition morphisms, in which, moreover, every graph C is labelled with a boolean operator $O^C \in \{\vee, \wedge\}$ and every morphism c with a quantor $Q^c \in \{\forall, \exists\}$.*

C is called closed *if $rt(C)$ is the empty graph.*

Satisfaction of a condition tree is once more expressed by a relation $C \vDash g$, where $dom(g) = rt(C)$, recursively defined as follows:

$$g \vDash C \quad \text{if} \quad O^{rt(C)}_{c \in out_C(rt(C))} \ Q^c \gamma \in [\![c]\!](g) : \gamma \vDash C[cod(c)]. \tag{8}$$

In this definition, we use a notational trick by which the quantors Q and logical connectives O are actually used in their natural-language meanings.

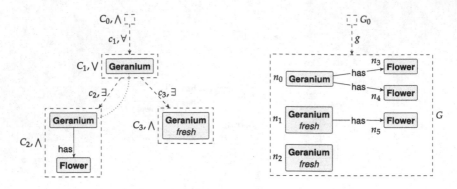

Fig. 3. Example condition tree C and morphism g such that $g \vDash C$

We call a **FOL** formula ϕ and a condition tree C *equivalent* if for any graph morphism $g \colon rt(C) \to G$:

$$G, g \circ \xi_{rt(C)}^{-1} \vDash \phi \quad \text{if and only if} \quad g \vDash C. \tag{9}$$

Example 3. Figure 3 shows a condition tree C that expresses the property "all geraniums either have a flower or are fresh", and a morphism g for which C is satisfied. Note that C_2 and C_3, which are childless in C, are labelled $\bigwedge$: this specifies that all their outgoing morphisms must be covered, which is vacuously satisfied. An equivalent **FOL** formula is:

$$\forall x : \mathbf{Geranium}(x, x) \to ((\exists y : \mathbf{Flower}(y, y) \land \mathsf{has}(x, y)) \lor \mathit{fresh}(x, x)).$$

A key result, reformulated from [25], is that conditions trees and **FOL** formulas are expressively equivalent. This generalises Proposition 2 to condition trees.

Theorem 1 (condition tree equivalence).

1. *For every **FOL** formula ϕ, there is an equivalent condition tree C_ϕ;*
2. *For every condition tree C, there is an equivalent **FOL** formula ϕ_C.*

3.4   Proof Trees

For the extension to set-based operators in the next section, it is useful to present an alternative characterisation of the satisfaction of condition trees defined in (8). Given a morphism $g \colon B \to G$ and a condition morphism $c \colon B \to C$ in a condition tree C, a set of morphisms $\Gamma \subseteq (C \to G)$ is said to *cover* c if $\mathsf{Q}^c = \exists$ and $|\Gamma \cap [\![c]\!](g)| > 0$, or $\mathsf{Q}^c = \forall$ and $[\![c]\!](g) \subseteq \Gamma$.

A *proof* of a condition tree C on a morphism $g \colon rt(C) \to G$ is itself a tree-shaped diagram P, with a mapping π to C that preserves all graphs and morphisms of P, and for every graph P a morphism $\gamma_P \colon P \to G$, such that

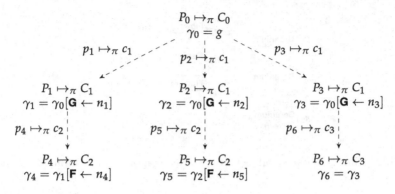

Fig. 4. Proof for $g \vDash C$ in Fig. 3. **G** is the **Geranium**-node in C_1 and **F** the **Flower**-node in C_2

(i) $\gamma_{rt(P)} = g$
(ii) $\gamma_{cod(p)} \circ p = \gamma_{dom(p)}$ for all edges p in $\boldsymbol{P}$
(iii) If $O^{\pi(P)} = \bigvee$ for P in $\boldsymbol{P}$, then $out_P(P)$ covers *some* $c \in out_C(\pi(P))$;
(iv) If $O^{\pi(P)} = \bigwedge$ for P in $\boldsymbol{P}$, then $out_P(P)$ covers *all* $c \in out_C(\pi(P))$.

$\boldsymbol{P}$ is called a *minimal proof* if it is no longer a proof when a single branch is removed. In practice, we always use minimal proofs.

Example 4. Figure 4 shows a proof $\boldsymbol{P}$ of the satisfaction $g \vDash \boldsymbol{C}$ in Example 3. The morphisms γ_i for the nodes P_i of $\boldsymbol{P}$ are constructed step by step, starting with the empty morphism ($\gamma_0 = g$) and adding images along the way. Note that this is not the only proof of $\boldsymbol{C}$ on g: from P_1, another mapping from **F** exists to the other flower n_3 of **Geranium**-node n_0, whereas from P_2, the fact that **Geranium**-node n_1 is *fresh* means that it is also possible to cover c_2 rather than c_3.

The following proposition states that a condition tree is satisfied by a morphism g if and only if there exists a proof of this kind. In other words, proofs are witnesses of the satisfaction of a condition tree.

Proposition 3. *Let $\boldsymbol{C}$ be a condition tree and g a morphism with $dom(g) = rt(\boldsymbol{C})$; then $g \vDash \boldsymbol{C}$ if and only if there exists a proof $\boldsymbol{P}$ for $\boldsymbol{C}$ on g.*

4   Set-Based Operators

All of the theory in Sect. 3 can be extended without any problem whatsoever to attributed graphs, with the understanding that condition graphs C are always attributed over $T_\Sigma(V_C)$ for some fixed $V_C \subseteq V$ and host graphs are attributed over $\mathbb{I}$, that $V \subseteq \mathcal{X}$ (all data variables are logical variables) and that ξ is the identity over V (hence every algebra variable stands for itself). To re-establish the connection to **FOL** (Theorem 1), all that is required is to extend basic predicates

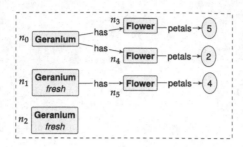

Fig. 5. Flowering geraniums, subject to the price computation $\mathsf{sum}(\mathsf{mul}(2, x) \mid x, f_0 : \mathsf{has}(g_0, f_0) \wedge \mathsf{petals}(f_0, x))$

to range over terms rather than just variables, i.e., so that they are of the form $a(t_1, t_2)$, and to extend the semantics accordingly to

$$I, \alpha \models a(t_1, t_2) \qquad \text{if } (h_\alpha(t_1), a, h_\alpha(t_2)) \in E_I$$

where $h_\alpha \colon \mathbb{T}(V_I) \to \mathbb{I}$ is uniquely determined by the assignment α.

This sets the stage for the introduction of set-based operators. Essentially, these arise from commutative and associative binary operators in Σ; essentially, they are operators that can be applied to arbitrary finite (in some case only non-empty) multisets of operands without regard for their ordering. Examples are:

- card, which just returns the number of operands;
- sum and mul, which compute the product, respectively sum;
- max and min, which compute the maximum, respectively minimum.

We use $\Sigma^\mathbb{O}$, ranged over by $\mathbb{O}$, to denote the collection of set-based operators. Clearly, each of the $\mathbb{O}$ has a corresponding operation $F^\mathbb{O} \colon 2^\mathbb{I} \to \mathbb{I}$. The core idea of this paper is that the operands can be computed over sets of graphs that are themselves characterised through universal quantification. This gives rise to terms of the form $\mathbb{O}(t \mid X : \phi)$, which computes t for all assignments to the (hitherto free) variables in X that cause ϕ to be satisfied.

Example 5. Let $t = \mathsf{sum}(\mathsf{mul}(2, x) \mid x, f_0 : \mathsf{has}(g_0, f_0) \wedge \mathsf{petals}(f_0, x))$ be a term, to be computed over the graph in Fig. 5. Note that g_0 is a free variable in t, which should be assigned one of the **Geranium**-nodes in the graph before the term can be evaluated. If $\alpha : g_0 \mapsto n_0$, then $\mathsf{has}(g_0, f_0) \wedge \mathsf{petals}(f_0, x)$ can be satisfied by assigning n_3 to f_0 and 5 to x, or by assigning n_4 to f_0 and 2 to x; hence t evaluates to $2 * 5 + 2 * 2 = 14$. Alternatively, if $\alpha : g_0 \mapsto n_1$ then t evaluates to 8, and if $g_0 \mapsto n_2$ then t becomes 0.

To formalise this, we extend and combine the term grammar (2) and the *FOL* grammar (3):

$$t ::= x \mid o(t_1, \dots, t_{\nu(o)}) \mid \mathbb{O}(t \mid X : \phi)$$
$$\phi ::= a(t_1, t_2) \mid \mid \phi_1 \vee \phi_2 \mid \phi_1 \wedge \phi_2 \mid \neg\phi \mid \forall x : \phi \mid \exists x : \phi. \qquad (10)$$

The function fv is extended with $fv(\mathbb{O}(t \mid X : \phi)) = fv(t) \setminus X$. We use $\mathbb{S}$ to denote the set of terms according to this grammar, and $\mathbb{S}(V)$ for those terms that take their free variables from V; and we call the resulting logic *set-based operator logic* (**SBOL**).

Note that (10) has a recursive dependency between the rules for t and ϕ; hence, to interpret **SBOL**, we need to simultaneously extend the notion of homomorphism as well as the semantics of **FOL**. Clearly, to evaluate a set-based operator application, we need to have an interpretation available; hence we use "extended homomorphisms" $h_{I,\alpha}$ to map $\mathbb{S}$ to $\mathbb{I}$, where I is an interpretation and α an assignment:

$$h_{I,\alpha} : \mathbb{O}(t \mid X : \phi) \mapsto F^{\mathbb{O}} | h_{I,\alpha[\beta]}(t) \beta \colon X \to I, \ I, \alpha[\beta] \vDash \phi.$$

Here, β may assign any of the elements of the interpretation I to the variables in X. This should be compared to the semantics of universal quantification as in $\forall X : \phi$, where the assignment is likewise extended to all variables in X before ϕ is evaluated. The **SBOL** semantic rule for predicates is then straightforward:

$$I, \alpha \vDash a(t_1, t_2) \qquad \text{if } (h_{I,\alpha}(t_1), a, h_{I,\alpha}(t_2)) \in E_I.$$

$\mathbb{O}$-terms are encoded in condition trees by treating them as data variables with additional constraints, namely that the value they are assigned equals the outcome of the corresponding set-based operation. The tricky part is that the sub-term t in an $\mathbb{O}$-term $\mathbb{O}(t \mid X : \phi)$ must be evaluated in the same context as ϕ, which corresponds to a child of the condition tree node in which the $\mathbb{O}$-term itself appears. This is illustrated by the following example.

Example 6. Consider the following predicate, based on the term t from Example 5:

$$\phi = \mathsf{price}(g_0, \mathsf{sum}(\mathsf{mul}(2, x) \mid x, f_0 : \mathsf{has}(g_0, f_0) \wedge \mathsf{petals}(f_0, x))).$$

This formula is satisfied by a graph G if the node assigned to g_0 has a price-labelled edge to the value of the sum-term. However, the subterm $\mathsf{mul}(2, x)$ used in computing the sum must be evaluated in a child of the condition graph encoding ϕ itself, with a corresponding universal quantification of the variables x and f_0. This dependency is encoded by the additional, sum-labelled dotted line in the condition tree of Fig. 6.

Definition 6 (extended condition tree). *An extended condition tree $\mathbf{X}$ is a condition tree $\mathbf{C}$ with, for every $\wedge$-labelled graph C in $\mathbf{C}$, a partial mapping $\tau_C \colon V_C \to (\Sigma^{\mathbb{O}} \times \mathbb{T} \times \mathbf{Morph})$ mapping some of the variables in V_C to triples $\langle \mathbb{O}, t, c \rangle$, where $c \in out_{\mathbf{C}}(C)$ is $\forall$-labelled and $t \in N_{cod(c)}$.*

Thus, τ_C identifies which data nodes in C encode terms of the form $\mathbb{O}(t \mid X : \phi)$, indicating what is the operator $\mathbb{O}$, what is the term t and which child in the condition tree corresponds to the subformula ϕ. For instance, in Fig. 6, τ_B maps node $p \in N_B$ to $\langle \mathsf{sum}, \mathsf{mul}(2, x), c \rangle$.

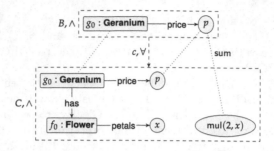

Fig. 6. Extended condition tree for $\mathsf{price}(g_0, \mathsf{sum}(\mathsf{mul}(2, x) \mid x, f_0 : \mathsf{has}(g_0, f_0) \wedge \mathsf{petals}\ (f_0, x)))$

The satisfaction of an extended condition tree $\boldsymbol{X}$ by a morphism g is determined by a minimal proof $\boldsymbol{P}$ of the condition tree $\boldsymbol{C}$ underlying $\boldsymbol{X}$ which should satisfy conditions (i)–(iv) in Sect. 3.4 and in addition

(v) For all nodes P in $\boldsymbol{P}$ and $x \in N_P$ such that $\tau_{\pi(P)}(x) = \langle \mathbb{O}, t, c \rangle$, if $\varGamma \subseteq out_{\boldsymbol{P}}(P)$ covers c then $\gamma_P(x) = F^{\mathbb{O}}|\gamma_{cod(p)}(t)p \in \varGamma$.

In other words, to evaluate a set-based operator node x in a given proof tree node P, where x is labelled by $\tau_{\pi(P)}$ as $\langle \mathbb{O}, t, c \rangle$, we collect the outgoing morphisms of P that cover (i.e., prove) the $\forall$-quantified condition morphism c, and for all of these we look up the value of t in the concrete host graph. The concrete operation $F^{\mathbb{O}}$ is applied to the resulting (multi)set. Thus, x effectively encodes the term $\mathbb{O}(t \mid X : \phi_{\boldsymbol{X}[cod(c)]})$, where $X = \xi(N_{cod(c)} \setminus N_P)$ is the set of variables fresh in $cod(c)$.

Example 7. Figure 7 shows a proof tree for the extended condition tree of Fig. 6. The two children of the root, P_1 and P_2, assign n_3, resp. n_4 to f_0, and accordingly, 5 resp. 2 to x; the term $\mathsf{mul}(2, x)$ hence evaluates to 10, resp. 4. Now condition (v) above kicks in, emposing the constraint

$$\gamma_0(p) = F^{\mathsf{sum}}\{\gamma_1(\mathsf{mul}(2, x)), \gamma_2(\mathsf{mul}(2, x))\} = F^{\mathsf{sum}}\{10, 4\} = 14.$$

It is interesting to note that where proof trees are ordinarily built from parents to children, condition (v) has a dependency in the other direction: the value of a set-based operation can only be computed after a covering set of children has been established.

This is the core ingredient in the following main theorem of this paper, extending Theorem 1, which we present here without proof.

Theorem 2 (extended condition tree equivalence).

1. *For every* **SBOL** *formula ϕ, there is an equivalent extended condition tree $\boldsymbol{X}_\phi$;*
2. *For every extended condition tree $\boldsymbol{X}$, there is an equivalent* **SBOL** *formula $\phi_{\boldsymbol{X}}$.*

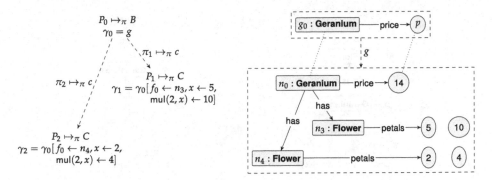

Fig. 7. Proof for the extended condition tree of Fig. 6

Both directions can be proved by induction, on (respectively) the structure of **SBOL** formulas and the depth of extended condition trees. The interesting case for Clause 1 is, obviously, how to deal with terms of the form $\mathbb{O}(t \mid X : \phi)$: this requires the introduction of a $\forall$-labelled child which a τ-mapping. Vice versa, for Clause 2, every τ-mapping gives rise to an $\mathbb{O}$-term.

5   The Geranium Experiment

The original motivation of this paper was not to develop a new theoretical concept but to extend the existing tool GROOVE [11] with a feature allowing the use of set-based operators. We will now illustrate the capabilities of the tool. It should be noted that, because the implementation preceded the theoretical foundation exposed in this paper, notations in the tool are not identical to the ones in the previous sections.

5.1   Two-Step Computation

Figure 8 shows two rules in GROOVE that specify, successively, the simultaneous computation of the price of all geraniums in the world, and the computation of the average price of geraniums with at least one flower. The applicability condition of these rules is given by condition trees with set-based operators.

The figure shows two nested rules in GROOVE syntax, the complete explanation of which is out of scope here. An important aspect is that the condition tree is flattened in that all graphs are combined; the structure of the tree is recovered through quantifier nodes.

- The root of the condition tree is always the empty graph—i.e., condition trees are always closed;
- The root has only a single child, called the *base*, which is existentially quantified and consists of all nodes without @-connector to any quantifier node, plus all edges between them;

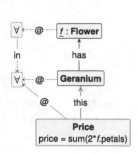

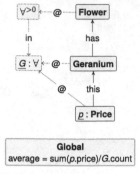

(a) Simultaneous computation of individual geranium prices

(b) Global average price of flowering geraniums

Fig. 8. Two-step computation of average geranium prices using multi-rules. (Color figure online)

- Quantifier nodes point to their parents in the condition tree through in-connectors; quantifier nodes without outgoing in-connectors are children of the base;
- Except for the base, every level of the condition tree consists of the nodes linked by @-connectors to the corresponding quantifier node or one of its ancestors, plus all edges between them;
- As an additional feature, not formalised in Definition 5, one of the quantifier nodes in Fig. 8b is labelled $\forall^{>0}$ rather than $\forall$. This indicates that, in a proof tree, a covering of this level should contain at least one element (corresponding to the fact that, in (1), we only want the average price of flower-bearing geraniums).

The green nodes and edges in Fig. 8 (the **Price**-node in Fig. 8a and the **Global**-node in Fig. 8b) are *created* when the rule is applied; if, as in the case of Fig. 8a, there is also a @-connector from such a creator node to a quantifier, that means an instance is that node is created for every match of the corresponding condition tree level.

The computation of the average price consists of applying these two rules in succession. Figure 9 shows an example computation, starting with the host graph in Fig. 9a; the application of the rule in Fig. 8a results in Fig. 9b, after which the rule in Fig. 8b results in Fig. 9c.

5.2   One-Step Computation

The above solution still does not actually express the whole expression (1) in a single go: instead, the function *price* is first computed, then used. A single rule that encodes the entire condition is given in Fig. 10.

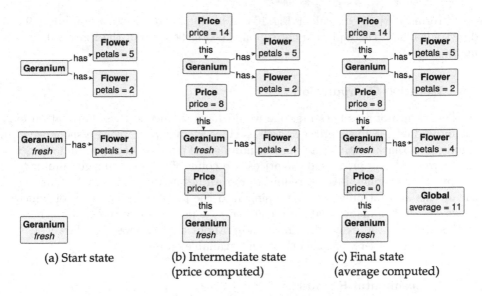

(a) Start state

(b) Intermediate state
(price computed)

(c) Final state
(average computed)

Fig. 9. Example average price computation

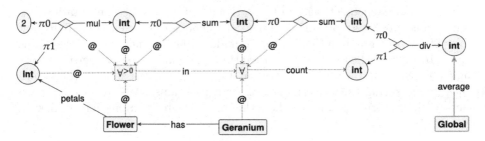

Fig. 10. One-step computation of average geranium prices

This rule uses more primitive syntax for expressions, which requires some further explanation.[2] Elliptical nodes are data nodes, which can be either data values or variables. Diamond-shaped ones correspond to operations: their outgoing π_i-labelled edges collect a list of arguments, and the remaining outgoing edge applies an operator to that list, depositing the result in its target node. Examples of such operators are: mul, which stands for multiplication (in this case, the multiplication of 2 to the number of petals of a **Flower**), 2 instances of sum, which is the set-based summation, and div, which divides the summed-up geranium prices by the number of geraniums involved—the latter being made available through an outgoing count-edge of the universally quantified level.

---

[2] The reason for reverting to more primitive syntax is simply that the GROOVE's expression parser cannot yet cope with the nested set-based operators used in this rule.

In terms of Fig. 9, the rule in Fig. 10 can be applied to the start graph Fig. 9a, directly leading to a graph that corresponds to Fig. 9c without the **Price**-labelled nodes.

5.3   Iterative Computation

In the absence of set operators, one would have to encode the computation of the individual geranium prices as well as their average price using a sequence of simple rules that iteratively add up the numbers of petals of each geranium to get the correct value of *price*, and the prices and count of the flowering geraniums to compute the average. Besides requiring more rules as well as a way to schedule them, this also introduces bookkeeping into the graph to keep track of which flowers or geraniums were already counted. We do not show the solution here, as this would entail explaining much more about the GROOVE tool; however, it is packaged together with the others and available online.[3]

5.4   Experimental Results

Table 1 reports the performance of the three implemented solutions: one-step (Sect. 5.2), two-step (Sect. 5.1) and iterative (Sect. 5.3). The computation has been applied on host graphs ranging in size from 60 nodes (essentially 10 disjoint copies of the start graph in Fig. 9a) to 600 nodes (100 disjoint copies of that same graph), by running the relevant rules 1000 times and taking the average time for a single computation. GROOVE is written in Java; to ged rid of some of the known issues in measuring the performance of Java programs, we started all experiments with a "warm-up run" to allow the Just-In-Time compilation to kick in.

Table 1. Performance of the geranium experiment

Graph size (#nodes)	One-step (ms)	Two-step (ms)	Iterative (ms)
60	0.59	0.72	5
120	0.99	1.29	17
180	1.32	1.57	37
240	1.44	2.40	67
300	1.48	2.90	108
360	1.71	3.18	140
420	1.96	3.52	190
480	1.90	3.99	249
540	2.11	4.64	316
600	2.39	5.15	395

---

[3] See groove.cs.utwente.nl/downloads/grammars/.

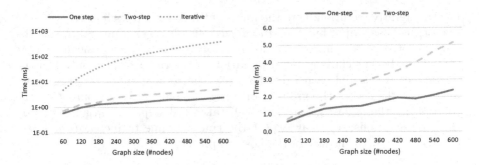

Fig. 11. Relative performance and scaling of the three implemented solutions

Even so, the precise run-time figures deviate within a margin of about 10% when repeating the same experiment, without, however, affecting the qualitative outcome and conclusions in any meaningful way.

The experiment has been conducted on a laptop with an Intel i5-6300U CPU running at 2.40 GHz, using Java 8 with sufficient memory to avoid major garbage collections. The GROOVE rule system used is available online and can be run in the newest version of the tool GROOVE.[4]

The results are shown graphically in Fig. 11. The left hand side compares all three approaches on a logarithmic scale, the second is limited to the one-step and two-step solutions that use the set operators and uses a linear time scale.

5.5   Evaluation

It can be seen from the data provided that not only are the one-step and two-step, set operator-based solutions several orders of magnitude faster than the iterative solution, they also scale much better: on the sample size of our experiment, the trend seems linear for the set operator-based solutions whereas the degradation in performance is clearly worse for the iterative solution.

A second observation is that the one-step solution performs better than the two-step solution, even at small problem sizes; the difference becomes more pronounced at larger sizes, seeing that the slope of the approximately linear trend is shallower for the former.

Both of these observations can be explained by a superficial analysis of the run-time effort involved. There are two effects in play when the graph size grows: matching becomes harder and transformation sequences become longer.

– For the set operator-based solutions: the *number* of matches remains the same (all rules have exactly 1 match) but the *size* of that match—which is nothing else than a proof tree—grows linearly. The length of the transformation sequence is not affected: it is always 1 for the one-step solution and 2 for the two-step solution. All in all, it makes sense that the running time of the computation increases linearly with the size of the host graph.

---

[4] See sf.net/projects/groove.

- For the iterative solution: here the *numer* of matches grows linearly with the size of the host graph, but the *size* of each match is constant. Since (for the purpose of this experiment) the exploration is set to linear (meaning that there is no backtracking in the exploration of the rule system), only 1 of the n matches is selected each time; however, the total number of steps grows linearly in the size of the graph. Concretely, in our solution, computing the solution for the largest graph (size 600) takes 703 steps. All in all, based on these observations, one may expect the running time to increase (at least) quadratically with the size of the host graph.

Besides a difference in performance, there is also a clear difference in conciseness of our three solutions: the single rule of Fig. 10 is (somewhat) smaller than the two rules of Fig. 8, whereas our iterative solution consists of 5 (smaller) rules plus a control program that schedules them. Moreover, all solutions except the one-step need to add elements for the graph for bookkeeping purposes: in the case of the two-step solution, this consists of the **Price**-nodes created by Fig. 8a and used by Fig. 8b, whereas the iterative solution does not only use such **Price**-nodes but also counted-markers for those flowers and geraniums that have already been taken into account.

Finally, we claim that there is also a difference in understandability. Though the primitive syntax of Fig. 10 is not ideal, this is a matter of supporting further syntactic sugar. The main difficulty in understanding the set-operator based solutions lies in the concept of condition trees, which can admittedly be tricky in practice, but once mastered is (to our opinion) quite usable. In contrast, the iterative solution requires an understanding of the way the 5 smaller rules work together, which is far from straightforward.

6 Conclusion

To summarise: the contribution reported in this paper consists of

- The extension of nested graph conditions to set-based operators such as sum, product and cardinality, increasing their expressiveness beyond first-order logic;
- The extension of first-order logic to set-based operator logic *SBOL*, which we claim to be expressively equivalent to the extended graph conditions;
- The implementation of set-based operators in GROOVE, leading to a clear gain in performance, conciseness and understandability in rule systems where set-based operators play a major role, as illustrated by a single case study.

6.1 Related Work

Within graph transformation, patterns and techniques to specify multi-rules have been studied for some time, leading to concepts such as *star operators* [19], *subgraph operators* [3], *collection operators* [13], *cloning rules* [15] and *set-valued transformations* [10]. More recently, *pattern rewriting* [17] has been developed and applied in the context of chemical reactions [1]. We believe that all these concepts can be seen as special forms of amalgamation as proposed first in [26] and generalised later in [12], as can our own nested rules from [24,25]. However, the treatment of set-based operators presented in this paper, though inspired by the mechanisms of amalgamation, goes beyond it in expressiveness.

On the tool front, many of the graph transformation tools that are currently being maintained support some form of multi-rules. Examples are FUJABA [21] which features *set nodes*, and HENSHIN [2] which knows the concept of an *amalgamation unit*. Again, we believe that these are limited to (essentially) the first-order level and cannot directly express set-based operators.

It should also be recognised that there are alternative ways to achieve the effect of multi-rules. For instance, VIATRA2 [4] allows the specification of recursive patterns through the control language, and FUJABA can specify some degree of parallel rule application through *storyboards*.

6.2   Future Work

In the theoretical exposition in this paper, we have kept things simple wherever we could. In particular, we have restricted our algebra to integers only, and our condition morphisms to injective ones. On the first count, we foresee no difficulty to extend to other datatypes, using multi-sorted algebras to ensure well-typedness. On the second count, we have already shown in [23] that allowing condition morphisms to be non-injective corresponds to introducing equality as a basic predicate in the logic; we have no reason to believe that the same correspondence fails to hold in the extended case of this paper.

On the logic side, it would be interesting to know whether **SBOL** as introduced in (10) actually corresponds to a known fragment of logic. Clearly it is well within monadic second-order logic, since all that can be done with sets in **SBOL** is applying set-based operators to them; this is far less than the ability to use sets as first-class values. As one reviewer suggested, the fact that the effect of set-based operators can be mimicked by an iterative solution justifies a hypothesis that the introduction of fixpoints of some kind into **FOL** may be sufficient to cover **SBOL**—although we feel that this will quite likely be more powerful, maybe even quite a bit so.

On the implementation side, the support of set-based operators in GROOVE can certainly be further improved, especially by providing further syntactic sugar for nested set-based operators as used in Fig. 10 (see Footnote 2). It should be noted that GROOVE does support other datatypes besides integers, and also supports non-injectivity in condition morphisms.

Acknowledgement. My scientific career got underway under the inspiring supervision of Ed Brinksma, who instilled and shared a fascination with the maths behind it all, without losing sight of intuition and pragmatics. Even if I do remember throwing a frustrated pen at him at one occasion, I am glad to have had Ed as mentor and friend.

References

1. Andersen, J.L., Flamm, C., Merkle, D., Stadler, P.F.: Inferring chemical reaction patterns using rule composition in graph grammars. CoRR abs/1208.3153 (2012). http://arxiv.org/abs/1208.3153
2. Arendt, T., Biermann, E., Jurack, S., Krause, C., Taentzer, G.: Henshin: advanced concepts and tools for in-place EMF model transformations. In: Petriu, D.C., Rouquette, N., Haugen, Ø. (eds.) MODELS 2010. LNCS, vol. 6394, pp. 121–135. Springer, Heidelberg (2010). doi:10.1007/978-3-642-16145-2_9
3. Balasubramanian, D., Narayanan, A., Neema, S., Shi, F., Thibodeaux, R., Karsai, G.: A subgraph operator for graph transformation languages. In: Ehrig and Giese [9]. http://journal.ub.tu-berlin.de/index.php/eceasst/article/view/72
4. Balogh, A., Varró, D.: Advanced model transformation language constructs in the VIATRA2 framework. In: Haddad, H. (ed.) Proceedings of the 2006 ACM Symposium on Applied Computing (SAC), pp. 1280–1287. ACM (2006)
5. Ehrig, H., Ehrig, K., Prange, U., Taentzer, G.: Fundamentals of Algebraic Graph Transformation. Monographs in Theoretical Computer Science. Springer, Heidelberg (2006). doi:10.1007/3-540-31188-2
6. Ehrig, H., Ehrig, K., Habel, A., Pennemann, K.: Theory of constraints and application conditions: from graphs to high-level structures. Fundam. Inform. **74**(1), 135–166 (2006). http://content.iospress.com/articles/fundamenta-informaticae/fi74-1-07
7. Ehrig, H., Mahr, B.: Fundamentals of Algebraic Specification, Part I and II. Monographs in Theoretical Computer Science. An EATCS Series, vols. 6 and 21. Springer, Heidelberg (1985, 1990). doi:10.1007/978-3-642-69962-7, doi:10.1007/978-3-642-61284-8
8. Ehrig, H., Pfender, M., Schneider, H.J.: Graph-grammars: an algebraic approach. In: Symposium on Switching and Automata Theory, pp. 167–180. IEEE Computer Society (1973). https://doi.org/10.1109/SWAT.1973.11
9. Ehrig, K., Giese, H. (eds.): Graph Transformation and Visual Modeling Techniques (GT-VMT). Electronic Communications of the EASST, vol. 6 (2007)
10. Fuss, C., Tuttlies, V.E.: Simulating set-valued transformations with algorithmic graph transformation languages. In: Schürr, A., Nagl, M., Zündorf, A. (eds.) AGTIVE 2007. LNCS, vol. 5088, pp. 442–455. Springer, Heidelberg (2008). doi:10.1007/978-3-540-89020-1_30
11. Ghamarian, A.H., de Mol, M., Rensink, A., Zambon, E., Zimakova, M.: Modelling and analysis using GROOVE. STTT **14**(1), 15–40 (2012)
12. Golas, U., Ehrig, H., Habel, A.: Multi-amalgamation in adhesive categories. In: Ehrig, H., Rensink, A., Rozenberg, G., Schürr, A. (eds.) ICGT 2010. LNCS, vol. 6372, pp. 346–361. Springer, Heidelberg (2010). doi:10.1007/978-3-642-15928-2_23
13. Grønmo, R., Krogdahl, S., Møller-Pedersen, B.: A collection operator for graph transformation. Softw. Syst. Model. **12**(1), 121–144 (2013). doi:10.1007/s10270-011-0190-3
14. Habel, A., Heckel, R., Taentzer, G.: Graph grammars with negative application conditions. Fundam. Inform. **26**(3/4), 287–313 (1996). doi:10.3233/FI-1996-263404
15. Hoffmann, B., Janssens, D., Eetvelde, N.V.: Cloning and expanding graph transformation rules for refactoring. In: Karsai, G., Taentzer, G. (eds.) Graph and Model Transformation (GraMoT). Electronic Notes in Theoretical Computer Science, vol. 152, pp. 53–67 (2006). https://doi.org/10.1016/j.entcs.2006.01.014

16. Junges, S., Guck, D., Katoen, J., Rensink, A., Stoelinga, M.: Fault trees on a diet: automated reduction by graph rewriting. Formal Asp. Comput. **29**(4), 651–703 (2017). doi:10.1007/s00165-016-0412-0

17. Kissinger, A., Merry, A., Soloviev, M.: Pattern graph rewrite systems. In: Löwe, B., Winskel, G. (eds.) International Workshop on Developments in Computational Models. EPTCS, vol. 143, pp. 54–66 (2014)

18. Kreowski, H.-J.: A comparison between petri-nets and graph grammars. In: Noltemeier, H. (ed.) WG 1980. LNCS, vol. 100, pp. 306–317. Springer, Heidelberg (1981). doi:10.1007/3-540-10291-4_22

19. Lindqvist, J., Lundkvist, T., Porres, I.: A query language with the star operator. In: Ehrig and Giese [9]. http://journal.ub.tu-berlin.de/index.php/eceasst/article/view/55

20. LOTOS: A formal description technique based on the temporal ordering of observational behaviour. ISO/IEC Infernational Standard 8807, International Organization for Standardization (1989). https://www.iso.org/standard/16258.html

21. Nickel, U., Niere, J., Zündorf, A.: The FUJABA environment. In: Ghezzi, C., Jazayeri, M., Wolf, A.L. (eds.) 22nd International Conference on on Software Engineering (ICSE), pp. 742–745. ACM (2000)

22. Plump, D.: Essentials of term graph rewriting. In: GETGRATS Closing Workshop. Electronic Notes in Theoretical Computer Science, vol. 51, pp. 277–289 (2001). https://doi.org/10.1016/S1571-0661(04)80210-X

23. Rensink, A.: Representing first-order logic using graphs. In: Ehrig, H., Engels, G., Parisi-Presicce, F., Rozenberg, G. (eds.) ICGT 2004. LNCS, vol. 3256, pp. 319–335. Springer, Heidelberg (2004). doi:10.1007/978-3-540-30203-2_23

24. Rensink, A.: Nested quantification in graph transformation rules. In: Corradini, A., Ehrig, H., Montanari, U., Ribeiro, L., Rozenberg, G. (eds.) ICGT 2006. LNCS, vol. 4178, pp. 1–13. Springer, Heidelberg (2006). doi:10.1007/11841883_1

25. Rensink, A., Kuperus, J.: Repotting the geraniums: on nested graph transformation rules. In: Boronat, A., Heckel, R. (eds.) Graph Transformation and Visual Modeling Techniques (GT-VMT). Electronic Communications of the EASST, vol. 18 (2009). http://journal.ub.tu-berlin.de/index.php/eceasst/article/view/260

26. Taentzer, G.: Parallel high-level replacement systems. Theor. Comput. Sci. **186**(1–2), 43–81 (1997). doi:10.1016/S0304-3975(96)00215-0

iDSL: Automated Performance Evaluation of Service-Oriented Systems

Freek van den Berg[1]([✉]), Boudewijn R. Haverkort[1], and Jozef Hooman[2,3]

[1] Design and Analysis of Communication Systems,
University of Twente, Enschede, The Netherlands
{f.g.b.vandenberg,b.r.h.m.haverkort}@utwente.nl
[2] TNO-ESI, Eindhoven, The Netherlands
[3] Radboud University, Nijmegen, The Netherlands
j.hooman@cs.ru.nl

Abstract. Service-oriented systems interconnect with other systems in a time critical manner, making their performance vital. For this purpose, we propose an automated performance evaluation approach for service-oriented systems which includes both performance measurement and prediction. The approach makes use of the iDSL language, a domain specific language tailored to modeling service-oriented systems, and the iDSL toolchain to evaluate iDSL models, as follows. First, discrete-event simulation yields many performance artifacts, e.g., latency breakdown charts, cumulative distribution graphs, and latency bar charts. Second, timed automata-based model checking yields absolute latency bounds. Third, probabilistic timed automata-based model checking leads to exact latency distributions for each service. We successfully validated our approach; several case studies on interventional X-ray systems displayed similar measured and predicted outcomes.

1 Introduction

An embedded system is a computer system that has a dedicated function within a larger system, often with real-time computing constraints [16,27]. Today, the majority of the commonly used devices are embedded systems, ranging from simple digital watches, to complex medical machines [19]. An embedded system is frequently used to perform safety critical tasks, which makes their malfunctioning prone to serious injury and fatalities, such as with medical systems. An embedded system interacts with its environments in a time critical way. Its safety is therefore predominantly determined by its performance, which is expressed in terms of response times, resource utilizations and queue sizes.

Many current practices only address the performance at the end of the development trajectory and only resort to tuning of the performance until the system is "good enough" [21]. Contrarily, we advocate that each design decision during system development should be evaluated for performance immediately, as it can have an increasing impact on performance later on. This prevents unexpected performance issues that are hard and costly to fix, especially the ones

© Springer International Publishing AG 2017
J.-P. Katoen et al. (Eds.): Brinksma Festschrift, LNCS 10500, pp. 214–236, 2017.
DOI: 10.1007/978-3-319-68270-9_11

that are detected late. On top of that, it is recommended to make use of performance predictions, which can provide early insight in the performance of different design alternatives, without having to realize an actual system yet. We claim that prediction-based performance evaluation should be an integral part of the design of complex embedded systems [18].

Good performance is hard to achieve, because embedded systems come with increasingly heterogeneous, parallel and distributed architectures [18]. At the same time, they are designed for many product lines and different configurations, which gives rise to many potential designs. Moreover, accurately predicting performance characteristics of embedded systems is hard, since the real system does not exist yet. Once the system has been built, measurements to gain insight in the performance tend to be expensive, because they require the system to run for quite some time, e.g., to detect rare performance outliers.

To narrow our scope, we constrain ourselves to so-called *service-oriented systems* [15, 23–26], a special class of embedded systems that have the following four properties. First, service-oriented systems provide services to their environment, accessible via so-called service requests. Second, a service request leads to exactly one service response. Third, individual service requests are isolated from each other in a service-oriented system and do, therefore, not affect each other's functionality. Fourth, service requests may negatively affect each other's performance by competing for the same resource in the service-oriented system.

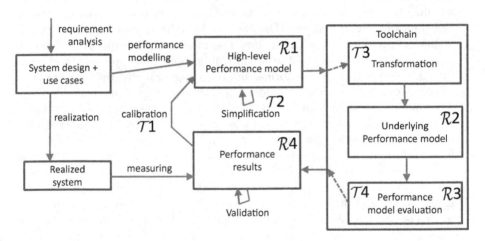

Fig. 1. System development including performance measurement and prediction.

We propose a framework for the performance evaluation of service-oriented systems (see Fig. 1), comprising performance measurement *and* prediction.

Performance measurement starts with the realization of a "system design + use cases", a blueprint of the system to be realized, resulting into a "realized system" via a realization. Performing measurements on this system then yield "performance results". Performance measurement comes with two downsides: (i) realizing a system is (often) very costly, let alone realizing many different systems only for testing purposes; and, (ii) since exhaustive performance measurement is impossible, assessing the performance of rare but important events is difficult.

Performance prediction starts with modeling the performance of a "system design + use cases", which may include the use of existing "performance results", i.e., measurements, for model calibration. The resulting "high-level performance model" enters the "toolchain" in which it is transformed into a "underlying performance model", and subsequently evaluated for performance, yielding "performance results". In this paper, performance prediction relies on measurements and can therefore only be used in addition to performance measurement. Also, it is model-based and thus inherently inaccurate. On the upside, however, a "high-level performance model" may represent many system designs and performing measurements on them can often be done at high speed. Hence, performance prediction is suitable for quickly evaluating the performance of many designs and thus enables design space exploration [5,11].

In this paper, we focus on performance prediction only. We do thereby assume that measurements for calibration purposes are readily available.

In the following, we address four requirements that a performance prediction approach should meet. For this purpose, Fig. 1 has been augmented with labels $\mathcal{R}1$, $\mathcal{R}2$, $\mathcal{R}3$ and $\mathcal{R}4$, respectively. We elaborate on them, as follows:

$\mathcal{R}1$ A high-level performance model should be expressive, yet concise. The model should allow for the use of different evaluation techniques. An integrated Development Environment (IDE) and/or graphical user interface (GUI) should be provided to ease modeling. The model should support calibration based on measurements and the Y-chart philosophy by supporting, and separating, the applications, platforms, and mappings. Finally, mechanisms such as compositionality, layers and hierarchies, and/or classes, are called for.

$\mathcal{R}2$ The underlying performance model should make it easy to analyze complex high-level performance models and also support the enabling and disabling of different properties, such as nondeterministic choices.

$\mathcal{R}3$ The performance evaluation process should be **fully** automated; a system designer creates a model, which is evaluated without any user interaction, and results are automatically returned. This includes Design Space Exploration [5,11] and post-processsing steps, e.g., visualizations. Also, multiple modes of analysis should be supported for models of reasonable complexity. Besides discrete-event simulations for quick results, model checking should be supported for more accurate results. Finally, evaluating the model should take a limited amount of time and scale well for models of complex systems.

$\mathcal{R}4$ Performance evaluations should lead to various results types, e.g., utilizations, latency breakdown charts, and latency distributions. Whenever possible, the results should be presented visually for easy human interpretation.

In previous work [22], many toolsets that support the performance evaluation process have been compared regarding these requirements; often their level of automation is limited, their models tend to be at a lower level of abstraction as called for, only one way of analysis is supported, and results are not visualized.

This paper's remainder is organized, as follows. Section 2 reveals so-called interventional X-ray systems, which are medical systems. Section 3 introduces the high-level iDSL language, followed by the iDSL tool chain in Sect. 4. Section 5 provides an extensive case study. Finally, Sect. 6 concludes the paper.

2 Interventional X-ray Systems

For a running example, we introduce interventional X-ray (iXR) systems, which are medical imaging systems that enable minimally-invasive surgeries.

An iXR system consist of a number of parts (as depicted in Fig. 2), as follows. It is used to assist a surgeon while performing surgery, during which a patient lies on a **table**. The iXR system displays a continuous stream of images of (the inside of) a patient on a display. These images are based on X-ray beams, generated in the **arc** and caught by the detector, whose task it is to extract raw images from X-ray beams. Via the control panel, the surgeon can move the arc and table in various ways and thereby change the angle of the recorded images of the patient, which are shown continuously on the display.

An iXR system needs to support different settings so that it can be customized for a specific patient, surgeon and procedure, for instance: (i) mono- or biplane, i.e., using either one or two X-Ray beams to generate and detect images, yielding 2D or 3D images; (ii) image resolution, e.g., images of 512^2, 1024^2 or 2048^2 pixels; and, (iii) image frame-rate, e.g., 5, 10 or 25 images per second.

Image Processing (IP) is an important subsystem of an iXR system. It turns raw X-ray images into high quality ones, in real-time; IP retrieves unprocessed images from the X-ray **detector**, processes them to enhance their quality, and delivers them to the **display** to be seen by the surgeon (see Fig. 2). IP comprises different kinds of operations, e.g., detecting so-called dead pixels, reducing spatial and temporal noise, and preparing an image for a particular display.

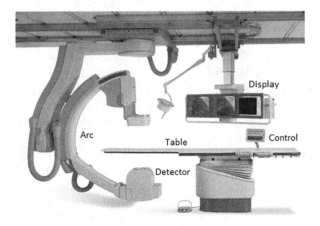

Fig. 2. The main parts that constitute an interventional X-ray system

IP is a trade-off between (i) constant quality and frame-rate of the images, (ii) average throughput, latency and jitter of individual images, (iii) amount of X-Ray a patient and surgeon get exposed to during a treatment, and (iv) required computational resources to process images.

The safety of IP is mainly determined by performance, viz., a surgeon needs to continuously receive high quality images to perform surgery on a patient. Hence, the image latency, the time between an image arriving on the detector and appearing on the display, needs to meet a strict requirement. Literature suggests an average latency below 165 ms for proper hand-eye coordination [12].

3   The iDSL Language

In this section, the iDSL language, which forms a conceptual model of a service-oriented systems, is defined [22,25]. It comprises six sections (see Fig. 3).

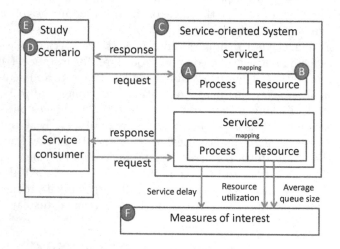

Fig. 3. A conceptual model of a service system.

A *service-oriented system* (see Fig. 3-C) provides one or more services to one or more *service users* (exterior to the service-oriented system), viz., a *service user* sends a request for a specific service at a given time, after which the system responds with some delay. A *service* is an entity that performs functions ranging from simple requests to computationally expensive processes.

Service-oriented systems do not only need to return the right answers to requests, but also face stringent performance constraints, e.g., the system has to reply to a request within a certain time, often referred to as *latency*. Service-oriented systems can particularly be hard to analyze when they handle many service requests in parallel, for multiple kinds of services, in a real-time manner.

A *service* is decomposed into one or more processes, resources and a mapping, in line with the Y-chart philosophy [14]. A *process* (see Fig. 3-A) decomposes high-level service requests into atomic tasks, each assigned to a resource via the *mapping* (not shown in the figure). Hence, the mapping connects the process to resource it relies on. A *resource* (see Fig. 3-B) is capable of performing one atomic task at a time. When multiple services are invoked of which the resources they rely on overlap, contention may occur, making performance analysis hard.

A *scenario* (see Fig. 3-D) comprises a number of invoked service requests over time to observe the performance behavior of the service system in specific circumstances over time. Service requests are functionally independent of each other, i.e., service requests do not affect each other's functional outcomes, but may affect each other's performance negatively due to contention.

A *study* (see Fig. 3-E) is a set of scenarios to be evaluated, so as to derive the system's underlying characteristics. Within a study, a *design space* is an efficient way to describe a large number of similar scenarios.

Finally, a *measure of interest* (see Fig. 3-F) defines an interesting performance metric, given a system and scenario, e.g., latencies and queue sizes.

In this section's remainder, we illustrate the meaning of the iDSL language via a running example of a so-called biplane iXR system (see Sect. 2).

The high-level Process decomposes a service into several atomic tasks, represented by a recursive data structure with layers of sub-processes. At the lowest abstraction level, an atomic task specifies a workload, e.g., some CPU cycles.

The example process of Table 1 combines hierarchies (curly brackets), sequential compositions (*seq*) and atomic tasks (*atom*). At its highest level, it consists of a sequential task "image_processing_seq" that decomposes into an atomic task "pre-processing" with (fixed) load 50, a sequential task "image_processing" and an atomic task "post-processing" with load 25. In turn, the sequential task "image_processing" decomposes into three atomic tasks named "motion compensation" with load 44, "noise reduction", and "contrast" with load 134. The load of "noise reduction" is drawn from a uniform distribution on [80, 140].

As in [3], iDSL also supports process algebra constructs for parallelism (*par*), nondeterministic (*alt*) and probabilistic choice (*palt*), mutual exclusion (*mutex*) to permit only one process instance to enter a certain subprocess at a time, and design alternative (*desalt*) to implement a subprocess that varies across designs.

Table 1. The code of an iDSL process

```
Section Process
  ProcessModel image_processing_application
    seq image_processing_seq {
      atom image_pre_processing load 50
      seq image_processing {
        atom motion_compensation load 44
        atom noise_reduction load uniform(80:140)
        atom contrast load 134 }
      atom image_post_processing load 25 }
```

The high-level Resource is decomposed into a number of atomic resources (*atom*) via different layers of decomposable resources (*decomp*). Each atomic resource has a constant rate that specifies how much load it can process per time unit, e.g., the number of CPU cycles per second. The example resource "image_processing_-decomp" of Table 2 is a composite resource which consists of two atomic resources, i.e., a "CPU" with rate 2 and a "GPU" with rate 5.

Table 2. The code of an iDSL resource

```
Section Resource
  ResourceModel image_processing_PC decomp
    image_processing_decomp { atom CPU rate 2, atom GPU rate 5 }
```

Table 3. The code of an iDSL system

```
Section System
  Service image_processing_service
    Process image_processing_application
    Resource image_processing_PC
    Mapping assign ( image_pre_processing, CPU )
      ( motion_compensation, CPU )( noise_reduction, CPU )
      ( contrast, CPU )( image_post_processing, GPU)
```

Table 4. The code of an iDSL scenario

```
Section Scenario
  Scenario image_processing_run
    ServiceRequest image_processing_service at time 0, 400, ...
    ServiceRequest image_processing_service
      at time dspace("offset"), (dspace("offset")+400), ...
```

The high-level System provides one or more services to its environment. The example system of Table 3 comprises one service which decomposes into a process (see Table 1), resource (see Table 2) and a mapping. This decomposition makes it easy to change a process and/or resource part of a service, e.g., to apply Design Space Exploration (DSE). Finally, the mapping assigns atomic task "image_post_processing" to "GPU", and the other atomic tasks to "CPU".

The high-level Scenario comprises several service requests to a system, each for a given service and at a certain time. The example *biplane* iXR system of Table 4 has two services types, viz., for frontal and lateral IP. They are modeled similarly, i.e., using the example service of Table 3. Frontal IP requests occur with fixed inter-arrival times of 400, without an initial delay. Lateral IP requests also have inter-arrival times of 400, but the initial delay is design dependent,

Table 5. The code of an iDSL study

```
Section Study
  Scenario image_processing_run
    DesignSpace ("offset" "0" "20" "40" "80" "120" "160" "260")
```

Table 6. The code of an iDSL measure

```
Section Measure
  Measure ServiceResponseTimes using 1 run of 250 requests
  Measure ServiceResponseTimes absolute
```

viz., the *dspace* operator with parameter "offset" refers to dimension "offset" in the design space (see Table 5), which varies from 0 till 260.

The high-level Study characterizes a set of designs to compare. A design space is a shorthand way to specify many designs; it consist one or more dimensions that each have several possible values. A design provides a unique valuation for each dimension. The example study of Table 5 encompasses a design space with one dimension "offset" that comprises seven values. The dimension is used to vary the degree of concurrency between both services in Table 4.

The high-level Measure defines, given a system and scenario, the metrics the system designer is interested in and how they are obtained.

The example measure of Table 6 consists of two measures that both return service response times. To this end, the first measure uses 1 discrete-event simulation run of 250 requests (see Sect. 4.4, discrete-event simulation) which provides insight in resource utilizations and latency breakdowns in one go. The second measure employs an iterative model checking approach (see Sect. 4.4).

4   The iDSL Toolchain

The iDSL toolchain takes an iDSL model (of Sect. 3) as input and automatically generates a wide array of performance artifacts. For this purpose, the iDSL toolchain subsequently executes the following four steps: (i) calibrate the model on the basis of measurements (see Sect. 4.1); (ii) simplify the model (see Sect. 4.2); (iii) transform the model into a low-level Modest model (see Sect. 4.3, [8–10]); and, (iv) evaluate the performance of the model (see Sect. 4.4). In Fig. 1, these steps are labeled $T1$, $T2$, $T3$ and $T4$, respectively.

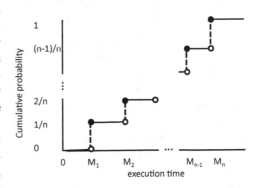

Fig. 4. The Empirical Distribution Function for n numerically-sorted measurements $m_1, m_2, \ldots, m_{n-1}, m_n$

4.1   Calibrating the Model on the Basis of Measurements

In Sect. 3, an atomic task load in a iDSL process (see Table 1) is either fixed or uniformly drawn from a certain interval. Next, we propose an Empirical Distribution Function (EDF) as a third possibility to enable model calibration on the basis of measurements. In Table 7, we observe that an EDF load has one parameter and comes in two flavors. Atomic task "edf_values" is initiated with a sequence of measurements values, whereas "edf_files" refers to an external file containing measurements.

The EDF for n numerically-sorted measurements $m_1, m_2, \ldots, m_{n-1}, m_n$ (see Fig. 4) is a step function that jumps up by $\frac{1}{n}$ at each of the n data points. Optionally, iDSL provides EDF prediction during which EDFs are predicted for designs for which no measurements have been performed, on the basis of existing EDFs. This is carefully explained in [22, 26], but beyond the scope of this paper.

Next, we show how model simplification is applied to an atomic task with an EDF load (in Sect. 4.2), after which it is transformed into a palt-construct as part of the transformation to Modest (in Sect. 4.3).

Table 7. The code of a small iDSL process with an EDF

```
Section Process
  ProcessModel image_processing_application seq {
    atom edf_values load EDF with values 6 8 10
    atom edf_files load EDF from file "measurements.dat" }
```

4.2   Simplifying the Model

Generally, an iDSL model is often too hard to analyze, especially when the iDSL processes have variable loads. To this end, iDSL comes with two model simplification techniques for EDFs in the iDSL process, viz., the clustering of loads and changing the model time unit.

The clustering of loads is applied to atomic processes that are defined as an EDF. Measurements are clustered into a number of clusters using K-means clustering [13]. Each cluster is summarized by the smallest interval of nondeterministic time containing all its measurements. These intervals are combined via a probabilistic choice, thereby reducing the number of probabilistic alternatives.

Figure 5 presents a small example based on three measurement values 6, 7 and 18. Figure 5(a) shows the original EDF, which assigns an equal weight of $\frac{1}{3}$ to each of the 3 measurements. When the number of given clusters is at least the number of measurements, this original EDF is returned since each measurement is assigned to its individual cluster. Figure 5(b) displays the result of K-means clustering with 2 clusters, viz., measurements 6 and 7 are grouped in one cluster due to their proximity, and 18 in the other. Hence, 6 and 7 are represented by a nondeterministic time interval, graphically depicted as a grey area covering

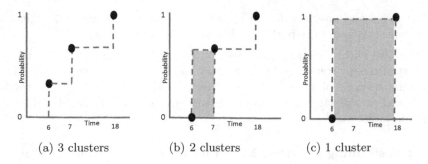

(a) 3 clusters   (b) 2 clusters   (c) 1 cluster

Fig. 5. EDFs based on measurements 6 μs, 7 μs and 18 μs that are simplified using K-means clustering.

time range [6 : 7], and probability range [0 : $\frac{2}{3}$]. This grey area represents an ambiguity, viz., all distributions that go through this area are possible. The result is accurate, which means that the real distribution goes through this area. [23] quantifies this ambiguity. Finally, Fig. 5(c) shows the one cluster case. All measurements end up in one cluster, yielding a nondeterministic time range [6 : 18] and probability range [0 : 1].

Changing the model time unit increases the global time unit of the iDSL model. It is, among others, applied to all EDF functions in the model: (i) the measurements are divided by the chosen time unit and rounded to the nearest integer value; (ii) performance evaluation is applied; and, (iii) the results are multiplied by the time unit again. Bigger time steps reduce the model complexity, whereas rounding reduces precision. In [23], this loss of precision is quantified. Note that rounding can both lead to conservative or overestimated results.

Figure 6 shows an example, again for measurements 6, 7 and 18. Figure 6(a) shows the case of time unit = 1, i.e., dividing measurements by 1 does not introduce rounding errors. Figure 6(b) highlights the case for time unit = 6. Measurements 6 and 18 are not rounded by being multiples of 6, but measurement 7 induces a rounding error, viz., an integer division of 7 by 6 followed by a multiplication by 6 yields 6 instead of 7. Effectively, measurement 7 is replaced by a 6,

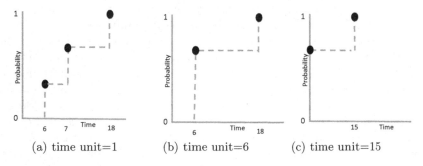

(a) time unit=1   (b) time unit=6   (c) time unit=15

Fig. 6. EDFs based on measurements 6 μs, 7 μs and 18 μs that are simplified by increasing the time unit.

yielding two 6 and one 18 values. Figure 6(c) the shows case for time unit $= 15$. Measurements 6 and 7 are both rounded to 0, and measurement 18 becomes 15.

Finding the right abstraction level of the model is achieved by systematically benchmarking iterations of MCSTA for models with different combinations of clusters and time units. It is the objective to find a model that computes fast enough and at the same contains enough level of detail. [22,23] describes the algorithm in detail.

4.3   Transforming the iDSL Model into Equivalent Modest Models

We explain how an iDSL model transforms into a set of Modest models [8–10] (as graphically depicted in Fig. 7). [25] provides a concrete example. On top, a Modest model comprises a parallel execution of interacting processes, i.e., services, resources and generators, implemented using a par-construct. This similar to a system in LOTOS [3].

For each ProcessModel in the iDSL process, a similar Modest process is generated. To this end, there are two types of processes. First, a compound process contains one operator, e.g., par, seq, alt and palt, and recursively refers to subprocesses. Furthermore, an atomic process with an EDF load is transformed into a palt-construct: an alternative is created for each jump in the cumulative distribution function with a weight corresponding to the jump size. For instance, Fig. 4 conveys a jump from $\frac{1}{n}$ to $\frac{2}{n}$ at time M_2, which translates to a palt-alternative with weight $\frac{2}{n} - \frac{1}{n} = \frac{1}{n}$ and time M_2. Note that each alternative is an atomic process. Second, atomic processes signal their ID and a load to a fixed resource queue, viz., the one defined in the mapping, and wait for a result.

For each ResourceModel in the iDSL resource, a Modest resource_queue and resource process are generated, which both repeat forever (as indicated by the repeat symbol) for FIFO scheduling. A resource_queue either receives an ID and load from a atomic process (a buffer addition), or forwards an ID and load to its resource (a buffer removal), each iteration. In turn, a Modest resource waits for a resource_queue to provide an ID and load, processes it using a delay (as indicated by the stopwatch), and returns the result to the atomic process with the given ID. A resource_queue is not generated in case of nondeterministic scheduling, since the order at which requests arrive is not relevant. In this case, the ID and a load an atomic process signals is directly connected to the resource process. We stress that other scheduling methods are not yet supported.

For each Service in the iDSL system, one or more Modest services are generated. Each service alternately waits for an incoming request trigger and activates the process that corresponds to the service. The number of created Modest services decide how many service instances the system can handle simultaneously, which is one by default to have a simple model. However, it can be overridden by the "numinstances" keyword. Moreover, the service mapping is used to connect the atomic processes and resource_queues (see the green circle in Fig. 7).

For each ServiceRequest in the iDSL Scenario, a Modest init_generator is generated that generates an initial delay, followed by a call to a Modest generator process that forever triggers a service at fixed inter-arrival times.

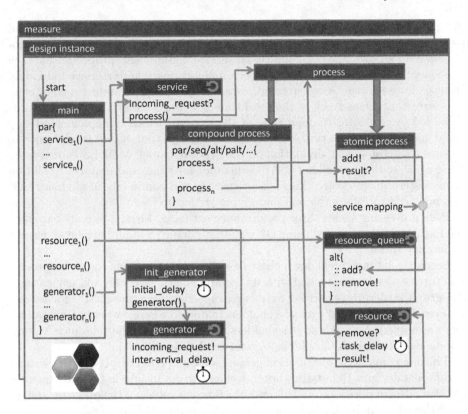

Fig. 7. The Modest processes that are generated given an iDSL model. (Color figure online)

Finally, similar Modest models are created for each design in the iDSL study and for each measure in the iDSL measure, as follows. First, a design instance provides a valuation for each dimension. It is used, among others, to replace the *dspace* operator by the actual value of the respective dimension in arithmetic expressions, e.g., the service request times in Table 4. Second, a measure specifies how a Modest model is analyzed. This requires measure specific adjustments to be made to the model (see Sect. 4.4), e.g., turning real values into integers.

4.4   Evaluating a Modest Model to Yield Performance Artifacts

In this section, Modest models of the previous section are evaluated for each design, using different evaluation techniques. Besides discrete-event simulation, there are four ways of model checking, viz., TA-based, PTA-based, and efficient PTA-based, and efficient & scalable PTA-based. Each technique comprises three execution steps: (i) the Modest model is modified to be compatible with the given technique; (ii) a Modest tool is applied to the Modest model at least once yielding performance numbers; and, (iii) post-processing turns the performance numbers into artifacts. Next, we explain these steps for each technique.

Discrete-event simulation yields latencies of services, subprocesses and resource utilizations. Latencies are obtained by enclosing each service and subprocess with stopwatches. An additional service counter and properties for each subsequent request of a given service then make it possible to retrieve individual latencies for a service. A resource utilization is obtained by adding a counter to a resource that keeps track of the total time it is processing. This counter value is divided by the total running time of the system, which is implemented as a global counter. For each run, MODES of the Modest toolset [10] is used once to perform a discrete-event simulation on the Modest model. MODES is instructed to use an as soon as possible (ASAP) scheduler for time, and uniform resolution for nondeterminism choice. This is a pragmatic and commonly used choice that does not need to reflect the real underlying structure [4].

Post-processing yields three performance artifacts. First, a latency bar chart (see Fig. 11(c)) is generated using GNUplot [20], which visually displays succeeding latency times.

Second, a latency breakdown chart (see Fig. 11(a)) conveys the static process structure of a service extended with its dynamics, i.e., latencies and utilizations. The graph structure is derived by recursively traversing the iDSL process and resource. It is augmented with placeholders in one go wherever performance numbers are needed. Next, these placeholders are replaced by the relevance Modest properties, after which GraphViz [6] renders the visualization.

Third, a cumulative distribution graph (see Fig. 11(b)) displays latency times for different designs. Hence, they are convenient to get insight in the consequences of certain design decisions. To this end, the latency values of the different designs are gathered, combined, and turned into a plot using GNUplot [20].

TA-based model checking yields absolute service latencies. To make the model finite, real values that concern time (including loads and rates) are rounded to their nearest integer values. Additionally, probabilistic choices and infinite distributions are replaced by nondeterministic choices. Latencies of services are obtained by enclosing each service with stopwatches that reset after registering one latency. To reduce the state space size, no service counter is added; we do not retrieve which latency is the maximum one. Combined, this leads to a finite, decidable model. TA-based model checking is performed using MCTAU [1]. Via a binary search algorithm of [25], i.e., recursive function lb (in Table 8), an initial range of possible values is halved iteratively until one value

Table 8. Function lb: compute lower bounds, pseudo code

```
lb ([lbound:ubound]){
    if (abs(ubound-lbound)<=1) return lbound          // case a
    check_value=(lbound+ubound)/2
    UPPAAL (p = probability(latency<check_value))
    if ( p=0 ) lb (check_value,ubound)                // case b
    else lb (lbound,check_value) }                    // case c
```

remains. This initial range is $[0 : n]$, where n is a deliberate overestimation of the latency. Each iteration, one of the following three cases occur: (a) there is only one possible value left, which is returned; (b) model checking conveys that the probability that the value is in the lower half of the values is 0 in which case the upper half of the values is returned; or, (c) the lower half of the values is returned. The complexity of the algorithm is $\mathcal{O}(log(n))$, where n is the chosen overestimation.

PTA-based model checking yields exact service latency distributions for each service; a Modest model is created for each service and both the minimum and maximum probability to compute the latency distribution of that particular service. In each Modest model, only the process of the given service is enclosed by stopwatches that record latencies of the service requests. The Modest models have one parameter time $t \in \mathbb{R}_{\geq 0}$, and return a probability p: the probability that the service completes within time t.

In iDSL, however, a service leads to an infinite stream of service requests, each with its individual latency. Ideally, the average of this infinite stream of latencies is a measure for the performance of the whole service. Put formally:

$$P_\Omega(t) = \lim_{k \to \infty} \frac{1}{k} \sum_{n=1}^{k} P_n(t), \tag{1}$$

where $P_\Omega(t)$ is the combined probability, n the service request number, t the latency time, $P_n(t)$ the probability that service request n finishes within time t.

This infinite sum cannot be directly computed. Instead, the computable *geometric distribution* [17] is proposed that is capable of detecting an absolute maximum latency, weighing service requests in an exponentially decreasing way:

$$P_\Omega(t) = \sum_{n=1}^{\infty} (1 - \rho)^{n-1} \rho \, P_n(t), \tag{2}$$

where $\rho \in (0 : 1)$ is the geometric distribution parameter. The distribution is similar to (1), for $\rho \approx 0$ and capable of finding the absolute latencies.

In Modest, the geometric distribution is implemented as a binary probabilistic choice every time a service request completes (as depicted in Fig. 8(a)): either the currently measured latency is returned, with probability ρ ($\frac{1}{10}$ in the figure), or the next service request is evaluated, with probability $1 - \rho$ ($\frac{9}{10}$ in the figure).

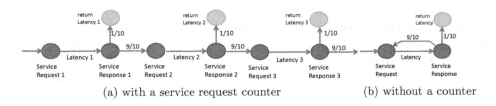

(a) with a service request counter   (b) without a counter

Fig. 8. Binary probabilistic choices induce the geometric distribution

The geometric distribution is memoryless, i.e., the binary choice does not rely on the service request number. It can thus be represented as a single reoccurring service request (as depicted in Fig. 8(b)). The figure conveys that a lower ρ-value yields a more complex model and more precise results, viz., for small values of ρ, the probability that state "Service Response" is followed by many occurrences of "Service Request" increases. In this paper, we empirically choose $\rho = \frac{1}{10}$; it leads to a state space that is large enough to deliver a reasonable amount of accuracy and which is moreover practically handleable.

The algorithm to compute a latency distribution of a service [22, 24] comprises three steps in which MCSTA, the explicit-state model checker for STA of the Modest toolset, is iteratively applied, as follows. First, the *initial scan* is used to obtain an upper bound on the latency. Second, the binary *lower & upper bound search* are binary searches, similar to TA-based model checking, to obtain a exact lower an upper bound. Third, the whole distribution is obtained by computing all values between the bounds in a *brute force* way.

Efficient PTA-based model checking provides the same functionality as its inefficient counterpart, but in a more efficient manner [22, 23]. The efficiency gain is the result of executing three lightweight techniques initially as shown in Fig. 9. Besides a so-called basic estimate function, we reuse the already introduced discrete-event simulation and four TA-based model checking techniques.

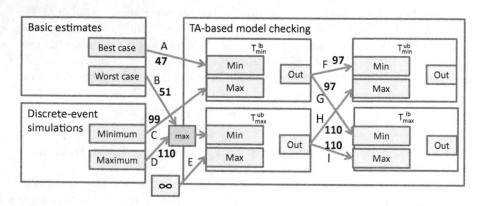

Fig. 9. The dataflow of three lightweight techniques. On the edges, execution times for service Frontal IP and offset $= 0$ are shown.

A basic estimate function returns, given a iDSL process, an optimistic but possibly inaccurate bound of either the minimum (maximum) latency. It is easy to compute. The result is optimistic because the concurrency between services and processing steps for resources are not taken into account. Hence, the best case can be used as a minimum for T_{min}^{lb} (**A**), a lower bound for T_{min}, and the worst case for T_{max}^{ub} (**B**), an upper bound for T_{max}. Table 9 conveys the recursive definition of the best case, as follows: (i) for an atomic process, the taskload is returned; (ii) for a (probabilistic) alternative process, the minimum of all recursively evaluated children processes is returned; (iii) for a parallel process, the maximum of the evaluated children processes is returned; and, (iv) for a sequential process, the sum of the evaluated children is returned. The worst case is defined analogously, but returns the maximum in case of a (probabilistic) alternative process.

Table 9. The recursive definition of the basic estimate (best case) function

```
                  BE: Basic estimate (best case) function
BE atom{p_1}         = p_1.taskload
BE alt{p_1,...,p_n}  = MIN { BE x | x in {p_1,...,p_n} }
BE palt{p_1,...,p_n} = MIN { BE x | x in {p_1,...,p_n} }
BE par{p_1,...,p_n}  = MAX { BE x | x in {p_1,...,p_n} }
BE seq{p_1,...,p_n}  = BE p_1 + BE p_2 + ... + BE p_n
```

Discrete-event simulations display average behavior, which means that the minimum outcome of all runs can be used as a maximum for T_{min}^{lb} (**C**), and the maximum outcome as a minimum for T_{max}^{ub} (**D**). Using the maximum of **B** and **D** for the minimum of T_{max}^{ub}, makes the range of T_{max}^{ub} as small as possible.

TA-based model checking T_{min}^{lb} and T_{max}^{ub} provide an absolute minimum and maximum, i.e., regardless of how nondeterminism is resolved, respectively. They are used as a minimum (**F+G**) and maximum (**H+I**) for t_{min}^{ub} and t_{max}^{lb}.

Efficient PTA-based model checking comprises five steps: (i) compute the basic estimates; (ii) perform multiple discrete-event simulation runs; (iii) perform TA-based model checking t_{min}^{lb} and t_{max}^{ub}; (iv) perform TA-based model checking t_{min}^{ub} and t_{max}^{lb}; and, (v) execute brute force PTA-based model checking.

Efficient and scalable PTA-based model checking is similar to the previous technique, but is applied to a model that is simplified using the algorithm of the Sect. 4.2. Overall, it aims to deliver a practical compromise between the amount of needed memory, amount of wall clock time, and quality of the results. In Sect. 5.2 (results), we illustrate the concrete efficiency gain.

5   Case Study on Interventional X-ray Systems

This section conveys two experiments in which various performance artifacts are returned (in Sect. 5.1) and exact results are computed (in Sect. 5.2).

5.1   Experiment I: Retrieving a Wide Array of Performance Artifacts

Experiment I focuses on generating many performance artifacts. This takes its toll on the high-level model quality which is simple, and moreover limits performance evaluation, viz., primarily discrete-event simulations are performed. For the sake of efficiency, the running example as introduced in Sect. 3 is reused.

Transformation. The resulting Modest code comprises a parallel process at its highest level, which contains service "image_processing_service", resources "CPU" and "GPU" that run forever, and two generators that call "image_processing_service". The service waits for incoming requests of either of the generators and triggers the process, similar to the iDSL process, in return. Atomic processes in the process call the respective resources, which perform a delay. Since nondeterministic scheduling is employed, the resources have no queues.

Evaluation. The iDSL measure (see Table 6) contains two measures, as follows. First, discrete-event simulation yields a single MODES execution that leads to latencies and utilizations in one go.

Second, TA-based model checking includes rounding the real values to integers. Since all but one values of the loads and rates are integers already, the model is not affected by this step. The uniform choice of atomic task "noise_reduction", however, is turned into a nondeterministic equivalent. Stopwatches are added to measure latencies. Given this model, a lower and upper bound latency are obtained via the binary search algorithm of Sect. 4.4 (TA-based model checking).

Results come in various kinds, as follows. First, the latency bar chart for offset $=0$ of Fig. 11(c) conveys that the latencies vary much, i.e., between 200 and 380, as a result of extreme concurrency. This variation is less for other offsets.

Second, the latency breakdown chart for offset $=0$ of Fig. 11(a) illustrates how the overall latency is dispersed over its subprocesses. Tasks "Noise_reduction" and "Contrast" account for 71% of the total latency. The utilization of "CPU" of 0.83 is high, but not alarming. The utilization of "GPU" is low, viz., 0.025.

Third, the cumulative distribution graph of Fig. 11(b) displays the cumulative latency functions for seven designs with offsets varying from 0 to 200. As anticipated, the offsets and latency times are negatively correlated, i.e., a smaller offset induces that the execution of services overlap more (see Table 13) and thus display more concurrency. In turn, this leads to a higher latency.

Fourth, Fig. 10 conveys, for a system with one service and obtained via TA-based model checking, the minimum and maximum absolute latency, viz., 159 and 189, respectively. It also shows a CDF of the same system based on discrete-event simulation. We observe that the bounds are valid, i.e., $s(159) = 0$ and $s(189) = 1$, and strict, i.e., $s(159 + \epsilon) > 0$ and $s(189 - \epsilon) < 1$,

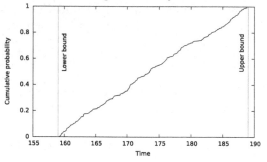

Fig. 10. The absolute lower and upper bound

where $\epsilon > 0$ and $s(n)$ is the probability that a latency equal to or below n based on discrete-event simulation.

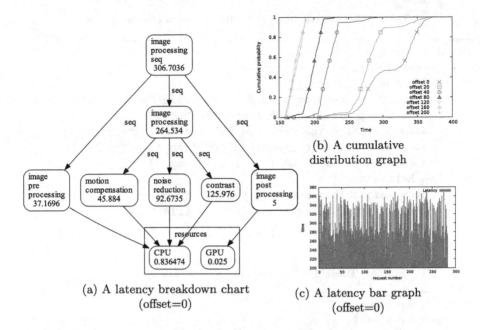

(a) A latency breakdown chart
(offset=0)

(b) A cumulative
distribution graph

(c) A latency bar graph
(offset=0)

Fig. 11. Three ways of representing latencies, generated from the iDSL code

5.2   Experiment II: Retrieving Exact Latency Distributions

Experiment II concerns generating *exact* latency distributions; the results generated using the model have to match the true values. This is accomplished by applying exhaustive methods based on model checking. Consequently, the model must be simple enough to deal with much complexity.

iDSL Model. The system (see Table 12) consists of two similar image processing services, a so-called frontal and lateral one. They are built up of the same process (see Table 10) and resource (see Table 11). The process encompasses successive high-level tasks "Noise_reduction" and "Refinement", which decompose into atomic tasks with EDF loads resulting from measurements. Notably, subprocess "Refinement" contains a nondeterministic choice, viz., atomic task "Refine" is executed either once or twice, which depends on the number of monitors connected to the iXR system. The resource (see Table 11) contains atomic resource "CPU" with rate 1 and buffersize 10 for FIFO scheduling, to which all atomic tasks are mapped. In the scenario (of Table 13), both frontal and lateral image processing are called with fixed inter-arrival times 40000. The offset of frontal is 0, the one of lateral depends on the "offset" dimension in the study (see Table 14).

Table 10. The code of an iDSL process with abstract loads

```
Section Process
  ProcessModel Image_Processing seq {
    seq Noise_reduction {
      atom Pre_processing load EDF from file "pproc"
      atom Decompose load EDF from file "dcomp"
      atom Spatial_noise_red load EDF from file "snr"
      atom Temporal_noise_red load EDF from file "tnr"
      atom Compose load EDF from file "comp" }
    seq Refinement { alt {
      atom Refine load EDF from file "ref"
        seq { atom Refine load EDF from file "ref"
      atom Refine load EDF from file "ref" } } } }
```

Table 11. The code of an iDSL resource

```
Section Resource
  ResourceModel Image_PC decomp { atom CPU rate 1 buffersize 10}
```

Table 12. The code of an iDSL system comprising two services

```
Section System
  Service Frontal_Image_Processing_Service
    Process Image_Processing
    Resource Image_PC
    Mapping assign  (all,CPU)  scheduling policy  (CPU, FIFO)
  Service Lateral_Image_Processing_Service
    Process Image_Processing
    Resource Image_PC
    Mapping assign  (all,CPU)  scheduling policy  (CPU, FIFO)
```

Table 13. The code of an iDSL scenario with two concurrent services

```
Section Scenario
  Scenario BiPlane_Image_Processing_run
    ServiceRequest FPontal_Image_Pnocessing_Serice
      at time 0, 40000, ...
    ServiceRequest Lateral_Image_Processing_Senvice
      at time dspace("offset"), 40000+dspace("offset"), ...
```

Table 14. The code of an iDSL study

```
Section Study
  Scenario BiPlane_Image_Processing_run
    DesignSpace (offset {"0" "10000" "20000" "30000"} )
```

Table 15. The code of an iDSL measure

```
Section Measure
  Measure ServiceResponseTimes PTA scalable
  Measure ServiceResponseTimes PTA scalable efficient
    ServiceResponseTimes using 1 run of 1000 requests
```

Transformation. The Modest code comprises a parallel process at its highest level, with services "Frontal_Image_Processing_Service" and a lateral equivalent, a resource "CPU", a resource queue "CPU_queue", and two generators that each call a different service. The two services alternately wait for incoming requests from different generators and call the same process. Atomic processes all call "CPU_queue", providing taskloads that Resource "CPU" processes.

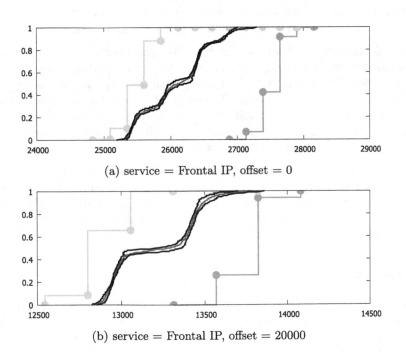

(a) service = Frontal IP, offset = 0

(b) service = Frontal IP, offset = 20000

Fig. 12. The lower (in purple) and upper bound CDF (in red), the simulation average (in blue), and $\alpha = 0.95$ confidence interval (in black) for two designs. (Color figure online)

Evaluation. The iSDL measure (of Table 15) encompasses two scalable Probabilistic Timed Automata measures, viz., an inefficient and efficient variant. The model is simplified using 256 cluster segments and time unit 4 (see Sect. 4.2). Additionally, a discrete-event simulation measure is added for validation.

Results. We compare the efficient approach with the inefficient one. The execution of basic estimates and discrete-event simulation takes only 27 s (<2%), but yields fairly tight bounds for model checking (as graphically depicted in Fig. 9), viz., [47 : 99], [110 : ∞], [97 : 110] and [97 : 110]. Hence, in return for little time, many expensive PTA-based model checking calls can be saved. Averagely, a TA-based model checking call takes 28 s and a PTA-based one 44 s. TA-based model checking is thus useful for the binary lower & upper bound search. Overall, the efficient approach takes (for offset = 0) 1589 s (50 calls), opposed to 1937 s (61 calls) for the inefficient one.

Validation is successful; the simulation confidence intervals (in black) are located between the lower (in purple) and upper bound (in red) in Fig. 12 for two offsets, despite the application of model simplifications (of Sect. 4.2).

6   Conclusion

This paper presents a method for performance evaluation of service-oriented systems which has been put into practice using two experiments, as follows.

The Performance Evaluation Process. To gain insight in the performance of embedded systems, we have proposed a framework for performance evaluation of service-oriented systems: A *high-level performance model* is obtained by modeling the performance of a system. Optionally, this model is simplified to make it scalable, after which it is transformed into a *underlying performance model* that adheres to a widespread formalism, e.g., Stochastic Timed Automata (STA, [2,7]). Applying *performance evaluation* yields *performance results*.

Two experiments have been conducted which exemplified a performance evaluation approach that: (i) provides a domain specific, high-level modeling language; (ii) allows for the automatic evaluation of a large number of complex designs; (iii) supports different ways of performance evaluation; and, (iv) presents its results intuitively via visualizations.

References

1. Bogdoll, J., David, A., Hartmanns, A., Hermanns, H.: MCTAU: bridging the gap between Modest and UPPAAL. In: Donaldson, A., Parker, D. (eds.) SPIN 2012. LNCS, vol. 7385, pp. 227–233. Springer, Heidelberg (2012). doi:10.1007/978-3-642-31759-0_16
2. Bohnenkamp, H., D'Argenio, P.R., Hermanns, H., Katoen, J.-P.: Modest: a compositional modeling formalism for hard and softly timed systems. IEEE Trans. Softw. Eng. **32**(10), 812–830 (2006)

3. Brinksma, H., Katoen, J.-P., Langerak, R., Latella, D.: Partial order models for quantitative extensions of LOTOS. Comput. Netw. ISDN Syst. **30**(9), 925–950 (1998)
4. D'Argenio, P.R., Hartmanns, A., Legay, A., Sedwards, S.: Statistical approximation of optimal schedulers for probabilistic timed automata. In: Ábrahám, E., Huisman, M. (eds.) IFM 2016. LNCS, vol. 9681, pp. 99–114. Springer, Cham (2016). doi:10.1007/978-3-319-33693-0_7
5. de Gooijer, T., Jansen, A., Koziolek, H., Koziolek, A.: An industrial case study of performance and cost design space exploration. In: Proceedings of the 3rd International Conference on Performance Engineering, pp. 205–216. WOSP/SIPEW, ACM (2012)
6. Ellson, J., Gansner, E., Koutsofios, L., North, S.C., Woodhull, G.: Graphviz— open source graph drawing tools. In: Mutzel, P., Jünger, M., Leipert, S. (eds.) GD 2001. LNCS, vol. 2265, pp. 483–484. Springer, Heidelberg (2002). doi:10.1007/3-540-45848-4_57
7. Hahn, E., Hartmanns, A., Hermanns, H.: Reachability and reward checking for stochastic timed automata. Electron. Commun. Eur. Assoc. Softw. Sci. Technol. **70**, 125–140 (2014)
8. Hahn, E., Hartmanns, A., Hermanns, H., Katoen, J.-P.: A compositional modelling and analysis framework for stochastic hybrid systems. Formal Methods Syst. Des. **43**(2), 191–232 (2012)
9. Hartmanns, A.: Model-checking and simulation for stochastic timed systems. In: Aichernig, B.K., de Boer, F.S., Bonsangue, M.M. (eds.) FMCO 2010. LNCS, vol. 6957, pp. 372–391. Springer, Heidelberg (2011). doi:10.1007/978-3-642-25271-6_20
10. Hartmanns, A., Hermanns, H.: The Modest toolset: an integrated environment for quantitative modelling and verification. In: Ábrahám, E., Havelund, K. (eds.) TACAS 2014. LNCS, vol. 8413, pp. 593–598. Springer, Heidelberg (2014). doi:10.1007/978-3-642-54862-8_51
11. Haveman, S., Bonnema, M.: Requirements for high level models supporting design space exploration in model-based systems engineering. In: Procedia Computer Science, vol. 16, pp. 293–302. Elsevier (2013)
12. Johnson, J.: Designing with the Mind in Mind: Simple Guide to Understanding User Interface Design Rules. Elsevier, Amsterdam (2010)
13. Kanungo, T., Mount, D., Netanyahu, N., Piatko, C., Silverman, R., Wu, A.: An efficient K-means clustering algorithm: analysis and implementation. IEEE Trans. Pattern Anal. Mach. Intell. **24**(7), 881–892 (2002)
14. Kienhuis, B., Deprettere, E.F., van der Wolf, P., Vissers, K.: A methodology to design programmable embedded systems. In: Deprettere, E.F., Teich, J., Vassiliadis, S. (eds.) SAMOS 2001. LNCS, vol. 2268, pp. 18–37. Springer, Heidelberg (2002). doi:10.1007/3-540-45874-3_2
15. Kontogiannis, K., Lewis, G., Smith, D., Litoiu, M., Muller, H., Schuster, S., Stroulia, E.: The landscape of service-oriented systems: a research perspective. In: Proceedings of the International Workshop on Systems Development in SOA Environments. IEEE Computer Society (2007)
16. Lee, I., Leung, J.Y., Son, S.H.: Handbook of Real-Time and Embedded Systems. CRC Press, Boca Raton (2007)
17. Philippou, A., Georghiou, C., Philippou, G.: A generalized geometric distribution and some of its properties. Stat. Probab. Lett. **1**(4), 171–175 (1983)
18. Pimentel, A., Hertzberger, L., Lieverse, P., van der Wolf, P., Deprettere, E.: Exploring embedded-systems architectures with Artemis. IEEE Comput. **34**(11), 57–63 (2001)

19. Prince, J., Links, J.: Medical Imaging Signals and Systems. Pearson Prentice Hall, Upper Saddle River (2006)
20. Racine, J.: GNUplot 4.0: a portable interactive plotting utility. J. Appl. Econom. **21**(1), 133–141 (2006)
21. Rosso, C.D.: Software performance tuning of software product family architectures: two case studies in the real-time embedded systems domain. J. Syst. Softw. **81**(1), 1–19 (2008)
22. van den Berg, F.: Automated performance evaluation of service-oriented systems. Ph.D. thesis, University of Twente (2017)
23. van den Berg, F., Haverkort, B.R., Hooman, J.: Efficiently computing latency distributions by combined performance evaluation techniques. In: Proceedings of the 9th EAI International Conference on Performance Evaluation Methodologies and Tools, VALUETOOLS 2015, pp. 158–163. ICST (2015)
24. van den Berg, F., Hooman, J., Hartmanns, A., Haverkort, B.R., Remke, A.: Computing response time distributions using iterative probabilistic model checking. In: Beltrán, M., Knottenbelt, W., Bradley, J. (eds.) EPEW 2015. LNCS, vol. 9272, pp. 208–224. Springer, Cham (2015). doi:10.1007/978-3-319-23267-6_14
25. van den Berg, F., Remke, A., Haverkort, B.R.: A domain specific language for performance evaluation of medical imaging systems. In: 5th Workshop on Medical Cyber-Physical Systems. OpenAccess Series in Informatics, vol. 36, pp. 80–93. Schloss Dagstuhl (2014)
26. van den Berg, F., Remke, A., Haverkort, B.R.: iDSL: automated performance prediction and analysis of medical imaging systems. In: Beltrán, M., Knottenbelt, W., Bradley, J. (eds.) EPEW 2015. LNCS, vol. 9272, pp. 227–242. Springer, Cham (2015). doi:10.1007/978-3-319-23267-6_15
27. Zurawski, R.: Embedded Systems Handbook. CRC Press, Boca Raton (2005)

Probabilities

Against All Odds:
When Logic Meets Probability

Johan van Benthem[1,2,3]($\boxtimes$)

[1] Institute for Logic, Language and Computation, University of Amsterdam,
Amsterdam, The Netherlands
[2] Department of Philosophy, Stanford University, Stanford, USA
[3] Changjiang Professors Program, Tsinghua University, Beijing, China
johan.vanbenthem@uva.nl

Abstract. This paper is a light walk along interfaces between logic and
probability, triggered by a chance encounter with Ed Brinksma. It is not
a research paper, or a literature survey, but a pointer to issues. I discuss
both direct combinations of logic and probability and structured ways
in which logic can be seen as a qualitative version of probability theory.
I end by sketching a concrete program for classifying qualitative scenarios
that would lend themselves to simple logical reasoning methods, but
I also acknowledge a challenge: the 'unreasonable effective of probability'.

1 Introduction

When I met Ed Brinksma recently in the "Glazen Zaal" in Den Haag, old memories came back of a very special student in Groningen, clearly 'a cut above the crowd', who wrote a pioneering thesis on interpolation in dynamic logic (still a live topic even today), and who turned my lecture notes on mathematical logic into a highly effective didactic manual that attracted many students over the years. I have followed Ed's career ever since, and find traces of encounters in my archive, such as our contributions printed side by side in a volume of the popular magazine "De Automatiseringsgids" in 1993, when, to some, computer science seemed to be in crisis, just as it was making a giant leap toward transforming our world. And there is of course his blazing trajectory as a Rector at the University of Twente, which I followed in the press, with, I confess, a tinge of pride in having contributed my bit to this higher flight.

But our conversation was about something else, namely, Ed's ideas on 'resonance' as a basis for communication, rather than elaborate logical models. This struck me since I had been thinking on similar lines, inspired by an introduction to cognitive science, [32], that made a distinction between two aspects of communication: 'transfer' of message content, and 'resonance' between the actors. The latter seems a precondition for the former to succeed.

I have thought a lot about this distinction, which seems real to me. I always tell my students who get a job interview that now is not the time to do still more transfer of information about how clever they are. It is not about touting their

© Springer International Publishing AG 2017
J.-P. Katoen et al. (Eds.): Brinksma Festschrift, LNCS 10500, pp. 239–253, 2017.
DOI: 10.1007/978-3-319-68270-9_12

latest papers, and their brilliant new projects, but rather, about establishing resonance with a committee trying to decide whether this (perhaps too) clever young person is someone they would like to have as a colleague.

But how to model resonance, real as it is? I can list many topics in my environment of logics of agency and philosophy of action that go a bit in this direction, such as common knowledge, opinion aggregation, or network dynamics, but they never seem to jell into one coherent picture, so all I have are accumulated notes in closed drawers. Now Ed seemed to think (it was a noisy reception, resonance by eye contact was easier than transfer) that all this presented a challenge to logic, and that we would need *probabilistic models*. So, here is my topic.

2   Logic and Probability

These are days of tension, or armed neutrality, between logical and statistical approaches to communication, language, and cognition. On the classical logical model of deliberative agents that communicate or interact, reasoning plays an important role, including complex 'theory of mind': what I believe about your beliefs about my beliefs, and upward. Much of my own work has been in this line, [34, 36], and the resulting logics of agency – also those by colleagues in computer science – are ever more sophisticated, but also, I am unhappy to say: ever more complex. It becomes a miracle that human interaction works at all. So, here is an alternative approach. We look for simple statistical patterns in human language and interaction, and explain observed behavior in terms of these. This contrast is sometimes cast in terms of 'high rationality' versus 'low rationality', [30]. Simple statistical models often explain emergent stable patterns in behavior just as well as complex logical theories with highly baroque sets of notions.

This is not just the usual sniping between competing academic disciplines. These issues are also potentially radical in their consequences for our daily lives. Take ethics and how we should behave. Classical ethical theory is reason-based, and the reasons why we engage in moral behavior toward others are cemented by complex logical and game-theoretic scenarios, a form of high rationality in the normative realm bequeathed to us by great minds like Immanuel Kant or John Rawls. Of course, there are people who do not play by the rules: criminals, or profiteers that play the system. But on the whole, society is in equilibrium. Now consider a low-rationality alternative without deep reasoning. There just happen to be two types of humans: predators (who do not follow the rules), and prey (those who do). Then a simple biological model for their encounters leads to an evolutionary game with probabilistic equilibria having stable percentages of predators and prey in the long run. Thus, stability has been explained in much simpler, and also less fragile, terms. And incidentally, those biological models do work on simple resonance (whether positive or negative) in terms of what the two types of beast do in their encounters.

The mathematics of the low rationality approach is statistics, dynamical systems, and evolutionary rather than classical game theory. And so a question arises, at least for someone like me. Is there any place left for logic? Well, the interface of logic and dynamical systems is an exciting new topic with old roots that I have discussed elsewhere, [37], and we are only at the beginning, [20].

But in this paper, I want to strike out in an even more general direction, focusing on just one aspect of dynamical systems. The rest of this little piece will try to paint a light picture of actual encounters between logic and probability, not in hostile or plaintive mode, but as serious paradigms treated on a par.

3   A Shared History

Qualitative deductive logic produces absolute certainty, but in a limited range, with its greatest triumphs perhaps in mathematics or automated deduction. In contrast, quantitative probability produces less certain conclusions, but it applies to all of life around us. But this way of phrasing the divide may create a spurious tension. It is important to realize that there is a good deal of harmony as well, and this section provides a few pointers.

Clearly, in our ordinary reasoning, probabilistic and logical steps proceed in tandem. One takes over where the other seems less appropriate. And indeed, this harmony can also be observed in the history of logic. Great logicians of the 19th century did not make sharp distinctions here. John Stuart Mill's highly influential "System of Logic" presents both logical and probabilistic rules for good reasoning, and it seems odd to say that he was confused between logic and probability theory, or between logic and methodology. Bernard Bolzano's "Wissenschaftslehre", another classical gem, even says that the task of logic is to chart all natural styles of human reasoning, which can be task-dependent, and he includes probabilistic reasoning among these. Similar views occur with Charles Saunders Peirce on the entanglement of deduction, induction (more probabilistic), and abduction (reasoning to the best explanation). And here is a title which says it all: George Boole's "An Investigation of the Laws of Thought on Which are Founded the Mathematical Theories of Logic and Probabilities". It is only with the birth of modern mathematical logic in Frege's "Begriffsschrift" that probability drops out, presumably because probability spaces live somewhere inside the set-theoretic universe, and thus have been 'dealt with' at the stratospheric abstraction level of the foundations of mathematics.

But even in a beginning modern logic course, numbers and probability come in naturally on top of the base structure. We normally give binary judgments of validity and non-validity for proposed inference patterns, say,

$$\neg B, A \to B \implies \neg A \text{ (valid) versus } \neg A, A \to B \implies \neg B \text{ (invalid)}$$

But there is more: among the non-validities, some seem worse than others. For instance, the inference $\neg A, A \to B \implies \neg B$ gets things wrong in half of the cases, but the invalid $A \vee B \implies \neg(A \wedge B)$ only in one of three cases. This is not yet probability, but it is natural numerical structure right inside logic.

This link continues into probability theory. A probabilistic axiom such as

$$P(A \vee B) = P(A) + P(B) - P(A \wedge B)$$

looks very much like propositional logic 'continued by other means'.

In fact, similar comments can be made about the simple almost propositional reasoning leading toward something as ubiquitous as Bayes' Rule:

$$P(A \mid B) = (P(B \mid A) * P(A))/P(B) \quad \text{if } P(B) \neq 0$$

Not surprisingly then, one of my favorite textbooks as a student (not on the official curriculum, but not on the Index either) was Suppes' "Introduction to Logic" from the 1950s which also included quantitative topics as a matter of course. It offers not just Venn Diagrams for syllogisms, but also Venn diagrams with numerical information about their regions – not just deductive logic, but also probability. And the same combinations can be seen in the creative work of major philosophical logicians. Carnap created 'inductive logic', [4], Hintikka developed numerical confirmation theory, [15], and Lewis moved happily from qualitative theories of conditionals to the principles of probabilistic update over time, [25]. This combination of interests is just natural, it will not go away.

With this in mind, let's now explore other encounters of logic and probability.

4   Logical Foundations of Probability

Here is an obvious first encounter that still may still need stating. One place where logic and probability can meet without conflict is at a meta-level, in the foundations of probability. Theorems in probability theory have standard mathematical proofs, and so there is a deductive logic to the theory of non-deductive reasoning. In this sense, Frege and the other founding fathers of mathematical logic were right. But there are also more intimate foundational contacts.

Consider our national classic, Johan De Witt's "Waerdije", [7], the founding document of modern insurance mathematics. At the start, the author gives an explanation of the laws of probability – which he may have learnt from a pamphlet by Christiaan Huygens – in terms of rational betting behavior. The betting connection is standard by now, and a famous version is the Dutch Book Theorem, [19]. This says that obeying the standard laws of probability is the only guarantee against having a 'Dutch book' made against you: that is, a system of bets that is systematically unfavorable to you. (This link between probability theory and financial gain is a pioneering instance of the 'valorization' so prized by our university leaders today.) There is more to be found in this line, witness [18] on justifications for qualitative probability. Indeed, I believe that one can also profitably give Dutch Book theorems for laws of logic, in terms of avoiding unsuccessful planning, but this theme would take me too far here.

And there is a deeper connection with logic as well. Pioneers of modern probability, such as De Finetti, [6], believed that probability rests on a qualitative notion, namely, a comparative binary connective between propositions:

$$A \leq B \quad B \text{ is more probable (more likely to be true) than } A \quad \cdot$$

De Finetti then proceeded to give axioms for this notion that allow for qualitative reasoning. In addition to obvious properties of a reflexive transitive order, these include intuitive laws of probability such as (with $-$ for set complement)

$A \leq B$ if and only if $(A - B) \leq (B - A)$

From these, other natural principles follow, such as the propositional monotonicity law saying that $A \leq B$ implies $A \wedge D \leq B \vee C$.

The aim of this approach was a set of intuitive qualitative laws of reasoning that would force the existence of a standard probability measure P such that

$$A \leq B \text{ iff } P(A) \leq P(B), \text{ for all propositions } A, B$$

Eventually, de Finetti's set of principles did not work out, as was shown in a famous technical counterexample in [21], a paper which also proposed necessary and sufficient qualitative principles for probabilistic representation. An accessible modern explanation of these matters can be found in [16].

Later on, Dana Scott gave a better-known streamlined version of necessary and sufficient logical principles for probability, [29], but still, their very complexity suggested by and large that this approach was a dead end. Much better to just calculate with probability values directly, and drop logical purism!

However, De Finetti's paradigm is not a closed chapter at the interface of logic and probability, and we will return to it in Sects. 6 and 7 below.

5   Probabilistic Patterns in Logic

Instead of looking for logical foundations for probability, we can also turn the tables, and look for probabilistic patterns in the foundations of logic. Here are a few strands that belong to this direction.

By the 1960s, the properties of first-order predicate logic, the logician's tool par excellence, had pretty much been discovered – and in 1969, Lindström's Theorem, [26], even stated a precise sense in which we had found a complete set that captured the essence of this system. History seemed at its end.

But in the 1970s, a striking discovery was the Zero-One Law, [9], and independently a Soviet team, which says the following. Take any first-order formula A, and compute the probability $P_n(A)$ of its being true on finite models of size n (there are only finitely many such models up to isomorphism). As n goes to infinity, the probability of $P_n(A)$ will go toward either 1 or 0. It is even decidable from the shape of the assertion A which of the two cases obtains. Many further such results have been discovered. In other words, underneath qualitative logical model theory, deep global statistical regularities have come to light – and in that sense, we probably do not know the meta-theory of classical logic at all yet.

Other examples of significant statistical behavior have been discovered as theorem provers started producing logs and outputs, making a vast store of experience available in how logical systems actually perform. One striking discovery were physical 'phase transitions' in computation time for propositional satisfiability problems, [27]: the average time toward an answer "satisfiable" or "not satisfiability" first increases with input size qua number of formulas, eventually it decreases, but the change is sharp for certain input sizes. These experiments have been replicated, also with other measures of input complexity, and the phenomenon seems robust: complexity of performance of logical systems has significant cliffs. Much progress has been made with analytical or logical explanations, but I am not aware of any definitive theory. Even so, we may conclude that the bulk behavior of proof systems, too, seems to hide important statistical structure for whose study we need to combine logic and probability.

My final example goes further, but is also more speculative. The great metatheorems of classical logic all have a limitative character. Basic problems are undefinable, non-axiomatizable, or undecidable. But how bad is this news really? The undecidability of first-order logic says that no single effective algorithm can decide validity correctly for arbitrary first-order formulas. But maybe there are methods that decide most first-order formulas, or even almost all of them except for a set of measure zero. Indeed, some results like this circulated in 2013, when a Bay Area-based group of computer scientists proposed a truth definition for arithmetic in a probabilistic first-order logic, [5], something that cannot be done classically by Tarski's Theorem. Of course, there is an all-important issue what sort of probability measure we are talking about, and I doubt that there is a consensus on the viability of these approaches. But there are versions which seem bona fide, witness the earlier paper [13] on the decidability of the Halting Problem on a set of asymptotic probability one. What I take from these results is that probability might make sense as a means of enriching results even in the heartland of mathematical logic. Even so, just in case: for a non-speculative and authoritative survey of established uses of probability in logic, cf. [23].

There are many further serious contacts between logic and probability than those enumerated here, starting from the 1960s until right today, in seminal work by Haim Gaifman, Jens Erik Fenstad, Jeff Paris, Michiel van Lambalgen, and many others. It would be tedious to bore the reader (and even worse, Ed) with huge bibliographies containing all of this work, so instead, I continue with just a few recent strands that I would like to highlight.

6   Mixed Practices in Language and Reasoning

Leaving polemics aside, there are good reasons for connecting up numerical probabilities and qualitative notions. In fact, this can be done in different ways.

One approach is modest, showing merely how logic and probability are not at odds, but can co-exist fruitfully in systems combining virtues of both. One such system is the 'probabilistic dynamic-epistemic logic' of [38], which has a logical component dealing with update of agents' knowledge and beliefs, and a probabilistic component providing fine-structure to the logical part. This is not just a case of living apart together. In the process of combining, perspectives enter from both sides, and in this particular combined system, the logic suggests new rules for update with new information, which distinguish three intuitively different sorts of probability: *prior probabilities* representing the agents' experience so far, *occurrence probability* representing what agents believe about the current process they are observing, and *observation probabilities* recording the quality, or the trust agents place in the new observation just made.

A more ambitious approach to our interface would establish some deeper functional connection between logical and probabilistic components in reasoning and problem solving. Perhaps the most obvious way of thinking about this is a division of labor: the logic is a qualitative counterpart for the probabilistic part, to which it stands in some precise definable relation.

This is not just a theorist's concern, there are indications that actual reasoning works in exactly this way. One such case rests on the fact that we use *natural language* all the time in phrasing our daily decisions, arguing for them, and even as academics, for explaining complex mathematical results, say quantitative insights about probability in more intelligible general terms.

Now the vocabulary of natural language has many notions that seem related to probability. The most striking examples are words like "probable" or "likely", though it would be naive, at least in my view, to suppose that these ordinary words stand directly for probabilistic notions. But even words that do not sound like this have been construed as having probabilistic content.

One famous example is that of natural language conditional statements

"if A, then B"

The influential book [1] proposed that these can be read as saying that the probability of the conditional equals the conditional probability $P(B \mid A)$, provided that $P(A) \neq 0$. There has been a spate of work on refining this intuition and rescuing it from counterexamples, and this perspective on natural language is very much alive, witness the relevant entry in the Stanford On-Line Encyclopedia of Philosophy: https://plato.stanford.edu/entries/logic-conditionals/. (Incidentally, the latter is also a great source for many other topics in this article.) Further probabilistic semantics have been given for so-called 'epistemic modals', such as the above words "probable" and "likely", or even "must" and "may" – cf. [17] for a modern take. Thinking in this way, many common expressions in natural language are surface manifestations of an underlying probabilistic reality, or probabilistic view of reality.

Here is another such line, this time not linguistic, but going back to philosophical epistemology in the 18th century. When we think about beliefs of humans (clearly, "know" and "believe" are typical natural language expressions that we use constantly to describe epistemic states of ourselves and others), probabilistic versions make sense, as these even allow for finer numerical degrees of belief. But at the same time, just speaking in terms of qualitative belief has never gone away, since it represents a stable and useful way of describing agents and their actions. But what is the connection with quantitative probability?

It has been proposed early on by Locke and Hume that belief in a proposition A would have an underlying probabilistic meaning

$$P(A) \geq k, \text{ where } k \text{ is some threshold in the interval } (0,1)$$

But there are well-known counterexamples to this view, which seems in conflict with the fact, usually assumed by philosophers, that beliefs of ideal agents are closed under conjunction. Now the recent study [24] has proposed an entirely new way to proceed here, by showing how each finite discrete probability space has a unique set of stable propositions whose probability remains above the given threshold when we get new consistent information. These propositions are a good candidate for our qualitative beliefs, as a stable core inside the probabilistic facts. At the same time, Leitgeb's analysis also provides an entirely new solution to the well-known Lottery Paradox, which I cannot go into here.

Finally, let us return to the foundations of probability. The discussion about De Finetti-style qualitative laws of reasoning with ordinary language expressions underpinning probability has been reopened recently in [16], whose authors show how a modified natural definition of qualitative comparative probability fits quite elegantly with representation in terms of sets of probability measures. The resulting logic is a subsystem of the original Scott-style qualitative probabilistic logic with independent interest as a means of drawing qualitative conclusions from qualitative premises that admit of probabilistic interpretation. Interestingly, this new analysis makes essential use of logics of qualitative probability in philosophy, [10] and in theories of agency in computer science [40].

These recent connections also suggest a more refined picture. We are not just investigating whether qualitative reasoning in logic fits with probabilistic reasoning by the precise canons of probability theory. One can look for a whole spectrum of numerical representations. Basic logical laws for comparative probability $A \leq B$ are valid if we just assume that propositions have numerical 'scores' that can be added and subtracted, cf. [31]. Other modes of reasoning, however, assume the probabilistic modus of normalizing everything to values in the interval $[0, 1]$ and allowing further numerical operations such as multiplication and division. We do not have to choose, but can see what fits the intended applications best. We will return to theses issues briefly in Sect. 7 below.

So, we live in exciting times. Old debates about the interface of qualitative reasoning and probability are being reopened, and boundaries seem less sharp and more flowing than before. I could add many more examples of this new phase of research, such as connections between probability and qualitative 'plausibility orders' for the semantics of belief, a popular tool in my own logical community, [39]. Also, a new wave of topological models for belief, evidence and learning is entering the fray, [2]. For a survey of the literature up to around 2000, and striking innovations far beyond my own community and including such powerful mixed probabilistic-qualitative calculi as Dempster-Shafer theory or Bayesian nets, I recommend Halpern's monograph "Reasoning about Uncertainty", [12].

I conclude with stating my own view on the matter. To me, it is a basic fact about cognition that we can approach language and reasoning at various levels of detail. Logical and mathematical languages 'zoom in', providing deep detail, and this has great virtues for utmost precision and computation. Natural language, on the other hand, 'zooms out', providing high-level qualitative descriptions that we can use to summarize our decisions and actions, and argue for or against them. Of course, traditional logicians tended to distrust natural language, as a cesspool of bad reasoning habits and naive or sloppy formulations. But I myself think in terms of harmony: both high zoom and low zoom seem important, and the real scientific task ahead is getting to grips with their constant interplay.

7   A Concrete Encounter

Finally, to complement the general picture painted in this paper, here is a concrete case for interfacing logic and probability. My starting point is a psychological study of patterns in natural language use, but I will also raise issues coming from other directions as we go along.

Here is an interesting psychological experiment, simplified a bit from [11].

Three Faces. People are shown three faces, one with a hat and glasses (1), one with glasses only (2), and one with neither (3). Now someone says: "My friend wears glasses." When asked who is that friend, most people say it is 2. Why?

Here is an explanation in terms of pragmatics using Grice's well-known maxims for conversation: "The friend must be 1 or 2. But if she were 1, there would be a more informative way of communicating this fact: namely, by saying "My friend has a hat". Therefore, the friend is 2." However, this style of analysis assumes that people are always maximally cooperative, so that the statement identifies the unique possibility of 'glasses only'. But this need not be the case in ordinary discourse, and we are merely talking tendencies, not certainty.

Accordingly, the analysis in the cited paper was probabilistic. To demonstrate this way of thinking, assume that all three possibilities are equally likely at the start. Now, qua empirical content the assertion "My friend wears glasses" rules out Case 3, leaving only Cases 1 and 2. But crucially, more information is available, viz. the fact that this particular assertion was used. We get at this surplus by assigning probabilities for two possible assertions to occur in Case 1. With any non-zero probability for "My friend has a hat", the sequence (Case 1, "Wears glasses") is less probable than (Case 2, "Wears glasses") (just compute the product of the prior probability of the case and the occurrence probability of the assertion), and this explains why we are more likely to be in Case 2.

Of course, there is freedom here in setting the occurrence probabilities for the two assertions in case 1. In fact, we can choose them so as to match the precise observed percentages of people choosing the 'correct' answer. But we can also view them as subjective probabilities that people have concerning linguistic behavior in the relevant community: the computation does not say.

Now for a logician's qualitative perspective. The probabilistic analysis given here seems overly specific. Agents do not have precise values for the probabilities of either statement in Case 1, and frankly, I am also somewhat suspicious of the statistics about respondents presented in these experiments, for various reasons that I will not go into here. In any case, the practical question at issue is qualitative about who is the friend, no finer measure is called for. Indeed, there seems to be a simple pattern at work here. The person hears that the friend wears glasses, which is still compatible with two faces: of persons 1 and 2. But she thinks it is more plausible that it is the face of person 2. Many decisions in daily life are driven by such simple judgments of comparative plausibility. How do these work, and can they be made to work simply and qualitatively?

There are two issues here. What, in fact, is the abstract underlying pattern of the *Faces*, and what sort of reasoning is appropriate to practical scenarios whose specifications are qualitative and so are the issues that need to be resolved?

Classifying the Structure of Problems. The above is not just one particular puzzle. Consider the much-discussed Monty Hall problem, [28]:

> "A car has been placed behind one of three doors. The car will be mine if I guess correctly where it is. Say, Door 1 is my guess. Now the quizmaster opens a door different from the one I chose and reveals there is no car behind it: say, he opens Door 3. He then asks if I want to switch my guess from Door 1 to Door 2. Should I?"

Many people, including professionals, have said I need not, since after the opening, the remaining two doors have equal probability. But again the point is that the quizmaster's opening Door 3 has surplus information: it is more likely that he did this with the car behind Door 2, where it was his only option, than with the car behind Door 1, where he had two options. And once more, the final issue is a qualitative "Yes/No": should I switch? Finally, I may not know the exact protocol followed by the quizmaster in opening doors when he has a choice. So, the core for this practical decision seems qualitative once more.

In fact, the key reasoning point of the Monty Hall scenario is *exactly* that of the Three Faces, as can be seen by drawing a diagram of the decision tree. This similarity can be made precise, and it raises an important general issue.

Many puzzles with probability seem to have the same structure, or at least, there are recurring general genres. This is seldom discussed in detail, but one often has a suspicion that different publications and communities discuss the same problem in different guises. This does not mean that there might not be differences in emphasis in such cases, say, in setting up the right probability space versus reasoning from a given probability space. But still, what would be very helpful here, for both theoretical and practical reasons, is having a classification from a higher standpoint. I believe that a good way to proceed here uses a known notion from the world of logic and computing, viz. *bisimulation*, of course in a version that fits a probabilistic setting, [22,38]. This could be the basis for a more systematic classification of probabilistic reasoning problems.

What Sort of Reasoning Fits Qualitative Problems? How can we do the reasoning in the Three Faces, or Monty Hall, qualitatively? One obvious candidate, in terms of our earlier discussion, are the earlier-mentioned logics for qualitative probability by Harrison-Trainor, Holiday & Icard. The most perspicuous formulation of this approach for our purposes in what follows may be that in [14].

> There are three relevant histories of events: *(friend is Person 1, "wears a hat"), (friend is Person 1, "wears glasses"), (friend is Person 2, "wears glasses")*. We know from the problem specification that the sets { *(friend is Person 1, "wears a hat"), (friend is Person 1, "wears glasses")*} and { *(friend is Person 2, "wears glasses")*} are equiprobable. We also know, or rather assume, that { *(friend is Person 1, "wears a hat")*} has non-zero probability, i.e., it is not equiprobable with the empty set. But then it *follows*, for instance in the probabilistic base logic of [16], that { *(friend is Person 1, "wears glasses")*} < { *(friend is Person 2, "wears glasses")*}.

Simple though this looks, there is an interesting problem here. In general, a qualitative specification of a probabilistic problem need not settle a comparative question. This is easy to see by varying on the *Faces*.

If we allow two assertions, say e, f, both if the friend is Person 1 (Case 1) and if she is Person 2 (Case 2), where we assume the two cases are equiprobable, and we observe event e, then it all depends on what we know about the relative plausibility of the events. Say, if we have $\{(1, e)\} > \{(1, f)\}$ and $\{(2, e)\} > \{(2, f)\}$, then we cannot conclusively compare the histories $(1, e)$ and $(2, e)$ unless we have more precise quantitative information. However, things are subtle. If we have $\{(1, e)\} > \{(1, f)\}$ and $\{(2, e)\} < \{(2, f)\}$, it follows necessarily that $\{(1, e)\} > \{(2, e)\}$.

A Numerical Calculus. I believe there is a simple numerical calculus behind the preceding observations, which acts as an intermediate level between full-fledged probabilistic computation and purely qualitative reasoning with binary comparative propositions. I will only sketch the idea, details are left to later work.

We merely need to assign variables to the relevant histories in some systematic way, and then use sums of such variables to describe relevant coherent sets of histories such as the ones that occurred in Monty Hall or the *Faces*. Then the available qualitative information in the problem at hand comes in the form of equalities and inequalities between terms that are sums of variables, with a constant 1 added for proper inequalities. And what we are asking is whether a particular inequality between relevant variables follows from the given information. I will not give concrete numerical examples here, but is easy to formulate the earlier problems and similar ones in this way.

Using standard ways of replacing inequalities by equations with additional variables as needed, this becomes an exercise in a small fragment of Presburger Arithmetic, namely, a satisfaction problem for algebraic terms, solvable by Gaussian elimination. The above examples represent very simple cases of such problems, driven by obvious properties such as monotonicity of addition, plus some slightly less obvious arithmetical inferences.

This numerical perspective on qualitative probability may be no more than an alternative notation for the more laborious formulations in [14] involving multisets, and it also seems related to the approach taken in [8,29]. Even so, I believe that analyzing the equational solution algorithm in the above manner might throw additional light on existing qualitative axiomatizations. Moreover, and much more ambitiously, I believe that we should look for such very simple (and often, simplistic) methods as the basis for a calculus of real practical use.

Of course, a more general issue remains, related to our earlier point about classification. Which kinds of qualitative problem can be solved in this way, and what makes them different from more complex scenarios where there is no alternative to biting the bullet, and doing the full probabilistic math?

Further Logical Features. There are also other logical perspectives on the examples discussed here. For instance, [35] analyzes the *Faces* in terms of information update and model-checking rather than inference. We have an initial probability space with equiprobable alternatives, events can occur which have different occurrence probabilities, and we want to know the relative probabilities of the resulting histories, perhaps after observing some particular event. This dynamics of constructing probability spaces seems important in clarifying puzzles in probabilistic reasoning, and [38] provides a mechanism for systematic construction.

But then, the issue of making qualitative comparisons in the final space becomes one of finding the right 'order merge' between prior plausibility order and plausibility order among events. And one difficulty for most current rules of order merge is the relevance of the eliminated history: in the *Faces* scenario, event $(1, f)$ did not occur, but it still influences our judgment of the relative plausibility of the case $(1, e)$ and $(2, e)$. As far as I know, no definitive update mechanism for qualitative probability has been found along these lines.

There are many further aspects to making probabilistic reasoning qualitative. What also seems relevant is the difference between *plausibility*, where we go for most prominent alternatives, an elitist epistemic perspective, versus *probability*, where many implausible possibilities may add up to one high-probability zone, a more democratic perspective. These are two valid styles of representing information in human reasoning. To see this co-existence in natural language, a sentence like "the candidate got most votes" can mean that she got more than half (the probabilistic view) but also that among the candidates, she received the largest vote (the plausibilistic view). Thus, we also need to disentangle the varieties of qualitative reasoning that are around in our daily practice.

The conclusion of my discussion is that natural qualitative viewpoints can be found on probabilistic reasoning toward qualitative conclusions, and that these may even have some chance of being practical, once we truly understand the mechanisms at work. I have made some concrete proposals to this effect, continuing on some recent literature, and pointing out further ways to go.

These concerns are not just a matter of purism but of practical importance. It is often said that 'people are bad at probabilistic reasoning'. Maybe this is just because they are performing other, more qualitative kinds of reasoning? This point is of course well-known, cf. [33], but I may have added some fuel.

Coda. Still, most of this is programmatic intentions, not proven achievements. Sometimes, one also has an opposite feeling. What we encounter in many scenarios is the 'unreasonable effectiveness of probability'. The numbers in one and the same probabilistic formula play distressingly different roles from a logician's point of view. A prior probability may record our accumulated experience in situations of similar kinds, or the strength of our prejudices unaffected by experience, while other probabilities measure features of an ongoing process such as likelihood of occurrence of events in certain states, there may also be numbers measuring the quality of our new observations, and so on. All these numbers, despite their different origins and meanings, are squashed together by numerical weights, and we freely apply arithmetical operations such as multiplication and division, even when these make little sense if we were to translate back to the intuitive meaning of the diversity notions involved. And yet it works!

8   Conclusion

I hope to have shown that the logic probability interface is very much alive. Even so, I have only scratched the surface. Innovative mixtures of probabilistic methods and more qualitative ones are everywhere today once you open your eyes, with some of them bubbling up right inside my own Amsterdam institute, such as the paradigm of data-oriented parsing, [3]. More generally, I think that, even in the current world of big data and deep learning, logic interfaces remain essential – and much more needs to be understood in general terms about productive mixtures of logic with probability and their general properties.

As for logic proper, I find it undeniable that my discipline has its place in the meta-theory of every scientific endeavor, including probability theory. But I would go further than this safe abstract sphere. Logic also has its place at object-level, so to speak, in our daily practices of deliberating, giving reasons, arguing, and making decisions. However, all this practice of our conscious minds takes place in a thin zone of rationality under our conscious control, hemmed in by sometimes turbulent seas of statistics on each side. There is the statistical behavior of society around us, and the statistical behavior of the neurons inside us. Logic finds itself surrounded by probability, but it holds it own. How?

I am not sure that the topics discussed in this light essay are anything like what Ed Brinksma had in mind in de Glazen Zaal. But I am sure that he will have interesting things to say about all of them once we meet again.

Acknowledgment. I thank Thomas Icard and two referees for helpful comments.

References

1. Adams, E.: The Logic of Conditionals. Reidel, Dordrecht (1975)
2. Baltag, A., Bezhanishvili, N., Özgün, A., Smets, S.: The topology of belief, belief revision and defeasible knowledge. In: Grossi, D., Roy, O., Huang, H. (eds.) LORI 2013. LNCS, vol. 8196, pp. 27–40. Springer, Heidelberg (2013). doi:10.1007/978-3-642-40948-6_3
3. Bod, R., Scha, R., Sima'an, K. (eds.): Data-Oriented Parsing. CSLI Publications, Stanford (2003)
4. Carnap, R.: The Continuum of Inductive Methods. University of Chicago Press, Chicago (1952)
5. Christiano, P., Yudkowsky, E., Herreshoff, M., Barasz, M.: Definability of "truth" in probabilistic logic. UC Berkeley and Google (2013)
6. de Finetti, B.: La prévision, ses lois logiques et ses sources subjectives. Annales de l'Institut Henri Poincaré **7**, 1–68 (1937)
7. de Witt, J.: Waerdije van lijfrenten naer proportie van losrenten. Letters to the Staten Generael, Den Haag (1671)
8. Delgrande, J., Renne, B.: The logic of qualitative probability. In: Yang, Q., Wooldridge, M. (eds.) Proceedings of the 24th International Joint Conference on Artificial Intelligence (IJCAI 2015), pp. 2904–2910. AAAI Press, Buenos Aires, Argentina (2015)
9. Fagin, R.: Probabilities on finite models. J. Symbolic Logic **41**(1), 50–58 (1976)

10. Gaerdenfors, P.: Qualitative probability as an intensional notion. J. Philos. Logic **4**, 171–185 (1975)
11. Goodman, N., Frank, M.: Predicting pragmatic reasoning in language games. Science **336**, 998 (2012)
12. Halpern, J.: Reasoning About Uncertainty. The MIT Press, Cambridge (2003)
13. Hamkins, J., Miasnikov, A.: The halting problem is decidable on a set of asymptotic probability one. Notre Dame J. Formal Logic **47**(4), 515–524 (2006)
14. Harrison-Trainor, M., Holliday, W.H., Icard, T.: Inferring probability comparisons. Mathematical Social Sciences, to appear
15. Hintikka, J.: Towards a theory of inductive generalization. In: Bar-Hillel, Y. (ed.) Proceedings of the 1964 Congress for Logic, Methodology and Philosophy of Science, pp. 274–288 (1965)
16. Holliday, W., Harrison-Trainor, M., Icard, T.: Preferential structures for comparative probabilistic reasoning. In: Proceedings of the Thirty-First AAAI Conference on Artificial Intelligence, pp. 1135–1141 (2017)
17. Holliday, W., Icard, T.: Measure semantics and qualitative semantics for epistemic modals. In: Proceedings of SALT, vol. 23, pp. 514–534 (2013)
18. Icard, T.: Pragmatic considerations on comparative probability. Philos. Sci. **83**(3), 348–370 (2016)
19. Kemeny, J.: Fair bets and inductive probabilities. J. Symbolic Logic **20**(3), 263–273 (1955)
20. Klein, D., Rendsvig, R.: Convergence, continuity and recurrence in dynamic-epistemic logic. University of Bamberg & University of Copenhagen (2017)
21. Kraft, C., Pratt, J., Seidenberg, A.: Intuitive probability on finite sets. Ann. Math. Stat. **30**(2), 408–419 (1959)
22. Larsen, K., Skou, A.: Bisimulation through probabilistic testing. Inf. Comput. **94**(1), 1–28 (1991)
23. Leitgeb, H.: Probability in logic. In: Hajék, A., Hitchcock, C. (eds.) The Oxford Handbook of Probability and Philosophy. Oxford University Press, Oxford (2014)
24. Leitgeb, H.: The stability theory of belief. Philos. Rev. **123**(2), 131–171 (2014)
25. Lewis, D.: A subjectivist's guide to objective chance. In: Studies in Inductive Logic and Probability, pp. 263–293. University of California Press, Berkeley (1980)
26. Lindström, P.: On extensions of elementary logic. Theoria **35**, 1–11 (1969)
27. Mézard, M., Montanari, A.: Information Physics and Computation. Oxford University Press, Oxford (2009)
28. Vos Savant, M.: The Power of Logical Thinking. St. Martin's Press, New York (1996)
29. Scott, D.: Measurement structures and linear inequalities. J. Math. Psychol. **1**(2), 233–247 (1964)
30. Skyrms, B.: The Dynamics of Rational Deliberation. Harvard University Press, Cambridge (1990)
31. Spohn, W.: Ordinal conditional functions: a dynamic theory of epistemic states. In: Harper, W., Skyrms, B. (eds.) Causation in Decision. Belief Change, and Statistics, vol. II, pp. 105–134. Kluwer, Dordrecht (1988)
32. Stenning, K., Lascarides, A., Calder, J.: Introduction to Cognition and Communication. The MIT Press, Cambridge (2006)
33. Tversky, A., Kahneman, D.: Probabilistic reasoning. In: Goldman, A. (ed.) Readings in Philosophy and Cognitive Science, pp. 43–68. The MIT Press, Cambridge (1993)
34. van Benthem, J.: Logical Dynamics of Information and Interaction. Cambridge University Press, Cambridge (2011)

35. van Benthem, J.: A problem concerning qualitative probabilistic update, Unpublished manuscript, ILLC, University of Amsterdam (2012)
36. van Benthem, J.: Logic in Games. The MIT Press, Cambridge (2014)
37. van Benthem, J.: Oscillations, logic and dynamical systems. In: Ghosh, S., Szymanik, J. (eds.) The Facts Matter, pp. 9–22. College Publications, London (2015)
38. van Benthem, J., Gerbrandy, J., Kooi, B.: Dynamic update with probabilities. Stud. Logica. **93**(1), 67–96 (2009)
39. van Benthem, J., Smets, S.: Dynamic logics of belief change. In: van Ditmarsch, H., Halpern, J., van der Hoek, W., Kooi, B. (eds.) Handbook of Logics of Knowledge and Belief, pp. 313–393. College Publications, London (2015)
40. van der Hoek, W.: Qualitative modalities. Int. J. Uncertainty Fuzziness Knowl.-Based Syst. **4**(1), 45–59 (1996)

FlyFast: A Scalable Approach to Probabilistic Model-Checking Based on Mean-Field Approximation

Diego Latella[1], Michele Loreti[2(✉)], and Mieke Massink[1]

[1] CNR-ISTI, Pisa, Italy
{D.Latella,M.Massink}@cnr.it
[2] Università di Firenze, Firenze, Italy
michele.loreti@unifi.it

Abstract. Model-checking is an effective formal verification technique that has also been extended to quantitative logics and models such as PCTL and DTMCs as well as CSL and CTMCs/CTMDPs. Unfortunately, the state-space explosion problem of classical model-checking algorithms affects also quantitative extensions. Mean-field techniques provide approximations of the mean behaviour of *large* population models. These approximations are *deterministic*: a *unique* value of the fractions of agents in each state is computed for each time instant. A drastic reduction of the size of the model is obtained enabling the definition of an efficient model-checking algorithm. This paper is a survey of work we have done in the last few years in the area of mean-field approximated probabilistic model-checking. We start with a brief description of FlyFast, an on-the-fly model checker we have developed for approximated bounded PCTL model-checking, based on mean-field population DTMC approximation. Then we show an example of use of FlyFast in the context of Collective Adaptive Systems. We also discuss two additional interesting front-ends for FlyFast; the first one is a translation from CTMC-based population models and (a fragment of) CSL that allows for approximate probabilistic model-checking in the continuous stochastic time setting; the second one is a translation from a predicate-based process interaction language that allows for probabilistic model-checking of models based on components equipped both with behaviour and with attributes, on which predicates are defined that can be used in component interaction primitives.

Keywords: Probabilistic on-the-fly model-checking · Mean-field approximation · Discrete time Markov chains · Time bounded probabilistic computation tree logic · Collective Adaptive Systems

1 Introduction and Related Work

Model-checking is an effective, powerful, and successful formal verification technique for concurrent and distributed systems that has also been extended to

© Springer International Publishing AG 2017
J.-P. Katoen et al. (Eds.): Brinksma Festschrift, LNCS 10500, pp. 254–275, 2017.
DOI: 10.1007/978-3-319-68270-9_13

quantitative logics and models. It consists of an efficient procedure that, given a model $\mathcal{M}$ of the system, typically composed of system states and related transitions, decides whether $\mathcal{M}$ satisfies a logical formula Φ, typically drawn from a temporal logic. Traditionally, model-checking approaches are divided into two broad categories: *global* approaches and *local* approaches.

In *global* model-checking approaches, the procedure determines the set of *all* states in $\mathcal{M}$ that satisfy Φ. Global model-checking algorithms are popular because of their computational efficiency and can be found in many model-checkers, both in a qualitative and in a probabilistic setting (see e.g. [2,3,11, 16,36]). The set of states that satisfy a formula is constructed recursively in a *bottom-up* fashion following the syntactic structure of the formula. Moreover, for stochastic model-checking, the global model-checking algorithm relies on existing and well-known algorithms for Markov Chains, such as those for transient and steady-state analysis (see e.g. [2]). Despite their success, the scalability of model-checking algorithms has always remained a concern due to the potential combinatorial explosion of the state space that needs to be searched.

This is unfortunate since current trends in information technology, like the Internet of Things (IoT), include specifically systems composed of a large number of components, often acting collectively and adapting to changing conditions, the so called *Collective Adaptive Systems*[1] (CAS), like, for instance gossip protocols, self-organised collective decision making, computer epidemic and smart urban transportation systems and decentralised control strategies for smart grids [4,10,12,49]. Given that large portions of the IoT are intrinsically (part of) critical infrastructures, with safety, security, and, in general, high dependability requirements, it is of great importance that system designers have the possibility to perform formal analysis before developing and deploying them.

In order to mitigate the state space explosion problem, in the qualitative analysis domain, *local* model-checking algorithms have been proposed that, given a state s in $\mathcal{M}$, determine whether s satisfies Φ. Local model-checking approaches use the so called 'on-the-fly' paradigm (see e.g. [5,17,26,32]) and follow a *top-down* approach that does not require global knowledge of the complete state space. For each state that is encountered, starting from a given state, the outgoing transitions are followed to adjacent states, constructing step by step local knowledge of the state space until it is possible to decide whether the given state satisfies the formula. For qualitative model-checking, local model-checking algorithms have been shown to have the same worst-case complexity as the best existing global procedures for the above mentioned logics. However, in practice, they have better performance when only a subset of the system states need to be analysed to determine whether a system satisfies a formula. Furthermore, local model-checking may still provide some results in case of systems with a very large or even infinite state space where global model-checking approaches would be impossible to use.

In the context of probabilistic model-checking several on-the-fly approaches have been proposed, among which [21,29,40]. In [21], a probabilistic

---

[1] See, e.g. www.focas.eu/adaptive-collective-systems.

model-checker is shown for the *time bounded* fragment of the Probabilistic Computation Tree Logic (PCTL) [30]. An on-the-fly approach for *full* PCTL model-checking is proposed in [40] where, actually, a specific *instantiation* is presented of an algorithm which is *parametric* with respect to the specific probabilistic processes modelling language and logic, and their specific semantics. Finally, in [29] an on-the-fly approach is used for detecting a maximal relevant search depth in an infinite state space and then a *global* model-checking approach is used for verifying bounded Continuous Stochastic Logic (CSL) [1,2] formulas in a continuous time setting on the selected subset of states.

An on-the-fly approach by itself however, does not solve the challenging scalability problems that arise in truly large parallel systems, such as CAS. To address this type of scalability challenges in probabilistic model-checking, recently, several approaches have been proposed. In [28,31] approximate probabilistic model-checking is introduced. This is a form of statistical model-checking that consists in the generation of random executions of an *a priori* established maximal length [37]. On each execution the property of interest is checked and statistics are performed over the outcomes. The number of executions required for a reliable result depends on the maximal error-margin of interest. The approach relies on the analysis of individual execution traces rather than a full state space exploration and is therefore memory-efficient. However, the number of execution traces that may be required to reach a desired accuracy may be large and therefore time-consuming. The approach works for general models, i.e. models where stochastic behaviour can also be non Markovian and that do not necessarily model populations of similar objects. On the other hand, the approach is not independent from the number of objects involved.

In [38], we presented a scalable model-checking algorithm, based on mean-field approximation, for the verification of time bounded PCTL properties of an individual[2] in the context of a system consisting of a large number of interacting objects. Also this algorithm is actually an instantiation of the above mentioned parametric algorithm for (exact) probabilistic model-checking [40]. In this case, the parametric algorithm is instantiated on (time bounded PCTL and) the *approximate*, mean-field, semantics of a population process modelling language. The approach is based on the idea of fast simulation, as introduced in [46]. More specifically, the behaviour of a generic agent with S states in a clock-synchronous system with a *large* number N of instances of the agent at given step (i.e. time) t is approximated by $\mathbf{K}(\boldsymbol{\mu}(t))$ where $\mathbf{K}(\mathbf{m})$ is the $S \times S$ probability transition matrix of a (inhomogeneous) DTMC and $\boldsymbol{\mu}(t)$ is a vector of size S approximating the mean behaviour of the global system at t; each element of $\boldsymbol{\mu}(t)$ is associated with a distinct state of the agent, say C, and gives an approximation of (the average of) the fraction of the instances of the agent that are in state C in the

---

[2] The technique can be applied also to a finite selection of individuals; in addition, systems with several distinct types of individuals can be dealt with. For the sake of simplicity, in the present paper we consider systems with many instances of a single individual only and we focus in the model-checking a single individual in such a context.

global system, at step t. Note that such an approximation is *deterministic*, i.e. μ is a *function* of the step t, computed iteratively, using (again) matrix $\mathbf{K(m)}$; the exact behaviour of the rest of the system would instead be a *large* DTMC in turn. Note furthermore, that $\mathbf{K(m)}$ does not depend on N; in other words, the cost of the analysis *is independent* from the number of objects involved, but only depends on the number of states of the single individual object. Our work is based on mean-field approximation in the *discrete time* setting; approximated mean-field model-checking in the *continuous time* setting has been presented in the literature as well. In the latter case, the deterministic approximation of the global system behaviour is formalised as an initial value problem using a set of differential equations. Preliminary ideas on the exploitation of mean-field convergence in continuous time for model-checking were informally sketched in a presentation at QAPL 2012[3] [34], but no model-checking algorithms were presented. Follow-up work on the above mentioned approach can be found in [33] which relies on earlier results on fluid model-checking by Bortolussi and Hillston [7], later published in [8]. Bortolussi and Hillston propose a *global CSL* model-checking procedure for the verification of properties of a selection of individuals in a population. The procedure relies on mean-field convergence and fast simulation results in a *continuous* time setting (see also [9,18,25] and references therein). The approach in [7,8] is based on an *interleaving* model of computation, rather than a clock-synchronous one. Furthermore, a *global* model-checking approach, rather than an on-the-fly approach is adopted; it is also worth noting that the treatment of nested formulas, whose truth value may change over time, turns out to be much more difficult in the interleaving, continuous time, global model-checking approach than in the clock-synchronous, discrete time, on-the-fly one.

We conclude this brief overview on related work by mentioning the approach of using techniques and tools developed for continuous signal monitoring as means for performing approximated global model checking of probabilistic models. In this approach, a deterministic, continuous, approximation of a population system model is first computed [9], and then monitoring techniques are applied on the resulting function of continuous time [23,24]. Recently, this approach has been extended in order to include also spatial features [50], as originally proposed in [13].

We finally note that one should keep in mind that mean-field/fluid procedures are based on *approximations* of the global behaviour of a system. Consequently, the techniques should be considered as *complementary* to other, more accurate analysis techniques for CAS, primarily those based on stochastic simulation, like for example statistical model-checking. In practice, given the high computational cost of simulation based techniques, especially when compared with the very low cost of the mean-field based techniques, the latter are more suitable for getting first ideas on the main features of the models at hand and a first screening

---

[3] Tenth Workshop on Quantitative Aspects of Programming Languages, March 31 - April 1, 2012, Tallinn, Estonia.

thereof. Then, when only a few options are left, more detailed analyses could be performed and more accurate techniques would be recommended.

In this paper, we present a survey of work we have carried out recently within the context of the EU project QUANTICOL[4] in the area of mean-field approximated probabilistic model-checking. We start with a brief description, in Sect. 2, of FlyFast, the on-the-fly model checker which implements the procedure we proposed in [38,42,43]. Then, in Sect. 3 we show a complete example of use of FlyFast in the context of Collective Adaptive Systems, taken from [39]. In Sect. 4 we discuss two additional interesting front-ends for FlyFast; the first one, originally presented in [41], is a translation to FlyFast from CTMC-based population models and (a fragment of) CSL that allows for approximate probabilistic model-checking in the continuous stochastic time setting; the second one, originally presented in [15], is a translation to FlyFast from a predicate-based process interaction language that allows for probabilistic model-checking of bounded PCTL formulas on models based on components equipped both with behaviour and with attributes; component interaction takes place via communication primitives using predicates over attributes for expressing the set of partners in multi-cast communication. We finally draw some conclusions in Sect. 5.

2   A Brief Overview of FlyFast

In this section we recall the main features of FlyFast.[5] The reader interested in details is referred to [38,42,43]. A FlyFast model specification characterises a system consisting of the *clock-synchronous product* of a (large) number of instances of a probabilistic process. Systems with several distinct types of processes can be specified as well; here we consider only the case of a single process type for the sake of simplicity. The size of the system is assumed constant during system evolution; FlyFast does not support explicit dynamic creation/deletion of processes. The behaviour of the probabilistic process is specified by a set Δ of state and action probability definitions. A state definition has the following syntax: **state** C $\{a_1.C_1 + \ldots + a_r.C_r\}$ where $a_i \in \mathcal{A}$—the set of FlyFast *actions*—C, $C_i \in$ —the set of FlyFast *states*—and, for $i,j = 1,\ldots,r$ $a_i \neq a_j$ if $i \neq j$; note that $C_i = C_j$ with $i \neq j$ is allowed instead. The informal meaning of the above definition is that, when in state C, the process can jump to state C_1, by executing (atomic) action a_1, or to state C_2, by executing (atomic) action a_2, and so on. Each action has a probability assigned by means of an action probability definition of the form **action a** : exp where exp is an expression involving constants and **frc** (C) terms. Constants are floating point values or names associated to such values using the construct **const name** = **value**—we let A denote the set of such auxiliary definitions; **frc** (C) denotes the element associated to state C

---

[4] http://www.quanticol.eu.

[5] FlyFast (https://quanticol.github.io/jSAM/flyfast.html) is provided within the jSAM (java StochAstic Model Checker) framework which is an open source Eclipse plugin (https://quanticol.github.io/jSAM/).

in the current occupancy measure vector—*o.m.v.* in the sequel—that is a vector with as many elements as the number of states of the individual process; the element associated to a specific state gives the fraction of the subpopulation currently in that state over the size of the overall population; the *o.m.v.* is a compact abstract representation of the system global state, where process identity is lost. Thus, the probability of executing a transition of a process in the system may depend on the global distribution of the processes in their local states within the system; process interaction is thus *probabilistic* and *indirect*, via transition probabilities, i.e. functions of the *o.m.v.*. Note that, whenever the exit probability p of a state is smaller than 1, FlyFast implicitly inserts a self-loop in the state, associated with the residual probability $1 - p$. The initial state of the system is specified by means of the **system** construct, followed by the name of the system model, and the vector $\mathbf{C_0}$ of the names of the initial state of all other instances, which implicitly specifies also the size N of the system. By convention, the first element $\mathbf{C_0}[1]$ of vector $\mathbf{C_0}$ refers to the individual process to analyse. In general more then one process can be specified for analysis; here we consider only the case of the single process for the sake of simplicity.

```
const N = 2000                          state S {inf_ext.E + inf_int.E}
const alpha_e = 0.1                     state E {activate.I}
const alpha_i = 0.2                     state I {recover.R}
const alpha_r = 0.2                     state R {loss.S}
const alpha_a = 0.4
const alpha_l = 0.1
action inf_ext : alpha_e
action inf_int : alpha_i * frc (I)
action activate : alpha_a               system SEIR = ⟨S[N], E[0], I[0], R[0]⟩
action recover : alpha_r
action loss : alpha_l
```

Fig. 1. A FlyFast specification of an epidemic model

Example 1 (An epidemic system model). In Fig. 1 the FlyFast specification of the epidemic model discussed in [38] is shown. The system is composed of 2000 instances of a process with four states; when in state S (susceptible) the process can become exposed (state E) either via an external infection, with probability **alpha_e**, or via internal infection, with a probability that is proportional to the fraction of processes in the system that are already infected, i.e. **alpha_i** * **frc (I)**. The infection activates in an exposed process with probability **alpha_a**, leading to state I. An infected process may recover with probability **alpha_r** and then loose immunity with probability **alpha_l**. Initially, all 2000 instances are in state S[6].

Given specification $\langle \Delta, A, \mathbf{C_0} \rangle$ for a system model of size N, FlyFast generates a transition probability matrix $\mathbf{K(m)}$ such that $\mathbf{K(m)}_{c,c'}$ is the probability for the (individual) probabilistic process to jump from state C to C′, given the

---

[6] In FlyFast, the notation C[n] is used for indicating n copies of state C.

current *o.m.v.* **m**. Thus, $\mathbf{K}(\mathbf{m})$ is a function of the *o.m.v.* **m**; strictly speaking, Δ characterises an inhomogeneous DTMC. In [38,42] the details of the formal operational semantics definition for the model specification language are provided as well as the procedure for generating $\mathbf{K}(\mathbf{m})$; in the sequel we recall only the main steps. Let Δ be the set of states defined in Δ, with $|\Delta| = S$, $\mathcal{U}^S = \{(m_1, \ldots, m_S) \in [0,1]^S | m_1 + \ldots + m_S = 1\}$ denote the unit simplex of dimension S, and $\mathcal{I} : \Delta \to \{1, \ldots, S\}$ be a bijection. For state $\mathsf{C} \in \Delta$, with $\mathcal{I}(\mathsf{C}) = c$, the interpretation $[\![\mathbf{frc}\,(\mathsf{C})]\!]_{\mathbf{m}}$ of $\mathbf{frc}\,(\mathsf{C})$ in the current *o.m.v.* $\mathbf{m} = (m_1, \ldots, m_S)$ is defined as expected: $[\![\mathbf{frc}\,(\mathsf{C})]\!]_{\mathbf{m}} = m_c$, i.e. $\mathbf{frc}\,(\mathsf{C})$ is the *fraction* of the subpopulation currently in state C over the size of the overall population, which, by definition of the *o.m.v.*, is exactly the element m_c of $\mathbf{m}$. The probability associated with an action **a** by action probability definition **action a** : E is a function $\pi_{\mathbf{a}}(\mathbf{m})$ of the *o.m.v.* **m**, defined as $\pi_{\mathbf{a}}(\mathbf{m}) = [\![E]\!]_{\mathbf{m}}$, where the interpretation function $[\![\cdot]\!]$ is defined recursively on arithmetic expressions E involving $\mathbf{frc}$ and constants, in the obvious way. More precisely, letting $\mathsf{C} \overset{\mathsf{a}}{\rightarrowtail} \mathsf{C}'$ represent an a-labelled transition in the operational semantics of the FlyFast modelling language and assuming $c = \mathcal{I}(\mathsf{C}) \neq c' = \mathcal{I}(\mathsf{C}')$, the probability matrix function $\mathbf{K} : \mathcal{U}^S \times \{1, \ldots, S\} \times \{1, \ldots, S\} \to [0,1]$ is defined as follows: $\mathbf{K}(\mathbf{m})_{c,c'} = \sum_{\mathsf{a}:\mathsf{C}\overset{\mathsf{a}}{\rightarrowtail}\mathsf{C}'} \pi_{\mathbf{a}}(\mathbf{m})$ and $\mathbf{K}(\mathbf{m})_{c,c} = 1 - \sum_{j \in \{1,\ldots,S\}\setminus\{c\}} \mathbf{K}(\mathbf{m})_{c,j}$. In other words, $\mathbf{K}(\mathbf{m})_{c,c'}$ is the *cumulative* probability of jumping from C to C', abstracting from the specific action performed by the process in the jump; this abstraction choice is typical of probabilistic, PCTL/DTMC-based approaches. Finally, note that, by construction, $\mathbf{K}(\mathbf{m})$ does *not* depend on N.

Example 2. It is easy to see that, for the model of Example 1, the resulting matrix is the following one, with $\mathbf{m} = (m_s, m_e, m_i, m_r)$ where m_s is the fraction of processes in state S, m_e is the fraction in state E, m_i is the fraction in state I, and m_r is the fraction in state R:

$$\mathbf{K}(m_s, m_e, m_i, m_r) = \begin{pmatrix} 1 - (0.1 + 0.2m_i) & 0.1 + 0.2m_i & 0 & 0 \\ 0 & 0.6 & 0.4 & 0 \\ 0 & 0 & 0.8 & 0.2 \\ 0.1 & 0 & 0 & 0.9 \end{pmatrix}$$

The exact probabilistic semantics of the complete system model is easily given as product of N instances of $\mathbf{K}$ with appropriate *o.m.v.* parameter and argument states. In other words, the transitions of different processes are intended as stochastically *independent*[7]. More precisely, for global system state $\mathbf{C} \in \Delta^N$, let the associated *o.m.v.* $\mathbf{M}(\mathbf{C})$ be defined as $\mathbf{M}(\mathbf{C}) = (M_1, \ldots, M_S)$ with $M_i = \frac{1}{N} \sum_{n=1}^{N} \mathbf{1}_{\{\mathsf{C}_{[n]}=\mathcal{I}^{-1}(i)\}}$ where $\mathbf{1}_{\{\alpha=\beta\}}$ is 1, if $\alpha = \beta$, and 0 otherwise. The probabilistic semantics of the system is the DTMC $X^{(N)}(t)$ with one-step transition probability $S^N \times S^N$ matrix $\mathbf{P}$ with $\mathbf{P}_{\mathbf{C},\mathbf{C}'} = \prod_{n=1}^{N} \mathbf{K}(\mathbf{M}(\mathbf{C}))_{\mathcal{I}(\mathsf{C}_{[n]}),\mathcal{I}(\mathsf{C}'_{[n]})}$

---

[7] It is worth stressing here that in the model of process interaction presented in [46], which FlyFast is based on, processes do *not* synchronize on actions explicitly (i.e. there is no notion of *randez-vous* here). Process interaction is only *indirect*, by means of the impact of the *o.m.v.* on individual transition probabilities.

and initial probability mass all in $\mathbf{C_0}$. FlyFast provides a standard stochastic simulation functionality based on the exact probabilistic semantics, namely matrix $\mathbf{P}$. In particular one can execute single runs or get averages of a user-specified number of runs. The output is given in the form of traces of the *o.m.v.* DTMC $\mathbf{M}^{(N)}(t) = \mathbf{M}(X^{(N)}(t))$. In addition, the tool can perform *exact*, on-the-fly (full) PCTL model checking using $\mathbf{P}$. FlyFast accepts state formulas built out of atomic propositions, negations, disjunctions and probabilistic quantification over path-formulas; the latter are next and until formulas. Of course, as opposed to approximate model-checking, exact PCTL model-checking of a formula can be used only if the portion of the state-space which needs to be generated and analysed for deciding satisfaction of the formula is not too large.

Example 3. For the epidemic model of Example 1, but with constant N set to 8, for a system with only 8 processes, we consider the following properties, where tt stands for *true*, LowInf is defined, using the **formula** construct of FlyFast, as follows: **formula** LowInf : (**frc** I) < 0.25, and I (E, respectively) labels all system states the first element of which is process state I (E, respectively):

P1 the worm will be active in the first component within k steps with a probability that is at most p: $\mathcal{P}_{\leq p}(\text{tt } \mathcal{U}^{\leq k} \text{ I})$;

P2 the probability that the first component is infected, but latent, in the next k steps while the worm is active on less then 25% of the components is at most p: $\mathcal{P}_{\leq p}(\text{LowInf } \mathcal{U}^{\leq k} \text{ E})$;

P3 the probability to reach, within k steps, a configuration where the first component is not infected but the worm will be activated with probability greater than 0.3 within 5 steps is at most p:

$$\mathcal{P}_{\leq p}(\text{tt } \mathcal{U}^{\leq k} (!\text{E} \wedge !\text{I} \wedge \mathcal{P}_{>0.3}(\text{tt } \mathcal{U}^{\leq 5} \text{ I}))).$$

In Fig. 2 the result of exact PCTL model-checking of Example 1 is reported. On the left the probability of the set of paths that satisfy the path-formulae used in the three formulae above is shown for k from 0 to 70. On the right the time needed to perform the analysis using PRISM [36] and using FlyFast exact PCTL model checking are presented[8].

More interestingly, FlyFast can compute the *deterministic* limit of the *o.m.v.* DTMC, for $N \to \infty$, and execute time bounded PCTL model-checking using such a deterministic approximation. The approach has been inspired by *Fast Simulation*, proposed in [46] and is based on Theorem 4.1 of [46], actually on a simplified version of the theorem, thanks to the specific syntax of the expressions used in FlyFast action probability definitions. Informally, let $\mathbf{C_0}^{(N)}$ be the initial state of the FlyFast specification of a system with N processes and assume there exists $\mu_0 \in \mathcal{U}^S$ such that almost surely $\lim_{N \to \infty} \mathbf{M}(\mathbf{C_0}^{(N)}) = \mu_0$. Let

---

[8] We used a 1.86 GHz Intel Core 2 Duo with 4 GB. State space generation time of PRISM is not counted. The experiments are available in the FlyFast web site, showing that the latter has comparable performance. Worst-case complexity of both algorithms are also comparable.

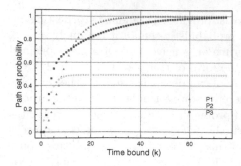

	PRISM	Exact on-the-fly
P1	108.479s	29.587s
P2	51.816s	3.409s
P3	216.952s	85.579s

Model parameter values:
$\alpha_e = 0.1$, $\alpha_i = 0.2$, $\alpha_r = 0.2$
$\alpha_a = 0.4$, $\alpha_l = 0.1$

Fig. 2. Exact model-checking results (left) and verification time (right).

function $\boldsymbol{\mu}(t)$ be defined as follows: $\boldsymbol{\mu}(0) = \boldsymbol{\mu_0}$ and $\boldsymbol{\mu}(t+1) = \boldsymbol{\mu}(t)^T \cdot \mathbf{K}(\boldsymbol{\mu}(t))$, where, as usual, $\mathbf{m}^T$ is the transpose of vector $\mathbf{m}$. Then, for any fixed time τ, almost surely $\lim_{N \to \infty} \mathbf{M}^{(N)}(\tau) = \boldsymbol{\mu}(\tau)$—cfr. Theorem 4.1 of [46]. So, the matrix $\mathbf{K}(\mathbf{m})$ generated by FlyFast can be conveniently (re)used also for *approximating* the *o.m.v.*, which, we recall, is an abstract representation of the global system state; it is important to stress here that the *o.m.v.* $\mathbf{M}^{(N)}(t)$ is a stochastic process, whereas the approximation we use, $\boldsymbol{\mu}(t)$, is *deterministic*, i.e. just a function of the step (time) t. We consider now the stochastic process $\mathcal{H}(t)$ the generic state of which, at time t, is a pair $(\mathtt{C}, \boldsymbol{\mu}(t))$. The first component $\mathtt{C}$ is the current state of the selected process in the system we are interested in, and the second component $\boldsymbol{\mu}(t)$ represents the current global system state. It is easy to see that $\mathcal{H}(t)$ is a DTMC and that the probability of a jump from state $(\mathtt{C}, \boldsymbol{\mu}(t))$ to $(\mathtt{C}', \boldsymbol{\mu}(t+1))$ is $\mathbf{K}(\boldsymbol{\mu}(t))_{\mathcal{I}(\mathtt{C}), \mathcal{I}(\mathtt{C}')}$. $\mathcal{H}(t)$ is the *approximated* probabilistic semantics of the system model. By performing on-the-fly model-checking on $\mathcal{H}(t)$—where state labels of the selected process are exported to pair states $(\mathtt{C}, \boldsymbol{\mu})$—FlyFast provides an approximated, mean-field based, efficient *time bounded* PCTL model-checking functionality. In other words, for any fixed time τ, sample $\mathbf{C}$ of $X(t)$ at time τ and safe formula[9] Φ the following holds: $\mathbf{C} \models_{X(t)} \Phi$ if and only if $(\mathbf{C}[1], \boldsymbol{\mu}(\tau)) \models_{\mathcal{H}(t)} \Phi$. In the case of mean-field model-checking, the set of atomic propositions is the set of states of the single agent or assertions on the components of the *o.m.v.*; in addition one can assign a name to a formula and use it in larger formulas. Finally, note that FlyFast can provide, as a by-product, the plot of $\boldsymbol{\mu}(\tau)$ for τ ranging in a user-specified range.

Example 4. Figure 3 shows the result of mean-field, approximated model-checking by FlyFast on the model of Example 1 with formulas as in Example 3, for the first object of a large population of 2000 objects, each initially in state S. In Fig. 3 (left) the same properties are considered as in Example 3. The analysis takes less than a second and is *insensitive* to the total population size. Figure 3 (right) shows how the probability measure of the set of paths satisfying the

---

[9] We refer to [38,42] for the characterisation of *safe* formulas and a related discussion.

formula tt $\mathcal{U}^{\leq k}$ (!E $\wedge$!I $\wedge$ $\mathcal{P}_{>0.3}$(tt $\mathcal{U}^{\leq 5}$ I)) of property P3 on page 8, (for $k = 3$), changes for initial time $t0$ varying from 0 to 10.

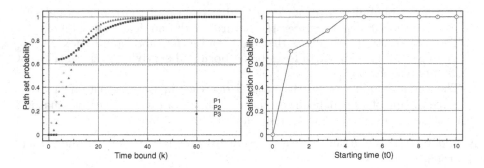

Fig. 3. Mean-field model-checking results.

We close this section by stressing that the exact full PCTL model-checker and the approximated mean-field time bounded PCTL model-checker are both instances of the *same* parametric implementation of an on-the-fly model-checking algorithm. Furthermore, the computation of the set of states to be analysed at the next step is a key operation of the on-the-fly procedure and, for exact model-checking, in the worst case the step returns S^N states, whereas for mean-field model-checking, the number of states returned in the worst case drops dramatically to S.

3   Predator-Prey Model of Lotka-Volterra in FlyFast

The next example we consider is a widely studied model for ecological competition, first independently investigated by the biophysicist Alfred Lotka and the Italian mathematician and physicist Vito Volterra in the twenties of the 19th century [48,51]. Since then, the model has been studied extensively by numerous other scientists and some of its elements are still at the basis of many population models that have been developed in the course of time, both in continuous time, e.g. [19,27] and references therein, and in discrete time settings, e.g. [22]. In its simplest form the model can be interpreted as a simplified and idealised description of two species in an ecosystem, often indicated as predator and prey, or foxes and rabbits for a concrete example.

In the variant we consider here we assume that each element of the two species can be in one of two states; it is either alive, or it is somehow 'dormant' waiting to get born again. We do this because the language we use does not provide explicit constructs for the dynamic creation of objects and is implicitly assuming that the total population size of all species remains constant. If we choose the size of the 'dormant' part of the population of each species large enough, this should not have any effect on the part of the population that is alive, since there are always enough dormant rabbits and foxes to get born.

As in the original version, we assume that the model depends on four parameters:

- The net probability 'a' of an increase in the size of the rabbit population which is the difference between the natural birth and death probabilities.
- The probability 'b' of rabbits that die because they are eaten by foxes
- The probability 'e' of extra foxes being born and surviving because they eat rabbits (efficiency).
- The net probability 'c' of the natural decrease in the population of foxes. Since the life of a fox depends on the availability of rabbits, there is a natural tendency of foxes to die when there a few or no rabbits.

A model in terms of difference equations of the populations of foxes and rabbits can then be given by:

$$RD(t+1) = RD(t) + b \cdot h \cdot RL(t) \cdot FL(t) - a \cdot h \cdot RL(t)$$
$$RL(t+1) = RL(t) + a \cdot h \cdot RL(t) - b \cdot h \cdot RL(t) \cdot FL(t) \qquad (1)$$
$$FD(t+1) = FD(t) - e \cdot h \cdot RL(t) \cdot FL(t) + c \cdot h \cdot FL(t)$$
$$FL(t+1) = FL(t) + e \cdot h \cdot RL(t) \cdot FL(t) - c \cdot h \cdot FL(t)$$

where t ranges over the set of the natural numbers, RD and RL are the fractions of 'dormant' and 'alive' rabbits, respectively, and FD and FL the fractions of 'dormant' and 'alive' foxes, respectively. The factor h is a rescaling factor for the duration of steps and $0 < h < 1$. The smaller the value of h the smaller the relative probabilities of the different events and the more accurate the results, but at the cost of an increase of the number of steps per time-unit in the model-checking procedure, which takes more time. For the model in this section we chose $h = 0.125$. Note that when this discrete model is interpreted as an approximation of the well-known continuous time model, i.e. in terms of differential equations, this approximation is not perfect, in the sense that the solution of the differential equations would give a perfect oscillating behaviour, whereas the solution of the difference equations will result in a small error in each step. This error has a cumulative effect resulting in oscillations with ever higher peaks, as can easily be observed in the results. A better approximation of the continuous model could be reached by using a more sophisticated integration method instead of the Euler method that is used implicitly in this case study.

The FlyFast specification of the Lotka-Volterra model is shown in Fig. 4. Assuming $\mathcal{I}(\text{RD}) = 1$, $\mathcal{I}(\text{RL}) = 2$, $\mathcal{I}(\text{FD}) = 3$, $\mathcal{I}(\text{FL}) = 4$, the 4×4 matrix $\mathbf{K} : \mathcal{U}^4 \times \{1, \ldots, 4\} \times \{1, \ldots, 4\} \to [0, 1]$ generated by FlyFast is shown below, noting that the matrix is stochastic for the time interval of interest (and in particular $m_1 \neq 0 \neq m_3$):

$$\mathbf{K}(m_1, m_2, m_3, m_4) = \begin{pmatrix} 1 - a \cdot h \cdot \frac{m_2}{m_1} & a \cdot h \cdot \frac{m_2}{m_1} & 0 & 0 \\ b \cdot h \cdot m_4 & 1 - b \cdot h \cdot m_4 & 0 & 0 \\ 0 & 0 & 1 - e \cdot h \cdot m_2 \cdot \frac{m_4}{m_3} & e \cdot h \cdot m_2 \frac{m_4}{m_3} \\ 0 & 0 & c \cdot h & 1 - c \cdot h \end{pmatrix}$$

```
const a = 0.04                            state RD {rborn.RL}
const b = 0.5                             state RL {rdies.RD}
const c = 0.05                            state FD {fborn.FL}
const e = 0.2                             state FL {fdies.FD}
const h = 0.125
action rborn : a * h * frc (RL)/frc (RD)  system LoVo = ⟨RD[5000], RL[1000], FD[3000], FL[1000]⟩
action rdies : b * h * frc (FL)
action fborn : e * h * frc (RL) * frc (FL)/frc (FD)
action fdies : c * h
```

Fig. 4. A FlyFast specification of the Lotka-Volterra model

It is easy to see that by computing $\boldsymbol{\mu}(t+1)$ as $\boldsymbol{\mu}(t+1) = \boldsymbol{\mu}(t)^T \cdot \mathbf{K}(\boldsymbol{\mu}(t))$, where $\boldsymbol{\mu}(t) = (\mu_1(t), \mu_2(t), \mu_3(t), \mu_4(t))$, one obtains again the difference Eq. (1) of page 11, where, of course, $\mu_1(t)$ stands for $RD(t)$, $\mu_2(t)$ for $RL(t)$, $\mu_3(t)$ for $FD(t)$, and $\mu_4(t)$ for $FL(t)$.

As it is well known, the global behaviour of the (idealised) model shows oscillations in the populations of rabbits and foxes for certain values of the model parameters. In fact, the model has very interesting behaviour and is therefore widely studied, but in this paper we focus mainly on the illustration of the application of fast mean field model checking of an individual rabbit or fox in the context of the overall oscillating behaviour. For example, for the values of the parameters and initial state as in Fig. 4, we obtain the results for the occupancy measure varying over time shown in Fig. 5, which is the plot of the limit o.m.v. $\boldsymbol{\mu}(\tau)$ produded by FlyFast.

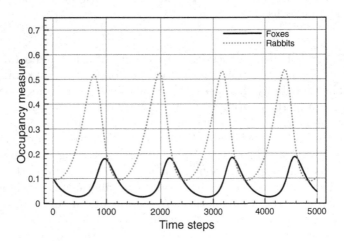

Fig. 5. Fraction of rabbit and fox populations.

In the predator-prey model one could furthermore be interested to know what is the probability that a rabbit survives for a certain amount of time, and how this probability changes over time with the oscillation of the population of foxes. Figure 6 shows the probability that a fox gets born or dies within time bound t

ranging from 0 to 3000 time steps. It also shows the results for a rabbit getting born or dying. The formula for the probability that a rabbit gets born within t time steps is $\mathcal{P}_{=?}(\text{RD } \mathcal{U}^{\leq t} \text{ RL})$. The other formulas are similar. Figure 6 shows that both foxes and rabbits eventually get born and die when given enough time and starting from the initial state of the overall system. The curves also reflect the oscillations in the populations over time and consequently the change in probability to get born or die.

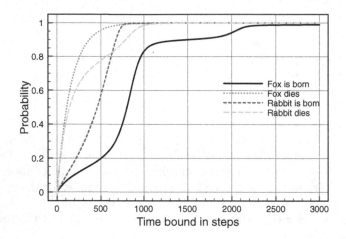

Fig. 6. Probability that a fox (rabbit) gets born or dies within time bound t ranging from 0 to 3000 time steps.

Figure 7 shows the time-dependent probability of a fox and a rabbit to get born or die in the next 10 time steps, starting from initial times ranging from 0 to 5000. The probability that a rabbit dies within 10 time units is obtained by evaluating the property $\mathcal{P}_{=?}(\text{RL } \mathcal{U}^{\leq 10} \text{ RD})$, for different initial times. The other formulas are similar. In this oscillating system the time-dependence of these probabilities can be observed very well. The probabilities of a rabbit getting born (dying respectively) within 10 time units and a fox getting born follow closely the oscillations in the respective population sizes. The probability that a fox dies in this model is constant. The amplitude of the oscillations is slowly increasing. This is likely due to the accumulation of small errors in the computation due to the constant step size used in the computations. In fact it is well-known that a mean-field approximation may become less accurate on the longer run, in a discrete time setting. See e.g. [19] for a study of this aspect of the Lotka-Volterra model in the continuous time setting. We will come back to these issues in Sect. 4.1.

Finally, Fig. 8 shows the time dependent probability of reaching a state, within 100 time steps, in which the probability of an individual rabbit to die within 10 time steps is higher than 0.2. This probability is shown for different

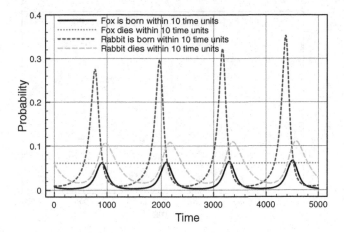

Fig. 7. Time dependent probability to get born or die in the next 10 time steps for different initial times from 0 to 5000.

initial times ranging from 0 to 5000. This is a typical example of a 'nested' formula involving two occurrences of the until operator. The formula is:

$$\mathcal{P}_{=?}(\text{tt } \mathcal{U}^{\leq 100} \ (\ \text{RL } \wedge \ \mathcal{P}_{>0.2}(\ \text{RL } \mathcal{U}^{\leq 10} \ \text{RD})))$$

The figure shows that there are indeed relatively short periods in which such states can be reached within 100 time steps. Nested formulas are relatively easy to handle due to the iterative and recursive way in which the FlyFast model-checker works.

4   Extending the Applicability of FlyFast

In the previous sections we have shown examples of the expected use of FlyFast, namely the development of a probabilistic, discrete time, population model of the system of interest and its analysis, mainly via bounded PCTL model-checking based on mean-field semantics. In this section we briefly describe two extensions of the applicability of the tool, both designed as additional *front-ends* for FlyFast, so that no modifications are required of the tool itself. The first extension concerns on-the-fly fluid CSL model-checking of *continuous* time population models; the second extends the FlyFast modelling language, and its underlying agent interaction paradigm, by adding *predicate* based communication primitives. Details on the first extension can be found in [41] while the second front end is described in detail in [15, 44].

4.1   FlyFast **Front-end for Fluid Model-checking of Continuous Time Population Models**

Fluid model checking [7, 8, 33] relies on a global model checking approach for time-inhomogeneous Continuous Time Markov Chains (ICTMC) representing

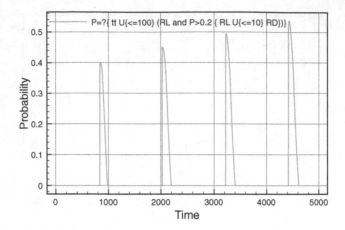

Fig. 8. Time dependent probability of reaching a state, within 100 time steps, in which the probability of an individual rabbit to die within 10 time steps is less than 0.2 for different initial times ranging from 0 to 5000.

an individual object in the context of a large CTMC population model. The rates of the individual may depend on the fraction of the population that is in a particular state. The algorithm relies on the deterministic approximation of the average stochastic behaviour of the system in *continuous time*, i.e. a fluid approximation [9,35]. Although the technical and mathematical foundations of the continuous time case are obviously different from those in the discrete case, at the intuitive/conceptual level, the two cases are similar.

Suppose you have system of N agents, each modelled by a ICTMC with states in $\{1,\ldots,S\}$, and $S \times S$ infinitesimal generator matrix $\mathbf{Q}^{(N)}(\boldsymbol{x})$ that may depend on the current *o.m.v.* $\boldsymbol{x} \in \mathcal{U}^S$; the *o.m.v.* process is a CTMC on the space $[0,1]^S$ with initial state $\boldsymbol{x}_0^{(N)}$ equal to the fraction of agents in each local state, in the initial global state. The average infinitesimal variation of the *o.m.v.* process, given that it is in state $\boldsymbol{x}$ is $F^{(N)}(\boldsymbol{x}) = \boldsymbol{x}^T \cdot \mathbf{Q}^{(N)}(\boldsymbol{x})$. If, for $N \to \infty$, $\mathbf{Q}^{(N)}(\boldsymbol{x})$ converges uniformly to the Lipschitz continuous generator matrix $\mathbf{Q}(\boldsymbol{x})$, and $\boldsymbol{x}_0^{(N)}$ to $\boldsymbol{x}_0$, and, furthermore, if $\boldsymbol{x}(t)$ is the solution of the ODE $\frac{d\boldsymbol{x}}{dt} = F(\boldsymbol{x}) = \boldsymbol{x}^T \cdot \mathbf{Q}(\boldsymbol{x})$ for initial condition $\boldsymbol{x}(0) = \boldsymbol{x}_0$, then, almost surely, in the limit, the *o.m.v.* process behaves the same as $\boldsymbol{x}(t)$, for any finite time horizon T [18,35].

This fundamental result has given rise to a *fast simulation* approach also in the continuous case. Assuming, again by convention and without loss of generality, that we are interested in the first of the N agents, let $Z^{(N)}(t)$ be the ICTMC on space $\{1,\ldots,S\}$ modelling the behaviour of such an agent. Let us furthermore consider the ICTMC on $\{1,\ldots,S\}$ $z(t)$ such that $\Pr\{z(t+dt) = j|z(t) = i\} = q_{i,j}(\boldsymbol{x}(t))dt$, and let $\mathbf{Q}_z(\boldsymbol{x}(t)) = (q_{i,j}(\boldsymbol{x}(t)))$. We then have that for any finite horizon T and $t \leq T$ the behaviour of the single object $Z^{(N)}(t)$ tends to the behaviour of the object that senses the rest of the system only through its limit behaviour given by x, i.e. $z(t)$. On the basis of these results, in [7,8] a model-checking algorithm has been proposed for CSL robust[10] formulas.

In [41] we took an alternative approach, showing that, under suitable convergence and scaling assumptions[11], and for models that are not too stiff[12], fluid model checking can be performed exploiting on-the-fly mean field model checking. In particular, in [41] a mechanical translation is defined which derives a time-inhomogeneous DTMC and a bounded PCTL formula from the input ICTMC model and bounded CSL formula. FlyFast can then be used for performing on-the-fly mean-field model-checking of the derived formula on the derived IDTMC.

Our approach starts from the idea that we can interpret the difference equations obtained from a discrete time population model as an instance of the Euler forward method for approximating the solution of a set of ODEs. The set of ODEs we are interested in solving are those of a corresponding continuous population model. This, in turn, means that we need to derive suitable values for the probabilities from the rates in the continuous model. What we are actually interested in is to transform an ICTMC model of an individual (from which the ODEs can be derived) into an IDTMC model, with the same local states and jump structure as the ICTMC; from this IDTMC we get the set of difference equations that can be used to approximate the solution of the ODEs. Intuitively, the IDTMC is obtained from the ICTMC using an approach which is similar to CTMC uniformisation[13]; we define a probability matrix $\mathbf{K}$ such that $\mathbf{K} = \mathbf{I} + \frac{1}{q} \cdot \mathbf{Q}$, where $\mathbf{Q}$ is the infinitesimal rate matrix—which is a function of $x(t)$—and q must not only satisfy the standard requirements for uniformisation, but also be such that absolute stability of the method as well as acceptable accuracy are guaranteed [47]. This procedure produces a discretisation of the continuous-time model; of course, also the logical formulas must be translated by consistently discretising them—and in particular the time bound of the bounded until operator.

We refer to [41] for the detailed definition of the translations and their correctness proof. Here we point out that such global fluid model checking algorithms, as described in [7,8], require the *a priori* calculation of discontinuity points, i.e. points in time in which the truth values of time-dependent (sub)-formulas of an until formula change. This is a non-trivial task and consists in finding all zeros of an analytic function. In the on-the-fly setting, instead, such points are detected automatically during the computation of the probabilities, up to a difference that is in the order of a small discrete step size; moreover, on-the-fly approaches are particularly efficient when verifying conditional reachability properties because in that case much fewer states need to be generated.

---

[10] We refer to [7,8] for the definition of formula robustness.

[11] See Theorem 5 of [7].

[12] Stiff models are those whose rates differ several orders of magnitude.

[13] More specifically, we use only the discretisation phase of uniformisation, and not the transient analysis part, that would require a further composition with a Poisson process.

On the other hand, our approach is ultimately based on an Euler forward method to solve differential equations. This poses certain limitations on the continuous time models that can be analysed efficiently this way, in particular they should not be too stiff. For non stiff models the results are promising as shown in [41] for the available benchmark models for which also some results for global fluid model checking and statistical model checking are available in the literature.

4.2   FlyFast Front-End for Predicate-Based Coordination

Recent proposals for CAS modelling and programming languages, like [6,20], typically assume any such a system be composed of a set of independent *components* where a component is a process equipped also with a set of *attributes* describing features of the component. Attributes can be used in *predicates* appearing in the language input/output primitives. *Predicate-based* output/input *multicast*, originally proposed in [45], forms the basis of interaction schemes in languages like SCEL [20] and CARMA [6]. In [15] we proposed PiFF—Predicate-based Interaction for FlyFast—a front-end modelling language for Fly-Fast inspired by CARMA, that provides *predicate-based* input/output *multicast* actions.

In PiFF, each component consists of a behaviour—modelled, like in Fly-Fast, as a DTMC-like agent—and a set of attributes. The attribute name-value correspondence is kept in the current *store* of the component. Associated to each action there is also an (atomic) probabilistic store-update. For instance, assume components have an attribute named loc which takes values in the set of points of a space, thus recording the current location of the component. The following action models a multi-cast via channel α to all components in the same location as the sender, making the latter change its location randomly: $\alpha^*[\text{loc} = \mathbf{my}.\text{loc}]\langle\rangle$ Jump. Here Jump is assumed to randomly update the store and, in particular attribute loc. The computational model of PiFF is *clock-synchronous*, as in FlyFast, but at the component level. In addition, each component is equipped with a local *outbox*. The effect of an output action $\alpha^*[\pi_r]\langle\rangle\sigma$ is to deliver output label $\alpha\langle\rangle$ to the local outbox, together with the predicate π_r, which (the store of) the receiver components will be required to satisfy, as well as the current store of the component executing the action; the current store is then updated according to update σ. Note that output actions are *non-blocking* and that successive output actions of the same component overwrite its outbox. An input action $\alpha^*[\pi_s]()\sigma$ by a component will be executed with a probability which is proportional to the *fraction* of all those components whose outboxes currently contain the label $\alpha\langle\rangle$, a predicate π_r which is satisfied by the component, and a store which satisfies predicate π_s in turn. If such a fraction is zero, then the input action will not take place (input is blocking), otherwise the action takes place, the store of the component is updated via σ, and its outbox cleared.

A PiFF model specification is compiled into a FlyFast model specification by means of a (purely mechanical) translation and related bounded PCTL formulas are mechanically translated as well. For the sake of simplicity, we do not describe the translation here; the interested reader can find its definition in [15], where the formal stochastic semantics of PiFF are also given and the translation is shown correct with respect to such semantics; optimisation of the translation is dealt with in [44]. In particular, in [44], a bisimilarity based state-reduction strategy for the target model specification is proposed.

5 Conclusions

Model-checking has proven to be an effective and successful formal verification technique. Initially developed for *qualitative* models and logics, it has been extended also to quantitative models and logics such as DTMCs and PCTL as well as CTMCs and CSL. It is well known that model-checking suffers from the state-space explosion problem, which makes the technique non-scalable and thus poorly applicable to large scale systems. On the other hand, current trends in information technology, like the Internet of Things, include systems composed of a large number of components, often acting collectively and adapting to changing conditions, the so called *Collective Adaptive Systems*. In this paper we have briefly described the work we have been carrying out in the area of approximated bounded PCTL model-checking of Population DTMC models. In particular we have given an introductory description of FlyFast, a mean-field, on-the-fly bounded PCTL model-checker, including an overview of its theoretical foundation, its main functionalities and a detailed example of application. A couple of extensions of the applicability of the tool have been shown as well, in the form of specific additional front-ends to the original tool; thus, the tool applicability is extended without actually modifying the tool.

There are several lines of future work of our interest. First of all, following approaches similar to those presented in [46], we plan to investigate the extension of the model-checking technique to systems with memory/rewards. Space and the spatial distribution of agents play a major role in CAS and, consequently, it should be a "first class" component of the modelling language and the underlying framework. For this reason, we have investigated *Closure Spaces*, a generalisation of Topological Spaces that includes discrete, graph-like, space structures, for which we have developed the *Spatial Logic for Closure Spaces*, SLCS and a specific model-checking algorithm [13,14]. A subject for future research is thus to incorporate a notion of space in the FlyFast modelling language and to integrate FlyFast and **topochecker**, the spatial model-checker for SLCS and its extensions. The investigation of different classes of interaction probability specifications in the FlyFast modelling language and of their implications on issues like model-reduction (see e.g. [44]) is also a promising subject for future research.

Acknowledgments. In the late 80's of the previous century, Diego met Ed, who was chairing a Work Package of the EU Lotosphere project, in which Diego participated as well. At that time, Diego was fascinated by the early work on probabilistic process algebras by Scott Smolka, Kim Larsen and others and he was applying similar ideas to LOTOS, together with Paola Quaglia. At the same time, he was loving the work of Rom, supervised by Ed, on Bundle Event Structures as a mathematical model underlying a truly concurrent semantics for LOTOS. The obvious step was to start thinking of probabilistic extensions of Bundle Event Structures. Accidentally, Diego and Mieke had met at a Lotosphere workshop in The Hague and they found themselves nicely synchronised in their professional interests, and beyond . . .

Not surprisingly, Diego moved to Twente where he spent 12 months, from july 1992 to june 1993, and together with Ed, Rom and Joost-Pieter, started investigating probabilistic, deterministically timed and stochastically timed Bundle Event Structures. This was the start of a lively friendship of the four of them as well as of a series of headaches when trying to find finite graph-like representations of such structures suitable for analysis. They have been struggling together for years, searching for *cut-off* events in those slippery structures. Eventually, Mieke moved to Italy and joined the group of cut-off events hunters. It was fun! Maybe we did not manage to completely master the analysis of quantitative Bundle Event Structures, but we are aware of a couple of things: our current work on probabilistic systems is rooted back to those days (and headaches . . .) and our friendship too. All this thanks to Ed, who accepted having Diego around in Twente in 1992–93.

References

1. Aziz, A., Sanwal, K., Singhal, V., Brayton, R.: Model checking continuous time Markov chains. ACM Trans. Comput. Log. **1**(1), 162–170 (2000)
2. Baier, C., Haverkort, B., Hermanns, H., Katoen, J.P.: Model-checking algorithms for continuous-time Markov chains. IEEE Trans. Softw. Eng. IEEE CS **29**(6), 524–541 (2003)
3. Baier, C., Katoen, J.P.: Principles of Model Checking. The MIT Press, Cambridge (2008)
4. Bernardo, M., De Nicola, R., Hillston, J. (eds.): Formal Methods for the Quantitative Evaluation of Collective Adaptive Systems. LNCS, vol. 9700. Springer, Heidelberg (2016). ISBN 978-3-319-34095-1 (print), 978-3-319-34096-8 (online), ISSN 0302-9743(2016)
5. Bhat, G., Cleaveland, R., Grumberg, O.: Efficient on-the-fly model checking for CTL*. In: LICS, pp. 388–397. IEEE Computer Society (1995)
6. Bortolussi, L., De Nicola, R., Galpin, V., Gilmore, S., Hillston, J., Latella, D., Loreti, M., Massink, M.: CARMA: collective adaptive resource-sharing Markovian agents. In: Bertrand, N., Tribastone, M. (eds.) Proceedings Thirteenth Workshop on Quantitative Aspects of Programming Languages and Systems, QAPL 2015, London, UK, 11th–12th April 2015, EPTCS, vol. 194, pp. 16–31 (2015). http://dx.doi.org/10.4204/EPTCS.194.2
7. Bortolussi, L., Hillston, J.: Fluid model checking. In: Koutny, M., Ulidowski, I. (eds.) CONCUR 2012. LNCS, vol. 7454, pp. 333–347. Springer, Heidelberg (2012). doi:10.1007/978-3-642-32940-1_24
8. Bortolussi, L., Hillston, J.: Model checking single agent behaviours by fluid approximation. Inf. Comput. **242**, 183–226 (2015)
9. Bortolussi, L., Hillston, J., Latella, D., Massink, M.: Continuous approximation of collective system behaviour: a tutorial. Perform. Eval. **70**(5), 317–349 (2013). http://www.sciencedirect.com/science/article/pii/S0166531613000023
10. Bradley, J.T., Gilmore, S.T., Hillston, J.: Analysing distributed internet worm attacks using continuous state-space approximation of process algebra models. J. Comput. Syst. Sci. **74**(6), 1013–1032 (2008)

11. Buchholz, P., Hahn, E.M., Hermanns, H., Zhang, L.: Model checking algorithms for CTMDPs. In: Gopalakrishnan, G., Qadeer, S. (eds.) CAV 2011. LNCS, vol. 6806, pp. 225–242. Springer, Heidelberg (2011). doi:10.1007/978-3-642-22110-1_19

12. Chaintreau, A., Le Boudec, J.Y., Ristanovic, N.: The age of gossip: spatial mean field regime. In: Douceur, J.R., Greenberg, A.G., Bonald, T., Nieh, J. (eds.) SIG-METRICS/Performance, pp. 109–120. ACM (2009)

13. Ciancia, V., Latella, D., Loreti, M., Massink, M.: Specifying and verifying properties of space. In: Diaz, J., Lanese, I., Sangiorgi, D. (eds.) TCS 2014. LNCS, vol. 8705, pp. 222–235. Springer, Heidelberg (2014). doi:10.1007/978-3-662-44602-7_18. ISBN 978-3-662-44601-0 (print), 978-3-662-44602-7 (online), ISSN 0302-9743

14. Ciancia, V., Latella, D., Loreti, M., Massink, M.: Model checking spatial logics for closure spaces. Log. Methods Comput. Sci. 12(4), 1–51 (2016). doi:10.2168/LMCS-12(4:2)2016. Published online: 11 October 2016. ISSN 1860-5974

15. Ciancia, V., Latella, D., Massink, M.: On-the-fly mean-field model-checking for attribute-based coordination. In: Lluch Lafuente, A., Proença, J. (eds.) COORDINATION 2016. LNCS, vol. 9686, pp. 67–83. Springer, Cham (2016). doi:10.1007/978-3-319-39519-7_5. ISSN 0302-9743, ISBN 978-3-319-39518-0 (print), 978-3-319-39519-7 (online)

16. Clarke, E.M., Emerson, E.A., Sistla, A.P.: Automatic verification of finite-state concurrent systems using temporal logic specifications. ACM Trans. Program. Lang. Syst. 8(2), 244–263 (1986)

17. Courcoubetis, C., Vardi, M., Wolper, P., Yannakakis, M.: Memory-efficient algorithms for the verification of temporal properties. Form. Methods Syst. Des. 1(2–3), 275–288 (1992)

18. Darling, R., Norris, J.: Differential equation approximations for Markov chains. Probab. Surv. 5, 37–79 (2008)

19. Dayar, T., Mikeev, L., Wolf, V.: On the numerical analysis of stochastic Lotka-Volterra models. In: IMCSIT, pp. 289–296 (2010)

20. De Nicola, R., et al.: The SCEL language: design, implementation, verification. In: Wirsing, M., Hölzl, M., Koch, N., Mayer, P. (eds.) Software Engineering for Collective Autonomic Systems. LNCS, vol. 8998, pp. 3–71. Springer, Cham (2015). doi:10.1007/978-3-319-16310-9_1. ISBN 978-3-319-16309-3 (print), 978-3-319-16310-9 (online), ISSN 0302-9743

21. Della Penna, G., Intrigila, B., Melatti, I., Tronci, E., Zilli, M.V.: Bounded probabilistic model checking with the Muralpha verifier. In: Hu, A.J., Martin, A.K. (eds.) FMCAD 2004. LNCS, vol. 3312, pp. 214–229. Springer, Heidelberg (2004). doi:10.1007/978-3-540-30494-4_16

22. Din, Q.: Dynamics of a discrete Lotka-Volterra model. Adv. Diff. Equ. 95, 1–13 (2013)

23. Donzé, A., Ferrère, T., Maler, O.: Efficient robust monitoring for STL. In: Sharygina, N., Veith, H. (eds.) CAV 2013. LNCS, vol. 8044, pp. 264–279. Springer, Heidelberg (2013). doi:10.1007/978-3-642-39799-8_19

24. Donzé, A., Maler, O.: Robust satisfaction of temporal logic over real-valued signals. In: Chatterjee, K., Henzinger, T.A. (eds.) FORMATS 2010. LNCS, vol. 6246, pp. 92–106. Springer, Heidelberg (2010). doi:10.1007/978-3-642-15297-9_9

25. Gast, N., Gaujal, B.: A mean field model of work stealing in large-scale systems. In: Misra, V., Barford, P., Squillante, M.S. (eds.) SIGMETRICS, pp. 13–24. ACM (2010)

26. Gnesi, S., Mazzanti, F.: An abstract, on the fly framework for the verification of service-oriented systems. In: Wirsing, M., Hölzl, M. (eds.) Rigorous Software Engineering for Service-Oriented Systems. LNCS, vol. 6582, pp. 390–407. Springer, Heidelberg (2011). doi:10.1007/978-3-642-20401-2_18

27. Goel, N.S., Maitra, S.C., Montroll, E.W.: On the volterra and other nonlinear models of interacting populations. Rev. Mod. Phys. **43**, 231–276 (1971). http://link.aps.org/doi/10.1103/RevModPhys.43.231

28. Guirado, G., Hérault, T., Lassaigne, R., Peyronnet, S.: Distribution, approximation and probabilistic model checking. In: PDMC 2005. LNCS, vol. 135. pp. 19–30. Springer, Heidelberg (2006)

29. Hahn, E.M., Hermanns, H., Wachter, B., Zhang, L.: INFAMY: an infinite-state Markov model checker. In: Bouajjani, A., Maler, O. (eds.) CAV 2009. LNCS, vol. 5643, pp. 641–647. Springer, Heidelberg (2009). doi:10.1007/978-3-642-02658-4_49

30. Hansson, H., Jonsson, B.: A logic for reasoning about time and reliability. Formal Aspects of Comput. **6**, 512–535 (1994)

31. Hérault, T., Lassaigne, R., Magniette, F., Peyronnet, S.: Approximate probabilistic Model checking. In: Steffen, B., Levi, G. (eds.) VMCAI 2004. LNCS, vol. 2937, pp. 73–84. Springer, Heidelberg (2004). doi:10.1007/978-3-540-24622-0_8

32. Holzmann, G.J.: The SPIN Model Checker - Primer and Reference Manual. Addison-Wesley, Boston (2004)

33. Kolesnichenko, A., de Boer, P.T., Remke, A., Haverkort, B.R.: A logic for model-checking mean-field models. In: DSN13 (2013)

34. Kolesnichenko, A.V., Remke, A.K.I., de Boer, P.T., Haverkort, B.: A logic for model-checking of mean-field models. Technical report TR-CTIT-12-11 (2012). http://doc.utwente.nl/80267/

35. Kurtz, T.: Solutions of ordinary differential equations as limits of pure jump Markov processes. J. Appl. Probab. **7**, 49–58 (1970)

36. Kwiatkowska, M., Norman, G., Parker, D.: Probabilistic symbolic model checking using PRISM: a hybrid approach. STTT **6**(2), 128–142 (2004)

37. Larsen, K.G., Legay, A.: Statistical model checking: past, present, and future. In: Margaria, T., Steffen, B. (eds.) ISoLA 2016. LNCS, vol. 9952, pp. 3–15. Springer, Cham (2016). doi:10.1007/978-3-319-47166-2_1

38. Latella, D., Loreti, M., Massink, M.: On-the-fly fast mean-field model-checking. In: Abadi, M., Lluch Lafuente, A. (eds.) TGC 2013. LNCS, vol. 8358, pp. 297–314. Springer, Cham (2014). doi:10.1007/978-3-319-05119-2_17

39. Latella, D., Loreti, M., Massink, M.: On-the-fly PCTL fast mean-field model-checking for self-organising coordination - preliminary version. Technical report TR-QC-01-2013, QUANTICOL (2013)

40. Latella, D., Loreti, M., Massink, M.: On-the-fly probabilistic model checking. In: Lanese, I., Sokolova, A. (eds.) Proceedings of the 7th Interaction and Concurrency Experience (ICE 2014), 6 June 2014, Berlin, Germany. EPTCS, vol. 166, pp. 45–59 (2014). doi:10.4204/EPTCS.166.6, http://cgi.cse.unsw.edu.au/~rvg/eptcs/, ISSN 2075-2180

41. Latella, D., Loreti, M., Massink, M.: On-the-fly fluid model checking via discrete time population models. In: Beltrán, M., Knottenbelt, W., Bradley, J. (eds.) EPEW 2015. LNCS, vol. 9272, pp. 193–207. Springer, Cham (2015). doi:10.1007/978-3-319-23267-6_13. ISSN 0302-9743

42. Latella, D., Loreti, M., Massink, M.: On-the-fly PCTL fast mean-field approximated model-checking for self-organising coordination. Sci. Comput. Program. **110**, 23–50 (2015). doi:10.1016/j.scico.2015.06.009, ISSN 0167-6423

43. Latella, D., Loreti, M., Massink, M.: FlyFast: a mean field model checker. In: Legay, A., Margaria, T. (eds.) TACAS 2017. LNCS, vol. 10206, pp. 303–309. Springer, Heidelberg (2017). doi:10.1007/978-3-662-54580-5_18. ISSN 0302-9743

44. Latella, D., Massink, M.: Design and optimisation of the FlyFast front-end for attribute-based coordination. In: de Vink, E.P., Wiklicky, H. (eds.) Proceedings of the Fifteenth Workshop on Quantitative Aspects of Programming Languages (QAPL 2017). Electronic Proceedings in Theoretical Computer Science, EPTCS (2017, to appear). Available also as QUANTICOL Technical report TR-QC-01-2017 (2017)

45. Latella, D.: Comunicazione basata su proprietà nei sistemi decentralizzati [property-based inter-process communication in decentralized systems], December 1983. Graduation thesis. Istituto di Scienze dell'Informazione. Univ. of Pisa (in italian)

46. Le Boudec, J.Y., McDonald, D., Mundinger, J.: A generic mean field convergence result for systems of interacting objects. In: QEST07, pp. 3–18. IEEE Computer Society Press (2007). ISBN 978-0-7695-2883-0

47. LeVeque, R.J.: Finite Difference Methods for Ordinary and Partial Differential Equations. SIAM, Philadelphia (2007)

48. Lotka, A.J.: Elements of Mathematical Biology. Williams and Wilkins Company, Philadelphia (1924)

49. de Oca, M.A.M., Ferrante, E., Scheidler, A., Pinciroli, C., Birattari, M., Dorigo, M.: Majority-rule opinion dynamics with differential latency: a mechanism for self-organized collective decision-making. Swarm Intell. 5(3–4), 305–327 (2011)

50. Nenzi, L., Bortolussi, L., Ciancia, V., Loreti, M., Massink, M.: Qualitative and quantitative monitoring of spatio-temporal properties. In: Bartocci, E., Majumdar, R. (eds.) RV 2015. LNCS, vol. 9333, pp. 21–37. Springer, Cham (2015). doi:10.1007/978-3-319-23820-3_2

51. Volterra, V.: Fluctuations in the abundance of a species considered mathematically. Nature 118, 558–560 (1926)

The Road from Stochastic Automata to the Simulation of Rare Events

Pedro R. D'Argenio[1,2,3]([✉]), Carlos E. Budde[4], Matias David Lee[1],
Raúl E. Monti[1,2], Leonardo Rodríguez[1], and Nicolás Wolovick[1]

[1] Universidad Nacional de Córdoba, Córdoba, Argentina
dargenio@famaf.unc.edu.ar
[2] CONICET, Córdoba, Argentina
[3] Saarland University, Saarbrücken, Germany
[4] University of Twente, Enschede, The Netherlands

Abstract. We report in the advances on stochastic automata and its
use on rare event simulation. We review and introduce an extension of
IOSA, an input/output variant of stochastic automata that under mild
constraints can be ensured to contain non-determinism only in a spurious manner. That is, the model can be regarded as fully probabilistic
and hence amenable for simulation. We also report on our latest work
on fully automatizing the technique of rare event simulation. Using the
structure of the model given in terms a network of IOSAs allows us to
automatically derive the importance function, which is crucial for the
importance splitting technique of rare event simulation. We conclude
with experimental results that show how promising our technique is.

1 Introduction

Stochastic automata were introduced by D'Argenio et al. in [10] as the semantics
basis for the compositional modeling of stochastically timed systems where the
occurrence time of events responds to continuous distributions. They can be
seen as a variant of timed automata [1] where clocks are initialized randomly
and run backwards, enabling transitions as soon as their value become 0. Based
on LOTOS [2] and other process algebras, the first ideas for compositionality
for stochastic automata were introduced through the process algebra $\lozenge$. Thus,
stochastic automata and $\lozenge$ provide a natural generalization of generalized semi-
Markov processes (GSMP) oriented to compositional modeling.

However, this framework came with the usually unavoidable non-determinism
introduced by concurrency. This is a drawback, since, when deterministic, this
type of general models could be only analyzed through discrete event simulation for the big majority of quantitative or even qualitative properties. (Model
checking stochastic automata can only provide a rough over approximation and
even though, with the usual limitation given by the state space explosion [19].)
Unfortunately, simulation and non-determinism are incompatible since simulation requires that all possible execution choices are resolve through randomiza-
tion. This is partly solved in stochastic automata by the races on random clocks

J.-P. Katoen et al. (Eds.): Brinksma Festschrift, LNCS 10500, pp. 276–294, 2017.
DOI: 10.1007/978-3-319-68270-9_14

enabling the transitions. Yet situations like the same clock enabling two different transitions may happen which yields a non-deterministic choice. Notwithstanding this situation, [12] presented a first approach to the simulation of stochastic automata where a scheduler indicating how the non-determinism should be resolved is explicitly required as input.

Notice however that the scheduler is an artifact that becomes part of the model and should be provided by an expert that understands the intricacies of the model. This task is clearly prone to error. Therefore, we sought instead for a way to ensure that the model is fully probabilistic (or deterministic, meaning here that all choices are resolved randomly) by construction. In [13] we introduced input/output stochastic automata (IOSA), a variant of stochastic automata that splits actions into inputs and outputs and let them behave in a reactive and generative manner respectively (see [18] for the concepts of reactive and generative transitions), following ideas proposed in [33]. Since outputs behave generatively, we let their occurrence time be controlled by a random variable (encoded in a clock). As inputs are reactive, they are passive and hence their occurrence time can only depend on their interaction with outputs. Thus, IOSA combines in a single model the two interpretations of stochastic automata (either as open or as closed systems [8,9].) It turns out that after all components are synchronized and the system is closed (i.e. all interactions are resolved), the whole model becomes fully probabilistic (i.e., it does not contain non-determinism).

This variant, however, turned to be a little too restricting for modeling. Decoupling stochastic behavior and synchronization as in [20] may simplify considerably compositional modeling. Thus, in this paper we extend IOSA by allowing certain non-determinism so that we can easily check whether it is spurious, that is, any possible path on the non-deterministic choice will converge to the same state without changing the value of the property. We do this by including urgent or committed transitions that do not take time, allowing that they are non-deterministic, but requesting that they are also confluent (with the standard notion of confluence in concurrency theory [24]). Having obtained a deterministic model, we are in conditions to simulate a closed IOSA with committed actions.

Since, nowadays, systems are required to have a high degree of resilience and dependability, determining properties that fail with extremely small probability in complex models can be computationally very demanding. However, standard Monte Carlo simulation is impractical when the probability of the event under analysis is extremely low: it will easily require an enormous amount of sampling to obtain an acceptable confidence level of the estimated probability, in order to compensate for the high variance induced by the rare occurrences of such event.

To reduce this considerable need for simulation runs, efficient Monte Carlo simulation techniques have been tailored to deal with rare events. These can be largely divided into two conceptually different techniques: *importance sampling* and *importance splitting* methods. We focus on *importance splitting* techniques, see e.g. [23,29,30]. Importance splitting works by decomposing the state space in multiple levels where, ideally, the rare event is at the top level and the probability of (reaching) the rare event increases for each increasing level. The estimation of the rare probability is obtained as the product of the estimates of the (not so rare) conditional probabilities of moving one level up. As a consequence, the effectiveness of this technique crucially depends on an adequate grouping of states into levels. *Importance functions* are the means to assign a value to each state so that, if perfect, such value is directly related to the likelihood of reaching the rare event. It is desirable that a state in the rare set receives the highest importance and the importance of a state decreases according to the probability of reaching a rare state from it. Usually, an expert in the area of the system provides the importance function in an *ad-hoc* manner. A badly chosen function can deteriorate the effectiveness of the technique. With some notable exceptions [4,16,21,25], automatic derivation of importance functions has received scarce attention.

In the same way that we eliminate the need for an expertise in the modeling of a scheduler, we have looked for techniques to automatically derive such importance functions. The overall aim thus is that the task of rare event simulation becomes a single push button technique after the modeling of the system and the property under study. In [4] we presented preliminary results on an effective technique to derive automatically an importance function. The algorithm works by applying inverse breadth first search (BFS) on the underlying graph of the stochastic process, labeling each state with the shortest distance to a rare state. The importance of each state is then defined as the difference between the maximum distance and its actual distance. This technique still requires a finite graph which fits in the computer memory. Unfortunately such graph grows exponentially with the number of components in the model of the system. To overcome this problem, in [5] we improve on this technique by obtaining the importance function in a compositional manner. We consider the system modeled as a network of IOSAs. The technique then works by applying the previous method per component, previous analysis on how the local states relate to the property under study, and the final importance function is obtained by composing the modular functions. Contrarily to the first technique, this way of calculating the importance function grows linearly with the number of modules that conform the system model. In this paper, we also report on these techniques and show experimental studies that demonstrate how promising our ideas are.

2 Input/Output Stochastic Automata

Stochastic automata [8–10] use continuous random variables called clocks to observe the passage of time and control the occurrence of events. This variables are set to a value according to their associated probability distribution, and as time evolves, they count down at the same rate. When a clock reaches zero, it may trigger some action. This allows the modeling of systems where events occur at random continuous time stamps.

Following ideas from [33], input/output stochastic automata (IOSA for short) restrict stochastic automata by splitting actions into input and output actions which will act in a reactive and generative way respectively [18]. This splitting reflects the fact that input actions are considered to be controlled externally, while output actions are locally controlled. Therefore, we consider the system input enabled. Moreover, output actions could be stochastically controlled or instantaneous. In the first case output actions are controlled by the expiration of a single clock while in the second case the output actions take place as soon as the enabling state is reached. We called these instantaneous actions *committed*. A set of restrictions over IOSA will ensure that, almost surely, no two non committed outputs are enabled at the same time.

Definition 1. *An input/output stochastic automaton with committed actions (IOSA for short) is a structure $(\mathcal{S}, \mathcal{A}, \mathcal{C}, \rightarrow, C_0, s_0)$, where $\mathcal{S}$ is a (denumerable) set of states, $\mathcal{A}$ is a (denumerable) set of labels partitioned into disjoint sets of input labels $\mathcal{A}^I$ and output labels $\mathcal{A}^O$, from which a subset $\mathcal{A}^{co}$ of them are marked as committed, $\mathcal{C}$ is a (finite) set of clocks where each $x \in \mathcal{C}$ has associated a continuous probability measure μ_x on $\mathbb{R}$ s.t. $\mu_x(\mathbb{R}_{>0}) = 1$, $\rightarrow \subseteq \mathcal{S} \times 2^\mathcal{C} \times \mathcal{A} \times 2^\mathcal{C} \times \mathcal{S}$ is a transition function, C_0 is the set of clocks that are initialized in the initial state, and $s_0 \in \mathcal{S}$ is the initial state.*

In addition, a IOSA should satisfy the following constraints, where we write $s \xrightarrow{C,a,C'} s'$ instead of $(s, C, a, C', s') \in \rightarrow$:

(a) *If $s \xrightarrow{C,a,C'} s'$ and $a \in \mathcal{A}^I \cup \mathcal{A}^{co}$, then $C = \emptyset$.*

(b) *If $s \xrightarrow{C,a,C'} s'$ and $a \in \mathcal{A}^O \setminus \mathcal{A}^{co}$, then C is a singleton set.*

(c) *If $s \xrightarrow{\{x\},a_1,C_1} s_1$ and $s \xrightarrow{\{x\},a_2,C_2} s_2$ then $a_1 = a_2$, $C_1 = C_2$ and $s_1 = s_2$.*

(d) *If $s \xrightarrow{\{x\},a,C} s'$ then $x \in \bigcup \text{safe}(s)$, where safe is the least fixed point of F defined as:*

$$\mathbf{F}(\mathsf{X})(s) = \{C_0 \mid s = s_0\} \cup \{C' \cup (\{y \mid \hat{s} \xrightarrow{\{y\},\_,\_} \_\} \setminus C) \mid \hat{s} \xrightarrow{C,a,C'} s \wedge a \notin \mathcal{A}^{co}\}$$
$$\cup \{C \cup C' \mid \hat{s} \xrightarrow{\emptyset,a,C} s \wedge a \in \mathcal{A}^{co} \wedge C' \in \mathsf{X}(\hat{s})\}$$

(e) *For every $a \in \mathcal{A}^I$ and state s, there exists a transition $s \xrightarrow{\emptyset,a,C} s'$.*

(f) *For every $a \in \mathcal{A}^I$, if $s \xrightarrow{\emptyset,a,C_1'} s_1$ and $s \xrightarrow{\emptyset,a,C_2'} s_2$, $C_1' = C_2'$ and $s_1 = s_2$.*

The occurrence of a transition is controlled by the expiration of clocks. $s \xrightarrow{C,a,C'} s'$ indicates that there is a transition from state s to state s' that can be taken only when all clocks in C have expired and, when taken, it triggers action a and sets all clocks in C' to a value sampled from their associated probability distribution. We write _ to replace parameters when they are not relevant.

These restrictions ensure that any *closed* IOSA without committed actions is deterministic [13]. An IOSA is closed if all its synchronizations have been resolved, that is, the IOSA resulting from a composition does not have input actions ($\mathcal{A}^I = \emptyset$).

Restriction (a) is two-folded: on the one hand, it specifies that input actions are reactive and their time occurrence can only depend on the interaction with an output, on the other hand, committed output actions must occur as soon as the state enables them. The difference will be more clear when we define the concrete semantics. Restriction (b) specifies that each non-committed output is locally controlled and has a single associated clock which controls its occurrence. Restriction (c) ensures that different non-committed output actions leaving the same state cannot be controlled by the same clock. Restriction (e) ensures input enabling. Restriction (f) determines that IOSAs are input deterministic. Therefore, the same input action in the same state can not jump to different states, nor set different clocks.

Finally, restriction (d) restricts enabling clock x to clocks that have not yet expired when reaching s. That is, either x has been reset during the transition to s, or during a path of committed transitions reaching s, or x is not used as enabling clock of a transition to s but it is an enabling clock on the immediately preceding state. By means of the least fixed point of $\mathbf{F}$ we are able to accumulate clocks that are reset along paths of committed transitions. Furthermore, this restriction allows a clock x to be an enabling clock at an initial state s if x is an initial clock, i.e. $x \in C_0$.

Note that since clocks are set by sampling from a continuous random variables, the probability that the values of two different clocks are equal is 0. This fact along with restriction (c) and (d) guarantees that almost never two different non-committed output transitions are enabled at the same time.

In the following we define parallel composition of IOSAs. Since we intend outputs to be autonomous (or locally controlled), we do not allow synchronization between them. Besides, we need to avoid name clashes on the clocks, so that the intended behavior of each component is preserved and moreover, to ensure that the resulting composed automaton is indeed an IOSA. Furthermore, synchronizing IOSAs should agree on committed actions in order to ensure their immediate occurrence. Thus we require to compose only *compatible* IOSAs.

Definition 2. *Two IOSAs $\mathcal{I}_1$ and $\mathcal{I}_2$ are said to be compatible if they do not share output actions nor clocks, i.e. $\mathcal{A}_1^O \cap \mathcal{A}_2^O = \emptyset$ and $\mathcal{C}_1 \cap \mathcal{C}_2 = \emptyset$, and moreover they agree on committed actions, i.e. $\mathcal{A}_1 \cap \mathcal{A}_2^{co} = \mathcal{A}_2 \cap \mathcal{A}_1^{co}$.*

Definition 3. *Given two compatible IOSAs $\mathcal{I}_1$ and $\mathcal{I}_2$, the parallel composition $\mathcal{I}_1 \| \mathcal{I}_2$ is a new IOSA $(\mathcal{S}_1 \times \mathcal{S}_2, \mathcal{A}, \mathcal{C}, \rightarrow, C_0, s_0^1 \| s_0^2)$ where (i) $\mathcal{A}^O = \mathcal{A}_1^O \cup \mathcal{A}_2^O$, (ii) $\mathcal{A}^I = (\mathcal{A}_1^I \cup \mathcal{A}_2^I) \setminus \mathcal{A}^O$, (iii) $\mathcal{A}^{co} = \mathcal{A}_1^{co} \cup \mathcal{A}_2^{co}$, (iv) $\mathcal{C} = \mathcal{C}_1 \cup \mathcal{C}_2$, and (v) $C_0 = C_0^1 \cup C_0^2$, and $\rightarrow$ is the smallest relation defined by rules in Table 1 where we annotate $s \| t$ instead of (s, t).*

Table 1. Parallel composition on IOSA

$$\frac{s_1 \xrightarrow{C,a,C'}_1 s_1'}{s_1 \| s_2 \xrightarrow{C,a,C'} s_1' \| s_2} \quad a \in \mathcal{A}_1 \setminus \mathcal{A}_2 \quad (1) \qquad \frac{s_2 \xrightarrow{C,a,C'}_2 s_2'}{s_1 \| s_2 \xrightarrow{C,a,C'} s_1 \| s_2'} \quad a \in \mathcal{A}_2 \setminus \mathcal{A}_1 \quad (2)$$

$$\frac{s_1 \xrightarrow{C_1,a,C_1'}_1 s_1' \quad s_2 \xrightarrow{C_2,a,C_2'}_2 s_2'}{s_1 \| s_2 \xrightarrow{C_1 \cup C_2, a, C_1' \cup C_2'} s_1' \| s_2'} \quad (3)$$

It can be proven that the parallel composition preserves IOSAs. That is, the parallel composition of two IOSAs is also an IOSA.

Following ideas from Milner [24] we say that an IOSA is confluent with respect to actions a and b if the occurrence of one of them does not prevent the other one from occurring in the future. More precisely, an IOSA $\mathcal{I}$ is confluent with respect to committed actions a and b in $\mathcal{A}$ if for every state s in $\mathcal{S}$ we can complete the diagram from Fig. 1.

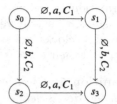

Fig. 1. Confluence in IOSA.

Notice that confluent actions do not alter the stochastic behavior of the system: by considering a and b silent actions (i.e. $a = b = \tau$ with τ interpreted as in Milner's work [24]) the IOSA of Fig. 1 behaves like the single transition $s_0 \xrightarrow{\emptyset, \tau, C_1 \cup C_2} s_3$. Thus, the non-determinism introduced by confluent committed actions is spurious.

It can be shown that parallel composition preserves confluence. Thus, if all IOSA components are confluent for all committed action, so is their parallel composition.

3 Semantics of IOSA

The semantics of IOSA is defined in terms of non-deterministic labeled Markov processes (NLMP) [14,32]. A NLMP is a generalization of probabilistic transition systems with continuous domain. In particular, it extends LMP [15] with *internal* non-determinism.

The foundations of NLMP is strongly rooted in measure theory, hence we recall first some basic definitions. Given a set S and a collection Σ of subsets of S, we call Σ a *σ-algebra* iff $S \in \Sigma$ and Σ is closed under complement and denumerable union. We call the pair (S, Σ) a *measurable space*. A function $\mu : \Sigma \to [0,1]$ is a *probability measure* if (i) $\mu(\bigcup_{i\in\mathbb{N}} Q_i) = \sum_{i\in\mathbb{N}} \mu(Q_i)$ for all countable family of pairwise disjoint measurable sets $\{Q_i\}_{i\in\mathbb{N}} \subseteq \Sigma$, and (ii) $\mu(S) = 1$. In particular, for $s \in S$, δ_s denotes the Dirac measure so that $\delta_s(\{s\}) = 1$. Let $\Delta(S)$ denote the set of all probability measures over (S, Σ). Let (S_1, Σ_1) and (S_2, Σ_2) be two measurable spaces. A function $f : S_1 \to S_2$ is said to be *measurable* if for all $Q_2 \in \Sigma_2$, $f^{-1}(Q_2) \in \Sigma_1$. There is a standard construction by Giry [17] to endow $\Delta(S)$ with a σ-algebra as follows: $\Delta(\Sigma)$ is defined as the smallest σ-algebra containing the sets $\Delta^B(Q) \doteq \{\mu \mid \mu(Q) \in B\}$, with $Q \in \Sigma$ and $B \in \mathscr{B}([0,1])$, where $\mathscr{B}([0,1])$ is the usual Borel σ-algebra on the interval $[0,1]$. Finally, we define the *hit σ-algebra* $H(\Delta(\Sigma))$ as the minimal σ-algebra containing all sets $H_\xi = \{\zeta \in \Delta(\Sigma) \mid \zeta \cap \xi \neq \emptyset\}$ with $\xi \in \Delta(\Sigma)$.

Definition 4. *A non-deterministic labeled Markov process (NLMP for short) is a structure $(\mathbf{S}, \Sigma, \{\mathcal{T}_a \mid a \in \mathcal{L}\})$ where Σ is a σ-algebra on the set of states $\mathbf{S}$, and for each label $a \in \mathcal{L}$ we have that $\mathcal{T}_a : \mathbf{S} \to \Delta(\Sigma)$ is measurable from Σ to $H(\Delta(\Sigma))$.*

The formal semantics of an IOSA is defined by a NLMP with two classes of transitions: one that encodes the discrete steps and contains all the probabilistic information introduced by the sampling of clocks, and another describing the time steps, that only records the passage of time synchronously decreasing the value of all clocks. For simplicity, we assume that the set of clocks has a particular order and their current values follow the same order in a vector.

Definition 5. *Given an IOSA* $\mathcal{I} = (\mathcal{S}, \mathcal{A}, \mathcal{C}, \rightarrow, C_0, s_0)$ *with* $\mathcal{C} = \{x_1, \ldots, x_N\}$, *its semantics is defined by the NLMP* $\mathcal{P}(\mathcal{I}) = (\boldsymbol{S}, \mathscr{B}(\boldsymbol{S}), \{\mathcal{T}_a \mid a \in \mathcal{L}\})$ *where*

- $\boldsymbol{S} = (\mathcal{S} \cup \{\text{init}\}) \times \mathbb{R}^N$, $\mathcal{L} = \mathcal{A} \cup \mathbb{R}_{>0} \cup \{\text{init}\}$, *with* init $\notin \mathcal{S} \cup \mathcal{A} \cup \mathbb{R}_{>0}$
- $\mathcal{T}_{\text{init}}(\text{init}, \boldsymbol{v}) = \{\delta_{s_0} \times \prod_{i=1}^{N} \mu_{x_i}\}$,
- $\mathcal{T}_a(s, \boldsymbol{v}) = \{\mu_{\boldsymbol{v}, C', s'} \mid s \xrightarrow{C, a, C'} s', \bigwedge_{x_i \in C} \boldsymbol{v}(i) \leq 0\}$, *for all* $a \in \mathcal{A}$, *where* $\mu_{\boldsymbol{v}, C', s'} = \delta_{s'} \times \prod_{i=1}^{N} \overline{\mu}_{x_i}$ *with* $\overline{\mu}_{x_i} = \mu_{x_i}$ *if* $x_i \in C'$ *and* $\overline{\mu}_{x_i} = \delta_{\boldsymbol{v}(i)}$ *otherwise, and*
- $\mathcal{T}_d(s, \boldsymbol{v}) = \{\delta_s \times \prod_{i=1}^{N} \delta_{\boldsymbol{v}(i)-d}\}$ *if* $s \xrightarrow{b} /$ *for all committed* $b \in \mathcal{A}^O \cap \mathcal{A}^{co}$ *and* $0 < d \leq \min\{\boldsymbol{v}(i) \mid \exists_{a \in \mathcal{A}^O, C' \subseteq \mathcal{C}, s' \in S} : s \xrightarrow{\{x_i\}, a, C'} s'\}$, *and* $\mathcal{T}_d(s, \boldsymbol{v}) = \emptyset$ *otherwise, for all* $d \in \mathbb{R}_{\geq 0}$.

The state space is the product space of the states of the IOSA with all possible clock valuations. A distinguished initial state init is added to encode the random initialization of all clocks (it would be sufficient to initialize clocks in C_0 but we decided for this simplification). Such encoding is done by transition $\mathcal{T}_{\text{init}}$. The state space is structured with the usual Borel σ-algebra. The discrete step is encoded by $\mathcal{T}_a$, with $a \in \mathcal{A}$. Notice that, at state $(s, \boldsymbol{v})$, the transition $s \xrightarrow{C, a, C'} s'$ will only take place if $\bigwedge_{x_i \in C} \boldsymbol{v}(i) \leq 0$, that is, if the current values of all clocks in C are not positive. For the particular case of the input or committed actions this will always be true. The next actual state would be determined randomly as follows: the symbolic state will be s' (this corresponds to $\delta_{s'}$ in $\mu_{\boldsymbol{v}, C', s'} = \delta_{s'} \times \prod_{i=1}^{N} \overline{\mu}_{x_i}$), any clock not in C' preserves the current value (hence $\overline{\mu}_{x_i} = \delta_{\boldsymbol{v}(i)}$ if $x_i \notin C'$), and any clock in C' is set randomly according to its respective associated distribution (hence $\overline{\mu}_{x_i} = \mu_{x_i}$ if $x_i \in C'$). The time step is encoded by $\mathcal{T}_d(s, \boldsymbol{v})$ with $d \in \mathbb{R}_{>0}$. It can only take place at d units of time if there is no output transition enabled at the current state within the next d time units (this is verified by condition $0 < d \leq \min\{\boldsymbol{v}(i) \mid \exists_{a \in \mathcal{A}^O, C' \subseteq \mathcal{C}, s' \in S} : s \xrightarrow{\{x_i\}, a, C'} s'\}$). In this case, the system remains in the same symbolic state (this corresponds to δ_s in $\delta_{(s, \boldsymbol{v})}^{-d} = \delta_s \times \prod_{i=1}^{N} \delta_{\boldsymbol{v}(i)-d}$), and all clock values are decreased by d units of time (represented by $\delta_{\boldsymbol{v}(i)-d}$ in the same formula). Note the difference from the timed transitions semantics of pure IOSA [13]. This is due to the maximal progress assumption, which forces to take committed transition as soon as they get enabled. We encode this by not allowing to make time transitions in presence of committed actions, i.e. $s \xrightarrow{b} /$ for all committed $b \in \mathcal{A}^O \cap \mathcal{A}^{co}$ (thus $\mathcal{T}_d(s, \boldsymbol{v}) = \emptyset$ whenever $s \xrightarrow{C, b, C'} s'$ with $b \in \mathcal{A}^O \cap \mathcal{A}^{co}$.) Instead, notice the *patient* nature of a state $(s, \boldsymbol{v})$ that has no output enabled.

That is, $\mathcal{T}_d(s, \boldsymbol{v}) = \{\delta_s \times \prod_{i=1}^{N} \delta_{\boldsymbol{v}(i)-d}\}$ for all $d > 0$ whenever $s \overset{b}{\nrightarrow}$ for all output action $b \in \mathcal{A}^O$.

In a similar way to [13], it is possible to show that $\mathcal{P}(\mathcal{I})$ is indeed a NLMP, i.e. that $\mathcal{T}_a$ maps into measurable sets in $\Delta(\mathcal{B}(\mathbf{S}))$, and that $\mathcal{T}_a$ is a measurable function for every $a \in \mathcal{L}$.

4   Rare Event Simulation

Assuming that the IOSA is closed and confluent on all committed actions and it does not contain loops of only committed transitions, from the semantics of IOSA (Definition 5) we can extract an algorithm for discrete event simulation which we give in Fig. 2.

Given that the IOSA is confluent for committed actions, the arbitrary choice of a committed transition in line 6 is irrelevant since, after finishing the while loop of line 5, the same set of clocks will be sampled whichever path of committed transitions is taken. Moreover, the while loop is ensured to finish since no loop of committed transition is allowed. Also, the restrictions imposed by Definition 1 guarantee the uniqueness of the transition in line 11 [13].

When a parameter is estimated using the usual Monte Carlo simulation (as described in Fig. 2), the speed and overall efficiency of the method is highly dependent on the precision required for the estimate. Confidence intervals are commonly used to convey a notion of how far the produced estimate may be from the actual value. As a general rule, whichever the confidence interval construction method, the simulations "length" grows with the tightness desired for

1: **for** all clock $x \in C_0$ **do**
2:     Sample a value $v(x)$ according to the distribution μ_x
3: Set s_0 as current state s.
4: **repeat**
5:     **while** s has an outgoing committed transition **do**
6:         Choose any committed transition $s \xrightarrow{\varnothing,a,C} s'$.
7:         **for** all clock $x \in C_0$ **do**
8:             Sample a value $v(x)$ according to the distribution μ_x
9:         Set s' as current state s.
10:     Let $x \in C$ be the clock with the smallest positive value.
11:     Let $s \xrightarrow{\{x\},a,C} s'$ be the unique transition enabled by x.
12:     **for** all clock $y \notin C$ **do**
13:         $v(y) = v(y) - v(x)$
14:     **for** all clock $y \in C$ **do**
15:         Sample a value $v(y)$ according to the distribution μ_y
16:     Set s' as current state s.
17:     Collect the relevant statistical data.
18: **until** sufficient statistical data was collected

Fig. 2. Simulation of a closed confluent IOSA

the interval. In particular several rare event scenarios are known to require a number of samples which grows exponentially on the model size [22].

Importance splitting (IS for short) aims to speed up the occurrence of a rare event without modifications on the system dynamics (see [23] and references therein.) The general idea in IS is to favor the "promising runs" that approach the rare event by saving the states they visit at certain predefined checkpoints. Replicas of these runs are created from those checkpoint states, which continue evolving independently from then on. Contrarily, simulation runs deemed to steer away from the rare event are identified and killed, avoiding the use of computational power in fruitless calculi. The likelihood of visiting a goal state from any other state s is called the *importance* of s. Variations in such importance determine when should a simulation run be split or killed, as the importance value crosses some given *thresholds* up or down, respectively.

We focus on the RESTART method, a version of IS with multiple thresholds, fixed splitting and deterministic discards of unpromising simulations [26,28–31]. A RESTART run can be depicted as in Fig. 3 where the horizontal axis represents the simulation progress and the vertical axis the importance value of the current state. The run starts from an initial state and evolves until the first threshold T_1 is crossed *upwards*. This takes the path from zone Z_0 below threshold T_1 into zone Z_1 between T_1 and T_2. As this happens the state is saved and $s_1 - 1$ replicas or *offsprings* of the path are created. See A in Fig. 3, where the *splitting* for T_1 is $s_1 = 3$. This follows the idea of rewarding promising simulations: up-crossing a threshold suggests the path heads towards a goal state. From then on the s_1 simulations will evolve independently. As they continue, one of them may hit the upper threshold T_2, activating the same procedure: $s_2 - 1$ offsprings are generated from it and set to evolve independently. See B in Fig. 3; here, the splitting is $s_2 = 2$.

However, it could also happen that some simulation hits T_1 again, meaning the path is leading *downwards*. This simulation steers away from the goal set and RESTART deals with it discarding the run right away (see C in Fig. 3). In each zone Z_i there exists nonetheless an *original simulation*, which crossed threshold T_i upwards generating the $s_i - 1$ offsprings. This run is allowed to survive a down-crossing of threshold T_i (see D in Fig. 3).

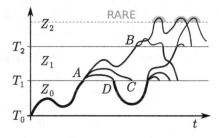

Fig. 3. RESTART importance splitting

In this setting all simulations reaching a goal state went through the replication procedure, which stacked up on every threshold crossed. Simply counting these hits would introduce a bias, because the *relative weight* of the runs in upper zones decreases by an amount equivalent to the splitting of the thresholds. In consequence, each rare event observed is pondered by the relative weight of the simulation from which it stemmed. If all the goal states exist beyond the uppermost threshold like in Fig. 3, then it suffices to divide the observed quantity of rare events by $\text{SPLIT}_{\text{MAX}} \doteq \prod_{i=1}^{n} s_i$. Otherwise more involved labeling mechanisms are needed.

In this work we study transient and long run properties. *Transient* properties are used to calculate the probability of reaching a set G of *goal states* before visiting any *reset state* from the (disjoint) set R. (For simulation purposes the probability of reaching a state in $G \uplus R$ has to be 1.) Following PCTL, we denote this probability by $\mathsf{P}(\neg R \cup G)$. *Long run* analysis focuses on the quantification of a property once the system has reached an equilibrium. In particular, the steady state probability of a set G of *goal states* is the portion of time in which any state in G is visited in the long run. Using CSL notation, we write $\mathsf{S}(G)$.

5   Automatic Derivation of the Importance Function

Notice that a simulation using importance splitting is entirely guided by the *importance function* which defines the importance of each state. This function conveys the states where the simulation effort should be intensified. Importance functions are defined in most situations in an *ad-hoc* fashion by an expert in the field of the particular system model. With a few exceptions in some specific areas [16,21,25,35] automatic derivation of importance functions is still a novel field for general systems and this has been our later concern [3–5].

Consider a single IOSA and any of the properties $\mathsf{P}(\neg R \cup G)$ or $\mathsf{S}(G)$. The rare event is precisely the set G of *goal states*. In [4], we propose a distance based on the length of the shortest path on the IOSA leading to a state in G: a state s is more important than other state s' if its shortest path to a state in G is shorter than the shortest path of s'. This can be implemented with the help of a breadth-first search algorithm that follows the backwards direction of the transitions in the given IOSA. The algorithm, which is given in Fig. 4, has complexity $\mathcal{O}(n \cdot k)$, where n is the size of the state space and k is the branching degree of the underlying graph of the IOSA.

Input: a IOSA model and
       the goal state set $G \neq \varnothing$
$g(G) \leftarrow 0$
queue.push(G)
repeat
    $s \leftarrow$ **queue.pop()**
    for all $s' \xrightarrow{C,a,C'} s$ **do**
        if s' not visited **then**
            $g(s') \leftarrow g(s) + 1$
            queue.push(s')
until queue.is_empty() or s_0 visited
$g(s) \leftarrow g(s_0)$ for every non visited state s
$f(s) \leftarrow g(s_0) - g(s)$ for every state s
return importance function f

Fig. 4. Basic importance function derivation

Using this strategy one can indeed obtain in very short computational time a good importance function to use with the IS technique of choice [4]. The thresholds can then be selected either arbitrarily, using e.g. some fixed approach ("*set one every three importance values*"), or adaptively by means of an algorithm that exercises the model dynamics [6,7].

However, this approach does not scale. The BFS algorithm requires an explicit representation of the state space of the composed IOSA (and actually of the whole adjacency matrix), which grows exponentially with the number of modules involved in the composition. This is clearly not in the spirit of simulation which scales nicely since it only requires to save only the current state been explored.

Taking advantage of the compositional nature of IOSA, in [5] we presented a compositional approach to automatically produce importance functions. The solution reuses our previous idea:

(i) identify the set G_i of local states in each IOSA component $\mathcal{I}_i$ that are part of the global set G of goal states,

(ii) apply the algorithm of Fig. 4 in each component $\mathcal{I}_i$ to obtain a *local importance function* f_i, and

(iii) compose the family of functions $\{f_i\}_i$ to obtain the *(global) importance function* f.

This brings two challenges: obtaining the local goal states sets G_i and composing the family of functions $\{f_i\}_i$ to obtain the importance function f.

For the first challenge, we require that the set G of goal states is given in terms of a propositional formula in *disjunctive normal form (DNF)*, i.e. a disjunction of *clauses*, each of which is a conjunction of *literals* (i.e. of atomic propositions or negated atomic propositions). As a restriction, we impose that each atomic proposition can only be changed or tested in a single IOSA component. This approach imposes no restriction on the description of the rare event, since any propositional formula can be equivalently written in DNF.

To obtain the set G_i of local goal states for component $\mathcal{I}_i$, we "project" the DNF formula $\bigvee_{n \in N} \bigwedge_{m \in M_n} \ell_{nm}$ defining G as follows. For each $n \in N$ define $L_n = \{\ell_{nm} \mid m \in M_n \text{ and } \ell_{nm} \text{ contains a proposition in } \mathcal{I}_i\}$. Then, define the local goal DNF formula by $\bigvee\{\bigwedge L_n \mid n \in N \text{ and } L_n \neq \emptyset\}$ which defines the set G_i of states of $\mathcal{I}_i$ in which such a formula is valid.

For composing the family of functions $\{f_i\}_i$ into the importance function f, we have experimented with several proposals. One option is to let the user settle the matter via an *ad-hoc* choice. He would have to provide an algebraic expression using the local importance which would be used at every step of the simulation to combine the local importance values. For example, consider a system of three IOSAs composed in parallel. If $s|_i$ denotes the projection of the global state s into the local state of component $\mathcal{I}_i$, possible definitions for f are $f(s) = f_1(s|_1) + f_2(s|_2) + f_3(s|_3)$ or $f(s) = \max(0.3 f_1(s|_1) + 0.7 f_2(s|_2), f_3(s|_3))$.

Since we request the properties to be expressed in DNF, we could exploit the structure of the formula to identify specific arithmetical operands or even algebraic structures to associate to each logical operand. We are currently investigating a way to automatically map the disjunctions and conjunctions to their best-match arithmetical counterparts. Our last studies are leading us towards the use of semi-rings such as (`max`,`+`) and (`+`,`*`), which could be thought of as naturally corresponding to the $(\vee, \wedge)$ structure of DNF formulas. For example, consider a system of three IOSAs composed in parallel, where p_i is a propositional formula in the component $\mathcal{I}_i$. If the goal DNF formula is $(p_1 \wedge p_2) \vee (p_1 \wedge p_3)$, the importance function could be defined by $f(s) = (f_1(s|_1) * f_2(s|_2)) + (f_1(s|_1) * f_3(s|_3))$ or $f(s) = \max((f_1(s|_1) + f_2(s|_2)), (f_1(s|_1) + f_3(s|_3)))$.

As a final remark notice that using the product to combine local importance functions could lead to problems whenever a null importance value is encountered. As a workaround in such cases the functions where updated after construction, replacing every importance value i with 2^i (e.g. the values $0, 1, 2, \ldots$ map into $1, 2, 4, \ldots$) This solved the issue and set the computed importance values further apart, with interesting consequences in the IS simulations.

6   Experimental Results

We have developed the software tool FIG, which implements the compositional approach to multilevel splitting described above. It is written in C++ and is a standalone software. FIG stands for *Finite Improbability Generator* as a homage to Douglas Adam's masterpiece and it is freely available at http://dsg.famaf. unc.edu.ar/fig.

In the following we report several case studies that validate our approach. All experiments were run in a computer with a 12-cores 2.40 GHz Intel Xeon E5-2620v3 processor, and 128 GiB 2133 MHz of available DDR4 RAM. More details of these and other case studies can be found in [3].

Tandem Queue. This system consists of a Jackson tandem network with two sequentially connected queues, where the rates of arrival, first service and second service are respectively $(\lambda, \mu_1, \mu_2) = (3, 2, 6)$, and for which transient and steady-state properties were evaluated.

Notice this tandem queue is Markovian. Therefore, we were able to validate that the results yielded by FIG because the IOSA model agree with those yielded by PRISM for an equivalent model written in the PRISM language. (We remark that the FIG input language is very much alike the PRISM input language.)

For this case study, we have performed transient and steady state analysis. For the transient analysis, the property of interest is $\mathsf{P}(q_2 > 0\, \mathsf{U}\, q_2 = C)$, i.e. the likelihood of observing a saturated second queue before it becomes empty, which we estimate starting from the state $(q_1, q_2) = (0, 1)$. We tested maximum queue capacities $C \in \{8, 10, 12, 14\}$, for which the values calculated with PRISM are respectively 5.62e−6, 3.14e−7, 1.86e−8, and 1.14e−9. Estimations were set to achieve 90% confidence interval with 20% of relative error. The execution time-out was 2.5 h, which FIG converged for each configuration producing intervals containing the values reported by PRISM.

The average of the wall times measured in three experiments are shown in Fig. 5. Three different importance functions were tested in the importance splitting simulations. The function denoted `amono` was automatically built by FIG using the monolithic approach of [4]. Instead, `acomp` stands for the function built following the compositional strategy, which in this case employed summation as composition operand (i.e., the global function is the summation of the local functions). The third importance function tested with RESTART was one of the

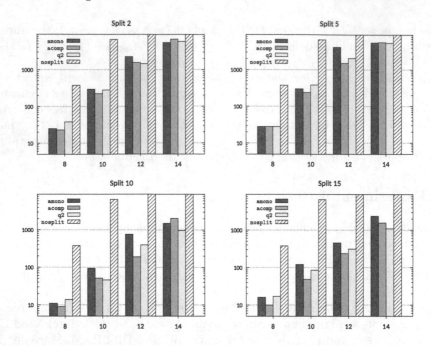

Fig. 5. Times for the transient analysis of the tandem queue

best known *ad-hoc* candidates viz. counting the number of packets in the second queue, which we denote q2. Standard Monte Carlo simulations are denoted nosplit. In Fig. 5, we display one chart per splitting value, with the outcomes of the nosplit simulations repeated in all four charts. The maximum queue capacity C, tuned to variate the rarity of the event, spans along the x-axis.

Regarding long run simulations we are interested in the property $S(q_2 = C)$, i.e. the proportion of time that the second queue spends in a saturated state. We tested maximum queue capacities $C \in \{10, 13, 16, 18, 21\}$, for which the values calculated with PRISM are respectively 7.25e−6, 2.86e−7, 1.12e−8, 1.28e−9, and 4.94e−11.

Estimations were set to achieve 90% confidence with 20% of relative error and expected to converge within 6 h of wall time execution. Again we corroborated that these estimations converged to the values yielded by PRISM. The same importance functions than in the transient case were employed.

The results obtained from an average among three experiments are presented in Fig. 6, following the same format than in the transient case.

Triple Tandem Queue. Consider a non-Markovian tandem network operating under the same principles than the previous tandem queue, but consisting of *three* queues with *Erlang-distributed* service times. The shape parameter α is the same for all servers, but the scale parameters $\{\mu_i\}_{i=1}^3$ differ from one queue to the next. Arrivals into the system are exponential with rate $\lambda = 1$.

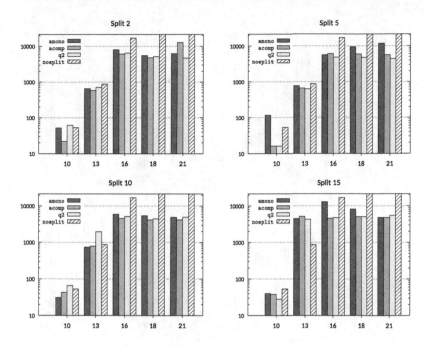

Fig. 6. Times for the steady-state analysis of the tandem queue

The long run behavior of this non-Markovian triple tandem queue was studied in [26] starting from an empty system. The shape parameter is $\alpha \in \{2, 3\}$ in all queues and the load at the third queue is kept at $1/3$. This means that the scale parameter μ_3 in the third queue takes the values $1/6$ and $1/9$ when α is 2 and 3 respectively. The scale parameters μ_1 and μ_2 of the first and second servers, as well as the thresholds capacity C at the third queue, are chosen to keep the steady-state probability in the same order of magnitude for all case studies.

The property of interest is the steady-state probability of a saturation in the third queue, i.e. $\mathsf{S}(q_3 = C)$. Following the same approach from [26] we choose the parameters so that the estimated value is in the order of $5 \cdot 10^{-9}$. Thus the values of $(\alpha, \mu_1, \mu_2, C)$ for the six case studies I–VI are respectively $(2, 1/3, 1/4, 10)$, $(3, 2/3, 1/6, 7)$, $(2, 1/6, 1/4, 11)$, $(3, 1/9, 1/6, 9)$, $(2, 1/10, 1/8, 14)$, and $(3, 1/15, 1/12, 12)$.

Estimations were set to achieve 90% confidence interval with 20% of relative error and expected to converge within 4 h of wall time execution. Four importance functions were tested in the importance splitting simulations: the monolithic (**amono**) and compositional (**acomp**) functions which FIG can build automatically, using summation as composition operand for **acomp**; an *ad-hoc* function which just counted occupation in the third queue (**q3**); and the *ad-hoc* approach from [26] (denoted **jva**), which also considers the occupancy in the other queues with weight coefficients specific to each case, taking values in the interval $[0.2, 0.9]$.

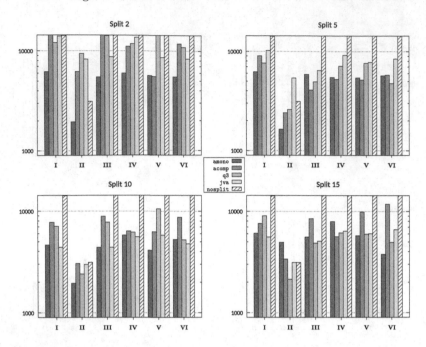

Fig. 7. Times for the steady-state analysis of the triple tandem queue

Results are presented in Fig. 7. This experiment was also run three times; the values in the plots show the average of the convergence times measured. Case studies I–VI span along the x-axis of each plot.

Oil Pipeline. Consider a consecutive-k-out-of-n: F system $(C(k, n : F))$. This consists of a sequence of n components *ordered sequentially*, so that the whole system fails if k or more *consecutive* components are in a failed state. For a more down-to-earth mental picture consider an oil pipeline where there are n equally spaced pressure pumps. Each pump can transport oil as far as the distance of k pumps and no further. Thus if $k > 1$, the system has certain resilience to failure and remains operational as long as no k consecutive pumps have failed.

Several generalizations exist to the original setting; we are interested in the non-Markovian and repairable systems analyzed in e.g. [27,34]. Those works assume the existence of a repairman which can take one failed component at a time and leave it "as good as new", after a log-normal distributed repair time has elapsed [34]. In particular [27] consider also the existence of non-Markovian failure times (namely, sampled from the Rayleigh—or Weibull—distribution) and measure the steady-state unavailability of the system.

We will limit here to the oil pipeline of the type $C(5, 20 : F)$, i.e. where there is a total of $n = 20$ pressure pumps, and $k = 5$ consecutive failed pumps cause a general system failure. This was the most difficult case we run, where the estimated probability are in the order of 2.62e−9 and 7.49e−9 for the exponential and Rayleigh, case respectively. Other parameters are studied in [3]. In this

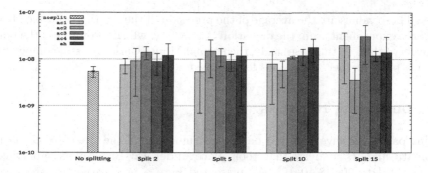

Fig. 8. Exponential-failures oil pipeline; intervals precision for 3 h timeout

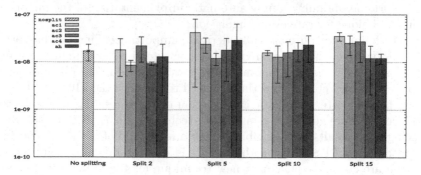

Fig. 9. Rayleigh-failures oil pipeline; intervals precision for 3 h timeout

setting, the steady-state system unavailability is given by the property query: $S(\bigvee_{i=1}^{15}(b_i \wedge b_{i+1} \wedge b_{i+2} \wedge b_{i+3} \wedge b_{i+4}))$, where b_i indicates that component i is broken.

Also, we present a variation of the original model by changing the policy of repair, since the policy used in [27] is quite singular and cannot be modeled with FIG input language. Instead, we chose a priority policy where lower numbered components have more priority than higher numbered components.

The large number of components of this model prevents us to use the monolithic approach to derive the important function. Therefore the automatic importance functions tested are only compositional. The naïve strategy of composing the local functions with summation as composition operand is denoted ac1. Similarly, ac2 uses product as composition operand and an exponentiation postprocessing. Taking advantage that the propositional formula is in DNF, we use the $(\max, +)$ and $(+, *)$ semirings composition strategies and we denote them by ac3 and ac4 respectively. Last, ah implements an *ad-hoc* function with the $(\max, +)$ semiring, using the variables of the modules rather than the local importance functions which the tool could compute if requested. This is the approach followed in [27] and denoted $\Phi(t) \doteq cl - oc(t)$ in that work.

Due to the fact that this model takes too long to simulate, we decided to run it for 3 h and compare the resulting precision of the intervals for a confidence of 90%. We run three independent experiments. The results are presented in Figs. 8

and 9. These values are the average of the precision of the intervals obtained from the three experiments run; the deviation is shown as whiskers on top of the bars. We observe that, in this case study, the normal Monte Carlo was still competitive and postpone further discussions for the next section.

7   Concluding Remarks

In this paper we have reported on the continuation of the work on stochastic automata and its analysis that took place under Ed Brinksma's supervision during the late 90s [8,10–12]. We presented here a new variant of stochastic automata, named IOSA, amenable for simulation, and moreover, we reported on our efforts on obtaining a fully automatic implementation of the importance splitting technique for rare event simulation.

Our technique on automatically deriving importance function has proven highly competitive when compared with known good *ad-hoc* importance functions. This is evident in all experimental results reported in the previous section as well as in [3–5]. Yet, we know that we need to improve the FIG tool. Particularly, we need a better automatic construction of the thresholds where splitting is produced. We are currently using known techniques [6,7] that are not always producing good results when combined with our method of deriving importance function and the RESTART method. This is evident in the oil pipeline case study. We are currently busy on a new technique for the automatic derivation of thresholds that we expect to report soon.

References

1. Alur, R., Dill, D.L.: A theory of timed automata. Theor. Comput. Sci. **126**(2), 183–235 (1994). https://doi.org/10.1016/0304-3975(94)90010-8
2. Bolognesi, T., Brinksma, E.: Introduction to the ISO specification language LOTOS. Comput. Netw. **14**, 25–59 (1987). https://doi.org/10.1016/0169-7552(87)90085-7
3. Budde, C.E.: Automation of importance splitting techniques for rare event simulation. Ph.D. thesis. Universidad Nacional de Córdoba, Argentina (2017)
4. Budde, C.E., D'Argenio, P.R., Hermanns, H.: Rare event simulation with fully automated importance splitting. In: Beltrán, M., Knottenbelt, W., Bradley, J. (eds.) EPEW 2015. LNCS, vol. 9272, pp. 275–290. Springer, Cham (2015). doi:10. 1007/978-3-319-23267-6_18
5. Budde, C.E., D'Argenio, P.R., Monti, R.E.: Compositional construction of importance functions in fully automated importance splitting. In: Puliafito, A., Trivedi, K.S., Tuffin, B., Scarpa, M., Machida, F., Alonso, J. (eds.) Proceedigns of VALUE-TOOLS 2016. ACM (2017). https://dx.doi.org/10.4108/eai.25-10-2016.2266501
6. Cérou, F., Del Moral, P., Furon, T., Guyader, A.: Sequential Monte Carlo for rare event estimation. Stat. Comput. **22**(3), 795–808 (2012). https://dx.doi.org/10.1007/s11222-011-9231-6
7. Cérou, F., Guyader, A.: Adaptive multilevel splitting for rare event analysis. Stoch. Anal. Appl. **25**(2), 417–443 (2007)

8. D'Argenio, P.R.: Algebras and automata for timed and stochastic systems. Ph.D. thesis. University of Twente, Enschede (1999)
9. D'Argenio, P.R., Katoen, J.P.: A theory of stochastic systems part I: Stochastic automata. Inf. Comput. **203**(1), 1–38 (2005)
10. D'Argenio, P.R., Katoen, J., Brinksma, E.: An algebraic approach to the specification of stochastic systems. In: Gries, D., de Roever, W.P. (eds.) PROCOMET 1998. IFIP Conference Proceedings, vol. 125, pp. 126–147. Chapman & Hall (1998)
11. D'Argenio, P.R., Katoen, J.P., Brinksma, E.: A compositional approach to generalised semi-Markov processes. In: Proceedings of WODES 1998, pp. 391–387. IEE (1998)
12. D'Argenio, P.R., Katoen, J., Brinksma, E.: Specification and analysis of soft real-time systems: quantity and quality. In: Proceedings of 20th RTSS, pp. 104–114. IEEE Computer Society (1999). https://doi.org/10.1109/REAL.1999.818832
13. D'Argenio, P.R., Lee, M.D., Monti, R.E.: Input/output stochastic automata. In: Fränzle, M., Markey, N. (eds.) FORMATS 2016. LNCS, vol. 9884, pp. 53–68. Springer, Cham (2016). doi:10.1007/978-3-319-44878-7_4
14. D'Argenio, P.R., Sánchez Terraf, P., Wolovick, N.: Bisimulations for non-deterministic labelled Markov processes. Math. Struct. Comput. Sci. **22**(1), 43–68 (2012)
15. Desharnais, J., Edalat, A., Panangaden, P.: Bisimulation for labelled Markov processes. Inf. Comput. **179**(2), 163–193 (2002)
16. Garvels, M.J.J., Van Ommeren, J.K.C.W., Kroese, D.P.: On the importance function in splitting simulation. Eur. Trans. Telecommun. **13**(4), 363–371 (2002). https://dx.doi.org/10.1002/ett.4460130408
17. Giry, M.: A categorical approach to probability theory. In: Banaschewski, B. (ed.) Categorical Aspects of Topology and Analysis. LNM, vol. 915, pp. 68–85. Springer, Heidelberg (1982). doi:10.1007/BFb0092872
18. van Glabbeek, R.J., Smolka, S.A., Steffen, B.: Reactive, generative and stratified models of probabilistic processes. Inf. Comput. **121**(1), 59–80 (1995)
19. Hahn, E.M., Hartmanns, A., Hermanns, H.: Reachability and reward checking for stochastic timed automata. ECEASST, vol. 70 (2014). http://journal.ub.tu-berlin.de/eceasst/article/view/968
20. Hermanns, H. (ed.): Interactive Markov Chains. LNCS, vol. 2428. Springer, Heidelberg (2002). doi:10.1007/3-540-45804-2
21. Jegourel, C., Legay, A., Sedwards, S.: Importance splitting for statistical model checking rare properties. In: Sharygina, N., Veith, H. (eds.) CAV 2013. LNCS, vol. 8044, pp. 576–591. Springer, Heidelberg (2013). doi:10.1007/978-3-642-39799-8_38
22. Kroese, D.P., Nicola, V.F.: Efficient estimation of overflow probabilities in queues with breakdowns. Performance Eval. **36**, 471–484 (1999)
23. L'Ecuyer, P., Le Gland, F., Lezaud, P., Tuffin, B.: Splitting techniques. In: Rare Event Simulation using Monte Carlo Methods, pp. 39–61. Wiley (2009). http://dx.doi.org/10.1002/9780470745403.ch3
24. Milner, R.: Communication and Concurrency. Prentice-Hall Inc., Upper Saddle River (1989)
25. Reijsbergen, D., de Boer, P.-T., Scheinhardt, W., Haverkort, B.: Automated rare event simulation for stochastic petri nets. In: Joshi, K., Siegle, M., Stoelinga, M., D'Argenio, P.R. (eds.) QEST 2013. LNCS, vol. 8054, pp. 372–388. Springer, Heidelberg (2013). doi:10.1007/978-3-642-40196-1_31
26. Villén-Altamirano, J.: RESTART simulation of networks of queues with Erlang service times. In: Winter Simulation Conference (2009), WSC 2009, pp. 1146–1154 (2009). http://dl.acm.org/citation.cfm?id=1995456.1995616

27. Villén-Altamirano, J.: RESTART simulation of non-Markov consecutive-k-out-of-n: F repairable systems. Rel. Eng. Sys. Safety **95**(3), 247–254 (2010). https://dx.doi.org/10.1016/j.ress.2009.10.005
28. Villén-Altamirano, M., Martínez-Marrón, A., Gamo, J., Fernández-Cuesta, F.: Enhancement of the accelerated simulation method restart by considering multiple thresholds. In: Proceedings of 14th International Teletraffic Congress, pp. 797–810 (1994)
29. Villén-Altamirano, M., Villén-Altamirano, J.: RESTART: a method for accelerating rare event simulations. In: Queueing, Performance and Control in ATM (ITC-13), pp. 71–76. Elsevier (1991)
30. Villén-Altamirano, M., Villén-Altamirano, J.: The rare event simulation method RESTART: efficiency analysis and guidelines for its application. In: Kouvatsos, D.D. (ed.) Network Performance Engineering. LNCS, vol. 5233, pp. 509–547. Springer, Heidelberg (2011). doi:10.1007/978-3-642-02742-0_22
31. Villén-Altamirano, J.: Asymptotic optimality of RESTART estimators in highly dependable systems. Reliab. Eng. Syst. Saf. **130**, 115–124 (2014). www.sciencedirect.com/science/article/pii/S0951832014001227
32. Wolovick, N.: Continuous probability and nondeterminism in labeled transition systems. Ph.D. thesis. Universidad Nacional de Córdoba, Argentina (2012)
33. Wu, S., Smolka, S.A., Stark, E.W.: Composition and behaviors of probabilistic I/O automata. Theor. Comput. Sci. **176**(1–2), 1–38 (1997)
34. Xiao, G., Li, Z., Li, T.: Dependability estimation for non-Markov consecutive-k-out-of-n: F repairable systems by fast simulation. Reliab. Eng. Syst. Saf. **92**(3), 293–299 (2007). https://dx.doi.org/10.1016/j.ress.2006.04.004
35. Zimmermann, A., Maciel, P.: Importance function derivation for RESTART simulations of Petri nets. In: RESIM, pp. 8–15 (2012)

System Dynamics

Discretization of Continuous Dynamical Systems Using UPPAAL

Stefano Schivo and Rom Langerak$^{(\boxtimes)}$

Formal Methods and Tools Group, Faculty of EEMCS,
University of Twente, Enschede, The Netherlands
`r.langerak@utwente.nl`

Abstract. We want to enable the analysis of continuous dynamical systems (where the evolution of a vector of continuous state variables is described by differential equations) by model checking. We do this by showing how such a dynamical system can be translated into a discrete model of communicating timed automata that can be analyzed by the UPPAAL tool. The basis of the translation is the well-known Euler approach for solving differential equations where we use fixed discrete value steps instead of fixed time steps. Each state variable is represented by a timed automaton in which the delay for taking the next value is calculated on the fly using the differential equations. The state variable automata proceed independently but may notify each other when a value step has been completed; this leads to a recalculation of delays. The approach has been implemented in the tool ANIMO for analyzing biological kinase networks in cells. This tool has been used in actual biological research on osteoarthritis dealing with systems where the dimension of the state vector (the number of nodes in the network) is in the order of one hundred.

Keywords: Discretization · Euler method · Model checking · Timed automata · Systems biology

1 Introduction

In this introduction we first motivate our interest in discretizing continuous systems using UPPAAL, then we give a short characterization of our approach, and finally we give an overview of the paper.

Many important and interesting phenomena in nature and technology can be adequately modeled as continuous dynamical systems where the evolution of a vector of real state variables is governed by differential equations. The mathematical theory of continuous dynamical systems is a mature field with a history of centuries, and occupies a firm position in any science or engineering curriculum.

The last decades have seen a great interest in the analysis of continuous dynamical systems using techniques from computer science developed in the context of discrete systems. A prominent example of such a technique is model

© Springer International Publishing AG 2017
J.-P. Katoen et al. (Eds.): Brinksma Festschrift, LNCS 10500, pp. 297–315, 2017.
DOI: 10.1007/978-3-319-68270-9_15

checking as originated in the 80's [10,15], where properties (often given in some kind of logical formalism) are checked against a model of a system, usually in the form of a discrete state transition system. The attractiveness of model checking lies in the fact that large and complex systems can be automatically and exhaustively checked. Model checking has fruitful applications to scheduling and control synthesis: reachability analysis may yield witness traces that contain the relevant information for a schedule or a control strategy. Our interest in model checking dynamical systems theory is aimed at biological applications; we refer to [5,25] for an overview of model checking biological systems.

Systems where timing aspects are critical can be modeled by enhancing state transition systems by real time clocks, leading to the timed automata model [1]. The application of symbolic techniques to (networks of) timed automata has led to effective model checking tools, most notably UPPAAL [22]. The UPPAAL website [38] contains an ample collection of applications of UPPAAL to e.g. protocol analysis, hardware verification and model checking, controller design, and scheduling. The fact that UPPAAL is a mature and powerful tool that is widely used makes it an attractive infrastructure for model checking continuous dynamical systems.

When modeling continuous dynamical systems by timed automata two problems have to be addressed. Firstly, timed automata can directly model only very simple dynamics: clock variables with a slope of 1. And secondly, timed automata are basically a discrete model. So some abstraction technique has to be found in order to represent continuous dynamics and values by using simple clocks and discrete values. The literature on abstractions of continuous dynamics is too vast to be dealt with here (we refer to [2] for an early overview); moreover, here we are primarily interested in those approaches that aim at timed automata as a target model. We identify two possible types of approaches.

One type of approach is to exploit knowledge of special properties of the dynamics (possibly restricted to a special class of dynamics) in order to obtain a discrete abstraction of the dynamical system. An example of this approach is given by [35,36,40] where the state space is partitioned by level sets of a kind of Lyapunov function. Another recent example is [4] where an abstraction technique based on time-varying regions of invariance (so-called control funnels) is applied to linear systems.

A second type of approach takes as a starting point a partitioning of the state space into rectangular cells and uses the differential equations to obtain information about reachability between cells. Examples of this approach are [6, 9,17,24,34] (they will be discussed in Sect. 2 of this paper). The approach in this paper falls in this category: we assume a discretization of a bounded part of the state space, even if we do not explicitly create cells in our approach. Conceptually our approach is just a slight modification of the well-known Euler approach for solving differential equations, where we take fixed value steps instead of fixed time steps. This leads to an arbitrary precision approximation of the dynamical system.

Our approach originated in the context of a biological application, viz. the analysis of kinase networks in living cells [31,32,39]. This means that we should be able to model check dynamical systems with dimensions in the order of 50–100. We do not just want to use model checking for the purpose of analyzing our systems (along the lines of e.g. [25]) but we also want to use generated counterexamples for extracting useful information (similar to the schedule synthesis of [16]). Suppose we model a network with all possible stimuli on the network, and we express a certain therapy target as a property on the network. Now model checking that the target cannot be reached may lead to a counterexample, representing exactly the stimuli leading to the desired target. In this way model checking is being used for drug synthesis, which is becoming even more important in the context of personalized therapies. Prerequisite for this is that our models are amenable to model checking in an efficient way. Many of the existing approaches in the literature are mathematically sophisticated but do not (yet) scale up to systems where the state vector has a high dimension. Our approach is conceptually simple, but has proven to be very efficient for a range of biological network models.

The field of nonlinear dynamical systems is complex and challenging. We would like to stress that our aim is not primarily to develop theory leading to a better understanding of this field. Instead, we obtain a discretization of a system using the Euler method, after which UPPAAL does most of the work. This tool-based approach works for an interesting application area (biological networks); it will be interesting to see whether it will work for other applications as well.

This paper is structured as follows. In Sect. 2 we describe the problem and discuss related approaches. In Sect. 3 we discuss the Euler method and our adaptation of it. In Sect. 4 we implement our version of the Euler method using timed automata and show an example. In Sect. 5 we discuss the correctness and make our implementation efficient. In Sect. 6 we describe how our approach has been implemented into the tool ANIMO that has already been used in biological research [28–30,33], and Sect. 7 contains conclusions and directions for further research.

2   Problem Statement and Related Work

We assume a dynamical system has a state vector $\mathbf{x} \in \mathbb{R}^n$, with $\mathbf{x} = (x_1, \ldots, x_n)$; x_i $(1 \leq i \leq n)$ is called a component of $\mathbf{x}$. We consider $\mathbf{x}$ as a function of time, and assume the dynamics of $\mathbf{x}$ to be governed by the differential equation

$$\frac{d\mathbf{x}}{dt} = \mathbf{f}(\mathbf{x}) \quad (*)$$

The function $\mathbf{f} : \mathbb{R}^n \to \mathbb{R}^n$ defines a vector field, i.e. it associates a vector $\mathbf{f}(\mathbf{x}) = (f_1(\mathbf{x}), \ldots, f_n(\mathbf{x}))$ to each point in $\mathbb{R}^n$ (note that $\mathbf{f}$ does not explicitly depend on t).

A *trajectory* of the dynamical system starting in initial state $\mathbf{x}_0$ is a function $\mathbf{x}(t) : \mathbb{R}_{\geq 0} \to \mathbb{R}^n$ such that $\mathbf{x}(0) = \mathbf{x}_0$ and $\frac{d\mathbf{x}(t)}{dt} = \mathbf{f}(\mathbf{x}(t))$ for all $t \geq 0$.

In this paper we are only interested in a bounded (and closed) part $\mathbf{M}$ of $\mathbb{R}^n$; for convenience we assume $\mathbf{M} = [0, max_1] \times \ldots \times [0, max_n]$. This restricts trajectories to remain within $\mathbf{M}$, which means that the time domain on which a trajectory is defined may be restricted: if a trajectory tries to leave $\mathbf{M}$ it has to be truncated (but we will show in Sect. 4 a pragmatic way of dealing with this).

We assume $\mathbf{f}$ is continuously differentiable on $\mathbf{M}$, which is sufficient to guarantee the existence of a unique solution of the differential equation $(*)$ for each initial value in $\mathbf{M}$.

We define a grid on $\mathbf{M}$ by defining a grid step d_i for each component of the state. We assume that $max_i/d_i = m_i$ is an integer. Let $\mathbf{k} = (k_1, \ldots, k_n)$ be a vector of integers with $0 \leq k_i \leq m_i$ for all i; we denote a cell in the grid by

$$C(k_1, \ldots, k_n) = [k_1 \cdot d_1, (k_1 + 1) \cdot d_1] \times \ldots \times [k_n \cdot d_n, (k_n + 1) \cdot d_n]$$

The possibility to have different grid steps for different components is quite convenient (and this is what we have implemented); however, for ease of exposition we assume we have a step size $d_i = 1$ for all components. By a slight abuse of notation we denote a cell $C(k_1, \ldots, k_n)$ by $(k_1, \ldots, k_n)$ or $\mathbf{k}$. Two cells are called neighbors if their difference is 1 in exactly one component, so e.g. $(k_1, \ldots, k_i, \ldots, k_n)$ and $(k_1, \ldots, k_i + 1, \ldots, k_n)$ are neighbors.

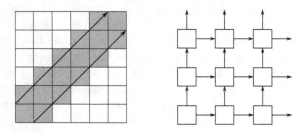

Fig. 1. A simple dynamical system with naive abstraction

Now the most simple idea for a discrete abstraction of the dynamical system would be to create a transition system with cells as locations, and transitions $\mathbf{k}_p \to \mathbf{k}_q$ between neighboring cells if there is a trajectory going from cell $\mathbf{k}_p$ to cell $\mathbf{k}_q$. A simple example (taken from [24]) shows that this naive abstraction contains too much spurious behavior (i.e. behavior that does not correspond to behavior in the original dynamical system) to be useful. Consider the simple dynamical system in Fig. 1 with state in $\mathbb{R}^2$ and dynamics given by $\frac{d\mathbf{x}}{dt} = (1, 1)$. Trajectories starting in cell $(0, 0)$ may only reach the gray area, but in the abstracted transition system all cells are reachable from $(0, 0)$.

Moreover, this is independent from the granularity of the grid: no matter how small the grid step, the entire state space will always be reachable from cell $(0, 0)$. The reason for this inherent spurious behavior is that time has been completely disregarded in the abstraction. For instance, when going from cell

$(0, 0)$ to $(0, 100)$ at least 99 grid steps are taken in the vertical direction, and not even 1 grid step in the horizontal direction, which is impossible since the horizontal and vertical speeds are the same. This observation lies at the basis of [24]. In order to solve the problem, to each dimension of a cell a maximum dwell time is associated. This maximum dwell time is obtained by calculating the extremal values of the components of the derivative function (which can be efficiently calculated for the class of functions considered in [24]), an idea already presented in [37]. This may considerably reduce spurious behavior; however, as the authors remark, problems may arise when components of the derivatives are zero. In that case no bound on dwell times can be given, which still allows spurious behavior. Some of these problems have been solved in [9] in the context of inevitability analysis, but only for linear systems and low dimensions.

A different approach is presented in [6] where an analysis is made on the facets of a cell: by analyzing from which parts of facets other facets are reachable (taking the dynamics into account) cells are refined and spurious behavior is greatly reduced. The method is sophisticated but scaling it to our intended applications (with cells having dimensions in the order of 100) would lead to an explosion of refined cells. Using reachability between facets is also the basis of [12] where control theory is used in order to influence the reachability of facets from other facets as studied in [18,19].

In our approach we do not explicitly create cells or transition relations between cells. Instead, we create a network of timed automata implementing the Euler approach for approximating a solution of a differential equation, and leave it to the UPPAAL tool to create a finite transition system as the underlying symbolic UPPAAL semantics. This approach has evolved from the IKNAT tool in [3] which models biological signaling networks. The timed automata created by IKNAT used a priori calculated delays between discrete activity levels of enzymes (a similar idea (but only for a one-dimensional system) has been used in [20] in the context of modeling battery lifetime). The IKNAT approach has been used by [17] in order to improve the quantitative modeling of gene regulatory networks in [34], thereby solving some instability problems of IKNAT. However, that approach is tied to a specific application and rather ad-hoc, conceptually not very clear, and the resulting timed automata are complicated and not efficient enough for effective model checking. The Euler-based approach we present in the next sections does not have these drawbacks.

3   The Euler Method for Solving Differential Equations

The Euler method is a well–known numerical procedure for solving differential equations. It can be found in most introductory books on calculus; for an extensive treatment we refer to [7].

The idea behind the Euler method is best illustrated on the one-dimensional case. Suppose we have a differential equation $\frac{dx}{dt} = f(x)$ and suppose we take time steps of size h. If at time t_n we have an approximation x_n of $x(t_n)$ we obtain the next approximation at time $t_{n+1} = t_n + h$ by $x_{n+1} = h \cdot f(x_n)$, see Fig. 2 (left).

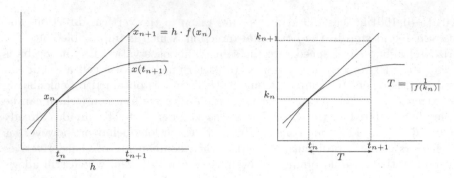

Fig. 2. The Euler method for a fixed time step (left) and for a fixed value step (right).

Starting at some initial value x_0 and then repeating this procedure yields a piecewise linear approximation of a trajectory of the dynamical system. The approximation error $|x(t_{n+1}) - x_{n+1}|$ goes to zero if the time step h goes to zero, so this is an arbitrary precision approximation.

We use a variant of the Euler method where we take a fixed value step, and then calculate the time T needed to arrive at this next value. This is illustrated in Fig. 2 (right).

If the starting point is the discrete value k_n, then the next discrete value is $k_n + 1$ if $f(k_n) > 0$, and $k_n - 1$ if $f(k_n) < 0$; in both cases $T = 1/|f(k_n)|$.

We explain the procedure in higher dimensions on the case $\mathbb{R}^2$ (since it is easiest to depict), so we have equation $\frac{d\mathbf{x}}{dt} = (f_1(\mathbf{x}), f_2(\mathbf{x}))$:

- suppose we start at point (p, q) with p and q integers
- the time T to reach the next cell: $T = min\{1/|f_1(p, q)|, 1/|f_2(p, q)|\}$
- if $T = 1/|f_1(p, q)|$ the next cell (p', q') reached will be $(p \pm 1, q)$ (depending on the sign of $f_1(p, q)$); otherwise $(p, q \pm 1)$ (depending on the sign of $f_2(p, q)$)
- now repeat this from the point where the next cell is entered, with vector $\mathbf{f}(p', q')$

This is illustrated in Fig. 3. Note that when the procedure starts from a point $\mathbf{x}$ that has just been reached on the cell boundary of cell $\mathbf{k}$ we use the vector value $\mathbf{f}(\mathbf{k})$ instead of the value of $\mathbf{f}(\mathbf{x})$, since we also want to obtain a discretization of the state space. When the step size tends towards zero, $\mathbf{f}(\mathbf{x})$ tends towards $\mathbf{f}(\mathbf{k})$, so this does not harm the arbitrary precision property of our approximation.

This version of the Euler method easily generalizes to dimension n:

Initialization:
Suppose we start at point $\mathbf{k}$. The waiting time for each component i:
$T_i = 1/|f_i(\mathbf{k})|$ (the time needed for reaching the next value $k_i \pm 1$, depending on the sign of $f_i(\mathbf{k})$). Note that if $f_i(\mathbf{k}) = 0$, $T_i = \infty$.

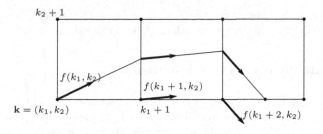

Fig. 3. Example of the Euler-based method in two dimension

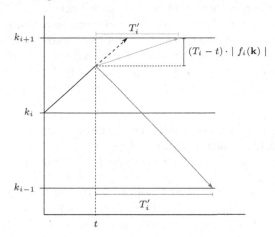

Fig. 4. Calculating a new delay time

Repeat Step:
 begin
   For all j for which $T_j = min\{T_1, \ldots, T_n\} = t$:
   $- k'_j = k_j + 1$ if $f_i(\mathbf{k}) > 0$
   $- k'_j = k_j - 1$ if $f_i(\mathbf{k}) < 0$
   Update all waiting times, based on t and $\mathbf{k}'$, as indicated below.
 end
 Each waiting time T_i is updated in one of the following ways:

- if $T_i = min\{T_1, \ldots, T_n\}$ or $f_i(\mathbf{k}) = 0$ or $f_i(\mathbf{k}') = 0$:
  $T'_i = 1/|f_i(\mathbf{k}')|$
- otherwise, if $f_i(\mathbf{k}')$ and $f_i(\mathbf{k})$ have the same sign:
  This situation is represented in Fig. 4 for a positive $f_i(\mathbf{k})$. At time t a distance $(T_i - t) \cdot |f_i(\mathbf{k})|$ still needs to be covered before reaching $k_i + 1$, so the new delay time becomes $T'_i = (T_i - t) \cdot |f_i(\mathbf{k})|/|f_i(\mathbf{k}')|$. Similar reasoning leads to the same formula if $f_i(\mathbf{k})$ is negative.
- otherwise, if $f_i(\mathbf{k}')$ and $f_i(\mathbf{k})$ have opposite sign: Suppose $f_i(\mathbf{k})$ is positive (see Fig. 4). At time t a distance $(T_i - t) \cdot |f_i(\mathbf{k})|$ would still have to be covered before reaching $k_i + 1$. But now the direction is changed, so an extra $1 - (T_i - t) \cdot |f_i(\mathbf{k})|$ has to be covered before $k_i - 1$ is reached, so a total of $2 - (T_i - t) \cdot |f_i(\mathbf{k})|$.

So the new delay time becomes $T_i' = (2 - (T_i - t) \cdot |f_i(\mathbf{k})|)/|f_i(\mathbf{k}')|$. Similar reasoning leads to the same formula if $f_i(\mathbf{k})$ is negative.

4   Translation into Timed Automata

We implement the Euler method of the previous section by a network of communicating timed automata. We first describe this implementation in an abstract way using pseudo-code and without worrying about syntactical and semantical issues. Then we show how to concretely implement this in UPPAAL, taking into account syntactical, semantical, and performance issues.

For each dimension i of the state space we create a timed automaton A_i containing a discrete state component k_i and a clock variable c_i. Clock c_i counts up to time $T_i = 1/|f_i(\mathbf{k})|$ which is the delay time for reaching next integer value $k_i \pm 1$, depending on the sign of $f_i(\mathbf{k})$. If $f_i(\mathbf{k}) = 0$ the component is for the time being quiescent, so $T_i = \infty$. While an automaton is waiting, two things may happen:

1. $c_i = T_i$, so the component has reached the new integer grid value $k_i' = k_i \pm 1$ (we call this *reaching*). Now all other automata are notified of this fact, and a new delay time T_i' is calculated for reaching the next grid value: $T_i' = 1/|f_i(k_1, \ldots, k_i', \ldots, k_n)|$, and clock c_i is reset.
2. a notification is received from automaton A_j that it has reached a new grid value k_j'. Now a new delay T_i' has to be calculated, based on the new value $f_i(k_1, \ldots, k_j', \ldots, k_n)$ and the time that has already been waited, i.e. the current value of clock c_i, in exactly the same way as in the Euler algorithm in the previous section. The clock c_i is reset.

An abstract version of automaton A_i with pseudo-code is given in Fig. 5.

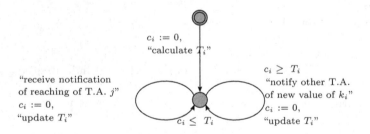

Fig. 5. Automaton A_i in pseudo code

We now change the abstract timed automaton with pseudo-code of Fig. 5 into a concrete UPPAAL automaton. The result is given in Fig. 6; from now on we assume the automaton A_i corresponding to component x_i has id i (and we often blur the distinction between components and their corresponding automata).

We explain step by step the various issues in this automaton.

Notifying When Reaching. When automaton A_i reaches the grid-point, it is not the case that all other automata have to be notified. Only those components

x_j have to be notified whose derivate f_j may change as a result of a change in x_i, i.e. $\frac{\partial f_j(\mathbf{x})}{\partial x_i} \neq 0$ for some value of $\mathbf{x}$. This can usually be detected at syntactic level: if variable x_i does not occur in the mathematical formula for f_j, then x_j is not dependent on x_i.

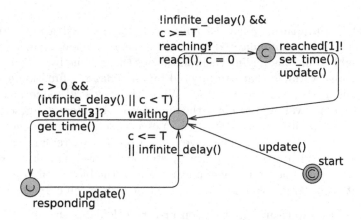

Fig. 6. The resulting UPPAAL automaton with id $= 1$

In Fig. 6 the depicted automaton A_1 is dependent on A_2 and A_3 so there are transitions from location `waiting` labeled `reached[2]?` and `reached[3]?`. Note that these transitions have been depicted in an overlapping fashion to enhance readability of the picture. These transitions then reach urgent location `responding` from which a transition is taken to update the delay time T_1.

Multiple Automata Reaching. It may happen that several automata reach a new grid-point at the same time. In order to guarantee a consistent resulting update of the global state we want the resulting sequence of updates to be atomic. To achieve this we synchronize all reaching transitions from location `waiting` by having two transitions labeled with `reaching!` and `reaching?` (again these two transitions are depicted overlappingly). Then a committed location is reached from which a transition `reached[id]!` is performed to notify the dependent automata. Note that this location is committed so the transition takes precedence over transitions in automata leaving urgent location `responding`.

If an automaton has just performed a `reached[id]!` transition and reached location `waiting` we do not want it to receive to a notification of another automaton that has just reached. Therefore we add predicate `c>0` to the guard on the transitions leaving location `waiting`.

Calculating the Clock Time. We saw in the last section that the value of clock c_i needs to be known at the moment the delay time T_i needs to be updated. However, UPPAAL does not allow the clock time to be read. Therefore we perform some global time administration in order to extract the clock time. We introduce a global variable `currentTime` that records the global time. Each automaton has a local variable `lastUpdate` that records the global time at the last delay update. Now if an automaton A_i reaches a new grid value this means it has waited the full delay time T_i. Therefore the variable `currentTime` is set to `lastUpdate` + T_i; this happens in function `set_time()`. When a notification is received, the current clock time is `currentTime` - `lastUpdate`; this is calculated in function `get_time()`.

The `reach()` Function. When an automaton has reached a new grid value this value should be communicated to the dependent automata. Since UPPAAL does not enable value passing in synchronizations this is done by writing the new value in a global variable that can be used by an `update()` function elsewhere. This happens in the function `reach()`. When the new grid value has reached one of the extremal values 0 or max_i the automaton A_i enters a quiescent mode by setting T_i to infinite. It may leave this quiescent mode when changes in other components make the component move away from the extremal value (so we do not need to truncate the trajectory by stopping time). This is a pragmatic solution that makes sense in many applications (e.g. the biological application in Sect. 6), but needs to be evaluated in the light of each specific application area.

The `update()` Function. The function `update` calculates the new time delay for reaching the next grid value, as described in the previous section. It is used in different contexts: when initializing, after reaching, and after having received a notification. In the latter case it has to make use of the old delay time, in the other two cases (characterized by the clock value being 0) it does not need the old delay time.

Dealing with Infinite Waiting Times. When the derivative of a component is 0 the waiting time is infinite. This could be modeled by a very large number, but it is not a good idea to put very large numbers in UPPAAL clock guards. Therefore a boolean function `infinite_delay()` has been defined that is true when the waiting time is (conceptually) infinite. This function is updated by function `update()`.

Numerical Representations. Our real number computations would require floating-point precision. Since UPPAAL only provides integer variables and operators, we use a significand-and-exponent notation with 4 significant figures, which allows for an error in the order of 0.1% while avoiding integer overflow in UPPAAL's engine. For example, the floating point number $a = 1.23456$ will be represented as the pair $\langle 1235, -3 \rangle$, which is translated back as $a = 1235 \times 10^{-3} = 1.235$. The interested reader can find the UPPAAL definitions and functions needed to compute rate and time values together with all other functions such as update() and react(), inside any UPPAAL model file generated by ANIMO [1].

This completes our explanation of our UPPAAL implementation. The resulting UPPAAL specification can be used for simulation.

---

[1] Models generated by ANIMO are saved in the system's temporary directory. Further details are available in the ANIMO manual at http://fmt.cs.utwente.nl/tools/animo/content/Manual.pdf.

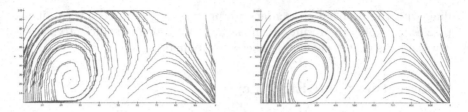

Fig. 7. Phase plane (x vs y plot) of the system in (1) obtained with the model from Fig. 6 on the intervals $[0, 100]$ (left) and $[0, 1000]$ (right), consequently adapting the equations to fit the $\mathbb{R}^2$ subsets. Starting values for x and y are defined on the $[0, 100]$ interval by the equations $x_0 = 5 + 10 \cdot j$, $y_0 = 5 + 10 \cdot k$, with $j, k = \{0, 1, \ldots, 9\}$.

In Fig. 7 we show a phase plane representation of a simulation of following non-linear system with two unstable equilibrium points:

$$\begin{cases} \frac{dx}{dt} = x - y \\ \frac{dy}{dt} = 1 - 16(x - 0.5)^2 \end{cases} \tag{1}$$

We produced the graphs in Fig. 7 directly in ANIMO, by translating the equations back into relations between nodes and edges in ANIMO's user interface and analyzing them with multiple initial values for x and y. Computing the resulting 100 simulation runs took about 11 s for the first graph in Fig. 7 and 17 s for the second.

For comparison we show in Fig. 8 the phase-plane representation of the same system obtained using the **pplane** software [26]. Note that the UPPAAL simulation succeeds in faithfully capturing the qualitative behavior.

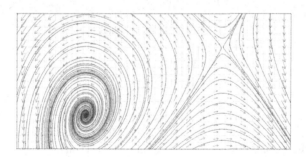

Fig. 8. Phase plane of the system in (1) obtained using the **pplane** software.

It is difficult to say something a priori about the accuracy of the Euler approximation; theoretical bounds on the truncation errors are not very helpful for this (as they depend on properties of the differential equation that may be hard to establish). What these theoretical bounds do show is that the approximation error is linear in the step size [7]. However, rounding errors caused by the representation of numbers further complicate the picture. As a pragmatic way of dealing with the problem of accuracy we propose to experiment with different step sizes, and plot the resulting simulations, until one is sufficiently satisfied (when the plots do not change significantly anymore).

5   Correctness and Efficiency

The translation of the previous section yields a set of n timed automata (one for each component of the state vector) that synchronize via channels. We first discuss the correctness of this translation by showing how one step of the Euler algorithm in Sect. 3 relates to a sequence of transitions in the product of the timed automata.

We assume each automaton is in state `waiting`. Suppose an automaton A_j has waited the allowed waiting time T_j in state `waiting`, so $T_j = min\{T_1, \ldots, T_n\}$. Note that this may happen for several automata at the same moment; we call these automata the *reaching* automata.

Now the following sequence of transitions is performed (this is illustrated in Fig. 9):

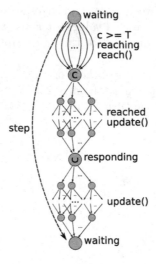

Fig. 9. Relation between timed automata transitions and Euler step.

– all the reaching automata synchronize on the **reaching** channel. Nondeterministically one of them performs **reaching!** and the others perform **reaching?**, leading to several possible transitions that all end up in the same global state. In this global state all the reaching automata are in a committed state, and all non-reaching automata are still in state `waiting`. The value of **k** has been updated via the **reach()** function.

- then all transitions from the committed states are executed in an interleaved way. These transitions may synchronize via channel reached with non-reaching automata, while updating the waiting times of the reaching automata. When all reached transitions are finished each reaching automaton is in state waiting, and each non-reaching automaton is in the urgent state responding.
- finally all transitions from the urgent states responding are performed in an interleaved way, thereby updating the waiting times in the non-reaching automata. After this each automaton is in the state waiting.

So the three phases of transitions in Fig. 9 taken together correspond to one step of the Euler algorithm in Sect. 3, showing the correctness of the translation.

The automaton in Fig. 6 has all the required functionality and can satisfactorily be used for simulation. However, it is not yet suitable for model checking (especially for higher dimensional systems): because of interleavings of transitions in different automata, the resulting system would contain too many states. If in each automaton there is one transition that interleaves with the corresponding transitions in the other automata, and if the system is n-dimensional, then just that transition generates 2^n interleavings. Since it is our ambition to deal with systems where n is in the order of 100, it is important to solve these problems. The problems, together with their remedies, are the following:

- from the start location: all update transitions interleave.
  Remedy: all update transitions are synchronized. The automaton with id 1 performs do_update! and all the other automata do_update?.
- from the responding location: all update transitions interleave.
  Remedy: all update transitions are synchronized. The automaton with the smallest id performs do_update! and all the other automata do_update?. The smallest responding id is established by enter_responding() and written into global variable minIDresponding. The automaton with the smallest id performs do_update! and all the other automata do_update?.
- all transitions from the committed location interleave.
  Remedy: all reaching transitions are enqueued in a priority queue (implemented by a boolean array) by the function enqueue(id). The reached[i]! transitions are performed by always choosing the minimum id in the queue, and removing the id from the queue by the function exit_queue(id). In this way one interleaving is picked out of the exponentially many.

The resulting timed automaton is given in Fig. 10. We will show in Sect. 6 that this model is amenable to model checking even for higher dimensions.

In many applications (like the biological application we deal with in Sect. 6) it is desirable to inject some imprecision in a model. This may be because of inherent nondeterminism in the modeled phenomena, it may be because model parameters are not precisely known, or it may be because we want our model checking results to be robust against small perturbations in the behavior.

A simple pragmatic way of doing this is by turning the calculated delay times T_i into intervals of possible delay times $[TL_i, TU_i]$ (where L stands for Lower

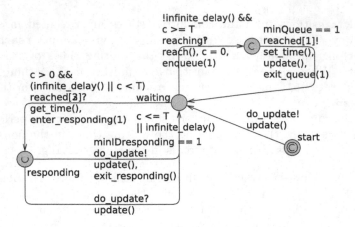

Fig. 10. Timed automaton with efficiency optimizations

and U stands for Upper). One might interpret such an interval as a uniform distribution of delay times (this approach was used for performance analysis in [41]). In the ANIMO tool in Sect. 6 such intervals are created by asking the user to specify an uncertainty percentage, say 10%, and then defining $TL = 0.9 \cdot T$ and $TU = 1.1 \cdot T$.

6   Application: ANIMO, a Tool for Analyzing Kinase Pathways

In this section we show how the approach has been implemented in the biological research tool ANIMO.

A signaling network in a biological cell describes the chain of reactions occurring between the reception of a signal and the response with which the cell reacts to such signal. The target of a signaling pathway is usually a transcription factor, a molecule with the task of controlling the production of some protein. Active molecules relay the signal inside the cell by activating other molecules until a target is reached. We define the activity level to represent the percentage of active molecules over an entire molecular species.

ANIMO (Analysis of Networks with Interactive MOdeling) [28–30,33] is a software tool that supports the modeling of biological signaling pathways by adding a dynamic component to traditional static representations of signaling networks. ANIMO allows to compare the behavior of a model with wet-lab data, and to explore such behavior in a user-friendly way. In order to achieve a good level of user-friendliness for a public of biologists ANIMO is accessible via the Cytoscape [11,21] user interface (see Fig. 11). A user may insert a node for each molecular species and an edge for each reaction. The occurrence of a reaction modifies the activity level of its target reactant; the rate with which a reaction

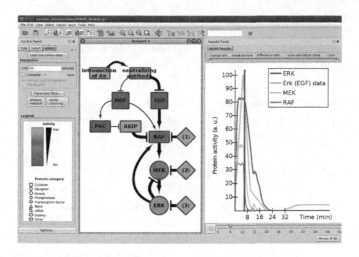

Fig. 11. The Cytoscape 3 interface for ANIMO

occurs depends on a formula selected by the user. For a more precise explanation on how reaction rates are computed in ANIMO, we refer to [29], for parameter setting in ANIMO to [27].

Once the user has created a model, this model is transformed into an UPPAAL model applying the discretizations described in the previous sections to the system of differential equations derived from the ANIMO network model. This model can then be analyzed via the Cytoscape/ANIMO interface that has facilities for model checking templates. ANIMO has also been used as a front-end for statistical model checking [13].

The ANIMO tool has been validated on several realistic biological case studies for which experimental data was available in the literature, and it has been demonstrated how to create models that faithfully fit experimental data [28–30, 33]. Moreover, ANIMO is being used in on-going research on chondrocyte signaling in relation to osteoarthritis, where the final objective is to enhance cartilage tissue engineering strategies [31, 32, 39].

Table 1 shows a comparison between some variants of the timed automata model when performing model checking on the model from [32] in UPPAAL. All the timed automata model variants contain 82 automata, i.e. they are a discretization of an 82-dimensional continuous dynamical system. "Approx. $\pm 5\%$" is the approximated variant with a setting of 5% uncertainty level in the original ANIMO model.

The model was initially configured so that a large change in the node activities on the whole network would take place. We then asked a query to understand whether such change is inevitable. In the UPPAAL query language, this is written as A<> R77 >= 80 (R77 being the most interesting readout in the particular experiment). The answer was positive, except for the non-optimized models where the computation could not terminate after several hours.

Table 1. Performance comparison of different model versions

Model version	Time (s)	Memory (peak KB)
Standard	-	-
Approx. ±5%	-	-
Standard + optimizations	139.61	3 880 040
Approx. ±5% + optimizations	63.13	1 107 552

7   Conclusions and Future Work

We have presented an arbitrary precision discretization of a continuous dynamical system as a network of UPPAAL timed automata. The implementation is conceptually based on the Euler method for solving differential equations. Mathematically this method is less sophisticated than many other discretizations in the literature; the main contribution of our approach is that is has been able to handle systems with dimensions in the order of 100. This efficiency is a prerequisite for the use of model checking of biological systems, especially with the objective of using the generation of counterexamples as a tool for aiding drug synthesis.

The approach has been used in the tool ANIMO for biological signal network analysis. ANIMO has been (and currently is being) used by biologists in actual biological research. The user interface (based on the tool Cytoscape) enables biologists to create their own models, perform analysis and interpret the results, all without intervention from computer scientists. Current research concentrates on automatic model generation from libraries, on analyzing parameter sensitivity, and on generating model improvements automatically from experimental data.

Our approach is based on an arbitrary precision approximation. However, the approximation error is hard to quantify, and it seems hard to qualify the approximation as an abstraction (in terms of either an over or under approximation). A CEGAR [23] type approach seems recommended: if model checking produces a trace, then this trace should be checked against a refined version of the model, i.e. an approximation with a smaller step size. In addition, it would be interesting to try to apply error estimation techniques like the one in [14].

The Euler method is known to have potential stability problems, especially for so-called stiff equations. The analysis of stiffness properties is a notorious difficult problem in mathematics; in the future we would like to evaluate (and possibly improve) the stability properties of our implementation, possibly by using more advanced versions of the Euler method. In addition we would like to try to optimize the number of differential equations using a form of preprocessing proposed in [8].

We certainly do not expect our approach to be applicable to the whole universe of nonlinear dynamical systems. The biological applications we have encountered so far could be described by multiaffine systems that posed no difficulties to our tools. In the future we would like to see whether our approach can be applied succesfully to other application areas. In addition we would like to obtain a better idea of the apriori limitations of our method.

Acknowledgements. We thank Arend Rensink for an important comment on an earlier version of this work. We thank Wim Bos, Liesbeth Geris, Marcel Karperien, Johan Kerkhofs, Jaco van de Pol, Janine Post, Jetse Scholma, Ricardo Urquidi Camacho, Paul van der Vet, and Brend Wanders for the fruitful and pleasant collaboration leading to ANIMO.

References

1. Alur, R., Dill, D.L.: A theory of timed automata. Theoret. Comput. Sci. **126**, 183–235 (1994)
2. Alur, R., Henzinger, T.A., Lafferriere, G., Pappas, G.J.: Discrete abstractions of hybrid systems. In: Proceedings of the IEEE, pp. 971–984 (2000)
3. Bos, W.: Interactive signaling network analysis tool. Master's thesis, University of Twente (2009)
4. Bouyer, P., Markey, N., Perrin, N., Schlehuber-Caissier, P.: Timed-automata abstraction of switched dynamical systems using control funnels. In: Sankaranarayanan, S., Vicario, E. (eds.) FORMATS 2015. LNCS, vol. 9268, pp. 60–75. Springer, Cham (2015). doi:10.1007/978-3-319-22975-1_5
5. Brim, L., Češka, M., Šafránek, D.: Model checking of biological systems. In: Bernardo, M., de Vink, E., Di Pierro, A., Wiklicky, H. (eds.) SFM 2013. LNCS, vol. 7938, pp. 63–112. Springer, Heidelberg (2013). doi:10.1007/978-3-642-38874-3_3
6. Brim, L., Fabriková, J., Drazan, S., Safránek, D.: Reachability in biochemical dynamical systems by quantitative discrete approximation. CoRR, abs/1107.5924 (2011)
7. Butcher, J.: Numerical Methods for Ordinary Differential Equations, 2nd edn. Wiley, Chichester (2008)
8. Cardelli, L., Tribastone, M., Tschaikowski, M., Vandin, A.: ERODE: a tool for the evaluation and reduction of ordinary differential equations. In: Legay, A., Margaria, T. (eds.) TACAS 2017. LNCS, vol. 10206, pp. 310–328. Springer, Heidelberg (2017). doi:10.1007/978-3-662-54580-5_19
9. Carter, R., Navarro-López, E.M.: Dynamically-driven timed automaton abstractions for proving liveness of continuous systems. In: Jurdziński, M., Ničković, D. (eds.) FORMATS 2012. LNCS, vol. 7595, pp. 59–74. Springer, Heidelberg (2012). doi:10.1007/978-3-642-33365-1_6
10. Clarke, E.M.: Model checking. In: Ramesh, S., Sivakumar, G. (eds.) FSTTCS 1997. LNCS, vol. 1346, pp. 54–56. Springer, Heidelberg (1997). doi:10.1007/BFb0058022
11. Cytoscape 3 ANIMO app. http://apps.cytoscape.org/apps/animo
12. David, A., Grunnet, J.D., Jessen, J.J., Larsen, K.G., Rasmussen, J.I.: Application of model-checking technology to controller synthesis. In: Aichernig, B.K., de Boer, F.S., Bonsangue, M.M. (eds.) FMCO 2010. LNCS, vol. 6957, pp. 336–351. Springer, Heidelberg (2011). doi:10.1007/978-3-642-25271-6_18
13. David, A., Larsen, K.G., Legay, A., Mikučionis, M., Poulsen, D.B., Sedwards, S.: Statistical model checking for biological systems. Int. J. Softw. Tools Technol. Transfer **17**(3), 351–367 (2015)

14. Donzé, A., Krogh, B., Rajhans, A.: Parameter synthesis for hybrid systems with an application to simulink models. In: Majumdar, R., Tabuada, P. (eds.) HSCC 2009. LNCS, vol. 5469, pp. 165–179. Springer, Heidelberg (2009). doi:10.1007/978-3-642-00602-9_12

15. Emerson, E.A., Clarke, E.M.: Characterizing correctness properties of parallel programs using fixpoints. In: de Bakker, J., van Leeuwen, J. (eds.) ICALP 1980. LNCS, vol. 85, pp. 169–181. Springer, Heidelberg (1980). doi:10.1007/3-540-10003-2_69

16. Fehnker, A.: Scheduling a steel plant with timed automata. In: Proceedings of the Sixth International Conference on Real-Time Computing Systems and Applications, RTCSA 1999, p. 280. IEEE Computer Society, Washington, DC (1999)

17. Goethem, S.V., Jacquet, J.-M., Brim, L., Šafránek, D.: Timed modelling of gene networks with arbitrarily precise expression discretization. Electron. Notes Theoret. Comput. Sci. **293**, 67–81 (2013). Proceedings of the Third International Workshop on Interactions Between Computer Science and Biology (CS2Bio 2012)

18. Habets, L.C.G.J.M., van Schuppen, J.H.: Control of piecewise-linear hybrid systems on simplices and rectangles. In: Di Benedetto, M.D., Sangiovanni-Vincentelli, A. (eds.) HSCC 2001. LNCS, vol. 2034, pp. 261–274. Springer, Heidelberg (2001). doi:10.1007/3-540-45351-2_23

19. Habets, L.C.G.J.M., van Schuppen, J.H.: Control to facet problems for affine systems on simplices and polytopes - with applications to control of hybrid systems. In: Proceedings of the 44th IEEE Conference on Decision and Control, pp. 4175–4180, December 2005

20. Jongerden, M., Haverkort, B., Bohnenkamp, H., Katoen, J.: Maximizing system lifetime by battery scheduling. In: 39th Annual IEEE/IFIP International Conference on Dependable Systems and Networks, DSN 2009, Los Alamitos. IEEE Computer Society Press, June 2009

21. Killcoyne, S., Carter, G.W., Smith, J., Boyle, J.: Cytoscape: a community-based framework for network modeling. Methods Mol. Biol. (Clifton, N.J.) **563**, 219–239 (2009)

22. Larsen, K.G., Pettersson, P., Yi, W.: UPPAAL in a nutshell. Int. J. Softw. Tools Technol. Transf. (STTT) **1**, 134–152 (1997)

23. Clarke, E., Grumberg, O., Jha, S., Lu, Y., Veith, H.: Counterexample-guided abstraction refinement. In: Emerson, E.A., Sistla, A.P. (eds.) CAV 2000. LNCS, vol. 1855, pp. 154–169. Springer, Heidelberg (2000). doi:10.1007/10722167_15

24. Maler, O., Batt, G.: Approximating continuous systems by timed automata. In: Fisher, J. (ed.) FMSB 2008. LNCS, vol. 5054, pp. 77–89. Springer, Heidelberg (2008). doi:10.1007/978-3-540-68413-8_6

25. Monteiro, P.T., Ropers, D., Mateescu, R., Freitas, A.T., de Jong, H.: Temporal logic patterns for querying dynamic models of cellular interaction networks. Bioinformatics **24**(16), i227–i233 (2008)

26. PPlane. http://math.rice.edu/~dfield/dfpp.html

27. Schivo, S., Scholma, J., Karperien, H.B.J., Post, J.N., van de Pol, J.C., Langerak, R.: Setting parameters for biological models with ANIMO. In: André, E., Frehse, G. (eds.) Proceedings 1st International Workshop on Synthesis of Continuous Parameters, Grenoble, France. Electronic Proceedings in Theoretical Computer Science, vol. 145, pp. 35–47. Open Publishing Association, April 2014

28. Schivo, S., Scholma, J., van der Vet, P.E., Karperien, M., Post, J.N., van de Pol, J., Langerak, R.: Modelling with ANIMO: between fuzzy logic and differential equations. BMC Syst. Biol. **10**(1), 56 (2016)

29. Schivo, S., Scholma, J., Wanders, B., Urquidi Camacho, R., van der Vet, P., Karperien, M., Langerak, R., van de Pol, J., Post, J.: Modelling biological pathway dynamics with Timed Automata. IEEE J. Biomed. Health Inform. **18**(3), 832–839 (2013)

30. Schivo, S., Scholma, J., Wanders, B., Urquidi Camacho, R.A., van der Vet, P.E., Karperien, H.B.J., Langerak, R., van de Pol, J.C., Post, J.N.: Modelling biological pathway dynamics with timed automata. In: 12th IC on Bioinformatics and Bioengineering (BIBE 2012), pp. 447–453. IEEE Computer Society (2012)

31. Scholma, J., Kerkhofs, J., Schivo, S., Langerak, R., van der Vet, P.E., Karperien, H.B.J., van de Pol, J.C., Geris, L., Post, J.N.: Mathematical modeling of signaling-pathways in osteoarthritis. In: Lohmander, S. (ed.) 2013 Osteoarthritis Research Society International (OARSI) World Congress, Philadelphia, USA, vol. 21, Supplement, p. S123. Elsevier, Amsterdam, April 2013

32. Scholma, J., Schivo, S., Kerkhofs, J., Langerak, R., Karperien, H.B.J., van de Pol, J.C., Geris, L., Post, J.N.: ECHO: the executable chondrocyte. In: Tissue Engineering & Regenerative Medicine International Society, European Chapter Meeting, Genova, Italy, vol. 8, p. 54. Wiley, Malden, June 2014

33. Scholma, J., Schivo, S., Urquidi Camacho, R., van de Pol, J., Karperien, M., Post, J.: Biological networks 101: computational modeling for molecular biologists. Gene **533**(1), 379–384 (2014)

34. Siebert, H., Bockmayr, A.: Temporal constraints in the logical analysis of regulatory networks. Theoret. Comput. Sci. **391**(3), 258–275 (2008). Converging Sciences: Informatics and Biology

35. Sloth, C., Wisniewski, R.: Verification of continuous dynamical systems by timed automata. Formal Methods Syst. Des. **39**(1), 47–82 (2011)

36. Sloth, C., Wisniewski, R.: Complete abstractions of dynamical systems by timed automata. Nonlinear Anal.: Hybrid Syst. **7**(1), 80–100 (2013). (IFAC) World Congress 2011

37. Stursberg, O., Kowalewski, S., Engell, S.: On the generation of timed discrete approximations for continuous systems. Math. Comput. Modell. Dyn. Syst. **6**(1), 51–70 (2000)

38. UPPAAL. www.uppaal.org

39. Urquidi Camacho, R.: Modeling osteoarthritic cartilage with ANIMO: an executable biology approach to osteoarthritic signaling and gene expression. Master's thesis, University of Twente, The Netherlands, July 2013

40. Wisniewski, R., Sloth, C.: Abstraction of dynamical systems by timed automata. Model. Ident. Control **32**(2), 79 (2011)

41. Xing, J., Theelen, B.D., Langerak, R., van de Pol, J., Tretmans, J., Voeten, J.P.M.: UPPAAL in practice: quantitative verification of a RapidIO network. In: Margaria, T., Steffen, B. (eds.) ISoLA 2010. LNCS, vol. 6416, pp. 160–174. Springer, Heidelberg (2010). doi:10.1007/978-3-642-16561-0_20

Analysis and Design of Interconnected Systems: A Systems and Control Perspective

Arjan van der Schaft[✉]

Jan C. Willems Center for Systems and Control,
Johann Bernoulli Institute for Mathematics and Computer Science,
University of Groningen, Groningen, The Netherlands
a.j.van.der.schaft@rug.nl
http://www.math.rug.nl/~arjan/

Abstract. Hybrid and cyber-physical systems are at the intersection of the theory of concurrent processes and of systems and control theory. This paper reviews some ideas from systems and control theory, which can be considered to be fruitful for the study of such systems. Particular emphasis is on the use of dissipative systems theory for the analysis of interconnected systems, and on the 'control by interconnection' problem using an extension of the notion of (bi-)simulation to the realm of continuous dynamics. Furthermore, the paper surveys a definition of hybrid systems, which treats the continuous and discrete dynamics on an equal footing.

Keywords: Interconnected systems · Dissipative systems · Control by interconnection · Bisimulation

1 Introduction

The theories of 'concurrent processes' and of 'systems and control' are both concerned with the modelling, analysis, control and design of *interconnected systems*. Despite conceptual similarities, these two areas have evolved rather independently of each other. One of the reasons for this was the difference in employed mathematical concepts and tools: from logic and automata theory in concurrent processes, to differential equations and transfer functions in systems and control theory. More abstractly, the distinction was between the use of *discrete* mathematics versus the use of *continuous* mathematics, both in variables and time.

At the end of the 1990s, stimulated among others by the theory of embedded systems in computer science and digital complexity in control, there was a strong move towards approachment of both areas, under the heading of 'hybrid systems' ('hybrid' referring to the combination of 'discrete' and 'continuous'). From the systems and control theory perspective this has led to new developments incorporating ideas from the formal methods realm into the theory of analysis and control of hybrid systems, and even of purely continuous systems. Further momentum was gained with the rise of the notion of cyber-physical

© Springer International Publishing AG 2017
J.-P. Katoen et al. (Eds.): Brinksma Festschrift, LNCS 10500, pp. 316–332, 2017.
DOI: 10.1007/978-3-319-68270-9_16

systems, where next to the hybrid system aspects the complexity and network aspects are emphasized.

In this paper I will briefly review some techniques from systems and control theory for interconnected systems analysis and design, whose extension to hybrid systems seems promising. One is the theory of *dissipative systems*, which is at the core of robust feedback control as well as of physical system modeling and control, including port-Hamiltonian systems theory. The other is the theory of *control by interconnection*, and its resulting necessary and sufficient conditions for achievable system behavior.

2   Dissipative Systems Theory

Dissipative systems theory was developed in the 1960/70s motivated by, among others, input-output stability theory and electrical network synthesis. A key step in the development was the two-part paper by Willems in 1972 [21], which still provides stimulating reading. One way of looking at the theory of dissipative systems is to consider it as a generalization of *Lyapunov function* theory for investigating the stability of dynamical systems. In this latter theory one wants to find scalar-valued functions of the state vector of the dynamical system that are monotonously decreasing (more precisely, non-increasing) along each solution trajectory of the system, for any initial condition. Under certain conditions this provides a guarantee for stability, possibly asymptotic, of equilibria of the system. Extensions to stability of periodic orbits, or of invariant sets, and to instability statements, are also possible. Thus in some sense Lyapunov function theory aims at *abstracting* the dynamics of the whole state vector to a *scalar* dynamics (the value of the Lyapunov function), in order to assess its stability. (We will briefly return to the abstraction interpretation in Sect. 5.)

The *strength* of Lyapunov function theory is that one does not need to compute the solutions of the differential or difference equations describing the dynamics of the system (which in the nonlinear case is usually not possible analytically). Instead one needs to verify algebraic inequalities in terms of the partial derivatives of the Lyapunov function and the right-hand sides of the differential (respectively, difference) equations.

The main *weakness* of Lyapunov function theory, on the other hand, is twofold. First, constructing a Lyapunov function is in many cases some kind of art (although in physical examples the total *energy* of the system and/or other conserved quantities are often guiding). Secondly, Lyapunov function theory is confined to *closed* dynamical systems (no interaction with other systems), and there is no clear way to build up the Lyapunov function from functions of subvectors of the full state vector.

Dissipative systems theory comes in to remedy this second weakness, and, eventually, will address the first weakness as well. Dissipativity of an open system entails the construction of a function of the state vector, now called a *storage function*, together with the construction of a function of the external interaction variables (e.g., inputs and outputs), called a *supply rate*, and verifying that along all solutions of the open system the rate of increase of the storage function at any moment of time is bounded from above by the value of the supply rate at this moment of time. Formally, for an input-state-output system the definition is as follows.

Definition 1 [21]. *Consider an input-state-output system*

$$\Sigma \; : \; \begin{array}{l} \dot{x} = f(x,u), \;\; u \in \mathcal{U} \\ y = h(x,u), \;\; y \in \mathcal{Y} \end{array} \tag{1}$$

where $x = (x_1, \ldots, x_n)$ *are local coordinates for an n-dimensional state space manifold* $\mathcal{X}$, *and* $\mathcal{U}$ *and* $\mathcal{Y}$ *are the linear input and output spaces, of dimension m, respectively p. Consider on the total space* $\mathcal{U} \times \mathcal{Y}$ *of external variables a function*

$$s \; : \; \mathcal{U} \times \mathcal{Y} \to \mathbb{R}, \tag{2}$$

called the supply rate. *Denote* $\mathbb{R}^+ = [0, \infty)$. *The system* Σ *is said to be dissipative with respect to the supply rate s if there exists a function* $S : \mathcal{X} \to \mathbb{R}^+$, *called the* storage function, *such that for all* $x \in \mathcal{X}$ *and* $u \in \mathcal{U}$

$$\frac{d}{dt}S(x) = S_x(x)f(x,u) \leq s(u, h(x,u)), \tag{3}$$

where $S_x(x)$ *denotes the row vector of partial derivatives of S.*

Note that dissipativity depends on the choice of the supply rate s. The two most common choices for s will be discussed below. The inequality (3) is called the *dissipation inequality*. In case the external variables u, y are absent (a closed system), the dissipation inequality reduces to the requirement $S_x(x)f(x) \leq 0$, $x \in \mathcal{X}$, which means that the storage function is a Lyapunov function for the closed dynamical system $\dot{x} = f(x)$.

Remark 1. In many cases of complex systems modeling the system is not of the input-state-output form (1), but more generally described by *differential-algebraic equations* $F(x, \dot{x}, w) = 0$, with w the total vector of external variables (not necessarily split into inputs and outputs). Definition 1 is directly generalized to this case by requiring that $S_x(x)\dot{x} \leq s(w)$ for all $x, \dot{x}, w$ satisfying the equations $F(x, \dot{x}, w) = 0$. Furthermore, dissipativity can be also defined for *static* systems $F(w) = 0$ by simply requiring that $s(w) \geq 0$ for all w satisfying $F(w) = 0$.

Like for Lyapunov functions the search for storage functions may seem to be an art. However, we have the following variational characterization of dissipativity and existence of a storage function for a given supply rate [16, 21].

Theorem 1. *Consider the system* Σ *with supply rate* $s(u, y)$. *Then* Σ *is dissipative with respect to s if and only if*

$$S_a(x) := \sup_{\substack{u(\cdot) \\ T \geq 0}} - \int_0^T s(u(t), y(t))dt, \qquad x(0) = x, \tag{4}$$

is finite for all $x \in \mathcal{X}$. Furthermore, if S_a is finite for all $x \in \mathcal{X}$ and differentiable then it defines a storage function, called the available storage. All other possible storage functions S satisfy

$$S_a(x) \leq S(x) - \inf_x S(x), \qquad x \in \mathcal{X} \tag{5}$$

Thus the presence of input and output variables (u, y) and the choice of a supply rate $s(u, y)$ leads immediately to the characterization of dissipativity and the construction of the minimal storage function (although the actual computation of S_a may be hard). Without giving any details we note that, under additional assumptions, there also exists a variational characterization of the *maximal* storage function; cf. [16,21] for details.

Dissipative systems theory leads to a modular construction of Lyapunov functions by variations of the following basic idea. Consider k systems Σ_i of the form (1) with state, input, and output spaces $\mathcal{X}_i, \mathcal{U}_i, \mathcal{Y}_i, i = 1, \cdots, k$. Suppose Σ_i are dissipative with respect to the supply rates

$$s_i(u_i, y_i), \quad u_i \in \mathcal{U}_i, \ y_i \in \mathcal{Y}_i, \tag{6}$$

and storage functions $S_i(x_i)$, $i = 1, \cdots, k$. Now consider an interconnection of $\Sigma_i, i = 1, \cdots, k$, defined through an *interconnection subset*

$$I \subset \mathcal{U}_1 \times \mathcal{Y}_1 \times \cdots \times \mathcal{U}_k \times \mathcal{Y}_k \times \mathcal{U}^e \times \mathcal{Y}^e, \tag{7}$$

where $\mathcal{U}^e, \mathcal{Y}^e$ are spaces of external input and output variables u^e, y^e. This defines an interconnected system Σ_I with state space $\mathcal{X}_1 \times \cdots \times \mathcal{X}_k$ and external variables u^e, y^e, by imposing the interconnection equations

$$((u_1, y_1), \cdots, (u_k, y_k), (u^e, y^e)) \in I \tag{8}$$

A special case occurs when the interconnection equations amount to setting the inputs of each i-th system equal to the outputs of another system. In physical network modeling this is, however, not the most common type of interconnection. As a consequence, the interconnected system Σ_I is often a *differential-algebraic equation* system; that is, a mixture of differential and algebraic equations.

The following result is immediate.

Proposition 1. *Suppose the supply rates $s_1, \cdots, s_k$ and the interconnection subset I are such that there exists a supply rate $s^e : \mathcal{U}^e \times \mathcal{Y}^e \to \mathbb{R}$ for which*

$$\begin{aligned} s_1(u_1, y_1) + \cdots + s_k(u_k, y_k) \leq s^e(u^e, y^e), \\ \text{for all } ((u_1, y_1), \cdots, (u_k, y_k), (u^e, y^e)) \in I \end{aligned} \tag{9}$$

Then the interconnected system Σ_I is dissipative with respect to the supply rate s^e, with storage function

$$S(x_1, \cdots, x_k) := S_1(x_1) + \cdots + S_k(x_k) \tag{10}$$

An extra degree of freedom results from noting that if Σ_i is dissipative with respect to the supply rate $s_i(u_i, y_i)$ with storage function $S_i(x_i)$, then so it is with respect to the supply rate $\alpha_i s_i(u_i, y_i)$ and storage function $\alpha_i S_i(x_i)$, for any $\alpha_i > 0$.

The two most commonly employed choices for the supply rate $s(u, y)$ are the following; see [16] for more information. For simplicity of exposition identify throughout the linear input and output spaces $\mathcal{U}$ and $\mathcal{Y}$ with $\mathbb{R}^m$, respectively $\mathbb{R}^p$, equipped with the standard Euclidean inner product and norm.

Definition 2. *A state space system Σ with $\mathcal{U} = \mathcal{Y} = \mathbb{R}^m$ is passive if it is dissipative with respect to the supply rate $s(u, y) = u^T y$.*

A state space system Σ with $\mathcal{U} = \mathbb{R}^m$, $\mathcal{Y} = \mathbb{R}^p$ has L_2-gain $\leq \gamma$ for a certain $\gamma \geq 0$ if it is dissipative with respect to the supply rate $s(u, y) = \frac{1}{2}\gamma^2 ||u||^2 - \frac{1}{2}||y||^2$.

These definitions take a particularly explicit form for systems which are *affine* in the input u (as is often the case in applications)

$$\Sigma_a : \begin{array}{l} \dot{x} = f(x) + g(x)u \\ y = h(x), \end{array} \tag{11}$$

with $g(x)$ an $n \times m$ matrix. In case of the passivity supply rate $s(u, y) = u^T y$ the dissipation inequality then takes the form

$$S_x(x)[f(x) + g(x)u] \leq u^T h(x), \quad x \in \mathcal{X}, u \in \mathcal{U}, \tag{12}$$

which can be seen to be equivalent to the conditions

$$S_x(x)f(x) \leq 0, \quad h^T(x) = S_x(x)g(x), \quad x \in \mathcal{X} \tag{13}$$

This implies that S is a Lyapunov function for the uncontrolled system, while the output map is determined by the input matrix g together with the storage function. The passivity supply rate has a strong physical background, with $s(u, y) = u^T y$ denoting the external power supplied to the system, and S the energy stored in the system. This can be further generalized to the theory of port-Hamiltonian systems; see e.g. [16, 17].

In case of L_2-gain $\leq \gamma$ the dissipation inequality becomes

$$S_x(x)[f(x) + g(x)u] - \frac{1}{2}\gamma^2 ||u||^2 + \frac{1}{2}||h(x)||^2 \leq 0, \quad x \in \mathcal{X}, u \in \mathcal{U} \tag{14}$$

This can be simplified by computing the maximizing u^* (as a function of x) for the left-hand side, i.e., $u^* = \frac{1}{\gamma^2}g^T(x)S_x^T(x)$, and substituting this into (14) to obtain the *Hamilton-Jacobi inequality*

$$S_x(x)f(x) + \frac{1}{2}\frac{1}{\gamma^2}S_x(x)g(x)g^T(x)S_x^T(x) + \frac{1}{2}h^T(x)h(x) \leq 0, \quad x \in \mathcal{X} \tag{15}$$

The L_2-gain supply rate underlies much of *robust control theory*, while mathematically it is related to contraction theory.

Actually, these two classical supply rates are closely connected by what is called the *scattering* transformation. Start from the passivity supply rate $s(u, y) = u^T y$, and define the new set of external vectors (sometimes called *wave vectors*)

$$s^+ = \frac{1}{\sqrt{2}}(u + y), \quad s^- = \frac{1}{\sqrt{2}}(-u + y) \tag{16}$$

Then $\|s^+\|^2 - \|s^-\|^2 = u^T y$. Hence, if the system with inputs u and outputs y is passive, then the system with inputs s^+ and outputs s^- has L_2-gain ≤ 1. This obviously generalizes to L_2-gains $\leq \gamma$ for any $\gamma > 0$.

An interesting application of the scattering transformation is the following passivity interpretation of pure *time-delays*. Consider two pairs of equally dimensioned input-output vectors u_0, y_0 and u_1, y_1. Consider as above the wave vectors

$$\begin{aligned} s_0^+ &= \tfrac{1}{\sqrt{2}}(u_0 + y_0), \quad s_0^- = \tfrac{1}{\sqrt{2}}(-u_0 + y_0) \\ s_1^+ &= \tfrac{1}{\sqrt{2}}(u_1 + y_1), \quad s_1^- = \tfrac{1}{\sqrt{2}}(-u_1 + y_1) \end{aligned} \tag{17}$$

Then $\|s_0^+\|^2 - \|s_0^-\|^2 = u_0^T y_0$ and $\|s_1^+\|^2 - \|s_1^-\|^2 = u_1^T y_1$. Consider now the time-delay systems

$$\begin{aligned} s_1^-(t) &= s_0^+(t - \Delta_0) \\ s_0^-(t) &= s_1^+(t - \Delta_1) \end{aligned} \tag{18}$$

with Δ_0, Δ_1 arbitrary nonnegative time-delays. Then for any $T \geq \max(\Delta_0, \Delta_1)$

$$\begin{aligned} &- \int_0^T [u_0^T(t)y_0(t) + u_1^T(t)y_1(t)]dt \\ &= \int_0^T (\|s_0^-(t)\|^2 - \|s_0^+(t)\|^2 + \|s_1^-(t)\|^2 - \|s_1^+(t)\|^2)dt \\ &= \int_0^T (\|s_0^+(t - \Delta_0)\|^2 - \|s_0^+(t)\|^2)dt + \int_0^T (\|s_1^+(t - \Delta_1)\|^2 - \|s_1^+(t)\|^2)dt \\ &= \int_{-\Delta_0}^0 \|s_0^+(t)\|^2 dt - \int_{T-\Delta_0}^T \|s_0^+(t)\|^2 dt \\ &\quad + \int_{-\Delta_1}^0 \|s_1^+(t)\|^2 dt - \int_{T-\Delta_1}^T \|s_0^+(t)\|^2 dt \\ &\leq \int_{-\Delta_0}^0 \|s_0^+(t)\|^2 dt + \int_{-\Delta_1}^0 \|s_1^+(t)\|^2 dt, \end{aligned}$$

where the terms in the last line are independent of the behavior on $[0, \infty)$ (and can be interpreted as the initial state of the infinite-dimensional system of the time-delay system). Hence the map (u_0, u_1) to (y_0, y_1) is *passive*! This observation has been used in the literature in a number of contexts, see e.g. [6] and the references quoted therein.

2.1   Network Versions of Passivity and Small-Gain Theorems

An important specialization of the above interconnection theory of dissipative systems concerns the interconnection of passive or finite L_2-gain systems via a network defined by a *graph*. In the passivity case a powerful scenario is the following, cf. [16] for more details and other possibilities. Consider a directed graph with N vertices and M edges, specified by its $N \times M$ *incidence* matrix [2], and associate passive systems both to its *vertices*, as well as to its *edges*. Thus to each i-th vertex of the graph there corresponds a passive system with scalar input and output (see Remark 2 for generalizations)

$$\begin{aligned}
\dot{x}_i^v &= f_i^v(x_i^v, u_i^v), \quad x_i^v \in \mathcal{X}_i^v, \ u_i^v \in \mathbb{R} \\
y_i^v &= h_i^v(x_i^v), \qquad y_i^v \in \mathbb{R}
\end{aligned} \tag{19}$$

with storage function $S_i^v, i = 1, \cdots, N$, and to each j-th edge of the graph there corresponds a passive single-input single-output system

$$\begin{aligned}
\dot{x}_i^b &= f_i^b(x_i^b, u_i^b), \quad x_i^b \in \mathcal{X}_i^b, \ u_i^b \in \mathbb{R} \\
y_i^b &= h_i^b(x_i^b, u_i^b), \quad y_i^b \in \mathbb{R}
\end{aligned} \tag{20}$$

with storage function $S_i^b, i = 1, \cdots, M$. Also static passive systems can be considered. Collecting the scalar inputs and outputs into vectors

$$\begin{aligned}
u^v &= [u_1^v, \cdots, u_N^v]^T, \ y^v = [y_1^v, \cdots, y_N^v]^T \\
u^b &= [u_1^b, \cdots, u_M^b]^T, \ y^b = [y_1^b, \cdots, y_M^b]^T
\end{aligned} \tag{21}$$

these passive systems are interconnected to each other by the interconnection equations

$$\begin{aligned}
u^v &= -Dy^b + e^v \\
u^b &= D^T y^v + e^b
\end{aligned} \tag{22}$$

where $e^v \in \mathbb{R}^N$ and $e^b \in \mathbb{R}^M$ are external inputs, and D is the $N \times M$ incidence matrix. Since the interconnection (22) satisfies the power conservation property

$$(u^v)^T y^v + (u^b)^T y^b = (e^v)^T y^v + (e^b)^T y^b$$

the following result is immediate.

Proposition 2. *Consider a graph with incidence matrix D, with passive systems (19) with storage functions S_i^v associated to the vertices and passive systems (20) with storage functions S_i^b associated to the edges, interconnected by (22). Then the interconnected system is again passive, with inputs e^v, e^b and outputs y^v, y^b, and total storage function*

$$S_1^v(x_1^v) + \cdots + S_N^v(x_N^v) + S_1^b(x_1^b) + \cdots + S_1^b(x_M^b) \tag{23}$$

This interconnection scenario of passive systems occurs abundantly in physical networks, from classical mass-spring-damper systems, multi-body systems, to power networks; see [16]. A further 'geometrization' of the network interconnection structure can be obtained within the theory of port-Hamiltonian systems; see again [16, 17].

Remark 2. The set-up is easily generalized to multi-input multi-output systems with $u_i^v, y_i^v, u_j^b, y_j^b$ all in $\mathbb{R}^m$ by simply replacing the incidence matrix D by the Kronecker product $D \otimes I_m$ and D^T by $D^T \otimes I_m$, with I_m denoting the $m \times m$ identity matrix.

In the L_2-gain one may formulate the following network result [4,16]. Consider a multi-agent system, corresponding to a directed graph with N vertices and input-state-output systems $\Sigma_i, i = 1, \cdots, N$, associated to these vertices. Furthermore, assume that the edges of the graph are specified by an $N \times N$ *adjacency matrix* [2] $\mathcal{A}$ with elements $0, 1$, corresponding to interconnections

$$u_i = y_j \tag{24}$$

if and only if the (i, j)-th element of $\mathcal{A}$ is equal to 1, with each row in the $\mathcal{A}$ matrix containing only one 1. Now assume that the systems Σ_i have L_2-gain $\leq \gamma_i, i = 1, \cdots, N$. This means that there exist storage functions $S_i : \mathcal{X}_i \to \mathbb{R}^+$ such that

$$\dot{S}_i \leq \frac{1}{2}\gamma_i^2 \|u_i\|^2 - \frac{1}{2}\|y_i\|^2, \quad i = 1, \cdots, N \tag{25}$$

Then define the following weighted adjacency matrix

$$\Gamma = \operatorname{diag}(\gamma_1^2, \cdots, \gamma_N^2)\mathcal{A} \tag{26}$$

Using the Perron-Frobenius theorem we obtain the following network version of the classical small-gain theorem [16], extending [4].

Theorem 2. *Consider a directed graph $\mathcal{G}$ and associated to its vertices systems Σ_i, which have L_2-gains $\leq \gamma_i$ with storage functions S_i, $i = 1, \cdots, N$, and which are interconnected through the adjacency matrix $\mathcal{A}$ defined by (24). Define the matrix Γ given by (26). Then if the spectral radius $r(\Gamma) < 1$, there exists $\mu > 0$ such that $\mu^T \Gamma < \mu$ and the non-negative function $S(x_1, \cdots, x_N) := \sum_{i=1}^N \mu_i S_i(x_i)$ satisfies along trajectories of the interconnected system*

$$\dot{S} \leq -\varepsilon_1\|y_1\|^2 - \varepsilon_2\|y_2\|^2 \cdots - \varepsilon_N\|y_N\|^2 \tag{27}$$

for certain positive constants $\varepsilon_1, \cdots, \varepsilon_N$.

In case of the feedback interconnection $u_1 = y_2, u_2 = y_1$ of two systems Σ_1, Σ_2 with L_2-gain $\leq \gamma_1$, respectively $\leq \gamma_2$, application of Theorem 2 leads to the consideration of the matrix

$$\Gamma = \begin{bmatrix} 0 & \gamma_1^2 \\ \gamma_2^2 & 0 \end{bmatrix}, \tag{28}$$

which has spectral radius < 1 if and only if $\gamma_1 \cdot \gamma_2 < 1$; thus recovering the classical *small-gain theorem* [16].

2.2   Converse Passivity and Small-Gain Theorems

Dissipative systems theory can be also used as some sort of *contract-based design* in the following sense. Consider for simplicity two systems $\Sigma_i, i = 1, 2$, in negative feedback interconnection $u_1 = -y_2, u_2 = y_1$. Now, let Σ_1 be the system under consideration, and Σ_2 an unknown environment. Suppose one wants to guarantee stability of the interconnected system for such unknown Σ_2. An attractive theorem is the following. Suppose that Σ_2 is unknown but passive. Then, under suitable conditions, it can be shown [7,8,19] that the interconnected system is stable if and only if Σ_1 is passive. The 'if' direction of this theorem just follows from the interconnection theory of passive systems discussed before, but the 'only if' direction is new (see [3] for an earlier result). This theorem has interesting applications e.g. in robotics, with Σ_1 being the controlled robot, and Σ_2 the unknown, but supposedly passive, environment. It implies that in order to guarantee stable operation with an unknown environment the controlled robot seen from the interaction port with the environment should be a passive system; see [3,19].

A similar statement holds in the L_2-gain case: the interconnection of the given system Σ_1 with an unknown perturbation system Σ_2 with L_2-gain $\leq \gamma$ is stable if and only the L_2-gain of Σ_1 is $\leq \frac{1}{\gamma}$; see e.g. [24]. This converse small-gain theorem quantifies the maximal allowable uncertainty in the feedback loop.

3   Control by Interconnection and Bisimulation

In this section we briefly discuss the control by interconnection problem as a 'correct by design' approach from control theory. Given a system, traditionally called the *plant*, and a *specification* system, describing the desired behavior, when does there exist a *controller* system, such that the plant system interconnected with the controller system is equivalent to the specification system?

Here 'equivalence' will be understood in the sense of *bisimulation* of continuous systems, as extended in [10,13] from concurrent processes to the continuous dynamics realm. Consider two linear input-state-output systems Σ_i, $i = 1, 2$, given as

$$\begin{aligned}\dot{x}_i &= A_i x_i + B_i u_i + G_i f_i, \quad x_i \in \mathcal{X}_i, f_i \in \mathcal{F} \\ z_i &= H_i x_i, \quad\quad\quad\quad\quad z_i \in \mathcal{Z}\end{aligned} \quad (29)$$

with f_i denoting external input functions, while u_i are *internal* input functions, modeling for example *non-determinism*.

Definition 3. *A bisimulation relation between Σ_1 and Σ_2 is a linear subspace $\mathcal{R} \subset \mathcal{X}_1 \times \mathcal{X}_2$ with the following property. Take any $(x_{10}, x_{20}) \in \mathcal{R}$ and any joint input function $f_1 = f_2$. Then, for any input function u_1 there should exist an input function u_2 such that the resulting state trajectories $x_1(\cdot)$ with $x_1(0) = x_{10}$ and $x_2(\cdot)$ with $x_2(0) = x_{20}$ satisfy*

$$(x_1(t), x_2(t)) \in \mathcal{R}, \quad z_1(t) = z_2(t), \quad \text{for all } t \geq 0, \quad (30)$$

and conversely, for any input function u_2 there should exist a function u_1 such that the state trajectories $x_1(\cdot)$ and $x_2(\cdot)$ satisfy (30).

Σ_1 and Σ_2 are said to be bisimilar, denoted $\Sigma_1 \approx \Sigma_2$, if there exists a bisimulation relation $\mathcal{R} \subset \mathcal{X}_1 \times \mathcal{X}_2$ such that $\pi_1(\mathcal{R}) = \mathcal{X}_1$ and $\pi_2(\mathcal{R}) = \mathcal{X}_2$, where $\pi_i : \mathcal{X}_1 \times \mathcal{X}_2 \to \mathcal{X}_i$, $i = 1, 2$, denote the canonical projections.

A bisimulation relation can be characterized by the following linear-algebraic conditions on the matrices describing the two systems [13].

Proposition 3. *A subspace* $\mathcal{R} \subset \mathcal{X}_1 \times \mathcal{X}_2$ *is a bisimulation relation between* Σ_1 *and* Σ_2 *if and only if*

$$\mathcal{R} + \text{im} \begin{bmatrix} B_1 \\ 0 \end{bmatrix} = \mathcal{R} + \text{im} \begin{bmatrix} 0 \\ B_2 \end{bmatrix} =_{\text{def}} \mathcal{R}_e$$

$$\begin{bmatrix} A_1 & 0 \\ 0 & A_2 \end{bmatrix} \mathcal{R} \subset \mathcal{R}_e \qquad (31)$$

$$\text{im} \begin{bmatrix} G_1 \\ G_2 \end{bmatrix} \subset \mathcal{R}_e$$

$$\mathcal{R} \subset \ker \begin{bmatrix} H_1 & -H_2 \end{bmatrix}$$

It is important to emphasize that bisimulation is thus fully characterized by the *equations* of the system, and no solution trajectories need to be computed. (This even extends to *nonlinear* input-state-output systems [12].) Furthermore, there is an effective linear-algebraic algorithm [13] for computing the *maximal* bisimulation relation between Σ_1 and Σ_2, and thus for checking bisimilarity.

The one-sided version, called 'simulation', is defined as follows [13].

Definition 4. *A simulation relation of* Σ_1 *by* Σ_2 *is a linear subspace* $\mathcal{S} \subset \mathcal{X}_1 \times \mathcal{X}_2$ *with the following property. Take any* $(x_{10}, x_{20}) \in \mathcal{S}$ *and any joint input function* $f_1 = f_2$. *Then, for any input function* u_1 *there should exist an input function* u_2 *such that the resulting state trajectories* $x_1(\cdot)$ *with* $x_1(0) = x_{10}$ *and* $x_2(\cdot)$ *with* $x_2(0) = x_{20}$ *satisfy*

$$(x_1(t), x_2(t)) \in \mathcal{S}, \quad z_1(t) = z_2(t), \text{ for all } t \geq 0 \qquad (32)$$

System Σ_1 *is said to be simulated by system* Σ_2, *denoted* $\Sigma_1 \preccurlyeq \Sigma_2$, *if there exists a simulation relation* $\mathcal{S}$ *of* Σ_1 *by* Σ_2 *such that* $\pi_1(\mathcal{S}) = \mathcal{X}_1$.

Analogous to the linear-algebraic conditions for bisimulation, a subspace $\mathcal{S} \subseteq \mathcal{X}_1 \times \mathcal{X}_2$ is a simulation relation of Σ_1 by Σ_2 if and only if [13]

$$\mathcal{S} + \text{im} \begin{bmatrix} B_1 \\ 0 \end{bmatrix} \subset \mathcal{S} + \text{im} \begin{bmatrix} 0 \\ B_2 \end{bmatrix} =_{\text{def}} \mathcal{S}_e$$

$$\begin{bmatrix} A_1 & 0 \\ 0 & A_2 \end{bmatrix} \mathcal{S} \subset \mathcal{S}_e \qquad (33)$$

$$\text{im} \begin{bmatrix} G_1 \\ G_2 \end{bmatrix} \subset \mathcal{S}_e$$

$$\mathcal{S} \subset \ker \begin{bmatrix} H_1 & -H_2 \end{bmatrix}$$

Again, this also yields a linear-algebraic algorithm for computing the maximal simulation relation of Σ_1 by Σ_2.

All this theory has been generalized from input-state-output systems (29) to linear differential-algebraic equation systems in [9]; see also [15].

The *control by interconnection* problem can now be formulated as follows. Let P denote the *plant* system with inputs f_P, u_P, outputs z_P and y_P, and state x_P. Let S denote the *specification* system, with inputs f_S, outputs z_S and state x_S. Furthermore, consider *controller* systems C with state x_C, which share the variables u_C and y_C with the inputs and outputs u_P, y_P of the plant, leading to an *interconnected* system $P \parallel C$ with inputs f_P and outputs z_P. Given P and S, the problem is now to give necessary and sufficient conditions for the existence, and explicit construction, of a C such that $P \| C$ is *bisimilar* to S.

The plant system P is thus represented as

$$\dot{x}_P = A_P x_P + B_P u_P + G_P f_P$$
$$\begin{bmatrix} y_P \\ z_P \end{bmatrix} = \begin{bmatrix} C_P \\ H_P \end{bmatrix} x_P \tag{34}$$

and the specification system S as

$$\dot{x}_S = A_S x_S + G_S f_S$$
$$z_S = H_S x_S \tag{35}$$

Finally, a controller system is taken to be of the form

$$\dot{x}_C = A_C x_C + B_C u_C$$
$$y_C = C_C x_C \tag{36}$$

In the solution of the control by interconnection problem an important role is played by the following system, which is derived from the plant system P by setting u_P and y_P to zero. The resulting system, denoted by N_P, is thus given by the differential-algebraic equations

$$\dot{x}_P = A_P x_P + G_P f_P$$
$$\begin{bmatrix} 0 \\ z_P \end{bmatrix} = \begin{bmatrix} C_P \\ H_P \end{bmatrix} x_P \tag{37}$$

Sharing of the external variables (u_P, y_P) of the plant and (u_C, y_C) of the controller is defined by

$$\begin{bmatrix} u_P \\ y_P \end{bmatrix} = \Pi \begin{bmatrix} u_C \\ y_C \end{bmatrix} \tag{38}$$

where Π is a *permutation* matrix to be chosen. The equations for $P \parallel_\Pi C$ are thus given by the differential-algebraic equations

$$\dot{x}_P = A_P x_P + B_P u_P + G_P f_P$$
$$\dot{x}_C = A_C x_C + B_C u_C$$
$$\begin{bmatrix} u_P \\ C_P x_P \end{bmatrix} = \Pi \begin{bmatrix} u_C \\ C_C x_C \end{bmatrix} \tag{39}$$
$$z_P = H_P x_P$$

We are now ready to formally state the control by interconnection problem and its solution [20].

Control by Interconnection Problem: Given P and S, find necessary and sufficient conditions for the existence of a controller C and permutation matrix Π such that $P \parallel_\Pi C \approx S$.

Theorem 3. $\exists C, \Pi$ *such that* $P \parallel_\Pi C \approx S \Leftrightarrow N_P \preccurlyeq S \preccurlyeq P$.

The necessary and sufficient conditions on the righthand side are referred to as *sandwich conditions* (like in the behavioral version of this problem [22, 23]): the specification system S should be 'sandwiched' between N_P and P. The condition $S \preccurlyeq P$ is rather obvious, while the condition $N_P \preccurlyeq S$ stems from the fact that by linearity N_P is the part of P that will not be influenced by any controller C.

A key ingredient in proving the $\Leftarrow$ direction in Theorem 3 is the notion of the *canonical controller* as introduced in [14] in a behavioral setting. This canonical controller is simply defined as $C_{\mathrm{can}} := P \parallel S$ where the interconnection is with respect to the variables f and z. In fact, the $\Leftarrow$ direction of Theorem 3 is proved by taking $C = C_{\mathrm{can}}$ and Π equal to the identity matrix.

As noted before, the conditions $N_P \preccurlyeq S$ and $S \preccurlyeq P$ can be checked without too much difficulty by a linear-algebraic algorithm. On the other hand we note that the condition $N_P \preccurlyeq S$ does not easily generalize to a nonlinear system context; see also the discussion in the behavioral context provided in [14].

4   Hybrid Systems

In this section we will indicate the extension of the theory of bisimulation to a *hybrid system* context. Let us start from the definition of a hybrid system as given in [18], modifying the definition of a hybrid automaton in [1] by symmetrizing the role of continuous and discrete dynamics.

Definition 5. *A hybrid system Σ^{hyb} is defined as a six-tuple $(\mathcal{L}, \mathcal{X}, \mathcal{A}, \mathcal{W}, E, F)$, where*

- $\mathcal{L}$ *is a discrete set, called the set of discrete states (or, locations).*

- $\mathcal{X}$ *is a finite-dimensional manifold called the continuous state space.*

- $\mathcal{A}$ *is a discrete set of symbols called the set of discrete communication variables (or, actions).*

- $\mathcal{W}$ *is a finite-dimensional linear space called the space of continuous communication variables. Often the vector $w \in \mathcal{W}$ can be partitioned into an input u and an output vector y.*

- E *is a subset of $\mathcal{L} \times \mathcal{X} \times \mathcal{A} \times \mathcal{L} \times \mathcal{X}$ specifying the event conditions. A typical element of E is denoted by (l^-, x^-, a, l^+, x^+), with $^-$ denoting the value just before and $^+$ denoting the value just after the event.*

- F *is a subset $\mathcal{L} \times T\mathcal{X} \times \mathcal{W}$ specifying the flow conditions. Here $T\mathcal{X}$ is the tangent bundle of $\mathcal{X}$. A typical element of F is denoted by $(l, x, \dot{x}, w)$.*

A hybrid trajectory or *run* of the hybrid system Σ^{hyb} on the time-interval $[0, T]$ consists of the following ingredients. First, such a trajectory involves a discrete set $\mathcal{E} \subset [0, T]$ denoting the set of *event times* $t \in [0, T]$ associated with the trajectory. Secondly[1], there is a function $l : [0, T] \rightarrow \mathcal{L}$ which is constant on every subinterval between subsequent event times $t_a, t_b \in \mathcal{E}$, and which specifies the location of the hybrid system for $t \in (t_a, t_b)$. Thirdly, the trajectory involves admissible time-functions $x : [0, T] \rightarrow \mathcal{X}$, $w : [0, T] \rightarrow \mathcal{W}$, satisfying for all $t \notin \mathcal{E}$ the dynamics

$$(l, x(t), \dot{x}(t), w(t)) \in F \tag{40}$$

with l the location between subsequent event times $t_a, t_b \in \mathcal{E}$. Finally, the trajectory includes a discrete function $a : \mathcal{E} \rightarrow \mathcal{A}$ such that for all $t \in \mathcal{E}$

$$(l(t^-), x(t^-), a(t), l(t^+), x(t^+)) \in E \tag{41}$$

Here $x(t^-)$ and $x(t^+)$ denote the limit values of the variables x when approaching t from the left, respectively from the right. (Thus we throughout assume that the class of admissible functions x is chosen in such a way that these left and right limits are defined.) Furthermore, $l(t^-)$ and $l(t^+)$ denote the values of l *before* and *after* the event time t. Hence a hybrid run r is specified by a five-tuple

$$r = (\mathcal{E}, l, x, a, w) \tag{42}$$

with l, x, a, w time-functions defined on $\mathcal{E}$, as specified above.

Note that the subset F (the *flow* conditions) specifies the continuous dynamics of the hybrid system depending on the location the system is in. On the other hand, E (the *event* conditions) stands for the event behavior at the event times, entailing the discrete state variables $l \in \mathcal{L}$ and the discrete communication variables $a \in \mathcal{A}$, together with a possible reset of the continuous state variables x. Furthermore, the flow conditions F incorporate the notion of *location invariant*, while the event conditions E include the notion of *guard*.

In terms of the hybrid runs a natural definition of hybrid bisimulation can be given as follows, cf. [12]:

Definition 6. *Consider two hybrid systems* $\Sigma_i^{hyb} = (\mathcal{L}_i, \mathcal{X}_i, \mathcal{A}_i, \mathcal{W}_i, E_i, F_i), i = 1, 2$, *as above. A hybrid bisimulation relation between* Σ_1^{hyb} *and* Σ_2^{hyb} *is a subset*

$$\mathcal{R} \subset (\mathcal{L}_1 \times \mathcal{X}_1) \times (\mathcal{L}_2 \times \mathcal{X}_2)$$

with the following property. Take any $(l_{10}, x_{10}, l_{20}, x_{20}) \in \mathcal{R}$. *Then for every hybrid run* $r_1 = (\mathcal{E}_1, l_1, x_1, a_1, w_1)$ *of* Σ_1^{hyb} *with* $(l_1(0), x_1(0)) = (l_{10}, x_{10})$ *there should exist a hybrid run* $r_2 = (\mathcal{E}_2, l_2, x_2, a_2, w_2)$ *of* Σ_1^{hyb} *with* $(l_2(0), x_2(0)) = (l_{20}, x_{20})$ *such that for all times* t *for which the hybrid run* r_1 *is defined*

$-\ \mathcal{E}_1 = \mathcal{E}_2 =: \mathcal{E}$

$-\ w_1(t) = w_2(t)$ *for all* $t \geq 0$ *with* $t \notin \mathcal{E}$

---

[1] Note that in the sequel we will also use the notations l, x, a, w for *time-functions*, mapping for each time instant t to elements $l(t) \in \mathcal{L}, x(t) \in \mathcal{X}, a(t) \in \mathcal{A}, w(t) \in \mathcal{W}$, respectively.

- $a_1(t) = a_2(t)$ *for all $t \geq 0$ with $t \in \mathcal{E}$*

- $(l_1(t), x_1(t), l_2(t), x_2(t)) \in \mathcal{R}$ *for all $t \geq 0$ with $t \notin \mathcal{E}$,*

and conversely for every hybrid run r_2 of Σ_2^{hyb} there should exist a hybrid run r_1 of Σ_1^{hyb} with the same properties.

A more checkable version of hybrid bisimulation is obtained [12] by merging the algebraic characterization of bisimulation relations for dynamical systems as discussed in the previous section with the common notion of bisimulation for concurrent processes. Hereto we throughout assume that the continuous state space parts of the bisimulation relation $\mathcal{R}$, namely all sets

$$\mathcal{R}_{l_1 l_2} := \{(x_1, x_2) \mid (l_1, x_1, l_2, x_2) \in \mathcal{R}\} \subset \mathcal{X}_1 \times \mathcal{X}_2 \tag{43}$$

are submanifolds.

Definition 7. *Consider two systems $\Sigma_i^{hyb} = (\mathcal{L}_i, \mathcal{X}_i, \mathcal{A}_i, \mathcal{W}_i, E_i, F_i)$, $i = 1, 2$, as above. A structural hybrid bisimulation relation between Σ_1^{hyb} and Σ_2^{hyb} is a subset*

$$\mathcal{R} \subset (\mathcal{L}_1 \times \mathcal{X}_1) \times (\mathcal{L}_2 \times \mathcal{X}_2)$$

with the following property. Take any $(l_1^-, x_1^-, l_2^-, x_2^-) \in \mathcal{R}$. Then for every l_1^+, x_1^+, a for which

$$(l_1^-, x_1^-, a, l_1^+, x_1^+) \in E_1,$$

there should exist l_2^+, x_2^+ such that

$$(l_2^-, x_2^-, a, l_2^+, x_2^+) \in E_2$$

while $(l_1^+, x_1^+, l_2^+, x_2^+) \in \mathcal{R}$, and conversely.
Furthermore, take any $(l_1, x_1, l_2, x_2) \in \mathcal{R}$. Then for every $\dot{x}_1, w$ for which

$$(l_1, x_1, \dot{x}_1, w) \in F_1$$

there should exist $\dot{x}_2$ such that

$$(l_2, x_2, \dot{x}_2, w) \in F_2$$

while $(\dot{x}_1, \dot{x}_2) \in T_{(x_1, x_2)} \mathcal{R}_{l_1 l_2}$, and conversely.

It is easily seen that any structural hybrid bisimulation relation is a hybrid bisimulation relation in the sense of Definition 6. The basic observation is that the invariance condition $(\dot{x}_1(t), \dot{x}_2(t)) \in T_{(x_1(t), x_2(t))} \mathcal{R}_{l_1 l_2}$ for all $t \geq 0$ implies that the trajectory $(l_1, l_2, x_1(t), x_2(t)), t \geq 0$ remains in $\mathcal{R}$. For the converse statement (a hybrid bisimulation relation is a structural hybrid bisimulation relation) additional conditions are necessary. For the specific case of *switching linear systems* see [11].

A logical next step for further research is to extend the control by interconnection problem as studied in the previous section to hybrid systems as defined above.

5   Conclusions and Outlook

In this paper we have discussed two approaches from systems and control theory to the analysis and design of interconnected systems. The first one is the theory of *dissipative systems*, which is primarily aimed at addressing stability and robustness problems. The second one is the *control by interconnection* problem, formulated through the extension of (bi-)simulation theory to continuous linear systems.

Abstractly, these two approaches are linked as follows. Given an input-state-output system Σ, the dissipation inequality $\frac{d}{dt}S(x) \leq s(u, y)$, with storage function S and supply rate s, can be interpreted as an *abstraction* of Σ in the following sense. Define, based on the storage function S and the supply rate s, the mapping

$$z = S(x), \; v = s(u, y),$$

from the product of the state space $\mathcal{X}$ and the total space of inputs and outputs $\mathcal{U} \times \mathcal{Y}$ to the product of a scalar state space $z \in \mathcal{Z} = \mathbb{R}^+$ and a scalar space of external variables $v \in \mathbb{R}$. This mapping can be seen to define a *simulation relation* in the following, generalized, sense. Dissipativity of Σ is equivalent to the pair (z, v) satisfying the *differential inequality*

$$\Sigma_s: \quad \dot{z} \leq v$$

Thus, the system Σ_s can be regarded as a (generalized) specification system, and the mapping $(z, v) = (S(x), s(u, y))$ as a generalized simulation relation between Σ and Σ_s. 'Generalized' in the sense that apart from the mapping $z = S(x)$ between the state spaces of Σ and Σ_s (as in the common definition of a simulation relation) also the additional mapping $v = s(u, y)$ between the external variables of both systems is considered. From a future research point of view this motivates the exploration of a theory of control by interconnection where the specification system is of a more general type than (35); at least including *inequalities*.

Finally in Sect. 4 we have reviewed a general definition of hybrid system, which places the continuous and discrete dynamics on a more equal footing than the definition of a hybrid automaton [1], or, alternatively, the definition of a hybrid system in [5]. This more general definition could serve as a useful starting point for further developments; e.g. concerning the control by interconnection problem for hybrid systems. In general, we believe that the combination of concepts from, one the one hand, systems and control theory, and, on the other hand, concurrent processes, may lead to promising developments; especially when it comes to hybrid systems.

Acknowledgements. After my collaboration with Hans Schumacher at the CWI on the topic of hybrid systems, I was very fortunate to be close to the *Formal Methods and Tools* group at the Computer Science department of the University of Twente, headed by Ed Brinksma. I happily remember the enjoyable and very stimulating conversations with especially Ed Brinksma, Rom Langerak and Joost-Pieter Katoen, also involving

Jan Willem Polderman from the mathematics side. Among others this led to the celebrated NWO-CASH project. I still regard this collaboration as an exemplary case of open and fruitful collaboration. It is a great pleasure to dedicate this paper, which is heavily inspired by this collaboration, to Ed at the occasion of his 60th birthday. Happy birthday Ed!

References

1. Alur, R., Courcoubetis, C., Henzinger, T.A., Ho, P.-H.: Hybrid automata: an algorithmic approach to the specification and verification of hybrid systems. In: Grossman, R.L., Nerode, A., Ravn, A.P., Rischel, H. (eds.) HS 1991–1992. LNCS, vol. 736, pp. 209–229. Springer, Heidelberg (1993). doi:10.1007/3-540-57318-6_30
2. Bollobas, B.: Modern Graph Theory, Graduate Texts in Mathematics, vol. 184. Springer, Heidelberg (1998). doi:10.1007/978-1-4612-0619-4
3. Colgate, J.E., Hogan, N.: Robust control of dynamically interacting systems. Int. J. Control **48**(1), 65–88 (1988)
4. Dashkovskiy, S., Ito, H., Wirth, F.: On a small-gain theorem for ISS networks in dissipative Lyapunov form. Eur. J. Control **17**(4), 357–365 (2011)
5. Goebel, R., Sanfelice, R.G., Teel, A.R.: Hybrid Dynamical Systems: Modeling, Stability, and Robustness. Princeton University Press, Princeton (2012)
6. Hatanaka, T., Chopra, N., Fujita, M., Spong, M.W.: Passivity-Based Control and Estimation in Networked Robotics. Springer, Heidelberg (2011)
7. Khong, S.Z., van der Schaft, A.J.: Converse passivity theorems. In: Proceedings of the IFAC World Congress, pp. 9983–9986, Toulouse (2017)
8. Khong, S.Z., van der Schaft, A.J.: The converse of the passivity and small-gain theorem for nonlinear input-output maps. Submitted for publication (2017). arXiv:1707.00148
9. Megawati, N.Y., van der Schaft, A.J.: Bisimulation equivalence of differential-algebraic systems. Int. J. Control (2016). doi:10.1080/00207179.2016.1266519
10. Pappas, G.J.: Bisimilar linear systems. Automatica **39**, 2035–2047 (2003)
11. Pola, G., van der Schaft, A.J., Di Benedetto, M.D.: Equivalence of switching linear systems by bisimulation. Int. J. Control **79**, 74–92 (2006)
12. van der Schaft, A.: Bisimulation of dynamical systems. In: Alur, R., Pappas, G.J. (eds.) HSCC 2004. LNCS, vol. 2993, pp. 555–569. Springer, Heidelberg (2004). doi:10.1007/978-3-540-24743-2_37
13. van der Schaft, A.J.: Equivalence of dynamical systems by bisimulation. IEEE Trans. Autom. Control **49**, 2160–2172 (2004)
14. van der Schaft, A.J.: Achievable behavior of general systems. Syst. Control Lett. **49**, 141–149 (2003)
15. van der Schaft, A.J.: Equivalence of hybrid dynamical systems. In: Proceedings of the 16th International Symposium on Mathematical Theory of Networks and Systems (MTNS 2004), Leuven, Belgium, July 2004
16. van der Schaft, A.: L_2-Gain and Passivity Techniques in Nonlinear Control. Springer, Cham (2017). doi:10.1007/978-3-319-49992-5. 3rd Revised and Enlarged edn. (1st edn. (1996), 2nd edn. (2000)), p. xviii + 321
17. van der Schaft, A.J., Jeltsema, D.: Port-Hamiltonian systems theory: an introductory overview. Found. Trends Syst. Control **1**(2–3), 173–378 (2014). Now Publishers, Boston-Delft
18. van der Schaft, A.J., Schumacher, J.M.: An Introduction to Hybrid Dynamical Systems. LNCIS, vol. 251. Springer, London (2000). doi:10.1007/BFb0109998

19. Stramigioli, S.: Energy-aware robotics. In: Camlibel, M.K., Julius, A.A., Pasumarthy, R., Scherpen, J.M.A. (eds.) Mathematical Control Theory I. LNCIS, vol. 461, pp. 37–50. Springer, Cham (2015). doi:10.1007/978-3-319-20988-3_3

20. Vinjamoor, H., van der Schaft, A.J.: The achievable dynamics via control by interconnection. IEEE Trans. Autom. Control **56**(5), 1110–1117 (2011)

21. Willems, J.C.: Dissipative dynamical systems, part I: general theory. Arch. Ration. Mech. Anal. **45**(5), 321–351 (1972)

22. Willems, J.C.: On interconnections, control, and feedback. IEEE Trans. Autom. Control **42**, 326–339 (1997)

23. Willems, J.C., Trentelman, H.L.: Synthesis of dissipative systems using quadratic differential forms, part I. IEEE Trans. Autom. Control **47**, 53–69 (2002)

24. Zhou, K., Doyle, J.C., Glover, K.: Robust and Optimal Control. Prentice-Hall, Englewood Cliffs (1996)

Applications

Runtime Monitoring Based on Interface Specifications

Ivan Kurtev[1], Jozef Hooman[2,3]($\boxtimes$), and Mathijs Schuts[4]

[1] Altran, Eindhoven, The Netherlands
[2] Embedded Systems Innovation by TNO, Eindhoven, The Netherlands
`jozef.hooman@tno.nl`
[3] Radboud University, Nijmegen, The Netherlands
[4] Philips, Best, The Netherlands

Abstract. Unclear descriptions of software interfaces between components often lead to integration issues during development and maintenance. To address this, we have developed a framework named ComMA (Component Modeling and Analysis) that supports model-based engineering of components. ComMA is a combination of Domain Specific Languages (DSLs) for the specification of interface signatures, state machines to express the allowed interaction behaviour, and constraints on data and timing. From ComMA models a number of artefacts can be generated automatically such as proxy code, visualizations, tests, and simulation models. In this paper, the focus is on the generation of runtime monitors to check interface conformance, including the state machine behaviour and the specified data and time constraints. We report about the development of this approach in close collaboration with the development of medical applications at Philips.

1 Introduction

Precise interface descriptions are crucial in the development of complex systems with many components, including third-party components. Unclarity about interfaces is a frequent source of errors. This does not only concern the signature of messages exchanged between components, but also the expected order of messages, assumptions on timing behaviour, and constraints on the exchanged data values. During system development, proper interface definitions are essential to prevent integration issues. During later phases of the system life cycle, continuous monitoring of interfaces is important to prevent system failures due to component changes. For instance, a supplier might deliver an improved version of a component which, however, has different timing characteristics.

The focus of this paper is on the automatic generation of monitoring support from interface specifications. This is done in the context of the development of minimally-invasive interventional X-ray systems of Philips. An example of such a system is depicted in Fig. 1.

© Springer International Publishing AG 2017
J.-P. Katoen et al. (Eds.): Brinksma Festschrift, LNCS 10500, pp. 335–356, 2017.
DOI: 10.1007/978-3-319-68270-9_17

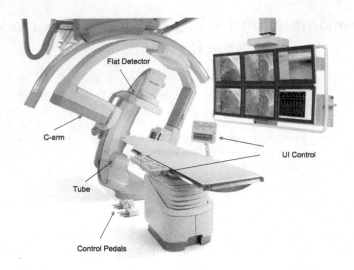

Fig. 1. Interventional X-ray system

In order to support the development and usage of precise interface specifications we proposed a framework named ComMA (Component Modeling and Analysis). ComMA enables model-based engineering of high-tech systems by formalizing interface specifications. It provides a family of domain-specific languages (DSLs) that integrates existing techniques from formal behavioural and time modeling and is easily extensible. The most important analysis tool in ComMA allows monitoring and checking of component executions against interface specifications. The monitoring can be performed for already existing logs with execution traces or by monitoring executions at runtime.

While developing ComMA and its monitoring capabilities we used the *industry-as-laboratory* approach [12]. This means that tools and techniques are developed in close interaction (e.g. on a daily basis) with real industrial projects. A similar approach has been applied in an earlier industry-as-lab project on runtime awareness [2].

The first version of ComMA was a basic domain-specific language and a few generators for glue code, visualisations and very basic monitoring. This provided immediate benefits for the industrial projects and created interest for further applications. It also led to a stream of feature requests which have been incorporated based on user priorities. For instance, inspired by the usefulness of monitoring timing constraints, users asked for monitoring of advanced data constraints. We also added document generation based on requests of users. By gradually increasing the number of generators and features, we incrementally add more value to the projects using the ComMA framework.

As part of our industry-as-lab approach, we had to refactor ComMA based on new insights we obtained while executing industrial cases. In addition, we refactored the framework to improve maintainability. The initial monolithic language has been split into a composition of DSLs for types, expressions, state machines, etc.

The initial component monitoring supported checking of conformance between interfaces and their implementations and checking timing constraints expressed as rules. The rules give the admissible time intervals between events in different contexts. Apart from timing behaviour, users were also interested in monitoring data values. For example, client requests for a given system mode with certain parameters have to match the parameters communicated later by the system. We developed a new small DSL for expressing only data constraints. It is known from the literature on runtime verification that time information in the form of event timestamps can be treated in the same way as the data values carried by events; they are just data fields associated to events. This observation motivated the unification of data and timing constraints into an underlying generic language which is used to generate the monitoring infrastructure. These changes in the DSLs infrastructure were executed iteratively and remained invisible for the users. Users could keep using the basic front-end notations for data and timing constraints and stayed isolated from the changes in the implementation.

The main contribution of this paper is the description of the syntax and semantics of the generic constraints language. In addition, we also present how the two existing languages for time and data constraints relate to the generic language.

This paper is organized as follows. Section 2 gives an overview of the related work. An industrial case that provided a motivation and insights for our work is presented in Sect. 3. Examples from the case are used to explain the DSLs in ComMA (Sect. 4), and the support for monitoring time and data constraints (Sect. 5). Section 6 presents the syntax and semantics of the generic constraints language. Section 7 concludes the paper.

2   Related Work

Runtime verification [7,9] is a technique for monitoring the behaviour of software during its execution and checking if the behaviour conforms to a specification. The literature contains a large number of methods to annotate programs with specifications and the use of these annotations for runtime checks. Examples are design by contract in Eiffel [10] and the Java Modeling Language (JML) [4]. As a unifying approach, monitor-oriented programming [6] supports runtime monitoring by integrating specifications in the program via logical annotations, where a particular specification formalism can be added as a logic plug-in. Actual monitoring code is automatically synthesized from these annotations and integrated at appropriate places in the program, according to user-defined configuration attributes of the monitor.

The approach of ComMA is independent of the hardware or software implementation of a component. In our working context, the implementation of many third-party components is not directly available. The properties are specified over traces of component executions. Traces can be obtained via sniffing the network traffic or from logs (if available).

Properties checked during monitoring can be expressed in various formalisms. Examples are logic formulas, automata, and context free grammars. The constraint languages in ComMA are inspired by constructs available in Linear Temporal Logic (LTL) and its real-time extension Metric Temporal Logic (MTL) [11]. Furthermore, our framework follows the ideas behind the languages RuleR and Eagle [1] with respect to formulating properties as a set of rules and it adapts the algorithms from the same work.

Interface signatures and behaviour can be defined in general-purpose modeling languages like UML and SysML [8] for which many commercial tools exist. Engineers usually need only a subset of these rich languages. In addition, tools require tailoring for a given problem area via profiles which is in effect a domain-specific extension. ComMA provides a set of standalone DSLs instead of extending an existing modeling language.

3 Industrial Case

With the interventional X-ray systems of Philips, X-ray movies of a patient's body can be made in real-time while executing a medical procedure. An example procedure is placing a stent into the aorta of a patient. The physician uses the system to navigate the stent through the patient's arteries to the target position. The arteries can be made visible by injecting a contrast medium. The physician positions the X-ray beam with respect to the patient in such a way that she/he can see the region of interest. This can be done by moving the table on which the patient lies, and by moving the C-arm which holds the X-ray generator and the X-ray detector. The table and C-arm can be maneuvered by means of a user interface.

A patient table has multiple axes of movement that can be controlled by a software interface. An example is the vertical movement that changes the height of the table with respect to the table base. During movements, the patient and the table can get in close proximity to the C-arm. This is controlled by safety mechanisms to prevent hitting the patient. Examples of these mechanisms are limiting the movement speed when the distance between table and C-arm is reduced and to stop all movements when the communication between table and system is lost.

Figure 1 shows an example of the system with a table developed at Philips. Besides Philips tables, the system also supports tables of third-party vendors. We applied ComMA to model a new interface between the interventional X-ray system and a third-party table. The communication between the system and the table uses an Ethernet connection and a proprietary protocol. The table has its own User Interface (UI) that can be used to change the positions. The X-ray system is treated as another UI for the table. From the perspective of the X-ray system this means that movements can originate from other sources. Thus, the system needs to observe the position of the table and to act when the distance between table and C-arm becomes too close.

Table movements are controlled by a joystick. The joystick has to be constantly leaned to a certain direction during the movement until the target position is reached. If the joystick is released the movement stops. While moving, the table notifies the system about its position and the movement status (moving, position is reached, position is not reached).

ComMA was used to model the software interface of the table by defining the signatures of the messages and the behaviour of the table by means of a state machine. In addition, several time and data constraints related to safety mechanisms were specified and checked.

In the following sections we explain the ComMA framework with a focus on support for monitoring time and data constraints. The presentation is based on simplified examples derived from the industrial case.

4   Overview of ComMA

4.1   ComMA Framework: Languages and Tools

The ComMA framework is based on a family of DSLs and allows users to specify the interface of a server towards its clients by two main ingredients:

- The interface signature, consisting of groups of synchronous & asynchronous calls and asynchronous notifications.
- The interface behaviour which is defined by:
  - State machines that describe the allowed interactions between clients and server, e.g., the allowed order of calls of clients and the allowed notifications by the server in any state.
  - Constraints on data and time, such as the allowed response time, the periodicity of notifications, and data relations between the parameters of subsequent calls.

Based on a ComMA model, the framework supports a number of generators, as shown in Fig. 2:

- Visualization and documentation. ComMA generates PlantUML[1] files that visualize state machines. In addition, constraints can be intuitively represented as annotated UML sequence diagrams. Also MS Word documents that are compliant with the company standard can be generated, based on the M2Doc framework[2]. This transformation extracts definitions and comments from models and inserts them in a document template. This process also utilizes the diagrams obtained from state machines and constraint rules.
- Interface proxy code. Interface signatures can be transformed to interface proxy code (C++ and C#) that can be incorporated in the company-specific platform for transparent component deployment.

---

[1] http://plantuml.com/.
[2] https://github.com/ObeoNetwork/M2Doc.

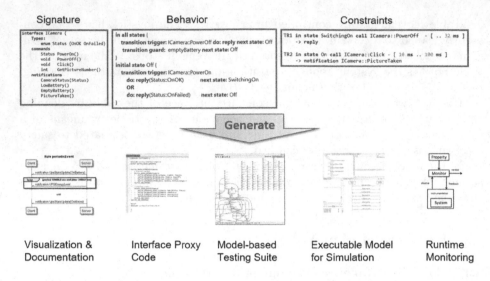

Fig. 2. Overview of ComMA and generators

- Model-based testing. Based on the state machines, models can be generated for various model-based testing tools such as SpecExplorer[3]. This allows test generation and on-line testing.
- Simulation. Simulation of a model helps in receiving an early feedback and detecting errors. State machine models are transformed to POOSL programs (Parallel Object Oriented Specification Language) [14]. Engineers can use the step-by-step visual execution facilities of POOSL[4].
- Runtime monitoring. A modified version of the transformation to POOSL produces an executable monitor for runtime verification. This feature is explained in details in Sect. 5.

4.2 Specifying Component Interfaces with ComMA

ComMA provides a DSL for defining interface signatures. Here we present a simplified version of the interface of the operating table.

```
interface ITable{
    types
    enum Status {PosReached PosNotReached InMove}

    commands
    bool start
    void stop
```

---

[3] https://www.microsoft.com/en-us/research/project/model-based-testing-with-spec
explorer/.

[4] http://poosl.esi.nl/.

```
    signals
    alive
    moveVertical(int moveId, int pos)

    notifications
    verticalPosition(int pos, Status moveStatus)
}
```

We distinguish between two types of calls: *commands* that may be called synchronously and always reply a result and asynchronous *signals*. Notifications are asynchronous messages sent from a server to the clients. Commands, signals, replies and notifications are referred to as *events*.

The interface above defines commands for starting and stopping the table operational mode and a signal for moving the table in the vertical axis. Every movement has an unique identifier (parameter *moveId*) and a target position (parameter *pos*). The table can notify the system about its current position in the vertical axis and the movement status. The status is encoded as a value of an enumeration and denotes if the table is moving, has reached the target position or the movement is interrupted and the target position is not reached. Once the table is operational, the X-ray system has to send periodic signals to it to indicate that the client side is alive. A signal is either a move request or an alive signal (if no move is needed).

In ComMA, the behaviour of interfaces is specified by state machines. A state machine is associated with at least one provided interface. Commands and signals are triggers for state transitions. The machines have disjoint sets of transition triggers and may share variables. Only one transition can be fired at a given moment across all machines. The DSL allows only flat machines: nested states are forbidden. All state transitions must be observable: either a transition is triggered by a command/signal or the transition effect is observable, for example, by sending a notification.

The following listing is a simplified specification of the externally visible behaviour of the table interface.

```
machine Main provides ITable {

variables
int currentMoveId

init
currentMoveId := 0

initial state Inactive {
  transition trigger: start
    do: reply(true) next state: PositionReached
    OR
    do: reply(false) next state: Inactive
}
```

```
state PositionReached {
  transition trigger: moveVertical(int moveId, int target)
    guard: moveId != currentMoveId
    do: currentMoveId := moveId
  next state: Moving

  transition trigger: moveVertical(int moveId, int target)
    guard: moveId == currentMoveId
  next state: PositionReached

  transition trigger: alive next state: PositionReached

  transition
    do: verticalPosition(*, Status::PosReached)
  next state: PositionReached

  transition trigger: stop do: reply
  next state: Inactive
}

state PositionNotReached {
...
}

state Moving {
  transition trigger: moveVertical(int moveId, int target)
    do: currentMoveId := moveId
  next state: Moving

  transition
    do: verticalPosition(*, Status::PosReached)
  next state: PositionReached

  transition
    do: verticalPosition(*, Status::PosNotReached)
  next state: PositionNotReached

  transition
    do: verticalPosition(*, Status::InMove)
  next state: Moving
}
}
```

The command *start* tries to activate the table. The result is indicated in the return value. If the activation is successful, the table assumes a reached position state. It can receive a move request with a given identifier (signal *moveVertical* with a positive integer as identifier and a target position). If it is a new move request, the table starts moving (represented by state *Moving*). The table is moving as long as it receives move requests. The movement status is continuously reported via notifications *verticalPosition*. The listing shows three different transitions that send *verticalPosition* as a notification: one for each possible status. The notation '*' denotes a value that is unknown in the state machine. The state *PositionNotReached* is not elaborated. It is similar to state *PositionReached*.

If the table stops receiving the signal *moveVertical*, the movement is interrupted and a notification for 'position not reached' status is sent. The machine then moves to *PositionNotReached* state. The machine above does not capture this logic. It just states that at any moment a transition to a non-moving state is possible. The described behaviour is captured in a timing constraint explained in the next section.

5 Monitoring of Time and Data Constraints

Issues at system level are often traced back to issues related to the conformance of components (possibly supplied by a third party) to their interface specifications. Many issues of this kind are manifested during the interaction of several components and it is difficult to detect them if a component is tested in isolation. Monitoring and checking component interactions can reveal the problems at an earlier phase and help in analyzing logs harvested from systems in the field. We applied available runtime verification techniques (mainly inspired by [1]) to support specification and monitoring of interface behaviour and constraints on timing and data.

5.1 General Scheme for Component Monitoring

Generally, runtime verification is a technique for checking system behaviour against a property during the execution of the system. The general scheme [7] is given in Fig. 3.

The property may be given in a formal specification language (automata, logic formula, grammar), as a set of rules or a program. A monitor is derived

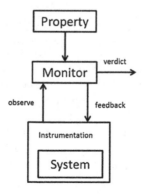

Fig. 3. General scheme of runtime verification

from a set of properties. The task of the monitor is to observe the execution of the system and to produce a verdict, that is, a statement if the observation satisfies the properties. The observation may be a series of system states or a series of input and output events. Monitoring is executed either step by step along with the system execution or over a log that contains the observations.

Figure 4 shows how this general approach is applied in ComMA. The behavioral model of the interfaces (state machines, timing and data rules) plays the role of properties. The monitor processes events observed during component executions. Currently the events are obtained in two ways: by logging during executions or by monitoring network traffic when the component is deployed on the company-specific middleware. It should be noted that currently the execution trace is checked after it is finished, that is, the check does not happen at runtime. The implementation of the monitor, however, is agnostic about the exact moment when events are supplied (during or after component execution). Monitoring at runtime can be performed if instrumentation is applied to components or to the middleware layer.

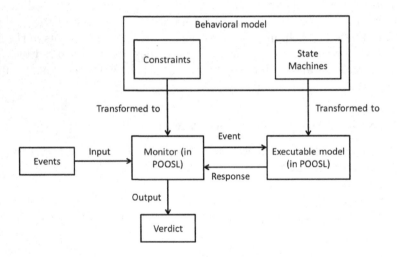

Fig. 4. Monitoring in ComMA

The monitor is a POOSL program that is partially synthesized from the constraint rules. It receives the events in the execution trace and sends them to an executable model (also a POOSL program) derived from the state machines. The state machine responds with events that are compared to the events in the trace. The monitor also checks if the constraints hold for the trace. Verdicts can be errors and warnings. Errors are violations of the state machine logic. Warnings are violations of constraints. Errors stop the monitoring process, after a warning the monitoring continues.

In the following subsections we elaborate on the support for specifying and monitoring constraints.

5.2   Timing Constraints

The first type of constraints are timing constraints defined as timing rules. They give the admissible intervals between events in different contexts. There are four rule types.

Interval rules constrain the allowed time interval for observing an event if a given preceding event was observed. The example rule named *timeForReply* states that if the command *stop* is observed then the reply must be observed between 10 and 20 ms after the command. The rule is checked on the first occurrence of reply after the command. Before checking timing rules, static checks ensure that every command is properly matched by a reply. Pairs of commands/replies are reconstructed in the order of their handling by the component.

```
timeForReply
command stop -[10.0 ms .. 20.0 ms] -> reply
```

The second rule type is called conditional interval. It states that if two events are observed without observing the first event in between then the interval between them lies within a certain boundary. The next example states that the interval between *start* and a positive reply is 30 ms. The rule will not be applied if the reply is false.

```
intervalBetweenEvents
command start
and
reply(true)
-> [ .. 30.0 ms] between events
```

The third rule type allows specifications of periodic events. The following rule states that after starting the system the connection should be kept alive by sending signals every 100 ms. It is also possible to specify a jitter for the expected period.

```
continousCommunication
reply(true) to command start then
any signal with period 100.0 ms jitter 10.0 ms
until
command stop
```

The fourth rule type allows stating that if a certain event is observed then another event must be absent during a given interval after the observation. The four types of rules can be combined in groups that form a scenario. Scenarios and the rule for absence of an event are illustrated in the following example. It is based on the safety mechanisms implemented in the table control. One of them states that if a move request is delayed for more than 200 ms during movement, the table must stop moving. The time for stopping after detecting the delay is also constrained. The scenario specifies this constraint. The first rule acts as a precondition: it detects if a move request is absent within 200 ms after receiving the previous move request. If this happens then the table must stop within 1 s after the delay is detected. The stop is manifested by the notification *verticalPosition* with the corresponding status value.

```
group intervalForStopping
in state Moving signal moveVertical
-> absent signal moveVertical in [.. 200.0 ms]
- [.. 1000.0 ms] ->
notification verticalPosition(*, Status::PosNotReached)
end group
```

This rule illustrates also the possibility to specify state information in timing rules. The rule will be triggered only if the signals are received in state *Moving*. This is possible because the rules are evaluated over events that are already accepted by the state machine, that is, state information is available.

5.3   Data Constraints

Apart from detecting delayed requests, other safety mechanisms in our industrial case check the distance that the table is allowed to move after detecting the absence of move requests. The distance should not exceed a certain value. This is schematically given below by showing the expected sequence of events when the table stops if move requests are no longer received:

```
verticalPosition(X, InMove)
moveVertical //The last moveVertical
... no more moveVertical signals ...
...
verticalPosition(Y, PosNotReached)
```

In order to check the distance we need to identify the last reported vertical position (say X) in the *verticalPosition* notification just before the last *moveVertical* signal. The fact that the table stops is indicated by a notification *verticalPosition* with status PosNotReached and position Y. The absolute value of Y-X must not exceed a certain limit.

We introduced a simple language for specifying data constraints. At an intuitive level, the meaning of a data constraint rule is: if a certain sequence of events is observed then the observed data values must satisfy a given condition. The monitoring algorithm should allow the observed data values to be bound to variables and then used in conditions. The specification of an expected event sequence can be done by using a regular expression-like notation. It should be possible to assert both the presence and the absence of events.

The following example shows the constraint expressed in the data constraints language.

```
stoppingDistance //name of the constraint
notification verticalPosition(X, Status::InMove);
in state Moving signal moveVertical;
no [signal moveVertical]
```

```
until
notification verticalPosition(Y, Status::PosNotReached)
where abs(X-Y) <= 100
```

The rule is checked as follows. Given a sequence of observed events, the following sub-sequence is searched:

- notification *verticalPosition* with status InMove. The reported position (as the first parameter) is kept as value of variable X;
- signal *moveVertical* that follows immediately after the previously observed notification;
- a sequence of events that do not contain *moveVertical* and the event specified in the **until** clause. In this way we capture the fact that move requests are no longer received;
- notification *verticalPosition* with status PosNotReached. This event marks the end of the sequence to be matched. The position is kept in variable Y.

If such a sequence in the trace is detected then the condition in the **where** clause is checked. It states that the distance should be less than 100 units. If the sequence is not detected then the rule precondition is not fulfilled and the rule holds for the given trace.

Considering the implementation options for checking the data constraints, several factors played a role. First, we were aware that time and data constraints can be treated uniformly: timestamps are just data fields associated to events. This brought the option to replace the existing dedicated engine for checking time rules with a more generic engine applicable to both types of constraints. Second, there exist formalisms for expressing properties used in runtime monitoring. However, these formalisms are complex and it is preferable to shield the engineers from directly using complex notations.

We decided to define a generic constraints language and engine while keeping two separate 'surface' languages: for time rules and for data constraints. Specifications in these languages are transparently translated to the underlying generic language. In this way, the surface languages can be kept simple and easily extensible if needed. Extensions would require only a syntactical translation to the more expressive generic language and no changes in the engine.

The language for generic constraints is the main contribution of this paper and is explained in the following section.

6   Language for Generic Constraints

The main construct in our solution allows specifying patterns for sequences of timestamped events observed in execution traces. Sequence patterns (called here just *sequence*) are used to construct formulas which are evaluated during monitoring.

A sequence is a concatenation of steps. Each step matches one or more observed events in a trace. There are three kinds of steps: event selector, a disjunction of event selectors, and two until operators (weak and strong) inspired by the similar constructs in LTL. Informally, the matching process starts from the first step in a sequence and tries to match it with the first event in a given trace. If successful, the process continues with the next steps that are matched against the remaining events in the trace. During this process free variables in the pattern are bound to matched values and become available in the next steps. The following example shows the formulation of the *stoppingDistance* data constraint rule of Sect. 5.3 in the generic language.

```
stoppingDistance
<t1, in state Moving
     notification verticalPosition(X, InMove)>;
<t2, in state Moving signal moveVertical>;
<t3, not [signal moveVertical]>
until
<t4, notification verticalPosition(Y, PosNotReached)>
where
abs(X-Y) <= 100
```

This rule has a name and a formula. The formula specifies a sequence (the part before the **where** keyword) and a condition that uses variables in the sequence (the part after **where**). The main difference with the syntax of the same rule expressed in the data constraints language is the presence of timestamp variables ($t1$, $t2$, ...).

The first step in the example sequence is an event selector. It has a variable named $t1$ that is bound to the event timestamp. The **until** construct with a general form *Selector*1 **until** *Selector*2 matches a sequence of events in which the last event matches *Selector*2 and all the preceding events match *Selector*1. As can be seen in the example, event patterns can be negated. Selectors may also have a boolean condition that is evaluated if the event pattern matches (this is shown in the following examples). The remaining part of this section defines the syntax and semantics of the generic constraints language.

6.1 Language Syntax

The syntax rules of the language are given in Table 1. In these rules some nonterminals are left undefined: S is a set of states, *Cond* is a Boolean expression defined by the ComMA grammar, *Var* denotes a variable, and $\bar{P}$ (event parameters) is a vector of variables and constants of types supported by ComMA. States, conditions and parameters can be omitted. For simplicity, the type of the event (command, signal, etc.) is skipped and **in state** is abbreviated to **in**. We assume that every variable appears at most once in all event selectors. The usage of variables in conditions has to be well-formed: no forward variable references are allowed.

From the rules it can be seen that event selectors have two forms. The first one was already explained by the example rule *stoppingDistance*. The second one has an extra variable called *occurrence counter*. The value of the variable is

Table 1. Syntax of the generic constraints language

Formula	$F ::= Seq \mid Seq \textbf{ and } Cond \mid Seq \textbf{ cf } F \mid \textbf{not } F \mid F \textbf{ or } F$
Sequence	$Seq ::= Step \mid Step \textbf{ until } Step \mid Step \textbf{ wuntil } Step \mid Seq \; ; \; Seq$
Step	$Step ::= ES \mid ES \textbf{ or } ... \textbf{ or } ES$
Event Selector	$ES ::= \langle Var, E, Cond \rangle \mid \langle Var, Var, E, Cond \rangle$
Event Pattern	$E ::= \textbf{in } S \; EvDes(\bar{P}) \mid \textbf{not } [\textbf{in } S \; EvDes(\bar{P})]$
Event Designator	$EvDes ::= eventName \mid *$

incremented every time the event selector is successfully matched in a sequence. Consider the following example that uses an occurrence counter:

```
<t1, i, in state s A>
or
<t2, not[in state s A]>
until
<t3, B>
```

If this sequence is evaluated against a trace, the counter i will be incremented every time an event A is observed in state s until event B is observed. The usage of counters is exemplified further in the context of periodic time rules.

Operator **cf** stands for *conditional follow* and expresses a common case in which the match of a sequence is a precondition for checking a formula over the remaining part of the trace. For example, the formula:

```
<t1, A>;
<t2, not[in state s B]>
until
<t3, C>
cf
<t4, D>
```

is used to check if all sequences of events that start with A, end with C and do not contain event B occurring in state s, are immediately followed by event D.

Some useful logical operations are defined as the following abbreviations:

- F1 **and** F2 $\equiv$ **not** (**not** F1 **or not** F2)
- F1 **implies** F2 $\equiv$ **not** F1 **or** F2
- Seq **where** Cond $\equiv$ **not** Seq **or** (Seq **and** Cond)

6.2 Language Semantics

Formulas are evaluated on traces of events. An event Ev is a tuple $\langle t, s, e(\bar{D}) \rangle$ where

- t is a non-negative real number denoting the timestamp of the event. Timestamps form an increasing sequence;

- s is the state in which the event occurs. The event occurs in exactly one state due to the constraints on the state machine syntax and semantics;
- e is event name and $\bar{D} = (d_1, \ldots, d_n)$ is a possibly empty vector of constants (event parameters).

A trace is obtained from a monitored sequence of timestamped events that satisfies the state machine behaviour. The process of monitoring adds state information to the events. Trace T is a sequence of events $Ev_0, Ev_1, \ldots, Ev_i, \ldots$. For an integer i ≥ 0, we denote $T^i = Ev_i, Ev_{i+1}, \ldots$ and $T(i) = Ev_i = \langle t_i, s_i, e_i(\bar{D}_i) \rangle$.

Bindings of variables in event selectors are captured in environments. We define an environment $\Gamma = \{[v_1 \mapsto d_1], \ldots\}$ as a set of *mappings* from variables to values. $\Gamma[\Gamma']$ is the familiar operation of updating Γ with the mappings in Γ' and $\Gamma(v)$ gives the value of v in Γ.

For an environment Γ and a boolean expression $Cond$, we denote $\Gamma \models Cond$ if $Cond$ evaluates to true for the valuations in Γ.

When a sequence is matched in a trace, the environment with bound variables and the remaining part of the trace are propagated to the possible next steps. This is formalized as a partial function $Cont : Trace \times Env \times Seq \to Trace \times Env$. Env is a set of environments and $Trace$ is a set of traces.

We define a satisfaction relation between events, environments and event patterns as follows:

- $(\langle t, s, e(\bar{D}) \rangle, \Gamma) \models \mathbf{in}\ S\ EvDes(\bar{P})$ iff $EvDes = e$ or $EvDes = *$, $s \in S$, for every constant c_i in $\bar{P}$, $c_i = d_i$ and for the list of variables $v_1 \ldots v_k$ in $\bar{P}$ we have $\Gamma = \{[v_1 \mapsto d_1], \ldots, [v_k \mapsto d_k]\}$
- $(\langle t, s, e(\bar{D}) \rangle, \varnothing) \models \mathbf{not}[\mathbf{in}\ S\ EvDes(\bar{P})]$ iff for all Γ, $(\langle t, s, e(\bar{D}) \rangle, \Gamma) \not\models \mathbf{in}\ S\ EvDes(\bar{P})$

If the set of states S and parameters $\bar{P}$ are not used in the event pattern, the corresponding checks are skipped.

The semantics of formulas is defined as satisfaction relation between formulas, traces and environments. We start with the semantics of sequences.

- $(T, \Gamma) \models \langle Var, E, Cond \rangle$ iff $(T(0), \Gamma_m) \models E$ and $\Gamma' \models Cond$, where $\Gamma' = \Gamma[\Gamma_m][Var \mapsto t_0]$
  $Cont(T, \Gamma, \langle Var, E, Cond \rangle) = \langle T^1, \Gamma' \rangle$
- $(T, \Gamma) \models \langle Var_1, Var_2, E, Cond \rangle$ iff $(T, \Gamma) \models \langle Var_1, E, Cond \rangle$
  $Cont(T, \Gamma, \langle Var_1, Var_2, E, Cond \rangle) = \langle T^1, \Gamma'[Var_2 \mapsto \Gamma(Var_2) + 1] \rangle$ where $Cont(T, \Gamma, \langle Var_1, E, Cond \rangle) = \langle T^1, \Gamma' \rangle$. Every occurrence counter takes initial value 0 before a formula is evaluated on a trace.
- $(T, \Gamma) \models ES_1\ \mathbf{or} \ldots \mathbf{or}\ ES_n$ iff there exist i such that $1 \leq i \leq n$, $(T, \Gamma) \models ES_i\ Cont(T, \Gamma, ES_1\ \mathbf{or} \ldots \mathbf{or}\ ES_n) = \langle T^1, \Gamma[\bigcup_k (\Gamma_k \setminus \Gamma)] \rangle$, for all k such that $(T, \Gamma) \models ES_k$ and $Cont(T, \Gamma, ES_k) = \langle T^1, \Gamma_k \rangle$

It should be noted that $\bigcup_k (\Gamma_k \setminus \Gamma)$ cannot contain two different bindings for the same variable because a variable can occur at most once in all ES_k.

– $(T, \Gamma) \models Step_1$ **until** $Step_2$ iff there exist i such that $i \geq 0$, $(T^i, \Gamma^i) \models Step_2$ and for each k, $0 \leq k < i$, $(T^k, \Gamma^k) \models Step_1$ and $(T^k, \Gamma^k) \not\models Step_2$ where environments are defined as:
  • $\Gamma^0 = \Gamma$
  • $Cont(T^k, \Gamma^k, Step_1) = \langle T^{k+1}, \Gamma^{k+1} \rangle$ for all k, $0 \leq k < i$ $Cont(T, \Gamma, Step_1$ **until** $Step_2) = Cont(T^i, \Gamma^i, Step_2)$
– $(T, \Gamma) \models Step_1$ **wuntil** $Step_2$ iff:
  • $(T, \Gamma) \models Step_1$ **until** $Step_2$
    $Cont(T, \Gamma, Step_1$ **wuntil** $Step_2) = Cont(T, \Gamma, Step_1$ **until** $Step_2)$
  or
  • $(T^i, \Gamma^i) \models Step_1$, for all $i \geq 0$ and Γ^i defined as in the case of **until**.
    $Cont$ is undefined
– $(T, \Gamma) \models Seq_1; Seq_2$ iff $(T, \Gamma) \models Seq_1$, $Cont(T, \Gamma, Seq_1)$ is defined and has value $\langle T^i, \Gamma' \rangle$ for some $i \geq 1$, and $(T^i, \Gamma') \models Seq_2$
    $Cont(T, \Gamma, Seq_1; Seq_2) = Cont(T^i, \Gamma', Seq_2)$
– $(T, \Gamma) \models Seq$ **and** $Cond$ iff $(T, \Gamma) \models Seq$, $Cont(T, \Gamma, Seq)$ is defined and has value $\langle T^i, \Gamma' \rangle$ and $\Gamma' \models Cond$
– $(T, \Gamma) \models Seq$ **cf** F iff
  • $(T, \Gamma) \models$ **not** Seq
  or
  • $(T, \Gamma) \models Seq$, $Cont(T, \Gamma, Seq) = \langle T^i, \Gamma' \rangle$ is defined and $(T^i, \Gamma') \models F$
– $(T, \Gamma) \models$ **not** F if $(T, \Gamma) \not\models F$
– $(T, \Gamma) \models F_1$ **or** F_2 if $(T, \Gamma) \models F_1$ or $(T, \Gamma) \models F_2$

We state that a formula F **holds** in a trace T and an initial environment Γ if for every i ≥ 0, $(T^i, \Gamma) \models F$. The initial environment gives 0 as a value of all occurrence counter variables. For the other variables the user can supply an initial value or a default value is assumed.

During monitoring, time and data constraints are translated to formulas in the presented generic language. The translation is automatic and transparent to the users. Hence, the users do not need to work directly with the generic formulas which are often more verbose and more difficult to grasp than the source constraints. We first show how time rules are translated.

6.3   Translation of Timing Constraints

In this section we show how different types of timing rules are translated into formulas in the generic constraints language.

Timing rules use a simplified event selectors of the form **in** $Se(\bar{P})$, where $\bar{P}$ is a possibly empty vector of constants. The set of states S and the parameters can be omitted. The translation of event selectors in timing rules to the selectors in the generic language is trivial and will not be discussed. Selectors will be given in capital letters A, B,...

Interval Rule. The general form is:

```
A -[p..q] -> B
```

A and *B* are selectors, [p..q] denotes a time interval with an obvious constraint $0 \leq p < q$. q may be infinity. The interval rule is translated to the following formula:

```
<t1, A>
cf
<t2, not[B]>
until
<t3, B, (t3-t1) in [p..q]>
```

The formula states that if a match of *A* is observed then there must be an occurrence of event that matches *B* and the first such occurrence is in the interval $[p, q]$.

Conditional Interval Rule. The rule gives two events as a premise of the rule and an expected interval.

```
A and B -> [p..q] between events
```

The rule is translated to:

```
<t1, A>; <t2, not[A]> until <t3, B>
where (t3-t1) in [p..q]
```

Absence of Event. The rule specifies an event that is a condition for not observing a follow up event in a certain interval.

```
A -> absent B in [p..q]
```

The corresponding formula is:

```
not
(<t1, A>;
<t2, *, t2-t1 <= q>
until
<t3, B, (t3-t1) in [p..q]>)
```

Periodic Event Rule. The rule specifies a triggering event *A* as a condition for a periodic observation of *B* with a period *p* and jitter *j* until a stop event *C* is observed.

```
A then B with period p and jitter j until C
```

The meaning of the rule is that if an event *A* is observed at time *t* then the i-th occurrence of event *B* after *A* and before *C* must be in the time interval $[t + i * p - j, \ t + i * p + j]$. The formula for this rule is:

```
<t, A>
cf
(<t1, i, B, t1 in [t + (i + 1)*p -j, t + (i + 1)*p + j]>
or
<t2, not[B], t2 <= t + (i + 1)*p + j>)
wuntil
<t3, C, t3 <= t + (i + 1)*p + j>
```

The rule uses an event selector with occurrence counter i. If an event A is observed then we check if the formula after 'cf' is satisfied for the events following A. The timestamp of A is bound to the variable t. There are three cases:

- we observe event B with timestamp $t1$. The condition of the first step in the disjunction checks if $t1$ is in the allowed interval. If it is not, the formula is not satisfied. If the condition is true (i.e. the occurrence is in the expected interval) the value of i is incremented and used to calculate the time interval of the eventual next occurrence of B;
- we observe an event different from B and C. In this case, the second component of the disjunction matches the event and we check the condition. If the condition is false this means that after the last occurrence of B we have not observed an event B and we have just observed an event that is already after the allowed interval. Therefore the formula is not satisfied;
- we observe event C. The condition checks if C is observed within the expected time upper bound for the event B. If the condition is false we have the situation in the previous case: B is not found in the expected interval and we have an event after this interval.

The semantics of the rule admits the case when C is never observed. **wuntil** is used to handle this.

The translation of periodic time rules illustrates that the resulting generic formulas may be more complex and more difficult to read than the original time constraint. We recall that users do not work with generic formulas directly. They use the more compact syntax of the surface languages.

Group Time Rule. This rule type allows specifying a rule that is a precondition for a series of interval rules thus allowing a scenario of several events. We will only show the case when an absence of event may be followed by other events with given time intervals. An example was shown in the previous section. The general form is:

```
group
A -> absent B in [0 .. p]
- [p1 .. q1] -> C
- [p2 .. q2] -> D
...
end group
```

This rule is translated to the formula:

```
<t1, A>;
<t2, not[B], (t2-t1) <= p>
wuntil
<t3, *, (t3-t1) > p>

implies

<t4, A>; <t5, *> until <t6, C, t6-t4-p in [p1..q1]>;
<t7, not[D]> until <t8, D, t8-t6 in [p2..q2]>;
....
```

6.4   Translation of Data Constraints

The grammar for data constraints rules is in Table 2. This language is as a subset of the generic constraints language following the same semantics.

Table 2. Syntax of data constraints language

Data Constraint DConstraint ::=	*Seq* **where** *Cond*
Sequence	*Seq* ::= *Step* | *Step* **until** *Step* | *Seq* ; *Seq*
Step	*Step* ::= **in** *S EvDes*($\bar{P}$) | **not** [**in** *S EvDes*($\bar{P}$)]
Event Designator	*EvDes* ::= *eventName* | *

6.5   Implementation Considerations

The definition of semantics for the generic constraints allows a proof that the initial semantics of time rules is preserved by the translation to the generic language. Generally, the development of the formalization enabled better understanding of the subtle details and greatly supported the software implementation.

An important aspect of the implementation is the fact that in a practical setting we deal with finite traces whereas the semantics of the formulas is given over infinite traces. This affects the evaluation of formulas. Consider an interval timing rule. In the trace we may observe the first event and according to the rule we must observe the second event within certain period of time. If the trace ends before passing this period and no event is observed the rule evaluates to false. However, we cannot conclude if the second event will never appear because the information is not complete (monitoring has stopped). For situations like this we do not give a yes/no verdict for the rule. Instead, a warning is produced that states the rule has not been fully evaluated due to the termination of monitoring. As an alternative, the semantics can be defined for finite traces. This is a subject of future investigation.

6.6   Application of Monitoring on the Industrial Case

Component monitoring was applied during the development of the client software for the operating table. The examples shown here are simplifications of the actual models. The real model and constraints are more complex and take into account the complete interface and its behaviour. Several issues were revealed. For instance, movement requests with negative identifiers were sent by the client and accepted by the component. This was detected as a violation of the model and corrections were implemented in the software. The availability of explicit timing constraints allowed to experiment with different values for the allowed delays. The experiments revealed situations in which some events occur earlier than expected.

Generally, the process of modeling the intended behaviour of the interface based on textual documentation supported the engineers to explore cases in which the documentation was missing or the interpretation of the information was not clear. We also faced situations when the data constraints language was not expressive enough. In these cases, the constraints were successfully expressed in the generic language.

7   Concluding Remarks

The availability of precise component interface specifications enables early detection of defects and ultimately supports the development of software with higher quality. In this paper we presented ComMA, a framework for interface behaviour specification and focused on the support for runtime monitoring of timing and data constraints. The DSLs in ComMA integrate techniques and results from different research areas and provide a single entry point for engineers to specify and develop component interfaces.

The development of ComMA follows the industry-as-laboratory approach. DSLs are based on the concrete needs of the engineers and evolve following these needs. The developed languages are not business-specific and are not restricted to the medical domain. They are aimed at problems that are found in other domains as well and utilize general techniques thus making the framework easily generalizable.

Acknowledgements. The anonymous reviewers are thanked for useful suggestions for improvement. We would like to thank Dirk-Jan Swagerman for his support and the collaborating teams at Philips for constructive feedback.

The second author is grateful to Ed Brinksma for the very pleasant collaboration when Ed was the scientific director of the Embedded Systems Institute (currently TNO-ESI). With his very broad knowledge he was able to discuss any topic with experts and he created an excellent environment for productive industry-as-lab projects. Moreover, Ed is thanked for the stimulating role in the career development of the second author.

References

1. Barringer, H., Rydeheard, D.E., Havelund, K.: Rule systems for run-time monitoring: from Eagle to RuleR. In: Sokolsky and Taşıran [13], pp. 111–125

2. Brinksma, E., Hooman, J.: Dependability for high-tech systems: an industry-as-laboratory approach. In: Design, Automation & Test in Europe (DATE 2008), pp. 1226–1231. European Design and Automation Association (EDAA) (2008)

3. Broy, M., Peled, D.A., Kalus, G. (eds.): Engineering Dependable Software Systems. NATO Science for Peace and Security Series, D: Information and Communication Security, vol. 34. IOS Press (2013)

4. Burdy, L., Cheon, Y., Cok, D.R., Ernst, M.D., Kiniry, J.R., Leavens, G.T., Leino, K.R.M., Poll, E.: An overview of JML tools and applications. STTT **7**(3), 212–232 (2005)

5. Cassez, F., Jard, C. (eds.): FORMATS 2008. LNCS, vol. 5215. Springer, Heidelberg (2008)

6. Chen, F., D'Amorim, M., Roşu, G.: A formal monitoring-based framework for software development and analysis. In: Davies, J., Schulte, W., Barnett, M. (eds.) ICFEM 2004. LNCS, vol. 3308, pp. 357–372. Springer, Heidelberg (2004). doi:10.1007/978-3-540-30482-1_31

7. Falcone, Y., Havelund, K., Reger, G.: A tutorial on runtime verification. In: Broy et al. [3], pp. 141–175

8. Kim, H., Fried, D., Menegay, P., Soremekun, G., Oster, C.: Application of integrated modeling and analysis to development of complex systems. Procedia Comput. Sci. **16**, 98–107 (2013)

9. Leucker, M., Schallhart, C.: A brief account of runtime verification. J. Logic Algebraic Program. **78**(5), 293–303 (2009)

10. Meyer, B.: Object-Oriented Software Construction, 1st edn. Prentice-Hall Inc., Upper Saddle River (1988)

11. Ouaknine, J., Worrell, J.: Some recent results in metric temporal logic. In: Cassez and Jard [5], pp. 1–13

12. Potts, C.: Software-engineering research revisited. IEEE Softw. **19**(9), 19–28 (1993)

13. Sokolsky, O., Taşıran, S. (eds.): RV 2007. LNCS, vol. 4839. Springer, Heidelberg (2007)

14. Theelen, B., Florescu, O., Geilen, M., Huang, J., van der Putten, P., Voeten, J.: Software/hardware engineering with the parallel object-oriented specification language. In: Proceedings of MEMOCODE 2007, pp. 139–148. IEEE (2007)

From Lotosphere to Thermosphere

Holger Hermanns[✉]

Saarland University – Computer Science,
Saarland Informatics Campus, Saarbrücken, Germany
`hermanns@cs.uni-saarland.de`

Abstract. This paper reflects on the influential nature of some of the many scientific achievements linked to Ed Brinksma on the occasion of his 60th birthday. We in particular discuss pioneering contributions in the contexts of constraint-oriented specification, model-based testing, and cost-optimal timed reachability, as well as with respect to tools and algorithms for the construction and analysis of systems. We shed light on these achievements by linking a historical perspective with recent and very applied research directly rooted in these contributions.

1 Introduction

The scientific œuvre of Ed Brinksma has many facets. We here focus on four of them, since we consider those to be characteristic cornerstones of his work and because we do feel they have notable impact on the world we live in. We discuss how the pioneering work of Ed Brinksma on (i) model-based testing, on (ii) constraint-oriented specification, and on (iii) cost-optimal reachability analysis is having impact on today's scientific forefront. We conclude by putting them into the greater context of his dedication to (iv) tools and algorithms for the construction and analysis of systems. The selection of facets considered naturally has a personal bias.

2 Model-Based Testing

This section reviews how model-based testing has made its way from the university labs in Twente to customer appliances that assist in everyday life.

Testing Theory. Formal theories for testing were pioneered by Rocco De Nicola and Matthew Hennessy [12], originally motivated by the desire to characterise interesting formalisations of the notion of observable behaviour for transition systems, using an idealised but intuitive formalisation of testing. The first attempts to use this theory for automatic test derivation from formal specifications were made by Ed Brinksma in [7], and further developed in Twente jointly with Kars, Tretmans and coworkers [25]. This work was the nucleus for what is nowadays known as model-based testing, a technique with manifold and very practical applications.

© Springer International Publishing AG 2017
J.-P. Katoen et al. (Eds.): Brinksma Festschrift, LNCS 10500, pp. 357–367, 2017.
DOI: 10.1007/978-3-319-68270-9_18

Input-Output Conformance. Using a formal model as the specification of desired behaviour, *model-based testing* provides means to generate and carry out a suitable set of experiments on the implementation under test (IUT). This is done in an automated manner, with the goal to assert some notion of conformance of the IUT with respect to the model. The most prominent conformance relation in use is *input-output conformance* [24], developed by Jan Tretmans under the guidance of Ed Brinksma. It is defined for systems interacting *synchronously* with their environment, and especially with the model-based testing tool. The models are represented as input-output transitions systems (IOTS). In IOTS the transitions between states have a certain structure: each of them carries a name of an action occurring and an identifier whether it is to be interpreted as an input (stimulus) to the implementation or an output (response) of the implementation (or an internal step).

Test Case Execution. A model-based testing tool performs automated inspection of the possible inputs and outputs while stepping through the states of a model. In each state of such a test case it either provides an input to or records an output from the IUT and accordingly updates its knowledge of what the current state of the model is. The test cases are executed on the actual software, system or device to be tested by translating the abstract transitions to concrete interactions with the IUT. Such a concrete execution of a test case (or of several test cases) ends in a test verdict of the form "pass", respectively "fail". Specifically, whenever an unexpected output of the IUT occurs, i.e. an output which is not foreseen by the current knowledge of the model state, the IUT is refuted with the verdict "fail".

Embedded Energy Managment Software. Embedded control software has become a major driver of industrial innovation, encompassing many critical, and sometimes safety-critical, application domains. A particularly delicate domain is the management of electric power: Embedded power management software has been traced to be the root of unintended and partly dangerous malfunctionings of laptops [27], smart phones [28], smart watches [29], pacemakers [30], and light electric vehicles [31]. The proper handling of electric power by software is obviously intricate. At the same time, electric power is the base commodity needed to innovate formerly all-mechanical systems.

EnergyBus. The ENERGYBUS is an emerging industrial standard for electric power transmission and management tailored to light electric mobility. At its core is an open specification for interoperability of the electrical components of e-bikes and other light electric vehicles, encompassing batteries, chargers, motors, sensors, and the human interface. The specification is based on the CANOPEN field bus. Its development is driven by EnergyBus e.V., an association formed by major industrial stakeholders in the e-bike domain. The ENERGY-BUS specification itself is the nucleus for the joint IEC/ISO standardisation IEC/IS/TC69/JPT61851-3 and European Norm (EN) 50604, aiming at eventually enabling a single charger to be used across all light electric vehicles. By mid 2018, this safety standard is scheduled to become a binding standard in Europe, thereby enabling effective public charging infrastructures for light electric mobility.

Applying Model-Based Testing. State-of-the-art formal methods and tools have been and are being applied in the ENERGYBUS context to assure the general correctness and safety of ENERGYBUS protocol specifications [16], as well as to support implementers of ENERGYBUS in designing correct and safe implementations. For the latter, we have lately developed a tool platform for automated conformance testing of ENERGYBUS implementations against their formal specification. The tool platform is based on the MODEST modelling language [17] and its accompanying MODEST TOOLSET [18], which we extended with support for effective model-based testing against the ENERGYBUS protocol specification.

Asynchrony in Conformance Testing. The ENERGYBUS testing process itself motivated us to extend the supported conformance relation to asynchronous testing, especially in order to eliminate spurious errors. This is because the ENERGYBUS protocol uses CAN-based communication primitives. This setting however violates the synchrony hypothesis, just as many other settings do. In order to nevertheless provide testing facilities we were required to come up with a new and effective approach to model-based testing under asynchrony. By waiving the need to guess the possible output state of the IUT, we indeed manage to reduce the computational effort of the test generation algorithm while preserving soundness and conceptual completeness of the testing procedures. In addition, no restrictions on the specification model need to be imposed [14].

Industrial Uptake and Integration. In order to foster both, the application of formal methods in industry, as well as the quality and interoperability of ENERGYBUS devices reaching the consumer market, we have made our testing platform available to all industrial members of EnergyBus e.V. free-of-charge. This means that ENERGYBUS members can freely operate with the tool, so as to test conformance of their implementations directly against the formal specification of the ENERGYBUS protocol [15]. At the same time, we are ourselves performing tests of prototype devices, as soon as they are made available to us by members of the association. Our contributions in the context of the ENERGYBUS standardization efforts support the entire process from specification, modelling, verification and certification including both traditional test case programming and model-based testing. Specification inaccuracies as well as programming bugs have been found in tested prototype and retail devices. Based on our insights, documentation and implementations have been improved. We are not aware of any other standardization procedure with a similarly tight integration of formal methods.

3   Constraint-Oriented Specification

This section discusses the constraint-oriented specification style, originally coined by Ed Brinksma, in the light of constraints on real-time behaviour. What may look like a surprising angle at first sight, is actually a natural and useful extension.

Behavioural Constraints by Composition. In the late 80ies of the last century, Ed Brinksma introduced *constraint-oriented specification* [8]. This specification style harvests features of multiway parallel composition operators as they are found in process languages such as LOTOS or CSP. Indeed, these operators can "implement" the power of logical conjunction with respect to sets of traces. The constraint-oriented specification style has shown its merits as an extremely useful tool in realistic applications, where it is used to carry out successive steps of logical refinement in specifications [13].

Timing by Composition. One particular manifestation of its usefulness is its adoption to the time domain, in the form of *time constraints*. Together with multiway synchronisation, time constraints can gradually turn a untimed specification into one where certain occurrences of actions are to be delayed. These constraints are added by composition. In the context of timed automata, this idea is implicitly present for instance in some of the modelling work related to the Bang & Olufsen audio/video power control protocol [19]. A full proposal has been developed in [21] in the context of interactive Markov chains [20]. There, it has been used to turn an untimed specification of a plain-old telephone system protocol into a timed specification, solely by the use of composition with time constraints. We here sketch the essence of time constraints recast into the setting of *timed automata* [1].

Timed Automata. Timed automata are a standard modelling formalism for real time systems. A timed automaton is an extension of finite state machines with non-negative real valued variables called *clocks* in order to capture timing constraints. Thus, a timed automaton is an annotated directed graph over a set of clocks C where vertices (called *locations*) are connected by edges, and both are decorated with conjunctions of clock constraints of the form $c \leq k$ or $c \geq k$ with c being a clock and $k \in \mathbb{N}$. For edges such constraints are called *guards*, for locations they are called *invariants*. Edges are additionally decorated with *reset sets* of clocks. Intuitively, taking an edge causes an instantaneous change of location and a reset to 0 for each clock in the reset set. However an edge may only be taken if its guard and the target location's invariant evaluate to true. It does not have to be taken however. As long as permitted by the invariant of the current location, time can advance there, meaning that all clocks increase continuously with their assigned rates, thus modelling the passing of time. Figure 1 depicts a small example of a timed automaton.

Fig. 1. A simple timed automaton *TA*. The invariant $c \leq t_{\max}$ in location ℓ_0 and the guard $c \geq t_{\min}$ on the edge together impose a nondeterministic delay of at least $t_{\min}$ and at most $t_{\max}$ before action d may occur. No clocks are reset, due to the reset set being $\varnothing$.

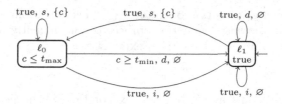

Fig. 2. A time constraint TC for $S = \{s\}$, $I = \{i\}$, and $D = \{d\}$ extending the timed automaton TA from Fig. 1. The delay on action d is started upon occurrence of action s and can be interrupted by action i.

Time Constraints. Now assume we are given a (possibly entirely untimed) system, which encompasses (not necessarily disjoint) sets of actions S, D, and I. Furthermore assume that we want to ensure a delay of some duration for occurrences of actions in D (to be delayed) after occurrence of any action in S (starting the delay), unless an action of I (interrupting the delay) occurs in the meanwhile. The delay we want to ensure has a duration of at least $t_{\min}$ and at most $t_{\max}$. So, we concretely assume

- an interval $[t_{\min}, t_{\max}] \subset \mathbb{R}^{\geq 0}$ of real time that determines the possible duration of the time constraint,
- a set of actions S (start) that determines when a delay starts,
- a set of actions D (delay) that are to be delayed, and
- a set of actions I (interrupt) each of which may interrupt the delay.

Based on this information, a simple two-location timed automaton needs to be constructed which operates with a single fresh clock c. The locations are ℓ_1 and ℓ_0. The invariant of ℓ_1 is true, the one of ℓ_0 is $c \leq t_{\max}$ (as already seen in Fig. 1). Location ℓ_1 serves as initial location. Furthermore,

- for each $s \in S$ we have $\ell_1 \xrightarrow{\text{true},s,\{c\}} \ell_0$ and $\ell_0 \xrightarrow{\text{true},s,\{c\}} \ell_0$;
- for each $d \in D$ we have $\ell_1 \xrightarrow{\text{true},d,\emptyset} \ell_1$ and $\ell_0 \xrightarrow{c \geq t_{\min},d,\emptyset} \ell_1$;
- for each $i \in I$ we have $\ell_1 \xrightarrow{\text{true},i,\emptyset} \ell_1$ and $\ell_0 \xrightarrow{\text{true},i,\emptyset} \ell_1$.

For singleton sets S, D, and I the result of the above construction is sketched in Fig. 2. The construction needs slight adjustments if the three sets are not disjoint [20, 5.5].[1] The main functionality of the above construction is that it does insert a delay for actions of D, but otherwise does not interfere with actions of $S \cup D \cup I$.

Incorporating Time Constraints. It is precisely the constraint-oriented specification style originally proposed by Ed Brinksma [8] that enables us to incorporate such a constraint TC into a system SY by composition. All that is needed is

---

[1] Notably, choosing the reset set to include c in $\ell_0 \xrightarrow{\text{true},s,\{c\}} \ell_0$ makes the delay restart should another action s occur while the delay is running. Another option would be to drop c from this set. This might be preferable dependent on the context.

a multiway parallel composition operator $\|_A$ which synchronizes precisely the actions in A and otherwise lets actions proceed independently [6,9]. With this operator the time-constrained system is expressed as

$$SY \,\|_{S \cup D \cup I} \, TC.$$

This system behaves just as SY behaves, except that whenever an action from S occurs in SY, all actions from D in SY are assured to be delayed at least by an amount of time that lies in the interval $[t_{min}, t_{max}]$ unless an action from I occurs in SY in the meanwhile. Further time constraints can be added to the system in the very same manner, as in

$$(\cdots ((SY \,\|_{S_1 \cup D_1 \cup I_1} \, TC_1) \,\|_{S_2 \cup D_2 \cup I_2} \, TC_2) \cdots \|_{S_n \cup D_n \cup I_n} \, TC_n).$$

Analysis. Overall, this approach can turn an untimed specification into a timed specification in a compositional manner. This makes the final system amenable to quantitative analysis, including real-time model checking and the like. A complete case study in this regard has been carried out in a setting with soft real-time [21]. It can also be combined with induction and data independence [11].

4 Cost-Optimal Timed Reachability

This section elaborates on the concepts of cost-optimal scheduling, originally co-developed by Ed Brinksma, and how they are finding their way into tiny objects orbiting the earth.

Priced Timed Automata. In order to reason about resource consumption, Ed Brinksma and his collaborators have enriched timed automata with non-negative integer *costs* and non-negative *cost rates* in the form of annotations for edges and locations respectively [22]. The result are *priced timed automata* (PTA). The intuition is that cost accumulates continuously in a proportional manner to the sojourn time of locations and increases in a step upon taking an edge as specified by the respective annotations.

Cost-Optimal Reachability. The original problem considered in the context of PTA is that of computing the minimum cost to reach a certain target location in a given PTA. This so-called *cost-optimal reachability analysis* (CORA) has received dedicated attention and is implemented in a number of tools, most prominently UPPAAL CORA [26]. As input UPPAAL CORA accepts networks of PTAs extended by discrete variables, and thus allows for modular formalisation of individual components. The set of goal states is characterised by formulae over the variables in the network of PTAs.

Schedule Synthesis. One of the most prominent applications of this technique, explored in particular within the EU-funded AMETIST project, is schedule synthesis. The main strength of this approach is that the expressiveness of timed automata allows - unlike many classical approaches - the modelling of scheduling problems of very different kinds. Furthermore, the models are robust against changes in the parameter setting and against changes in the problem specification. A milestone in practical applicabilitly of this technique is a case study originally provided by AXXOM: an intricate scheduling problem for lacquer production [2]. A number of problems needed to be addressed for the modelling task, including information transfer from the industrial partner, the derivation of a timed automaton model for the case study, and the heuristics that have to be added in order to reduce the search space.

Robustness of Schedules. This analysis had to ignore two dimensions of the original problem specification as provided by AXXOM. These relate to quantitative stochastic influences due to failures, repairs, cleaning periods and other unforeseeable (and thus unplannable) events. To attack thesem the timed automata model of the production units has been refined into a stochastic timed automata model [4] in order to faithfully represent the stochastic perturbations and to assess the robustness of the system in light of these perturbations. The robustness of the schedules is assessed on the basis of estimates obtained by a discrete-event simulation-based analysis [5,23]. This two-step analysis approach, which combines timed automata-based verification with stochastic robustness analysis is a very striking and effective way to exploit the benefits of formal verification.

Scheduling in Thermosphere. Lately, we have applied this very same approach to a very challenging domain, the domain of *low-earth orbiting satellites*. This work was coined as part of the EU-funded SENSATION project, and continues as part of the ERC Advanced grant POWVER. For a satellite in low orbit all resources are sparse and the most critical resource of all is power. It is therefore crucial to have detailed knowledge on how much power is available for an energy harvesting satellite in orbit at every time – especially when in eclipse, where it draws its power from onboard batteries.

GOMX–3 *Mission.* The GOMX–3 CubeSat was a 3 l ($30 \times 10 \times 10$ cm, 3 kg) nano-satellite designed, delivered, and operated by Danish sector leader GomSpace. GOMX–3 was the first ever In-Orbit Demonstration (IOD) CubeSat commissioned by ESA. The GOMX–3 system used Commercial-off-the-shelf (COTS) base subsystems to reduce cost, enabling fast delivery so as to focus on payload development and testing. GOMX–3 was launched from Japan aboard the HTV–5 on August 19, 2015. It successfully berthed to the ISS a few days later. GOMX–3 was deployed from the ISS into thermosphere on October 5, 2015, it deorbited in October 2016. Figure 3(left) shows the satellite at the time of deployment from ISS.

In-Orbit Scheduling. The heterogeneous timing aspects and the experimental nature of this application domain pose great challenges, making it impossible to use traditional scheduling approaches for periodic tasks. Our approach harvests work on schedulability analysis with (priced) timed automata, and is distinguished by the following features: (i) The timed automata modelling is very flexible, adaptive to changing requirements, and particularly well-suited for discussion with space engineers, since easy-to-grasp; (ii) A dynamic approach to the use of cost decorations and constraints allows for a split scheduling approach

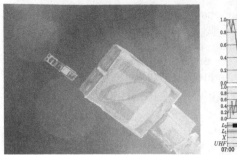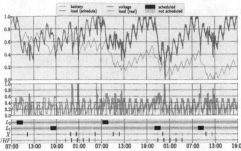

Fig. 3. The GoMX–3 nanosatellite deployment from the ISS (left, picture taken by Astronaut Scott Kelly), and schedule effectuated March 20, 2016 7 AM to March 22, 2016 7 PM (right).

optimising over intervals, at the (acceptable) price of potential sub-optimality of the resulting overall schedules; (iii) A linear battery model is employed while computing scheduling, but prior to shipping any computed schedule is subjected to a quantitative validation on the vastly more accurate stochastic kinetic battery model, and possibly rejected. This last aspect is very close in spirit to the robust scheduling approach [23] discussed above. The stochastic validation step however is not based on simulation, but instead is exact (or conservative) up to discretisation. The procedure has been in use for the automatic and resource-optimal day-ahead scheduling of GoMX–3. One of the schedules computed by the approach, and effectuated in by GoMX–3 is displayed in Fig. 3(right).

Results. The GoMX–3 in-orbit experiments have demonstrated an indeed great fit between the technology developed and the needs of the LEO satellite sector. The schedules generated are of unmatched quality: It became apparent that relative to a comparative manual scheduling approach, better quality schedules with respect to (i) number of experiments performed, (ii) avoidance of planning mistakes, (iii) scheduling workload, and (iv) battery depletion risk are provided. At the same time, the availability of scheduling tool support flexibilises the satellite design process considerably, since it allows the GomSpace engineers to obtain answers to what-if questions, in combination with their in-house tools. This helps shortening development times and thus time-to-orbit. In fact, GomSpace will launch a constellation consisting of two spacecrafts (GoMX–4 A and B) soon and is actively pursuing several projects with much larger constellations. Deploying constellations of a large number of satellites (2 to 1000) brings a new level of complexity to the game. The need to operate a large number of satellites asks for a larger level of automation to be used than has previously been the case in the space industry. For larger constellations tools for optimization, automation and validation are not only a benefit, but an absolutely necessity for proper operations.

5   Conclusion

This paper has reviewed high-impact pioneering contributions of Ed Brinksma in the contexts of constraint-oriented specification, of model-based testing, and of cost-optimal timed reachability. These are manifestations of a general theme overarching his scientific work, namely *software tools supporting the application of formal methods*. Before being promoted to Rector Magnificus at Universiteit Twente he for many years held the Chair for Formal Methods and Tools ("Formele Methoden en Gereedschappen"). During this period, he heavily invested in tool support for formal methods, including tools for formal testing, verification of soft- and hard-real time systems, algebraic specifications, and many more. And very many of his projects of national, European and international scale have had a distinguished focus on the advancements on the software support side, notably including LOTOSPHERE, SVC, VHS, ARTIST, AMETIST, and QUASIMODO. Together with Kim Larsen (co-founder of UPPAAL [3]), Bernhard Steffen, and Rance Cleaveland (co-founders of the Concurrency Workbench [10]) he founded an international conference on tools and algorithms for the construction and analysis of systems (TACAS). This conference is nowadays simply *the* conference on tools and algorithms for the construction and analysis of systems.

Acknowledgments. We gratefully acknowledge insightful comments by Sadie Creese (University of Oxford) on an early draft of this paper. This work is supported by the ERC Advanced Investigators Grant 695614 (POWVER), and has profited from the EU-funded projects SENSATION, QUASIMODO, and AMETIST.

References

1. Alur, R., Dill, D.L.: A theory of timed automata. Theoret. Comput. Sci. **126**, 183–235 (1994)
2. Behrmann, G., Brinksma, E., Hendriks, M., Mader, A.: Production scheduling by reachability analysis - a case study. In: 19th International Parallel and Distributed Processing Symposium (IPDPS 2005), CD-ROM/Abstracts Proceedings, Denver, CO, USA, 4–8 April 2005. IEEE Computer Society (2005)
3. Bengtsson, J., Larsen, K., Larsson, F., Pettersson, P., Yi, W.: UPPAAL—a tool suite for automatic verification of real-time systems. In: Alur, R., Henzinger, T.A., Sontag, E.D. (eds.) HS 1995. LNCS, vol. 1066, pp. 232–243. Springer, Heidelberg (1996). doi:10.1007/BFb0020949
4. Bohnenkamp, H.C., D'Argenio, P.R., Hermanns, H., Katoen, J.-P.: MODEST: a compositional modeling formalism for hard and softly timed systems. IEEE Trans. Softw. Eng. **32**(10), 812–830 (2006)
5. Bohnenkamp, H.C., Hermanns, H., Klaren, R., Mader, A., Usenko, Y.S.: Synthesis and stochastic assessment of schedules for lacquer production. In: 1st International Conference on Quantitative Evaluation of Systems (QEST 2004), Enschede, The Netherlands, 27–30 September 2004, pp. 28–37. IEEE Computer Society (2004)
6. Bolognesi, T., Brinksma, E.: Introduction to the ISO specification language LOTOS. Comput. Netw. **14**, 25–59 (1987)

7. Brinksma, E.: A theory for the derivation of tests. In: Aggarwal, S., Sabnani, K.K. (eds.) Protocol Specification, Testing and Verification V, Proceedings of the IFIP WG6.1 Eighth International Conference on Protocol Specification, Testing and Verification, pp. 171–194. North-Holland (1988)
8. Brinksma, E.: Constraint-oriented specification in a constructive formal description technique. In: de Bakker, J.W., de Roever, W.-P., Rozenberg, G. (eds.) REX 1989. LNCS, vol. 430, pp. 130–152. Springer, Heidelberg (1990). doi:10.1007/3-540-52559-9_63
9. Brookes, S.D., Hoare, C.A.R., Roscoe, A.W.: A theory of communicating sequential processes. J. ACM **31**(3), 560–599 (1984)
10. Cleaveland, R., Parrow, J., Steffen, B.: The concurrency workbench: a semantics-based tool for the verification of concurrent systems. ACM Trans. Program. Lang. Syst. **15**(1), 36–72 (1993)
11. Creese, S.J., Roscoe, A.W.: Verifying an infinite family of inductions simultaneously using data independence and FDR. In: Wu, J., Chanson, S.T., Gao, Q. (eds.) Formal Methods for Protocol Engineering and Distributed Systems, FORTE XII/PSTV XIX 1999, IFIP TC6 WG6.1 Joint International Conference on Formal Description Techniques for Distributed Systems and Communication Protocols (FORTE XII) and Protocol Specification, Testing and Verification (PSTV XIX), IFIP Conference Proceedings, Beijing, China, 5–8 October 1999, vol. 156, pp. 437–452. Kluwer (1999)
12. De Nicola, R., Hennessy, M.: Testing equivalences for processes. Theoret. Comput. Sci. **34**, 83–133 (1984)
13. Garavel, H., Serwe,W.: The unheralded value of the multiway rendezvous: illustration with the production cell benchmark. In: Hermanns, H., Höfner, P. (eds.) Proceedings 2nd Workshop on Models for Formal Analysis of Real Systems, MARS@ETAPS 2017, EPTCS, Uppsala, Sweden, 29 April 2017, vol. 244, pp. 230–270 (2017)
14. Graf-Brill, A., Hermanns, H.: Model-based testing for asynchronous systems. In: Petrucci, L., Seceleanu, C., Cavalcanti, A. (eds.) FMICS 2017, AVoCS 2017. LNCS, vol. 10471, pp. 66–82. Springer, Cham (2017). doi:10.1007/978-3-319-67113-0_5
15. Graf-Brill, A., Hartmanns, A., Hermanns, H., Rose, S.: Modelling and certification for electric mobility. In: 15th IEEE International Conference on Industrial Informatics, INDIN 2017, Emden, Germany, 24–26 July 2017. IEEE (2017)
16. Graf-Brill, A., Hermanns, H., Garavel, H.: A model-based certification framework for the EnergyBus standard. In: Ábrahám, E., Palamidessi, C. (eds.) FORTE 2014. LNCS, vol. 8461, pp. 84–99. Springer, Heidelberg (2014). doi:10.1007/978-3-662-43613-4_6
17. Hahn, M.E., Hartmanns, A., Hermanns, H., Katoen, J.-P.: A compositional modelling and analysis framework for stochastic hybrid systems. Formal Methods Syst. Des. **43**(2), 191–232 (2013)
18. Hartmanns, A., Hermanns, H.: The modest toolset: an integrated environment for quantitative modelling and verification. In: Ábrahám, E., Havelund, K. (eds.) TACAS 2014. LNCS, vol. 8413, pp. 593–598. Springer, Heidelberg (2014). doi:10.1007/978-3-642-54862-8_51
19. Havelund, K., Larsen, K.G., Skou, A.: Formal verification of a power controller using the real-time model checker UPPAAL. In: Katoen, J.-P. (ed.) ARTS 1999. LNCS, vol. 1601, pp. 277–298. Springer, Heidelberg (1999). doi:10.1007/3-540-48778-6_17
20. Hermanns, H.: Interactive Markov Chains: And the Quest for Quantified Quality. LNCS, vol. 2428. Springer, Heidelberg (2002). doi:10.1007/3-540-45804-2

21. Hermanns, H., Katoen, J.-P.: Automated compositional Markov chain generation for a plain-old telephone system. Sci. Comput. Program. **36**(1), 97–127 (2000)

22. Larsen, K., Behrmann, G., Brinksma, E., Fehnker, A., Hune, T., Pettersson, P., Romijn, J.: As cheap as possible: effcient cost-optimal reachability for priced timed automata. In: Berry, G., Comon, H., Finkel, A. (eds.) CAV 2001. LNCS, vol. 2102, pp. 493–505. Springer, Heidelberg (2001). doi:10.1007/3-540-44585-4_47

23. Mader, A., Bohnenkamp, H.C., Usenko, Y.S., Jansen, D.N., Hurink, J., Hermanns, H.: Synthesis and stochastic assessment of cost-optimal schedules. STTT **12**(5), 305–318 (2010)

24. Tretmans, J.: Model based testing with labelled transition systems. In: Hierons, R.M., Bowen, J.P., Harman, M. (eds.) Formal Methods and Testing. LNCS, vol. 4949, pp. 1–38. Springer, Heidelberg (2008). doi:10.1007/978-3-540-78917-8_1

25. Tretmans, J., Kars, P., Brinksma, E.: Protocol conformance testing: a formal perspective on ISO IS-9646. In: Kroon, J., Heijink, R.J., Brinksma, E. (eds.) Protocol Test Systems IV, Proceedings of the IFIP TC6/WG6.1 Fourth International Workshop on Protocol Test Systems, IFIP Transactions, Leidschendam, The Netherlands, 15–17 October 1991, vol. C-3, pp. 131–142. North-Holland (1991)

26. UPPAAL CORA (2005). http://people.cs.aau.dk/~adavid/cora/introduction.html. Accessed 31 July 2017

27. Catastrophic Surface Pro 3 battery life finally has its firmware fix (2016). http://arstechnica.com/?p=945575. Accessed 31 July 2017

28. Samsung recalls Galaxy Note 7 worldwide due to exploding battery fears (2016). http://theverge.com/2016/9/2/12767670. Accessed 31 July 2017

29. Basis Peak watches recalled (2016). http://techcrunch.com/2016/08/03/basis-peak-watches-recalled-due-to-overheating/. Accessed 31 July 2017

30. Important: Medical device correction, EnRhythm pacemakers (2010). http://www.medtronic.com/enrhythm-advisory/downloads/enrhythm-battery-issues_physician-letter.pdf. Accessed 31 July 2017

31. Qualitätsprobleme bei E-Bikes: Schlappe Akkus, anfällige Elektronik (2011). http://www.spiegel.de/auto/aktuell/a-790142.html. Accessed 31 July 2017

Boosting Fault Tree Analysis by Formal Methods

Joost-Pieter Katoen[1,2]([✉]) and Mariëlle Stoelinga[2]

[1] RWTH Aachen University, Aachen, Germany
katoen@cs.rwth-aachen.de
[2] University of Twente, Enschede, The Netherlands

Abstract. Fault trees are a key technique in safety and reliability engineering. Their application includes aerospace, nuclear power, car, and process engineering industries. Various fault tree extensions exist that increase expressiveness while yielding succinct models. Their analysis is a main bottleneck: techniques do not scale and require manual effort. Formal methods have an enormous potential to solve these issues. We discuss a mixture of formal method techniques resulting in a fully automated and scalable approach to analyze Dugan's dynamic fault trees.

1 Introduction

Fault Trees are Ubiquitous. Fault trees were developed in 1961 at Bell Labs. A few years later Boeing started to use fault tree analysis (FTA, for short) for civil aircraft design. The U.S. Nuclear Regulatory Commission published the NRC Fault Tree Handbook in 1981. Several other industries followed later with their FTA standards. Since the Challenger accident in 1986, NASA considers FTA as a key system reliability and safety analysis technique. The U.S. Federal Aviation Administration's System Safety Handbook (2000) advocates the use of FTA. Fault trees are used on a daily basis by millions of engineers around the world. For example, after the explosion of the (unmanned) Falcon-9 rocket in 2015, the SpaceX CEO posted the following on Twitter [42]:

> "That's all we can say with confidence right now. Will have more to say following a thorough fault tree analysis."

What are Fault Trees? They are directed acyclic graphs. Leaves model individual component failures or human errors. As errors in FTA are assumed to happen randomly, leaves are equipped with a continuous probability distribution. Internal vertices (a.k.a.: nodes), commonly referred to as gates, model how component failures lead to system failures. Gates are like logical elements in circuits such as AND and OR (but no inverters). FTA amounts to determine the failure probability of the root of the fault tree, called the top-level event. Fault trees that only contain logical gates such as AND and OR are called *static*. Static fault tree analysis can be efficiently done using binary decision diagrams[1].

---

[1] BDDs are succinct representations for switching functions. In 1990, their use in formal methods, in particular formal verification, has been introduced [11].

© Springer International Publishing AG 2017
J.-P. Katoen et al. (Eds.): Brinksma Festschrift, LNCS 10500, pp. 368–389, 2017.
DOI: 10.1007/978-3-319-68270-9_19

The key step in the analysis is determining a minimal cut set. This is a set of leaves of minimal cardinality whose failures together causes the top-level event to fail. The analysis of static fault trees is simple as the ordering of failure is irrelevant; it only matters whether a leaf has failed or not.

Dynamic Fault Trees. Static fault trees are too simple for practical systems. This has led to several extensions; for a recent survey see [49]. Dugan's *dynamic* fault trees [16] (DFTs, for short) are the most well-known and commonly used. The behaviour of a DFT not only depends on the set of failed leaves, but also on their order. Thus, DFTs have a richer set of gates and are more expressive than static fault trees. This, however, comes at a price. Their analysis can no longer be done using minimal cut sets. Instead, their behaviour is state-dependent. DFT analysis is typically done by distilling a stochastic process, mostly a continuous-time Markov chain (CTMC, for short), from the DFT. Markov chain analysis is used to obtain information about the probability of the top-level event to fail.

The Challenge. Conceptually, this sounds simple. In practice it is not. This leads to the belief that DFT analysis is a difficult problem. For instance, [54] and [43] argue that a state-based approach for dynamic gates is not "realistic" due to the state-space explosion on increasing the DFT size. Indeed, DFTs in practice are large. Hundreds of nodes is not an exception. Their Markov chains consist of millions or even billions of states. State-space generation is a major bottleneck in DFT analysis. This complicates their analysis considerably. As [20] argues:

> "Although DFTs are powerful in modeling systems with dynamic failure behaviors, their quantitative analyses are pretty much troublesome, especially for large scale and complex DFTs."

Or, in the most recent survey paper on fault tree analysis [32]:

> "Although many extensions of fault trees have been proposed, they suffer from a variety of shortcomings. In particular, even where software tool support exists, these analyses require a lot of manual effort."

Model Checking. In our opinion, this common belief is way too pessimistic! We know that formal methods are not a panacea. However, we argue in this paper that probabilistic and statistical model checking can alleviate the above mentioned "problems" and "shortcomings" to a very large extent. Model checking [4] is a systematic way to analyze the state space with powerful algorithms. It is heavily used in hardware industry to verify IC designs, and the founding fathers of model checking won the prestigious ACM Turing award in 2007.

Probabilistic model checking combines standard model checking techniques with clever stochastic methods to obtain efficient numerical algorithms. Statistical model checking, a state-of-the-art Monte Carlo simulation technique, is more widely applicable and is far less dependent on the state space size. However, it is not an exhaustive technique and requires special treatment of rare events and nondeterminism. In this paper, we show that due to unremitting improvements of state-space generation techniques in the field of probabilistic and statistical model checking, extremely large state spaces can nowadays be treated, both numerically and statistically. In particular, we show how techniques like compositionality, abstraction, partial order reduction, graph rewriting, and abstraction-refinement can be exploited to analyse large DFTs in a matter of minutes.

Take-Home Message. As such, this paper argues that *FTA is a playground par excellence for formal methods.* Formal methods boost dynamic fault tree analysis significantly and result in a fully automated and software-supported approach.

2   Dynamic Fault Trees in a Nutshell

What are DFTs? Dynamic fault trees (DFTs) [16] are directed acyclic graphs consisting of gates and leaves. A DFT has a distinguished root node, called the top-level event (TLE, for short). DFT leaves represent component failures, called basic events (BEs, for short). DFTs describe how component failures propagate through the system. Gates, depicted in Fig. 1, model failure propagation. The static gates OR, AND, VOT(k) fail if respectively one, all or k (out of $n \geq k$) of their inputs fail. The PAND, SPARE, and FDEP are dynamic gates. A PAND-gate fails if the inputs fail from left to right; if the components fail in any other order, then no failure occurs. A SPARE-gate contains one primary, and one or more spare inputs. If the primary input fails, then the leftmost dormant spare takes over its functionality, putting the spare from dormant into active mode. If all spares have failed too, then the SPARE-gate fails. Primary and spares can be entire DFTs, and spares can be shared among several gates. An FDEP-gate contains a trigger input, which instantaneously triggers the failure of all its dependent events.

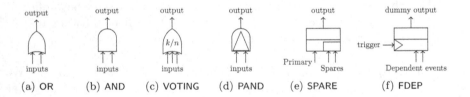

(a) OR   (b) AND   (c) VOTING   (d) PAND   (e) SPARE   (f) FDEP

Fig. 1. Gates in dynamic fault trees

DFT leaves can be either dormant, active, or failed. Component failures are governed by continuous distribution functions, e.g., exponential probability distributions. Dormant leaves fail less frequently as they are not in use. Their failure rate λ is reduced by a dormancy factor d in the interval $[0, 1]$. The probability for an active component to fail within time t is $1 - e^{-\lambda \cdot t}$ and $1 - e^{-d \cdot \lambda \cdot t}$ for a dormant component. Figure 2(a) depicts a simple sample DFT.

The DFT's Markov Chain. DFTs have an internal state, e.g., the order in which failures occur influences the internal state, and thus whether the designated top

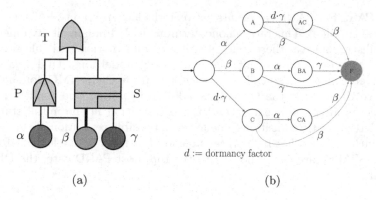

$d :=$ dormancy factor

(a)   (b)

Fig. 2. A (a) sample DFT with three leaves, an OR-gate (top-level event T) and a PAND-gate P and a SPARE-gate S (T's children), and (b) its CTMC.

event has failed. The behaviour of DFTs can be naturally described by CTMCs, where transitions correspond to the failure of a basic event. Figure 2(b) depicts the CTMC of our sample DFT. Initially, any of the leaves can fail with failure rates α, β, and γ, respectively. As the rightmost leaf is dormant, its failure rate is reduced by d. Once this leaf becomes active, e.g., in CTMC state B, its failure rate becomes γ. In the rightmost CTMC state F, the TLE and thus the entire DFT has failed. Due to the expressive power of DFTs, their interpretation is not always clear; an in-depth discussion on this can be found in [31].

Nondeterminism. Most DFTs are fully probabilistic. They do not exhibit any nondeterminism. Their behaviour can adequately be described by CTMCs. Some DFTs give rise to nondeterminism. An example is provided in Fig. 3(a). The two SPARE gates share a spare. Once the rightmost leaf fails first, the primary child

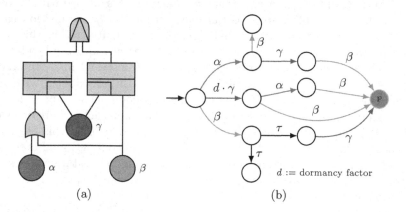

(a)   (b)

Fig. 3. A (a) sample DFT with three leaves, a PAND-gate (top-level event), two SPARE-gates, and an OR-gate, arranged to create nondeterminism, (b) its IMC (assuming the PAND fails on simultaneous failures of its children). (Color figure online)

of each SPARE fails. A "race" occurs between the left and right SPARE to use the middle leaf (in blue). This race is nondeterministic. It fundamentally differs from a probabilistic choice as there is no quantitative information available about how to resolve this race. As a result, the underlying model for a DFT is a CTMC with nondeterminism, a so-called *interactive* Markov chain (IMC, for short) [28, 29]. Figure 3(b) depicts the IMC of the DFT in Fig. 3(a). The nondeterministic choice occurs after the occurrence of the β-transition in the initial state. The two nondeterministic transitions, one for each possible resolution of the race, are labeled with τ. Note that if the race is resolved in favor of the left SPARE-gate, the right SPARE-gate fails, and due to the top-most PAND-gate, the DFT can never fail.

3   Compositional State-Space Generation

A crucial step in DFT analysis is to generate the state space underlying a DFT. Each state records for each BE its status, i.e., whether it is up or down and whether it is operational or not. Key result in [6,7] is to perform this via *compositional aggregation*, a.k.a. iterative minimization. Rather than generating the whole state space at once—leading to a procedure that is difficult to understand and modify—[6,7] generate a Markov model for each DFT element. Recently, Ammar *et al.* [1] advocated the use of compositional model generation combined with probabilistic model checking for DFTs using Markov decision processes (MDPs). The whole state space is then obtained by composing these Markov models in a smart way.

IOIMCs. Standard Markov models cannot be composed in a natural way; i.e., there are no adequate notions to build a larger Markov model from smaller ones. Hence, [5–7] use input/output interactive Markov chains (IOIMCs) [5]. IOIMCs combine CTMCs and labeled transition systems, see Fig. 4 for an example. They feature two types of transitions: *Markovian* transitions are labeled with the parameter λ (a.k.a.: rate) of an exponential distribution. Such a transition can be taken after an exponential waiting time, i.e., the probability to take this transition before time t is given by $1 - e^{-\lambda \cdot t}$. *Interactive* transitions are labeled with action labels and can be used to synchronize two or more IOIMCs. Interactive transitions feature three types of action labels: transitions labeled with *input* labels a? indicate that the IOIMC waits for another component to provide a corresponding output label $a!$. Transitions labeled with input actions are delayable, meaning that the IOIMC can wait as long as needed to take this transition. *Output* actions $a!$ are immediate; i.e., as soon as the output action $a!$ is enabled, it has to be taken. In particular, this means that whenever a state enables both an output action and a Markovian action, the Markovian action is never taken as its probability to be taken immediately is zero. *Internal transitions* are like output actions, and hence immediate, with the difference being that the action label is not visible to the environment. Thus, internal actions are used to model steps that are internal to the component.

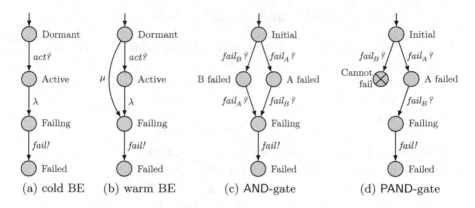

Fig. 4. Examples of the IOIMCs underlying DFTs.

Example 1. Figure 4(a) depicts the IOIMC underlying a cold BE, a basic event that cannot fail in dormant mode. In the initial state, the IOIMC waits to be activated, i.e., it waits until it has received an input signal *act?* from its environment. If so, it moves to the state named Active. This state has a Markovian transition labeled with λ, indicating that the BE's failure rate is exponentially distributed with parameter λ. After failing, the IOIMC moves to state Failing, which has an outgoing transition labeled with *fail!*. As soon as the BE has failed, the IOIMC sends out a *fail!* signal, so that other components can update their state.

Figure 4(b) depicts the IOIMC of a warm BE, i.e., a basic event that can fail in dormant mode, but with a reduced rate $\mu = d \cdot \lambda$. Now, in the initial state, two things may happen: Either the component is activated, and moves to state Active and the behavior is as before. Alternatively, the component fails before activation, which happens with a reduced failure rate μ, as modeled by the transition Dormant $\xrightarrow{\mu}$ Failing.

The IOIMC for an AND-gate C with children A and B is given in Fig. 4(c). When it has received failure signals from both its children, the IOIMC sends out a *fail!* signal. Finally, the IOIMC for the PAND-gate is given in Fig. 4(d): if the IOIMC receives a failure signal from A first, and then from B, then the IOIMC sends out a *fail!* signal; otherwise it moves to a sink state (indicated by X) from which it can never fail.

The IOIMCs for the other gates are similar, but more complex.

Smart Composition. The CTMC underlying a DFT is obtained by composing all DFT-element IOIMCs via composition aggregation. That is, rather than composing all IOIMCs in one shot, all DFT-element models are composed one-by-one, in an iterative way. After each step, the models are reduced. Thus, the compositional aggregation procedure iteratively performs the following three steps: (1) Pick two IOIMCs and compose these. (2) Hide all actions that are not relevant for other components; i.e., actions that are not used for synchronization by

Table 1. Results of CORAL and Galileo (taken from [7]).

Case study	Approach	Max # of states	Max # of transitions	Unreliability	Run time (sec)
CPS	Galileo	4,113	24,608	0.00135	490
	CORAL	133	465	0.00135	67
CPS	Galileo	8	10	0.65790	1
	CORAL	36	119	0.65790	94
CAS-PH	CORAL	40,052	265,442	0.112826	231
FTPP-4	Galileo	32,757	426,826	0.01922	13111
	CORAL	1,325	13,642	0.01922	65
FTPP-5	CORAL	43,105	643,339	0.00306	309
FTPP-6	CORAL	1,180,565	22,147,378	0.000453	1989
FTPP-C	CORAL	653,303	12,220,653	0.02136	1806
FTPP-A	Galileo	32,757	426,826	0.0167	13111
	CORAL	19,367	154,566	0.0167	240
NDPS	CORAL	61	169	[0.00586, 0.00598]	266

other IOIMCs are made internal. (3) Reduce the model just obtained via minimization techniques such as weak bisimulation [5] or confluence reduction [51]. Action hiding makes that more states are equivalent, enabling stronger reductions. Minimization means that one replaces the model by an equivalent one that is smaller, for instance by grouping states that exhibit the same behavior. The order in which the models are composed does not matter for the end result; however, it impacts the memory footprint, i.e., the size of the intermediate Markov models. Heuristics have been developed to obtain a low peak memory usage [13].

This procedure has been implemented in the tool CORAL and its successor DFTCalc [2]. An advantage of this technique is its flexibility: adding new gates for instance, is easy, since one only has to provide the IOIMC for that new gate. For example, cyber attacks can easily be incorporated in this way [3,36], and the same holds for maintenance strategies [24,25]. A further improvement over existing methods is that the compositional approach is more liberal on the DFTs it can analyze. Earlier methods make rather severe assumptions on the DFTs to analyze, which limits the ability to model and analyze realistic systems. For example, dependent events of FDEP-gates could only be BEs, and the same holds for the spare inputs of a SPARE-gate. CORAL was the first tool to alleviate these restrictions.

Experiments. Several experiments have been carried out comparing DFTCalc's predecessor CORAL to Galileo [50], the state-of-the-art tool at that time. The following case studies were used: Cascaded PAND system (CPS), Cardiac assist system (CAS), fault tolerant parallel processors (FTPP) [16], and a pump system with inherent nondeterminism (NDPS). Table 1 shows the benchmark results in terms of memory footprint (i.e., maximum number of states and transitions encountered during the analysis process) and in terms or running time. It also indicates the DFT's unreliability of the DFT, i.e., the probability that the DFT fails within a deadline. Except for the CAS system which has a very small state space, compositional analysis outperforms Galileo, both in time and memory usage. CORAL could analyze several variants of the FTPP case where Galileo ran out of memory. Note that the NDPS system cannot be modeled in Galileo, since it does not support nondeterminism. Due to the nondeterminism, the unreliability of the NPDS system is an interval and not a single value as for the other cases.

4   Reduce, Reduce, and Reduce More

The previous section described a compositional approach for distilling a CTMC from a DFT. Its main advantage is that each DFT gate and leaf results in a relatively simple CTMC. These CTMCs can be reduced individually and in a pairwise fashion after being put in parallel. This reduces the peak memory consumption. The price is that the CTMC of a DFT gate needs to be equipped with extra transitions to enable its parallel composition with CTMCs of other DFT gates. They thus are slightly more complex due to the fact that they need to be composed. Another drawback is that the CTMCs of each DFT gate are "context free". That is to say, their behaviour does not take into account the context in which they are put. This is good on the one hand, as it means equal gates yield equal CTMCs, which can be exploited. On the other hand, it is bad as certain parts of the CTMCs might not be reachable if the context would be taken into account. For instance, if a given sub-tree can only become active once other parts of the DFT have failed, then parts of the sub-tree might not be relevant any more.

Revive the Original Approach. An alternative is to take the original Galileo [50] approach—the first tool for DFT analysis; it treats a DFT as monolithic entity—and modernise it using techniques to shrink the state space prior or during its generation. Techniques that can be adopted are: *symmetry reduction, partial-order reduction,* and *don't care detection.* Symmetry reduction recognises isomorphic sub-trees and stochastic independences among sub-trees by a static analysis of the DFT. It thus is *not* a symmetry reduction at state-space level, but rather at the DFT level. Sub-trees that become obsolete (don't care) after the occurrence of some failures in the DFT are pruned. Finally, one can detect superfluous nondeterminism such that certain failure orderings are irrelevant. A detailed account of this approach is given in [52,53].

Monolithic State-Space Generation with Don't Care Propagation. The principle is rather straightforward. Each gate and leaf in the DFT is provided with a status such as e.g., operational (OP), failed (F), fail-safe (FS), or don't care (X). For each SPARE-gate, one has to do some extra bookkeeping. One needs to keep track of the currently used child (a.k.a.: spare) (CUC). In addition, for each spare one needs information about whether it is active (A) or dormant (D). All this information together constitutes the state space of a DFT. A state is thus the status of each gate and leaf, plus some extra information for each SPARE-gate and its spares. State changes originate from the failure of one of the DFT leaves[2]. These state changes not only involve a status change of the just failed BE. It may affect the CUC of a SPARE-gate, may give rise to gates to become fail-safe (FS) as they cannot fail in the future anymore, and involves don't care propagation—a top-down pass over the DFT determining whether nodes have become don't care (X) as all their parents are F or FS.

Partial-Order Reduction. In many DFTs, the actual order in which subsets of leaves fail is not crucial. This is exploited for FDEP-gates, where instead of exploring all interleavings over the triggered events one aims to only explore a single order. This can be done applying static partial order reduction [4, Ch. 8.2.4] to DFTs. A static analysis of the DFT identifies which dependencies can be executed in arbitrary order. If so, only a canonical order is expanded.

Symmetry Reduction. The symmetry in a DFT, i.e., the presence of isomorphic sub-trees, can be exploited [12]. Faults in isomorphic sub-trees have the same effect if they are only connected to the remaining DFT via a single static node, i.e., an AND, OR, or a VOT(−) gate. The states of symmetric sub-trees can then be swapped. Thus it is not important to administer which nodes in symmetric sub-trees have failed, but only how many and reduces the number of states.

Experiments. Together with compact bit-level state representations and manipulations, bisimulation minimisation of the resulting CTMC, and modularisation, the above approach results in a well-performing modern version of Galileo. Modularisation [26] is a DFT technique that identifies independent sub-trees in the DFT, analyses them separately, and combines the results to a final result. Experiments show that intermediate state spaces are often ten times smaller compared to the compositional approach. This results in boosting the state-space generation by up to several orders of magnitude[3]. For some case studies, the compositional approach yields a smaller peak memory usage. For 164 problem instances, this approach solved 11% more cases (for analysing the DFT's reliability) than the compositional approach. Plots indicating the difference between the compositional and the revived Galileo approach are provided in Fig. 5. These are log-log scale plots. Figure 5(a) compares the time consumption (which includes state-space generation and analysis). The lower dashed line indicates an advantage of our tool by a factor ten, the upper of a factor 100. The outer lines indicate time-outs (TO) and memory-outs (MO), respectively. Figure 5(b) indicates the peak memory consumption. Here one sees that for several benchmarks

---

[2] As failure probabilities are continuous probability distributions, the probability that two or more leaves fail simultaneously is zero.

[3] It is fair to say, that some of these effects are also due to a different implementation of the state-space generation process; the compositional approach as realised in the tool DFTCalc [2] is based on the CADP tool-box [19], whereas the monolithic approach is implemented [52] on top of the storm model checker [15].

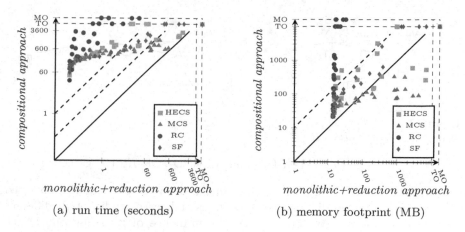

(a) run time (seconds)   (b) memory footprint (MB)

Fig. 5. Overview of the experimental results on four different benchmark sets (taken from [52,53]).

it is beneficial to employ compositional state-space generation and reduction, whereas for others it is not. The following benchmarks were used: Hypothetical Example Computer System (HECS) from the NASA FT handbook, Multiprocessor Computing System (MCS) [40], Railway Crossing (RC) [24] and the Sensor Filter (SF) [8]. The sizes of the corresponding CTMCs vary to up to one million states.

5   Fault Tree Rewriting and All That

Whereas the previous reductions work on the underlying CTMC or IOIMC, one can also reduce the DFT before any state is generated, thus obtaining a "slim" fault tree. This is the idea behind the paper *Fault trees on a diet* [30]: one rewrites a DFT into another one that is equivalent—in the sense that important measures-of-interest such as reliability and mean time-to-failure are preserved, but whose state space is much smaller. Note that this does not necessarily mean that the fault tree itself is smaller.

Since fault trees are graphs, it is natural to use graph transformation systems for that. Graph transformation systems rewrite one graph into another one via transformation rules. These rules look for patterns in a graph, and if such a pattern is found, then it can be replaced by another pattern. In this way, nodes and edges can be removed or added, and attributes such as failure rates can be changed. For example, if two OR-gates are stacked on top of each other, then these gates can be glued into one large OR-gate as depicted as follows: In total, [30] has developed a set of 29 transformation rules, which have been implemented in the graph transformation tool GROOVE [22], and can be used in combination with any DFT analysis tool.

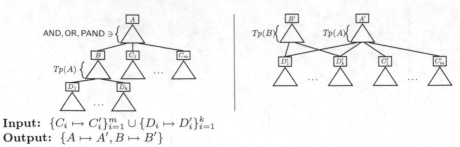

Input: $\{C_i \mapsto C_i'\}_{i=1}^m \cup \{D_i \mapsto D_i'\}_{i=1}^k$
Output: $\{A \mapsto A', B \mapsto B'\}$

Rewrite rule 1: Left-flattening of AND-/OR-/PAND-gates

Experiments. The effect of rewriting was analyzed on 183 benchmarks, obtained by instantiating seven different, mostly industrial, case studies with different parameter values [30]. We investigated the influence of rewriting on (1) the

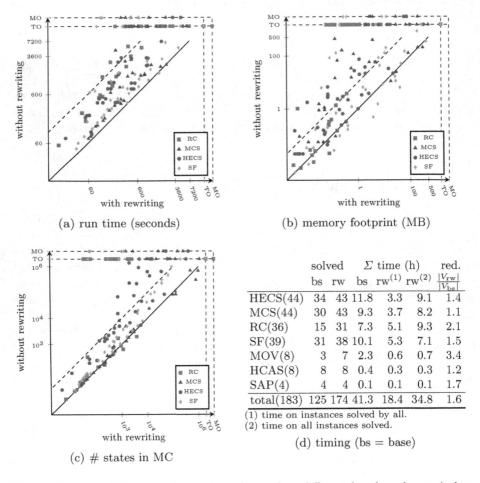

	solved		Σ time (h)			red.
	bs	rw	bs	$\mathrm{rw}^{(1)}$	$\mathrm{rw}^{(2)}$	$\frac{|V_{\mathrm{rw}}|}{|V_{\mathrm{bs}}|}$
HECS(44)	34	43	11.8	3.3	9.1	1.4
MCS(44)	30	43	9.3	3.7	8.2	1.1
RC(36)	15	31	7.3	5.1	9.3	2.1
SF(39)	31	38	10.1	5.3	7.1	1.5
MOV(8)	3	7	2.3	0.6	0.7	3.4
HCAS(8)	8	8	0.4	0.3	0.3	1.2
SAP(4)	4	4	0.1	0.1	0.1	1.7
total(183)	125	174	41.3	18.4	34.8	1.6

(1) time on instances solved by all.
(2) time on all instances solved.

(a) run time (seconds)   (b) memory footprint (MB)

(c) # states in MC   (d) timing (bs = base)

Fig. 6. Overview of the experimental results on four different benchmark sets (taken from [30]). (Color figure online)

number of nodes in the DFT, (2) the peak memory consumption, (3) the total analysis time (including model generation, rewriting, and analysis), as well as (4) the size of the resulting Markov chain, see Fig. 6(a)–(d). The base setting is the compositional minimization approach as realised in the tool DFTCalc without rewriting. These plots clearly show that rewriting DFTs improves the performance for all these criteria in almost all cases. Improvements of upto several orders of magnitude were obtained. In particular, 49 cases could be analysed that yielded a time-out (TO, two hours) or out-of-memory (MO, 8000 MB) in the base setting without rewriting. A more detailed analysis reveals that the graph rewriting with GROOVE is very fast, typically between 7 and 12 s. Most time is devoted to the Markov chain construction and bisimulation minimisation. The analysis time of the resulting Markov chain using probabilistic model checking (see Sect. 3) is negligible.

6   Abstract, Check, and Refine

Partial State-Space Generation. The approaches so far focused on the analysis of the DFT after the entire CTMC has been generated. This has the advantage that all information is available to get an exact[4] account of the DFT's measures-of-interest. In many cases, however, one is not interested in the exact mean time to failure (MTTF) or the exact probability that the top-level event fails within a certain time deadline (a.k.a.: reliability). Instead, in practice one often wants to know whether the reliability is below a given threshold or, similarly, whether the MTTF is beyond a certain value. To answer these queries, it suffices to analyse DFTs by considering their *partial* state space only. The simple idea is to generate only a—hopefully small—fragment of the DFT's CTMC. This goes along the way described in Sect. 4 except that one stops the state-space generation at a certain point, e.g., if a certain fraction of the DFT has been considered, a certain size of the CTMC has been reached, or similar. Inspired by the ISO 26262 standard where "high-order" failures are ignored, bounded depth exploration is a good possible termination criterion: any states encoding up to k-point failures are considered. This CTMC fragment is now used to obtain lower and upper bounds on the measure-of-interest, say MTTF. A detailed account of this approach can be found in [53].

Pessimistic Abstraction. To obtain a lower bound on the MTTF, the DFTs failure probability is overestimated. Correspondingly, it is assumed that the failure of *any* additional leaf results in a TLE failure. This is easily realised by mildly adapting the state space fragment: a transition is added in the CTMC from each unexplored state to a failed state on the failure of any additional DFT leaf. The rate of such transition is the sum of the failure rates of the operational leaves. The resulting CTMC can be viewed as a *pessimistic abstraction* of the DFT. This results in a lower bound on the MTTF as it corresponds to the worst possible scenario. The true MTTF can not be worse. The lower bound thus is safe.

---

[4] Up to some numerical or simulative evidence.

Optimistic Abstraction. Symmetrically, an optimistic view is obtained by assuming that *all* of the unconsidered DFT leaves have to fail to cause the TLE to fail. This uses the mild assumption that the TLE always fails if all (fallible) leaves fail regardless of the order in which they fail[5]. This yields a safe upper bound, as the true MTTF can not be larger. The realisation of this optimistic perspective is somewhat more involved though. The failure rate of the DFT is given by the maximum of all failure rates of the operational leaves. We add a transition to each state in the CTMC fragment. Its rate μ is chosen such that the expected time of an exponential distribution with rate μ equals the expected time of the maximum over the failure distributions of the operational leaves. The resulting CTMC can be viewed as an *optimistic abstraction* of the DFT.

Refinement. So far, so good. Assume now the DFT's MTTF is required to exceed some threshold M, say. If the lower bound lb is at most M, the DFT satisfies the requirement; if the upper bound ub is below M, it refutes. In all other cases, the result is inconclusive. In that case, a heuristic can be employed to refine the two abstractions. This can be done such that earlier analysis results can be partially re-used. The MTTF analysis by means of probabilistic model checking (see Sect. 7), provides bounds on the MTTF for each state. This can be exploited in a simple heuristic: states that are reachable with a high probability and whose gap between lower and upper bound is wide, are explored first.

Abstract-Reduce-Refine. Altogether, this results in an iterative abstraction-refinement approach. It stops whenever it can be decided whether the MTTF is beyond or below M. Or, if one is nonetheless interested in more precise information about the MTTF, one can also terminate the abstraction-refinement process whenever the gap between lower and upper bound is sufficiently tight. While obtaining the partial state spaces, symmetry and partial-order reduction, as well as don't care propagation (see Sect. 4) can be exploited.

Experiments. This approach works very well for larger models: some DFTs which result in an out-of-memory for the monolithic approach of Sect. 4 are now solved within minutes. Results are provided in Fig. 7a where a precision of 10% is used. That is to say, the abstract-reduce-refine algorithm terminates with lower bound lb and upper bound ub if $ub - lb < 0.1 \cdot \frac{ub+lb}{2}$. The approximation comes at some overhead. It requires some internal bookkeeping for the state-space generation and constructing the upper bound is costly. Whenever the upper bound is too pessimistic, an almost complete state space is required leading to a decreased performance. Lower bounds are easier to estimate and are not really influenced by low probability paths. The on-the-fly algorithm updates the approximation after each iteration, and the lower bounds quickly becomes accurate. Let x be the true MTTF: For Fig. 7b the runtime until the (unchanged) procedure certified that the MTTF was at least $0.95 \cdot x$ is given. This is *always* very fast. Thus, 90% to 99% of the computation time is spent making the upper bound tighter.

---

[5] It can be automatically checked whether a DFT satisfies this assumption by encoding it in difference logic, a fragment of linear integer arithmetic, and check this encoding using SMT solvers; for further details see [53].

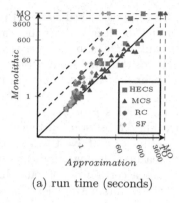

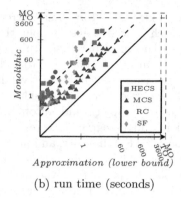

(a) run time (seconds)   (b) run time (seconds)

Fig. 7. Abstract-reduce-refine versus the monolitic approach on four different benchmark sets (taken from [53]).

7   Probabilistic Model Checking

The quantitative analysis of the resulting DFT's CTMC can be done using probabilistic model checking [34,37]. This is *not* the branch of computer-aided verification that exploits randomized algorithms for verification but rather the area that focuses on the model checking of probabilistic models such as Markov chains and variations thereof. This field is not new. Soon after the birth of model checking in 1981, the first papers on probabilistic model checking (though not called that way) appeared. Whereas initial works focused on almost-sure events – does a phenomenon happen with probability one? – later quantitative queries could be handled by combining model-checking algorithms with algorithms from numerical mathematics and operations research. Powerful tools such as Prism [38], MRMC [35] and storm [15] together with the development of various efficient verification algorithms have led to an enormous impulse to the field. It is fair to say that probabilistic model checking extends and complements long-standing analysis techniques for Markov processes.

Model Checking DFTs. Probabilistic model checking can be directly applied to the CTMCs underlying DFTs. This does not require any additional means. It can be used as a black box. Measures-of-interest such as MTTF and reliability can be readily cast as formulas in stochastic temporal logics such as some form of probabilistic CTL. Alternatively, automata can be used. In fact, this is not quite right. Logics allow for specifying constraints on such measures. Examples are e.g., the MTTF is at least M, or the probability that the TLE fails is below 10^{-9}. Verifying these logical formulas is typically very fast and requires a negligible amount of time compared to the state-space generation for DFTs. The aforementioned tools enable the automated verification of models with several millions of states within a couple of minutes.

The Benefits of Probabilistic Model Checking DFTs. Is that all? Not quite. Given the rich plethora of functional correctness properties that can be described in temporal logics, the functional correctness of DFTs can be checked as well. Properties such as: can it ever happen that gates A and B both fail? or: if the leaves fail in a certain order, does that cause a TLE failure? can be automatically checked using model checking too. No dedicated algorithms are needed for that. Using the same machinery for validating the measures of interest, many functional properties can be checked.

The use of logics and automata for specifying DFT's properties offers, in addition, a high degree of expressiveness and flexibility. Most standard measures such as MTTF, reliability, and availability are readily covered. Nesting formulas yields a simple mechanism to specify complex measures in a succinct manner. A complex property like "the probability that once a certain set of gates have failed soon with high probability (say, within 10 time units with at least probability 0.99), the TLE will fail within 1,000 time units when in addition gates A and B have failed is low" can be captured by a succinct formula. The main benefit though is the use of model checking as a fully algorithmic approach toward measure evaluation. Even better, it provides a single computational technique for any possible measure that can be written. This applies from simple properties to complicated, nested, and possibly hard-to-grasp formulas. This is radically different from common practice in DFT evaluation where tailored and new algorithms are developed for "new" measures.

Measure-Specific Computation. All algorithmic details, all detailed and nontrivial numerical computation steps are hidden to the user. Without any expert knowledge on, say, numerical analysis techniques for CTMCs, measure evaluation is possible. Even better: the algorithmic analysis is measure-driven. That is to say, the stochastic process can be tailored to the measure of interest prior to any computation, avoiding the consideration of parts of the state space that are irrelevant for the property of interest. In this way, computations must be carried out only on the fragments of the state space that are relevant to the property of interest.

Nondeterminism. Finally, probabilistic model checking is applicable to models with nondeterminism. This is relevant for DFTs too, as some DFTs may give rise to nondeterminism, see Fig. 3 (left). In these models the future behaviour is not always determined by a unique probability distribution, but by selecting one from a set of them. Rather than providing exact probabilities, the measures are subject to the resolution of the nondeterminism. As a result, bounds on the measures are obtained: lower bounds typically correspond to the "worst" possible resolution of nondeterminism, whilst upper bounds correspond to the most favourable resolution of the nondeterminism. For DFTs, the recent advances in model checking of Markov automata [17], a nondeterministic extension of CTMCs is of relevance. Efficient algorithms have been developed for objectives such as expected reward (and time, a.k.a.: MTTF), long-run rewards, timed reachability, and combinations of such objectives; for algorithmic details we refer to [23].

8   Statistical Model Checking

Statistical model checking [39] relies on Monte Carlo simulation, and can be seen as a modern form of discrete event simulation. Rather than exploring the whole state space and numerically computing the probability on a certain event, statistical model checking takes (a large number of) random samples from a statistical model and estimates the metric of interest.

Advantages. Statistical model checking has two important advantages over numerical model checking. First, it can handle very large state spaces, enabling the analysis of DFTs with many and/or complex elements, which cannot be tackled with numerical methods due to the size of the underlying state space. The memory footprint of statistical techniques is extremely low, and this method can trivially be parallelized on multi-core computer clusters.

Second, statistical methods can handle (almost) any probability distribution. Numerical computations of models with non-exponential probability distributions is difficult, especially when various types of distributions are combined. One can however, approximate arbitrary distributions with combinations of exponentials, using (acyclic) phase type distributions, but this comes at the cost of a larger state space. This is particularly true for the frequently occurring deterministic distributions and Gaussian distributions. Statistical methods do not suffer from this problem of combining different probability distributions. Therefore, they have been fruitfully applied in a number of case studies. These include the evaluation of complex maintenance strategies and their effect on system reliability [44–46]. Here, the failure rates are Erlang-distributed, whereas repair times and inspection frequencies are deterministic.

Drawbacks and Remediations. Statistical methods have also their drawbacks. First, they yield a stochastic estimate upto a certain confidence level, rather than an exact value. It is, however, a subject of debate whether this is a true disadvantage, since the failure rates and other numerical values appearing in DFTs are often estimates themselves, obtained via measurements or expert opinions. Second, statistical methods have a hard time supporting nondeterminism, however, recent progress has been made in [14].

Finally, statistical methods require many samples for rare events, i.e., events whose probability is low, which is typically the case for safety-critical systems. For example, if the probability for a failure to happen is $\frac{1}{1000}$, we need 1,000 samples on average to see the event once, and for statistically significant results, even more samples are needed, e.g., 10,000. To remedy this problem, rare event simulation techniques have been invented [33]. These techniques increase the probability for the rare events to happen, and then compensate the end result for it. Two major classes of rare event simulation exist: importance sampling [27] and importance splitting [41], and both have also been applied to DFTs, respectively in [47] and [10].

9   Industrial Applications

Railway Engineering. We have conducted a series of case studies [24,44,46,48] in close collaboration with stakeholders from railroad engineering, namely asset manager ProRail, rolling stock maintenance company NS/NedTrain, and consultancy firm Movares. All these case studies focussed on maintenance and studied the effect of different maintenance policies in terms of their performance benefits (i.e., increased availability or reliability) and costs (broken down into cost for planned and unplanned downtime, and corrective and preventive maintenance).

More specifically, the maintenance strategies were modeled in the leaves of the fault trees, leading to fault maintenance trees [45]. Both probabilistic and statistical model checking were deployed.

The paper [24] analyzed a railway safety system of a railroad trajectory a major crossing-points in the Netherlands. The goal of the analysis is to verify that the rail trajectory fulfils the railway system specifications. Here, the focus lies on the availability of the systems on the rail trajectory, defined by three failure categories: Severe disruption in both directions, such that no train can ride; severe disruption in one direction, such that no train can ride; and minor disruption which leads to dispunctuality. These yield fault trees containing 25 to 350 BEs.

The paper considers two different repair strategies: a dedicated repair procedure for each component, i.e., each component can be repaired at any time. This is the strategy Movares has considered for their analysis. A second strategy considers one repair per group of components, which is more realistic in practice.

The paper [44] studies the effect of different maintenance strategies on a pneumatic compressor, which produces compressed air used to operate, among other things, the doors and brakes of trains. This compressor is critical to the operation of the train, and a failure can lead to a lengthy and expensive disruption. Within the rolling stock maintenance company NedTrain, [44] modelled this compressor as a fault maintenance tree (FMT), i.e., a fault tree augmented with maintenance aspects. We have shown how this FMT naturally models complex maintenance plans including condition-based maintenance with regular inspections. The analysis demonstrates that FMTs can be used to model the compressor, a practical system used in industry, including its maintenance policy. We validate this model against experiences in the field, compute the importance of performing minor services at a reasonable frequency, and find that the currently scheduled overhaul may not always be cost-effective.

The paper [46] studies the effect of different maintenance strategies on the electrically insulated railway joint (EI-joint), a critical asset in railroad tracks for train detection, and a relative frequent cause for train disruptions. Together with experts in maintenance engineering, [46] modeled the EI-joint as a fault maintenance tree (FMT). Again, complex maintenance concepts, such as condition-based maintenance with periodic inspections, were naturally modeled by FMTs, and several key performance indicators, such as the system reliability, number of failures, and costs, can easily be analysed.

The analysis shows that the current maintenance policy is close to cost-optimal. It is possible to increase joint reliability, e.g., by performing more inspections, but the additional maintenance costs outweigh the reduced cost of failures.

The faithfulness of quantitative analyses heavily depends on the accuracy of the parameter values in the models. Here, we have been in the unique situation that extensive data could be collected, both from incident registration databases, as well as from interviews with domain experts from several companies. This made that we could construct a model that faithfully predicts the expected number of failures at system level.

Automotive Industry. For the car manufacturer BMW, we have carried out a large case study on the design-phase safety analysis of vehicle guidance systems [21]. Its aim is to model a variety of safety concepts and E/E architectures for drive automation. Several DFTs have been automatically generated from system descriptions and combined (in an automated manner) with hardware failure models for several mappings of functions on hardware. The DFT statespace generation has been done according to the monolithic approach using abstraction-refinement to obtain bounds. The DFT analysis focused on investigating the effect of different hardware partitionings on a range of metrics. These metrics include e.g., the mean time from degradation to failure and the minimal degraded reliability. DFTs with more than 300 nodes resulting in a CTMC of about 4 million states and 66 million transitions have been generated and successfully analysed in a matter of minutes.

Aerospace Industry. This paper focused on exploiting formal methods in statespace generation and DFT analysis. Formal methods can however also help to *synthesise* fault trees from system description languages such as AADL or SysML, see the recent survey [32]. The key idea here is to exploit the structure of the system architecture so as to generate a fault tree in a fully automated manner. In a case study with ESA [18], this technique has been successfully applied to obtain a (static) fault tree of 66 nodes explaining the behaviour of a severe failure in a complex satellite. The interesting aspect here is that the satellite design team developed this FT manually, whereas using the `compass` tool-set [8] that supports AADL, it could be generated in a fully automated manner within two hours. The FT generation algorithm is described in detail in [9].

10   Epilogue

Summary. This paper concentrated on the *analysis* of (dynamic) fault trees. This includes the generation of stochastic state-based models from DFTs as well as their quantitative analysis. We argued why formal methods can substantially boost this. In a nutshell, the main benefits are: (1) probabilistic model checking is mostly faster than competitive DFT analyses especially when several dynamic gates are involved; (2) it enables the treatment of a larger class of DFT, namely also those giving rise to nondeterminism; (3) it supports a large set of measures of interest that go beyond the classical DFT measures; (4) compositionality, abstraction, and reduction techniques improve the scalability of DFT analysis; and (5) flexibility: attack trees can be treated in a similar way, extensions with maintenance aspects, and other DFT elements are possible.

Future Work. This paper concentrated on state-space generation for DFTs and the analysis of the resulting stochastic (decision) processes. Open research challenges are to improve the process of obtaining DFTs for systems at hand. There are effective ways to obtain fault trees from architecture description languages such as AADL and SysML in an automated manner. Formal methods play an important role here too as recently surveyed in [32]. The current approaches do however not support the full expressiveness of DFTs but rather concentrate on a subclass of DFTs. More importantly though is how to obtain trustworthy information about the system at hand, such as failure rates, repair strategies and so on. We believe that big data analysis can be exploited to help out. An alternative direction is to consider parametric DFTs in which rates or even the redundancy of components is left open. The key issue is then to synthesize parameter values for which the resulting DFT ensures to satisfy a given reliability.

Acknowledgement. We thank the anonymous reviewers for their valuable feedback. A big thanks goes to our co-workers on fault trees in academia: Hichem Boudali, Pepijn Crouzen, Dennis Guck, Sebastian Junges, Viet Yen Nguyen, Bart Postma, Enno Ruijters, and Matthias Volk, and to our industrial partners: Peter Drolenga (NS/NedTrain), Jaap van Ekris (Delta Pi), Bob Huisman (NS), Madji Ghadhab (BMW), Gea Kolk (Movares), Matthias Kuntz (BMW), Martijn van Noort (ProRail), Margot Peters (NS/NedTrain), Wietske Postma (Nuclear Research Group), Judi Romijn (Movares), and Yuri Yushstein (ESA).

We thank Ed Brinksma for his guidance and inspiration over the many years. This survey paper is a birthday salute to him. His belief in formal methods, especially the elegance of compositionality and his strong view on narrowing the gap between formal methods and industrial practice have influenced our work to an enormous extent. About 25 years ago, Ed was one of the creative minds to aim at developing a framework for the *integrated* modelling and analysis of functional and performance aspects of reactive systems. This survey gives a short account about what one can achieve along these lines in a by tradition completely different research field—reliability analysis. Last but not least, we thank Ed for his eloquence, his view on culture, art, books, and good food. And, as a Rector Magnificus of the University of Twente, his role in establishing a branch of Starbucks on campus, almost next to our offices.

References

1. Ammar, M., Hamad, G.B., Mohamed, O.A., Savaria, Y.: Efficient probabilistic fault tree analysis of safety critical systems via probabilistic model checking. In: Proceedins of FDL. IEEE (2016)
2. Arnold, F., Belinfante, A., Van der Berg, F., Guck, D., Stoelinga, M.: DFTCALC: a tool for efficient fault tree analysis. In: Bitsch, F., Guiochet, J., Kaâniche, M. (eds.) SAFECOMP 2013. LNCS, vol. 8153, pp. 293–301. Springer, Heidelberg (2013). doi:10.1007/978-3-642-40793-2_27

3. Arnold, F., Guck, D., Kumar, R., Stoelinga, M.: Sequential and parallel attack tree modelling. In: Koornneef, F., van Gulijk, C. (eds.) SAFECOMP 2015. LNCS, vol. 9338, pp. 291–299. Springer, Cham (2015). doi:10.1007/978-3-319-24249-1_25

4. Baier, C., Katoen, J.-P.: Principles of Model Checking. MIT Press, Cambridge (2008)

5. Boudali, H., Crouzen, P., Stoelinga, M.: A compositional semantics for dynamic fault trees in terms of interactive Markov chains. In: Namjoshi, K.S., Yoneda, T., Higashino, T., Okamura, Y. (eds.) ATVA 2007. LNCS, vol. 4762, pp. 441–456. Springer, Heidelberg (2007). doi:10.1007/978-3-540-75596-8_31

6. Boudali, H., Crouzen, P., Stoelinga, M.I.A.: Dynamic fault tree analysis using input/output interactive Markov chains. In Proceedings of DSN, pp. 708–717 (2007)

7. Boudali, H., Crouzen, P., Stoelinga, M.I.A.: A rigorous, compositional, and extensible framework for dynamic fault tree analysis. IEEE Trans. Dependable Secure Comput. **7**(2), 128–143 (2010)

8. Bozzano, M., Cimatti, A., Katoen, J.-P., Nguyen, V.Y., Noll, T., Roveri, M.: Safety, dependability and performance analysis of extended AADL models. Comput. J. **54**, 754–775 (2011)

9. Bozzano, M., Cimatti, A., Tapparo, F.: Symbolic fault tree analysis for reactive systems. In: Namjoshi, K.S., Yoneda, T., Higashino, T., Okamura, Y. (eds.) ATVA 2007. LNCS, vol. 4762, pp. 162–176. Springer, Heidelberg (2007). doi:10.1007/978-3-540-75596-8_13

10. Budde, C.E., D'Argenio, P.R., Hermanns, H.: Rare event simulation with fully automated importance splitting. In: Beltrán, M., Knottenbelt, W., Bradley, J. (eds.) EPEW 2015. LNCS, vol. 9272, pp. 275–290. Springer, Cham (2015). doi:10.1007/978-3-319-23267-6_18

11. Burch, J.R., Clarke, E.M., McMillan, K.L., Dill, D.L., Hwang, L.J.: Symbolic model checking: 10^{20} states and beyond. In: Proceedings of LICS, pp. 428–439. IEEE Computer Society (1990)

12. Clarke, E.M., Emerson, E.A., Jha, S., Sistla, A.P.: Symmetry reductions in model checking. In: Hu, A.J., Vardi, M.Y. (eds.) CAV 1998. LNCS, vol. 1427, pp. 147–158. Springer, Heidelberg (1998). doi:10.1007/BFb0028741

13. Crouzen, P., Lang, F.: Smart reduction. In: Giannakopoulou, D., Orejas, F. (eds.) FASE 2011. LNCS, vol. 6603, pp. 111–126. Springer, Heidelberg (2011). doi:10.1007/978-3-642-19811-3_9

14. D'Argenio, P.R., Hartmanns, A., Legay, A., Sedwards, S.: Statistical approximation of optimal schedulers for probabilistic timed automata. In: Ábrahám, E., Huisman, M. (eds.) IFM 2016. LNCS, vol. 9681, pp. 99–114. Springer, Cham (2016). doi:10.1007/978-3-319-33693-0_7

15. Dehnert, C., Junges, S., Katoen, J.P., Volk, M.: A STORM is coming: a modern probabilistic model checker. In: Majumdar, R., Kunĉak, V. (eds.) CAV 2017. LNCS, vol. 10427, pp. 592–600. Springer, Cham (2017). doi:10.1007/978-3-319-63390-9_31

16. Dugan, J.B., Bavuso, S.J., Boyd, M.A.: Dynamic fault-tree models for fault-tolerant computer systems. IEEE Trans. Reliab. **41**(3), 363–377 (1992)

17. Eisentraut, C., Hermanns, H., Zhang, L.: On probabilistic automata in continuous time. In: Proceedings of LICS, pp. 342–351. IEEE CS (2010)

18. Esteve, M.-A., Katoen, J.-P., Nguyen, V.Y., Postma, B., Yushtein, Y.: Formal correctness, safety, dependability, and performance analysis of a satellite. In: Proceedings of ICSE, pp. 1022–1031. IEEE Computer Society (2012)

19. Garavel, H., Lang, F., Mateescu, R., Serwe, W.: CADP 2011: a toolbox for the construction and analysis of distributed processes. Int. J. Softw. Tools Technol. Transfer **15**(2), 89–107 (2013)
20. Ge, D., Lin, M., Yang, Y., Zhang, R., Chou, Q.: Quantitative analysis of dynamic fault trees using improved sequential binary decision diagrams. Reliab. Eng. Syst. Safe **142**, 289–299 (2015)
21. Ghadhab, M., Junges, S., Katoen, J.P., Kuntz, M., Volk, M.: Model-based safety analysis for vehicle guidance systems. In: Tonetta, S., Schoitsch, E., Bitsch, F. (eds.) SAFECOMP 2017. LNCS, vol. 10488, pp. 3–19. Springer, Cham (2017). doi:10.1007/978-3-319-66266-4_1
22. Ghamarian, A.H., de Mol, M., Rensink, A., Zambon, E., Zimakova, M.: Modelling and analysis using GROOVE. STTT **14**(1), 15–40 (2012)
23. Guck, D., Hatefi, H., Hermanns, H., Katoen, J.-P., Timmer, M.: Analysis of timed and long-run objectives for Markov automata. LMCS, **10**(3) (2014)
24. Guck, D., Katoen, J.-P., Stoelinga, M.I.A., Luiten, T., Romijn, J.: Smart railroad maintenance engineering with stochastic model checking. In: Proceedings of RAIL-WAYS. Civil-Comp Proceedings, vol. 104, pp. 299–314. Civil-Comp Press (2014)
25. Guck, D., Spel, J., Stoelinga, M.: DFTCalc: reliability centered maintenance via fault tree analysis (tool paper). In: Butler, M., Conchon, S., Zaïdi, F. (eds.) ICFEM 2015. LNCS, vol. 9407, pp. 304–311. Springer, Cham (2015). doi:10.1007/978-3-319-25423-4_19
26. Gulati, R., Dugan, J.B.: A modular approach for analyzing static and dynamic fault trees. In: Proceedings of RAMS, pp. 57–63 (1997)
27. Heidelberger, P.: Fast simulation of rare events in queueing and reliability models. ACM Trans. Model. Comput. Simul. **5**(1), 43–85 (1995)
28. Hermanns, H.: Interactive Markov Chains: The Quest for Quantied Quality. LNCS, vol. 2428. Springer, Heidelberg (2002)
29. Hermanns, H., Katoen, J.-P.: The how and why of interactive Markov chains. In: de Boer, F.S., Bonsangue, M.M., Hallerstede, S., Leuschel, M. (eds.) FMCO 2009. LNCS, vol. 6286, pp. 311–337. Springer, Heidelberg (2010). doi:10.1007/978-3-642-17071-3_16
30. Junges, S., Guck, D., Katoen, J.-P., Rensink, A., Stoelinga, M.: Fault trees on a diet: automated reduction by graph rewriting. Formal Asp. Comput. **29**(4), 651–703 (2017)
31. Junges, S., Guck, D., Katoen, J.-P., Stoelinga, M.I.A.: Uncovering dynamic fault trees. In: Proceedings of DSN, pp. 299–310. IEEE CS (2016)
32. Kabir, S.: An overview of fault tree analysis and its application in model based dependability analysis. Expert Syst. Appl. **77**, 114–135 (2017)
33. Kahn, H., Harris, T.E.: Estimation of particle transmission by random sampling. In: Monte Carlo Method; Proceedings of the Symposium National Bureau of Standards Applied Mathematics Series, 29, 30 June and 1 July 1949, vol. 12, pp. 27–30 (1951)
34. Katoen, J.-P.: The probabilistic model checking landscape. In: Proceedings of LICS, pp. 31–45. ACM (2016)
35. Katoen, J.-P., Zapreev, I.S., Hahn, E.M., Hermanns, H., Jansen, D.N.: The ins and outs of the probabilistic model checker MRMC. Perform. Eval. **68**(2), 90–104 (2011)
36. Kumar, R., Stoelinga, M.: Quantitative security and safety analysis with attack-fault trees. In: Proceedings of HASE, pp. 25–32. IEEE (2017)
37. Kwiatkowska, M.Z.: Model checking for probability and time: from theory to practice. In: Proceedings of LICS, pp. 351–360. IEEE Computer Society (2003)

38. Kwiatkowska, M., Norman, G., Parker, D.: PRISM 4.0: verification of probabilistic real-time systems. In: Gopalakrishnan, G., Qadeer, S. (eds.) CAV 2011. LNCS, vol. 6806, pp. 585–591. Springer, Heidelberg (2011). doi:10.1007/978-3-642-22110-1_47

39. Larsen, K.G., Legay, A.: On the power of statistical model checking. In: Margaria, T., Steffen, B. (eds.) ISoLA 2016. LNCS, vol. 9953, pp. 843–862. Springer, Cham (2016). doi:10.1007/978-3-319-47169-3_62

40. Montani, S., Portinale, L., Bobbio, A., Codetta-Raiteri, D.: Automatically translating dynamic fault trees into dynamic Bayesian networks by means of a software tool. In: Proceedings of ARES, pp. 804–809 (2006)

41. Morio, J., Pastel, R., Le Gland, F.: An overview of importance splitting for rare event simulation. Eur. J. Phys. **31**(5), 1295–1303 (2010)

42. Musk, E.: (2015). https://twitter.com/elonmusk/status/615185689999765504

43. Durga Rao, K., Gopika, V., Sanyasi Rao, V.V.S., Kushwaha, H.S., Verma, A.K., Srividya, A.: Dynamic fault tree analysis using Monte Carlo simulation in probabilistic safety assessment. Reliab. Eng. Syst. Safe **94**(4), 872–883 (2009)

44. Ruijters, E., Guck, D., Drolenga, P., Peters, M., Stoelinga, M.: Maintenance analysis and optimization via statistical model checking. In: Agha, G., Van Houdt, B. (eds.) QEST 2016. LNCS, vol. 9826, pp. 331–347. Springer, Cham (2016). doi:10.1007/978-3-319-43425-4_22

45. Ruijters, E., Guck, D., Drolenga, P., Stoelinga, M.: Fault maintenance trees: reliability centered maintenance via statistical model checking. In: Proceedings of RAMS. IEEE (2016)

46. Ruijters, E., Guck, D., van Noort, M., Stoelinga, M.: Reliability-centered maintenance of the electrically insulated railway joint via fault tree analysis: a practical experience report. In: Proceedings of DSN, pp. 662–669. IEEE (2016)

47. Ruijters, E., Reijsbergen, D., de Boer, P.T., Stoelinga, M.: Rare event simulation for dynamic fault trees. In: Tonetta, S., Schoitsch, E., Bitsch, F. (eds.) SAFECOMP 2017. LNCS, vol. 10488, pp. 20–35. Springer, Cham (2017). doi:10.1007/978-3-319-66266-4_2

48. Ruijters, E., Stoelinga, M.: Better railway engineering through statistical model checking. In: Margaria, T., Steffen, B. (eds.) ISoLA 2016. LNCS, vol. 9952, pp. 151–165. Springer, Cham (2016). doi:10.1007/978-3-319-47166-2_10

49. Ruijters, E., Stoelinga, M.I.A.: Fault tree analysis: a survey of the state-of-the-art in modeling, analysis and tools. Comput. Sci. Rev. **15–16**, 29–62 (2015)

50. Sullivan, K.J., Dugan, J.B., Coppit, D.: The Galileo fault tree analysis tool. In: Proceedings of FTCS, pp. 232–235 (1999)

51. Timmer, M., Katoen, J.-P., van de Pol, J., Stoelinga, M.: Confluence reduction for Markov automata. Theoret. Comput. Sci. **655**, 193–219 (2016)

52. Volk, M., Junges, S., Katoen, J.-P.: Advancing dynamic fault tree analysis - get succinct state spaces fast and synthesise failure rates. In: Skavhaug, A., Guiochet, J., Bitsch, F. (eds.) SAFECOMP 2016. LNCS, vol. 9922, pp. 253–265. Springer, Cham (2016). doi:10.1007/978-3-319-45477-1_20

53. Volk, M., Junges, S., Katoen, J.-P.: Fast dynamic fault tree analysis by model checking techniques. IEEE Trans. Ind. Inform. (2017 to appear). doi:10.1109/TII.2017.2710316

54. Yuge, T., Yanagi, S.: Quantitative analysis of a fault tree with priority AND gates. Reliab. Eng. Syst. Safe **93**(11), 1577–1583 (2008)

Author Index

Printed in the United States
By Bookmasters